Milde's International Air Law and ICAO

Milde's International Air Law and ICAO

Revised by Attila Sipos

Fourth edition

eleven

Published, sold and distributed by Eleven
P.O. Box 85576
2508 CG The Hague
The Netherlands
Tel.: +31 70 33 070 33
Fax: +31 70 33 070 30
e-mail: sales@elevenpub.nl
www.elevenpub.com

Sold and distributed in USA and Canada
Independent Publishers Group
814 N. Franklin Street
Chicago, IL 60610, USA
Order Placement: +1 800 888 4741
Fax: +1 312 337 5985
orders@ipgbook.com
www.ipgbook.com

Eleven is an imprint of Boom uitgevers Den Haag.

ISBN 978-94-6236-622-0
ISBN 978-94-0011-261-2 (E-book)

© 2023 Attila Sipos | Eleven

This publication is protected by international copyright law.
All rights reserved. No part of this publication may be reproduced, stored in a retrieval system, or transmitted in any form or by any means, electronic, mechanical, photocopying, recording or otherwise, without the prior permission of the publisher.

Table of Contents

About the Fourth Edition, as Revised by Attila Sipos	ix
Author's Reminiscences by Michael Milde (1931-2018)	xi

1 Air Law – Concept and Definitions ... 1

2 Historical Evolution of Air Law ... 5
- 2.1 Paris Conference 1910 ... 8
- 2.2 Paris Convention 1919 ... 11
- 2.3 The Madrid Convention 1926 ... 13
- 2.4 The Havana Convention 1928 ... 14
- 2.5 The Chicago Conference 1944 ... 15

3 Convention on International Civil Aviation (Chicago, 1944) ... 19
- 3.1 Depositary ... 20
- 3.2 Authentic Texts of the Convention ... 21
- 3.3 Amendment of the Convention ... 24
- 3.4 Parties to the Convention ... 32
- 3.5 Expulsion of a State Party ... 33

4 International Legal Regime of the Airspace ... 35
- 4.1 Territory ... 37
- 4.2 Airspace over the Sea ... 39
  - 4.2.1 High Seas ... 40
  - 4.2.2 Contiguous Zone ... 41
  - 4.2.3 Straits Used for International Navigation ... 41
  - 4.2.4 Archipelagic Waters ... 42
  - 4.2.5 Exclusive Economic Zone (EEZ) ... 42
  - 4.2.6 Continental Shelf ... 44
- 4.3 Polar Regions ... 44
- 4.4 Specific Rights of States in the Sovereign Airspace ... 45
- 4.5 International Duties of States in Their Airspace ... 50
- 4.6 Protection of the Sovereign Airspace ... 53
- 4.7 Justifiable Use of Force against Civil Aircraft? ... 62

5 International Legal Regime of Aircraft and Its Operation — 65
- 5.1 Civil Aircraft and State Aircraft — 66
  - 5.1.1 Evolution of the Legal Regime for Civil and State Aircraft — 68
  - 5.1.2 Chicago Convention on Civil and State Aircraft — 69
  - 5.1.3 Other International Instruments Relating to Civil and State Aircraft — 71
  - 5.1.4 Applicability of ICAO Standards, Recommended Practices and Procedures — 73
  - 5.1.5 "Definition" of Civil and State Aircraft — 76
  - 5.1.6 De Lege Ferenda … — 81
- 5.2 Nationality and Registration of Aircraft — 83
- 5.3 Joint and International Registration of Aircraft — 86
- 5.4 Functions of the State of Registry — 88
- 5.5 Transfer of Functions and Duties from the State of Registry to the State of the Operator — 93
- 5.6 "Nationality" of an Airline and "Substantive Ownership…" Clause — 96
- 5.7 Aircraft Accident Investigation — 100
- 5.8 Aircraft in Distress — 107
- 5.9 Documents Carried in Aircraft — 109

6 Legal Regime of International Air Transport — 111
- 6.1 General — 111
- 6.2 Non-Scheduled International Flight — 113
- 6.3 Scheduled International Air Service — 115
  - 6.3.1 International Air Services Transit Agreement — 115
  - 6.3.2 International Air Transport Agreement — 117
- 6.4 Bilateral Agreements on Air Services — 119
- 6.5 Code-Sharing of Air Services — 127
- 6.6 Computer Reservation Systems (CRS) — 127
- 6.7 Air Transport as "Trade in Services"? — 129

7 International Civil Aviation Organization (ICAO) — 133
- 7.1 History — 133
- 7.2 PICAO — 134
- 7.3 ICAO — 136
  - 7.3.1 Aims and Objectives — 136
  - 7.3.2 Permanent Seat — 138
  - 7.3.3 Legal Status of ICAO — 139
  - 7.3.4 Specialized Agency of the UN System — 141

	7.3.5	Organs of ICAO	144
		7.3.5.1 ICAO Assembly	145
		7.3.5.2 ICAO Council	156
		7.3.5.3 ICAO Secretariat	190
		7.3.5.4 ICAO Legal Committee	196
		7.3.5.5 Settlement of Differences in ICAO	204
7.4	Does the Chicago Convention Require Modernization?		217

8 Legal Management of Aviation Security — 231

8.1	Unlawful Seizure of Aircraft	231
8.2	Tokyo Convention on Offences and Certain Other Acts Committed on Board Aircraft 1963	235
8.3	The Hague Convention for the Suppression of Unlawful Seizure of Aircraft 1970	244
	8.3.1 Definition of the "Offence"	246
	8.3.2 Jurisdiction of Courts and Extradition of Offenders	249
8.4	Montreal Convention for the Suppression of Unlawful Acts Against the Safety of Civil Aviation 1971	253
8.5	Montreal Protocol for the Suppression of Unlawful Acts of Violence at Airports Serving International Civil Aviation 1988, Supplementary to the Convention for the Suppression of Unlawful Acts Against the Safety of Civil Aviation 1971	262
8.6	Montreal Convention on the Marking of Plastic Explosives for the Purpose of Detection 1991	265
8.7	Annex 17 – Security	270
8.8	Unruly/Disruptive Passengers	275
	8.8.1 Montreal Protocol to Amend the Tokyo Convention 1963	278
8.9	MANPADS	280
8.10	"Bonn Declaration" 1981	282
8.11	Other Acts or Offences of Concern Addressed after "911"	284

9 International Unification of Private Air Law through ICAO — 291

9.1	Geneva Convention on the International Recognition of Rights in Aircraft 1948	292
	9.1.1 Background	292
	9.1.2 Outline of the Convention	294
9.2	"Warsaw System" and the Montreal Convention 1999	297
	9.2.1 Background of the Warsaw Convention 1929	297
	9.2.2 Basic Elements of the Warsaw Convention	298

		9.2.2.1	The Format and Legal Significance of the Documents of Carriage (Passenger Ticket, Baggage Check, Air Waybill)	298
		9.2.2.2	Regime of Liability	299
		9.2.2.3	Limitation of Liability	300
		9.2.2.4	Jurisdiction of Courts	301
	9.2.3	Steps in the Amendment of the Warsaw Convention		302
		9.2.3.1	The Hague Protocol 1955	302
		9.2.3.2	Guadalajara Convention 1961	304
		9.2.3.3	Montreal Agreement 1966	306
		9.2.3.4	Guatemala City Protocol 1971	307
		9.2.3.5	Additional Protocols of Montreal Nos. 1-3 and Montreal Protocol No. 4 1975	309
		9.2.3.6	Japanese Initiative 1992	311
9.3	Montreal Convention 1999			313
9.4	Rome Convention on Damage Caused by Foreign Aircraft to Third Parties on the Surface 1952			316
	9.4.1	After "9/11"		321
9.5	Cape Town Convention on International Interests in Mobile Equipment 2001			326

Appendices 333

Appendix 1	Convention on International Civil Aviation, Chicago 1944	333
Appendix 2	Standing Rules of Procedure for the Assembly of ICAO	370
Appendix 3	Rules of Procedure for the ICAO Council	393
Appendix 4	Rules for the Settlement of Differences	443
Appendix 5	List of the Nationality Marks of Aircraft	455
Appendix 6	ICAO Illustration of the "Freedoms of the Air"	460

Bibliography of Documents 461

1	General Public Law Treaties	461
2	ICAO Public and Private Air Law Treaties	461
3	Internet Links	464
4	General Bibliography of Air Law	465

Index 467

About the Fourth Edition, as Revised by Attila Sipos

> *"Habent sua fata libelli…"*
> Terentianus Maurus, De litteris

Books have their own destiny. This book has a special one and Prof. Michael Milde did his utmost to achieve excellence. The author has presented us with such unique knowledge which draws on practice and becomes vivid in style and comprehensible because of personal experiences. The book engages the reader because an outstanding expert cultivating jurisprudence as well as shaping the aviation industry familiarises us with and guides us in the labyrinth of aviation law. The author dedicated his years of retirement to writing a significant volume on international air law and ICAO, via which he created unassailably venerable value in a classic work.

The book was first published by the Eleven International Publisher in early 2008 in the series "Essential Air and Space Law" founded and edited by Dr Marietta Benkö. Currently, the reader holds the 4th edition in hand. Its success is described most vividly by the fact that the 2nd edition was published in Chinese (Law Press China, Beijing), Russian (Aerohelp, St. Petersburg) and Korean (Bobmunsa Publishing House, Paju Book City). The translation into Arabic and Chinese (China International Book Trading Corporation) of the 3rd edition is in progress.

The volume has achieved a great deal and it continues its undiminished progress. If the question arises why this book has become compulsory reading for aviation experts and jurisprudents, the answer is simple: all the knowledge and experience manifested by the author accounts for it, which he shared with his reader to the most minute detail professionally and impressively.

With regard to the interest kindled by the book, its update and revision was inevitable. I was delighted by the fact that Dr Benkö together with the publisher Eleven commissioned me with this time-consuming but professionally imposing work. I got acquainted with Michael Milde primarily via his books, but we used to meet in Montreal at McGill University, then at international conferences, where he enthralled me with his wits and extraordinarily confident knowledge, revolutionary approach and argument. It is elevating that owing to the work of meticulous revision, while contemplating on each sentence, I could get closer to the author, gained a better understanding of his professional grandeur and style.

About the Fourth Edition, as Revised by Attila Sipos

I can only hope that the revised version will further serve the reader and promote an insight into the rigorous regulatory world of aviation, thanks to which the reader will have a good grip thereof.

Michael Milde is and has stayed forever with us via his numerous works and this last masterpiece.

Dr Attila Sipos, LL.M.
University of Sharjah (UAE)
Sharjah, December 2022
United Arab Emirates

About Attila Sipos
He is currently a Faculty Member of the Master's Program in Air and Space Law at the College of Law of the University of Sharjah (UOS). Having studied international air and space law at Leiden University (IIASL), he graduated with an Adv. Master's Degree in 2002. He worked for MALÉV Hungarian Airlines in various positions such as Flight Operation and Navigation Officer, Chief Advisor to CEO and Legal Director. Subsequently, Sipos was the Permanent Representative of Hungary on the Council of ICAO (2004-2007) and the Vice-President of the Council of ICAO (2006-2007). As a lawyer, he was employed by the Hungarian Air Navigation Service Provider (HungaroControl) as Legal Director, Alliance Director and Legal Advisor to the CEO (2008-2014). His scholarly career commenced at the International Law Department of the Faculty of Law of ELTE University in Hungary in 2008, lecturing as Honorary Professor and Associate Professor. Attila Sipos has been a Committee Member of the European Air Law Association (EALA) since 2004 and a member of the Space Law Committee of the International Law Association (ILA) since 2020.

Author's Reminiscences by Michael Milde (1931-2018)

Et in Arcadia ego

In the 85th year of his life the ageing author may be permitted to look back and review what aviation meant for him and reveal what he believes has been his motivation to write this book.

Over more than 65 years I have been privileged to fly a multitude of different aircraft types – from the rickety second-hand DC-3, workhorse of the immediate post-war period, to the current wide-bodied behemoths bridging distant continents. Thanks to aviation, I could visit 73 countries on all continents, many of them repeatedly, logging many flight hours and covering vast distances. Yet none of my grandparents ever flew in an aircraft – times have changed most dramatically in the past three generations.

Much has changed in international air travel, and the younger generation would not remember the time of the bumpy and noisy flights – when the airlines competed in serving delicious food and drinks, when most passengers nervously smoked on board or when a fountain pen in the breast pocket leaked during the unpressurized flight and ruined the smart shirt, tie and jacket that was *de rigeur* for men on international flights. Like a story from a different world must sound the experience of my first flight from Europe to the US (16 hours with refuelling stops in Ireland and New Foundland) when prior to the flight the dashing commander of the aircraft and an elegant stewardess stood at the bottom of the boarding steps and shook hands with every passenger, addressing him or her by name. Today's mass transportation has long since dispensed with such personalized courtesies, but has become so much faster and by far more affordable. I recall that in the late 1950s the return ticket from Europe to US cost the equivalent of the price of a basic VW Beetle – a dream of every European student at that time. Today the cost of air travel is far more affordable, but any premium comfort above the spartan "economy" class still commands a premium price. The rapid progress of aviation during a single generation is overwhelming: in 2014, 3.3 billion passengers were carried by air – almost a half of mankind; by 2015, according to the World Bank Group, the number of passengers rose by an additional 6.7%, and long-term forecasts are not below 5% growth per year. Low prices of fuel and the proliferation of low-cost carriers could make these estimates conservative.

Air law presented an attractive subject for research in the early years of aviation, and as a law student more than 60 years ago, I was fascinated by the potential plurality of "foreign elements" (and conflicts of laws) in international carriage by air and the need for unification of law and its uniform interpretation. While to me international aviation initially meant only an illustration of the more general problems of private and public international law in the broad spectrum, it soon became the real focus of my attention, and some of my early publication efforts were noted in Montreal. McGill University's Law Dean Maxwell Cohen – then also Director of the McGill Institute of Air and Space Law – invited me to the Institute for the academic year 1964-1965 with a generous Canada Council grant and Ford Foundation scholarship to broaden my horizons in the field of air law and to bring me into contact with ICAO.

After 11 years as Associate Professor of private international law at the Charles University (Prague), I was privileged to be recruited as a Legal Officer in the ICAO Secretariat in Montreal; there I spent 25 years (1966-1991) fast progressing to the positions of Senior Legal Officer, Principal Legal Officer and finally Director of the Legal Bureau responsible for the legal work programme of the Organization, and on a few occasions serving briefly as Acting Secretary General of ICAO. Those years presented distinct challenges in international law-making, whether in the interminable efforts to modernize the antiquated 1929 Warsaw Convention, the 1952 Rome Convention or the novel pressing priorities to prevent and suppress unlawful acts against aviation security (for a long time it was not permissible to use the word "terrorism" within the United Nations system). In the history of ICAO those were perhaps the most dynamic years in the successful progressive development and codification of international law, the need for security of aviation marshalling consensus among States despite the zenith of the Cold War. Some of the most respectable experts in the field of international law took part in the ICAO meetings at the time, and I had the unique opportunity to have a direct insight into the process of international law-making and perhaps to add my own modest fingerprints to that process. ICAO itself changed dramatically during those years, its membership increased by scores of newly independent States, the new presence of two permanent members of the UN Security Council (USSR and People's Republic of China) brought a new political dimension and Cold-War controversies to ICAO, and the responses to international terrorism against civil aviation became a high priority.

In 1989 I was appointed Professor of Law and Director of the McGill Institute of Air and Space Law. It was a singular honour to follow in the footsteps of Dr Eugene Pepin, the legendary aviation pioneer and first Director of ICAO Legal Bureau and later Director of the McGill Institute of Air and Space Law. In 1991 I retired from the ICAO Secretariat, after 25 years of service, and came fully to McGill University; however, my close cooperation with ICAO continued in numerous consulting projects in several States. The academic detachment from ICAO gave me a new perspective and freedom to express views and critical comments from which an active international civil servant must refrain so as not to compromise his duty to serve with impartiality.

Author's Reminiscences by Michael Milde (1931-2018)

I took as my principal task at McGill a radical revision of the teaching curriculum and teaching methods, the pursuit of high academic respectability of the Institute's programme and reorientation of the research and publications of the Institute. The multinational classrooms of graduate students at the McGill Institute proved to be stimulating, and until 2006 I enjoyed the inspiring company of bright young lawyers with their endless curiosity and motivation. In 1996 the Institute obtained from the Council of ICAO the prestigious *Edward Warner Award* – often called the "Nobel Prize" of aviation – for its contribution to the development of air law. It belongs to the alumni of the Institute, many of whom now occupy prominent positions in international organizations, governments, airlines, judiciary, legal practice and academia. The McGill "family" is ubiquitous and faithful to the McGill traditions.

Dr Marietta Benkö – the Editor of the growing series "Essential Air and Space Law" – invited me in 2007 to contribute a volume on international air law and ICAO to her series. I remain grateful to Dr Benkö for her initiative and encouragement – she has created in the series a valuable platform not only for an academic discourse but also for works of practical relevance that found readership on all continents.

Having addressed the history and motivation for writing this book, I must thank my wife, Maria, for her continuing support, understanding and inspiration in the 62nd year of our married life, and also our children and grandchildren. All of them deserve my gratitude and love. This edition is specifically dedicated to my first granddaughter, Clara Marie Milde, who has chosen law as her profession and was just this month called to the Bar of Ontario, Canada.

Professor Dr Michael Milde
Emeritus Director, Institute of Air and Space Law
McGill University
London, Ontario, June 2016

1   AIR LAW – CONCEPT AND DEFINITIONS

Nomina sunt consequentia rerum

The very term "air law" *(droit aerien, derecho aereo, Luftrecht, vozdushnoye pravo)* is controversial and imprecise but it has been used in practice for over a century. It was arguably coined, in its French form, by Professor Ernest Nys of the University of Brussels in 1902 in his report to the *Institute de Droit International* on the subject "droit et aerostats".[1] In his time – a year before the Wright brothers flew their first heavier-than-air machine – the growing operation of balloons, dirigibles and Zeppelins attracted the attention of the leading legal scholars around the world.

Even the earliest legal authors did not apply their thinking to the gaseous substance known as "air" but rather to the space above the Earth that appeared in their time usable for aeronautical activities. It was not within their imagination to consider any navigational activities beyond the airspace and without the buoyancy given by air to the flying machines. It is transparent that even the earliest thinkers did not believe that "air law" would govern the air as a substance or the airspace or the flying machines as such but solely the social relations among different subjects that may take place in or with respect to the gaseous envelope surrounding the Earth. That is a very basic axiom – law does not govern "objects" as such but only the social relations, in some cases associated with specific "objects".

From the beginning of legal thinking relating to "air law" it was obvious that the term was to be used exclusively for the regulation of such social relations in the airspace that are related to or generated by the aeronautical uses of that space. None of the early authors thought to include under the term "air law" also the regulation of wireless transmissions or any other aspects of the propagation of electromagnetic waves through the space; neither did they consider the issues of the use of wind power to generate electricity. The problem of air pollution and environmental protection was not yet recognised as a subject calling for legal regulation or that had any relevance to aviation. Again, the term "outer space", *i.e.*, space beyond the navigable airspace, was not yet even imagined and "air law" in its development did not foresee its relevance to the possibility of space flight.

It is safe to conclude that the term "air law" from its inception was confined only to the legal regulation of social relations generated by the aeronautical uses of the airspace. The term "aeronautical law" would be more precise but a century of common use of the term "air law" should be respected and any terminological doubts, disputes or preferences are of no practical relevance. However, it is interesting to note that the International Law

---

1   Annuaire de l'Institut de Droit International, Session de Bruxelles, Septembre 1902, Vol. 19. p. 88 ss.

Commission of the United Nations has in its current work programme the subject "protection of the atmosphere" and that potential development and codification of international law would well deserve the title "air law" as it would address the gaseous substance "air".[2]

The term "air law" may indicate – and many authors support this approach – that it is an independent branch in the system of law. This author does not accept the independence or "autonomy" of air law in the system of law. The aviation-related social relations could be governed by private law (property, contracts, torts), labour law (contract of employment), administrative law (licensing, certification), criminal law (prevention and suppression of aviation terrorism) public international law (air traffic agreements, unification of law), private international law (conflict of laws or interpretation of unified private law), etc. Consequently, the "air law" is not an autonomous branch in the system of law but rather a pragmatic conglomeration – a selection and grouping of rules from different branches of law relevant for aviation – a selection for a systematic classification and analysis, professional specialization and pedagogical purposes.

One single book cannot possibly encompass the entire spectrum of "air law" that would cover all aviation-related aspects of national law, comparative law and international law. This book has a modest aim to deal only with "international air law", *i.e.*, with such sources of aeronautical regulations that are created by treaties concluded by sovereign States, by States' practice or through the mechanism of international intergovernmental bodies. Special attention is given to the constitutional framework and work of the International Civil Aviation Organization (ICAO), the focus of international law-making in the aviation field. The book does not deal with the regional legal arrangements, such as the vast body of aeronautical regulations and laws generated within the European Union that would deserve a separate and extensive monographic treatment.

The only universally accepted axiom of international law is the sovereignty and equality of States. International law has the undisputed character of "law" only to the degree that it governs the conduct of States under international treaties freely entered into by them or under the "international custom" accepted by them as "law". This approach may be criticized as "positivism" by those who base their consideration on international law "as it should be" rather than on "what it is". Ideas based on so-called "natural law" or "natural justice" or concepts of "soft law" may appear to introduce attractive and lofty principles into international law, but they are not based on reality. Journalists (and some politicians and even legal thinkers) are often quick in labelling some events as "lawful" or "contrary" to international law, but would not be able to prove the true legal source/authority of their statements. International law must be understood as the minimum common denominator

---

2 See Peter H. Sand and Jonathan B. Wiener, *"Towards a New International Law of the Atmosphere"*, Gottingen Journal of International Law 7 (2), prepublication 2016.

of the political will of States expressed in treaties or international custom and it is important to ascertain the positive (real) content of international law from its proper sources and not to confuse it with wishful thinking about the "desirable" legal concepts.

Aviation helps to shrink the distances of the world and frequently crosses the national boundaries. This international nature of aviation underlines the importance of international air law. The International Civil Aviation Organization (ICAO) is a central focus of the international community through which the international law is not only applied but also created. The creation of ICAO it appears also useful to analyse the constitutional structure of ICAO and the rules governing its working methods and the impact of ICAO on the development of international air law.

After a brief overview of the historical development of air law, the subjects of international air law addressed in this book will include the general analysis of the Chicago Convention (1944), which is the fundamental source of current international air law; then attention will also be drawn to

- the legal regime of the airspace;
- legal issues relating to aircraft and air navigation;
- legal regulation and practice of international air transport;
- case study of the ICAO and its law-making functions;
- international legal responses to unlawful acts against the safety of civil aviation; and
- introduction to the international instruments for the unification of private air law.

Law must be understood as a dynamic discipline that changes with the changing needs of the society and does not remain static. This applies to aviation in particular since here, law must also follow rapid technological development.

Law must also be understood as an integral and powerful tool of the management process. Any management/policy decision must take into account the applicable legal ramifications, comply with them and make the best use of the potential they offer; that may be called *management by law*. However, another equally essential aspect is the *management of law* – legal regulation has to be adjusted and updated according to the changing needs of the society, and the academic analysis may help in that process.

In this connection, international civil aviation may serve as a prime example for such a regulatory mechanism being one of the most regulated industry, as well as "create and preserve friendship and understanding among the nations and peoples of the world", by all means may also "promote co-operation between them upon which the peace of the world depends".[3]

---

[3] Convention on International Civil Aviation, Chicago, 7 December 1944, Preamble.

2   Historical Evolution of Air Law

In omni historia curiosus

It is always interesting to trace the roots and historic evolution of a legal discipline. The context of its origin and the causes of its evolution help to illustrate the social and cultural framework and could assist in better understanding and interpretation of the rules. However, in a modern treatise of air law these issues hardly deserve more than a brief comment.

Common sense dictates that air law – *i.e.*, law governing the aeronautical uses of the airspace – could not have existed before mankind learned the art of aerial navigation and before the practice of that art created social relations and possible social conflicts of interests that required legal regulation. By analogy, highway codes did not exist before the automobile was invented and before a high number of cars appeared on the roads creating possible social conflicts and requiring regulation – need for a "certification", licensing of drivers, registration and insurance, to drive on the right or left side, any speed limit, how to behave on intersections…?

If we assume that law does not govern the technology but only the social relations created by the technology, we will agree that air law cannot have a long history.

It appears misguided to comb the legal history and claim that the "Roman law" concept *cuius est solum eius est usque ad coelum et ad inferos* (whoever owns the land owns it all the way to the sky and to the depth of the Earth) was a nascent principle of air law. On all counts, that would be an erroneous submission. In the first place, the principle *cuius est solum* cannot be found in the classical (royal, republican and early imperial) Roman law. It cannot be found even in the Byzantine 6th century A. D. Justinian's codification in *Digesta seu Pandectae* (525 A. D.) much later named *Corpus Iuris Civilis*.[1] The concept was apparently used for the first time only in the 13th century by the Bolognese Professor Accursius in a *"glossa ordinaria"* or comment on the ancient Roman texts. Whatever the true origins of this term, it had nothing to do with the aeronautical uses of the airspace and it only more closely defined the property rights of the owner of the land against any incursions (protruding construction or tree branches, etc.) by the owner of the neighbouring land; originally it probably meant protection of the public roads against any incursions above them. Practically the ancient Roman jurisprudents divided the object of law into two parts: air and airspace. The air *(aer)* we all freely breathe is not a negotiable

---

1   Corpus Iuris Civilis (Corpus of Civil Law) is the collective title of the body of ancient Roman law. It is not only preserved in Roman law but it also provided the basis of law for emerging European nations.

object *(res extra commercium)*, while the airspace above the estate *(coelum)* is negotiable *(res in commercio)* as it belongs to the soil *(solum)*, to the estate, which the owner may dispose of.

A real historical curiosity is the doctoral thesis of a certain Johannes Stephan Dancko presented in 1687 to University Viadrina (Frankfurt/Oder). It was re-discovered by Andreas Kadletz and edited by Marietta Benkoe and Bernhard Schmidt-Tedd as a facsimile of the original Latin text "*De jure principis aereo*" (The Jurisdiction of the Prince over the Air) with a German and English translation in 2002.[2] The author of the thesis admits the *res omnium communis* quality of the air (the air belongs to everyone) but preserves for the ruler (Prince) special *patrimonium* prohibiting the general population to hunt birds or to use wind for windmills without authorization or even to display fireworks in the air. It would be a daring conclusion to state that the *patrimonium* of the ruler (special inherent right) in the air is a precursor of the concept of territorial sovereignty; however, the thesis is interesting for its scholarly attempt to address the legal issues of the air and of the airspace.

It was only in the second half of the 18th century that mankind experienced the first manned flight. It is hardly known but the first balloon flight was effected even 74 years before the Brothers Montgolfier – namely on 8 August 1709 by Bartholameu Laurenço Gusmao in Lisbon with the support of King João V of Portugal. Gusmao was even granted the King's protection for his invention which according to legal terms of today could be considered as the first patent in the history of human flight. Unfortunately, though, even the King could not protect the inventor from the wrath (and ignorance) of the Holy Inquisition which argued that "man cannot fly", except in league with Lucifer. So, Batholomeu Gusmao was forced to renounce his work in exchange for his life.[3]

The "first" well-known manned flight was just years before the French revolution and the American war of independence. The hot air balloon constructed by the brothers Josef-Michel and Etienne-Jacques Montgolfier took off in Annonay on 4 June 1783, in Versailles on 19 September 1783 (with a "crew" of a sheep, a rooster and a duck) and in Paris on 21 November 1783 with a human crew. While the brothers Montgolfier believed that they invented a new gas ("Montgolfier gas") produced by the fire that lifted the balloon, the

---

2   Johannes Stephanus Dancko, "*De Iure Principis Aereo*", (The Jurisdiction of the Prince over the Air). Anhalt-Zerbst, 1867, Latin–English Synopsis, Editors, Marietta Benkoe and Bernhard Schmidt-Tedd; Translators, Marty H. Heitz and Peter Kertész, Cologne 2002, pp. 1-79. See www.researchgate.net/profile/Marietta-Benkoe/publication, also available at http://heinonline.org.

3   *Historical Manuscripts Relating to the Invention of the First Balloon and Its Maiden Flight in Lisbon, August 8, 1709*. Edited by Marietta Benkoe and Bernhard Schmidt-Tedd in co-operation with Denise Digrell. Translations by Abilia Scheidl, Peter Kertész and Marietta Benkoe, Cologne 2002. www.researchgate.net/publication/327906130_Historical_Manuscripts_Relating_to_the_Invention_of_the_First_Balloon_and_its_Maiden_Flight_in_Lisbon_August_8_1709_Synopsis_of_the_Portugese_Original_with_an_English_and_a_German_Translation and http://heinonline.org.

buoyancy was in fact created by the physical reality that hot air is much lighter than the surrounding atmosphere; the ages old Archimedes principle explains that the balloon is supported in the atmosphere by a force equal to the weight of air displaced by the balloon. The hot air balloon was a primitive contraption built of fabric, paper, ropes and a wicker basket and the hot air was generated by an open fire pit fed with wood, straw and paper. The balloon was not dirigible or controllable and was essentially at the mercy of the prevailing wind. In a densely populated city with flammable wooden structures a possible fiery landing of a balloon represented a major hazard. It is not surprising that on 23 April 1784 – not even one year after the first experiment – a lieutenant of police in Paris issued a directive that balloons must not be operated in the city without prior police permission. That seems to be the very first real trace of aviation law in history – a prohibition aimed at protecting the safety of persons and property on the ground.[4]

Hot air balloons were soon followed by balloons filled with hydrogen, then "dirigibles" and air ships ("Zeppelins") and history was made on 17 December 1903 when the brothers Orville and Wilbur Wright accomplished a 12 seconds' powered, heavier-than-air controlled sustained flight covering the distance of 36.6 metres (120 feet) with a pilot aboard at Kitty Hawk, North Carolina. No legal framework existed that would have preceded and governed this historic achievement.[5]

On 25 July 1909, French aviator Louis Bleriot crossed the English Channel between Les Barraques, France and Dover, England – a distance of 38 km flown in 37 minutes. His aircraft, which he helped to design, was powered by a 25-horsepower three-cylinder engine. No legal steps were taken to authorize the flight and its landing in a foreign territory and Bleriot did not even carry his French passport or any other identification paper![6] While the newspapers of the day rejoiced that "England is no longer an island", concern was also evident that England could be one day open to an air attack, an obvious sign that the new technological achievement had a potential impact on the social relations. Bleriot was welcomed as a hero both in England and France and won the 1,000 pounds prize offered by the British *Daily Mail* for the first flight across the Channel in a heavier-than-air machine. Another contender for the prize – Hubert Latham – made an attempt to cross the Channel on 19 July 1909, but his engine failed, and he had to be rescued from the sea by a French ship.

---

4   P.H. Sand, G. Pratt and J.T. Lyon, *A Historical Survey of the Law of Flight*, Institute of Air and Space Law, McGill University, Montreal, 1961, p. 5.

5   However, the Wright Brothers were involved in a patent dispute with another aviation pioneer – Glen Curtiss – inventor of the ailerons.

6   This is recorded according to a personal discussion of this book's original author, Michael Milde, with Eugene Pepin, the first Director of the Legal Bureau of ICAO and the second Director of the McGill Institute of Air and Space Law – in both positions a predecessor of M. Milde. E. Pepin also recalled that he was personally present at Bleriot's historic take-off and push-started the propeller of his aircraft.

In fact, military interests in aviation appeared at a very early stage. Military observation balloons were used at the time of the French Revolution by the end of the 18th century, during the Napoleonic wars, US Civil War 1861-1865 and the Franco-Prussian War 1870-1871.[7] Apart from the observation and communication purposes, the military soon realised the potential of the nascent aviation for the bombardment of enemy targets. The First International Peace Conference in 1899 at The Hague "prohibited launching of projectiles and explosives from balloons" but it applied as a "moratorium" only for a period of five years.[8]

The practice of States in the early 20th century is convincingly illustrated by the shooting down of foreign military balloons that were alleged to have crossed the national boundary for "espionage" purposes (*e.g.*, taking photographs of fortifications, etc.) – the tsarist Russia having the primacy in defence against "intruders" by shooting down German military balloons in 1904 and 1910.[9] Similar incidents occurred on the German/Belgian and German/French border before World War I (1914-1918).

2.1 PARIS CONFERENCE 1910

It is recorded that between April and November 1908 "at least ten German balloons crossed the frontier and landed in France carrying over twenty-five aviators at least half of whom were German officers".[10] The government of France wished to avoid international confrontations and proposed to convene an international conference that would attempt to regulate the operational issues of flight into and over a foreign territory. The *Paris International Air Navigation Conference* in 1910 represents the first diplomatic effort to formulate the principles of international law relating to air navigation.[11]

---

7   The Prussians (Germans) laid siege to Paris in 1870. Both sides were using hot-air balloons (defined as an aircraft). Under Bismarck's signature warning was issued to France that any balloon that would fly over the territory occupied by Prussians would be dealt with as an intruder and will be shot down. These balloons were treated as belligerent forces behind its lines. This was the first harbinger of the attitude of the nation States. States asserted special rights in the airspace and did not accept "strangers" flying over their territories without permission.

8   "Hague IV", 29 July 1899, see www.yale.edu/lawweb/avalon/lawofwar/hague994.htm accessed 31 December 2022.

9   J. Kroell, *Traite de Droit International Aerien*, Tome I L'aeronautique en temps de paix, Paris, Editions Internationales, 1934, p. 36, footnote (4).

10 Quoted in J.C. Cooper, "The International Air Navigation Conference Paris 1910" in *Explorations in aerospace Law, Selected essays by John Cobb Cooper, Edited by I. A. Vlasic*, McGill University Press, Montreal 1968, pp. 105-156.

11 The records of the Conference held in Paris from 8 May to 28 June 1910 will be found in *Conference Internationale de Navigation Aerienne, Paris 8 mai-28 juin 1910, Procès-verbaux des seances et annexes*, Paris, Imprimerie Nationale (1910). This publication is now very rare but is readily accessible in the Nahum Gelber Law Library (McGill University, Montreal) under call number KLQAC C 762.

Many States responded to a detailed questionnaire formulated by the French Government in 1909 and the Conference was attended by Austria-Hungary, Belgium, Bulgaria, Denmark, France, Germany, Great Britain, Italy, Luxemburg, Monaco, Netherlands, Portugal, Rumania, Russia, Serbia, Spain, Sweden, Switzerland and Turkey – a fairly universal representation of Europe. The USA and States from other continents were not invited since their geographic distance made the operation of their aircraft in European airspace unrealistic.

The academic thinking of that time concentrated its attention on the legal status of the airspace, *i.e.*, whether the airspace is "free" as the high seas and whether States have some special rights up to a certain altitude (with analogy to the territorial sea) and whether other States enjoy the right of "innocent passage", etc.; only few authors advocated at that time the principle of complete sovereign rights of States over the airspace above their territory.[12] However, the Conference carefully avoided the issues relating to the general legal status of the airspace or, more specifically, whether the airspace was part of the sovereign territory of the subjacent States or whether it was free to be used by any State without any limitations.[13]

The Conference did not succeed in the effort to draft an international convention, but their work was the first real source and influenced the development of public international air law as it said in the very first statement something very dramatic and revolutionary, vastly different from the previous thinkers that the "national airspace should be an area of 'restricted access'". In addition to this, it managed to identify and address several issues essential for the future regulation of international air navigation and in the fifty-five draft articles and two annexes it formulated rules relating to the nationality of aircraft and their registration, certification of aircraft (airworthiness), licensing of the flight crew, rules of the air, customs procedures, permission required for the carriage of explosives or munitions of war, photographic and radio equipment, etc. The draft texts dealt with the distinction between public and private aircraft, agreed that States can declare prohibited zones above their territory and recognized that cabotage should be reserved to national aircraft. In the prevailing "vacuum" in international law of that time this represented a very respectable progress – in particular by the explicit recognition that there should be uniform international rules on aviation and that aircraft cannot be subject to different rules whenever they cross the national boundary.

---

12 The most explicit advocate of the principle of absolute sovereignty was the British Professor of international law John Westlake, see "*Annuaire de l'Institut de droit international*", Vol. 21, 1906, p. 297.
13 Edmund Faller, "The Historical Significance of a Diplomatic Failure: The Paris Air Navigation Conference of 1910" in *Beitraege zum Luft- und Weltraumrecht, Festschrift zu Ehren von Alex Meyer*, Carl Heymans Verlag 1975, pp. 83-102. E. Faller corrects the view of J.C. Cooper (*Ibid.* 10) that the Conference in fact accepted the principle of state sovereignty over the airspace – on the contrary, this aspect was expressly avoided.

The crucial disagreement among the States concerned the right of foreign aircraft to overfly the national territory – Germany and France advocating wide freedom and "national treatment" of foreign aircraft while Great Britain, Austria-Hungary and Russia stressed territorial sovereign's right to limit such overflights for national security and unlimited protection of their persons and security. It should be noted that by that time Germany enjoyed unique technical advantage in their Zeppelins and other dirigibles for civil and military purposes and would have benefited from a wide freedom of flight.

The Conference should have reconvened at a later session but the war 1914-1918 interrupted any international cooperation in that field. However, theoretical debates continued in a most divisive manner while the practice of States became more and more consistent.

Some of the leading legal thinkers of the time met at the 27th Conference of the International Law Association (ILA)[14] held in Paris from 27 May to 1 June 1912 and an absolute stalemate was reached between the advocates of the freedom of the air[15] and those advocating complete sovereignty of States over their airspace;[16] it is of interest to note that they paid no attention whatsoever to the results of the abortive Paris Conference (1910).

On the other hand, already prior to the outbreak of the war in 1914 the practice of States was unmistakable – they *de facto* protected their airspace, protested against its violations and used force for the assertion of their rights.

During the devastating World War I (1914-1918) – "the war to end all wars" – aviation technology marked a tremendous progress and proved to be a new and potent weapon. From the initial tentative use of aircraft for aerial reconnaissance of the enemy positions with the pilot equipped only with a pistol for personal defence[17] aviation soon progressed to heavily armed fighter aircraft involved in daring dog fights and to bombers capable of inflicting major damage on the ground. It is also recorded that during that war the first "air-to-air missile" was used: French Lieutenant Yves Le Prieur invented a simple rocket (called Le Prieur Rocket) that was successfully used by French fighter aircraft to destroy enemy observation balloons.[18] During the war both the belligerents and the neutral States vigorously protected the airspace above their territory and the general perception of aviation became closely linked to national security. It is to be admitted that the subsequent

---

14   ILA was founded in Brussels in 1873 and its headquarters are in London. This is one of the oldest continuing organisation in the field of international law in the world. www.ila-hq.org/en.
15   Paul Fauchille, author of the seminal "La Domaine Juridique des Aerostats" in *Revue Generale de Droit International Public*, 1901, pp. 414-485; his position formulated at the 27th ILA Conference in 1912. See 27 *Int'l L.Ass. Rep*, pp. 239-260. http://heinonline.org.
16   H.D. Hazeltine, "State Sovereignty in the Air-Space", 27 *Int. L.Ass. Rep*. 1912, pp. 261-270.
17   Personal recollections of E. Pepin: *Ibid*. 6.
18   http://firstworldwar.com/atoz/leprieur.htm.

rapid development of international air law occurred in the shadow of the war and reflected the security concerns of States.

2.2 PARIS CONVENTION 1919

The Paris Peace Conference of 1919 created an Inter-Allied Aeronautical Commission that was to consider the limits on commercial aviation to be allowed to the defeated Germany.[19] Moreover, the Commission was invited to prepare a Convention on international aerial navigation in the time of peace – recognition that aviation had become a growing technology requiring specific international legal regulation "to prevent controversy" and "to encourage the peaceful intercourse of nations by means of aerial communications".[20] It is typical for the period that almost all delegates formulating the principles of international air law were military officers.

On 13 October 1919 the following States signed the instrument called *Convention Relating to the Regulation of Aerial Navigation*:[21] Belgium, Bolivia, Brazil, The British Empire, China, Cuba, Czechoslovakia, Ecuador, France, Greece, Guatemala, Haiti, The Hedjaz (Saudi Arabia), Honduras, Italy, Japan, Liberia, Nicaragua, Panama, Peru, Poland, Portugal, Roumania, The Serb-Croat-Slovene State, Siam, Uruguay and the United States. Although the United States signed the Paris Convention, they never ratified it.[22]

The Convention is historically the first multilateral instrument of international law relating to air navigation. It also helped to formulate the principles of the domestic law of contracting States, many of whom did not have any laws governing aviation in 1919.

The Paris Convention is no longer in force and has become part of history.[23] However, its pioneering contribution to the formulation of some basic concepts of air law survives and maintains its relevance.

In its very first Article the Convention puts an end to almost two decades of academic discussions whether the airspace is "free" like the high seas or whether it forms a part of the sovereign territory of the subjacent State. In the shadow of the wartime experience States firmly and unequivocally confirmed the complete and exclusive sovereignty of

---

19 "The armed forces of Germany must not include any military or naval air forces". See Article 198 of the Treaty of Peace with Germany, Versailles, Part V, Section III, Air Clauses, 28 June 1919.
20 See, Preamble of the Convention. The text of the Convention is in the *League of Nations Treaty Series* Vol. XI, p. 173; more readily in *Annals of Air and Space Law* Vol. XXX (2005), pp. 5-15.
21 For an authoritative analysis of the Convention, see *Albert Roper, Secretaire generale de la CINA, La Convention internationale du 13 octobre 1919 portant sur la reglementation de la navigation aerienne, These de Paris 1930*.
22 The reason was the amending process (Article 34) of the Paris Convention and its Annexes by the International Commission for Air Navigation.
23 In Article 80 of the Chicago Convention on International Civil Aviation (1944) the States undertook to denounce the Paris Convention (1919) upon entry into force of the Chicago Convention.

States over their airspace. This principle has become an axiom and a backbone of international air law ever since. Undoubtedly, *Bar in parem non habet imperiu*; an equal does not have any power over an equal.

> The High Contracting Parties recognize that every Power has *complete* and *exclusive* sovereignty over the airspace above its territory.

The formulation of that principle in the Paris Convention deserves an analysis as its terms, "complete" and "exclusive" sovereignty implies an absolute right to take whatever action the offended state deems appropriate. However, according to customs and agreements responses are dependent on whether the aircraft was civil or military; whether it was in distress, hostile or peaceful; in a state of war or peace; and also take into account the existing political climate. The political will of States must reassess the legal axiom of sovereignty and its practical interpretation and application. Aviation must no longer be perceived primarily as a potential menace to the national security, it is an essential public service. Its safety, regulatory and economic efficiency should be the guiding principles of regulations, taking priority over national pride, prestige and wasteful protectionism.

It is noteworthy that the Paris Convention does not *create* the principle of air sovereignty but *recognizes* it; moreover, it recognizes it not only for the Parties of the Convention among themselves but for *every Power* as a rule that is generally applicable for all States. It can be concluded that in the light of the practice of States protecting their airspace and in the light of the war time experience as belligerents or as neutrals, the Paris Conference considered the principle of State sovereignty to be a firm part of the customary international law that was to be only formally recognised by a codified instrument. International custom is defined as "evidence of a general practice accepted as law".[24] The theory requires not only this *opinio juris ac necessitatis* – conviction of the legal nature or necessity of a rule – but also *usus longaevus* – long practice in observing such a rule. There is no agreement in theory on what constitutes this *usus longaevus* and the formulation in the Paris Convention is based on the observable practice of States shorter than two decades.

The contracting States granted themselves in time of peace "freedom of innocent passage" on a non-discriminatory basis.[25] Other provisions that influenced the further development of international air law included prohibited zones, provisions on nationality

---

24 Article 38 d. of the Statute of the International Court of Justice.
25 Vincent Correia, "The Legacy of the 1919 Paris Convention Relating to the Regulations of Aerial Navigation. Behind and Beyond the Chicago Convention. The Evolution of Aerial Sovereignty" (*Aerospace Law and Policy*), Wolters Kluwer, 2019, p. 14, pp. 16-19.

and registration of aircraft, certificates of airworthiness and competency, establishment of international airways, cabotage and special regime for "State aircraft".

The Paris Convention also established the International Commission for Air Navigation (ICAN or CINA for *Commission Internationale de la Navigation Aerienne*) – a permanent Commission placed under the direction of the League of Nations. One of the legally important duties of ICAN was the amendment of Annexes A-H to the Convention that contained more detailed provisions on nationality and registration of aircraft, certificates of airworthiness and competency, rules of the air, signals to be used, etc.[26]

The Annexes were given the same force as the Convention itself. The Convention thus created the first international organization specialized in civil aviation. The idea of "Annexes" to the Convention that could be flexibly amended or updated by the Commission itself without the laborious and time-consuming formalities of a Diplomatic Conference indicated the understanding of States that the aviation technology and procedures will develop rapidly and their legal regulation must be adjusted accordingly without the laborious process of amendment of the Convention.

The Paris Convention shared the fate of the entire "Versailles" peace system. In the USA, the defeat of the visionary President W. Wilson resulted in increasing isolationist policies and the USA did not become a member of the League of Nations and did not ratify the Paris Convention. The Convention thus never achieved universal acceptance. It was also partly due to the fact that by 1919 aviation could not cover trans-oceanic distances and the transcontinental cooperation and coordination was not urgently relevant anywhere else than in Europe. A specific legal reason for the United States non-ratification of the Paris Convention quite likely was also the provision giving the Annexes the same legal status as the Convention itself while leaving their amendment within the mandate of the Commission – thus the ratification would be in fact signing a "blank cheque" and automatically accepting any future amendments without exception and without the specific consent of the appropriate constitutional authorities of States.

2.3   THE MADRID CONVENTION 1926

Another attempt at international legal regulation of civil aviation was initiated in 1926 by Spain and was motivated by political ambitions and rivalry of Spain with the League of

---

26   The Convention Relating to the Regulation of Aerial Navigation signed at Paris on 13 October 1919 had eight Annexes elaborated by the Technical Sub-Committee: Annex (A): The Marking of Aircraft; Annex (B): Certificates of Airworthiness; Annex (C): Log Books; Annex (D): Rules as to Lights and Signals. Rules of the Air; Annex (E): Minimum Qualifications Necessary for Obtaining Certificates as Pilots and Navigators; Annex (F): International Aeronautical Maps and Ground Markings; Annex (G): Collection and Dissemination of Meteorological Information; Annex (H): Customs Regulations.

Nations and with ICAN. Under the dictator Primo de Rivera, Spain withdrew from the League of Nations where Spain was not granted a permanent seat on the League's Council. Spain did not adhere to the Paris Convention (1919) because it was not offered the same voting power as France or Italy. In October 1926, Spain invited all Latin American States to an "Ibero-American Aviation Congress" that met in Madrid on 25-30 October 1926 and adopted the Ibero-American Air Navigation Convention, generally referred to as the *Madrid Convention* (1926).[27] The Convention was not a success and was eventually ratified only by Argentina, Costa Rica, the Dominican Republic, El Salvador, Mexico and Spain. Argentina and Spain renounced the Convention by 1933 and joined the Paris Convention, thus the Madrid Convention never came into force. It did not bring about any innovations in legal terms and practically repeated *verbatim* the text of the Paris Convention, while omitting all references to the League of Nations and the Permanent Court of International Justice. It was no more than the result of political posturing of Spain trying to assert its leadership in Latin America.

2.4 THE HAVANA CONVENTION 1928

Another attempt at the codification of air law on a regional basis was made by the Commercial Aviation Commission of the Pan-American Union. The convention was adopted at the sixth Pan-American Conference in Havana on 20 January 1928 and has been known as the *Convention on Commercial Aviation – the Havana Convention* 1928. It differs considerably from the Paris (1919) and Madrid (1926) Conventions, which dealt with the technical and operational aspects of aviation and left the establishment of international routes and the granting of traffic rights to particular bilateral or multilateral negotiations. The Havana Convention dealt in a most liberal manner with the traffic rights and provided that aircraft of a contracting State are to be permitted to discharge passengers and cargo at any airport – authorized as a port of entry – in any other contracting State, and to take on passengers and cargo destined to any other contracting State. The practical impact of this provision would amount to multilateral granting of the "five freedoms of the air", a concept to be addressed later. The Havana Convention – unlike the Paris Convention (1919) – did not provide for the establishment of a permanent body and did not contain any technical Annexes. The Havana Convention attracted sixteen States – the USA and all Latin American States except Argentina, Paraguay and Peru, members of the ICAN. The main beneficiary of the Convention was the USA with its fast advancing aviation technology and growing international network of regular flights. The Convention is no

---

27   CIANA – Convencion Ibero-Americana de Navegacion Aerea.

longer applicable,[28] but its liberal handling of the traffic rights still inspires partisans of the "open skies" and free competition of air transport services in a borderless world.

2.5   THE CHICAGO CONFERENCE 1944

During World War II (1939-1945) aviation technology developed rapidly and became a primary tactical and strategic weapon of destructive efficiency. New large multi-engine bombers fittingly called "flying fortresses" could carry heavy loads over long distances and were the technological forerunners of the post-war large transport aircraft capable to cross the oceans and vast continents with heavy load. Before the end of the war both sides of the conflict introduced jet-powered fighter aircraft indicative of the future potential of the jet technology. It is a sad fact that the military conflagration, the worst man-made catastrophe in human history, accelerated the development of aviation technology and possibly telescoped decades of research and development into a short period. The cost of this "progress" in human lives and suffering is hard to measure.

Many parts of the world were devastated by the war, communications were disrupted, and starvation, diseases and general chaos could be expected by the end of the war. The Allies fighting the Powers of the Axis (Berlin-Rome-Tokyo) subscribed to the aims of the Atlantic Charter signed between the USA and UK on 14 August 1941 "somewhere in the Atlantic" (Placentia Bay, Newfoundland, Canada) and confirmed their aims in the "Declaration of the United Nations" signed in Washington, D.C. on 1 January 1942. These "United Nations"[29] engaged in series of consultations during the war concerning the post-war arrangements, reconstruction and guarantees of lasting peace. The Conference in Dumbarton Oaks (Washington, D.C.) prepared the Charter of the United Nations eventually signed at San Francisco on 26 June 1945 creating a universal organization for the safeguarding of world peace and security. At the Conference of Bretton Woods in July 1944, the Allies agreed on the establishment of the International Bank for Reconstruction and Development and of the International Monetary Fund to secure the needs of reconstruction and prevent the devastating hyperinflation and other monetary crises that plagued Europe after the World War I. The conference at Hot Springs in May-June 1943 dealt with the agricultural production to assure post-war nutrition and led to the creation of the Food and Agriculture Organization (FAO). While the war was still raging in the European and Pacific battlefields, the Allies were earnestly arranging for the peace time needs. Restoring and regulating the post war air transport was also perceived

---

28   The States undertook to denounce it upon entry into force of the Chicago Convention (1944). "As between contracting States, the Chicago Convention supersedes the Paris and Habana Conventions" (Article 80).
29   This is the title assumed by the war-time allies fighting the powers of the Axis; it is not to be confused with the United Nations Organization created by the UN Charter only with effect from 24 October 1945.

as an urgent priority since aviation appeared to be the most effective and first available means of transport in the world of disrupted railway lines and destroyed roads.

On 11 September 1944 the President of the United States invited the representatives of 54 nations to meet at Chicago from 1 November to 7 December 1944 at an International Civil Aviation Conference to "make arrangements for the immediate establishment of provisional air routes and services" and "to discuss the principles and methods to be followed in the adoption of a new aviation convention".[30]

Of the fifty-four invited States only Saudi Arabia did not accept the invitation, while the USSR, although it accepted, their presence had been withdrawn before the Conference started. The absence of the USSR was felt as a major disappointment since the it represented the largest land territory in the world and was expected to play an important role in the post-war arrangements. This negative attitude of the USSR was perhaps an early sign of the "Cold War," mistrust and isolation, and the secretive USSR was not ready to open its airspace to international cooperation. The official reason given for the non-participation was that "among the nations taking part in the Conference are Switzerland, Spain and Portugal, countries which, for a number of years have subscribed to a hostile policy towards the Soviet Union".[31]

Since the occupied Denmark and Thailand were represented only by their Ministers with the rank of Ambassadors attending in their personal capacity, the total number of participating delegations was fifty-two.

The Chicago Conference represents a major landmark in the development of international air law and its results are up to the present time the fundamental source of law in the field of international civil aviation.

Many extensive commentaries have been published on the dynamics and final achievements of the Chicago Conference, the majority of them focusing on the aspects of political science and economics, in particular the competing philosophies of free competition or national protectionism in air transport services. These aspects are illustrative of the deeply conflicting interests of the States that were otherwise closely cooperating in the wartime aims.

The most noticeable cleavage of interests and proposals was manifest between the United States and the United Kingdom. The United States' economy and aviation production were robust while the United Kingdom was severely weakened by the war and

---

30 See *Proceedings of the International Civil Aviation Conference, Chicago, Ill, November 1 – December 7, 1944*, The Department of State, Vol. I and Vol. II, at Vol. I, pp. 11-13 (further referred to as "Proceedings").

31 *The Times*, London, 30 October 1944; cited in J. Schenkman, *International Civil Aviation Organization*, Librarie E. Droz, Geneva, 1955, p. 75. The Union of Soviet Socialist Republics (USSR) continued its boycott of the Convention and of ICAO until 1969 – some 13 years after the initial "destalinization" of the USSR and 25 years after the date of the Convention. The USSR finally became the 120th member of ICAO on 14 November 1970.

faced a collapse of its colonial empire. The United States developed during the war mammoth industrial capacity to build large bomber aircraft – a technology easily convertible to civilian design and use; the United Kingdom's industry produced efficient fighter aircraft but lagged behind in the production of large air transport equipment. The competing interests predictably influenced the competing proposals.

The United States favoured the freedom of air transport very much along the lines of the Havana Convention and the creation of an international aviation authority, the mandate of which would be limited to technical and consultative issues. Under such a scenario the US air carriers would have easily dominated the world air transport without facing, at least in the immediate post-war period, any substantial competition.

This "liberal" approach faced strong objections, in particular from the United Kingdom that wished to protect its vast colonial airspaces all around the globe. In extreme opposition to the US liberalism and free competition was the joint proposal by Australia and New Zealand for international State ownership and operation of civil air services on world trunk routes. The United Kingdom proposed to establish an international authority that would have discretionary power to allocate routes, fixing rates and determining frequencies. Canada's proposal was close to the UK approach of international regulation of the commercial rights. Briefly, the policy debates at the Chicago Conference confronted economic liberalism with national protectionism. Even at the present time – decades after the Chicago Conference – this fundamental dichotomy persists although the main players and characteristics may have changed.

No compromise could be found between the vastly different approaches and the Conference could have failed. After weeks of private discussions in the hotel rooms and with skilful diplomacy of the Canadian delegation chaired by C.D. Howe (Minister of Reconstruction) a way out of the impasse was found: the Convention would not govern the granting of traffic rights in international scheduled carriage by air but there would be two separate and distinct instruments, in addition to the main Convention, through which the States would mutually exchange, on a multilateral basis, reciprocal commercial rights referred to as "Freedoms of the Air".[32] It was sometimes claimed in the press of the period that the Chicago Conference was a "failure" because it did not reach an agreement on the granting of traffic rights. However, it is fair to say that the issue of traffic rights is a general problem of trade policies that go far beyond aviation alone and reflects the policy attitudes of States to economic cooperation and competition.

In the historic perspective it is clear that the Chicago Conference on International Civil Aviation was a significant success and that it prepared the legal regulation of international civil aviation for its remarkable development not only for the post-war period but in many respects till the present time.

---

32 See Appendix 6 to the book.

The Conference is to be credited with the preparation and adoption of the following instruments:
1. The Convention on International Civil Aviation opened for signature at Chicago on 7 December 1944.
2. The International Air Services Transit Agreement ("two freedoms agreement") opened for signature on the same date.
3. The International Air Transport Agreement ("five freedoms agreement") also opened for signature on the same date.
4. Recommendations, for example, a standard form of bilateral agreements for the exchange of air routes that assisted States in their bilateral negotiation and brought a high degree of consistency and uniformity into the practice.
5. An Interim Agreement on International Civil Aviation that bridged over the period before the entry into force of the Convention on International Civil Aviation and served as a constitution for the Provisional Civil Aviation Organization (PICAO).
6. Extensive "Drafts of Technical Annexes" (12 Annexes) documenting the scope of international consensus and cooperation in operational and technical matters of civil aviation.

"In the light of this record of achievement, it can safely be said that the International Civil Aviation Conference at Chicago was one of the most successful, productive, and influential international conferences ever held."[33]

---

33   Proceedings, Vol. I, p. 4; this statement was valid in its time, but several UN or ICAO-sponsored law-making Conferences were at least of equal importance and reached wide international acceptance.

3   Convention on International Civil Aviation (Chicago, 1944)

Pacta inter gentes omnimodo observanda sunt

This chapter will deal with the Convention as a multilateral instrument of international law and with its characteristics related to the
- depositary;
- authentic texts of the Convention;
- procedure for the amendment of the Convention;
- Parties to the Convention; and
- expulsion of a Member State.

The Convention commonly called the "Chicago Convention" is the primary source of public international air law. Adopted at the Chicago Conference on International Civil Aviation on 7 December 1944 by 52 States, it is currently in force for 193 States. It thus belongs to the most generally accepted multilateral law-making conventions (for example, the UN Charter has also been ratified by 193 Member States). The Convention is a monumental piece of international law-making drafted with great foresight. Nevertheless, it is only a product of balancing conflicting interests of its authors in the given historic time-frame and, like all international conventions, embodies the achievable common denominator of the political will of the negotiating States at the time of its drafting.

As an international instrument it is subject to the international law of treaties. The Vienna Convention on the Law of Treaties,[1] which codifies mainly the existing customary international law, sets forth the following provision relevant to the Chicago Convention:

> Article 5
> Treaties constituting international organizations and treaties adopted within an international organization.
> The present Convention applies to any treaty which is the constituent instrument of an international organization and to any treaty adopted within an international organization without prejudice to any relevant rules of the organization.

---

1   Signed on 23 May 1969, in force since 27 January 1980, text in 1155 U.N.T.S. 331, 8 I.L.M 679.

The Chicago Convention is a constituent instrument of the International Civil Aviation Organization (ICAO); the "relevant rules of the organization" mentioned in Article 5 of the Vienna Convention (1969) would be those referring to the procedure for the amendment of the Convention[2] through the mechanism of the ICAO Assembly under its applicable rules. The general rules of the law of treaties, including questions of interpretation, apply to the Chicago Convention.

The Chicago Convention basically consists of 4 major parts (Air Navigation, The International Civil Aviation Organization, International Air Transport and Final Provisions), and within these it contains 22 Chapters and 96 Articles. The Convention and its 19 Annexes exceed a total of 4,000 pages.

It is noteworthy that the Chicago Convention is almost symmetrically divided into two separate segments: the first (roughly Article 1 to 42, PART I; Chapters I to VI) represents an exhaustive codification and unification of public international law that replaces all previous sources of international law – the Paris Convention of 1919 and the Havana Convention of 1928. The second part (roughly Articles 43 to 96, PARTS II, III and IV; Chapters VII to XXII) represents a constitutional instrument of the International Civil Aviation Organization (ICAO) – a charter under which the organization was created and under which it is obliged to act.

The provisions of the Convention are mandatory since there is no provision permitting any reservations to the Convention.[3] The mandatory nature of the Convention is underlined by Article 82, in which the contracting States committed themselves to abrogate any inconsistent obligations and understandings and not to enter into any such obligations or understandings.

3.1 Depositary

The Government of the United States – the host of the Chicago Conference – is the depositary of the Convention. The depositary functions are performed by the Department of State of the US government that keeps custody of the original signed copy of the Convention, sends its certified true copies to the signatories and new parties and receives instruments of accession or of ratification and informs other parties of such actions. The

---

2 Amendment of the Chicago Convention regulated in Article 94 of the Chicago Convention and the Standing Rules of Procedure for the Assembly, ICAO Doc 7600/5.
3 The practice confirms that: on 15 February 1954 Yugoslavia deposited an instrument of ratification containing a reservation to Article 5 of the Convention; in view of many protests the depositary government did not accept the instrument and ICAO did not take any action to recognize Yugoslavia as a Member State. A new instrument of ratification without any reservation was deposited by Yugoslavia on 9 March 1960.

functions of the depositary are international in character and must be performed impartially.[4]

With the development of the UN system of international organizations it is becoming more and more common that the multilateral instruments elaborated within the framework of such organizations are not deposited with a State (it used to be customary to deposit an instrument with the government of the State hosting a conference that adopted it) but with the Chief Executive Officer (Director General or Secretary General) of the organization concerned. That stresses even more the international character of the depositary functions. All ICAO Assembly decisions since 1947 on the amendment of the Convention have been adopted in the form of Protocols deposited with the Secretary General of ICAO.

3.2 Authentic Texts of the Convention

Latin used to be historically the diplomatic language of conferences and conventions but starting with the Congress of Vienna in 1815 after the defeat of Napoleon's armies French became the exclusive language of diplomacy. After World War I with the creation of the League of Nations, the International Labour Organization (ILO) and of other bodies the English language emerged as a working language but did not reach an equal level of acceptance as French. (For instance, the first international private air law treaty, the Warsaw Convention [1929] was drafted only in French language.)

The Chicago Conference on International Civil Aviation is one of the turning points when the French international influence was weakened during the war and the States using the English language started to be internationally dominant. It was taken as a fact of life that the documentation for the Chicago Conference was prepared only in English and that all opening statements and discussions were also only in English.

At the second Plenary Session on 2 November 1944, the head of the Delegation of France, Mr. Max Hymans, speaking in French, regretted that [the rules and regulations] "did not recognize the historic right of the French language in failing to consider it one of the two official languages of the Conference. All international conventions since 1815 have been drawn up in French, the universal language of diplomacy". The presiding Adolf A. Berle, Assistant Secretary of State of the United States, politely listened to the statement, but through a possible misunderstanding took it for a motion seconded by China and put it to vote. A chorus of "AYES" approved the report that only English would be the language of the Conference and the point raised by France met with "silence".[5] *Sic transit gloria…*

---

4 See Articles 76 and 77 of the Vienna Convention on the Law of Treaties (1969).
5 See Proceedings, Vol. I., p. 52.

and further developments continue to establish English as the international language of aviation but – without any nationalistic overtones – the "English" used in aviation operations and international meetings is not necessarily the language of Shakespeare but just a simplified convenient means of communication that does not possess any "nationality".

It is a historic fact that the Convention on International Civil Aviation and other instruments were prepared by the Conference and opened for signature on 7 December 1944 only in the English version. The Conference did not enjoy the luxury of staffing and time available to the Dumbarton Oaks negotiation[6] that was preparing the Charter of the United Nations at that time in five languages: English, French, Spanish, Russian and Chinese as equally authentic versions.

The Chicago Conference was well aware of the need to prepare authentic texts of the Convention in other languages but "deferred" the action. The final clause of the Convention reads:

> DONE at Chicago the seventh day of December 1944, in the English language. A text drawn up in the English, French and Spanish languages, each of which shall be of equal authenticity, shall be open for signature at Washington, D.C. Both texts shall be deposited in the archives of the Government of the United States of America, and certified copies shall be transmitted by that Government to the governments of all States which may sign or adhere to this Convention.

This provision relating to the French and Spanish texts proved to be less than understandable. For many years it was not clear who should prepare the French and Spanish texts of the Convention and make sure that such texts are "authentic". The US government as the depositary had a working text in French and Spanish prepared but had no means to guarantee its "authenticity". In fact, the Convention was not clear about who was to prepare such an authentic text, only that it should be open for signature in Washington, D.C. After years of hesitation it was agreed that a text can be truly authenticated only by an international Conference of plenipotentiaries in the form of a Protocol that would be subject to ratification by States. Such a Diplomatic Conference was convened in conjunction with the 16th Session of the ICAO Assembly in September 1968 in Buenos Aires – almost 24 years after the Chicago Conference. On 24 September 1968 the Conference adopted "Protocol on the Authentic Trilingual Text of the Convention on

---

6   The Dumbarton Oaks (a mansion in Georgetown, Washington D.C.) conversations held from 21 August to 7 October 1944, were the first concrete steps taken towards an international organization for the maintenance of peace and security.

International Civil Aviation (Chicago 1944)".[7] The Protocol came into force the very same day because a sufficient number of signatories signed "without reservation as to acceptance".

In 1969, the USSR adhered to the Chicago Convention and one of their first pressing policy demands was to have an authentic text of the Convention in the Russian language and to introduce the Russian language as a working language of the organization. The USSR prepared a Russian text and the question was raised how to have it authenticated. The 21st Session of the ICAO Assembly in September 1974 requested the Council of ICAO "to undertake the necessary measures for the preparation of the authentic text of the Convention on International Civil Aviation in the Russian language, with the aim of having it approved not later than the year 1977".

It soon became clear that the precedent of the Buenos Aires Protocol of 1968 could not be fully followed. In the case of the French and Spanish texts there was an explicit provision in the final clause of the Convention foreseeing the existence of such texts. However, with respect to the Russian text there was no constitutional basis in the Convention itself and it was essential to create it first by amending the final clause of the Convention to provide for the existence of the authentic Russian text.

A Diplomatic Conference held in conjunction with the 22nd Session of the Assembly adopted, on 30 September 1977 a "Protocol on the Authentic Quadrilingual Text of the Convention on International Civil Aviation (Chicago, 1944)".[8] The Protocol stipulated for its entry into force a cumulative condition that twelve States sign it without reservation as to acceptance or accept it "and after entry into force of the amendment of the final clause of the Convention which provides that the text of the Convention in the Russian language is of equal authenticity".[9] It took full twenty-two years before the Protocol came into force on 16 September 1999, long after the USSR ceased to exist, the Russian Federation became its international successor and the ex-Soviet republics became independent States, several of them abandoning the use of the Russian language at international meetings.

An identical procedure had to be followed with regard to the Arabic authentic text of the Convention – the Final Clause of the Convention was amended by the 31st Session of the ICAO Assembly on 29 September 1995 to refer also to the existence of an Arabic authentic text[10] and a "Protocol on the Authentic Quinqueligual Text of the Convention on International Civil Aviation (Chicago, 1944)"[11] was opened for signature on that date.

---

7   Text in ICAO Doc 7300/9, pp. 45-47.
8   Text in ICAO Doc 7300/9, pp. 48-51.
9   Article IV, 1) of the Protocol; that Assembly also adopted an amendment of the final clause of the Chicago Convention to provide for the existence of a Russian authentic text.
10 ICAO Doc 9664.
11 ICAO Doc 9663.

The Protocol is not yet in force since the required number of ratifications was not yet obtained for that amendment of the Final Clause of the Convention.[12]

Finally, the same process took place with respect to the Chinese authentic text of the Convention: the Final Clause of the Convention was again amended by the 32nd Session of the Assembly on 1 October 1998 to provide for a legal basis to the existence of the Chinese authentic text.[13] A Diplomatic Conference held in conjunction with the 32nd Session of the Assembly from 28 September to 1 October 1998 adopted "Protocol on the Authentic Six-Language Text of the Convention on International Civil Aviation (Chicago, 1944)".[14] Again, this Protocol is not yet in force.[15]

The proliferation of the authentic texts of the Convention hardly serves other purpose than national pride and status of the countries requesting the existence of such texts. The texts are not universally accepted since under Article 94 a) of the Convention the amendments of the Convention come into force only "with respect of States which have ratified such amendments". So far no disagreement has been recorded on the meaning of any provision in different language versions.

3.3 Amendment of the Convention

The Convention on International Civil Aviation is a multilateral international treaty and its amendment is governed in general by the international law of treaties; however, since the Convention is a constituent instrument of an international organization, the Vienna Convention on the Law of Treaties applies to it "without prejudice to any relevant rules of the organization".[16] What are those "relevant rules of the organization"? This question was never formally raised or answered in the practice of ICAO. There is no doubt that Article 94 of the Convention which specifically deals with the amendment of the Convention is one such "rule". It states:

> *Article 94*
> Amendment of Convention: a) Any proposed amendment to this Convention must be approved by a two-thirds vote of the Assembly and shall then come into force in respect of States which have ratified such amendment when

---

12 The Final Clause as amended requires 122 ratifications; by December 2022 only 76 ratifications have been deposited.
13 ICAO Doc 9722.
14 ICAO Doc 9721.
15 This Final Clause requires 124 ratifications; by December 2022 only 57 ratifications have been deposited.
16 "The present Convention applies to any treaty which is the constituent instrument of an international organization and to any treaty adopted within an international organization without prejudice to any relevant rules of the organization". Vienna Convention on the Law of Treaties (1969), Article 5.

ratified by the number of contracting States specified by the Assembly. The number so specified shall not be less than two-thirds of the total number of contracting States. b) If in its opinion the amendment is of such a nature as to justify this course, the Assembly in its resolution recommending adoption may provide that any State which has not ratified within specified period after the amendment has come into force shall thereupon cease to be a member of the Organization and party to the Convention.

The words "relevant rules of the organization" in Article 5 of the Vienna Convention (1969) cannot be interpreted narrowly as referring only to a provision or provisions of the Convention itself relating to the process of amendment; the Vienna Convention on the Law of Treaties does not refer to a "provision" of the treaty which is a constituent instrument of an international organization but in general to the "relevant rules of the organization" – i.e., any regulatory rules adopted by the organization separately from the text of the Convention itself. Thus, the process of an amendment of the Chicago Convention must comply with the Standing Rules of Procedure of the ICAO Assembly[17] and with the policies adopted by the Organization. Article 94 of the Convention clarifies that an amendment is not to be adopted by a Diplomatic Conference but by the supreme body of the organization – the Assembly.

The wording of Article 94 a) of the Convention caused considerable difficulties in interpretation which were to a large degree clarified by subsequent changes of the Standing Rules of Procedure of the Assembly of ICAO.[18] The expression "two-thirds vote of the Assembly" is to be construed as meaning "two-thirds of the total number of Contracting States represented at the Assembly and qualified to vote at the time the vote is taken". For the purpose of establishing this total, all Delegations are counted if they presented valid credentials except those Delegations who had given notice, in writing or otherwise, of their departure or withdrawal from the Assembly prior to the time when the vote is taken as well as Delegations of States whose voting power is under suspension at the time the vote is taken. These provisions are to be read in the context of Article 48 c) of the Convention, according to which "a majority of the contracting States is required to constitute a quorum for the meetings of the Assembly". With the current membership of ICAO standing at 193, the quorum of the Assembly is 97 States; the two-thirds majority of those States (65) would be, in theory, entitled to approve an amendment to the Convention

---

17   ICAO Doc 7600, see Appendix 2 to this book.
18   Rule 10 d) on the time-limits ("at least ninety days before opening the Session") for the inclusion of a proposal for an amendment of the Convention into the Provisional Agenda of the Session; Rule 53 governs the interpretation of the expression "two-thirds vote" in Article 94 of the Convention.

even if such a majority represents just one-third of the total membership of the Organization.

It should be noted that the ICAO Assemblies never used the provision of paragraph b) of Article 94 to compel States to ratify an amendment under the threat of ceasing to be party to the Convention and member of the Organization – evidence of the predominant interest in the universality of the membership in ICAO and need for universal application of the legal framework created by the Convention.

"Approval" of an amendment by the Assembly does not lead automatically to its entry into force. Any amendment to the Convention comes into force only when ratified by the number of Contracting States specified by the Assembly; the number so specified must not be less than two-thirds of the total number of Contracting States. In the history of ICAO, the Assembly without exception always specified exactly two-thirds of the total number of Contracting States, the constitutional minimum, and never required a higher number of ratifications. Over the years the absolute number of ratifications so required varied in accordance with the growing membership of the Organization; this leads to a paradoxical result that some amendments to the Convention are "in force" although they have not been ratified by two-thirds of the current number of Contracting States.

An amendment to a multilateral instrument of almost universal character is becoming in practice more and more difficult. The Paris Convention on the Regulation of Aerial Navigation (1919) – the direct predecessor of the Chicago Convention– required that any amendments be ratified by all Parties.[19] This principle of unanimity is clearly impracticable in the current circumstances and was rightly rejected in the deliberations of the Chicago Conference. However, the principle of unanimity still survives in a modified form and no State can be bound by an amendment to which it did not give its specific consent. Article 94 a) spells out clearly that an amendment comes into force only "in respect of States which have ratified such amendment"; the principle *pacta tertiis nec nocent nec prosunt*[20] is thus fully respected. The consequences of this "concealed unanimity"[21] rule are far-reaching because the subsequent amendments of the Convention may result in its atomization into different instruments binding upon different groups of States and lead in fact to an institutionalized disunification of law.

The question whether amendments apply for consenting States *inter se* or *erga omnes* was raised in the practice of the Organization with respect to those amendments of the Convention which refer to the constitutional structure of the Organization, specifically to the composition of the Council. The original text of the Convention provides for twenty-

---

19 Article 34 of the Paris Convention (1919).
20 "A treaty does not create either obligations or rights for a third State without its consent". Vienna Convention on the Law of Treaties (1969), Section 4, General rule regarding third States, Article 34.
21 M. Milde, "Chicago Convention – 45 Years Later: a Note on Amendments", *Annals of Air and Space Law*, Vol. XIV (1989), p. 207.

one Members of the Council; the dramatic growth in the membership of the Organization required more effective representation of different groups of States and the number of Council Members was increased to twenty-seven,[22] then to thirty,[23] then to thirty-three,[24] then to thirty-six,[25] and finally, to forty.[26]

None of the amendments of Article 50 a) of the Convention on the composition of the Council is in force for all Contracting States of the Organization. This could lead to a paradoxical conclusion that for some States the Council is still composed of twenty-one Members, for others, of twenty-seven or thirty, and for further others, of thirty-three or thirty-six (even the decision on forty seats has not yet entered into force); furthermore, a problem could arise whether a State which had not ratified an amendment increasing the membership of the Council could vote or be a candidate in the election of an enlarged Council. This problem has been addressed only once in a most informal fashion at the 14th Session of the Assembly in 1962 when the Plenary accepted without vote and without a recorded objection the view of the Executive Committee that any State participating in the Assembly could be a candidate in the election of the enlarged Council and is entitled to vote in the election, whether or not it had ratified the amendment to the Convention.[27] Never thereafter was this issue addressed in ICAO and it would be unjustified to refer to it as to "established practice".

This pragmatic experience which in some respects has been perpetuated since 1962 leads some to a conclusion that amendments of the Convention dealing with the institutional problems of the Organization as such could be deemed to come into force *erga omnes* and not only *inter se* in respect of States which have ratified the amendment. However, such a conclusion would be legally incorrect. The Convention in Article 94 clearly stipulates that the amendments do not come into force for States that have not ratified them. Political convenience could have motivated the presiding officer of the Assembly (then President of the Council and a jurist himself) and his legal assistants not to raise the issue prior to the act of voting.[28] However, a repeated "wrong" cannot create a rule of law. The President of the Council and other members of the ICAO Secretariat are obliged to draw the attention of delegations to the applicable rules and prevent any violations of the Convention or other rules.

---

22 13th (Extraordinary) Session of the Assembly, 19 June 1961.
23 17th (A) (New York) (Extraordinary) Session of the Assembly, 12 March 1971.
24 21st Session of the Assembly, 14 October 1974.
25 28th (Extraordinary) Session of the Assembly, 22-26 October 1990.
26 39th Session of the Assembly, 1 October 2016, Resolution A39-4.
27 14th Session of the Assembly, Minutes of the Plenary, Doc 8269, A14-P/21, paragraph 31, September 1962.
28 M. Milde, "Chicago Convention at Sixty – Stagnation or Renaissance?", *Annals of Air and Space Law*, Vol. XXIX (2004), pp. 443-471, at p. 453; See also C-WP/12594 and the discussion in C-MIN 177/5, 13/4/06.

If there is a wish that institutional amendments to the Convention should be applicable *erga omnes*, a good precedent for an amendment of Article 94 could be found in Article 316 (5) of the UN Convention on the Law of the Sea of 1982[29] that states:

> 5. Any amendment relating exclusively to activities in the Area and any amendment to Annex VI shall enter into force for all States Parties one year following the deposit of instrument of ratification by three fourths of the State Parties.

The procedure for the amendment of the Chicago Convention is thus the "classic" (and now somewhat antiquated) *consensual* method; the amendment does not come into force for *all* States once it is ratified by the prescribed constitutional majority; the amendment does not have an *erga omnes* effect and comes into force only "with respect of States which have ratified such amendment". In theory it may be argued that the classical *consensual* method fully respects the sovereignty of States and that States cannot be bound by the amendment unless they specifically ratify it; this method also appears to respect the principle of the law of treaties that treaties do not create either obligations or rights for a third State without its consent. While this principle is fully justifiable for the multilateral treaties in general, the specific nature of the treaties which are constituent instruments of international organizations require a different approach: the very substance of an international organization requires a unity of will to create a functioning mechanism, a "club" of States following the shared aims, principles and expectations in a particular field of activities and in such an organization the States willingly accept a certain limitation of their sovereign powers by accepting the rule of a constitutional majority in the decision-making. The requirement of unanimity in multilateral decision-making was the feature of congresses and conferences of the 19th century and survived to some degree in the League of Nations[30] (and was possibly one of the reasons of the League's inefficiency and eventual collapse).

The Charter of the United Nations was adopted only six months after the Chicago Convention but the provision on its amendment is decidedly more modern and responsive to the needs of a global international organization; it is based on the *erga omnes* principle and an amendment comes into force "for all Members of the United Nations" when adopted by a vote of two thirds of the members of the General Assembly and ratified by two thirds of the Members of the United Nations, including all the permanent members of the Security Council.[31] The application of the *erga omnes* principle is a better safeguard

---

29 See below, at Section 4.1.
30 Covenant of the League of Nations, Article 5; text in LNTS Volume 1, Geneva, 1920.
31 Article 108 of the Charter of the United Nations.

of the continuing homogenous nature of the organization; it does not contravene the axiomatic principle of sovereignty of States when the States in the interests of continuing efficiency of their common organization expressly and freely accepted the *erga omnes* effect of a majority decision.

A similar provision reflecting the legislative (rather than consensual) nature of the amendments adopted by the defined constitutional majority will be found in the Statute of the International Atomic Energy Agency (IAEA),[32] the Constitution of the International Labour Organization (ILO),[33] the Convention on the International Maritime Organization (IMO),[34] the Articles of Association of the International Monetary Fund (IMF),[35] the Articles of Agreement of the International Bank for Reconstruction and Development (IBRD),[36] the Constitution of the United Nations Educational, Scientific and Cultural Organization (UNESCO),[37] the Constitution of the World Health Organization (WHO),[38] the Constitution of the Food and Agriculture Organization (FAO)[39] and the Constitution of the United Nations Industrial Development Organization (UNIDO).[40]

The consensual principle regarding the amendment of an international treaty which is a constituent instrument of an international organization appears to be obsolete and harmful; if certain amendments are in force for some States and not for others, the unity and homogeneity of the organization itself is jeopardized and the practical result is dis-unification of law and splitting the organization into groups of States governed by different rules.

The ICAO experience well illustrates this point: since 1947 the ICAO Assemblies adopted numerous amendments to the Chicago Convention; most of them have come into force but none of them is in force for all contracting States of ICAO. Moreover, since the two-thirds majority of contracting States whose ratification is required under Article 94 of the Convention has changed with the growing membership of the organization over the years, some of these amendments are now in force for a number of States which does not represent the statutory majority of the two thirds of the current membership. This could, at least in theory, lead to absurd results that for some States the Council should still be

---

32 Article XVIII C (i) and (ii), text in 276 UNTS 3, however, a State may withdraw from the Agency whenever it is unwilling to accept an amendment (Article XVIII D).
33 Article 36, text in 15 UNTS 35.
34 Article 66 and Article 71, text in 289 UNTS 48, Part XVIII (signature and acceptance).
35 Article XXVIII, text in 2 UNTS 39; the required majority is three-fifth of the members having 85% of the total voting power; however, in some defined cases acceptance by all members is required.
36 Article VIII, with the same majorities and exceptions as the IMF; text in 2 UNTS 1.
37 Article XIII, text in 4 UNTS 275.
38 Article XVII, text in 14 UNTS 185.
39 Article XX, (1-4), text in FAO Basic Texts, Vol. I (2017).
40 Article 23 (1-3), Chapter VI, text in UNIDO Basic Texts.

composed of twenty-one or twenty-seven or thirty or thirty-three members, that the Assembly should still hold an annual session, etc.

Another serious problem in the practice of ICAO is the fact that the amendments require an inordinately long time to come into force. The amendment introducing new Article 93*bis* took nearly fourteen years to come into force; the amendment of Article 48 a) of 1962 came into force thirteen years later; the amendment of the final clause of the Convention (to create a legal basis for the existence of an authentic Russian text of the Convention) was adopted in 1977 and came into force only twenty-two years later in 1999.

With the growing membership of ICAO the situation is bound to become more and more difficult since under the terms of Article 94 a higher number of ratifications is required to correspond to the two-thirds majority; with the current membership of 193 the minimum number of ratifications required under Article 94 is 129; to meet the parliamentary or other constitutional requirements for ratification in at least 129 States is a difficult and time consuming task under the best of circumstances when the amendment is uncontroversial and is supported by the political will of States as necessary and urgent. The likelihood of a speedy ratification will dramatically decrease if the amendment is controversial in nature or deemed to be only "cosmetic" or not urgent.

The procedure for the amendment will itself determine whether any initiatives for a major revision of the Convention are realistic and practicable. The experience of ICAO indicates that it would be desirable to amend Article 94 to bring it into harmony with the Charter of the United Nations and the constitutional instruments of many other specialized agencies by introducing the "legislative" (*erga omnes*) effect of all amendments. Furthermore, ICAO can learn from the practice of other agencies that amendments which do not create new specific obligations for Member States (*e.g.*, modification of the membership in different bodies, frequency of sessions and similar internal "institutional" elements of the organization) would come into force automatically upon approval by the Assembly without a requirement of ratification.[41]

Any proposed amendment of Article 94 would, of course, face all the current difficulties and would require long time to come into force before it would provide any tangible benefit for the organization. With respect to the procedure for the amendment of the Convention it would appear interesting to learn from the experience of the International Telecommunications Union (ITU); the International Telecommunications Convention is revised by the Plenipotentiary Conference when necessary and the revised text replaces the previous text of the Convention in its totality; thus the International Telecommunications Convention is kept up-to-date with the technology and policy and operational requirements by relatively frequent major revisions which maintain the unity and

---

41 This practice is embodied in the constitutional instruments of UNESCO (Article XIII. 1), FAO (Article XX. 2) and WMO (Part XV, Article 28 (b)).

homogeneity of the legal framework. A similar practice has been followed by the Universal Postal Union (UPU) where the Acts of the Congress upon their entry into force abrogate and replace all previous Acts and thus the unity of the modernized provisions is maintained.

The Charter of the United Nations[42] and the Statute of the International Atomic Energy Agency (IAEA)[43] foresee the convening of a General Conference for the revision of these instruments – a farsighted provision recognizing that the multilateral instruments will require a major general review at any appropriate time or at periodic intervals; the Chicago Convention does not contain a similar provision but there is no constitutional obstacle for the ICAO Assembly to convene such a general Conference or to prepare for it by studies in the Legal Committee or other body.

The leading policy of ICAO with respect to amendments of the Convention is reflected in Assembly Resolution A4-3 adopted at the 4th Session of the Assembly in 1950 – one of the very few resolutions of that period some two human generations ago that are still in force. That resolution reflected a very specific situation of that time when there were numerous competing proposals for the amendment of the Convention with respect to air transport, attempting to revisit the matters that did not marshal consensus at the Chicago Conference. In the given situation the Assembly felt that these matter were not "ready for immediate action" and "that no plans should be initiated in the near future for a general revision of the Convention". The Council was directed by the Assembly that it "should not itself initiate any proposals for amendment to the Convention for submission to the Assembly unless in the opinion of the Council it is urgent in character".

Resolution A4-3 also resolved that

> an amendment of the Convention may be appropriate when either or both of the following tests are satisfied: when it is proved necessary by experience, and when it is demonstrably desirable or useful.

Resolution A4-3 has been serving as a sacred "mantra" for decades and as an excuse for the entrenched leadership of ICAO for inaction and spurious claims that the Convention is untouchable and sacred. Such attitude also explains that the Organization for many decades in the past did not see any fresh blood in the leadership and that any attempt at innovation was deemed undesirable for the perpetuation of that situation. Yet, it must be recognized that the Convention adopted in 1944 by 52 of the current 193 Member States reflects only the historic time-frame of 1944 and cannot take account of the vast geopolitical, technical and economic changes that have taken place since 1944. Updating

---

42 Amendments, Chapter XVIII, Articles 108-109.
43 Amendments and withdrawals, Article XVIII, A-B-C.

and modernization of the Convention should become a priority in the work plans of ICAO.[44]

3.4 Parties to the Convention

The Chicago Convention was adopted by the war-time allies calling themselves "the United Nations", by States associated with them and by invited States that remained neutral during the war. It was signed at Chicago on behalf of 52 States and came into force by the ratification of twenty-six signatories.[45] Signatories could accept the Convention by ratification, others only by adherence.

The Convention was not generally open to adherence by all States but only by "members of the United Nations",[46] States associated with them and States that remained neutral during the war conflict.[47] Thus the Convention defined a "closed club" of potential parties. The States so defined could adhere to the Convention and thus become members of the Organization without any special admission procedure.[48]

The Convention enabled admission of "other States" – a term that designated essentially the "enemy States".[49] Admission of such States required

i) "approval by any general international organization set up by the nations to preserve peace" (this was so formulated in anticipation of the creation of the United Nations Organization); and

ii) four-fifth vote of the Assembly and subject to conditions prescribed by the Assembly; and

iii) with a further provison that in each case the assent of any State invaded or attacked "during the present war" by the State seeking admission shall be necessary.

The Convention contained strict safeguards against the "enemy States", including the requirement of unanimity of all States invaded or attacked.

---

44   See paragraph below 7.4: "Does the Chicago Convention Require Modernization?"; M. Milde, "Chicago Convention at Sixty: Stagnation or Renaissance?", *Annals of Air and Space Law*, Vol. XXIX (2004), pp. 1-4.
45   Article 91 of the Chicago Convention.
46   Article 92 a) – in 1944 the expression "United Nations" referred to the war-time alliance of States and must not be confused with the United Nations Organization established by the UN Charter signed at San Francisco on 26 June 1945 and coming into force on 24 October 1945 – after the Chicago Conference.
47   The scores of newly independent States in the decolonization process were accepted to facilitate accession to the Convention without any formalities because they were deemed to be "neutral" in the sense of Article 92.
48   Compare the practice of the United Nations (among others) where admission is effected by a decision of the General Assembly on the recommendation of the Security Council (requiring unanimity of permanent members) – Article 4 (2) of the UN Charter.
49   Article 93 of the Chicago Convention.

The practical application of these "admission" procedures varied over the time: in 1947 Italy – a former ally of Germany – was admitted by resolution A1-5 without any conditions. Austria and Finland were admitted in 1948 by Resolutions A2-3 and A2-4, respectively, with a statement that the special proviso on States attacked or invaded did not apply to them. In 1953 by Resolution A7-2 the Assembly admitted Japan without any objections.

In 1955 the Federal Republic of Germany (FRG) applied for admission – at a time of advanced Cold War when the USSR had its client puppet State in East Germany. It was feared that at the 10th Assembly (1956) in Caracas, the delegations of Poland and Czechoslovakia – then the only East European Member States of ICAO and both under USSR influence – would block the admission of the FRG as States "invaded" by Germany. However, to a general surprise a colossal "diplomatic blunder" changed the outcome – Poland failed to send a delegation to the Caracas Assembly and the Czechoslovak delegation had its voting power suspended under Article 62 of the Convention since it failed to discharge its financial obligations to the Organization for more than two years. The FRG was thus admitted by Resolution A9-1 without even a mention of the specific proviso in Article 93.

With the passage of time the terms of Article 93 became more and more obsolete – former "enemy States" became members of the United Nations and the reasons for their special treatment lost their relevance. The admission of Romania – also a former "enemy State" – in 1965 did not even call for an Assembly Resolution. Romania by that time was a member of the United Nations and the Executive Committee of the Assembly simply declared that – if and when the delegation of Romania arrives, they will be seated as a contracting State.[50] Shortly thereafter, the delegation of Romania entered the conference hall and was welcomed by applause. A similar treatment was accorded in 1971 to Hungary and Bulgaria – the last "ex-enemy" States. It could now be concluded that Article 93 of the Convention is a historic relic that has no further legal relevance. In any future revision of the Convention Article 93 should be deleted.

3.5   EXPULSION OF A STATE PARTY

The Convention did not originally contain any provision on the possibility to debar a State from membership or to expel it from the Organization. That became a problem in 1947 when negotiations started about ICAO – that just came into existence on 4 April 1947 – being brought into relationship with the United Nations Organization as a "specialized agency" under Article 57 of the UN Charter. In the United Nations strong political objections were raised about the membership of "fascist" Spain in international

---

50   ICAO Doc 8516, A15-P/5, p. 124.

organizations and ICAO was compelled to initiate an amendment of the Chicago Convention at its very first Assembly Session on 27 May 1947.

The new Article 93*bis*[51] provides that a State shall automatically cease to be a member of ICAO if the UN General Assembly recommends it to be debarred from international agencies or if such State is expelled from the United Nations. It must be noted that ICAO is not entitled to act on its own but must strictly follow the UN directives. This amendment came into force, in respect of States which ratified it, only on 20 March 1961 by which time Spain was fully integrated in the UN and ICAO. At present (December 2022), 119 ICAO Member States have ratified this amendment – a paradox when the current two-thirds majority would be 129. Article 93*bis* of the Convention was never applied in the practice of ICAO. There were occasional attempts to ostracize a Member State (South Africa for its policy of apartheid, Israel in Middle East conflicts) but there was never a specific action by the United Nations that would have permitted ICAO to act. It should be noted that, under Articles 5 and 6 of the UN Charter, an action could be taken against a Member State by the General Assembly upon recommendation of the Security Council; the requirement of unanimity of the permanent members of the Security Council under Article 27 of the UN Charter thwarted any action proposed within the United Nations.

The very idea of expelling a State from a general international organization goes contrary to the needs for universality of the international body and the requirements of global international cooperation.

---

51 The designation "*bis*" is often misunderstood. In Latin it means "twice" or "for the second time" and it is used in the legal drafting to avoid renumbering of numerous provisions when a new provision is inserted. Any additional inserted articles would be marked *ter, quatter, quinquies, sexies,* …

4   International Legal Regime of the Airspace

A iure nemo recedere praesumitur

While the legal regime of the airspace was the subject of extensive theoretical studies and discussion in the early 20th century, the governments of States remained for a long time uncommitted and did not define their position. This was evident at the abortive Paris Conference (1910) where the delegations of States carefully avoided any discussion of the general legal status of the airspace – specifically the question whether the airspace is to be "free" by analogy with the high seas or whether it should be subject to the sovereignty of the territorial power.

For some period of time the leading academic theory was that formulated in 1901 by the French jurist Paul Fauchille in his pioneering article "Le domain aerien et le regime juridique des aerostats"[1] and thereafter further developed by him in the fora of the *Institute de Droit International* and of the *International Law Association* until the outbreak of World War I.

In substance, Fauchille's views were that the airspace should be "free" as the high seas and that the territorial powers should have reserved powers up to a certain altitude above their territory – initially set at 300 m (the height of the Eiffel Tower – the tallest building of that time), later 330 m, still later 1500 m as a "buffer" by analogy with the territorial sea to protect the special interest of the State. There were other jurists – admittedly a minority – who advocated complete sovereignty of States over the airspace above their territory.

As always, it was not the legal theory that created the rules of international law but the interests and the political will of sovereign States. Regardless of any legal theories States forcefully protected their territories against incursions of foreign military aircraft well before World War I. That war proved the vulnerability of States to aerial attacks and the airspace was strongly defended by the belligerents as well as neutrals and aircraft were perceived as a potential danger to the security of the State.

As seen above, the Paris Conference (1919) without much discussion and without any objection "recognized" the complete and exclusive sovereignty of "every" State (not only "contracting" State) over the airspace above its territory. It is a historic reality that this principle of international law which is the leading axiom of international air law was born in the shadow of a major armed conflict and carries the marks of that conflict.

---

1   *Revue generale de droit international public*, 1901, p. 414 *et seq.*

At the 1944 Chicago Conference no discussion was recorded on this principle and the Convention on International Civil Aviation in its Article 1 proclaims:

Article 1
The contracting States recognize that every State has complete and exclusive sovereignty over the airspace above its territory.

Again, the spectre of the devastating World War II (1939-1945) looms over this principle that has been the cornerstone of all aspects of international air law. The obvious concern for security expressed in this principle can be used to protect also other interests of a State; it can become one of the arguments attempting to justify economic protectionism.

This leading principle of international air law must be read in the context of other peremptory rules of the general international law, among them the fundamental principles embodied in the UN Charter:
– sovereign equality of States;
– fulfilment of obligations in good faith;
– settlement of differences by peaceful means;
– cooperation among States;
– duty to refrain in their international relations from the threat or use of force;
– duty to give assistance to the UN in actions taken in accordance with the Charter.[2]

Again, this basic principle is to be interpreted and applied in the spirit of the Preamble to the Chicago Convention that stresses the role of international civil aviation in the preservation of friendship and understanding among nations and peoples, urges States to avoid friction and to promote that cooperation between nations and peoples upon which the peace of the world depends and calls for the development of international civil aviation in a safe and orderly manner and on the basis of equality of opportunity to operate soundly and economically.

In this wider legal framework it appears justified to interpret the principle of complete and exclusive territorial sovereignty over the airspace not as a restrictive and self-centred entitlement but rather as a right that is to be exercised for mutual international benefit and cooperation.

The concept of complete and exclusive air sovereignty means in the first place the *exclusive jurisdiction* of the State concerned to adopt laws and regulations relating to the status and uses of its airspace and to implement such laws by administrative decisions and sanctions – all to the exclusion of any other State's jurisdiction. There is no "freedom to fly"

---

2   Chapter I, Articles 1-3 of the UN Charter.

– every aspect of aviation is regulated in great detail – and foreign aircraft have no right to enter the airspace of another State otherwise than in conformity with the applicable laws and regulations.

International air transport is possible only on the basis of special legal arrangements between the States of origin, overflight and destination – either in the form of bilateral or multilateral treaties as a "concession" or "privilege" and on a reciprocal basis. Even the forms of such reciprocity may vary – from the equality of opportunity to a strictly balanced equality of advantage. The questions of international air transport will be dealt with in Chapter 6 below.

4.1 Territory

The term "territory" as used in Article 1 of the Convention is not self-explanatory and its definition is partially given in Article 2:

> Article 2
> For the purposes of this Convention the territory of a State shall be deemed to be the land areas and territorial waters adjacent thereto under the sovereignty, suzerainty, protection or mandate of such State.

The reference to "suzerainty, protection or mandate" is a vestige of the colonial times or the system of the League of Nations mandates and has no legal relevance at present. The "land area" includes not only the land mass but also all islands, internal waters and lakes.

The territorial waters under the Convention are an integral part of the "territory" and the airspace above them is subject to complete and exclusive sovereignty of the coastal State. The drafters of the Convention, basing themselves on the uncodified customary law of the sea as it existed in 1944, felt compelled to draft this provision as a legal "fiction" ("shall be deemed" and "for the purposes of this Convention"). The Convention does not offer a definition of "territorial waters" and we have to look for explanation into the international law of the sea. The current international law of the sea is codified in the United Nations Convention on the Law of the Sea (UNCLOS)[3] signed on 10 December 1982 in Montego Bay, Jamaica and in force as of 16 November 1994.

In Article 2 the UNCLOS states:

---

3   UN Treaty Series, Vol. 1833, p. 3.

> *Article 2*
> *Legal status of the territorial sea, of the airspace over the territorial sea and of its bed and subsoil*
> (1) The sovereignty of a coastal State extends, beyond its land territory and internal waters and, in the case of an archipelagic State, its archipelagic waters, to an adjacent belt of sea, described as the territorial sea. (2) This sovereignty extends over the airspace over the territorial sea as well as to its bed and subsoil. (3) The sovereignty over the territorial sea is exercised subject to this Convention and to other rules of international law.

UNCLOS gives us, in the first place, a definition of the territorial sea and confirms that the coastal State possesses sovereignty over that territorial sea, including the airspace over it. In paragraph 3 of Article 2 UNCLOS refers to "other rules of international law" with respect to the exercise of sovereignty and that includes the Chicago Convention – an important reference since the Chicago Convention does not grant the "right of innocent passage" to foreign aircraft over the territorial sea while the UNCLOS gives that right to all foreign ships, including the military ships.

The extent of the territorial sea was traditionally deemed to be three nautical miles from the coastline – the range of naval cannons of the past. However, the breadth of the territorial sea was lately disputed among several States and some of them made excessive demands of up to 200 miles to protect their fisheries interests. The UNCLOS took care of the special economic interests by creating the Exclusive Economic Zone (EEZ) up to 200 miles but put a restriction on the extent of the territorial sea – under Article 13 of UNCLOS every State has the right to establish the breadth of its territorial sea up to a limit not exceeding twelve nautical miles,[4] measured from the defined baselines. There was no consensus at the UN Conference on the exact breadth of the territorial sea and only the maximum limit was defined. In some cases, however, the twelve miles' limit would not be practicable where the coasts of two States are opposite or adjacent to each other. In such cases a median line is to be determined, which is equidistant from the base lines of each of the two States.[5]

To determine the frontiers of the sovereign airspace of a State one has to draw an imaginary perpendicular line from each point of the frontier of the land mass and of the territorial sea leading to the centre of the Earth. The resulting irregular cone defines the national airspace.

A logical question then arises: how high does the national airspace reach? Is there a horizontal limit of that airspace? Many views have been expressed on this issue that

---

4 One nautical mile is 1,852.2 metres long, that is, 12 nautical miles equal 22.2 kilometres.
5 Article 15 of UNCLOS.

transcends air law and touches upon the field of the law of space applications. There is no answer to this question in the positive international law since States have not found it necessary so far to formulate rules on the delimitation of the airspace and outer space.

A pragmatic view should be that this question has no practical relevance at present since it did not attract a decision by the international community. Air law deals with aviation – *i.e.*, with the aeronautical uses of the airspace. Hence, the interest of current air law should be limited to such human activities that use the buoyancy given to flying machines by the air. Beyond that "supportive" airspace the current aviation activities do not reach. However, we cannot fail to remember that the development of technology facilitated suborbital flight, which makes this demarcation issue once again topical. In the near future commercial flights will be carried out via suborbital flights by the specialised operators.[6] The working definition of "suborbital flight" proposed by ICAO[7] and the "suborbital spaceflight activity" can be defined as: "any activity [intended to operate in outer space] involving a parabolic flight that is not intended to complete an orbit around Earth".[8]

4.2 Airspace over the Sea

The water (seas and oceans; in law: sea) covers about 70% of the Earth's surface, and a substantial portion of today's air navigation takes place in the airspace above the sea. The airspace superjacent to the vast areas of the sea shares and reflects the legal regime of the different areas and zones of the sea. It is therefore unavoidable to study the sources of maritime law to understand the legal regime of the airspace above the different areas and zones of the sea – since the Chicago Convention itself does not contain the answers.

The general source of the modern maritime law is the United Nations Convention on the Law of the Sea (UNCLOS) which is not only a codification of the general customary law of the sea but contains also substantive "progressive development" of international law in the spirit of the UN Charter.[9] Further to the subject of the territorial sea that is specifically mentioned in Article 2 of the Chicago Convention the UNCLOS is relevant for the application of the Chicago Convention.

---

6   See Virgin Galactic's SpaceShipTwo Unity 22 launched with Richard Branson on 12 July 2021. www.space.com/virgin-galactic-richard-branson-unity-22-launch-explained.
7   ICAO defines suborbital flight as a "flight up to a very high altitude which does not involve sending the vehicle into orbit". ICAO Council – 175th Session, Concept of Sub-orbital Flights, Working Paper C-WP/12436, 5 May 2005, p. 2.
8   Concept of Suborbital Flights: Information from the International Civil Aviation Organization (ICAO), paper A/AC.105/C.2/2010/CRP.9, presented at the 49th Session of the Legal Subcommittee of UNCOPUOS, 19 March 2010.
9   UN Charter, Article 13, 1. a.

4.2.1   High Seas

The largest area of the world seas and oceans is defined only indirectly in Article 86 of the UNCLOS as follows:

> The provisions of this Part apply to all parts of the sea that are not included in the exclusive economic zone, in the territorial waters of a state, or in the archipelagic waters of an archipelagic State.

The freedom of the high seas includes freedom of navigation and freedom of overflight[10] and no State may validly purport to subject any part of the high seas to its sovereignty. Consequently, the high seas and the airspace above are beyond the jurisdiction of any State. Nevertheless, there cannot be a legal vacuum in the airspace over the high seas and the "rules of the air" must safeguard the safety of aircraft sharing that airspace. Article 12 of the Chicago Convention in its third sentence stipulates that *"Over the high seas, the rules in force shall be those established under this Convention"*. It is within the law-making power of the ICAO Council (see 7.3.5.2) to determine, in the form of International Standards embodied in Annex 2 to the Chicago Convention, the regulation relating to the flight and manoeuvre of aircraft over the high seas, and the contracting States cannot validly depart from such standards. This is a unique situation when the executive body of a Specialized Agency can legislate, with a binding power for all States; but another practical solution is hardly imaginable – there is a need for a globally applicable standard, and at the same time no State could validly exercise its jurisdiction and issue its own standards over the high seas.

UNCLOS contains two references to "aircraft" in Part VII dealing with the high seas. One of them deals with *piracy* (Articles 100-107) and the other with *hot pursuit* (Article 111). Both these terms have no relevance to the Chicago Convention but it is worth noting that an act of piracy can be theoretically committed on the high seas or in the place outside the jurisdiction of any State by the crew or passengers of a private aircraft against another ship or aircraft. No such act has ever been recorded. "Hot pursuit" is even less relevant for civil aviation because this right may be exercised only by a warship or military aircraft or other aircraft clearly marked as being on governmental service.

---

10   Article 87, 1 (a-b).

4.2.2 Contiguous Zone

In a zone contiguous to its territorial sea and not extending beyond 24 nautical miles from the baselines from which the breadth of the territorial sea is measured, the coastal State may exercise control necessary to prevent infringements of its customs, fiscal, immigration or sanitary laws and regulations within its territory or territorial waters and punish such infringement.[11]

The practical meaning of this provision has not been addressed in theory or practice. The formulation of this provision would not rule out an action against a foreign aircraft (hydroplane) on the surface of the waters within the contiguous zone or even an interception of an aircraft in flight in that zone and requesting its landing at a suitable airport. There is no recorded experience concerning the relevance of the contiguous zone for civil aviation.

4.2.3 Straits Used for International Navigation

The UNCLOS formulated a delicately balanced regime for international straits where States have an interest in securing for themselves the freedom of navigation and overflight through or over the straits while the States bordering the straits have an interest to protect their territorial sea (which encompasses part or the totality of such straits) and to protect their security in these often strategically important geographic locations. The Convention has coined a new term in international law – "*regime of transit passage*" in straits used for international navigation, a compromise between "free transit" and "right of innocent passage".

Ships and *aircraft* enjoy the right of unimpeded transit passage in straits used for international navigation between one part of the high seas or an exclusive economic zone and another part of the high seas or an exclusive economic zone.[12] Transit passage means the freedom of *overflight* solely for the purpose of continuous and expeditious transit of the strait.

Aircraft in transit passage must "observe the *Rules of the Air* established by the International Civil Aviation Organization (ICAO) as they apply to civil aircraft" and must "at all times monitor the radio frequency assigned by the competent internationally designated air traffic control authority or the appropriate international distress radio frequency".[13] (The "international distress radio frequency" is the VHF emergency

---

11 Article 33 of UNCLOS.
12 Articles 38, 2 of UNCLOS (Transit Passage, Section 2, Articles 37-44).
13 Article 39, 3 (a-b) of UNCLOS.

frequency 121.5 MHz referred to in Annex 10 – Aeronautical Communications – to the Chicago Convention and also in other Annexes.)

4.2.4   Archipelagic Waters

UNCLOS introduced, in Part IV (Articles 46-54) a profound innovation in international law that will have a direct impact on the application of the Chicago Convention- the concept of *archipelagic States* and *archipelagic waters*. "Archipelagic State" means a State constituted wholly by one or more archipelagos, *i.e.*, a group of islands, interconnecting waters and other features that form an intrinsic geographical, economic and political entity. "Archipelagic waters" are the parts of the sea enclosed by archipelagic baselines joining the outermost points of the outermost islands of the archipelago.

The essential innovation is that the sovereignty of the archipelagic State is extended by UNCLOS to waters enclosed by the archipelagic baselines and this sovereignty extends to the airspace over the archipelagic waters. Ships (but not aircraft!) of all States enjoy the right of innocent passage through archipelagic waters in the same way and under the same conditions as through the territorial sea. Moreover, in Article 53 UNCLOS provides for the "archipelagic sea lanes passage" – an archipelagic State may designate sea lanes and air routes there above, suitable for continuous and expeditious passage of foreign ships and aircraft through or over its archipelagic waters and adjacent territorial sea.

The implications for international air law are important: vast areas of the sea that were part of the high sea and free for air navigation will become "archipelagic waters" over which the archipelagic State will have sovereignty extending also to the airspace. Without any need for the textual amendment of the Chicago Convention, its Article 2 will have to be read as meaning that the territory of a State shall be the land areas, territorial waters adjacent thereto and *its archipelagic waters*. Any events taking place in the archipelagic waters (*e.g.*, an aircraft accident) will have to be considered as having occurred in the territory of the archipelagic State.

"Right of archipelagic sea lanes passage" becomes a new concept of public international law.

4.2.5   Exclusive Economic Zone (EEZ)

In the second half of the 20th century some coastal States attempted to extend their jurisdiction well beyond the limits of the traditional territorial sea to protect their fisheries and other natural resources. There were instances of unilateral declarations claiming territorial sea up to 200 nautical miles – claims that were vigorously contested by other

States interested in the freedom of navigation and overflight and safeguarding of other traditional freedoms of the high seas.

UNCLOS found a compromise in the concept of the *"exclusive economic zone"* (EEZ) with a specific legal regime. The EEZ is an area beyond and adjacent to the territorial sea in which the coastal States enjoy specific rights and jurisdiction and other States enjoy rights and freedoms. The breadth of the EEZ shall not exceed 200 nautical miles from the baselines from which the breadth of the territorial sea is measured.

In the EEZ the coastal State has *sovereign rights* for the purposes of exploring and exploiting, conserving and managing the natural resources, whether living or non-living, of the waters superjacent to the sea-bed and its subsoil; it also has sovereign rights with regard to other activities for the economic exploitation and exploration of the zone, such as the production of energy from water, currents and winds. Furthermore, in the EEZ the coastal State has *jurisdiction* with regard to the establishment and use of artificial islands, installations and structures, marine scientific research and protection and preservation of the marine environment.

All other States, including the land-locked States, enjoy in the EEZ the freedoms of the high seas with respect to navigation and overflight, laying of submarine cables and pipelines and other related freedoms, such as those related to the operation of ships or aircraft, etc.

The EEZ is an area of the sea which was given by UNCLOS a *specific legal regime*. It is a zone *sui generis* with special economic rights reserved for the coastal State and the traditional freedoms of the high seas (minus the rights reserved for the coastal State) maintained for other States. The *"sovereign rights"* of the coastal State relate only to the natural resources of the sea and the coastal State cannot interfere with the traditional freedoms of the high seas, in particular the right of navigation and overflight.

The coastal State has jurisdiction with regard to the establishment and use of artificial islands, installations and structures in the EEZ. In that context a question has arisen whether a coastal State could build an international airport in the EEZ adjacent to its coast. Nothing can be ruled out in the future if there is an appropriate agreement of the States concerned but the current text of the UNCLOS would seem to stand in the way of such a project: such an airport would not be in the "territory" of the coastal State but on the high seas; it could present an obstacle to the freedom of navigation and overflight; the airspace above such an airport would be "over the high seas" and not subject to the jurisdiction of the coastal State. It means under applicable international law, operationally it would be a free port, as no sovereignty is involved and the rule of the high seas prevails. The coastal State is not granted any sovereign rights external to its territorial waters, the artificial island will not be part of its territory if it is in the EEZ.

The future growing needs of international civil aviation may in due course necessitate the construction of airports beyond the territorial limits of States, *e.g.*, within the EEZ.

There were some preliminary considerations of such a project in the Netherlands that may urgently need additional airport and lacks the suitable land territory. An appropriate legal framework for such a project has not yet been defined and would have to be agreed by the States of the international community.

Conflicting claims as to the extent and location of the EEZ and activities within such zones are the subject of open disputes among States; one such area is the East and South China Sea where some excessive claims by China are challenged by its neighbouring States. (Note: Japan does have an airport on the sea. Kansai International Airport is located on an artificial island, but it is within the territorial sea.)

4.2.6   Continental Shelf

The coastal States exercise sovereign rights over the continental shelf with respect to the exploitation of the natural resources possibly up to 350 nautical miles from the baselines from which the breadth of the territorial sea is measured. This is a substantial concession to the economic interests of the coastal States since it gives them exclusive access to the natural resources of the sea bed and its subsoil, in particular oil, gas and important minerals. The rights of the coastal State over the continental shelf do not affect the legal status of the superjacent waters or of the airspace above those waters.[14] Consequently, the airspace above the continental shelf beyond the territorial sea has the same legal status as the airspace over the high seas.

4.3   POLAR REGIONS

In the analysis of the term "territory" or "sea" the polar areas do not seem to fit the usual pattern due to the vast areas either covered by permanent ice or floating icebergs, hardly suitable for human habitation.

The extensive area of the North Pole covered by solid ice or floating icebergs is the Arctic Ocean and the airspace above it has the regime of the airspace over the high seas open to overflight by all States. In fact, since the most recent part of the 20th century many air routes have been used by scheduled international air lines over the polar area between Asia, North America and Europe substantially shortening the flight time and shrinking the distances between different parts of the northern hemisphere. In spite of the inhospitable character of the area and its severe climatic conditions there is no record of an accident of a scheduled commercial flight in the Arctic area. Environmental damage attributable to the global warming progressively decreases the amount of ice in the Arctic

---

14   Article 78 of UNCLOS.

regions and aviation will face the challenge to minimize the effects of engine emissions and counter-trails. Early in the 21st century specific sovereignty claims have been raised in the Arctic region by some States and strongly contested by others – the conflicting interests involve strategic security, as well as the potential oil and other mineral reserves on the Arctic seabed.

On the other hand, the Antarctic area is mostly a vast land mass with high mountains and covered by mammoth layers of ice. Historically, quite a few countries have claimed sovereign rights over several segments of the Antarctic continent while other countries were denying such claims. The legal situation was not fully clarified by the Antarctic Treaty[15] signed at Washington, D.C. on 1 December 1959. Under its Article IV 1 (a-c) nothing in the Treaty is to be interpreted as renunciation of previously asserted rights or claims or prejudicing the position of States as regards recognition or non-recognition of any other State's rights or claims. In other words, the status of the Antarctica has not been determined and the uncertain *status quo* prevails. Hence, it appears justified, on balance, to consider the Antarctica as a territory of *undetermined sovereignty* comparable to the status of the high seas. However, it is to be expected that some States claiming sovereign rights in "their" sectors would vocally object to this conclusion.

Antarctica is of lesser importance for civil aviation since no major air routes used by scheduled airlines cross its airspace at present. In general, the southern hemisphere is much less populated than the North and generates less traffic but in the future flights over the Antarctica (for tourism or just transit) may increase. Antarctica recorded one major aviation disaster: on 28 November 1979 a DC-10 of Air New Zealand on a sightseeing flight crashed at Ross Island on the slopes of Mount Erebus with the loss of 257 lives.[16]

4.4   Specific Rights of States in the Sovereign Airspace

The sovereignty of a State in its airspace is complete and exclusive, *i.e.*, all-encompassing. However, the Chicago Convention spells out specific attributes of that sovereignty – not in an exhaustive manner but perhaps for greater clarity and stipulation of specific conditions.

> – *Scheduled air services* – Article 6: any scheduled air service over or into the territory of a contracting State is subject to the special permission or other authorization of that State.

---

15   Text at www.ats.aq/e/antarctictreaty.html.
16   Report at http://aviation-safety.net/database/record.php?id=19791128-0.

This is a provision of critical importance for international air transport and has been seen as an obstacle to the global liberalization of air transport services. As will be seen later,[17] in practice such "special permission or other authorization" is usually reciprocally exchanged between States in the form of a bilateral air services agreements (ASAs).

> – *Cabotage* – Article 7: each contracting State has the right to refuse permission to the aircraft of other contracting States to take on in its territory passengers, mail and cargo carried for remuneration or hire and destined for another point within its territory.

It is frequently believed that the Chicago Convention "prohibits" cabotage, *i.e.*, domestic carriage by foreign aircraft. However, international law does not "prohibit" cabotage as such but stresses the right of each State to "refuse" to permit cabotage. Article 7 imposes a condition that the granting or obtaining of such a special privilege must not be made "specifically… on an *exclusive basis*". On two occasions a futile attempt has been made to amend Article 7 by deleting this condition;[18] the current practice within the European Union amounts to considerable liberalization of cabotage.

> – *Pilotless aircraft* – Article 8: no aircraft capable of being flown without a pilot is permitted to fly over a territory of a contracting State without a special authorization of that State. Contracting States also undertake to insure that pilotless aircraft in regions open to civil aircraft shall be so controlled as to obviate danger to civil aviation.

Most pilotless aircraft are currently in use by the military – sometimes as "drones" equipped for surveillance or combat; their flight over a foreign territory would be already prohibited – because of its military or state characteristics – by Article 3, paragraph 3. Even a "civil" pilotless aircraft represents a hazard of a collision with other aircraft if not effectively controlled. At the 6th meeting of its 40th Council Session on 13 June 1960, the ICAO Council adopted a resolution relating to the flight of uncontrolled balloons and declared that uncontrolled balloons may constitute "a definitive hazard to safety of air navigation" and urged contracting States "to take whatever action they may deem appropriate or necessary…"; this super cautiously worded decision was taken in the heightened tension of Cold War when a protest was lodged against the "propaganda balloons" allegedly launched into the airspace of East Europe. The use of remotely piloted

---

17 See Chapter 6 below.
18 16th Session of the Assembly in 1968 and 18th Session in 1971. See ICAO Doc 8771, A16-EX, Report, p. 43, A16-Min. P/7 (1968) and A18-Min. P/12 (1971).

aircraft systems (RPAS in ICAO usage) are increasing in both the military and civilian fields and will create many technical and operational problems. Even miniature vehicles (drones) widely available on the market and used for observation or photography could create problems in the vicinity of airports and will require domestic legislation; security against terrorist attacks must not overlook the potential use of such instruments to carry explosives or even nuclear material. Nevertheless, there is no apparent need to amend Article 8 of the Convention.[19] National legislations gradually introduce a requirement that any RPAS be registered and its operator specifically licensed.[20]

> *Prohibited areas* – Article 9: each contracting State may, for reasons of military necessity or public safety, restrict or prohibit uniformly the aircraft of other States from flying over certain areas of its territory; no distinction must be made between own aircraft engaged in international scheduled airline service and foreign aircraft likewise engaged.

The prohibited area must be of "reasonable extent and location" so as not to interfere unnecessarily with air navigation. Description of such areas must be promptly communicated to other contracting States and to ICAO. In exceptional circumstances or during a period of emergency or in the interest of public safety, and with immediate effect, each State reserves the right temporarily to restrict or prohibit flying over the whole or any part of its territory; such restriction must apply without distinction of nationality to aircraft of all other States. Moreover, each contracting State may require landing within its territory at a designated airport of an aircraft that has entered a prohibited or restricted area. The destruction by a ground-to-air missile of the Malaysian aircraft on flight MH17 over Ukraine on 17 July 2014 highlights the need for effective action by States to protect civil flights over "conflict zones" by appropriate warning or by closing the airspace, if necessary.[21]

The right of a State to restrict or prohibit overflights of designated areas or of the entire national territory is a natural aspect of the complete and exclusive sovereignty of the State. The Convention, however, stipulates some conditions and limitations to the exercise of that right – non-discrimination between aircraft of different nationalities, "reasonable extent and location" of the prohibited or restricted area not to interfere "unnecessarily"

---

19   ICAO Secretariat study in LC/36-WP/2-4.
20   Ronald Schnitker and Dick van het Kaar, *Drone Law and Policy*, Eleven, The Hague, Chapter 5, Safety Requirements of UAS Operations, 2021, pp. 254-268. Commission Implementing Regulation (EU) 2019/947 of 24 May 2019 on the rules and procedures for the operation of unmanned aircraft, C/2019/3824, OJ L 152, 11.6.2019, pp. 45-71.
21   ICAO Council action in C-WP/14325; ICAO Assembly, 39th Session Working Paper, A39-WP/108TE/32, 19/8/2016.

with air navigation, duty to communicate description of the areas to States and to ICAO. The terms are too vague and not self-explanatory and could lead to disagreements. In September 1967, the United Kingdom initiated a dispute settlement procedure before the Council of ICAO against Spain relating to the establishment by Spain of a prohibited area in the Bay of Algeciras facing Gibraltar – the allegation was that the area was not of "reasonable extent and location" and that it "interfered unnecessarily" with the flights to and from the Gibraltar airport.[22]

To clarify the terms of Article 9, the Council of ICAO defined, in Annex 2,[23] Annex 4[24] and Annex 15[25] the following terms:

> *Prohibited Area* – an airspace of defined dimensions above the land area or territorial waters of a State, within which the flight of aircraft is prohibited.
>
> *Restricted Area* – an airspace of defined dimensions above the land areas or territorial waters, within which the flight of aircraft is restricted in accordance with certain specified conditions.
>
> *Danger Area* – a specified area within which activities dangerous to flight may exist at specified times.

International frictions have arisen in some occasions when States purported to restrict air navigation over the high seas for their military exercises, testing of missiles or nuclear tests but the clearly political impact of such situations kept these issues out of the purview of ICAO.

It will be recalled that on 11 September 2001 and for three days thereafter the US government prohibited all civil air operations in the US airspace.

In this context it is also relevant to note Article 89 of the Convention under which States have "freedom of action" (*i.e.*, are free to disregard the provisions of the Convention) in case of war, whether as belligerents or neutrals; the same principle applies if a contracting State declares a State of national emergency and notifies the fact to the Council of ICAO. That could lead to the restriction or prohibition of flights of civil aircraft.

> *Landing at customs airport* – Article 10: contracting States have the right to require that foreign aircraft land at an airport designated for the purpose of

---

22 The Council of ICAO never took a decision on this subject. ICAO Annual Report of the Council to the Assembly for 1969 (Doc 8869 A18-P/2 June 1970).
23 Annex 2 – Rules of the Air.
24 Annex 4 – Aeronautical Charts.
25 Annex 15 – Aeronautical Information Service.

customs and other examinations. On departure from the territory, such aircraft have to depart from a similarly designated customs airport.

Applicability of air regulations – Article 11: the laws and regulations of a contracting State relating to admission to or departure from its territory of aircraft engaged in international air navigation, or the operation and navigation of such aircraft within its territory shall be applied to the aircraft of all contracting States without distinction as to nationality and they must be complied with by such aircraft upon entering or departing from or while within the territory of that State.

Entry and clearance regulations – Article 13: the laws and regulations of a contracting State as to the admission to and departure from its territory of passengers, crew or cargo of aircraft, such as regulations relating to entry, clearance, immigration, passports, customs, and quarantine must be complied with by or on behalf of such passengers, crew or cargo upon entrance into or departure from, or while within the territory of that State.

Search of aircraft – Article 16: the authorities of each contracting State have the right to search aircraft of the other contracting States on landing or departure, and to inspect the certificates and other documents prescribed by the Convention; it should be done "without unreasonable delay".

Articles 11, 13 and 16 of the Convention confirm the complete jurisdiction of the State within its territorial airspace and only set some conditions or limits to its exercise (non-discrimination as to nationality, speedy search). They also clarify that an aircraft in the airspace of another State does not enjoy any "exterritorial" status but is fully subject to the laws and regulations of that State. Only over the high seas is the aircraft fully subject to the jurisdiction of the State of its registry. Essentially, two jurisdictions prevail in the case of foreign aircraft crossing the national airspace, that of the sovereign state in its airspace and that of the registering State over the aircraft, while on the high seas solely one jurisdiction prevails, that of the State registering the aircraft.

In this context it should be also noted that all aircraft have to observe the *rules of the air* of the State in which they operate (Article 12). States have the duty to insure that all aircraft within its territory and every aircraft of their own nationality – wherever such aircraft may be – shall comply with the rules of the air there in force and also have the duty to prosecute all persons violating the applicable regulations. The "rules of the air" could be compared to a "highway code" of the air and govern the flight and manoeuvre of the aircraft. States accepted an undertaking to keep their own regulations uniform, to the greatest possible extent, with those established under the Convention – *i.e.*, the Standards adopted by the Council of ICAO and embodied in the Annexes to the Convention (Article 54 *l*).

Over the high seas no State is entitled to exercise its jurisdiction or extend to that area the application of its laws and regulations relating to the rules of the air; yet, there is need for uniformity in the rules of the air over the high seas for safety reasons. The Convention stipulates – in the third sentence of Article 12 – that "Over the high seas, the rules in force shall be those established under this Convention".

In adopting the text of Annex 2 – Rules of the Air – in April 1948 and Amendment 1 thereto in November 1951, the Council of ICAO resolved that "the Annex constitutes *Rules relating to the flight and manoeuvre of aircraft* within the meaning of Article 12 of the Convention. Over the high seas, therefore, these rules apply without exception".[26] That, in practice, means that States cannot file a difference under Article 38 of the Convention to Standards of Annex 2 as they apply to the high seas. The Council of ICAO is thus the sole "legislator" of the rules of the air over the high seas – a unique feature among the specialized agencies of the UN system.

4.5 International Duties of States in Their Airspace

The rights of States under international law must be understood in the context of corresponding duties that international law imposes upon States.

In the first place States have to observe the obligations under the Convention on International Civil Aviation and other relevant international instruments in the spirit of the international law of treaties as formulated in the Vienna Convention on the Law of Treaties (1969):[27]

> *Article 26*
> *Pacta sunt servanda*
> Every treaty in force is binding upon the parties to it and must be performed by them in good faith.

---

26 Foreword to Annex 2 – Rules of the Air, Chapter 2, 2.1.1.
27 UN Treaty Series, Vol. 1155, 1980, p. 331.

Article 27
Internal law and observance of treaties
A party may not invoke the provisions of its internal law as justification for its failure to perform a treaty. This rule is without prejudice to Article 46.[28]

The following are some illustrative examples of the specific duties of States under the Chicago Convention as they relate to matters of air navigation:

Article 3 c): not to permit its State aircraft to enter foreign airspace without authorization;

Article 3bis: refrain from the use of weapons against civil aircraft in flight;

Article 4: not to use civil aviation for any purpose inconsistent with the aims of the Convention.[29]

Article 8: not to permit use of pilotless aircraft over foreign territory without authorization of that State.

Article 9: to give equal treatment to foreign aircraft as to its own with respect to prohibited areas.

Article 12: enforce the observance of the rules of the air in its territory and by its aircraft of such rules wherever they may be; over the high seas the applicable rules are those of Annex 2 to the Chicago Convention.

Article 14: take effective measures to prevent the spread by means of air navigation of communicable diseases.

Article 15: keep its public airports open to aircraft of other contracting States under uniform conditions and not to discriminate with regard to the charges for airports and air navigation services between foreign and own aircraft; the charges are to be published and communicated to ICAO and are subject to review and recommendations by the Council

---

28   Article 46 of the Vienna Convention (1969) refers to the invalidity of a treaty if the consent of the State to be bound by the treaty has been expressed in violation of a provision of its internal law regarding the competence to conclude treaties.
29   This prohibition of the "misuse of civil aviation" was based on the regulation of the Briand-Kellogg Pact (also known as Pact of Paris) of 27 August 1928 outlawing resort to war as an instrument of national policy. This provision must be interpreted as applying to the acts of States, not to acts of individuals. See also Proceedings, Vol. II, p. 1381.

of ICAO. Expressly – no fees, dues or other charges must be imposed by any contracting State in respect solely of the right of transit over or entry into or exit from its territory of any aircraft of a contracting State or persons or property thereon.[30]

Article 21: supply to ICAO or any contracting State on demand information concerning the registration and ownership of any particular aircraft registered in that State.

Article 22: adopt all practicable measures to facilitate and expedite air navigation between the territories of contracting States and to prevent unnecessary delays to aircraft, crews, passengers and cargo.

Article 23: establish customs and immigration procedures, as far as practicable, in conformity with practices that may be recommended pursuant to the Chicago Convention.

Article 25: provide all practicable assistance to aircraft in distress in its territory and collaborate internationally in search for a missing aircraft.

Article 26: institute an inquiry in the event of an accident of a foreign aircraft in its territory.

Article 27: exempt foreign aircraft from seizure on patent claims.

Article 28: as far as practicable, provide in its territory airports, radio services, meteorological services and other air navigation facilities to facilitate international air navigation; adopt and put into operation standard systems of communications procedures, codes, markings, signals, lighting and other operational practices and rules that may be established pursuant to the Chicago Convention; collaborate in international measures to secure the publication of aeronautical maps and charts in accordance with standards which may be established pursuant to the Chicago Convention.

Article 33: recognize as valid certificates of airworthiness and certificates of competency and licenses issued or rendered valid by the contracting State in which the aircraft is registered – provided that the requirements under which such certificates or licenses were issued or rendered valid are equal to or above the minimum standards established pursuant to the Chicago Convention.

---

30 This provision was flagrantly and so far with impunity violated by the Russian Federation that granted the right to overfly the Trans-Siberian route on condition that the designated airline concludes a "commercial" agreement with AEROFLOT providing for payments for each overflight. See M. Milde, 'Some Question Marks about the Price of 'Russian Air'", 49 *ZLW (German Journal of Air and Space law)* 2000, p. 147.

Article 37: to collaborate in securing the highest practicable degree of uniformity in regulations, standards, procedures and organization in relation to aircraft, personnel, airways and auxiliary services in all matters in which such uniformity will facilitate and improve air navigation.

Article 38: give immediate notification to ICAO of any differences between its own practice and that established by international standard.

4.6   PROTECTION OF THE SOVEREIGN AIRSPACE

States legitimately protect their territories against unlawful incursions and against other activities perceived as dangerous – violation of customs regulations, smuggling of people or substances, violation of quarantine regulations, etc.

Protection of the airspace is an integral part of the protection of the national territory. In addition to the general protected interests of a State, the airspace is protected to safeguard safety and security of flight, observance of the aviation regulations and of the life and property on the ground.

The protection of the airspace may be vested in the national police forces or in the military, both using aircraft in performance of their functions. Aircraft used in military or police (state featured) functions are not within the scope of applicability of the Chicago Convention[31] which is applicable only to civil aircraft. However, the conduct of the "State aircraft" is governed by certain rules of the general international law and, under the Convention's Article 3 d), the contracting States have accepted a legal commitment "when issuing regulations for their State aircraft, that they will have due regard for the safety of navigation of civil aircraft".

The basic means in the protection of the airspace is the *interception* of the suspect aircraft in the air. The aircraft may be "suspect" by not identifying itself, appearing unexpectedly in the airspace contrary to the recorded flight plans or schedules, flying beyond the established air route or even over a prohibited or restricted area, by not communicating with the Air Traffic Services (ATS) or by appearing to perform improper operations or manoeuvres.

The "interception" of a civil aircraft is an interaction with a State aircraft; such State aircraft locates the civil aircraft and approaches it for purposes of identification and decision on a further action. "Interceptions of civil aircraft are, in all cases, potentially hazardous" – states a Note to Standard 3.8.1 in Annex 2. The flight safety requires a minimum horizontal and vertical separation between aircraft in the airspace to avoid the

---

31   Article 3 a).

danger of collision and minimize the effects of wake turbulence. However, in the case of interception the precautions of minimum separation are disregarded and the State aircraft approaches the intercepted aircraft to a distance sufficient for optical identification or optical signalling. It need not take any further action if the intercepted aircraft it satisfactorily identified, communication is restored and the aircraft returns to its proper course or proceeds to landing.

Appendix 2 to Annex 2 that deals with interception of civil aircraft States that "due regard shall be had by contracting States to the following principles when developing regulations and administrative directives:

a. interception of civil aircraft will be undertaken only as a last resort;
b. if undertaken, an interception will be limited to determining the identity of the aircraft, unless it is necessary to return the aircraft to its planned track, direct it beyond the boundaries of national airspace, guide it away from prohibited, restricted or danger areas or instruct it to effect a landing at a designated aerodrome;
c. practice interception of civil aircraft will not be undertaken;
d. navigational guidance and related information will be given to an intercepted aircraft by radiotelephony, whenever radio contact can be established; and
e. in the case where an intercepted civil aircraft is required to land in the territory overflown, the aerodrome designated for the landing is to be suitable for the safe landing of the aircraft type concerned.

These detailed and specific provisions were adopted by the ICAO Council in 1985 – in the wake of the shooting down of the Korean Airlines B-747 Flight 007 and after the adoption of a new Article 3*bis* to the Convention; the provisions do not foresee the use of force or weapons against the intercepted aircraft and in a *Note* recalls: "In the unanimous adoption by the 25th Session (Extraordinary) of the ICAO Assembly on 10 May 1984 of Article 3*bis* to the Convention on International Civil Aviation, the Contracting States have recognized that "every State must refrain from resorting to the use of weapons against civil aircraft in flight". The decision on the adoption of Appendix 2 to Annex 2 was not unanimous – some States maintained that ICAO was acting *ultra vires* when issuing regulations for State aircraft; however, the majority believed that the regulations were not aimed at State aircraft but governed the safety of civil aviation in the spirit of Article 3 d) of the Convention.

During the period of Cold War in the second half of the 20th century there were numerous incidents of use of weapons, mostly by the USSR military, against military and civil aircraft alleged to have violated the sovereign airspace. Many human lives were lost in the dubious and nearly paranoid protection of the "sacred fatherland" that did not make a distinction between civil and military aircraft. Among the more significant incidents involving civil aircraft are the following:

On 29 April 1952, an Air France aircraft on a flight through the Berlin corridor from Frankfurt to Berlin was attacked by two Soviet interceptors that opened fire with machine guns and cannons. The attack caused injuries to several passengers and one crew member. The Soviets claimed that the aircraft strayed from the corridor, intruded into the East German airspace and did not obey the orders to land. The French side denied the claim and stated that "quite apart from the questions of fact, to fire in any circumstances, even by way of warning, on an unarmed aircraft in time of peace, wherever the aircraft may be, is entirely inadmissible and contrary to all standards of civilized behaviour".[32]

On 23 July 1954, a Cathay Pacific aircraft on a flight from Bangkok to Hong Kong was fired at without warning by Chinese interceptors. The aircraft crash-landed in the sea and some passengers were killed on impact, some others drowned. The Chinese apologized for the incident, promised compensation and claimed that their military mistook the aircraft for a Chinese Nationalists' military aircraft. They implied, unlike the Soviets, that their military would not knowingly open fire against an unarmed civil aircraft.

On 27 July 1955, an Israeli El-Al aircraft strayed into the Bulgarian airspace and was shot down with the loss of lives of 51 passengers and 7 crew members. The Bulgarian government initially claimed that they were not able to identify the aircraft and that it was shot down by anti-aircraft artillery; later it had to be admitted that the aircraft was shot down by an interceptor that was in the position to visually identify the aircraft as an unarmed civil aircraft. The Bulgarian government initially offered compensation to the victims but later refused any responsibility and would consider only *ex gratia* payments[33] in local currency. Thereafter Israel, United Kingdom and United States filed an application to the International Court of Justice against Bulgaria but the case had to be dismissed since Bulgaria refused to accept the jurisdiction of the ICJ. The pleadings presented, in particular, by the United Kingdom offer a remarkable legal analysis proving the illegality, in international law, of the use of deadly force against an unarmed civil aircraft in the time of peace.[34]

On 21 February 1973, the Israeli air force shot down a civilian B-727 of Libyan airlines over the Israeli occupied Sinai – in the crash 106 people died. The aircraft was flying to Cairo but in a sandstorm lost its bearings and was almost 100 mile off course – allegedly flying over secret Israeli positions in occupied Sinai. The incident was investigated by the ICAO Council that *condemned* the Israeli action and Israel agreed to pay compensation to the victims. A politically charged discussion took place whether the Israeli action should

---

32   Oliver J. Lissitzyn, "The Treatment of Aerial Intruders in Recent Practice and International Law", 47 *AJIL* (1953), p. 674.
33   The essence of the payment of *ex gratia* character is that despite the provision of material compensation this act does not entail the admission of responsibility.
34   ICJ Pleadings 1959, Aerial Incident of 27 July 1955, *Israel v. Bulgaria, US v. Bulgaria, UK v. Bulgaria*.

be "condemned" or only "deplored"... The Council was explicit by labelling the Israeli action as a "flagrant violation of the principles enshrined in the Chicago Convention".

On 20 April 1978, a Korean Air B-707 on a flight from Paris to Seoul via the Polar route experienced a malfunction of the navigational avionics and, following the magnetic compass (where every direction at the Pole could be "South"...) entered the area of the Kola Peninsula and Murmansk in the USSR – an area of sensitive military installations and a submarine base. A Soviet interceptor was sent to locate the plane and it fired two air-to-air missiles at the plane and returned to its base, reporting that "the target was destroyed". It appears that the missiles were not "activated" and did not explode and only "impact" damage was caused to the aircraft. In fact, two passengers were killed and eleven wounded and the crippled aircraft managed to land on a frozen lake where it was located by the Soviet authorities some two days later. In the absence of diplomatic relations between the USSR and the Republic of Korea at that time the release of the passengers and of the crew was negotiated by the US authorities and no international protest was ever raised. There were anecdotal claims that the pilot who falsely reported the destruction of the plane and also his supervisor were court-marshalled and executed; if true, this fact would go a long way towards explaining the painstaking paranoid effort of the Soviet military in the area of Sakhalin some five years later to make sure that the Korean Airlines B-747 Flight 007 was actually destroyed…

The most extensively commented incident occurred on 1 September 1983 off the island of Sakhalin in the Far East of the USSR. An extensive comment has to be devoted to that incident due to its implications for the formulation of important legal principles.

However, after that tragic incident there were other cases of use of force against civil aircraft that have to be mentioned: in July 1988 an Airbus A300 of Iran Air Flight 655 was hit by a missile fired from the US naval ship *Vincennes* in the Gulf. The US authorities instantly admitted an accidental error due to erroneous identification of the aircraft as an attacking military aircraft, apologized for it and offered full compensation to the victims; on 14 July 1988 the Council "deplored" the accidental sequence of events that resulted in the tragedy – a conclusion that did not satisfy the government of Iran.

In February 1996 the Cuban air force interceptors shot down two US registered private light aircraft over the high seas – the ICAO Council then reaffirmed that the use of weapons against civil aircraft in flight was incompatible with the rules enshrined in the Chicago Convention.

On 17 July 2014, a Malaysian aircraft on flight MH17 was destroyed by a missile over the Ukrainian territory near Donetsk, and 283 passengers and 15 crew members died; it is disputed which party is responsible for the attack.[35] The authorities of the Netherlands lead the investigation and concluded that over the territory of Ukraine the aircraft

---

35 See LC/36-WP/8-1 for references to the report on the investigation.

progressed normally while it was hit by a (Russian) Buk surface-to-air missile system launched from the eastern part of Ukraine. The crime was committed by four known perpetrators and against them the Netherlands Public Prosecution Service instituted a criminal procedure.[36] The court finally found two Russians and one Ukrainian separatist guilty over downing of flight MH17 and sentenced all to life imprisonment on 17 November 2022.[37] Back to the case of KE007 that triggered important developments in international law: Korean Airlines B-747 Flight 007 (New York – Anchorage – Seoul) penetrated the Soviet airspace over the Kamchatka Peninsula and later over the island of Sakhalin – areas of heavy concentration of military forces and equipment and "prohibited areas" according to Soviet aeronautical maps. There were 246 passengers of different nationalities on board and 23 crew members. The investigation launched at the request of the ICAO Council by the Secretary General[38] concluded that the plane after leaving Anchorage started progressively deviating from its planned route 20 North followed a (erroneous) magnetic heading and at the critical point was about 500 kilometres beyond the expected track. All evidence indicates that the crew was completely unaware that they were off course and they were engaged in light-hearted banter while the cabin crew was preparing to serve breakfast to passengers. The Soviet air force located the plane on their radars but failed to intercept it while it was flying over Kamchatka or the Sea of Okhotsk. They increased their effort to intercept the aircraft which they took for a US military reconnaissance plane when it came over Sakhalin; they issued a categorical order to their interceptors "destroy the target". When the aircraft was about to leave the USSR airspace over Sakhalin, the Soviet General Kornukov became agitated and with an expletive enquired "… how long to get into attack position, he is already getting into neutral waters! Engage afterburners immediately!"[39] One Suchoi 15 interceptor (designated 805) with pilot Osipovich had the KE007 in sight by that time and on three separate occasions reported that he saw the navigational lights and the flashing strobe light of the aircraft – clear evidence that the plane was a civil aircraft and not engaged on a clandestine mission. General Kornukov was then heard "… cut the horseplay, I repeat the combat task: fire missiles, fire on target 60-65, destroy target 60-65".[40]

After firing some 200 rounds from his cannon, Osipovich reported "Launch, executed launch – the target is destroyed". The missiles fired were R-98 air-to-air missiles, one with a heat-seeking guidance system, the other radar guided with a proximity fuse. The aircraft

---

36 Dutch Safety Board: Crash of Malaysia Airlines (MH) Flight 17. The Hague, 13 October 2015, pp. 1-279; www.prosecutionservice.nl/topics/mh17-plane-crash/prosecution-and-trial.
37 www.courtmh17.com/en/.
38 C-WP/7764, attachment; *Destruction of Korean Air Lines Boeing 747 over the Sea of Japan, 31 August 1983: Report of ICAO Fact-Finding Investigation (1983)*.
39 M. Milde, "KE 007 – 'Final' Truth and Consequences", 42 ZLW, 4/1993, p. 364.
40 *Idem.*, p. 365.

was not instantly destroyed, the cockpit voice recorder (CVR) indicates surprised reaction of the crew who felt sudden decompression and contacted Tokyo HF with a message that due to decompression they initiate descend. There is not the slightest evidence that the crew was aware of the interception, there was no warning whatsoever, they did not realize that they were attacked by missiles and one minute and 44 second after the impact of the missiles the recording stopped. After some time, the aircraft hit the surface of the sea and 269 lives were lost. Some ten years later ICAO and the world learned that the debris of the plane was found 114 m below the surface some 17 miles off the coastline in international waters – suggesting the possibility that the aircraft was not attacked in the Soviet airspace but in the international airspace over the high seas (according to the report the airplane in the moment of its interception was at a distance of 21 nautical miles from the nearest Soviet continental baseline and it crashed at a distance of 30 miles from the coast of the Sakhalin Island).[41]

This incident evoked sharp reaction of the international community for its inhuman brutality and also due to the fact that for several days after the tragedy the Soviets kept denying any knowledge of the aircraft. The Soviet version eventually was that the aircraft was on an espionage mission and that they had taken a legitimate defensive action. However, there never was the slightest piece of evidence pointing to another scenario than accidental erroneous programming of the navigational avionics that caused the growing deviation from the proper route that was not noticed by the crew. No warning whatsoever was given to KE007; the interceptor's pilot saw and reported proper navigational lights and flashing strobe light of the plane but for the Soviet command the plane was from the very beginning an "enemy target" and the order was, without any verification, "destroy the target".

A draft resolution presented to the UN Security Council would have proclaimed that "use of armed force against civil aircraft is incompatible with the norms governing international behaviour and elementary considerations of humanity" – the resolution was defeated due to the predictable veto by the USSR.

The Council of ICAO held an Extraordinary Session on 15 and 16 September 1983 and adopted a resolution "deeply deploring the destruction of an aircraft in commercial international service resulting in the loss of 269 innocent lives' and "recognizing that such use of armed force against international civil aviation is incompatible with the norms governing international behaviour and elementary considerations of humanity and with the rules, standards and recommended practices enshrined in the Chicago Convention and its Annexes and invokes generally recognized international consequences".[42] This

---

41 *Destruction of Boeing 747-200 of Korean Air Lines on 31 August 1983. Report of the completion of the ICAO fact-finding investigation.* June 1993.
42 ICAO Doc 9416, C/1077, C-Min Extraordinary (1983).

resolution was adopted by a roll-call vote by 26 votes, 2 votes opposed (USSR and Czechoslovakia) with 3 abstentions (Algeria, China and India).

On 6 March 1984 the Council of ICAO adopted a resolution unique in its history – a resolution that is openly and strongly worded without any diplomatic niceties and that is hard-hitting, condemnatory and principled. It concludes that after Secretary General's investigation no evidence had been found that KE007 would have been involved in any premeditated deviation and that the crew was completely unaware of its incorrect position. The resolution continues that "such use of armed force constitutes violation of international law, and invokes generally recognized consequences". It also recognizes that "such use of armed force is a grave threat to the safety of international civil aviation and is incompatible with the norms governing international behaviour and with the rules, Standards and Recommended Practices (SARPs) enshrined in the Chicago Convention and its Annexes and with the elementary considerations of humanity". In a rare departure from the diplomatic tone the resolution

> CONDEMNS the use of armed force which resulted in the destruction of the Korean airliner and the tragic loss of 269 lives' and 'DEEPLY DEPLORES' Soviet failure to co-operate with the ICAO investigation of the incident by refusing to accept the visit of the investigating team appointed by the Secretary General and by failing to provide the Secretary General with information relevant to the investigation.[43]

The position of States and of the ICAO Council indicated a strong legal belief that the existing international law prohibits the use of weapons against civil aircraft in flight. Nevertheless, there was also a strong feeling that this principle should be clearly formulated in the form of codified international law and included directly in the Chicago Convention.

The 25th Session (Extraordinary) of the ICAO Assembly adopted – without a vote by consensus – on 10 May 1984 an amendment to the Chicago Convention[44] by adding a new Article 3*bis*; its critical paragraph a) reads as follows:

> a) The contracting States recognize that every state must refrain from resorting to the use of weapons against civil aircraft in flight and that, in case of interception, the lives of persons on board and the safety of aircraft must not be endangered. This provision shall not be interpreted as modifying in any way the rights and obligations of states set forth in the Charter of the United Nations.

---

43   C-Min 111/3-6 (1984).
44   ICAO Doc 9437, Resolutions A25-1, A25-2, A25-3; ICAO Doc 9438, A-25-EX.

This paragraph represents the real thrust of this amendment to the Convention. The remaining paragraphs b), c) and d) were inserted at the insistence mainly of the USSR and their allies to appear as partly mitigating the strength of paragraph a) by confirming the right of States to require landing of an aircraft if there are reasonable grounds to believe that the aircraft is being used for purposes inconsistent with the Convention and the corresponding duty of the States of registration to make the compliance by their aircraft with the request to land mandatory.

Some readers have been wondering about the meaning of the last sentence of paragraph a) and its reference to the Charter of the United Nations; it was inserted at the insistence of the French delegation to stress that the legitimate right of self-defence against armed attack under Article 51 of the Charter is not modified; from the legal point of view this addition was quite unnecessary since under Article 103 of the UN Charter the provisions of the Charter always prevail.[45]

A serious discussion has been going on among some legal commentators whether Article 3*bis* represents a new "progressive development" of international law or whether it amounts only to the confirmation of the existing general (customary) international law in a codified format. Such discussion has little practical meaning if the historic facts are not fully considered. As a direct participant of the preparations for and the course of the 25th Session (Extraordinary) of the ICAO Assembly the author can assert with full conviction what was the intention of the delegations at the Assembly:

- the Assembly shared the views expressed by the Council of ICAO in its Resolutions of 16 September 1983 and 6 March 1984 on the illegality of the USSR action under then applicable international law and were convinced that existing international law already ruled out the use of force against civil aircraft in flight; and
- the wording of Article 3*bis* a) – not accidentally but knowingly and intentionally – follows verbatim the introductory words of Article 1 of the Chicago Convention that does not *create* the concept of sovereignty over the national airspace but *recognizes* its existence under the general customary international law.

International custom is "evidence of a general practice accepted as law"[46] and that practice may be supported by the "general principles of law recognized by civilized nations".[47] The international custom and the principles of law do not exclude the use of force in general but require that its use be *proportional* to the level of danger caused by the act against which the force is to be applied.

---

45 "In the event of a conflict between the obligations of the Members of the United Nations under the present Charter and their obligations under any other international agreement, their obligations under the present Charter shall prevail."
46 Article 38. 1 (b) of the Statute of the International Court of Justice.
47 *Idem.*, Article 38. 1 (c).

The commentators agree that the decision of the US-Mexican General Claims Commission in the *García and Garza v. United States case*[48] confirms an important legal standard. The Mexican claim against the US referred to the case of a Mexican girl who was shot dead by US National Guardsman while trying illegally to cross the Rio Grande and to enter the US territory at a point where both US and Mexican laws strictly prohibited any crossing. The Commission confirmed that among the civilized nations there is a common standard that deadly force should not be used against a person if there are other means to prevent the "delinquency" and that there must be a proportion between the danger created by the delinquency and the level of force used. The crucial *dictum* of the case is that there must be a proportion between the force applied and the act against which the force is used. Under this dictum, it must to emphasise regarding of the armed attack (criterion of quantity), the conduct attributed to the aggressor and the circumstances related to the perpetrator (criterion of quality).[49]

The same principle applies in national laws. An owner of a garden has the right to protect his fruit trees against trespassers and thieves; however, would law justify his shooting the neighbourhood children who came to pick his apples? Would any law justify his shooting a child who is already running away and climbs out over the fence? Such trivial analogy would well compare with the case of KE007 that was fired at when it was almost or fully out of the Soviet airspace! While the violation of the Soviet airspace was "unlawful" (albeit unintentional), the deadly response killing 269 innocent people was grossly disproportionate and patently unlawful.

The International Court of Justice in its very first decision – the *Corfu Channel Case*[50] – formulated additional principle of international law relating to the protection of human life in general. In the disputed case the government of Albania placed or at least knew about the placement of anchored automatic mines positioned in its territorial waters between its territory and the Greek island of Corfu and intentionally did not issue any warning to passing British warships; on 22 October 1946 two warships were destroyed, forty-two British marines were killed and forty-two injured. The Court ruled that it was incumbent upon the Albanian authorities to warn all ships of the imminent danger to which the minefield exposed them and to prevent the tragedy. It mentioned The Hague Convention of 1907, No. VIII which even in time of war protects the civilians, prisoners of war and the shipwrecked or wounded "Such obligations are based … on certain general

---

48 *Teodoro García and M. A. Garza (United Mexican States) v. United States of America*, UN Report of International Arbitral Awards, Vol. IV, 3 December 1926, pp. 119-134.
49 Gábor Kajtár, "Fragmentation of Attribution in International Law" in Gábor Kajtár, Başak Çali and Marko Milanovic (Eds.), *Secondary Rules of Primary Importance – Attribution, Causality, Standard of Review and Evidentiary Rules in International Law*, Oxford University Press, 2022, pp. 283-301.
50 *UK. v. Albania*, ICJ Year 1949, *The Corfu Channel Case*, (Merits) Decision of 9 April 1949, p. 22.

and well-recognized principles, namely: elementary consideration of humanity, *even more exacting in peace than war.*"

It may be safely concluded that Article 3*bis* did not establish a new principle of international law but reflects the principles of existing general (customary) international law. From that point of view it is of little relevance whether a State has or has not ratified the amendment to the Convention introducing new Article 3*bis* – the duty to refrain from use of weapons against civil aircraft in flight has been in existence regardless of the amendment to the Convention. The end of the Cold War by 1990 will hopefully mark the end of State-sponsored attacks against civil aircraft. By December 2022, 157 States have ratified the amendment that includes a new Article 3*bis* into the Convention, and it may be safely assumed that the prohibition of the use of weapons against a civil aircraft in flight is a firm part of the general international law.

It may appear puzzling that the United States – a leading protagonist of safety and security of civil aviation and initiator of what became Article 3*bis* – never ratified this amendment to the Convention and objected vigorously to the inclusion of new provisions on interception of aircraft in Annex 2. While no official explanation was ever offered, it is known that the US authorities are strongly opposed to the method of settlement of disputes under Chapter XVIII of the Chicago Convention that includes the possibility of appeal and grants compulsory jurisdiction to the International Court of Justice. Any dispute relating to the application or interpretation of Article 3*bis* or of Annex 2 could involve the United States in a situation where they could not legitimately object to the jurisdiction of the International Court of Justice.

4.7 Justifiable Use of Force against Civil Aircraft?

Doubts seem to be continuing whether the prohibition of the use of weapons against civil aircraft is absolute. The intentions of the drafters are apparent from the deliberations of the 25th Session (Extraordinary) of the ICAO Assembly, although they may not have been expressed with absolute clarity.

The term "weapons" has not been defined but its interpretation in practice should not cause any difficulties when the ordinary meaning of the word is considered; it would include guns, machine guns, cannons, missiles or targeted drones or any other object or substance that can damage or destroy an aircraft in flight.

"Civil aircraft" is also not defined with any clarity but it was a clear intention of the drafters to apply Article 3*bis* only to "*foreign*" aircraft. However, it is difficult to argue that international law would not give an equal protection to all aircraft regardless of their registration and to human life regardless of nationality.

"In flight" could be interpreted, by analogy with Article 1.2 of the Rome Convention (1952),[51] as "from the moment when power is applied for the purpose of actual take-off until the moment when the landing run ends". It should cover the period when the aircraft is committed to a specific action of flying. It could be argued that States are "free" to use weapons against an aircraft on the ground but the test of the proportionality of force used to the alleged infraction cannot be avoided.

In the general discussions a question was raised whether a State could use deadly force against an aircraft – regardless of its registry – if there are serious reasons to believe that the aircraft is operated by "narco-traffickers" and carries illicit substances; the answer must be strongly negative because the use of weapons against such aircraft would amount not only to a disproportionate death sentence for all persons on board but also instant execution of the sentence without appeal; yet, no country is known to have an unconditional death sentence for a mere suspicion of trafficking in drugs and it is also most likely that totally innocent persons unconnected with the drug trade may be on board the aircraft, possibly against their will.

A sad example of overanxious use of weapons against alleged drug traffickers occurred on 20 April 2001: the Peruvian air force's interceptor of Russian manufacture (Sukhoi Su-22) shot down a private single engine Cessna 185 (Skywagon) that lost communication and was erroneously suspected of carrying drugs. The wife of a US missionary on board and her seven-month-old baby were killed.

A more complex question was raised by the tragedy of 11 September 2001 when civil aircraft were unlawfully seized in the United States and then intentionally crashed against the towers of the World Trade Centre in New York City and the Pentagon in Washington, D.C. What could or should be the action of the authorities if they suspect that an aircraft in flight is about to be misused for a physical impact against an important target and could cause an explosion, fire and a major loss of life? Could they shoot it down?

Article 3*bis* of the Convention was never intended to prevail over the lawful self-defence against an "armed attack" under Article 51 of the UN Charter or the natural right of each State to its own "self-preservation". No State is obliged to remain idle and follow the destruction of its vital interests by criminal acts. The use of force, even of weapons, in such case cannot be ruled out by international law. However, such use of force must observe the requirement of proportionality and the decision-making authority authorizing or ordering the use of force should be vested in a constitutionally designated body or person. Innocent lives may be sacrificed in order to prevent a perceived possibility of a much larger disaster – a most difficult decision to take and tremendous responsibility if the judgement proves to have been incorrect.

---

51   Rome Convention on Damage Caused by Foreign Aircraft to Third Parties on the Surface (1952), ICAO Doc 7364.

5   International Legal Regime of Aircraft and Its Operation

Lex spectat naturae ordinem

It is paradoxical that aircraft – an object that is central to aviation and that is subject to such extensive international regulation – is not defined in any primary source of international law. Only in the Annexes to the Chicago Convention do we find a definition. In Annex 7 – Aircraft Nationality and Registration Marks – the following definition is given:

> *Aircraft* – Any machine that can derive support in the atmosphere from the reactions of the air other than the reactions of the air against the earth's surface.

Definitions in the Annexes are used for terms which are not self-explanatory in that they do not have accepted dictionary meaning; the definition does not have an independent status but is an essential part of each Standard and Recommended Practice in which the term is used.[1]

It may sound surprising that the term "aircraft" does not have accepted dictionary meaning; however, in the regulatory field of aviation the term encompasses so many types of flying instruments that cannot be covered by the ordinary dictionary meaning. Table I – Classification of aircraft – to Annex 7 lists more than twenty different machines that are to be called "aircraft" – from a free balloon over dirigibles to heavier-than-air and power-driven aeroplanes and helicopters; for completeness, even a kite deserves the name "aircraft". Of course, for all practical purposes of international civil aviation, only aeroplanes and helicopters are relevant. Unmanned aircraft ("drones") shall include unmanned free balloons and remotely piloted aircraft. Drones have become widely available, and many are in private hands for "hobby" (*e.g.*, photography) or simply as toys – obviously, even the smallest drone qualifies as an "aircraft" and is subject to safety regulations. "Air cushion vehicles" or "hovercraft" also move above the surface of the earth or water but do not derive support in the atmosphere from the aerodynamic reactions of

---

1   Annex 7, Definitions 1, p. 1.

the air but from the pressure of air against the earth's surface – hence they are not classified as "aircraft".[2]

Missiles and rockets also travel through the airspace but do not derive support from the reactions of the air. Nevertheless, one type of space exploration vehicles – the US Space Shuttle – on return to Earth flew through the airspace like a glider deriving support in the atmosphere from the reactions of the air. It would appear logical to consider it an "aircraft" on that segment of the journey when it may cross the established air routes where it would be necessary to maintain the separation with other aircraft to prevent collision and otherwise comply with the rules of the air. The US NASA does not consider the Space Shuttle an aircraft but classifies it *sui generis* equipment; however, there are no practical international consequences of this classification of the Space Shuttle since it does not enter the territorial airspace of any country except the United States during any segment of its flight (it takes off from California or Florida over the Atlantic and returns over the Pacific to US territory) and the classification is a domestic matter of the United States.

5.1 Civil Aircraft and State Aircraft

International air law deals only with *civil* aircraft and specifically excludes from its scope of applicability the status and operation of other aircraft generally designated as "*State aircraft*". The main source of the current international air law – the Chicago Convention on International Civil Aviation – stresses the concept "civil" right in its title and in Article 3 states:

> *Article 3*
> (a) This Convention shall be applicable only to civil aircraft and shall not be applicable to State aircraft. (b) Aircraft used in military, customs and police services shall be deemed to be State aircraft. (c) No State aircraft of a contracting State shall fly over the territory of another State or land thereon without authorization by special agreement or otherwise, and in accordance with the terms thereof. (d) The contracting States undertake, when issuing regulations for their State aircraft, that they will have due regard for the safety of navigation of civil aircraft.

---

2 The words "other than" were added in 1967 to make it clear that the *Hovercraft* is not included in the definition of aircraft. However, for the UK, a registered hovercraft on international sailing for passengers: the hovercraft is classified as an aircraft and the carriage of passengers is governed by the Montreal Convention (1999). For the cargo, though, the hovercraft is a ship and it is governed by maritime law. Anyway, internationally the hovercraft is not an aircraft.

The airspace of the Earth is equally used by "civil" aircraft (whether "commercial" or "general aviation") and by "State aircraft" (a typical representative of which is the "military" aircraft). It is arguable that in the world there are as many "military" aircraft in actual operation and in the arsenals of the States as there are "civil" aircraft engaged in commercial operations. These different types of aircraft share the same airspace, may mutually interact and should be subject to similar or identical standardized rules to secure mutual safety of air navigation. However, the vast body of international air law deals exclusively with civil aircraft and their operations. The international governmental and non-governmental organizations dealing with aviation also have their mandate restricted to civil aviation.

The status of the military aircraft is not clearly determined by positive rules of international law and is not particularly transparent or unequivocal. The issue is not addressed in international law with any specificity, could not be located in any one single international instrument and only some fragmentary aspects can be deduced directly or indirectly from different sources of international law (international treaties). The identifiable rules are mostly "negative" – stating what does not apply to military aircraft or what such aircraft are not permitted to do. The practice of States that could form a basis for the development of customary law is also not transparent or uniform and is often shrouded in secrecy.

The problem has been also mostly ignored in the legal research and literature and in the process of teaching – the only dedicated monograph on the legal status of military aircraft was published in 1957 – more than half a century ago and only in French.[3] Much more attention has been paid in literature to the legal position of military aircraft during an armed conflict – as belligerent, neutral or on a humanitarian mission – than to its status in the time of peace.

Since the inception of aviation States have been openly hostile to the idea that their military aircraft – tools and symbols of their military power, sovereignty, independence and prestige – should be subject to international regulation. The concerns for national security have prompted the States to legally curtail the access of foreign military aircraft to their territory well before the outset of World War I when aviation was at its infancy.

Much of the current lack of transparency and precision concerning the status of military aircraft is attributable to the fact that aviation since its inception was perceived as a potential tool for belligerent activities. The military use of aviation has been a powerful primary catalyst in the rapid development of aviation technology in general and that technology was only later adapted to civilian use. The fundaments of codified international air law were created in the shadow of World War I and the current public international air

---

3   Ming-Min Peng, "*Le status juridique del'aeronef militaire*", Martinus Nijhoff, The Hague, 1957. See also M. Milde, "Status of Military Aircraft in International Law" in *Luft- und Weltraumrecht im 21. Jahrhundert*, Carl Heymans Verlag KG, 2001, pp. 152-165.

law in World War II during which aviation proved its devastating tactical and strategic potential.

5.1.1 Evolution of the Legal Regime for Civil and State Aircraft

The Paris Convention (1919) drew a distinction between "private aircraft" and "State aircraft". The following provisions are relevant:

> *Article 30*: The following shall be deemed to be State aircraft:
> a. Military aircraft;
> b. Aircraft exclusively employed in State service, such as posts, customs, and police.
>
> Every other aircraft shall be deemed to be a private aircraft.
> All State aircraft other than military, customs and police aircraft shall be treated as private aircraft and as such shall be subject to all the provisions of the present Convention.
>
> *Article 31*: Every aircraft commanded by a person in military service detailed for the purpose shall be deemed to be a military aircraft.

The Paris Convention was fairly liberal and each State granted, in time of peace, "*freedom of innocent passage*" above its territory to the aircraft of other contracting States without distinction of nationality.[4] However, Article 32 of the Convention provided that "no military aircraft of a contracting State shall fly over the territory of another contracting State nor land thereon without special authorization". Similarly, special arrangements between the States concerned were to determine in what cases police and customs aircraft may be authorized to cross the frontier. Thus, from the very inception of international air law military aircraft were given a special status restricting their freedom of operation in foreign sovereign airspace and making it subject to a "special authorization" of the State to be overflown.

It is noteworthy that Articles 30 and 31 of the Paris Convention do not give a definition of "*military aircraft*" but rather set a presumption what should be "deemed" to be a State or military aircraft.

Practical problems arose shortly after the adoption of the Versailles Peace Treaty when the Allies tried to confiscate some of the German aeronautical equipment as "military"

---

[4] Chapter I (General Principles), Article 2.

while Germany claimed it to be "civil". The Allied Supreme Council requested the Consultative Committee on Aeronautics to draft rules permitting to make a distinction between "civil" aviation and "military and naval aviation" prohibited by the Peace Treaty. The complex negotiations resulted in the formulation of "Nine Rules" which came into force on 5 May 1922.[5] These "Rules" made a futile attempt to define "military" aircraft strictly by the technical parameters known at that period which, by today's standards, sound not only outdated but outright ludicrous.[6] It appears evident that the civil or military character of an aircraft will never be meaningfully determined solely on the basis of its technical features. The absurdity of the technical criteria was soon proved when Germany made protests that much of the civil aviation equipment operated by the Allies over Germany in fact met the criteria of "military" aircraft. Another problem was not solved in the period between the two World Wars – the ease with which a civil aircraft could be converted to military use and *vice-versa*. Lufthansa planes were known to carry military supplies and drop military parachutists during World War II.

5.1.2   Chicago Convention on Civil and State Aircraft

By its very title the Convention is addressed to *civil* aircraft and *civil* aviation. Like its 1919 precursor, the Convention itself does not give a definition of "*aircraft*" and that definition will be found only in subsidiary legal sources.[7] In its Article 3, the scope of applicability of the Convention is restricted to "civil" aircraft:

The initial interpretation of this provision must lead to unequivocal conclusion that:

– the Chicago Convention as such does not apply to State aircraft (which includes *military* aircraft); hence, even the law-making power of the ICAO Council to adopt Standards and Recommended Practices (SARPs) and the overall mandate of the Organization is restricted only to civil aircraft; and
– State aircraft are not permitted to fly over or land in foreign sovereign territory otherwise than with express authorization of the State concerned; and
– State aircraft may fly within the territory of their own State (*i.e.*, within the land mass and territorial waters of that State), over the high sea and the areas of undetermined sovereignty; they may fly within a foreign sovereign territory on the basis of a special authorization and in harmony with the terms of such authorization; such authorization must be given by a special agreement "or otherwise" – the practice of States indicates

---

5   See J.C. Cooper, *op. cit.*, p. 306.
6   Any single-seat aircraft with engine power exceeding 60 horsepower (HP), aircraft which can reach an altitude beyond 4000 m with full load or exceed the maximum speed of 170 km per hour or carry more than 600 kg load, including the pilot, mechanic and instruments – all such aircraft were classified as "military aircraft".
7   See, *i.e.*, Annex 7, International Standards, 1. Definitions.

that the preferred form is a bilateral or multilateral agreement between the States concerned, or an "*ad hoc*" permission properly obtained through the diplomatic channels; a mere operational air traffic control (ATC) clearance for the flight would not appear sufficient to satisfy the terms of Article 3 (c).

What could be the consequences if a "State aircraft" enters the foreign sovereign airspace without a proper authorization? Such an aircraft may be
– intercepted for purposes of identification;
– directed to leave the violated airspace by a determined route;
– directed to land for the purpose of further investigation/prosecution; or
– forced to land for further investigation/prosecution.

The State of the violating aircraft would face international responsibility for the infraction; the nature and severity of such responsibility would much depend on the overall relations of the States concerned and could range from the duty to apologize, promise to penalize the individuals responsible, promise not to repeat such infraction … to more severe sanctions, including the forfeiture of the violating aircraft and imprisonment of the crew or other sanctions. The use of weapons against such an aircraft – "violator" – in time of peace would be reprehensible and contrary to all humanitarian concepts; it in fact would in most cases lead not only to the destruction of the aircraft but also would amount to a death sentence and immediate execution for all persons on board without due process of law or right to appeal – hardly a "proportionate" use of force. Nevertheless, the codified international law (new Article 3*bis* of the Chicago Convention) recognizes the general prohibition of the use of weapons only against *civil* aircraft in flight – the State (and in particular *military*) aircraft do not enjoy such a general protection in international law.

Article 8 – Pilotless aircraft: The Chicago Convention contains additional restrictions which in practice would be applicable in particular to State (military) aircraft:

> The arsenals of air forces of the world include aircraft capable of being flown without a pilot (balloons, drones – some of them of miniature size …). The flights of *pilotless aircraft* over foreign territory are expressly subject to special authorization of the State to be overflown and in accordance with the terms of such authorization. Moreover, contracting States have accepted a legal undertaking to insure that the flights of such pilotless aircraft in regions open to civil aircraft shall be so controlled as to obviate danger to civil aircraft.[8]

---

8   Article 8 of the Chicago Convention.

Article 35 – Cargo restrictions: No munitions of war or implements of war may be carried in or above the territory of a State in aircraft engaged in international navigation, except by permission of that State and each State may define by its regulations what constitutes implements of war.[9]

5.1.3 Other International Instruments Relating to Civil and State Aircraft

State aircraft are also expressly excluded from the scope of applicability of many multilateral conventions unifying the international air law: The scope of applicability of such Conventions is not predetermined by Article 3 a) and b) of the Chicago Convention; they define their scope of applicability independently

– The Geneva Convention *on the International Recognition of Rights in Aircraft* (1948)[10] has a provision, in Article XIII "This Convention shall not apply to aircraft used in military, customs or police services"; this text avoids the Chicago Article 3 a) term "State aircraft" and the presumption in Article 3 b) as to what is "deemed" to be "State aircraft". The same way in the Aircraft Protocol of the Cape Town Convention *on International Interests in Mobile Equipment* and its Protocol *on Matters Specific to Aircraft Equipment* (2001): the definition of aircraft engines, airframes, helicopters is "other than those in military, customs or police services".[11]

– The Rome Convention *on Damage Caused by Foreign Aircraft to Third Parties on the Surface* (1952)[12] in Article 26 stipulates "This Convention shall not apply to damage caused by military, customs or police aircraft". This wording departs even further from Article 3 of the Chicago Convention by omitting the expression "used in" and not helping in any manner to define the terms "military, customs or police aircraft". This Convention was amended by the *Montreal Protocol* (1978)[13] which would amend Article 26 to be closely aligned on Article 3 (b) of the Chicago Convention ("This Convention shall not apply to damage caused by aircraft used in military, customs or police services"). ICAO modernised the Rome Convention and made out the *Convention on Compensation for Damage Caused by Aircraft to Third Parties*, the so-called *"General Risk Convention"*,[14] and, due to unlawful acts, the *Convention on Compensation for Damage to Third Parties, Resulting from Acts of Unlawful Interference*

---

9 Article 35 a) of the Chicago Convention.
10 ICAO Doc 7620.
11 ICAO Doc 9794 – Protocol to the Convention on International Interests in Mobile Equipment on Matters Specific to Aircraft Equipment, 16 November 2001. Chapter I, Article I, 2. (b), (e), (l).
12 ICAO Doc 7364.
13 ICAO Doc 9257.
14 ICAO Doc 9919 – Montreal Convention on Compensation for Damage Caused by Aircraft to Third Parties (2009), Chapter I, Article 2, 4.

Involving Aircraft, the so-called *"Convention on the Compensation for Unlawful Acts"*.[15] These Conventions use the same terminology and follow the predecessor treaty as they "do not apply to damage caused by State aircraft".

- The Tokyo Convention *on Offences and Certain Other Acts Committed on Board Aircraft* (1963)[16] stipulates in Article 1, paragraph 4: "This Convention shall not apply to aircraft used in military, customs or police service". The Tokyo Convention was amended by the Montreal Protocol[17] but this provision remained unamended. Such standardized clause is further used in The Hague *Convention for the Suppression of Unlawful Seizure of Aircraft* (1970)[18] and the Montreal *Convention for the Suppression of Unlawful Acts Against the Safety of Civil Aviation* (1971).[19] The Beijing Convention *on the Suppression of Unlawful Acts Relating to International Civil Aviation*,[20] which replaced the Montreal Convention (1971) and its supplementary Protocol (1988) sets forth the same provisions. In the Beijing Protocol *Supplementary to the Convention for the Suppression of Unlawful Seizure of Aircraft*,[21] which supplemented The Hague Convention (1970), this part was not modified.

Less direct is the exclusion of State aircraft from the scope of applicability of the *Convention for the Unification of Certain Rules Relating to International Carriage by Air* (1929)[22] signed in Warsaw – the Convention is applicable to carriage performed by the State or by legally constituted public bodies.[23] However, the Additional Protocol to the Warsaw Convention gave parties the right to make a declaration that Article 2 (1) of the Convention shall not apply to carriage performed directly by the State. Under The Hague Protocol of 1955 amending the Warsaw Convention of 1929[24] States are entitled to make a declaration that the Convention as amended by the Protocol shall not apply to the carriage of persons, cargo and baggage for its military authorities on aircraft, registered in that State, the whole

---

15 ICAO Doc 9920 – Montreal Convention on Compensation for Damage to Third Parties, Resulting from Acts of Unlawful Interference Involving Aircraft (2009), Chapter I, Article 2, 4.
16 ICAO Doc 8364.
17 ICAO Doc 10034 – Protocol to Amend the Convention on Offences and Certain Other Acts Committed on Board Aircraft, Montreal, 4 April 2014; The Montreal Protocol took effect on 1 January 2020. Chapter I, Article 1, 4.
18 ICAO Doc 8920, Article 3, paragraph 2.
19 ICAO Doc 8966, Article 4, paragraph 1.
20 ICAO Doc 9960 – Beijing Convention on the Suppression of Unlawful Acts Relating to International Civil Aviation. (2010); The Beijing Convention took effect on 1 July 2018, Article 5.
21 ICAO Doc 9959 – Protocol Supplementary to the Convention for the Suppression of Unlawful Seizure of Aircraft. Beijing, 10 September 2010; The Beijing Protocol took effect on 1 January 2018.
22 II Conference Internationale de droit prive aerien, 4-12 October 1929, Varsovie (Warszawa 1930), pp. 220-233. [Note: the text of the Convention is authentic only in the French language].
23 Article 2 of the Warsaw Convention; in 1929 there were in fact no "private" airlines, except in the United States and possibly Japan. The airlines were State owned and controlled.
24 ICAO Doc 7632, Article XXVI.

capacity of which has been reserved by or on behalf of such authorities. Similar provisions will be found in further attempts at a revision of the "Warsaw system" – the *Guatemala City Protocol* (1971)[25] the *Additional Protocol of Montreal No. 2* (1975),[26] *Additional Protocol of Montreal No. 3* (1975)[27] and the *Montreal Protocol No. 4* (1975).[28] On 28 May 1999, a Diplomatic Conference convened under the auspices of ICAO at Montreal adopted and opened for signature a new *Convention for the Unification of certain Rules for International Carriage by Air*[29] which is intended to replace the "Warsaw system" of instruments. Under its Article 2, paragraph 1, the Montreal Convention (1999) applies to carriage performed by the State or by legally constituted public bodies; however, under Article 57, a State may at any time make the only reservations permitted by the Convention – to declare that the Convention shall not apply to

> a) international carriage by air performed and operated directly by that State Party for non-commercial purposes in respect to its functions and duties as a sovereign State; and/or b) the carriage of persons, cargo and baggage for its military authorities on aircraft registered in or leased by that State Party, the whole capacity of which has been reserved by or on behalf of such authorities.

It may be concluded that the unification of private air law in the "Warsaw system" and its successor of 1999 does not exclude carriage by State/ military aircraft but permits States to exclude by an explicit reservation any such carriage performed *iure imperii*, *i.e.*, in the exercise of the sovereign functions of the State.

5.1.4 Applicability of ICAO Standards, Recommended Practices and Procedures

In view of Article 3 a) of the Chicago Convention it could be argued that the extensive spectrum of "ICAO rules" – *i.e.*, the Standards and Recommended Practices (*SARPs*) adopted by the ICAO Council under Articles 37, 38, 54 l) and 90 of the Chicago Convention and designated as *Annexes* to the Convention – are not applicable to State/military aircraft.

---

25 ICAO Doc 8932; this document did not come into force and is now obsolete.
26 ICAO Doc 9146, Article XXVI.
27 ICAO Doc 9147, Article XI, paragraph 1 b); this document did not come into force and is now obsolete.
28 ICAO Doc 9148, Article XXI, paragraph 1 b).
29 ICAO Doc 9740.

The same must apply for guidance materials contained in the Procedures for Air Navigation Services (*PANS*)[30] or Regional Supplementary Procedures (*SUPPs*).[31]

However, the history of ICAO records a striking cleavage of opinions as to whether the Council of ICAO is entitled to "legislate" in the form of Standards and Recommended Practices on any issues relating to military aircraft. The issue arose in 1983-1986 in the wake of the 007 Korean Airlines disaster. The Extraordinary Session of the ICAO Council on 16 September 1983 decided "to review the provisions of the Convention, its Annexes and other related documents and consider possible amendments to prevent recurrence of such a tragic incident".[32] In 1984, the ICAO Air Navigation Commission initiated studies to amend Annex 2 to the Convention to include Standards governing the interception of civil aircraft by military aircraft and the related activities of the interception control. There were strong objections from several States that the adoption of such rules would exceed the mandate of ICAO which is restricted to civil aircraft. However, the majority of States were of the view that such regulation of interception was aimed at safeguarding the safety of civil aviation – the primary aim and purpose of ICAO – and did not purport to regulate the conduct of military aircraft but the conduct of States with respect to the safety of civil aviation foreseen in Article 3 d) of the Convention. Consultation with States through a State Letter[33] resulted in 54 responses, of which 46 supported the proposal or had no objections, while 8 expressed disagreement on the constitutional grounds.[34]

In the Council discussions the strongest opposition to the proposal came from the USA, USSR, Egypt and Pakistan who argued that the adoption of Standards on interception were aimed at military aircraft and as such were not within the purview of ICAO.[35] On 10 March 1986 a vote on the entire proposal resulted in 22 votes for, 4 opposed and 6 abstentions.[36] After the vote the US Representative Stated that his Government continued to hold that the adoption of the Standards relating to interception was *ultra vires* and would treat them accordingly; this view was vigorously echoed by the representative of the USSR.[37]

---

30 PANS provide operative guidance including practical regulations, which are too detailed in comparison with SARPs, therefore, they function as special rules for SARPs.
31 The regulatory scope of SUPPs coincides with the scope of SARPs, but their application is not wide-scale and their territorial scope applies only to one specific ICAO region.
32 C-Min Extraordinary (1983), 4, paragraph 24.
33 Resolution A13/38-84/72, 26 October 1984.
34 AN-WP/5736.
35 C-Min 116/5.
36 It should be noted that at that time the Council had 33 seats, so the 22 votes in favour represented just the bare two-thirds majority of the Council required under Article 90 of the Chicago Convention. Such a divided vote is unprecedented in the annals of ICAO – the adoption of new Standards is usually supported by a full consensus.
37 C-Min 117/12. It should be also noted that the United States so far did not ratify the Protocol introducing the new Article 3*bis*; while it never explicitly explained its hesitations thereon and its rejection of amend-

The ICAO experience in this matter indicates that the amendment to Annex 2 with respect to interception was adopted in a highly emotionally charged atmosphere following the destruction of KAL 007 and that there is a strong opinion – in particular among the States with powerful air forces – that ICAO has no jurisdiction whatsoever to deal with military aircraft.

However, it would be incorrect to believe that ICAO does not pay any attention to matters related to military aircraft. There is a solid tradition that each regular session of the ICAO Assembly adopts (without exception unanimously) an extensive Resolution entitled "Consolidated statement of continuing ICAO policies and associated practices related specifically to air navigation". An integral part of such a Resolution is Appendix P – *"Co-ordination of civil and military air traffic"*. That part of the resolution explicitly recognizes that the airspace as well as many facilities and services should be used in common by civil and military aviation and that full integration of the control of civil and military air traffic may be regarded as the ultimate goal. Most revealing is the second operative clause of the Resolution which states:

> The regulation and procedures established by Contracting States to govern the operation of their State aircraft over the high seas shall ensure that these operations do not compromise the safety, regularity and efficiency of international civil air traffic and that, to the extent practicable, these operations comply with the Rules of the Air in Annex 2.

This wording in fact, although in a cautious tone ("to the extent practicable"), asserts the need for State aircraft to comply with the rules of the air over the high seas in conformity with Annex 2 to the Convention.

The rules of the air represent the basic "highway code" in the air safeguarding safe and orderly flight, rules for collision avoidance, etc. Over the high sea no State can exercise jurisdiction to stipulate the rules of the air in a manner harmonized for all users. Annex 2 to the Chicago Convention has a very special status: it contains only Standards and no Recommended Practices – hence, in case of non-compliance States would have the legal duty to notify a "difference" under Article 38 of the Convention; moreover, in view of the third sentence of Article 12 of the Convention "over the high seas the rules in force shall be those established under this Convention". When adopting Annex 2, the Council of ICAO decided that the Annex constitutes "rules relating to flight and manoeuvre of

---

ment 27 to Annex 2. It is apparent that the real cause is the fact that the interpretation of the Chicago Convention and of the Annexes may, on appeal from the ICAO Council decision under Article 84 of the Convention, become open to compulsory jurisdiction of the International Court of Justice – a serious policy matter for the US government.

aircraft" within the meaning of Article 12 of the Convention and that "over the high seas, therefore, these rules apply without exception".[38] This means that no State can file a difference to Annex 2 with respect to the high seas and it gives a unique status to the Council of ICAO that it "legislates" Rules of the Air for some 43% of the surface of the Earth!

ICAO Assembly Resolution A36-13,[39] Appendix O goes in the right direction when it calls for the compliance with the ICAO rules of the air over the high seas by military aircraft. The "Associated Practice" attached to Appendix P further exhorts States to coordinate with all States responsible for the provision of air traffic services over the high seas in the area in question.

There are many other fields where the ICAO Standards and Recommended Practices contained in the 19 Annexes to the Convention should be made applicable to "State aircraft" in the interests of safety, standardization and uniformity of the legal regulation. However, this cannot be achieved without a profound amendment of the Chicago Convention in order to make it applicable also to "State aircraft" – a step that is most unlikely to marshal the political will and consensus of States.

On the other hand, nothing prevents the States themselves to accept or to approximate the ICAO Standards and Recommended Practices (SARPs) into their national legislation applicable to their "State aircraft" and thus achieve a better harmony and coordination between their civil and State aviation activities. Such a course of action seems to be imperative also because the distinction between a "civil" and "State" aircraft is in practice frequently obliterated, the same aircraft may be either "civil" or "State" aircraft depending on its actual "use", and there is no reliable and generally accepted legal definition of what is "civil" and what is "State" aircraft.

5.1.5 "Definition" of Civil and State Aircraft

Article 3 of the Chicago Convention singles out the concept of "*State aircraft*" for a special legal regime outside the scope of the Convention but does not give a definition of the term. Article 3 b) of the Convention only states that

> Aircraft used in military, customs and police services shall be deemed to be State aircraft.

---

[38] Annex 2 – Rules of the Air, 2.1.1 Note.
[39] See Resolutions A37-15, Appendix O, WP/11, 2010; A38-12, Appendix I, 2013; A40-4, Appendix I, 2019; A41-10, Appendix I, 2022.

This is not a definition but only a rebuttable presumption *(presumptio iuris)*. Many other types of aircraft may be involved in activities of the State *iure imperii* (in the State's "power" function), such as coast guard, search and rescue, medical services, mapping or geological survey services, disaster relief, VIP and Government transport, etc.; consequently, the examples given in Article 3 b) cannot be taken as all-comprehensive.

In the context of this study the definition of "military" aircraft is of critical importance. However, the Convention does not give any definition of "military ... services" and any effort at interpretation has to start with the "ordinary meaning to be given to the terms of the treaty in their context and in the light of its object and purpose".[40]

The ordinary meaning of the terms "military ... services" may seem to be a matter of "common sense" and probably was so treated by the drafters of the Convention at the Chicago Conference since the Proceedings of the Chicago Conference of 1944 fail to clarify in any manner the meaning of the expression. The original proposal of the US Delegation consisted of one single sentence stating that the Convention should be applicable only to civil aircraft (without defining the term). In later discussions (which are not recorded) it was suggested that the article be expanded to give a definition of military and State aircraft and defining their status with respect to the Convention. "After considerable consultations with the military authorities of the United States and United Kingdom ... "the text was adopted as it appears in Article 3.[41] Thus the drafting history does not assist in any manner in the interpretation. "A special meaning shall be given to a term if it is established that the parties so intended",[42] but there is no indication of any special intention of the parties with respect to the words "military ... services".

What characteristics could distinguish an aircraft to characterize it as a "military aircraft"? The following elements could be considered – not in isolation but in their mutual combination and may assist in the determination of the military nature of the aircraft:

– *design of the aircraft* and its *technical characteristics*: some aircraft by their design and characteristics (including their weaponry) are constructed exclusively for military combat, while other types may be readily converted for other purposes. As mentioned above, it does not appear reliable to define the nature of the aircraft solely on the basis of its technical characteristics;

– *registration marks*: the nationality and registration marks of an aircraft may designate the aircraft as "military" but that fact by itself is not a proof that the aircraft is "used in military services" in a particular situation;

---

40   Vienna Convention on the Law of Treaties (1969), Article 31, 1.
41   Proceedings, Vol. II, p. 1381.
42   Vienna Convention on the Law of Treaties. (1969), Article 31, 4.

- *ownership*: the fact that the aircraft is owned by the State or specifically by a military arm of the State is a valid indication of its status but in itself does not prove that it is "used in military services" in a particular situation;
- *type of operation*: the nature of the flight, documents carried on board, flight plan, communications procedures, composition of the crew (military or civilian?), secrecy or open nature of the flight, etc. could assist in the qualification of an aircraft as "military".

In the absence of any other guidance, it is proposed that the interpretation should focus on the expressions "used" and "services" in Article 3 b) of the Chicago Convention – aircraft *used in military, customs* and *police services*. This wording, in the absence of any other guidance, suggests that the drafters had in mind a *functional approach* to the determination of the status of the aircraft as civil and military: regardless of the design, technical characteristics, registration, ownership, the nature of the crew, documentations, etc., the status of the aircraft is determined by the *function* it actually performs at a given time. The insurance requirements are also not the issue, but it is good to know that there is mandatory insurance (hull and air carrier liability) requirements for civil aircraft and there is no insurance mostly for state aircraft since the State assumes underlying responsibility (*i.e.*, Air-Transat would be used for civil purposes but if it is used in a military/police mission, it may not be covered by their insurance policy).

Thus, it is conceivable that the same aircraft may be "State/military aircraft" in one situation and "civil aircraft" in another.[43] There is, *e.g.*, an undocumented story of an unarmed fighter plane F-18 piloted by a military officer cleared under a civil flight plan for a flight to another country's civil airport to deliver a rare serum for a critically ill person – this would be an example of a humanitarian "mercy flight" and the aircraft could claim civil status. It is well documented that military cargo planes piloted by air force officers were cleared as "civil flights" when delivering humanitarian assistance to victims of devastating earthquakes in Pakistan, Nepal, Macedonia or Georgia.

Conversely, there is a well-documented case of a civil aircraft (B-737, EgyptAir Flight 2843 from Cairo to Tunis) carrying, on the basis of charter by the Government, suspected terrorists out of the country under Military Police escort; that aircraft was intercepted by US F-14 Tomcat Jet fighter, and forced to land in Italy but no protest was raised in ICAO.[44]

---

43 Even the US Presidential Aircraft, the famous "Air Force One" has flown on a civilian flight plan as civil aircraft if the President of the United States was not on board. But if the President is on board of the aircraft, it would automatically be designated as a State aircraft.
44 *Achille Lauro* case: the Italian cruise ship, the MS Achille Lauro was hijacked on 7 October 1985 in the Mediterranean Sea of the coast of Alexandria, Egypt. The suspected terrorists after negotiations were released and travelled on board the aircraft to Tunis.

The US Government in a letter to IFALPA[45] stated: "It is our view that the aircraft was operating as a State aircraft at the time of interception. The relevant factors – including exclusive State purpose and function of the mission, the presence of armed military personnel on board and the secrecy under which the mission was attempted – compel this conclusion".[46]

Another illustration of the possibly complicated status of the same aircraft is the case of USAF CT-43A (a military version of B-737-200), registration 31149 which crashed, on 3 April 1996, at Dubrovnik, Croatia; it carried VIP passengers and the Croatian accident investigation report expressly recognized the aircraft as "civil aircraft in accordance with Article 3 of the Convention" and not "as a flight for military purposes".[47]

In practice the definition of "military aircraft" should be very narrow and should reflect the true military mission of the particular flight. A possible analogy could be found in the UN Convention on the Law of the Sea (1982), Article 29 of which gives the following definition of a *warship*:

> For the purpose of this Convention, "warship" means a ship belonging to the armed forces of a state bearing the external marks distinguishing such ship of its nationality, under the command of an officer duly commissioned by the government of the State and whose name appears in the appropriate service list or its equivalent, and manned by a crew which is under regular armed forces discipline.

A definition of a *military aircraft* along these lines would represent a progress compared with the vague stipulation of Article 3 b) of the Chicago Convention. However, even such wording would not be sufficient for all situations, because even a *military aircraft* covered by such a definition could perform, in a specific situation, functions which are not part of "military service" and could be qualified as *civil aircraft* under the terms of Article 3 of the Chicago Convention.

The need for an acceptable definition of "civil" and "state" aircraft was addressed at the 36th Session of the ICAO Legal Committee in November-December 2015. A working paper titled "State/civil aircraft definition and its impact on aviation"[48] was presented by Poland on behalf of ten Central-European Rotation Group [CERG] and other States (Bulgaria, the Czech Republic, Cyprus, Greece, Hungary, Lithuania, Poland, Romania, Slovenia and Slovakia). Recalling the 1993 Secretariat Study on Civil/State Aircraft,[49] the

---

45 International Federation of Air Line Pilots' Association.
46 Quoted in ICAO Doc LC/29-WP/2-1, pp. 11-12.
47 Accident Investigation Board Report, August 1996, p. 4.
48 LC36-WP/2-6.
49 A37-WP/80.

paper submitted "that the absence of clear and generally accepted international rules affects the order and safety of international civil aviation". Difficulties and uncertainties arise when an aircraft is not used in military, customs or police services but is used in other governmental services. As examples of such difficulties, the discussion cited the carriage by "detainees" – an obvious allusion to the cases of "extraordinary rendition flights" mentioned below. The US Delegation did not support this initiative,[50] cautioning against any efforts to regulate state aircraft through ICAO, because the Chicago Convention is not applicable to state aircraft. After an inconclusive debate the Legal Committee agreed that a questionnaire should be sent to States requesting information about possible difficulties with the concept of civil/state aircraft and the subject will again be considered at the 37th Session of the Legal Committee.

Any confusion in the actual legal status of an aircraft in a particular situation would have serious consequences and would raise doubts about the law applicable to such aircraft – e.g., the Chicago Convention and its Annexes, other international air law instruments, bilateral agreements on air services, validity of the hull and liability insurance policies and the life insurance policies of the crew if the aircraft is deemed to be *military*, etc.

Some critical attention has been attracted by "extraordinary rendition" flights – initially firmly denied but lately reluctantly confirmed acts of the US authorities during the years 2002-2005 in the wake of "911": suspected high-value terrorists were abducted in one territory and transported by aircraft to another territory for interrogation by US agents or delivered to security forces in other countries where they would not enjoy protection against torture or other abuses. Among such countries media mentioned Syria, Egypt, Uzbekistan, Afghanistan, Poland, Morocco, Jordan… The aircraft used for such "rendition" landed in several European countries and in the UK dependent territory Diego Garcia; they must have flown, without landing, through the sovereign airspace of several other countries.[51] The aircraft used for such flights were identified as "executive" passenger aircraft of the type Gulfstream (14 seat) and executive version of B-737 (32 seats), often not displaying the carrier's name or logo and all had US nationality marks ("N" – is represented by "November" in aviation "phony")[52] and registration numbers with history of frequent changes. While such aircraft were ostensibly civil aircraft by their design, markings, ownership and operating crew, they were "used" for police/security services in a clandestine manner and that clearly put them in the category of State aircraft. Flights of such State aircraft over a foreign territory or landing in such territory without a special authorization was a flagrant violation of an international legal obligation (Article 3 c) of

---

50   LC36-WP/2-8.
51   See M. Milde, "'Rendition Flights' and International Law", ZLW, 4/2008, pp. 477-486.
52   The communication in aviation has to take place according to the ICAO "phonetic alphabet". The ICAO phonetic alphabet has assigned the 26 code words to the 26 letters of the English alphabet in alphabetical order. The ICAO also offers guidance on pronouncing numbers.

the Chicago Convention); moreover, the operators of such flights misrepresented the nature of the flight and the nature of the aircraft when filing their "flight plan" as provided in Annexes 2 and 6 to the Chicago Convention and it is doubtful that they carried the journey log book and a list of passengers with their names and places of embarkation and destination as prescribed in Article 29 of the Chicago Convention. Any criticism of the US actions is veiled in the discrete diplomatic secrecy. Only the Parliamentary Assembly of the Council of Europe adopted, on 27 June 2007, Resolution 1562 (2007) "Secret detention and illegal transfers of detainees involving Council of Europe Member States" critical of the extraordinary renditions and of the apparent tolerance or even collusion of some Member States of the Council of Europe.[53]

Another controversial issue may be whether aircraft deemed to be *military* is liable to pay the charges for route air navigation services, airport charges, ATC, etc., although it is mostly recognized, as a matter of natural justice, that even military aircraft cannot be exempted from payment for services made available or actually rendered, unless there is an express agreement between the States concerned to the contrary. As a matter of international courtesy, such charges are not in practice imposed on an aircraft carrying a Head of State, although such a person is a commander-in-chief of the military forces of the State concerned, and his aircraft should be deemed to be "state aircraft".

5.1.6 De Lege Ferenda …

The analysis of the positive law and practice with respect to the status of a military aircraft in time of peace confirms a lack of clarity and certainty in the very concept and definition of *military aircraft*. The status of an aircraft is determined by the actual function that aircraft performs in a particular situation and most aircraft could perform either the civil or military function.

It is proposed that the status of each flight should be determined by the *approved flight plan* accepted by the State or States to be flown over and specifying the nature of the flight as either civil or military. It is quite conceivable in practice that the aircraft on a particular route would be once considered *military* (*e.g.*, when carrying military troops and supplies for exercises or combat mission), other time as *civil* (*e.g.*, when carrying humanitarian supplies to a disaster area).

The easy conversion of most aircraft types from one function to another makes it almost imperative that the international standards and recommended practices and procedures relating to the safety, regularity and economy of air navigation should be applicable equally to civil and State aircraft in the interest of global safety and security.

---

53   www.assembly.coe.int/Main.asp?link=Documents/Adoptedtext/ta07/ERES1562.htm.

However, the entrenched concerns for national sovereignty, security, prestige and pride make it most unlikely that States in the foreseeable future would be willing to subject their military equipment and its operations to international legal regulation, standardization and globalization, however convincing arguments may be presented.

Nevertheless, the global concerns for the safety of air navigation could and should lead the States to accept unilaterally, in their domestic legislation, the agreed benchmarks of the international standards, recommended practices and procedures elaborated by the international community through ICAO and applicable to civil aviation.

Among the priorities for the alignment of domestic regulation for military aircraft on the international standards could be the following:

- *personnel training* and *licensing*: the national standards for the health requirements, training and testing of pilots and other flight crews should at least meet the minimum standards of Annex 1 to the Chicago Convention, in particular in cases when such crews may be involved in the carriage of passengers.
- *rules of the air*: the aerial "highway code" in Annex 2 to the Chicago Convention is of primary importance for the safety of any air navigation, civil or military. In a foreign airspace, all aircraft must observe the Rules of the Air there in force. Over the high seas the standards of Annex 2 should be observed without exception, as strongly urged by ICAO Assembly Resolution A37-15, Appendix O.
- *aircraft operation*: the standards of Annex 6 to the Chicago Convention should be observed by military aircraft, in particular when carrying passengers [availability of cockpit voice recorder (CVR), flight data recorder (FDR), navigational equipment, oxygen, life vests…].
- *airworthiness*: the minimum standards of aircraft airworthiness under Annex 8 to the Chicago Convention should be required for the military aircraft engaged in the carriage of persons and cargo in the time of peace.
- *aeronautical communications*: military aircraft should be equipped with means of communication and procedures to interact safely with civil aircraft and should comply with the standards of Annex 10 to the Chicago Convention, be tuned always also to the civil emergency frequencies, etc.
- *air traffic services*: military aircraft should observe the existing air traffic services established and operating under Annex 11 to the Chicago Convention and should be capable to interact with the different flight information regions.
- *search and rescue*: the military aircraft in practice may be the main tool of any search and rescue operations; the standards of Annex 12 to the Chicago Convention should be applied to such operations regardless of the type of aircraft used.
- *accident investigation*: the procedures prescribed by Annex 13 to the Chicago Convention should be followed in cases of "military" accidents involving aircraft of the type also used for non-military purposes.

- *airports*: the standards of Annex 14 and of the related PANS should be made applicable to military airports open to transportation of persons and cargo.
- *environmental protection*: this could be one of the most difficult tasks for States to approximate the Standards of Annex 16 to the Chicago Convention to military aircraft with respect to curtailing their noise and engine emissions; however, it is unavoidable that in time of peace military aviation must make its contribution to the protection of the environment.

Aviation is a global activity and the interests of global aviation safety do justify balancing and harmonization of the rules, standards and procedures and making them applicable both to civil and State/military aircraft.

5.2 Nationality and Registration of Aircraft

An aircraft is not an ordinary moveable object. It is complex machinery and its possession and operation require special precautions and skills to prevent possible dangers to persons and property around. For that reason, States from the inception of aviation required, by domestic law, prescribed terms and conditions under which a person or corporation may own an aircraft and operate it.

One of the generally applied conditions was the registration of the aircraft – similar to the old practice of registering merchant ships or more recent one registering of motor vehicles. The national practice requiring registration of aircraft was soon adopted in the international regulation.[54] The Paris Convention (1919) contained substantial restrictions – no aircraft to be entered on the register of one of the contracting States unless it belongs wholly to nationals of such State; moreover, no incorporated company can be registered as the owner of an aircraft unless it possesses the nationality of the State in which the aircraft is registered, unless the president or chairman of the company and at least two-thirds of the directors possess such nationality, and unless the company fulfils all other conditions which may be prescribed by the laws of the said State.

What could have been the cause for such substantial restrictions? Perhaps the fierce opposition of States to "flags of convenience" from the early beginning of aviation, perhaps also an effort to block the defeated Germany from advancing its aviation development in other States.

The current international regulation based on the Chicago Convention is far less restrictive: Article 19 of the Convention states:

---

54 Article 6 of the Paris Convention (1919).

Article 19
National laws governing registration
The registration or transfer of registration of aircraft in any contracting State shall be made in accordance with its laws and regulations.

It is thus a sovereign power of each State to decide by its legislation who and under what conditions can register an aircraft in its register – perhaps not only a citizen but also a permanent resident, corporate body either registered or having its principal place of business in that State, etc. Such laws would also determine whether a foreign owned aircraft (*e.g.*, when the ownership title is retained by a foreign bank or other creditor, by a lessor of the aircraft, etc.) could be entered on the national register.

A limitation is imposed by international regulation in Article 18 of the Convention that prohibits dual registration:

Article 18
Dual registration
An aircraft cannot be validly registered in more than one State, but its registration may be changed from one State to another.

The Chicago Convention also imposes an international duty to report to ICAO on the registration and ownership of any aircraft registered in that State. The relevant Article 21 of the Convention is for all practical purposes a "dead letter" since there is no record that it has ever been applied.

Article 21
Report of registrations
Each contracting State undertakes to supply to any other contracting state or to the International Civil Aviation Organization, on demand, information concerning the registration and ownership of any particular aircraft registered in that State. In addition, each contracting State shall furnish reports to the International Civil Aviation Organization, under such regulations as the letter may prescribe, giving such pertinent data as can be made available concerning the ownership and control of aircraft registered in that State and habitually engaged in international air navigation. The data thus obtained by the International Civil Aviation Organization shall be made available by it on request to other contracting States.

The registration marks of an aircraft should be letters, numbers, or a combination of letter and numbers, and are to be assigned by the State of Registry.[55]

In international law more important than the registration of aircraft and the registration marks is the *nationality* of the aircraft and the nationality marks. The concept of nationality of aircraft has also its roots in the old concept of maritime law and practice. Nationality of a person denotes a legal relation between that person and a particular State – a relation from which legal consequences follow in the form of rights and duties.

The Paris Convention (1919) introduced into international law a provision that aircraft possess the nationality of the State on the register of which they are entered.[56] This principle is currently reflected in Article 17 of the Chicago Convention:

Article 17
Nationality of aircraft
Aircraft have the nationality of the State in which they are registered.

Annex 7 to the Chicago Convention prescribes the size, format and position of the nationality and registration marks on the hull of the aircraft and also the format of the Certificate of Registration that is to be carried in the aircraft at all times. Such certificate contains the name of the registering State, description of the nationality and registration mark, manufacturer's designation of the aircraft, aircraft serial number, name and address of the owner and the date of registration.

The nationality mark should precede the registration mark and consist of a character or group of characters; when the first character of the registration mark is a letter it shall be preceded by a hyphen.

The nationality marks are to be selected "from the series of nationality symbols included in the radio call signs allocated to the State of Registry by the International Telecommunications Union. The nationality mark shall be notified to the International Civil Aviation Organization".[57]

Some of the radio call signs have a long history going back to the 19th century and then either appear as an acronym of the name of the State (*e.g.*, F for France, D for Germany [Deutschland], I for Italy, G for Great Britain, etc.) or were easily used in the Morse code (*e.g.*, N= –. for the USA, B= –... for China, etc.) but mostly there is no such evident logic in the system of signs (*e.g.*, 7T for Algeria, UN for Kazakhstan, EX for Kyrgyzstan, etc.).

A list of the nationality marks is in the Supplement to ICAO Annex 7; for convenience it is attached to this publication as Appendix 5.

---

55 International Standards 3 (3.5), Annex 7 – Aircraft Nationality and Registration Marks.
56 Article 6 of the Paris Convention (1919).
57 International Standards 3 (3.3), Annex 7. See also Appendix 5 to this book.

5.3 Joint and International Registration of Aircraft

The high-technology aircraft represent an extremely high investment and their acquisition and economic operation could be facilitated, in particular among the developing countries, by establishing joint or international operating organizations or agencies in which the resources of two or more States could be combined and share. The establishment of such organizations or agencies is not only permitted by the Chicago Convention but is in fact encouraged. The relevant provisions are to be found in Chapter XVI, Articles 77-79:

> *Article 77*
> *Joint operating organizations permitted*
> Nothing in this Convention shall prevent two or more contracting states from constituting joint air transport operating organizations or international operating agencies and from pooling their air services on any routes or in any region, but such organizations or agencies and such pooling services shall be subject to all provisions of this Convention, including those relating to the registration of agreements with the Council. *The Council shall determine in what manner the provisions of this Convention relating to nationality of aircraft shall apply to aircraft operated by international operating agencies.* [Emphasis added]
>
> *Article 78*
> *Function of the Council*
> The Council may suggest to contracting States concerned that they form joint organizations to operate air services on any routes or in any regions.
>
> *Article 79*
> *Participation in operating organizations*
> State may participate in joint operating organizations or in pooling arrangements, either through its government or through an airline company or companies designated by its government. The companies may, at the sole discretion of the State concerned, be state-owned or partly state-owned or privately owned.

An early example of the cooperation of States in a jointly operating organization was the Scandinavian Airlines System (SAS) – a consortium of Danish, Norwegian and Swedish enterprises. However, there was no issue of a "common" nationality mark for the SAS aircraft since the entire fleet was divided into seven parts of which two were nationally registered in Denmark, two in Norway and three in Sweden.

The studies of the problems of joint operating organizations and the registration of their aircraft started already in 1948 when the 2nd Session of the Assembly adopted Resolution A2-13 requesting the Council to initiate studies of the legal and other problems involved in determining the manner in which the Convention's provisions on nationality of aircraft would apply to aircraft operated by international operating agencies. The studies continued for many years without a tangible result.[58] New life was brought into it in late 1959 when the League of Arab States informed ICAO of its intention to establish an international aviation enterprise open to all Arab States and requested Council's "determination" under the last sentence of Article 77. The creation of *Air Afrique* in 1961 added more urgency to the question, although no request was made to ICAO by the States of the Yaoundé Convention (1963).[59]

After studies in the ICAO Legal Committee and its Sub-Committees the Council finally adopted, on 14 December 1967, a resolution on "Nationality and Registration of Aircraft Operated by International Operating Agencies"[60] – the basis for the first stage of the Council's determination under the last sentence of Article 77 defining the criteria to be applied to *joint* or *international* registration. In both cases the registration is not on a national basis but the aircraft are to be inserted on a special non-national register kept by one of the States of the joint enterprise or, in the case of international registration, on the register of the appropriate international body.

It took sixteen more years before this "determination" was first used in the practice of ICAO. In 1983 the governments of Iraq and Jordan decided to create a joint air transport operating organization "*Arab Air Cargo*" and requested the Council's "determination" under the last sentence of Article 77.[61] Following the criteria approved in 1967, the Council determined, on 2 December 1983,[62] that the aircraft of that company shall bear a "common mark" 4YB and not any nationality mark; a joint (non-national) register will be kept by Jordan and its government shall perform all functions of the State of Registry.

"Arab Air Cargo" is long defunct and since that time no further determination has been made. Nevertheless, the laborious process of study at least confirmed that there is a possibility, if States wish, to provide for the registration of aircraft on a non-national basis, either in the form of joint or international registration.

---

58 M. Milde, "Nationality and Registration of Aircraft Operated by Joint Air Transport Operating Organizations or International Operating Agencies", *Annals of Air and Space Law*, Vol. X (1985), pp. 133-153.
59 The Convention was signed in the city of Yaoundé city (Cameroon) between the European Economic Community (EEC) and the AASM (Associated African States and Madagascar) in 1963 for five year term. After the term expired it was signed between EEC and ASMM (African States, Madagascar and Mauritius) in 1969.
60 Doc 8722, C/976.
61 C-WP/7746, annex C, pp. 11-23.
62 C-Min 110/11.

"International" registration (*i.e.*, with an international organization) also foreseen by the Council decision of 14 December 1967 has never been tested and was initially considered impractical: the international registering authority would have to possess the ability to actually perform the functions and duties of the State of Registry under the Convention (*e.g.*, issuing the certificates of competency and licenses, certificate of airworthiness, etc.) and by 1967 there was no such organization in existence. However, at present, with the progress of integration of State functions, *e.g.*, in the European Aviation Safety Agency (EASA), this solution cannot be excluded and a "common mark" may one day become a wide-spread reality.

5.4 Functions of the State of Registry

National laws define the functions of a State with respect of aircraft on its register. Moreover, international law attaches important functions and duties to the State of Registry.

The Chicago Convention contains the following five provisions that explicitly attach specific functions or duties to the State of registry:

> 1) *Article 12*
> *Rules of the air*
> Each contracting State undertakes to adopt measures to insure that every aircraft flying over or manoeuvring within its territory and that every *aircraft carrying its nationality mark*, wherever such aircraft may be, shall comply with the rules and regulations relating to the flight and manoeuvre of aircraft there in force. Each contracting State undertakes to keep its own regulations in these respects uniform, to the greatest possible extent, with those established from time to time under this Convention. Over the high seas, the rules in force shall be those established under this Convention. Each contracting State undertakes to insure the prosecution of all persons violating the regulations applicable.

Contracting States are thus responsible for adoption of such appropriate steps that would assure the compliance by aircraft of their nationality with the rules of the air wherever such aircraft may operate.

2) *Article 26*
Investigation of accidents
The *State in which the aircraft is registered* shall be given the opportunity to appoint observers to be present at the inquiry and the State holding the inquiry shall communicate the report and findings in the matter to that State.

The State of Registry is thus entitled, under international law, to participate by observers in the investigation of an accident of an aircraft of its registry anywhere in the world. Annex 13 elaborates then on the rights and functions of the observers from the State of Registry.

3) *Article 30*
Aircraft radio equipment
a. Aircraft of each contracting State may, in or over the territory of other contracting States, carry radio transmitting apparatus only if a license to install and operate such apparatus has been issued by the appropriate authorities of the *State in which the aircraft is registered*. The use of radio transmitting apparatus in the territory of the contracting State whose territory is flown over shall be in accordance with the regulations prescribed by that State.
b. Radio transmitting apparatus may be used only by members of the flight crew who are provided with a special license for the purpose, issued by the appropriate authorities of the *State in which the aircraft is registered*."

It is a sovereign right of each State to regulate the installation, possession and use of radio transmitters in its own territory. In a foreign airspace the communication equipment on board the aircraft must be properly licensed by the State of Registry of the aircraft, its use must comply with the regulations of the State overflown and the equipment must be operated by a flight crew member duly licensed by the State of Registry of the aircraft.

The law relating to aeronautical communications is extensively elaborated by the International Telecommunications Union (ITU) and by the voluminous Annex 10 to the Chicago Convention. The finite scope of available radio frequencies requires international harmonization of the competing interests to prevent mutual interference and aviation requires due priority for all its safety related communications.

"Private" telephone communications ("non-safety") from an aircraft in flight have been commercially available for a long time using terrestrial Very High Frequency (VHF) or Ultra High Frequency (UHF) radio services; later the satellite-based global commercial service was offered by INMARSAT[63] and other providers. A question did arise whether such private communications are compatible with Article 30 b) of the Chicago Convention. It was studied by the 28th Session of the ICAO Legal Committee[64] and conclusions were drawn in ICAO Assembly Resolution A29-19 that

> nothing in Article 30 b) of the Chicago Convention shall be taken to preclude the use by unlicensed persons of the radio transmitting apparatus installed upon an aircraft where that use is for non-safety related air-ground radio transmissions.

That resolution presupposes that the apparatus will remain under the control of the operator licensed by the State of Registry and the operation would avoid harmful interference with other services and respect the priority of aeronautical communications relating to distress, safety and regularity of flight.

Passengers thus can communicate from an aircraft in flight through the equipment provided and controlled by the operator of the aircraft. So far there are no international regulations concerning the possible use of personal cell phones during a flight. It could be argued that the terms of Article 30 of the Chicago Convention would not cover the use of personal cell phones and that such a problem would not even appear to be within the purview of ICAO. However, in practice most airlines expressly prohibit the use of personal cell phones on board and require that they be switched off during the take-off and landing to prevent a possible interference with the vital avionics. Violation of this prohibition should be made punishable by national laws as an act endangering the safety of flight and should empower the flight crew to restrain the unruly passenger.[65]

> 4) *Article 31*
> *Certificates of airworthiness*
> Every aircraft engaged in international navigation shall be provided with a certificate of airworthiness issued or rendered valid by the *State in which it is registered.*

The term "airworthiness" developed by analogy with the maritime term "seaworthiness" describing the ship's qualities as suitable for safe sailing. The benchmarks of airworthiness applicable for the design and manufacture of aircraft and its components and for the

---

63 British satellite telecommunications company.
64 Doc 9693-LC/190.
65 See the Tokyo Convention on Offences and Certain Other Acts Committed on Board Aircraft (1963) and Montreal Protocol to Amend the Convention on Offences and Certain Other Acts Committed on Board Aircraft (2014). The Montreal Protocol took effect on 1 January 2020.

suitability of the aircraft for air navigation are determined by national legislation – in particular in the industrialized countries actually capable to design and build aircraft. Strict government supervision of the compliance with established standards is at arm's lengths from the designer/manufacturer and safeguards fullest possible level of safety. A new model of an aircraft obtains its "type certification" to which all products of that series must comply. The type certificate defines the design of the aircraft type and certifies that this design meets the appropriate airworthiness requirements of the certifying State.

International regulation of airworthiness is contained in Annex 8 to the Chicago Convention that has been declared to constitute "the minimum standards for the purpose of Article 33".[66] Annex 8 does not replace the national legislation. It contains only broad standards or "objectives" rather than the means how to achieve them and must be supplemented as necessary by technical guidance material. The ICAO *Airworthiness Technical Manual*[67] represents such guidance material but Manuals are only for guidance and have no legally binding power.

Verification of continuing airworthiness is also the task of the State of Registry to ensure that the aircraft is duly maintained and that there are no new developments that would negatively reflect on the airworthiness of the aircraft.

Annex 8 must be read and interpreted in conjunction with Annex 6 – Operation of Aircraft[68] since the airworthiness must be considered in the context of different phases, configurations, operating limitations and conditions of the flight.

Under Article 31 of the Convention the certificate of airworthiness is to be either issued or rendered valid by the State of registry of the aircraft; in practice it is quite common that the initial certificate of airworthiness for a new aircraft is issued by the State of the manufacturer and then validated by the State of the owner/operator. Only few States have currently the capacity to manufacture large aircraft and components may be manufactured in several other States; thus, there is a limited number of States actually issuing a certificate of airworthiness.

A valid certificate of airworthiness by itself does not yet authorize its owner/operator to actually operate the aircraft. Under Annex 6 of the Convention the operator must obtain from its State (*i.e.*, State where the operator is resident or has the principal place of business) an Air Operators Certificate (AOC) giving the operator's name, date of issue, description of the operations authorized, type of aircraft authorized for use and authorized

---

66 Annex 8 – Airworthiness of Aircraft, 13th ed., July 2022, Foreword, p. viii; under Article 31 of the Chicago Convention certificates of airworthiness issued or rendered valid by the State of Registry must be recognized by other contracting States if they meet or exceed the minimum standards established pursuant to the Convention.
67 ICAO Doc 9051.
68 Annex 6 – Operation of Aircraft consists of three parts: I. International Commercial Air Transport – Aeroplanes; II International General Aviation; III. International Operation – Helicopters.

areas of operation.[69] The applicant for the AOC must comply with detailed conditions prescribed by the certifying State – including availability of airworthy equipment, properly licensed crews, financial guarantees and liability insurance and also evidence of an effective aviation security program. The specific detailed conditions for the issuance of an AOC differ from State to State but their common denominator is to safeguard public safety and security.

> 5) *Article 32*
> *Licenses of personnel*
> a. The pilot of every aircraft and the other members of the operating crew of every aircraft engaged in international navigation shall be provided with certificates of competency and licenses issued or rendered valid by the State in which the aircraft is registered.

Licensing of aviation personnel is regulated by national laws and the requirements differ from State to State. Annex 1 to the Chicago Convention formulates minimum international standards for personnel licensing and the compliance with such minimum standards carries with it the obligation of other contracting States to recognize such licenses.[70]

Licenses are issued for the flight crew (cockpit and cabin crew) and for other aviation personnel. The flight crew includes a
- private pilot – aeroplane;
- commercial pilot – aeroplane;
- airline transport pilot – aeroplane;
- private pilot – helicopter;
- commercial pilot – helicopter;
- airline transport pilot – helicopter;
- glider pilot;
- free balloon pilot;
- flight navigator;
- flight engineer;
- flight attendant.

---

69 Annex 6, paragraph 4.2.1.5 (a-e).
70 Article 33 of the Chicago Convention.

Other aviation personnel requiring a license include
- aircraft maintenance (technician/engineer/mechanic);
- air traffic controller;
- flight operations officer;
- aeronautical station operator.

Apart from the requirements of training, knowledge and experience the Annex 1 and the relevant national legislations deal with the medical fitness and continuing medical fitness of the aviation personnel. Guidance in the matters of medical fitness is contained in the ICAO *Manual of Civil Aviation Medicine*[71] that is updated from time to time. Safety requires absolutely drug free environment in all segments of aviation and strict rules forbid operation at any level if the person concerned could be under the influence of narcotic drugs or psychotropic substances. Guidance on matters of drug abuse prevention is in the ICAO *Manual on Prevention of Problematic Use of Substances in Aviation Workplace*.[72]

5.5 Transfer of Functions and Duties from the State of Registry to the State of the Operator

A large proportion of aircraft used in international transport is operated by an operator having his principal place of business in a country other than the State of Registry. There is a variety of reasons for this fact – an airline leases an aircraft from a foreign airline or from a leasing company and the registration of the aircraft remains unchanged, creditors retain the title to the aircraft and its registration while the aircraft is operated by an operator in another country, etc. It would be difficult to provide an exhaustive list of all situations where the aircraft is registered in one country while it is operated by an operator having his permanent place of business or residence in another country and the Convention in Article 83*bis* refers to "an agreement for the lease, charter or interchange of the aircraft or any similar arrangement".

A practical illustration may clarify the problem: at a certain time a Bulgarian airline leased a B-767 of French registry and operated it on regular flights Sofia-New-York-Sofia; the aircraft during the long period of the lease never entered the French territory. That situation creates a practical problem: international law attaches functions and duties with respect to the aircraft to the State of Registry but that State is far removed from the actual

---

71   ICAO Doc 8984.
72   ICAO Doc 9654.

operation of the aircraft and cannot effectively discharge its duties – *e.g.*, with respect to verification of continuing airworthiness.

The following example will illustrate how such a situation may reflect on the safety: On 7 June 1989 Suriname Airlines Flight 764 from Amsterdam to Paramaribo crashed on approach to Zandery International Airport, Paramaribo, Suriname. The airplane was totally destroyed on impact and 175 persons of 187 were fatally injured including the cockpit crew and cabin crew. The accident was fully attributed to a gross incompetence of the pilots and their disregard of all ground proximity warnings. The aircraft was a DC-8-62 manufactured in 1969 and registered in the United States with nationality and registration mark N1609E and was earlier operated by Braniff, later sold to McDonnell Douglas Finance Corporation, then leased back and at the time of the accident owned by a US Holding Company based in Coral Gables, Florida.[73]

The aircraft had a chequered history and on 14 October 1979 was involved in an accident in Panama City. There is no record that the aircraft was subject to continuing airworthiness verification by the US authorities as the State of Registry or that the pilots' licenses were properly extended by the same authorities. Both the pilots were American citizens and were not qualified by recent proficiency training and tests to perform the flight. Moreover, the captain was 66 years old – well beyond the 60 years limit under both US and Surinam regulatory requirements and the minimum international standards of Annex 1 for a pilot-in-command for international flights (this limit is 65 at present). Suriname Airways contracted the pilots on a week-to-week basis through Air Crews International Inc. who represented them as being properly licensed, qualified and meeting the proficiency requirements. The investigation into the captain's qualifications disclosed that he had received his last proficiency test on 16 April 1989 but only from a private company Flying Tigers, Inc. located in Marietta, PA. after a check conducted on a 4-seater Grumman Cougar powered by twin reciprocating engines, not on a jet DC-8. The name "Flying Tiger" was misleadingly similar to that formerly used by an international air carrier and Suriname Airways believed that the captain had received his proficiency test from a *bona fide* major carrier.

This tragic accident proves how damaging can be the absence of the due supervision by the State of Registry or its factual impossibility to perform the internationally prescribed functions and duties. The State of the Operator (Suriname) did not exercise the functions with respect of continuing airworthiness of the aircraft or verification of the continuing competence of the cockpit crew since those functions belong to the State of Registry of the aircraft. The lack of mutual communication permitted all errors and shortcomings to go unnoticed and uncorrected.

---

73 The facts are summarized from several Internet resources and from the National Transportation Safety Board's (NTSB) Safety Recommendation, dated 24 April 1990.

In ICAO the different legal aspects of the lease, charter and interchange of aircraft were studied for some 20 years – since the Guadalajara Conference on Air Law (1961) that dealt with issues of unified private law. At a later stage the study focused on the safety aspects involved in the lease, charter and interchange of aircraft and other similar arrangements and that study culminated in the adoption, on 6 October 1980, of the first substantive (*i.e.*, non-procedural) amendment of the Chicago Convention – new Article 83*bis*:[74]

> *Article 83bis*
> *Transfer of certain functions and duties*
> a) Notwithstanding the provisions of Articles 12, 30, 31 and 32 a), when an aircraft registered in a contracting State is operated pursuant to an agreement for the lease, charter or interchange of the aircraft or any similar arrangement by an operator who has his principal place of business or, if he has no such place of business, his permanent residence in another contracting state, the State of registry may, by agreement with such other State, transfer to it all or part of its functions and duties as State of registry in respect of that aircraft under Articles 12, 30, 31 and 32 a). The State of registry shall be relieved of responsibility in respect of the functions and duties transferred. b) The transfer shall not have effect in respect of other contracting States before either the agreement between States in which it is embodied has been registered with the Council and made public pursuant to Article 83 or the existence and scope of the agreement have been directly communicated to the authorities of the other contracting State or States concerned by a State party to the agreement. c) The provisions of paragraphs a) and b) above shall also be applicable to cases covered by Article 77.

The drafting of this provision is not very felicitous and may be difficult to understand without the knowledge of its background and rationale. The essential points may be summarized as follows:
– the provision is *permissive* and not obligatory; States *may* enter into an agreement on this subject but are not obliged to do so;
– the agreement is to be concluded between *States* – the State of Registry and the State of the operator, not by the air carriers;
– the functions and duties that may be transferred include Article 12 (observation of the rules of the air), Article 30 (aircraft radio equipment), Article 31 (airworthiness) and 32 a) (licenses of personnel);

---

[74] Came into force on 20 June 1997 in respect of States which ratified it and by December 2022, 176 States have ratified this amendment.

- by the transfer the State of Registry is relieved of its responsibility in respect of the functions and duties transferred;
- the transfer shall have effect with respect to other contracting States when the agreement is registered with the ICAO Council and made public or when it is directly communicated to the States concerned;
- Article 83*bis* applies equally to the non-national (joint or international) registration of aircraft under the last sentence of Article 77.

In spite of the years of effort to create a legal basis for the transfer of functions and duties of the State of Registry to the State of the operator, only few States avail themselves of the new opportunity – the ICAO registry of aeronautical agreements lists only 174 agreements under the terms of Article 83*bis*,[75] many of them most probably no longer in force.

5.6 "Nationality" of an Airline and "Substantive Ownership..." Clause

Airlines operating internationally are without exception corporate entities created by registration in a particular State and having their permanent place of business in a State. Corporate entities derive their legal existence and their rights and duties from the laws of the State where they have their principal place of business and they are deemed to have the "nationality" of that State. Such nationality of the airline is completely unrelated to the nationality of the aircraft they operate and it is not unusual that an airline operates aircraft registered in different States. In practice it is more and more evident that the State of the operator may have a closer and more effective relation to all safety and security related aspects of air navigation than the State of Registry of the aircraft. It is not unlikely that in the future development of international air law the basic functions and duties with respect to safety will attach to the State of the operator rather than to the State of registry.

Nationality of the airline has its international legal relevance in the context of agreements between States on air services. Under such agreements States mutually agree on an exchange of traffic rights and the conditions thereof and each of them designates an airline (single designation) or airlines (multiple designations) that are authorized to perform the agreed services.

The designation formula in most cases includes a *nationality clause* or *"substantial ownership clause"* under which a party of the agreement may refuse to grant to a carrier

---

75 On the basis of Article 83*bis* few agreements (altogether 174 before 2018) have been concluded. Legal Committee 37th Session, Safety aspect of economic liberalisation and Article 83*bis*, LC/37-WP/2-7, September 2018, p. 1.

designated by the other party the right to operate the agreed services, if it is not convinced that *substantial ownership* and *effective control* of that carrier is vested in the other State or its nationals. Such action is not automatic or obligatory but permissive and subject to the discretion of the State concerned.

At the roots of the "substantial ownership and effective control" clause is protectionism to make sure that operators essentially belonging to a third State would not benefit from the advantages mutually exchanged between the parties to the agreement.

The origins of the clause could be traced to the International Air Services Transit Agreement[76] and the International Air Transport Agreement[77] in their Articles I section 5 and 6, respectively, stipulate that

> Each contracting State reserves the right to withhold or revoke a certificate or permit to an air transport enterprise of another State in any case where it is not satisfied that *substantial ownership* and *effective control* are vested in the national of a contracting State, or in the case of failure of such air transport enterprise to comply with the laws of the State over which it operates, or to perform its obligations under this Agreement.

It should be noted that this provision refers to "national of "*a*" (*i.e.*, any) contracting State" and it is apparent that by 1944 the aim of the contracting States was to deny the benefits of the Agreements to non-contracting, *i.e.*, "enemy States". However, an identical wording was inserted by the Chicago Conference in Chapter VIII of the Final Act in the "Standard Form of Agreement for Provisional Air Routes"[78] as a model for future bilateral agreements. From there the clause found its way into "Bermuda I." – the bilateral agreement on air services between the USA and the UK of 11 February 1946[79] that for many years became the guiding model for hundreds of bilateral agreements on air services.

The clause could be justified by the general principle of international law that "a treaty does not create either obligations or rights for a third State"[80] (reflecting the axiom of Roman law *pacta tertiis nec nocent nec prosunt*). However, the clause is not imposed by international law and is only a creation of States' practice of protectionism. The continuing use of the clause is harmful for the global development of international air transport.

There is no accepted definition of what is to be considered "substantial ownership" – is it to be 51% (or 50%+1), *i.e.*, a majority share? Would not an, *e.g.*, 5% ownership in a major airline be considered to be "substantial"? Similarly, there is no agreed benchmark of what

---

76 ICAO Doc 7500.
77 U.S. Department of State Publication 2282.
78 Proceedings, Vol. I, p. 129, paragraph (7).
79 Text at http://en.wikisource.org/wiki/Bermuda_Agreement.
80 Article 34 of the Vienna Convention on the Law of Treaties (1969).

is "effective control" – a majority of the voting shares or a majority in the Board of Directors?

In summary,

- *substantial ownership* is a *primary, legal (de iure)* condition, which requires *quantitative* ownership (above 50%) by the State, its citizens or both in the designated airline;
- *effective control* is a *predominant, actual (de facto)* condition, under which the substantial national owner exercises the rights of ownership via *qualitative* management constituted by the citizens of the given State.

States are not obliged to invoke the clause and to revoke the permit if they believe that the conditions are not met, its use is fully discretionary and could be motivated by extraneous political or other considerations in either a positive or negative manner.

Except for aviation no other industry faces the restrictions with respect to foreign ownership or control. In fact, in view of the high cost of aviation equipment the airlines could benefit from the transborder flow of capital, foreign investment, cooperative schemes or mergers. This is particularly relevant in particular for the developing countries for which foreign investment may be the only way how to develop their aviation. A timid voice was raised in an ICAO Assembly Resolution[81] urging States "to accept the designation of airlines owned by one or more developing States belonging to a regional grouping". In 2010 the 37th Session of ICAO Assembly used more explicit wording of such recommendation in resolution A37-20.[82]

Air carrier ownership and control vested in a single State is "an anachronism in the global economy"[83] and liberalization of ownership and control is a necessary precursor of widespread liberalization.

Some States – arguably for reasons of security and defence – legally limit the foreign financial participation in their airlines; thus, in the US the foreign ownership must not exceed 49%[84] and it is required that US citizens control 25% – a sore point for the States of the European Community; again, the US airlines are handicapped in competition when they cannot draw foreign capital. The argument of security and defence is not convincing – regardless of the foreign ownership the State bodies would have overriding authority in all matters of security and defence. The true reason for the limitation of foreign ownership is more likely in the surviving economic protectionist attitudes.

---

81 Resolution A32-17.
82 Resolutions A37-20, Consolidated Statement of Continuing ICAO Policies in the Air Transport Field, Appendix A, Economic regulation of international air transport, Section II, Cooperation in regulatory arrangements, 3-4; A41-27, Appendixes A-E (2022).
83 ICAO Doc AT-WP/1939, p. A-7.
84 The limit of 25% on foreign ownership of the US airlines had been in force for a long time, it has been changed to 49% (the European Union limits non-EU ownership of the airlines of its Member States to 49%).

Within the EU the link between the substantial ownership/effective control and the traffic rights within the Community was removed by the creation of the new concept of "community carrier". The community carrier is an "air carrier with a valid operating license granted by a competent licencing authority".[85] Ownership and control are of no legal relevance for the determination of a community carrier[86] and this practice shows desirable direction of the future development. ICAO Assembly expressed itself in favour of a flexible policy and positive approach to use "alternative criteria" for airline designation and authorization" and "to liberalize air carrier ownership" and effective regulatory "control without compromising safety and security".[87] Within the EU the opposition to the "nationality clause" was stressed by a series of judgements of the European Court of Justice of 2002 in the "open skies" cases alleging that eight Member States of the EC have breached their duties under the EU Treaty by concluding with the USA "open skies" agreements containing the "nationality clause" rather than referring to any "Community carrier".[88] The European Parliament and Council adopted, on 29 April 2004, a Regulation on the Negotiation and Implementation of Air Services Agreements between Member States and Third Countries[89] implementing the decisions of the Court. Nevertheless, in 2010 and 2011 the European Commission launched infringement procedures against several Member States because their bilateral air services agreements with the Russian Federation "may hinder competition, breach EU rules on freedom of establishment, and provide a basis for Siberian overflight charges which may be illegal";[90] these agreements with the Russian Federation do not include "EU designation" clause contrary to the 2002 decision of the EU Court of Justice; moreover, the EU carriers are de facto forced into agreements with their competitor – Aeroflot – on the Siberian overflight charges which 2008 alone they paid total around USD 350 million.[91]

It is noteworthy that in the second phase of arrangements on "open skies" between the European Union and the United States[92] the parties expressly agreed that "Neither party shall exercise any available rights under air services arrangements with a third country to revoke, suspend or limit authorizations or permissions for any airline of that third country on the grounds that substantial ownership of that airline is vested in the other party, in its

---

85 Regulation (EC) No. 1008/2008 of the European Parliament and of the Council of 24 September 2008 on common rules for the operation of air services in the Community. OJ L 293, 31.10.2008, Definitions, 11.
86 Idem.
87 Resolution A35-18, Annex A, Section II, 4; Ibid. 224 (A37-20, A 41-27).
88 Series C-466/98, [2002] E.C.R. I-9427 and following.
89 [2004] O.J.L. 157/7 [Regulation (EC) No. 847/2004].
90 EU Memorandum MEMO/11/167.
91 European Parliament, Trans-Siberian overflights, Written Question E-6399/09, 10 December 2009. www.europarl.europa.eu/doceo/document/E-7-2009-6399_EN.html.
92 Protocol of 24 June 2010 signed at Luxembourg, Annex 6, see Chapter 6 below.

nationals, or both". This perhaps indicates a trend that the issue of "substantial ownership and effective control" in international aviation is finally becoming obsolete.

5.7 AIRCRAFT ACCIDENT INVESTIGATION

Civil air transport is considered to be the safest means of transport. Nevertheless, by its very nature air navigation is an activity facing many potential dangers – it counteracts the law of gravity, may encounter severely adverse weather conditions, carries a large load of flammable fuel, any of the multiple and complex mechanical or electrical components could fail, the human element controlling the aircraft could make a mistake or danger could be created by an act of unlawful interference.

National law governs the consequences of an aircraft accident and the actions to be taken by the appropriate authorities. Whenever there is an event with a loss of life, injuries or material damage States have a procedure for salvage and investigation that may include the police service, fire service, Coroner's investigation, insurer's investigation, judicial procedures to prosecute alleged violations of laws or decide on compensations, etc.

The international character of civil aviation necessitated such development of law that would make sure that any accident of an aircraft anywhere in the world would be subject to investigation. International law now contains specific provision on the investigation of accidents in Article 26 of the Chicago Convention:

> *Article 26*
> *Investigation of accidents*
> In the event of an accident to an aircraft of a contracting State occurring in the territory of another contracting State, and involving death or serious injury, or indicating a serious technical defect in the aircraft or air navigation facilities, the state in which the accident occurs will institute an inquiry into the circumstances of the accident, in accordance, as far as its laws permit, with the procedure which may be recommended by the International Civil Aviation Organization. The State in which the aircraft is registered shall be given the opportunity to appoint observers to be present at the inquiry and the state holding the inquiry shall communicate the report and findings in the matter to that State.

The "procedure which may be recommended by the International Civil Aviation Organization" is embodied in Annex 13 to the Chicago Convention. The ICAO Council felt compelled to clarify the relation between Article 26 of the Convention and Annex 13.[93] That Annex incorporates the wording of Article 26 and in its adoption the ICAO Council was concerned that States should not be permitted to file a difference, under Article 38 of the Convention, to the Annex with respect to the fundamental points of Article 26 – the duty of the state of occurrence to institute an inquiry, the right of the State of Registry of the aircraft to appoint observers to be present at the inquiry and the duty of the State holding the inquiry to communicate the report and findings to that State.

Annex 13 deals mostly with procedures of the investigation but it contains a number of points of legal significance which have to be stressed. While there could be different types of investigations for different purposes under the national laws, the investigation under the international Standards of Annex 13 is specific as defined in Standard 3.1:

Objective of the Investigation
3.1 The sole objective of investigation of accidents or incidents shall be the prevention of accidents of incidents. It is not the purpose of this activity to apportion blame or liability.

This provision is of critical importance – the sole purpose of the investigation under Article 26 and Annex 13 is to find the cause or causes (actions, omissions, events, conditions or combination thereof) which led to the accident or incident; it is to be done by gathering and analysis of information, the drawing of conclusions, including the determination of causes and, when appropriate, the making of safety recommendations. The purpose of the investigation is to prevent the repetition of similar accidents or incidents in similar situations and conditions in the future. Apportionment of blame or liability is specifically not the purpose of the investigation. It could also mean that the process of investigation should not be led in an adversarial spirit and should aim at establishing the essential facts with full objectivity to draw lessons for the future.

Annex 13 goes beyond the scope of Article 26 of the Convention in many respects and that is perfectly legitimate – the Convention stipulates the basic legal framework binding in the form of an international treaty and the Annex complements it in great detail. It is the outcome of the quasi-legislative activity of the ICAO Council under Articles 37, 54 (l) and 90 of the Convention and States are expected to comply "to the highest practicable degree".[94]

While Article 26 of the Convention refers to "accidents" Annex 13 refers to "accidents and incidents" and "serious incident". Their definitions follow:[95]

---

93 Council Resolution of 11 April 1951, 13th Meeting of its 12th Session.
94 See details below in Chapter 7.
95 Annex 13, 12th ed., July 2020, Chapter 1, Definitions.

Accident: An occurrence associated with the operation of an aircraft which, in the case of a manned aircraft, takes place between the time any person boards the aircraft with the intention of flight until such time as all such persons have disembarked, or in the case of an unmanned aircraft, takes place between the time the aircraft is ready to move with the purpose of flight until such time as it comes to rest at the end of the flight and the primary propulsion system is shut down, in which:

a. a person is fatally or seriously injured as a result of:
   - being in the aircraft, or
   - direct contact with any part of the aircraft, including parts which have become detached from the aircraft, or
   - direct exposure to jet blast,

except when the injuries are from natural causes, self-inflicted or inflicted by other persons, or when the injuries are to stowaways hiding outside the area normally available to the passengers and crew; or

b. the aircraft sustains damage or structural failure which:
   - adversely affects the structural strength, performance or flight characteristics of the aircraft, and
   - would normally require major repair or replacement of the affected component,

except for engine failure or damage, when the damage is limited to a single engine, (including its cowlings or accessories), to propellers, wing tips, antennas, probes, vanes, tires, brakes, wheels, fairings, panels, landing gear doors, windscreens, the aircraft skin (such as small dents or puncture holes), or for minor damages to main rotor blades, tail rotor blades, landing gear, and those resulting from hail or bird strike (including holes in the radome); or

c) the aircraft is missing or is completely inaccessible.

Incident: An occurrence, other than an accident, associated with the operation of an aircraft which affects or could affect the safety of operation.

Serious incident: An incident involving circumstances indicating that there was a high probability of an accident and is associated with the operation of an aircraft which, in the case of a manned aircraft, takes place between the time any person boards the aircraft with the intention of flight until such time as all such persons have disembarked, or in the case of an unmanned aircraft, takes place between the time the aircraft is ready to move with the purpose of flight until such time it comes to rest at the end of the flight and the primary propulsion system is shut down.

The "State of Occurrence" is obliged to institute an investigation into the circumstances of the accident both under Article 26 of the Convention and under Annex 13.[96] However, to "institute" does not necessarily mean "to conduct" an investigation. Such investigation under Annex 13 is a demanding and laborious process requiring considerable expenses (*e.g.*, for the retrieval of the wreckage from the territorial sea or other difficult locations, re-composition of the wreck, etc.) and also advanced expertise that may not be available to each contracting State. That is why Annex 13 permits the State of occurrence to delegate the whole or any part of the conducting of such investigation to another State by mutual arrangement and consent. The duty to investigate a serious incident is only a recommended practice, not a standard.[97]

Investigation of accidents and incidents outside the territory of any State (typically on the high seas) is to be instituted by the State of Registry of the aircraft; again, that State may delegate the whole or any part of the investigation to another State by mutual agreement and consent.[98]

So far there is no international legal regulation relating to the cost of accident investigation. The accident investigation may often require extremely high expenses, in particular when the debris of the aircraft are to be retrieved from the seabed; it is recorded that the disaster of Swissair Flight 111 on 2 September 1998 off the Peggy Cove, Nova Scotia, Canada took over 4 years and cost some 57 million Canadian dollars. Comparable and possibly higher costs must have been involved in the EgyptAir Flight 990 disaster in the Atlantic on 31 October 1998 or the Air France Flight 447 from Rio de Janeiro to Paris that disappeared in the Atlantic on 1 June 2009. The most expensive mission was the tragedy of Trans World Airlines Flight 800 on 17 July 1996, the wreckage of the B-747 aircraft was left sunk at 130 feet (approx. 40 m) under surface in the Atlantic Ocean. Many parts of the aircraft (nearly 1,600 pieces) were collected and it was rebuilt. Yet, the expense was absolutely necessary and justifiable for the identification of the cause or causes of the

---

96 Annex 13, Standard 5.1.
97 Annex 13, Recommendation 5.1.1.
98 Annex 13, Standard 5.3. Example: Egypt delegated to the United States the investigation of the disaster of EgyptAir Flight 990 from New York to Cairo on 31 October 1999 (Boeing 767-300ER, registration SU-GAP) some 60 miles south of Nantucket Island. The National Transportation Safety Board (NTSB) issued a report in March 2002 and the Egyptian Civil Aviation Authority strongly disagreed with the conclusions. The extensive reports offer an instructive example of the investigation process and its depth. See www.airsafe.com/flt990.htm.

accident and the prevention of similar occurrences in the future.[99] Such findings present a lesson that would greatly benefit not only the actual operator of the aircraft but all operators of similar equipment or in similar conditions everywhere in the world and also the manufacturers of the aircraft and the authorities involved in the certification of the aircraft and of the crew members. Few States possess the technical expertise and financial means for a thorough aircraft accident investigation. The global interest in the proper investigation of all aircraft accidents would justify the creation of an international body of the leading experts in all aspects of accident investigation and also the international financing or cost sharing of such investigations, possibly with substantial contribution from the aircraft manufacturers.

A legally sensitive aspect of aircraft accident investigation is the question whether the evidence presented by the persons directly involved should remain confidential or whether it should be made publicly available. The investigation is to be non-adversarial, the direct participants (flight crew, air traffic controllers, mechanics, etc.) are heard not as "accused" or "suspects" but as witnesses capable to clarify the events from their direct knowledge and thus help in preventing similar accidents in the future. However, it cannot be ruled out that such voluntarily given testimonies before the investigating body could be later used in some subsequent disciplinary proceedings, administrative or criminal proceedings or as a basis for financial liability. The organizations of pilots have long argued that only absolute confidentiality of the statements would guarantee that the participants would tell full truth about the events without fear of possible personal consequences. On the other hand, it was argued that publicity of the evidence freely given could jeopardize any future investigation and that the statements could not be expected to be fully candid.

The demand for full confidentiality is comparable to a claim of "immunity". Why should the aviation personnel enjoy such protection that is not provided, *e.g.*, to the medical profession, politicians or employees of other means of transport? Access to information or "freedom of information" and transparency are being heralded as axioms of modern legislation, sometimes as constitutional principles. In 1973, a Judge of the US District Court – J.J. Sirica – ruled that President R. Nixon was obliged to surrender the tapes recorded in the Oval Office of the White House relating to the Watergate case.[100] It would be rather difficult to argue that the testimonies of the aviation personnel during an aircraft accident investigation deserve a higher level of protection of confidentiality than the private tape recordings of the US President secretly recorded in the Oval Office!

---

99 "The wreckage itself would be able to teach future generations a lesson so that a similar occurrence can be prevented". Jim Hill, Chairman of the National Transportation Safety Board (NTSB). See www.apnews.com/article, TWA Crash Wreckage Spurs Arguments, 16 July 1999.
100 J.J. Sirica was declared "Man of the Year 1973" by the *TIME Magazine* – See www.time.com/time/subscriber/manoftheyear/archive/1973.html.

If some information is kept confidential and is not available as evidence in other proceedings (*e.g.*, a claim of a widow of a passenger killed in the accident), it may lead to grave denial of justice.

There is no convincing evidence that statements of the personnel involved would be more truthful and uninhibited – as forcefully claimed by the pilots' organizations – if the records are kept confidential; it is a human nature to withhold, even subconsciously, or modify information that could be leading to self-incrimination.[101] It is therefore quite surprising that the ICAO Assembly at its 36th Session in September 2007 adopted a resolution[102] appealing to States to further protect the confidentiality of the data from accident investigations. In 2010, that Resolution was replaced by another[103] that again recognizes the need to strike a balance between the need for the protection of safety information and the need for the proper administration of justice and urges States "to continue to examine, and if necessary, adjust their laws, regulations and policies to protect certain accident and incident records in compliance with paragraph 5.12 of Annex 13, in order to mitigate impediments to accident and incident investigations …". The pressure to keep the information of investigation "protected" comes from professional (pilots) circles, and States bring the issue to the Assembly regularly; however, even the unanimously adopted Assembly Resolutions do not create any legal obligation, and the practice of States differs according to their prevailing domestic laws.[104]

Annex 13 introduces in Standard 5.12 a delicate compromise between the access to information and confidentiality of the statements and data:

Non-disclosure of records
5.12 The State conducting the investigation of an accident or incident shall not make the following records available for purposes other than accident or incident investigation, unless the competent authority designated by that State determines, in accordance with national laws and subject to Appendix 2 and 5.12.5, that their disclosure or use outweighs the likely adverse domestic and international impact such action may have on that or any future investigations:
a. cockpit voice recordings and airborne image recordings and any transcripts from such recordings; and
b. records in the custody or control of the accident investigation authority being:

---

101 "Everybody has something to hide" was made classic by H. Poirot of Agatha Christie; the Beatles uplifted this pessimistic attitude in their song "Everybody's got something to hide, except me and my monkey … ."
102 Resolution A36-9.
103 Resolution A37-2.
104 See Resolutions A38-3 (2013) that superseded A37-2, and A39-WP/110 (TE/34) Protection on Safety Information (2016).

1. all statements taken from persons by the accident investigation authority in the course of their investigation;
2. all communications between persons having been involved in the operation of the aircraft;
3. medical or private information regarding persons involved in the accident or incident;
4. recordings and transcripts of recordings from air traffic control units;
5. analysis of and opinions about information, including flight recorder information, made by the accident investigation authority and accredited representatives in relation to the accident or incident; and
6. the draft Final Report of an accident or incident investigation.

Thus it would be for the court of law to decide what is more important for the proper course of justice – confidentiality of the records or access to relevant information. Very few States commented on Annex 13 and only the following filed expressly their difference under Article 38 of the Convention to Standard 5.12 of Annex 13: Austria, Denmark, Finland, Iceland, Netherlands, Sweden, Switzerland and United States;[105] their national legislation would not permit a restricted status of the information and would insist on full disclosure. National legislation relating to freedom of information may still enable access to the records, possibly after the passage of certain time.

The entire aviation community of the world has a vested interest in the results of any aviation accident investigation anywhere in the world. In many States identical types of aircraft are operated under identical operational procedures and techniques and such States may draw vital conclusions from the knowledge of the causes that led to an accident anywhere in the world

Annex 13 provides for Accident Data Report (ADREP)[106] – a detailed Final report of the investigation prepared by the State instituting the investigation and distributed with maximum dispatch to contracting States, together with any safety recommendations. Moreover, Annex 13 opens up the process of investigation far beyond the terms of Article 26 by admitting to the process of investigation, in different forms, the participation of experts from the State of the operator, State of design, State of manufacture, State having interest because of fatalities of its nationality and any State that provided information, experts or other form of assistance. The investigating team may be composed of many persons and is headed by an Investigator-in-charge – a person charged, on the basis of his or her qualifications, with the responsibility for the organization, conduct and control of an investigation.

---

105 Supplement to Annex 13.
106 Annex 13, Accidents to aircraft over 2,250 kg, Standard 7.5.

Aviation accidents are also addressed in Annex 9 to the Convention that deals with facilitation – it provides for the arrangements to facilitate the entry to the State of the occurrence for family members of the victims, for the relevant authorities, the authorized representatives of the operator to provide assistance to survivors and for making arrangements for transport and clearing customs in the repatriation of human remains, etc.

A detailed set of guidance material is contained in ICAO *Manual of Aircraft Accident and Incident Investigation*.[107]

5.8 Aircraft in Distress

"Distress" in air navigation means a situation where there is reasonable certainty that an aircraft and its occupants are threatened by grave and imminent danger or require immediate assistance.

Distress may have different forms – from a minor malfunction of the systems, loss of orientation to a critical threat of fire on board, engine failure, etc. Under all circumstances it is important that the aircraft crews communicate with the ground services and with other aircraft in nearby airspace their position and explain the difficulty and the type of assistance required. The typical emergency communication should be on the 121.5 MHz transmitter frequency which is reserved for aviation distress calls.[108]

Annex 12 – Search and Rescue governs the organization and procedures of the search and rescue (SAR) services in the territory and the region (including the parts of the sea allocated for SAR to the State concerned by the Regional Air Navigation Plan).

A specific rule of the current international law concerning aircraft in distress is in Article 25 of the Chicago Convention:

> *Article 25*
> *Aircraft in distress*
> Each contracting State undertakes to provide such measures of assistance to aircraft in distress in its territory as it may find practicable, and to permit, subject to control by its own authorities, the owners of the aircraft or authorities of the state in which the aircraft is registered to provide such measures of assistance as may be necessitated by the circumstances. Each contracting State, when undertaking search for missing aircraft, will collaborate in coordinated

---

107 ICAO Doc 9756, Part I. Organization and Planning, Part II. Procedures and Checklists, Part III. Investigation, Part IV. Reporting.
108 Prescribed in Annexes 6 and 10.

measures which may be recommended from time to time pursuant to this Convention.

In this Article States have accepted an international obligation to provide all "practicable" assistance to aircraft in distress. They also agreed to permit the owners or the authorities of the State of Registry to provide such assistance and to collaborate in coordinated measures now expressed in Annex 12 to the Convention.

A question did arise whether an aircraft subject to unlawful seizure (hijacking) is to be deemed to be in distress. On the technical and operational grounds, it is obvious that such an aircraft is in distress and needs any assistance available, in particular facilities to land as soon as possible at a convenient airport. However, on "policy" grounds some States were refusing such aircraft the right to land and even let the runways be blocked by obstacles to prevent such a landing – for fear that after the landing with the offenders on board a real "distress" would occur: the offenders might be asking for publicity for their statements, release of prisoners, etc. The matter had to be addressed in an ICAO Assembly resolutions[109] that noted that

> the safety of flight of aircraft subjected to an act of unlawful seizure may be further jeopardized by the denial of navigational aids and air traffic services, the blocking of runways and taxiways and the closure of airport.

Expressing the view that the safest place for an aircraft under unlawful seizure is on the ground, the Assembly stated that

> the safety of passengers and crew of an aircraft subjected to an act of unlawful seizure may also be further jeopardized if the aircraft is permitted to take off while still under seizure.

The Assembly then urged contracting States

> to provide assistance to an aircraft subjected to an act of unlawful seizure, including the provision of navigational aids, air traffic services and permission to land.

---

109 In 2010 the 37th Session of the ICAO Assembly integrated this issue in Resolution A37-17: Consolidated statement of the continuing ICAO policies relating to the safeguarding of international civil aviation against acts of unlawful interference, Appendix D: Action of States concerned with an act of unlawful interference. See Resolutions A39-18 (2016), A40-11 (2019), A41-18 (2022) (Appendix A).

The Assembly also urged the contracting States

> to ensure that an aircraft subjected to an act of unlawful seizure which has landed in its territory is detained on the ground unless its departure is necessitated by the overriding duty to protect human life.

5.9 Documents Carried in Aircraft

In Chapter V the Chicago Convention describes conditions to be fulfilled with respect to the aircraft. Among them is Article 29 which stipulates:

> *Article 29*
> *Documents carried in aircraft*
> Every aircraft of a contracting State, engaged in international navigation, shall carry the following documents in conformity with conditions prescribed in this Convention: Its certificate of registration; Its certificate of airworthiness; The appropriate licenses for each member of the crew; Its journey log book; If it is equipped with radio apparatus, the aircraft radio station license; If it carries passengers, a list of their names and places of embarkation and destination; If it carries cargo, a manifest and detailed declarations of the cargo.

The required documents have their legal basis in other provisions of the Convention relating to registration, airworthiness, licenses and radio apparatus. In practice, apart from the request of the Convention, it is necessary to keep on board the documents of Air Operator Certificate (AOC), the insurance agreements, the noise certificates, the declaration issued by the servicing technical organisation on the technical adequacy of the aircraft, etc.

> *Article 34*
> *Journey log books*
> There shall be maintained in respect of every aircraft engaged in international navigation a journey log book in which shall be entered particulars of the aircraft, its crew and of each journey, in such form as may be prescribed from time to time pursuant to this Convention.

The concept of a journey log book has its long tradition in the maritime navigation and it is meant to maintain a continuing detailed record of each journey. The form of the journey log book has not been prescribed by international standards but the ICAO Assembly at its 10th Session adopted a Resolution[110] that resolved that

> the General Declaration when prepared so as to contain all the information required by Article 34 with respect to the journey log book, may be considered by contracting states to be an acceptable form of journey log book; and the carriage and maintenance of the General Declaration under such circumstances may be considered to fulfil the purposes of Articles 29 and 34 with respect to the journey log book.

The Assembly took its decision in the interests of facilitation to simplify the documentary requirements. However, the more recent concern for aviation security against unlawful interference necessitates in practice more detailed documentation relating to the identities of the passengers and other data than would follow from Article 29 f).

Annex 6 – Operations of aircraft contains a recommendation (not a standard) concerning journey log book and it would appear that most aircraft operators comply with this recommendation:

> *11.4 Journey log book*
> 11.4.1 Recommendation. – The aeroplane journey log book should contain the following items and the corresponding roman numerals:
> I – Aeroplane nationality and registration.
> II – Date.
> III – Names of crew members.
> IV – Duty assignments of crew members.
> V – Place of departure.
> VI – Place of arrival.
> VII – Time of departure.
> VIII – Time of arrival.
> IX – Hours of flight.
> X – Nature of flight (private, aerial work, scheduled or non-scheduled).
> XI – Incidents, observations, if any.
> XII – Signature of person in charge.

It is further recommended that entries in the journey log book should be made currently and in ink or indelible pencil and that completed journey log book should be retained to provide a continuous record of the last six months' operations.

---

110 Resolution A10-16.

6 Legal Regime of International Air Transport

Iustitia est constans et perpetua voluntas ius suum cuique tribuendi
Digesta, 1.1.10

6.1 General

There are extensive rules of international law relating to the technical and operational aspects of air navigation. However, there are only sparse rules of general international law relating to air transport. The international carriage of passengers, baggage, cargo and mail is a commercial activity of highly competitive nature and States have not yet agreed on a general legal framework that would govern the global exercise of this economic activity. The complete and exclusive sovereignty of each State over the airspace above its territory is applied not only to the safety and security interests of each State but also becomes a protection of the State's economic interests to admit or not to admit foreign aircraft to perform transport from, to or through its territory.

The early efforts of the United States at the Chicago Conference in November-December 1944 to liberalize the international air transport clashed then with the economic interests of the weakening British Empire and several other countries and the Conference failed to adopt any general rules liberalizing air transport. The framework of the Chicago Convention with respect to international air transport remained unchanged since 1944 and does not respond to the needs of the current global economy.

The crucial provision of the Chicago Convention on scheduled international air transport is expressed in Article 6 that could be rightly described as a nail in the coffin of any concept of global liberal air transport:

> *Article 6*
> *Scheduled air services*
> No scheduled international air service may be operated over or into the territory of a contracting State, except with the special permission or other authorization of that State, and in accordance with the terms of such permission or authorization.

This means that there is no "freedom" of international air transport and any such "air service" requires "special permission or other authorization" of the sovereign State into or over whose territory the flight is to be performed. The language of this provision called for further clarification which is provided in Article 96 of the Convention among "definitions":

> Article 96
> For the purpose of this Convention the expression:
>
> a) "Air service" means any scheduled air service performed by aircraft for the public transport of passengers, mail or cargo.
> b) "International air service" means an air service which passes through the airspace over the territory of more than one State. "Airline" means any air transport enterprise offering or operating an international air service.
> c) "Airline" means an air transport enterprise offering or operating an international air service.

The "air service" is "international" when passing through the airspace over the territory of more than one State. Even if such service is only 'in transit" (overflight without landing in a foreign State) it still requires a special permission or other authorization.

The "air service" must be performed by aircraft "for the public transport", *i.e.*, it must be open to the general public for transport of passengers, mail or cargo – this condition would not be met by a charter flight reserved for a select group and not open to the public.

The "air service" is to be "scheduled". This expression is not defined in the Convention and its meaning could be open to interpretations. The French, Spanish and Russian authentic texts of the Convention are of little help since they render the English word "scheduled" as "regulier", "regular" and "regulyarnoe" although in English the words "scheduled" and "regular" are not fully co-extensive. The correct interpretation of this word is important because a special regime is foreseen in Article 5 of the Convention for "non-scheduled" flights.

The matter was addressed at the very first Session of the ICAO Assembly in 1947[1] which called for a further study and by the 2nd Session[2] that requested the Council to provide guidance to contracting States on the matter.

On 25 March 1952, the Council of ICAO, pursuant to the directive of the Assembly in Resolution A2-18, adopted the following definition of "scheduled international air service":

---

[1] Resolution A1-39: "Distinction between Scheduled and Non-scheduled Operations in International Civil Air Transport" – now obsolete.
[2] Resolution A2-18: "Definition of Scheduled International Air Service".

A scheduled international air service is a series of flights that possesses all of the following characteristics: a) it passes through the airspace over the territory of more than one State; b) it is performed by aircraft for the transport of passengers, mail or cargo for remuneration, in such a manner that each flight is open to use by members of the public; c) it is operated, so as to serve traffic between the same two or more points, (i) either according to a published timetable, or (ii) with flights so regular or frequent that they constitute a recognizable systematic series.[3]

This definition is just an interpretation of the terms used in Article 6 of the Chicago Convention as formulated by the ICAO Council more than half a century ago and need not be taken as rigid or definitive. The progress in liberalization of international air transport entering the 21st century may well obliterate any distinction between "scheduled" and "non-scheduled" air transport operations.

6.2 Non-Scheduled International Flight

Scheduled international air services are the main component of international air transport and are commercially by far the most important. However, there are other types of flights across national boundaries that do not meet the criteria of "scheduled air service" and which are subject to a different international legal regime. Article 5 of the Chicago Convention is the solitary provision that appears to grant a certain level of a "right to fly" internationally without the necessity of obtaining prior permission:

> *Article 5*
> *Right of non-scheduled flight*
> Each contracting State agrees that all aircraft of other contracting states, being aircraft not engaged in scheduled international air service shall have the right, subject to the observance of the terms of this Convention, to make flights into or in transit non-stop across its territory and to make stops for non-traffic purposes without the necessity of obtaining prior permission, and subject to the right of the state flown over to require landing. Each contracting State nevertheless reserves the right, for reasons of safety of flight, to require aircraft desiring to proceed over regions which are inaccessible or without adequate air navigation facilities to follow prescribed routes, or to obtain special permission for such flights.

---

3   See ICAO Doc 7278, C/841: "Definition of Scheduled International Air Service", 1952.

> Such aircraft, if engaged in the carriage of passengers, cargo, or mail for remuneration or hire on other than scheduled international air services, shall also, subject to the provision of Article 7, have the privilege of taking on or discharging passengers, cargo, or mail, subject to the right of any state where such embarkation or discharge takes place to impose such regulations, conditions or limitations as it may consider desirable.

The language of this provision is not very fortunate. "All aircraft" surely could not include "State aircraft" that are excluded from the scope of the Convention by its Article 3. The expression "aircraft of other contracting States" cannot refer to aircraft owned by those States but to aircraft registered in such States. The substance of this provision is that contracting States agree that any civil aircraft registered in another contracting State has the right – provided it is not engaged in "scheduled international air service" – to fly into or make non-stop transit across its territory or make stops for non-traffic purposes without the need to obtain a prior permission.

The expression "stop for non-traffic purposes" necessitated a definition in Article 96 paragraph d) as follows:

> d) "Stop for non-traffic purposes" means a landing for any purposes other than taking on or discharging passengers, cargo or mail.

Such stop for non-traffic purposes would include a landing for refuelling, repairs, rest of the crew, etc., but not for any commercial purpose of air transportation. The expression "without the necessity of obtaining prior permission" refers to the formal permission normally granted through the diplomatic channels but it does not mean a complete "freedom" to fly without any regulation – the flight has to observe the "terms of this Convention", must have an approved flight plan, determination where it is permitted to cross the national boundary, the State overflown may require landing and customs inspection or a search under Article 16 of the Convention, etc. It would be incorrect to conclude that the first paragraph of Article 5 grants a true and unfettered "freedom of flight".

The second paragraph of Article 5 refers to aircraft engaged in unscheduled commercial transport of passengers, cargo or mail – *e.g.*, a charter flight. Such flights do not require a formal prior permission through diplomatic channels but are fully subject to the laws, regulations, conditions and limitations of the State where they are to take on or discharge their passengers, cargo or mail. The "privilege" granted by this provision is fully subject to the national law of the granting State. The expression "also" in the second paragraph would suggest that the provision of the paragraph itself is additional to the first paragraph and that the State concerned would not be entitled to require a "prior permission".

The flights contemplated by Article 5 would include only a relatively small segment of civil aviation – general aviation (private flights), air-taxi service and different types of charter operations. Such flights are only seldom regulated by bilateral agreements on air services and are generally subject to the national laws.[4] The specific attitudes and decisions of the different States are a matter of national policy in the field of air transport and are influenced by the overall policy consideration on matters of international relations.

The overriding concept of national sovereignty gives States full latitude to adopt a liberal or restrictive policy with respect to non-scheduled flights and this aspect is no longer a matter of international law but a matter of the political will of the States concerned.

6.3   SCHEDULED INTERNATIONAL AIR SERVICE

The Chicago Conference failed to reach an agreement on the mutual granting of traffic rights for scheduled international air services among States on a multilateral basis. The peremptory language of Article 6 of the Convention makes the exercise of such traffic rights contingent on the special permission or other authorization of the State into or over whose territory the air service is to lead.

While a general consensus on the granting of traffic rights could not be reached, the Conference adopted and opened for signature, on 7 December 1944, two separate Agreements as a compromise dealing directly with scheduled air services – the International Air Services Transit Agreement[5] (generally referred to as "the two freedoms Agreement") and the International Air Transport Agreement[6] (referred to as the "the five freedoms Agreement"). These Agreements salvaged a modicum of positive multilateral approach to the granting of traffic rights in scheduled international air services and positively advanced international air law by formulating the concept and scope of the basic "freedoms of the air" that enjoys respectful application more than half a century later.

6.3.1   *International Air Services Transit Agreement*

By this *Transit Agreement* the parties thereto grant to other Parties the following "freedoms of the air" in respect of scheduled international air services:

---

4   See ICAO Doc 9587.
5   ICAO Doc 7500 or Proceedings, Vol. I, p. 175.
6   Proceedings, Vol. I, p. 179.

The privilege to fly across its territory without landing; The privilege to land for non-traffic purposes.

It is noteworthy that the 'freedoms" are referred to as "privileges" to stress their exceptional nature.

These two "freedoms" are an indispensable condition for any international flight of scheduled nature – they represent the basic and elementary proviso for the "right to fly" internationally.

However, even those basic "freedoms" that do not grant any commercial rights have not been accepted by all of ICAO 193 Member States. Only 134 States have ratified the agreement by December 2022 – some 69% of the ICAO membership. In fact – some of the States possessing the largest territories are not parties to this agreement. Among them are the Russian Federation, China, Canada, Brazil, Indonesia (with its vast archipelagic sea) and others.

Rather special is the case of Canada – the second largest land territory of the world and an active supporter of liberalized attitudes in international aviation. Canada was an original party to the Agreement but decided to denounce it on 12 November 1986 and with finality on 10 November 1987 with effect from 10 November 1988; the cause was an essentially commercial dispute with the authorities of the United Kingdom who planned to curtail some of the rights and space for Air Canada (at that time still a Crown corporation) at the Heathrow airport and to relegate its operations to Gatwick – an airport without convenient connections for flights beyond the UK. Since the dispute could not be solved by other means, Canada resorted to the denunciation of the Agreement that would have deprived the UK carriers of the right to overfly vast territories of Canada on their flights not only to Canada but also to such destinations as Boston, New York, Chicago, San Francisco, Los Angeles, Anchorage, etc. Faced with this threat the UK authorities instantly offered satisfactory accommodation for Air Canada at Heathrow and Canada continues to offer to the UK and any other State the "two freedoms" on a bilateral reciprocal basis. This illustrates how the "freedoms of the air" can play a tactical or strategic role in the mutual relations of States.

The Sessions of the ICAO Assembly regularly urge all contracting States that have not yet done so to become party to the Transit Agreement and such resolutions[7] are accepted by unanimous consensus. Nevertheless, 59 Member States of ICAO are still not ready to grant, on a multilateral basis, the two elementary "freedoms" of the air. They include , regretfully, five States with permanent representation among the 36 current Members of

---

[7] See Resolution A41.27, Consolidated statement of continuing ICAO policies in air transport field, Appendix A, October 2022.

the ICAO Council.[8] The "freedoms of the air" – even in their most elementary form of "two freedoms" could be a tool of national policies, sometimes even a source of unlawful profit.[9]

States that are not parties to the Transit Agreement have to seek permission for overflight of foreign territories in international scheduled air service by a series of bilateral agreements with other States; in practice it is not difficult to obtain such permission based on reciprocal treatment but the advantage of a multilateral arrangement approaching a global solution has not been achieved.

As in Article 5 of the Chicago Convention, the expression "landing for non-traffic purposes" means landing for any other purpose than taking on or discharging passengers, mail or cargo, *i.e.*, strictly for non-commercial purposes. However, there is a provision[10] that a State granting to airlines of another State the privilege to stop for non-traffic purposes may require such airlines to offer reasonable commercial service at the points at which such stops are made. This provision is mitigated by conditions that such requirements shall not involve any discrimination between airlines operating on the same route, shall take into account the capacity of the aircraft and shall be exercised in such a manner as not to prejudice the normal operations of the international air service concerned or the rights and obligations of a contracting State. There is no evidence that this provision has ever been invoked in the current practice of the States.

6.3.2 International Air Transport Agreement

This "five freedoms Agreement" has an important place in the fundaments of international air law for one single aspect: it pioneered the definition of the fundamental "freedoms of the air" that has been widely used in a large number of bilateral agreements between States. The Agreement proved otherwise to be of little significance since it attracted ratification by only eleven States,[11] almost all of them immediately in the euphoria of the post-war period and all with very limited air transport activities in their mutual relations, if any.

---

8   Brazil, Canada, China, Russian Federation and Saudi Arabia. The Russian Federation (in Part I: the States of chief importance in air transport) was not re-elected as Council member for the period of 2022-2025 at the 41th Assembly in Montreal. It was the first time in the history of ICAO that a country has been voted off from Part I on the Council of ICAO.
9   See Section 5.6, the comment above on Article 15 of the Convention and the unlawful practice of the Russian Federation in requiring cash payments from foreign airlines for the "use of Russian airspace".
10 Article I, Section 1, paragraph 2 of the Agreement.
11 Bolivia, Burundi, Costa Rica, El Salvador, Ethiopia, Greece, Honduras, Liberia, the Netherlands, Paraguay and Turkey.

By the International Air Transport Agreement (1944) each contracting State would grant to other contracting States the following "freedoms of the air" in respect of scheduled international air services:
1. The privilege to fly across its territory without landing.
2. The privilege to land for non-traffic purposes.
3. The privilege to put down passengers, mail and cargo taken on the territory of the State whose nationality the aircraft possesses.
4. The privilege to take on passengers, mail and cargo destined for the territory of the State whose nationality the aircraft possesses.
5. The privilege to take on passengers, mail and cargo destined for the territory of any other contracting State and the privilege to put down passengers, mail and cargo coming from any such territory.

There is a limiting condition that

> With respect to the privileges specified under paragraphs (3), (4) and (5) ..., the undertaking of each contracting State relates only to through service on a route constituting a reasonably direct line out from and back to the homeland of the State whose nationality the aircraft possesses.

The first two freedoms (or "privileges") are the non-commercial freedoms defined already in the International Air Services Transit Agreement. The remaining freedoms are of commercial nature and the Agreement attaches the privileges to the State of Registry of the aircraft. In the current practice of international civil aviation, the nationality (registration) of the aircraft may be of little relevance due to the operation of leased aircraft and other similar practices where the State of the operator is different from the State of registration. When these freedoms are defined in the bilateral agreements on air services the reference is in different form to the "nationality of the airline" based on the principal place of business and designated by a party to the agreement.

The *third freedom* permits the designated airline to unload in another State passengers, mail and cargo taken up in the home State of the air carrier.

> *Example 1*: Air Canada unloads in New York passengers, mail and cargo taken up in Toronto.
> *Example 2*: Lufthansa unloads in Cairo passengers, mail and cargo taken up in Frankfurt/M.

The third freedom by itself would be economically meaningless if the aircraft were to return to its home State empty; therefore, the third freedom is always paired with the *fourth freedom* which permits the designated airline to take on in another State passengers, mail and cargo destined to the home State of the air carrier.

> *Example 1*: Air Canada takes on in New York passengers, mail and cargo destined to Toronto.
> *Example 2*: Lufthansa takes on in Cairo passengers, mail and cargo destined to Frankfurt/M.

The combination of the third and fourth freedom has been the basic pattern of international air transport, "bread and butter" of the airlines. It continues to be the basic pattern more and more due to the long range of modern aircraft and the preference of the passengers for "point-to-point" transport without time-consuming intermediate landings in another State or States.

The *fifth freedom* has been historically considered the most important freedom from the economic point of view because it is not geographically limited to one pair of States but enables to take on and unload passengers, mail and cargo in any other State. Of course, all States concerned must be bound by agreements permitting such traffic rights.

> *Example 1*: Air Canada flies from Toronto to London and then via Bombay to Singapore and back. At all these points it can take on or unload passengers, mail and cargo. However, to exercise such rights, Canada has to have bilateral air services agreements with the UK, India and Singapore that would permit this type of carriage.
> *Example 2*: Lufthansa would fly from Munich to Cairo and then via Nairobi to Johannesburg and back. At all these points it would have the right to take on or unload passengers, mail and cargo. Again, the exercise of such rights Germany would have to conclude bilateral air services agreements with Egypt, Kenya and South Africa permitting this type of carriage.

6.4 Bilateral Agreements on Air Services

The commercial freedoms of the air are not generally offered on a multilateral basis and have to be negotiated on a bilateral basis by agreements on international air services. The parties of such agreements are sovereign States, and the agreements are "treaties" subject to the Vienna Convention on the Law of Treaties (1969). The national legislation of the States concerned would determine who is to sign such an agreement, whether it requires ratification, and how it comes into force, etc. The plenipotentiaries for the negotiations and signature are usually officials from the Department of Transport or from the Civil

Aviation Authority and the agreement comes into force either on the day of signature or day of ratification (if required) but there is also a practice of advance application of the agreement pending its formal entry into force.

Many States use a less formal method than an "agreement" in the form of a Memorandum of Understanding (MOU) on the mutual exchange of international air services. While the MOU may appear to be less formal from the point of the internal laws of the States concerned but in international law it would still have the status and force of a "treaty", regardless of its designation.[12]

The bilateral air services agreement (ASA) is typically concluded between two States but there could be also "joint bilateral talks" (historically practiced by Sweden, Denmark and Norway negotiating terms with other States for the joint SAS consortium) or one State with a group or an organization of other States.[13] The agreements are mostly the result of hard bargaining during which each party tries to achieve the most advantageous position or at least a fair balance of the competing interests.

The perspectives of the globalization of the international trade make it apparent that the complex network of hundreds of un-coordinated bilateral agreements is an obstacle to liberalization of this economic activity. There are no obstacles in the current international law to the liberalization, globalization and multilateral approach to international air services – all is a matter of policy, *i.e.*, the political will of States to abandon any protectionist strategies and to enable free competition.

It is a normal expectation that each State aims at "equality of opportunity" as proclaimed in the third paragraph of the Preamble to the Chicago Convention. Nevertheless, the "equality" may be interpreted differently by different parties – some would see it as a balance of "opportunity" (*e.g.*, equal access to the market, non-discrimination in all respects), others may look for "equality of advantage" or "balance of benefit" and calculate in economic detail that neither party draws a bigger benefit from the agreed international air service. It is obvious that a rigorous insistence on a 'balance of benefit" would not be conducive to a liberal competition on the market. That again is a matter of national policies that should not be confused with the international legal regulation of civil air transport.

A model of a bilateral international air services agreement was prepared in December 1944 by the Chicago Conference.[14] This format was followed by hundreds of agreements concluded shortly after the end of World War II. The main provision concerned

---

12 See Article 2, 1. a) of the Vienna Convention on the Law of Treaties (1969) according to which "treaty" means "an international agreement concluded between States in written form and governed by international law, whether embodied in a single instrument or in two or more related instruments and whatever its particular designation".
13 See for example the recent negotiations between the United States and the European Commission on Atlantic transport.
14 Standard Form of Agreement for Provisional Air Routes, Proceedings Vol. I., pp. 127-129.

the specific rights (determination of routes) the details of which were to be included in an Annex to the Agreement – that practice is followed until the present time. The agreement was to provide for the authorization (designation) of the airlines to perform the agreed services, airport and other facilities charges on a non-discriminatory basis and mutual recognition of certificates of airworthiness and licenses. Two common aspects of the later bilaterals were missing: there were no provisions on the applicable tariffs and no capacity clauses (that was probably of little relevance when the common model of aircraft was the DC-3 type of equal capacity).

The Standard Form also provided for the registration of the international air services agreements with ICAO – a clear sign of the need for international transparency and general access to information. That requirement is also stipulated in the Chicago Convention in Articles 81 and 83 requiring that all aeronautical arrangements are registered with the Council of ICAO "forthwith" and that the Council should make them available "as soon as possible". Regretfully, these are "imperfect" provisions that do not contain any sanction for non-observance. Many States fail to register their agreements – often through a confusion which of the parties should register the agreement – and it has become a practice that more recently – all aeronautical agreements contain a specific clause stipulating which of the contracting States accepts the obligation to register the document with the Council of ICAO. The Council of ICAO did not implement the provision to make the agreements available – it proved impracticable and excessively expensive if the hundreds and eventually thousands of agreements were to be reproduced and distributed. In Resolution A16-32 the ICAO Assembly resolved

> [...]
> c) that, in view of the expense involved, it is undesirable that ICAO should reproduce in ICAO treaty form agreements registered with it, but that the Council should issue periodically notices giving the titles of agreements registered;
> d) that it should be open to any contracting state to apply to ICAO for one or more copies of any agreement registered with the Organization and that the Organization should, within its existing resources, use its best endeavours to supply one or more copies to the state concerned, upon payment of a fee adequate to cover any costs involved in reproduction.

The registered agreements are deposited with the Legal Bureau of the ICAO Secretariat and copies can be made on request against payment of a fee. A reference guide to the main provisions of the agreements is published from time to time in the "Database of the World's Air Services Agreement".[15]

An electronic ICAO database "DAGMAR" lists over 5000 aeronautical agreements and arrangements.[16] It is common that authorities preparing for negotiation of a bilateral agreement study the agreements entered into by their negotiating partner to understand better the practice of that partner.

The ICAO Council adopted Rules for Registration with ICAO of Aeronautical Agreements and Arrangements that are from time to time updated.[17]

The main protagonists at the Chicago Conference in 1944 were the United States and the United Kingdom who had vastly different views on the organization of the post-war international air transport. Their compromise solution is reflected in their bilateral agreement on air services signed at Bermuda on 11 February 1946 and generally referred to as "Bermuda I".[18] This agreement has become the model for up to 3000 post-war air services agreements entered into not only by these two partners but many other pairs of States.

The brief text of the agreement mostly follows the Chicago standard form but the true essence is in the voluminous annexes. They define in great detail the routes that could be served within the territory of the parties and beyond (5th freedom) all over the world. Moreover, they stipulate that the applicable tariffs are to be determined by the International Air Transport Association (IATA) and be subject to the approval by the governments.[19] The volume of traffic (capacity) was to be coordinated by the designated airlines to suit the proven practical demands for transportation. It also addressed the issue of "change of gauge" – change of the size of the aircraft used for reasons of economy at different segments of the same route – limiting it strictly as a direct continuation of the previous segment and serving only such previous segment.

It should be noted that in the bilateral policy dealings some new terminology was developed to expand the definitions of the "five freedoms" to a total of nine! These "new freedoms" are not defined in any international instrument and their interpretation and relevance may differ from State to State. They are the following:

Sixth freedom: flight from a foreign State via the home State of the airline to another foreign State

---

15 ICAO Doc 9511. The Database is available in CD-ROM format.
16 Aeronautical Agreements and Arrangements (icao.int), www.cfapps.icao.int/dagmar/main.cfm.
17 ICAO Doc 6685.
18 Text at http://en.wikisource.org/wiki/Bermuda_Agreement; "Bermuda II" of 23 July 1977 went further in the direction of deregulation of air transport, prohibited predatory pricing and capacity dumping, etc.
19 Lasantha Hettiarachchi, *International Air Transport Association (IATA): Structure and Legitimacy of Its Quasi-International Regulatory Power*, Eleven International Publishing, The Hague, 2020, pp. 22-24.

Example 1: KLM flight from New York to Amsterdam and from there continues (perhaps under another flight number) to Moscow. It may be argued that KLM is in fact unlawfully exercising traffic rights from New York to Moscow; it may be equally argued that the segment New York/Amsterdam is operated in the exercise of the 4th freedom and Amsterdam/Moscow in the exercise of the 3rd freedom.

Example 2: Gulf Air flies from Sydney to Manama (Bahrain) and after luxurious overnight hospitality carries passengers from Manama to London. It may be argued they undercut the competition of British Airways and Quantas and allegedly unlawfully purport to exercise traffic rights Sydney/London; it may also be argued that the segment Sydney/Manama is in the exercise of the 4th freedom and Manama/London in the exercise of the 3rd freedom.

The so-called sixth freedom is disputed. While it can be interpreted as a combination of the fourth and third freedoms, it may offer some advantages to one party and a loss to the others. It is a matter of negotiation and mutual accommodation, *e.g.*, limited publicity to the "through" flights. Conflicting situations related to the sixth freedom are not rare; in early 2011 a conflict arose between the United Arab Emirates and Canada when Canada refused to authorize additional frequencies and destinations to *Emirates* and *Etihad*; Canada argued that the UAE airlines were taking most of the passengers to and from destinations beyond the UAE territory to the detriment of *Air Canada* and its partners in the *Star Alliance*. The UAE responded by abolishing Canada's use of an air force base in the UAE and introducing entrance visa for Canadian citizens; however, the visa requirement was later withdrawn.

Seventh freedom: operation from one foreign State to another foreign State without contact with the home State of the air carrier.

Example 1: a flight of the United States carries passengers between Hong Kong and Singapore and from Singapore to Hong Kong and does not go to the USA at all.

Example 2: Pan Am used to fly with a smaller plane between Berlin and London and London to Berlin to connect in London with other large capacity Pan Am flights to or from the USA. In other contexts, such arrangement is called "change of gauge".

In special circumstances (*e.g.*, very liberal or open skies policy) such operations are permitted by the States concerned even if they are generally available and do not represent only a change of gauge connected with flights from or to the USA.

> *Eighth freedom*: flight from a home State the air carrier is carrying local traffic (passengers, cargo or mail) between two points in the same foreign State.
>
> *Example*: (hypothetical!) Air France would fly from Paris to New York and embark there additional local passengers and carry them to Los Angeles. Such a flight would be cabotage subject to Article 7 of the Chicago Convention.

Cabotage is still a matter of controversy but in international law it is to be understood that Article 7 of the Chicago Convention does not prohibit cabotage as such – it gives the right to each State to refuse cabotage or permit it under special conditions of non-exclusivity.

> *Ninth freedom*: flights operating only within a foreign State
>
> *Example*: (hypothetical!) Lufthansa would establish a sister company that would operate, at the request and with full approval of the Egyptian government, the busy commercial tourist routes between Cairo and Aswan (Abu Simbel).

This scenario should not be listed as "freedom of the air" under international law. It would be a purely domestic matter of the State authorizing such type of operation. This alleged "freedom" is also called "stand alone cabotage".

Vastly new perspectives in bilateral agreements on international air services were introduced by the so called "open skies" agreements. The pioneering agreement of this nature was concluded in 1992 between the United States and the Netherlands and it provided free access to any routes between the two countries, no limitation on the number of carriers to be designated by each party, no limitation on the capacity and frequency; pricing was to be freely determined by the market forces (unless disapproved by both governments – so called "double disapproval"). The agreement also provided for the seventh freedom for cargo flights, *i.e.*, all cargo flights between the other country and a third country via flights not linked to the home State of the airline. This pattern of a bilateral agreement became popular and at present there are already scores of similar bilateral "open skies" agreements between many pairs of States. From the legal point of view there cannot be any reservations to such type of agreements expressing the aviation policy and the political will of the States concerned. The analysis of the merits or demerits of such agreements for a particular State or group of States is a matter of economic and policy considerations, not a legal analysis.

A multilateral progress towards the "open skies" has been achieved in the Agreement between the United States and all the States of the European Union that was signed in Brussels on 25 April 2007 and in Washington, D.C. on 30 April 2007.[20] This Agreement – came into force on 30 March 2008 and – permitted the EU and US airlines to fly on any route between any city in the US and any city in the EU; moreover, the EU airlines will be allowed to operate between any point in the US and a non-EU country like Switzerland. The "phase two" of the US-EU agreement was reached by the "Protocol to amend the air transport agreement between the United States of America and the European Community and its Member States signed on April 25 and 30, 2007" that was signed in Luxembourg on 24 June 2010.[21] European airlines did not achieve complete satisfaction – their wish would be to enjoy cabotage rights in the US domestic market – an unlikely scenario for the foreseeable future.

The bilateral agreements among different States differ in style and substance but there is a certain pattern common to them. To assist States in the drafting of the bilateral agreements ICAO prepared two templates (TASAs – template air services agreements), one for purely bilateral relations and the other for plurilateral or regional use.[22]

There are also similar structures to the bilateral agreements and typical provisions to be found in most of them. The examples include:[23]

> *Preamble*: the introductory paragraph of all agreements usually identifies the contracting parties and defines the purpose of the agreement or the aim of the parties. The preamble is an important part of any treaty for the purposes of interpreting the objectives intended by the parties. The Preamble is then followed by numbered Articles.
>
> *Definitions*: it is common for most agreements to list the terms used in the agreement if they have a special meaning for the purposes of the agreement or if they depart from the ordinary dictionary meaning.
>
> *Grant of rights*: the key provision of each agreement is a clause defining the rights that the parties mutually grant to each other. Details of technical nature (*e.g.*, the description of the routes authorized) may be relegated to an "annex"

---

20   http://ec.europa.eu/transport/air_portal/international/pillars/global_partners/doc/us/ec_us_openskies_agreement_24_4_07.pdf; formal text is in the OJ L/134/16.
21   Council of the EU, Interinstitutional file 2010/0113, 9913/10.
22   ICAO Doc 9587– Policy and Guidance Material on the Economic Regulation of International Air Transport, Appendix 5, 4th ed., 2017.
23   ICAO Doc 9626 – Manual for the Regulation of International Air Transport, Chapter 3, 3.2, 3rd ed., 2018.

or "schedule" that could be amended from time to time at a lower negotiating level without disturbing the structure of the agreement itself.

Agreed principles: under some such headings the agreements spell out the manner of mutual cooperation – non-discrimination, "equal opportunity", "fair competition", etc. Capacity clauses, if any, may be stipulated under this heading. It could be also seen that parties sometimes authorize the designated airlines only to "operate" or more freely to "compete".

Designation: the parties agree whether each of them will designate one single carrier to operate on the basis of the rights granted (single designation) or whether there may be two or more such designated carriers (double or multiple designation). There could be a separate provision on the revocation of the designation or suspension of the operating authorization.

Capacity: ICAO guidance speaks of "pre-determination" ruling in advance on the permitted capacity, "Bermuda I" type determination (determination by airline agreement according to actual demand for carriage) and "free determination". There could be also a separate provision on the authorized frequencies of flights.

Tariff: the regulation of pricing is one of the sensitive aspects and in most cases requires consent of both parties ("double approval"); other alternatives determine the pricing based on the country of origin.

Soft rights: apart from the "hard rights" (essentially the traffic rights) parties grant themselves mutually "soft rights" such as "doing business" (establishing offices in the partner country, hiring own staff …), ticket sales, own ground handling opportunity, to run the computer reservation system, availability of "slots" at the airports, etc.

Security: the attention paid to aviation security against unlawful interference is reflected also in the fact that the Council of ICAO prepared a model "security clause"[24] to be inserted in bilateral air services agreements as an integral part of the mutual exchange of the traffic rights. Annex 17 also recommends to States to set procedures to be followed by the parties in case of unlawful interference or threat thereof.

---

24 C-WP/11608.

Other typical clauses may deal with taxation, charges for airports and air navigation facilities, mutual recognition of the certificates of airworthiness and licenses, settlement of differences, entry into force of the agreement, termination of the agreement, determination of the authentic language or languages and date and place of signature.

Much of the substance of the air services agreements is a matter of government policy in economic regulation and is beyond the scope of this treatise.

6.5 CODE-SHARING OF AIR SERVICES

In international practice each flight of the airlines is identified by a two-letter airline code (*e.g.*, AF for Air France, AC for Air Canada, LH for Lufthansa, etc.) and a flight number. Thus AC 015 is the code for Air Canada flight from Toronto to Hong Kong and AC 016 for Hong Kong to Toronto (west-bound flights are designated by an odd number, east-bound by even number); LH 572 means Lufthansa flight from Frankfurt/M to Johannesburg and LH 573 for Johannesburg to Frankfurt/M (south-bound flights carry an even number, north-bound an odd number).

The code-sharing is a form of cooperation between airlines in which the aircraft of one airline (operating airline) performs the flight under its own code and adds to it the code of another airline (non-operating airline). This cooperation enables the non-operating airline to extend its route network and to sell the flight as its own without having to employ its own equipment. The sales of seats are coordinated and the non-operating airline may have a certain number of seats reserved for its own sales (blocked space). Domestic law in most cases requires that the passenger be informed which airline is actually to perform the carriage.

Code-shared flights are accepted by other States, but both the performing and non-performing airlines must be designated carriers of a State enjoying traffic rights between the relevant points under the applicable bilateral agreements.

6.6 COMPUTER RESERVATION SYSTEMS (CRS)

The management of airline marketing and sales found a powerful tool in electronic data processing – the computer reservation system (CRS). Its effect for the airline economy and competition was such that the system was soon considered in need of national and international regulation.

By its nature CRS is no more than an advanced, complex and constantly updated database for information storage, information correlation and information retrieval. CRS store information about thousands of flights, thousands of applicable fares and rates, can assign the seats for passengers, print the e-ticket and/or boarding pass, keep the accounting records and calculate the yield for each flight. It can also serve as departure record, crew planning and rotation, scheduling of maintenance, pro-rating the fares in successive interline carriage and it can also calculate and record the frequent flyer's points, arrange for hotel reservation, car rentals or other elements of the land segment of the trip and it can also keep record of the passengers' travel pattern and personal preferences for future marketing purposes. The CRS are owned and operated by major airlines or groups of airlines, and they become "vendors" of the services and have a global (transborder) reach. Among the major CRS have been *Apollo, Sabre, Amadeus, Galileo* and several others.

CRS can link practically all airlines and give them advantages in efficiency and reliability in marketing and considerable savings in labour costs. However, the system is also prone to anticompetitive practices – biased display in favour of the airline owning the system or otherwise controlling it while suppressing or lowering the prominence of the competitors, the CRS vendors have the sole control over the CRS booking fees that could lead to discriminatory practices for the same type of services, the vendor has a privileged access to the marketing data of the airlines, etc.

The need for regulation of the CRS became apparent soon after their introduction due to the perception of their easy abuse and distortion of the fair competition. However, international legal regulation of the CRS has not been achieved so far. A step in the direction of international legal regulation is the ICAO *Code of Conduct for the Regulation and Operation of Computer Reservation Systems* adopted by the Council on 17 December 1991 and revised on 25 June 1996.[25]

A "Code of Conduct", although the contracting States are "strongly urged … to follow the revised Code of Conduct … (of) 25 June 1996",[26] is not a source of international law, it is not an international treaty and does not have any legally binding force. It is no more than "Guidance Material" that States may or may not consider in their national practice. Since the CRS are global – regardless of the national boundaries – it would be desirable to provide a multilateral (or even global) legal basis for the CRS.

The aims of the ICAO Code of Conduct, as expressed in its Article 1, are transparency, accessibility, non-discrimination, fair competition and offering the air transport users the widest possible choice of options.

The obligation of States should be to ensure compliance with the Code, remove regulatory obstacles to investment in CRSs domiciled in their territories and allow system vendors to provide their CRS services in their territories and to treat all system vendors impartially.

---

25 http://www.icao.int/icao/en/atb/ecp/CodeOFConduct.htm.
26 Resolution A35-18, Appendix A, Section III; updated by Resolution A37-20 (2010), Consolidated statement of continuing ICAO policies in air transport field, Appendix A: Economic regulation of international air transport, Section III: Airline product distribution.

The system vendors are to permit participation in their CRS by any carrier prepared to pay the fees and meet the conditions, not require that their service be used exclusively and not to discriminate among the participating carriers

The European Union addressed the issue of CRS well before ICAO. The Council of the European Communities issued, on 24 July 1989, *Council Regulation (EEC) No. 2299/89*[27] *on a Code of Conduct for computerised reservation systems*. The regulation applies with the force of law to computerized reservation systems for air transport products, when offered for use and/or used in the territory of the Community and their essence is to provide equal access and non-discrimination. A revised version of the Regulation is in Regulation (ERC) No. 80/2009 that entered into force on 29 March 2009.[28]

As will be seen further, CRS has become one of the elements of the "trade in services" under GATS.[29]

6.7　Air Transport as "Trade in Services"?

The post-war efforts to facilitate and liberalize international trade found its expression in the General Agreement on Tariffs and Trade (GATT) – its aim was to reduce the customs barriers to international trade and to introduce the non-discriminatory attitudes through the "most favoured nation clause" (MFN clause – the very best commercial treatment offered to one State must be equally extended to all other commercial partners). GATT remained "provisional"[30] and the Havana Charter of the International Trade Organization of 24 March 1948[31] never entered into force. After years of stalemate States attempted, in the mid-sixties, the "Kennedy Round" of negotiations, between 1973 and 1979 the "Tokyo Round" followed, between 1986 and 1994, by the "Uruguay Round", which achieved the creation of the World Trade Organization (WTO) – on 15 April 1994 in Marrakech the Agreement Establishing the World Trade Organization was signed.[32]

Annex 1 to the Agreement contains a Multilateral Agreement on Trade in Goods and is of no direct relevance to aviation. However, Annex 1 B contains the General Agreement on Trade in Services (GATS) dealing with all internationally traded services – *e.g.*, banking, telecommunications, tourism, professional services, etc. – providing for the most favoured

---

27　Council Regulation (EEC) No. 2299/89 of 24 July 1989 on a code of conduct for computerised reservation systems. OJ L 220, 29/7/1989, pp. 1-7. This regulation is no longer in force, instead Regulation (EC) No. 80/2009 of the European Parliament and of the Council of 14 January 2009 on a Code of Conduct for computerised reservation systems, *OJ L 35, 4/2/2009, pp. 47-55*.
28　Idem.
29　General Agreement on Trade in Services.
30　UNTS, Vol. 55, p. 187.
31　E/CONF 2/78, UN Publication Sales No. 1948 II. D 4.
32　www.wto.org/english/docs_e/legal_e/04-wto_e.htm.

nation treatment and special machinery for the settlement of differences. Air transport services may appear to be a typical international "trade in services" but States have stopped short of that classification. The Annex on Air Transport Services applies to measures affecting trade in air transport services, whether scheduled or non-scheduled, and ancillary services; it confirms that any specific commitment or obligation assumed under the GATS shall not reduce or affect a Member's obligation under bilateral or multilateral agreements that are in effect on the date of entry into force of the WTO Agreement.

In its paragraph 2, the Annex stipulates that the Agreement, including its dispute settlement procedure, shall not apply to the "hard rights" in international air services, namely traffic rights however granted or services directly related to the exercise of traffic rights. Thus the bilateral or multilateral regime of the traffic rights remains untouched by the GATS and the MFN clause or settlement of differences under the WTO procedures are not available.

The GATS, however, applies to "soft rights" in aviation – specifically to aircraft repair and maintenance services, the selling and marketing of air transport services and the computer reservation system (CRS) services.

True and effective liberalization of international air services would be achieved by a full extension of the GATS to the "hard rights" that would replace the chaotic network of restrictive bilateral agreements by open competition.

In ICAO, there are no signs of support to relegate international air transport to WTO. The 35th Session of the ICAO Assembly in 2004 reaffirmed "the primary role of ICAO in developing policy guidance on the regulation of international air transport" and also requested the WTO "to accord due consideration to the particular regulatory structures and arrangements of international air transport…and the ICAO's constitutional responsibility for international air transport and, in particular, for its safety and security".[33]

Resolution A35-18 was superseded, in September 2007, by Resolution A36-16 which, in Appendix A, Part IV again strongly reaffirms the "primary role" of ICAO in developing guidance on the regulation of international air transport. No early change in the ICAO policies is likely. In 2010 the 37th Session of the Assembly in Resolution A37-20[34] and also in the other Resolutions (*e.g.*, 40th and 41st Sessions),[35] again strongly reasserted the "primary role" of ICAO.

This statement is not supported by the wording of the Chicago Convention or the results of the Chicago Conference in 1944 that failed to give to ICAO any strong mandate in the field of international air transport. In any case, these arguments of the Resolutions

---

33 Resolution A35-18, Appendix A, Section IV.
34 Also Appendix A, Section IV.
35 Resolutions A40-9 (2019) and 41-27 (2022), Consolidated statement of continuing ICAO policies in the air transport field. Appendix A, Economic regulation of international air transport. Section IV, Trade in services. Point 3.

are not convincing and give the impression of, perhaps subliminal, competition between ICAO and the WTO, as if WTO were endangering some ICAO's vested rights.

In fact ICAO does not possess any regulatory authority with respect to air transport (unlike its strong mandate in the field of air navigation) and cannot do more than provide debating forum and draft guidance materials without any legally binding force. It would appear logical that in due course the issues of international air transport will be recognized as international trade in services with all freedom and flexibility that the WTO and GATS can provide.

That will take nothing away from the continuing importance of ICAO – it will retain its primary role in regulating the issues of air navigation on a world-wide basis with special emphasis on the safety and security. The operators of airlines enjoying the air transport freedoms under the new GATS would, as a condition of their designation as carriers, be obliged to meet the safety and security standards originating in ICAO.

7 INTERNATIONAL CIVIL AVIATION ORGANIZATION (ICAO)

Societas suum cuiques tribuere debet

7.1 HISTORY

The proliferation of international intergovernmental organizations in the first half of the 20th century was a sign of growing international cooperation and interdependence and a trend towards multilateral diplomacy. The League of Nations established by the Versailles Peace Conference (1919) was an attempt to create a system of collective security and of the pacific settlement of international disputes.[1] Article 24 of the Covenant of the League of Nations attempted to bring under the umbrella of the League all existing and future international organizations for the regulation of matters of international interest. The article stated:

> *Article 24*
> There shall be placed under the direction of the League all international bureaux established by general treaties if the parties to such treaties consent. All such international bureaux and all commissions for the regulation of matters of international interest hereafter constituted shall be placed under the direction of the League. In all matters of international interest which are regulated by general conventions, but which are not placed under the control of international bureaux or commissions, the Secretariat of the League shall, subject to the consent of the Council and if desired by the parties, collect and distribute all relevant information and shall render any other assistance which may be necessary or desirable. The Council may include as part of the expenses of the Secretariat the expenses of any bureau or commission which is placed under the direction of the League.

The International Commission for Air Navigation (ICAN or CINA for *Commission internationale de la navigation aerienne*) created by the Paris Convention (1919) Relating

---

[1] The Covenant of the League of Nations was included in Articles 1-40 of the Versailles Peace Treaty signed on 28 June 1919; the entire text had 440 Articles and its Articles 387-399 contained the Constitution of the International Labour Organization (ILO).

to the Regulation of Aerial Navigation was one of such "commissions" placed under the coordinating direction of the League of Nations. The Paris Convention – like the Chicago Convention – also had a double function: codification of international law and at the same time establishing an international body vested with jurisdiction to perform specific functions under the Convention. However, the ICAN was a precursor of ICAO only in a limited measure – without the participation of the United States and other non-European States in the League and its institutions the ICAN could not achieve a world-wide scope.

The definitive agenda of the 1944 Chicago Conference as approved at the Second Plenary Session of the Conference on 2 November 1944 had as its first item

> Multilateral aviation convention and international aeronautical body ... (and) establishing such permanent international aeronautical body as may be agreed on, and determining the extent of its jurisdiction.[2]

This task has been accomplished by the adoption of the Convention on International Civil Aviation which is both an "aviation convention" unifying and codifying the basic principles of public international air law and a charter of an "international aviation body".

The timing of the Conference prior to the conclusions of the negotiations leading to the adoption of the Charter of the United Nations prevented the Conference from achieving a closer coordination with the drafting of the UN Charter and the Convention is in some respects more "old-fashioned" than the UN Charter

The Conference agreed on the establishment of the Provisional International Civil Aviation Organization (PICAO)[3] to act pending entry into force of the Convention on International Civil Aviation and creation of the International Civil Aviation Organization (ICAO). According to Section 2 of Article I of the Interim Agreement the seat of the Organization was Canada.

7.2 PICAO

The Interim Agreement entered into force on 6 June 1945 and on the invitation of the Government of Canada the Interim Council[4] met at Montreal on 15 August 1945 – the

---

2   Proceedings, Vol. I, p. 14.
3   "Interim Agreement on International Civil Aviation", Proceedings, Vol. I, p. 132.
4   The Interim Council was elected by the 4th Plenary Session of the Chicago Conference on 6 December 1944; only 20 Member States were elected instead of 21 leaving the vacancy open in case the USSR decided to join. At the Final Plenary Session on 7 December 1944 Norway, already elected to the Council, "placed at the disposal of the Conference" its seat to enable the election of India that failed to be elected; however, the Delegate of Cuba offered the resignation of his country in favour of India and asked Norway to withdraw

first international body initiating work in the post-war period. Edward Warner (USA) was elected President of the Interim Council and Albert Roper (France, Secretary General of ICAN) was appointed Secretary General of PICAO.

The role of PICAO was to be a provisional body of a technical and advisory nature for the purpose of collaboration in the field of international civil aviation. It was to be in existence until the new permanent body – ICAO – replaced it upon entry into force of the Convention on International Civil Aviation.

PICAO was composed of the Interim Assembly, Interim Council and the Secretariat. The Interim Council was to appoint three interim committees:[5]
a. Committee on Air Transport;
b. Committee on Air Navigation; and
c. Committee on International Convention on Civil Aviation.

The Committee on International Convention on Civil Aviation was created in response to a specific recommendation by the Chicago Conference to deal with matters on which it was impossible to reach agreement between the States represented at the Conference.[6] PICAO was thus charged to address the "unfinished business" of the Conference, in particular the contentious issues of air transport. It will come as no surprise that PICAO did not achieve any progress in this field either.

The PICAO Interim Assembly held its first and only Session in Montreal from 21 May to 7 June 1946. The only hotly discussed item was whether to fill the remaining 21st vacancy on the Interim Council – the seat reserved by the Chicago Conference for the USSR. By a very slim majority it was decided to fill the vacancy and Ireland was elected. It took another 23 years before the USSR decided to ratify the Chicago Convention…

PICAO is now only a part of history, but it is interesting to note this unique and unprecedented method of organized preparatory work pending the entry into force of the permanent arrangements. PICAO is to be credited with very useful work in preparation of the draft Rules of Procedure both for the Council and Assembly, setting up the working methods for the Council, creation of the Secretariat and selecting both the President of the Council and the Secretary General who would become eventually officials of the permanent body. It also sorted out the priorities for the preparation of the Standards and Recommended Practices and Procedures and prepared the agendas for the ICAO Council and the Assembly.

---

its offer and so it was done. Such sign of grace and nobility was not seen again in the history of international organizations. Proceedings, Vol. I., pp. 103-106.
5   Interim Agreement on International Civil Aviation, Section 5, paragraph 5 of Article III.
6   "Resolution X in the Final Act of the Conference", Proceedings, Vol. I, p. 130.

7.3 ICAO

On 4 April 1947 the Convention on International Civil Aviation came into force and thereby the PICAO ceased to exist. Instead, under Article 43 of the Convention a new organization came into being:

> *Article 43*
> *Name and composition*
> An organization to be named the International Civil Aviation Organization is formed by the Convention. It is made up of an Assembly, a Council, and such other bodies as may be necessary.

The new organization – ICAO – has all the main features of an international intergovernmental organization (IGO):
a. it is set up by an international treaty;
b. its members are sovereign States; and
c. the organization possesses clearly defined aims of international nature.

7.3.1 Aims and Objectives

The aims and objectives of the organization are set out in Article 44:

> *Article 44*
> *Objectives*
> The aims and objectives of the Organization are to develop the principles and techniques of international air navigation and to foster the planning and development of international air transport so as to a) Insure the safe and orderly growth of international civil aviation throughout the world; b) Encourage the arts of aircraft design and operation for peaceful purposes; c) Encourage the development of airways, airports and air navigation facilities for international civil aviation; d) Meet the needs of the peoples of the world for safe, regular, efficient and economical air transport; e) Prevent economic waste caused by unreasonable competition; f) Insure that the rights of contracting States are fully respected and that every State has a fair opportunity to operate international airlines; g) Avoid discrimination between contracting states; h) Promote safety of flight in international air navigation; i) Promote generally the development of all aspects of international civil aeronautics.

The aims and objectives are also reflected in the Preamble of the Convention that sets out the reasons for which the Parties concluded the Convention and that should serve as a tool for the interpretation of the Convention:

> WHEREAS the future development of international civil aviation can greatly help to create and preserve friendship and understanding among the nations and peoples of the world, yet its abuse can become a threat to the general security; and
>
> WHEREAS it is desirable to avoid friction and to promote the cooperation between nations and peoples upon which the peace of the world depends;
>
> THEREFORE, the undersigned governments having agreed on certain principles and arrangements in order that international civil aviation may be developed in a safe and orderly manner and that international air transport services may be established on the basis of equality of opportunity and operated soundly and economically;
>
> Have accordingly concluded this Convention to that end.

The Preamble and Article 44 define the aims, objectives and basic principles of the Convention and of the Organization in great detail and in a solemn language that is self-explanatory. A place of prominence is given to concepts of "safety", "regularity", "efficiency", "economy" and "equality of opportunity".

The concept of "general security" was related to international peace as the Convention, by 1944, did not foresee the problems of aviation security against unlawful interference. The aims, objectives and principles on which the Convention and the Organization were based in 1944 are fully valid at present but any future renewal of the Convention would most likely add to the aims and principles highlighted concern for security against unlawful acts and for the protection of the environment – issues that could not be identified in 1944.

The organization – ICAO – that carries the responsibility of implementing the aims and objectives of the Convention came into being in 1947 and reached a mature age of 76 years in 2023. It is now a different organization than the one of 1947 which then had a limited membership mostly of the "old" world. Today's 193 States give the Organization a global membership and to the Convention global applicability as general international law.

However, the Convention itself is a "snapshot" of the level of unity of the political will that could be reached by the 52 States that participated at the Chicago Conference while the additional 141 States joined the Convention and the Organization without having any influence on its drafting. Moreover, the technology of aviation of the present time is not comparable to that of 1944 and the present progress to globalized economy was not even foreseeable in 1944. Yet, the aims and objectives agreed decades ago under vastly different conditions maintain their validity.

7.3.2   Permanent Seat

The Interim Agreement on International Civil Aviation determined that PICAO shall have its seat in Canada. On the invitation of the government of Canada the Interim Council and the Interim Assembly met at Montreal. Article 45 of the Convention provides:

> Article 45
> Permanent seat
> The permanent seat of the Organization shall be at such place as shall be determined by the final meeting of the Interim Assembly of the Provisional International Civil Aviation Organization set up by the Interim Agreement on International Civil Aviation signed at Chicago on December 7, 1944. The seat may be temporarily transferred elsewhere by decision of the Council, and otherwise than temporarily by decision of the Assembly, such decision to be taken by the number of votes specified by the Assembly. *The number of votes so specified will not be less than three-fifths of the total number of contracting States.*[7]

The Interim Assembly had to consider competing candidacies for the permanent seat of ICAO – Canada, China, France and Switzerland. In a secret ballot on 6 June 1946, Montreal obtained 27 votes, China one, Paris 9 and Geneva 4.[8]

The original text of the Convention provided only for a temporary transfer of the seat elsewhere by decision of the Council. At the 8th Session the Assembly in 1954 amended

---

[7]   The text in italics was added by the amendment of the Convention approved by the 8th Session of the Assembly on 14 June 1954.

[8]   PICAO Doc 1826 A/44 – 4th meeting of the Plenary. The original premises were in downtown Montreal partly in the Sun Life building and some adjacent office buildings, the Assemblies, when held at Montreal, took place in the Ball Room of Hotel Windsor. Later a dedicated building was offered by the government of Canada at 1080 University Street in the block housing the Queen Elisabeth Hotel and the Central Station of the CNN; in 1975, ICAO moved to a larger building at 1000 Sherbrooke Street West and by 1996 ICAO moved to its current location at 999 University Street (on 15 March 2015 the street was renamed for Robert-Bourassa Boulevard) with some overflow in the adjacent Bell Tower. ICAO does not own the premises but uses them on the basis of a heavily subsidized lease or sub-lease from the Government of Canada. Paradoxically, Canada is paying not only 75% of the rental for the meeting rooms and secretariat offices, but also subsidizes 75% of the cost of the basic office accommodation of the permanent representatives of Member States on the Council in the building (extra to these basic space delegations have to pay at the market rate); the Canadian taxpayer thus subsidizes 35 national delegations who should be bearing their costs under the explicit provision of Article 69 of the Chicago Convention.

Article 45 to provide for "otherwise than temporary" transfer of the seat. However, the conditions for such a permanent transfer from Montreal would not be easy – it would require an Assembly decision taken by at least 60% vote of all members of the Organization (not just those present and voting, *i.e.*, 116 votes at least would be required for such a change). In the history of ICAO, no formal proposal for the transfer of the seat has ever been presented, although informal references to possible invitation were mentioned with respect to Vienna, Berlin, Bonn, Singapore, and a formal invitation was issued in 2013 by Qatar (later withdrawn). Any transfer of the Headquarters out of Montreal is highly unlikely – Canada offers to the Organization exceptional support and hospitality and on the local labour market is a rich pool of multilingual talent for the local recruitment of the clerical secretarial staff that in another place would have to be internationally recruited at much higher cost.

Over the years ICAO established the following Regional Offices:
– Asia and Pacific (APAC) Office – Bangkok, and its Sub-office (APAC RSO) – Beijing[9]
– Middle East (MID) Office – Cairo
– Western and Central African (WACAF) Office – Dakar
– South American (SAM) Office – Lima
– North American, Central American and Caribbean (NACC) Office – Mexico
– Eastern and Southern African (ESAF) office – Nairobi
– European and North Atlantic (EUR/NAT) Office – Paris

7.3.3 Legal Status of ICAO

International intergovernmental organization need to have a legal personality different from that of its Member States. They need it to perform their functions, to conclude in their own name contracts (lease, purchase of equipment…) and agreements with States or other organizations. The Convention addresses the legal capacity of ICAO in Article 47:

> *Article 47*
> *Legal capacity*
> The Organization shall enjoy in the territory of each contracting State such legal capacity as may be necessary for the performance of its functions. Full juridical personality shall be granted whenever compatible with the constitution and laws of the state concerned.

---

[9] The Secretary General of the ICAO with the consent of the ICAO Council decided on 5 November 2012 to open a regional sub-office in Beijing under the supervision of the regional office in Bangkok. C-WP/13854.

The status of the Organization in the Host State of its seat is of considerable importance. Few countries of the world have the privilege of hosting the headquarters of an international organization – in particular a specialized agency of the UN system.[10] The relations of an international organization with a host State are, as a rule, agreed in form of an agreement between the host State and the organization which determines the legal status, immunities and privileges of the Organization in the territory of the host State, as well as the status, immunities and privileges of the representatives of Member States and of its officials (Secretariat).

In the early years of the United Nations system it was believed that all such matters should be regulated uniformly in one single multilateral agreement.[11] The General Assembly of the United Nations adopted, on 21 November 1947 the *Convention on the Privileges and Immunities of the Specialized Agencies*[12] that did not achieve universal acceptance and was deemed to be too general for the bilateral relations of an international organizations and its host State. Only 130 of 193 ICAO Member States agreed to apply this agreement to ICAO.

Canada did not become party to the 1947 Convention but the "Headquarters Agreement between Canada and ICAO of 14 April 1951"[13] closely paraphrased the principles and the wording of that Convention. The 1951 Headquarters Agreement served both ICAO and Canada well for over four decades. On 16 September 1980, a Supplementary Agreement entered into force dealing with the (then) new ICAO premises for which the Government of Canada assumed 75% of the rental costs. On 20 February 1992, the 1951 Agreement was terminated and was superseded by a very generous new Agreement that entered into force on that day.[14] (However, the Supplementary Agreement of 1980 on the Headquarters premises remained in force). The new agreement enhanced the privileges and immunities of the representatives of State members and of the senior staff to the level of diplomatic agents in conformity with the Vienna Convention on Diplomatic Relations (1961) and also exempted Canadian staff from income tax on their ICAO salary and emoluments.[15]

---

10 Austria/Vienna: IAEA, UNIDO; Canada/Montreal: ICAO; France/Paris: UNESCO; Italy/Rome: FAO; Switzerland/Geneva, Bern: ILO, ITU, UPU, WHO, WMO, WIPO; United Kingdom/London: IMO; United States/New York, Washington, D.C.: UN, IMF, IBRD.
11 UN General Assembly Resolution of 13 February 1946 contemplated unification of the privileges and immunities enjoyed by the United Nations and by the various specialized agencies.
12 UNTS, Vol. 33, p. 261.
13 ICAO Doc 7147.
14 *Headquarters Agreement Between the Government of Canada and the ICAO*, E101905, CTS 1992 No. 7; supplementary E103232, CTS 1999 No. 20; Supplementary E 105390.
15 M. Milde, "New Headquarters Agreement between ICAO and Canada", in *Annals of Air and Space Law*, Vol. XVII, Part II (1992), pp. 305-322; Text of the Agreement and related correspondence is on pp. 571-594.

Under the Headquarters Agreement ICAO possesses juridical personality and has the legal capacity of a body corporate, including the capacity to contract, to acquire and dispose of immovable and movable property and to institute legal proceedings. The Organization, its property and assets enjoy the same immunity from suit and every form of judicial process as is enjoyed by foreign States. The Headquarters premises are inviolable and enjoy the same protection given to diplomatic missions in Canada. However, the organization is obliged to prevent the premises from becoming a refuge either for persons who are avoiding arrest or for persons who are endeavouring to avoid service or execution of legal process. The purpose of the privileges and immunities of the representatives and staff is not for personal benefit of the individuals themselves, but to safeguard the independent exercise of their functions with the organization. Member States and the Secretary General not only have the right but are under the duty to waive the immunity of such persons in any case the immunity would impede the course of justice. Laws and regulations of Canada must be respected by the beneficiaries of the immunities and privileges and they also have the duty not to interfere in the internal affairs of Canada. The Organization is obliged to facilitate the proper administration of justice, secure the observance of police regulations and prevent the occurrence of any abuse of the privileges and immunities.

In view of its immunity from the judicial process, the Organization is obliged to make adequate provision for the appropriate modes of settlement of disputes arising out of contract or other disputes to which the Organization is a party and disputes involving any officials of the organization if their immunity has not been waived. ICAO observes this provision by inserting an arbitration clause (compromise or "clause compromissoire") in all contracts of commercial nature.

As time flies the Headquarters Agreement between the Parties was required to be renewed. The new Supplementary Agreement was signed by the Secretary General of the ICAO, by Raymond Benjamin and the Canadian Minister of Foreign Affairs, by John Baird on 29 May 2013. The Agreement guarantees the operation of the ICAO in Montreal for the following 20 years until 30 November 2036 (as the new Agreement came into force at the end of 2016). This historic step allows Montreal – as the third most influential aerospace metropolis in the world – to continue "serving as a natural home to ICAO".[16]

7.3.4 Specialized Agency of the UN System

At the time of the Chicago Conference in November-December 1944 it was known that negotiations were proceeding between the allies in Dumbarton Oaks, Washington, D.C.

---

16 www.icao.int/Newsroom/Pages/ICAO-and-Canada-sign-new-supplementary-agreement.aspx.

on the establishment of a "general organization" to replace the League of Nations and to become eventually the United Nations Organization and on the drafting of the Charter of the United Nations. In anticipation, the Conference embodied Article 64 into the Convention:

> Article 64
> Security arrangements
> The Organization may, with respect to air matters within its competence directly affecting world security, by vote of the Assembly enter into appropriate arrangements with any general organization set up by the nations of the world to preserve peace.

This provision anticipated in 1944 what was later embodied in Article 57 of the Charter of the United Nations:

> Article 57
> 1. The various specialized agencies, established by intergovernmental agreement and having wide international responsibilities, as defined in their basic instruments, in economic, social, cultural, educational, health and related fields, shall be brought into relationship with the United Nations in accordance with the provisions of Article 63.
> 2. Such agencies thus brought into relationship with the United Nations are hereinafter referred to as specialized agencies.

The Charter of the United Nations provides in Article 63 that the Economic and Social Council may enter into agreements with any of the agencies referred to in Article 57, defining the terms on which the agency concerned shall be brought into relationship with the United Nations; such agreements are subject to approval by the General Assembly.

The PICAO Council negotiated a draft agreement on the relations between ICAO and the United Nations and submitted the text to the 1st Session of the ICAO Assembly in 1947. By Resolution A1-2 the Assembly approved the Agreement and authorized the President of the Council to sign it with an appropriate official of the United Nations.

On 14 December 1946, the Sixty-fifth plenary meeting of the First Session of the UN General Assembly adopted resolution 50 (1) *"Agreements with Specialized Agencies"* in which it resolved to approve the agreements with several organizations, including ICAO – but with a proviso that, in the case of the agreement with ICAO, "the Organization complies with any decision of the General Assembly regarding Franco Spain". In the United Nations Spain was ostracized from the very inception of the Organization for its "fascist" past and alliance with the Nazi Germany. The Charter of the United Nations also contains, in Articles 5 and 6, provisions on the suspension of membership of a Member State and on the expulsion of such a State. On the other hand, the Chicago Convention did not contain any provision to debar or expel a State and Spain participated in the Chicago Conference and ratified the Convention.

To comply with the UN General Assembly's condition, the First ICAO Assembly adopted, on 27 May 1947, Resolution A1-3 by which it amended the Chicago Convention by adding to it a new Article 93*bis* that enables the Organization to debar or expel a State member if such an action is first taken by the United Nations.[17] Spain then left the Assembly in protest but on 4 November 1950, the UN General Assembly revoked its decision on debarring Spain from the UN[18] and Spain continued its active participation in the UN, ICAO and other agencies.

The "Agreement between the United Nations and the International Civil Aviation Organization"[19] came into force on 13 May 1947. The UN recognizes in the agreement ICAO as a specialized agency "responsible for taking such action as may be appropriate under its basic instrument for the accomplishment of the purposes set forth therein". The Agreement provides for reciprocal representation and participation, without vote, in meetings of different bodies and ICAO accepts to put on the agenda of its Assembly and Council items proposed by the United Nations and to exchange information. ICAO is also committed to assist the UN Security Council in carrying out decisions of the Security Council for the maintenance of international peace and security. ICAO is also authorized to request advisory opinions from the International Court of Justice.

The UN and ICAO are to cooperate to establish a single unified international civil service, to develop common personnel standards and conditions of employment.

ICAO thus belongs to the "UN family" of organizations. The other specialized agencies at present are: Food and Agriculture Organization (FAO); International Bank for Reconstruction and Development (IBRD or "World Bank"); International Fund for Agricultural Development (IFAD); International Finance Corporation (IFC); International Labour Organization (ILO); International Monetary Fund (IMF); International Maritime Organization (IMO); International Telecommunications Union (ITU); United Nations Educational, Scientific and Cultural Organization (UNESCO); United Nations Industrial Development Organization (UNIDO); Universal Postal Union (UPU); World Intellectual Property Organization (WIPO); World Health Organization (WHO) and World Meteorological Organization (WMO). A special position is reserved to the International Atomic Energy Agency (IAEA) which has a direct link to the UN Security Council.

---

17   The amendment came into force on 20 March 1961 – long after Spain resumed full participation in the UN and ICAO.
18   Relations of States Members and specialised agencies with Spain, Resolution 386 (V), 4 November 1950.
19   ICAO Doc 7970, UNTS Vol. 8, pp. 315-343.

It is a common perception that the UN specialized agencies are "technical" bodies, *i.e.*, that their activities are non-political. That perception is incorrect – whenever sovereign States consider any specific question, they express their political will and defend their own interests against the competing interests of other States. Nothing in the mutual relations of States could be deemed to be "non-political". All international conflicts among States find their appropriate reflection in the agendas and attitudes within international organizations.

7.3.5   Organs of ICAO

Article 43 of the Convention states that the Organization

> is made up of an Assembly, a Council, and such other bodies as may be necessary.

All specialized agencies of the UN system have very similar structures (although using different terminology) made up of three basic components:
a. Assembly, General Assembly, General Conference, etc.: a body composed of all contracting States meeting at regular intervals and representing the supreme authority in the Organization;
b. Council, …: a body of limited membership elected by the Assembly and possessing specific jurisdiction and functions between the Sessions of the Assembly;
c. Secretariat: Secretary General (or Director General) as a chief executive/administrative officer of the Organization and the staff appointed by him.

This typical "tripartite" structure has evolved as the standard feature of all international intergovernmental organizations since the end of the 19th century. The comparison with the national structures of "parliament – government – civil service" seems to be logical but need not be proper in all cases and much depends on the wording of the specific constitutional instrument of the organization. In addition, several other subordinate bodies are created in each organization with a particular scope of functions.

The Assembly of ICAO is legally the supreme body of the Organization but it is not "absolute". Its functions and jurisdiction are determined and restricted by the Convention and over the years of practical experience its role seems to have been substantially eroded, and its sessions are shorter and far apart. Many important issues that should have been addressed by the Assembly (perhaps in an Extraordinary Session) have been relegated to bodies with fanciful names such as "Conferences", "World-wide Conferences" or "High Level Meetings" that have no constitutional justification in the Convention. On the other hand, the composition, role and power of the Council have increased, and it now appears to be the real focus of the ICAO decision-making. Much of this evolution was perpetuated to serve the personal preferences of a long-serving President of the Council.

7.3.5.1   ICAO Assembly

The first meeting of the ICAO Assembly was convened by the Interim Council of PICAO in conformity with Article 46 of the Convention. It met at Montreal from 6 to 27 May 1947, just four weeks after the Convention came into force.

The frequency of the Assembly Sessions is governed by Article 48 a) of the Convention that was amended twice in the history of ICAO. The original version provided that

> a) the Assembly shall meet annually and shall be convened by the Council at a suitable time and place. Extraordinary meetings of the Assembly may be held at any time upon the call of the Council or at the request of any ten contracting states addressed to the Secretary General.

The annual Session of the Assembly was beneficial for the Organization since it brought together the contracting States at frequent intervals to permit them to be in control of the program, budget and to follow the activities of the Council. However, at the 8th Session of the Assembly in Montreal on 1-14 June 1954 paragraph a) of Article 48 was amended to provide for triennial Sessions of the Assembly; the main justification of this step were the cost of the national delegations for attending the Sessions and the cost for the Organization. The amended text reads:

> a) The Assembly shall meet not less than once in three years and shall be convened by the Council at a suitable time and place. Extraordinary meetings of the Assembly may be held at any time upon the call of the Council or at the request of any ten contracting States addressed to the Secretary General.

This amendment came into force on 12 December 1956 and since 1959 the Assemblies meet only every three years. The duration of the sessions has been gradually shortened from the original more than three weeks to some twelve calendar days – all for the sake of "economy". The impact of this change was predictable – coupled with the almost quadrupling of the number of Member States since 1947 the duration of the Assemblies is not long enough to permit each Member State to address extensively any item of its special concern. The role of the Assembly has thus been weakened; much time of the sessions is wasted in protocolar matters and general statements and the main attention of the sessions focuses on the politically sensitive election of the Members of the Council and on the approval of the work program and budget for the next triennium.

In the history of ICAO there have been only nine Extraordinary Sessions,[20] most of them of very short duration and convened for either an urgent amendment of the Convention or to fill a vacancy on the Council. As the membership of the organization gradually rose to the current 193, it would not have been logical to permit "any ten contracting States" to force the convening of an extraordinary session. The text of paragraph a) of Article 48 of the Convention was again amended by the 14th Session of the Assembly on 15 September 1962; the amendment came into force on 11 September 1975. The text now reads:

> a) The Assembly shall meet not less than once in three years and shall be convened by the Council at a suitable time and place. An extraordinary meeting of the Assembly may be held at any time upon the call of the Council or at the request of not less than one-fifth of the total number of contracting states addressed to the Secretary General.

With the current membership at 193 States it would take at least 39 States to cause convening an extraordinary session. In the history of ICAO, the extraordinary sessions were always convened by the decision of the Council. However, the Organization could have resorted to more frequent extraordinary sessions of the Assembly rather than holding "meetings" or "conferences" of general character that are not foreseen in the Convention and have no constitutional basis in the Convention.

The "suitable place" for the session of the Assembly has been, since 1974, invariably ICAO's Headquarters in Montreal. In the previous years the sessions were sometimes held elsewhere, usually on the invitation of a State that agreed to defray any costs in excess of the costs of the session at Montreal. Sessions were held in Geneva (1948), Brighton (1953), Caracas (1956), San Diego (1959), Rome (1962 and 1973), Buenos Aires (1968), Vienna (1971) and New York (1971 and 1973).

Representation at the ICAO Assembly
All contracting States are entitled to participate in the Assembly and to vote there. Article 48 b) states about it:

> b) All contracting States shall have an equal right to be represented at the meetings of the Assembly and each contracting State shall be entitled to one vote. Delegates representing contracting States may be assisted by technical advisers who may participate in the meetings but shall have no vote.

---

20 13th, Montreal 1961; 17th, Montreal 1970; 17th, New York, 1971; 19th, New York 1973; 20th, Rome 1973; 25th, Montreal 1984; 28th, Montreal 1990; 30th, Montreal 1993; 34th, Montreal 2003.

This provision sets the principle of equality – all States regardless of their size or power are equal and have one vote; the principle of weighted vote does not apply in ICAO. The *Standing Rules of Procedure of the Assembly of the International Civil Aviation Organization*[21] specify further that in Rule 3,

> No person shall represent more than one State.

Rules 4, 5, 6 (a-b) and 7 of the Standing Rules of Procedure elaborate on delegations, observers and credentials:

> *Rule 4*
> Delegations of Contracting States may be composed of delegates, alternates and advisers. One of the delegates shall be designated as the Chief Delegate. In case of his absence the Chief Delegate may designate another member of his delegation to serve instead.

The Chief Delegates are frequently senior officials, such as Cabinet Ministers or Directors General of Civil Aviation, Ambassadors, etc. – at least for the first part of the Session until the election of the Council. Some Member States send to the Assemblies large delegations, but the seating arrangements admit only a limited number for each delegation to sit at the desk with a microphone. Overflow participants may have to follow the discussions from adjacent conference rooms through closed circuit TV.

The Standing Rules of Procedure also provide for participation by observers from duly invited non-contracting States and international organizations:

> *Rule 5*
> Non-Contracting States and international organizations duly invited by the Council, or by the Assembly itself, to attend a session of the Assembly may be represented by observers. Where a delegation consists of two or more observers, one of them shall be designated as "Chief Observer".

The Delegates and observers must be properly accredited to attend the Assembly. Rule 6 of the Standing Rules of Procedure stipulates:

> *Rule 6*
> Delegations shall be provided with credentials signed on behalf of the State or organization concerned, by a person duly authorized thereto, specifying the

---

21 ICAO Doc 7600/8 (2014), see Appendix 2 to this book.

name of each member of the Delegation and indicating the capacity in which he is to serve. The credentials shall be deposited with the Secretary General.

The "credentials" are usually much less formal than "full powers" required under the law of treaties; they must be signed "by a person duly authorized thereto" and that is usually a senior official of the Civil Aviation Authority, Minister of Transport or an Ambassador of the State concerned. One formality is, however, strictly required in practice: the credentials must be in the form of a written document, cables or facsimiles are accepted only temporarily subject to actual submission of the proper document. The credentials are examined by the Credentials Committee that is established, under Rule 6 b), at the beginning of the session and is composed of three delegates nominated by the President of the Assembly. The Credentials Committee should report to the Assembly "without delay" – in practice a preliminary report is presented on the second day of the session and the "final" just prior to the substantive votes, usually the election of the Council. The Assembly may bar from any further part in its activities any member of a delegation whose credentials it finds to be insufficient (Article 7).

Quorum and Voting in the Assembly
Paragraph c) of Article 48 of the Convention states:

> c) A majority of the contracting States is required to constitute a quorum for the meeting of the Assembly. Unless otherwise provided in this Convention, decisions of the Assembly shall be taken by a majority of the votes cast.

With the current 193 Member States at least 97 States must be represented to form the Assembly.[22] The "votes cast" means the positive and negative votes; as stated in Rule 45 of the Standing Rules an *"abstention shall not be considered as a vote"*. In theory this could lead to absurd results – if one or two delegations were to vote in favour of a motion and all others abstain, the motion would be adopted "unanimously"…

Voting is normally by voice, show of hands (name plate of the Delegation) or by standing. However, at the request of any single Delegation of a contracting State there shall be a roll-call vote taken in the alphabetical order of the names of the contracting States (always in the past in the English language) beginning with a State whose name is drawn by lot by the presiding officer; in a roll-call vote the vote of each delegation participating in the vote is recorded in the minutes.[23] By the 37th Session of the Assembly in 2010

---

22 It occurred in the history of ICAO that the opening meeting of the Assembly had to be postponed until a sufficient number of Delegations was summoned and had registered.
23 Rule 46 of the Standing Rules of Procedure of the Assembly of the ICAO.

electronic voting was introduced, initially for the election of the Council and only "on loan" (see below).

At the request of two or more Delegations of the contracting States and if that request is not opposed, there is to be a secret ballot (the vote to be marked on the ballot ticket and placed into the ballot box). However, if there is an opposition – even by one single Delegation of a contracting State – the question whether there should be a secret ballot is to be decided by a majority of votes cast in secret ballot. A decision to have a secret ballot prevails over any request for a roll-call vote.[24]

Until 2013, ICAO did not have an acceptable and reliable electronic system for the roll call or secret ballot, and such votes were extremely time-consuming and wasted the time allocated to the Assembly. For the secret ballot, delegates were called in the order (determined by a lot from the English alphabetical list of delegations), and one by one had to come to the head table and deposit their ballot sheet in the urn; that took considerable time, compounded further by the manual scrutiny and verification of the ballots prior to the announcement of the results; roll call voting was equally slow – calling the delegations one by one to say "yes" or "no" or "abstention", recording the answers and announcing the results. At the 37th Session of the Assembly in 2010, an electronic voting system has been made available on loan from the International Labour Organization (ILO) at the cost of CAD 90,000 and the Standing Rules of Procedure of the Assembly were amended in Rule 59 c) to enable electronic balloting.[25]

"Majority of the votes cast" is not sufficient where the Convention requires otherwise. Thus Article 94 a) of the Convention relating to the amendment of the Convention requires a two-third majority which is further qualified in the Standing Rules of Procedure "as meaning ... two-thirds of the total number of contracting States represented at the Assembly and qualified to vote at the time the vote is taken".[26] From that total are excluded States whose Delegation notified its departure from the Assembly or whose credentials or instructions deposited with the Secretary General expressly deprive them of the right to vote on the given subject or States whose voting power is under suspension at the time the vote is taken. Another example would be the vote under Article 93 of the Convention dealing with the admission of "ex-enemy" States and requiring four-fifth vote of the Assembly and non-objection by any State invaded or attacked during World War II by the State seeking admission; this provision is no longer relevant. Again, under Article 45 of the Convention a decision to transfer the permanent seat of the Organization would require "no less than three-fifth of the total number of contracting States".

---

24 Rule 47 of the Standing Rules of Procedure of the Assembly of the ICAO.
25 A37-WP/8, P/4, 29 June 2010.
26 Rule 53 of the Standing Rules of Procedure of the Assembly of the ICAO.

Languages of the Assembly

The Chicago Convention is silent on the working languages of the Organization and its bodies. The Standing Rules of Procedure of the Assembly provide that all documentation of the Assembly and its decisions shall be prepared and circulated in five languages – English, Arabic, French, Russian and Spanish. Six languages – English, Arabic, Chinese, French, Russian and Spanish – may be used in the deliberations of the Assembly and its bodies and speeches in any of these languages are interpreted into the other five languages.[27] The service in such multiplicity of languages substantially impacts on the ICAO's budget. The record of the last Assembly Session (41st, in 2022) shows that many documents were distributed only in one or two languages.

Powers and Duties of the ICAO Assembly

The Assembly is the supreme organ of the Organization and its powers and duties are extensively defined in eleven paragraphs a) to k) of Article 49 of the Convention.

> a) Elect at each meeting its President and other officers.

The President of the Assembly should be elected "as soon as practicable after the commencement of a session";[28] it usually takes some time to coordinate the geographic and political balance in the election of the officers of the Assembly and until such election the President of the Council acts as President of the Assembly. On numerous occasions between 1977 and 2004 the Assembly wished to avoid competing claims and frictions and agreed to keep the long-serving President of the Council as President of the Assembly. This may have been a "pragmatic" solution but such a practice is highly undesirable and the President of the Council should have categorically refused his candidacy: it could be perceived as a conflict of interest since the Council is subordinate and responsible to the Assembly; the President of the Council is a salaried official of the Organization, and the elevation of such single person to the two highest positions of the Organization creates a perception of concentration of power with some unsavoury characteristics of the "cult of personality".

The Assembly also elects four Vice-Presidents and the Chairmen of the Commissions of the Assembly. Under Rule 14 of the Standing Rules of Procedure, the Assembly should create the Executive Committee (to consider, in particular, matters of policy), a Co-ordinating Committee and the Administrative Commission. In well-established practice, the Assembly creates also the Technical Commission, Economic Commission and Legal Commission. The Assembly usually holds very few plenary meetings since the agenda

---

27 Rules 63 and 64 of the Standing Rules of Procedure of the Assembly of the ICAO.
28 Rule 8 of the Standing Rules of Procedure of the Assembly of the ICAO.

items are primarily discussed in the Executive Committee or in the various Commissions and come to the Plenary only for the final approval of the reports and of any draft resolutions.

> b) Elect the contracting States to be represented on the Council, in accordance with the provisions of Chapter IX.

The election of the Council members is the policy highlight of each regular triennial Session of the Assembly. The criteria and procedure of the election are rather involved and shall be addressed in the context of the ICAO Council below.

> c) Examine and take appropriate action on the reports of the Council and decide on any matter referred to it by the Council.

The Council prepares for the Assembly its Annual Reports which are presented in the Plenary by the President of the Council. Such reports are hardly ever "examined" but are just "noted". The voluminous reports for the last three calendar years and the part of the year of the Assembly amount to a few hundred pages and their thorough "examination" is not practicable due to the short duration of the Assembly. Yet, the study of the annual reports should be an essential part of the Assembly's prerogative to approve or disapprove the actions of the Council between the Sessions of the Assembly.

> d) Determine its own rules of procedure and establish such subsidiary commissions as it may consider necessary or desirable.

The Standing Rules of Procedure were created by the Assembly and amended several times. The thorough knowledge of the Rules is very essential for the efficient work of all Delegations. An oversight or ignorance of some Rule may thwart some initiatives. The Rules are subject to the Convention and cannot contradict the provisions of the Convention. The Rules may be amended, or any portion of the Rules may be suspended, at any time by the Assembly.[29] Since there is no requirement for a qualified vote, the decision may be taken by the majority of the votes cast. Under this rule on "subsidiary" bodies the Assembly established, *e.g.*, the Legal Committee of ICAO,[30] an important body of the Organization that is based only on an Assembly Resolution and does not have its constitutional basis in the Convention itself.

---

29 Rule 66 of the Standing Rules of Procedure of the Assembly of the ICAO.
30 Originally Resolution A1-46.

e) Vote annual budget and determine the financial arrangements of the Organization, in accordance with the provisions of Chapter XII.

This is the text as amended in 1954, when the Assembly decided on the triennial frequency of the Assembly Sessions; the original 1944 text referred to "*annual budget*". Chapter XII of the Convention comprises Article 61, 62 and 63 that deal with the finances of the Organization; the budgets are submitted to the Assembly by the Council together with annual statements of accounts and estimates of all receipts and expenditures. The Assembly votes the budgets with whatever modification it sees fit to prescribe and apportions the expenses of the Organization among contracting States on the basis which it determines from time to time.

The Regular Programme Budget for 2011, 2012 and 2013 was approved by the 37th Session of the Assembly in September 2010.[31] It was again very "innovative" in that it was conceived, in harmony with modern commercial methods of management, as a "result-based budget" (RBB). Another innovation is the expression of the budget in Canadian dollars (CAD) due to the instability of USD at that time and the fact that many expenses are incurred by ICAO in Canadian funds. It is hard to foresee how stable the Canadian dollar proves to be during the triennium and beyond it; by 2011 the Canadian dollar – contrary to its historic rate – stood higher than the US dollar, but by early 2016 the Canadian dollar fell temporarily below 70 US cents before a slow partial recovery! The stability of the budgets of international bodies would probably be best protected if they were expressed in the Special Drawing Rights (SDR)[32] of the International Monetary Fund that balances the "basket" of the leading currencies. The budget also provided for a rather massive reduction of the Secretariat staff – a costly proposition due to the duty to pay the termination indemnities and also a daring proposition because of the untested perspective how to secure the necessary services (in the language field in particular) with a limited staff. The 38th Session of the Assembly approved the budget for 2014, 2015 and 2016. Compared with other organizations of the UN system, the ICAO budget is rather moderate and in the past triennium stood at CAD 93-99 million. States contribute to the budget according to scales of assessment approved by the Assembly – the lowest contribution uniformly assessed to smaller or developing States is 0.06% of the annual budget; the United States contributes 25% of the budget, the maximum determined by the Assembly.

---

31   Resolution A37-26.
32   The determination of the SDR is effected by the unification of the major international currencies used in international transactions in a currency basket. The SDR (the currency code of which according to the ISO–4217 standards: XDR) derives its value from a basket of five currencies: the Euro, the Japanese Yen, the US Dollar, the British Pound Sterling and the Chinese Renminbi (yuan). The weight of the given currency manifest in SDR is determined by the weight the given national currency carries in international transactions. IMF Review of the Method of Valuation of the SDR. Executive Summary, July 2015, pp. 1-2.

The budget of the ICAO for 2020-2022 was a total amount of CAD 322.7 million (for the previous triennium it was CAD 302.1).[33] As the numbers are growing the amount of the contributions by the Member States are also changing, *i.e.*, the United States is still the principal contributor to the budget of the ICAO (20%), since it accounts for the largest civil air traffic, which is followed by China (about 15%).

Chapter XII of the Convention also refers to the suspension of the voting power in the Assembly and in the Council that may be decided by the Assembly if a contracting State fails to discharge within a reasonable period its financial obligations to the Organization – this power is discretionary and the Assembly is not obliged to suspend the voting power under any and all circumstances.[34] Article 63 of the Convention clarifies that each contracting State must bear the expenses of its own delegation to the Assembly and the remuneration, travel and other expenses of any person whom it appoints to serve on the Council, or of its nominees or representatives on any subsidiary committees or commissions of the Organization.

> f) Review expenditures and approve the accounts of the Organization.

Under this provision the Assembly notes and approves the accounts as audited by the External Auditor of the Organization. The Auditor General of Canada has been acting as the External Auditor of the Organization since 1952. But since the 36th Session of the Assembly in September 2007, the Member States appointed external auditors from different countries.[35]

> g) Refer, at its discretion, to the Council, to subsidiary commissions, or any other body any matter within its sphere of action.

Under this general provision the Assembly Resolutions may urge or request the Council, the Air Navigation Commission, the Legal Committee or any other body to take a specific action.

---

33 It was approved in October 2019 during the 40th Session of the Assembly.
34 Latest Assembly ruling is in Resolution A39-31 (2016).
35 For example: the 36th Session of the Assembly (2007) appointed the Cour des Comptes of France as External Auditor of ICAO for the accounts of the financial years 2008-2010, Resolution A36-WP/41; the 37th Session of the Assembly (2010) confirmed the appointment of the Cour des Comptes of France for the fiscal years 2011-2013, Resolution A37-31; the 38th Session of the Assembly (2013) appointed as External Auditor for the years 2014-2016 the Audit Chamber of the Community and International Affairs of the Corte dei Conti of Italy, Resolution A38-30, Doc 10022; The Italian Corte dei Conti remained the auditor for the triennium 2017-2019, Resolution A39-36; The Swiss Federal Audit Office (SFAO) became the ICAO's External Auditor for the financial years 2020-2022 and that has been extended for 2023-2025, Resolutions A40-33, A41-33.

> h) Delegate to the Council the powers and authority necessary or desirable for the discharge of the duties of the Organization and revoke or modify the delegation of authority at any time.

This provision is seldom used since the Council itself has very wide powers and does not require delegation of additional powers from the Assembly. In the early period of the Organization the Assembly delegated to the Council the function to conclude agreements with the United Nations, with other governmental organizations and with private international organizations.[36]

> i) Carry out the appropriate provisions of Chapter XIII.

Chapter XIII of the Chicago Convention contains Article 64, 65 and 66 dealing with international agreements to be entered into with the United Nations and other international organizations of what is currently referred to as the "UN common system". Under Article 66 of the Convention the Organization also carries out the functions conferred upon it by the International Air Services Transit Agreement (1944) and International Air Transport Agreement (1944);[37] members of the Assembly or of the Council who are not parties to the agreements shall not have the right to vote on any questions referred to the Assembly or to the Council under the provisions of the relevant Agreement.

> j) Consider proposals for the modification or amendment of the provisions of this Convention and, if it approves of the proposals, recommend them to the contracting States in accordance with the provisions of Chapter XXI.

The Assembly has the jurisdiction to approve any "modification or amendment" of the Chicago Convention both under Article 49 j) and Article 94. The approval of an amendment requires two-thirds majority vote of the Assembly, and the amendment comes into force upon ratification by not less than two-thirds of the total number of contracting States. So far, the Assembly considered and approved only "amendments" of the Convention and no "modification" of the Convention was ever proposed. If ever there were a proposal to replace, after a major review, the Convention in its entirety by a new Convention – would that be a "modification" of the existing Convention subject to the decision of the Assembly or would the new Convention have to be adopted by a new Diplomatic Conference? This

---

36 Resolutions A1-2, A1-10 and A1-11.
37 See Chapter 6 above, Legal Regime of International Air Transport.

question was never raised since the Chicago Convention, unlike the Charter of the United Nations,[38] does not foresee a general review Conference.

> k) Deal with any matter within the sphere of action of the Organization not specifically assigned to the Council.

This provision is of critical importance since it falsely seems to give to the Assembly such overall jurisdiction that really makes it the most powerful body of the Organization. However, the last six words of this paragraph in fact seriously restrict the jurisdiction of the Assembly – the Assembly is not entitled to deal with any matter that is "specifically" assigned to the Council and there are several such matters that are "specifically assigned" to the Council and they are of fundamental importance:

- the Assembly is to be convened by the Council, it cannot decide on its convening;[39]
- the President of the Council, rightly or wrongly considered to be the highest representative official of the Organization, is elected and his emoluments are determined by the Council;[40]
- the Secretary General is appointed by the Council;[41]
- membership of the Air Transport Committee and of the Air Navigation Commission is appointed by the Council;[42]
- adoption of International Standards and Recommended Practices (SARPs) – perhaps the most important function of ICAO – is exclusively within the purview of the Council;[43]
- "determination" in what manner the provisions of the Convention relating to nationality of aircraft apply to aircraft operated by international operating agencies[44] belongs to the Council;
- settlement of differences[45] is an exclusive competence of the Council.

This illustrative list of "matters specifically assigned to the Council" indicates that the Convention substantially empowered the Council compared with the Assembly; moreover, the Council is a permanent body practically in session without major interruption while the Assembly meets for a short period once in three years.

---

38   In Article 109, the UN Charter foresees a "General Conference of the Members of the United Nations for the purpose of reviewing the present Charter".
39   Article 48 a) of the Chicago Convention.
40   Articles 51 and 54 g) of the Chicago Convention.
41   Article 54 h) of the Chicago Convention.
42   Articles 54 d) and e) and 56 of the Chicago Convention.
43   Articles 54 l) and m), 37, 38 and 90 of the Chicago Convention.
44   Article 77 of the Chicago Convention.
45   Articles 84-88 of the Chicago Convention.

7.3.5.2 ICAO Council

The ICAO Council is a body of unique characteristics in the entire United Nations system of organizations. It possesses not only the typical administrative and management functions within the organization but it is endowed with functions of a law-making nature (frequently called "*quasi-legislative*") and functions in the settlement of differences (sometimes called "*quasi-judicial*").

Composition of the Council

The original text of the Chicago Convention provided for membership of twenty-one contracting States elected by the Assembly.

With the growth of the membership of the Organization resulting from the advancing progress of decolonization this number was increased to 27.[46]

In 1971, the number was again increased to thirty – essentially as a reaction to the fact that the USSR joined the Organization in 1970 and aspired for membership in the Council while the "established" members were anxious to keep their seats.[47]

Further amendment brought the membership to thirty-three States and was prompted by the restitution of the legitimate membership of the Peoples' Republic of China – a logical candidate for the Council membership that could have displaced another of the "established" members.[48]

The amendment in 1990 increased the Council membership to the present thirty-six.[49] The last amendment ensued in 2016 and the membership was raised by the Assembly to 40 (it is not in force yet).[50] The composition of the Council was thus subject to several amendments prompted by "ad hoc" pragmatic political considerations rather than by any long-term planning. There is a serious constitutional problem since the amendments are in force only for those States that have ratified the protocols of amendment[51] and none of the amendments has been ratified by all 193 Member States of the Organization; thus, technically for some States the Council is still composed of twenty-one members, for others of twenty-seven or thirty or thirty-three. Moreover, it is highly objectionable that those States that have not ratified the latest amendment were permitted by the President of the Assembly[52] to cast a vote in the Assembly for Council composition not covered by their ratification.

---

46   13th (Extraordinary) Session of the Assembly, 1961, in force as of 17 July 1962.
47   17th (A) (extraordinary) Session, 1971, in force as of 16 January 1973.
48   21st Session of the Assembly, 1974, in force as of 15 February 1980.
49   28th Session (Extraordinary) of the Assembly, 1990, entered into force on 28 November 2002.
50   39th Session WP/18, EX/6, 31/05/2016; Resolutions adopted by the ICAO Assembly A39-4, 1 October 2016.
51   Article 94 of the Chicago Convention.
52   On both such occasions it was the then President of the Council – himself a lawyer and well-aware of the implications. This is how "political convenience" proves stronger than law.

As a result of the series of *ad hoc* modifications the Convention presently states:

Article 50
Composition and election of Council
a) The Council shall be a permanent body responsible to the Assembly. It shall be composed of thirty-six contracting States elected by the Assembly. An election shall be held at the first meeting of the Assembly and thereafter every three years, and the members of the Council so elected shall hold office until the next following election.

The enlarged composition of the Council perhaps safeguards a wider representation of the 193 Member States but did not enhance its effectiveness – in a large body the discussions tend to take inordinate amount of time and may lead to repetitious statements but such is the trend in most international organizations. It is important to note that the members of the Council are sovereign States and that they are represented on the Council by their appointed Representatives; therefore, it would be incorrect to refer to these representatives as "Members" of the Council.

Election of the Council
The Convention stipulates specific criteria for the election of the members of the Council to give "adequate representation" to three different groups of States and the Standing Rules of Procedure then regulate the different stages of the election process. Paragraph b) of Article 50 reads:

b) In electing the members of the Council, the Assembly shall give adequate representation to 1) the States of chief importance in air transport; 2) the States not otherwise included which make the largest contribution to the provision of facilities for international air navigation; and 3) the States not otherwise included whose designation will ensure that all the major geographic areas of the world are represented on the Council. Any vacancy shall be filled by the Assembly as soon as possible; any contracting State so elected to the Council shall hold office for the unexpired portion of its predecessor's term.

The authors of the Convention apparently wished to keep an economic, technical and geographic balance in the composition of the Council. However, the Convention does not offer any guidance how to determine which States are of "chief importance" in air transport or which States make the largest contribution to the provision of facilities for international air navigation. Since there are no objective benchmarks or guidance, it is in the secret ballot in the Assembly where States express their political judgement whether a candidate

State meets the respective criteria. As an illustrative exaggeration, it may be said that even the smallest State may present its candidature in the first group and could be elected if a sufficient number of votes is cast for it. The classification of candidates into the three groups is relevant only for the process of voting in the election; once States are elected as members of the Council, there is no difference between the different elected members. However, for some States the placement in a particular group is a matter of prestige (and logic) – the Republic of Korea and the United Arab Emirates are traditionally elected in the third group, while they belong to States of chief importance in international air transport. The State of Qatar was also elected in the third group during the 41st Assembly the first time in its history.[53] Paragraph c) of Article 50 was meant to prevent a conflict of interest by ruling that

> c) No representative of a contracting State on the Council shall be actively associated with the operation of an international air service or financially interested in such a service.

There is no record that this provision had ever been invoked in the history of ICAO.

The Convention is also silent on an important question how many States should be elected in each of the three defined groups, *i.e.*, what is deemed to be "adequate representation". It posed no problem for the Assembly in the earlier years of the Organization – while there were twenty-one members of the Council the ratio was 8-7-6; when there were twenty-seven members of the Council the proportion was 9-9-9; when the membership was increased to thirty, the proportion was still equal 10-10-10. Later, when the membership was increased to thirty-three, there was political pressure to increase the share of the second and, in particular, the third group and the ratio was amended to 10-11-12. Finally, when the membership of the Council was increased to thirty-six, the 35th Session of the Assembly in 2004 agreed to distribute the three additional seats evenly among the three groups – 11-12-13 and that was maintained at the 36th Session in 2007, the 37th Session in 2010 and the 38th Session in 2013. This need not be a permanent solution since each Assembly must fix the number of contracting States to be elected in each group. On the 41st Assembly Session in 2022 the Russian Federation was not re-elected in the first Group due to lack of votes,[54] for this reason the composition of the ICAO Council changed to 10-12-14. Rule 55 b) of the Standing Rules of Procedure of the Assembly of the ICAO states:

---

53 www.icao.int/Meetings/a41/Pages/assembly-report-and-minutes.aspx.
54 86 votes are necessary to maintain representation in the ICAO Council, and the Russian Federation received 80 on 1 October 2022.

Rule 55
Principles of Adequate Representation
a) As early as possible after the opening of the Session, the assembly shall fix the maximum number of contracting States to be elected in each part of the election and fix also the day on which the first two parts of the election shall be held.

There are also strict procedural formalities and deadlines for the presentation of candidacies: Rule 56 a) states:

Rule 56
a) Each contracting State which desires to stand for election in either the first or the second part shall so notify the Secretary General in writing during the period of forty-eight hours following the opening of the Session.

It is not enough that a State may have advised the Secretary General of its candidacy well in advance of the Assembly – the State must be physically represented at the Assembly and must present its candidacy within the prescribed deadline. After the second part of the election the President of the Assembly declares an interval of approximately forty-eight hours after which the candidacies for the third part of the election are to be submitted.[55]

The election in each of the three parts is conducted by a secret ballot – the ballot papers containing the names of the candidate States and a statement of the maximum number of vacancies to be filled. The ballot papers are to be marked by a cross (X) against the name of the State for which the vote is cast; a ballot paper would be rejected if the number of affirmative votes in it exceeds the number to be elected in that vote. Starting from the 37th Session of the Assembly in 2010, electronic ballot was introduced for the process of election. However, there are still some views that the time-consuming secret ballot can hardly be replaced by electronic means since the secrecy would not be absolutely guaranteed. Further experience and technological developments in this field are essential for convincing conclusions.

It is a common part of the political strategy and tactics that States do not cast a vote for all vacancies but initially – after multilateral coordination – vote only for a preferred few States on the list assuring their election ("strategic voting"); only in the subsequent ballot or ballots they vote to fill the remaining vacancies.

---

55 Rule 57 of the Standing Rules of Procedure of the Assembly of the ICAO.

Sessions of the Council
The Council is by definition a permanent body available and ready to work in principle at any time. States Members of the Council have an obligation defined already at the 4th Session of the Assembly in 1950 in Resolution A4-1 as follows:

> A contracting State giving notice, in accordance with Rule 45 of the Standing Rules of Procedure of the Assembly of the ICAO,[56] of its desire to stand for election to the Council is understood to have indicated its intention, if elected, to appoint and support full-time representation at the Headquarters of the Organization to ensure the participation of the Council Member States in the work of the Organization.

Each Council Member State maintains a permanent delegation in Montreal on the premises of the Headquarters or the adjacent Bell Tower. While under Article 63 of the Convention each State must bear the expenses of any person whom it appoints to serve on the Council and its nominees or representatives on any subsidiary committees or commissions of the Organization, the Government of Canada subsidizes the basic office space of the delegations to the same degree that it subsidizes the space for the Secretariat and the meeting halls. Delegations needing more than the basic space have to obtain it at the prevailing market cost.

The sessions of the Council are held at regular intervals and throughout the calendar year there are usually three Council sessions. The sessions are divided into "Committee phase" and "Council phase". During the Committee phase there are sessions of the Air Navigation Commission (ANC) – a body consisting currently of nineteen members appointed by the Council from among persons nominated by contracting States; the candidates are selected from among persons of suitable qualification in the science and practice of aeronautics and the ANC acts as an expert body in the preparation of international Standards, Recommended Practices and Procedures.

Moreover, under Article 54 d) the Council must appoint an *Air Transport Committee* that works in several meetings during the Committee phase of the session and is composed of the representatives on the Council.

The *Finance Committee* is also composed of the representatives on the Council and is in charge of the functions imposed by the Financial Regulations of ICAO for the management and planning of ICAO's finances.[57]

---

56 Currently Rule 54. ICAO Doc 7600/8, 8th ed., 2014. See Appendix 2 to this book.
57 ICAO Doc 7515/16.

Since the request of the very first Assembly Session in 1947 the Council establishes a *Committee on Joint Support of Air Navigation Services*[58] that performs the functions accepted by ICAO with respect to the "Danish" and "Icelandic" Agreements on the joint financing of specified air navigation services over the North Atlantic.[59]

The *Edward Warner Committee* advises the Council on the selection of laureates of the "Edward Warner Award" – the highest distinction that the Council may bestow on an individual or institution of exceptional merit in the field of civil aviation named after the renowned first President of the ICAO Council.[60]

The *Personnel Committee* existed for some time to advise the Council on matters of staff recruitment, benefits and alignment with the UN common system.

The *Technical Cooperation Committee* considers the programs of technical assistance and cooperation.

The *Committee on Unlawful Interference with Civil Aviation and its Facilities* gained prominence and urgent agenda to assist in the formulation of ICAO policy, keeping up-to-date Annex 17 dedicated to aviation security and the ICAO Security Manual.

The work of the Committees often leads to duplication and repetition of debates in the forum of the Council and during both phases of the Council sessions the representatives are kept busy.

The practically permanent session of the Council and its subordinate bodies represent also considerable strain on the Secretariat services that produce masses of working papers at the request of the Council that lead to extensive translations and interpretations as well as a considerable workload for the entire Secretariat.

The "permanent" session of the Council may have been justified in the early years of the Organization when the Council faced an enormous workload to prepare the full spectrum of international standards and recommended practices. It would be an improvement of the working methods of the Council if it were to meet no more than twice a year for ten working days at a time – such an arrangement would save the costs of the resident delegations and could attract for such short and effective meetings high-level specialists or representatives of ministerial rank. There are successful examples of such practice in other international organizations[61] and ICAO could, after more than sixty years, modernize its working methods. Such a change would not even require an amendment of the Convention – just enough courage for innovation and progress.

---

58 Resolution A1-7.
59 ICAO Doc 9585-JS/681 Agreement on the Joint Financing of Certain Air Navigation Services in Greenland and ICAO Doc 9586-JS/682 Agreement on the Joint Financing of Certain Air Navigation Services in Iceland (as both amended in 1982 and 2008).
60 The most prestigious aviation award, the ICAO's Edward Warner Award was bestowed on the Institute of Air and Space Law of McGill University in 1996. See Author's Reminiscences in this book.
61 In the WMO, the governing body meets once per year; in the WHO twice a year; in ILO three times a year.

The Council is also expressly entitled to delegate authority with respect to any particular matter "to a committee of its members";[62] however, the Council never availed itself of this authority that could have often simplified and streamlined its work in specialized fields and avoid duplication of the discussions in the Council committees and the Council itself.

Functions of the Council
The Convention allocates to the Council *mandatory functions* that it is obliged to implement and *permissive functions* that it may implement. Taken together they open an extremely wide spectrum of issues that are within the jurisdiction of the Council. The mandatory functions are listed in Article 54 of the Convention, the permissive in Article 55. Moreover, there are additional references to the functions of the Council scattered in different other provisions of the Convention.

The Council's decisions shall require approval by a majority of its members[63] and a majority of the members of the Council constitutes a quorum for the conduct of business of the Council.[64] With the current Council membership at thirty-six, the quorum is nineteen members and a decision requires no less than nineteen affirmative votes. However, the *Rules of Procedure for the Council*[65] permit some flexibility:

> *Rule 62*
> In the case of any provision herein which does not specify the majority by which a decision shall be taken, it is understood that a majority of the votes cast will be sufficient, provided that if a member of the Council has requested that the decision be taken by a majority of Members of the Council, the latter majority shall apply.

Consequently, it has been the practice of the Council to approve some procedural matters by the majority of the votes cast unless prior to a vote any Member of the Council requests "statutory majority" foreseen by Article 52 of the Convention. By a majority of the votes cast the Council is to take decisions on procedural "priority motions" listed in Rule 41 – *e.g.*, motion to reverse a ruling of the President, motion to adjourn the meeting, etc. On such motions a request for "statutory majority" would not be applicable.

Under Article 53 *(Participation without vote)* of the Convention:

---

62 Article 52 of the Chicago Convention.
63 Idem.
64 Rule 33 of the Rules of Procedure for the Council. ICAO Doc 7559/11, 11th ed., 2022. See Appendix 3 to this book.
65 Idem.

Any contracting State may participate, without a vote, in the consideration by the Council and by its committees and commissions of any question which especially affects its interests. No member of the Council shall vote in the consideration by the Council of a dispute to which it is a party.

This article combines two profoundly different issues. First – the right of any contracting State (non-member of the Council) to participate without a vote in the consideration of any question of its special interest; the declaration of a "special interest" is a unilateral statement of the State concerned and there is no record that such a statement would have ever been challenged by other State. To "participate ... in the consideration" implies the right to make statements. Second – the principle that a party to a dispute must not vote[66] in the consideration by the Council of the dispute is a *verbatim* repetition of the second sentence of Article 84 of the Convention where it properly belongs; this was an apparent oversight in the drafting of the Convention.

A practice has developed over the years that several States – non-members of the Council – keep a permanent resident delegation at the ICAO Headquarters. However, it would be incorrect to call such delegations "observer delegations" since a State may participate as "observer" in the Council only upon invitation when it is recognized that a question under consideration especially affects its interests.

President of the ICAO Council
It is a historic anomaly not seen in any other organization of the UN system that ICAO has two leading officials – the President of the Council and the Secretary General – without a distinct delimitation of their jurisdictions that would convincingly justify this duality. The common practice is that the agencies have one single executive official named Secretary-General, Director or Director General.[67]

Unlike the "President" of other bodies (Assembly of ICAO, organs of other Organizations of the UN system), the President of the ICAO Council is a salaried official, by rank and salary the highest official/employee of ICAO.

In the history of ICAO there have been only five persons holding the position as Presidents of the Council. Each of them impressed his character and personality on the position and the office of the President became what the incumbent wished it to be.

The first President was Edward Warner (USA) in 1947-1956, an influential delegate to the Chicago Conference, scholar, gentleman and a wise statesman who took over the office from the very beginning with a clean slate and guided it to impressive development. The

---
66 *Nemo judex in re sua* – "nobody should be a judge in his own cause", an axiom rooted in Roman law.
67 Secretary-General in the UN and IMO; Director-General in the IMF, ITU, ETO, FAO, ILO, UNESCO and WHO.

Edward Warner Award was established in his honour and is awarded by the Council of ICAO for exceptional merit in the field of civil aviation.

The second President was Walter Binaghi (Argentina) in 1956-1976 – an extremely gifted and dynamic man of renaissance scope of knowledge and culture coupled with personal humility, commanding respect, harmony and efficiency; he led the Organization to the completion of standards and recommended practices in seventeen Annexes to the Chicago Convention, to its massive expansion and visible successes during the process of decolonization, brought to membership the former USSR and oversaw the restitution of the membership status of the Peoples' Republic of China; he also launched an enormous program in the untested field of aviation security. Walter Binaghi was a legendary man who made a permanent mark on the Organization and left the position at his chosen time refusing any medals or awards and has been missed.

The third President was Assad Kotaite (Lebanon) in 1976-2006 – who, in 1970-1976, was the Secretary General of ICAO, thus completing 36 years of service in top positions – an unparalleled longevity in top positions that is not matched by anybody else in the UN system of organizations for the number of unanimous re-elections (for the position of the President 10 times in a row) and service well beyond his 80th birthday. A. Kotaite proved to be an astute senior statesman, facilitator and politician, guardian of the "established practices" impressing the representatives by his commanding "institutional memory". As promised, after some pressure, in 2004 at the 35th Session of the ICAO Assembly, he resigned during his last term in 2006, and the Council elected for the remainder of his term Roberto Kobe Gonzales (Mexico).

On 21 November 2007, the Council elected Roberto Kobe Gonzales as President for a period of three years.[68] He was re-elected for a second term of three years on 15 November 2010.[69] In view of Assembly Resolution A36-28 (see below), he was not a candidate for a further election. From 1 January 2014 to 31 December 2016, the President of the Council was Olumuyiwa Benard Aliu (Nigeria), and he was re-elected for another 3 years. The current president is Salvatore Sciacchitano (Italy) elected for a three-year term beginning on 1 January 2020 and re-elected for a second three-year term in 2022. It appears that the Council's policy is to "rotate" the function of the President to satisfy all continents.

There could be different views as to whether the Organization benefitted from the fact that throughout its history there were only five Presidents of the Council between 1944-2006, one of them for 20 years (W. Binaghi) and another one (A. Kotaite) for an unprecedented 30 years. It could be a positive sign of stability and continuity. Nevertheless, each organization requires frequent input of "fresh blood", new dynamism, new

---

68 ICAO News Release, PIO 11/07.
69 ICAO News Release, PIO 15/10.

experiences, courage for a change and improvements, not the stagnation of the established order. Already in 1963, the Council approved a new policy on the appointment of Directors of the different Bureaus of the Secretariat and decided to limit the length of service of Directors to eight years – with a view to keep bringing into the Organization fresh blood and up-to-date expertise.[70] What applies to Directors should even more strongly apply to the President of the Council and to the Secretary General and they should be eligible for no more than two consecutive terms. Similarly, the established age of retirement of staff members (65 years)[71] should be equally applicable to the posts of the President of the Council and the Secretary General since "gerontocracy" could hardly benefit the organization. (W. Binaghi was the first to recognize this fact and resigned when he was at the peak of his efficiency.).

This was confirmed already in 1997 by a unanimous Resolution of the UN General Assembly[72] that uniform terms of four years, renewable once, should be introduced for the executive heads and this policy was specifically recommended to the specialized agencies – it is difficult to understand why this recommendation was never brought to the attention of the ICAO Council. There is no record that the UN Resolution was ever publicized within ICAO, brought to the attention of the Council or subject to any discussion.

However in 2006, the ICAO Council reformed the institutions of the election of the President and procedure of selection itself.[73] The 36th Session of the ICAO's Assembly in 2007 was asked to consider a proposal for the term limits for the offices of Secretary General and President of the Council.[74] Not wishing to amend Article 51 of the Convention, the Assembly decided[75] to urge States not to nominate candidates for the post of President who had that position for two terms and urged the Council not to accept such candidacies. Under Article 54 (b) of the Chicago Convention the Council is obliged to "carry out the directions of the Assembly". With respect to the position of Secretary General no action by the Assembly was necessary since under Article 54 (h) the decision on the term of office of the Secretary General was fully in the discretion of the Council, and the Council is obliged to follow the directions of the Assembly.

The Chicago Convention contains one single Article defining rather narrowly the powers of the President of the Council but in practice over the years the image and power of the President was permitted to grow out of proportion. In Article 51 the Convention states:

---

70   49th Session of the Council 1963, Doc 9352-C/947.
71   The age limit for staff recruited prior to 1 January 2014 was extended to age 65. ICAO Staff Regulation 9.15.
72   Resolution 51/241 "Strengthening the United Nations System".
73   Election of the President of the Council. Presented by Austria and Hungary, C-WP/12494, 2005.
74   A36-WP/3, EX/1, A36-WP/136.
75   Resolution A36-28.

> *Article 51*
> *President of Council*
> The Council shall elect its President for the term of three years. He may be re-elected. He shall have no vote. The Council shall elect from among its members one or more Vice Presidents who shall retain their right to vote when serving as acting President. The President need not be selected from among the representatives of members of the Council but, if a representative is elected, his seat shall be deemed vacant and it shall be filled by the State which he represented. The duties of the President shall be to: a) Convene meetings of the Council, the Air Transport Committee and the Air Navigation Commission; b) Serve as representative of the Council; and c) Carry out on behalf of the Council the functions which the Council assigns to him.

It has been the practice of the Council to elect three (First, Second and Third) Vice Presidents. However, when one of the Vice-Presidents chaired a meeting of the Council for the absent President took place in very rare instances. The Vice-President when acting in the absence of the President retains his right to vote.[76]

The Council determines by a "delegation of authority" to the President the tasks of representing the Council and carrying out the functions assigned by the Council. The format and content of the delegation of authority dated back to 1949 and minor amendments were introduced in 1950 and 1961.[77] That delegation of authority was too broad and gave an excessive discretion to the President of the Council who was entrenched in the position for thirty years while the Council did not exercise meaningful oversight of his performance. As of 1 August 2006, the Council approved a new format of delegation of authority to the President which is more restricted and subject to the Council's oversight.[78]

Mandatory Functions of the ICAO Council
The mandatory functions of the ICAO Council are set forth in Article 54 of the Chicago Convention and some of its fourteen paragraphs require more extensive comment:

> *Article 54*
> *Mandatory functions of the Council*
> The Council shall
> a) Submit annual reports to the Assembly.

---

[76] Rules of Procedure for the Council, Articles 3, 6, 8-11, 19 (b), 60, Appendix B.
[77] C-WP/12633.
[78] C-WP/12684.

For every calendar year following the last regular Assembly session the Council prepares a voluminous report giving an account to the Assembly of the highlights of the year in the work of the Organization, principal trends in civil aviation, projects given special attention, technical cooperation, constitutional and legal questions, regional activities and relations with other international organizations. The President of the Council presents to the Assembly under a separate agenda item a summary of the three annual reports and the Assembly usually "notes" the reports without comment and refers their parts to the Committees of the Assembly for consideration under Article 49 c) of the Convention.

> b) Carry out the directions of the Assembly and discharge the duties and obligations which are laid on it by the Convention.
> c) Determine its organization and rules of procedure.

The Council is legally subordinate to the Assembly, must implement the decisions of the Assembly and discharge the functions imposed upon it by the Chicago Convention. It has determined and can amend as necessary its establishment and organization of subordinate bodies, the pattern and frequency of its sessions and its Rules of Procedure.

> d) Appoint and define the duties of an Air Transport Committee, which shall be chosen from among the representatives of the members of the Council, and which shall be responsible to it.

On 24 June 1947, at its 1st Session the Council established the Air Transport Committee with the terms of reference to present to the Council studies and recommendations on air transport matters and prepare for the Council proposals for Standards and Recommended Practices relating to air transport – in particular facilitation of air transport by simplification of national regulations.[79] On 12 October 1948, the Council decided that the Air Transport Committee shall be composed of twelve members appointed by the Council from among the representatives on the Council.[80] On 23 June 1954, the Council suspended the provision on twelve members of the Air Transport Committee and since that time the Committee is in fact open to all representatives on the Council. One consequence seems to be that the debates are frequently duplicated among the same persons in the Committee and the Council. The Rules of procedure governing the Air Transport Committee are the *Rules for the Standing Committees of the Council*.[81]

---

[79] Doc 6808-C/791, pp. 20-21.
[80] Doc 6544-C/742, pp. 74-75.
[81] Doc 8146-C/930.

e) Establish an Air Navigation Commission, in accordance with the provisions of Chapter X.

Chapter X of the Chicago Convention consists of Articles 56 and 57 which deal with the appointment of the Air Navigation Commission (ANC) and its duties. The ANC is currently composed of nineteen members[82] appointed by the Council from among persons nominated by contracting States. At the 39th Assembly of the ICAO (2016), the Member States raised the number of the ANC members to 21, which will take effect following ratification by 128 Member States.[83] They act as experts and are expected to have suitable qualifications and experience in the science and practice of aeronautics. The President of the ANC is appointed by the Council. The primary duty of the ANC is to study and recommend to the Council the adoption and modification of the Annexes to the Convention. Over the years many leading experts nominated by States contributed to the work of the ANC and to the formulation of the principles embodied in the Standards, Recommended Practices and Procedures approved by the Council. The members of the ANC do not represent the State or States that have nominated them and ideally should act in their personal expert capacity. However, there is no record that a member of the Commission would depart from the fundamental policies of the State that nominated him.

f) Administer the finances of the Organization in accordance with the provisions of Chapters XII and XV.

Chapter XII (Articles 61-63) of the Convention deals with "finances" assigning to the Council, in Article 61, the task of submitting to the Assembly annual budgets, annual statements of accounts and estimates of all receipts and expenditures. Beyond that the Chapter does not refer to functions of the Council.

Chapter XV of the Convention has a title "Airports and Other Air Navigation Facilities" and became a focus of Organization's involvement in joint support (later referred to as "joint financing") of certain air navigation services.

Assembly Resolution A1-65 "Joint Support Policy" has been since 1947 the policy guidance for the actions under Chapter XV. The joint support of air navigation services had its early origin in the "Agreement on North Atlantic Ocean Weather Stations"

---

82   The original number of ANC members was twelve, increased by amendment of Article 56 in 1971 to fifteen; the current text originates in the amendment of 1989 that entered into force in 2005.
83   At the 39th Assembly the ANC membership was raised to 21 members. To get this number of ratifications takes a long time. Resolution A39-6, October 2016.

concluded in London on 25 September 1946 – then accepted by the ICAO Council "on behalf of ICAO" on 28 November 1948.[84]

Next step was the "Agreement on North Atlantic Ocean Stations" (generally referred to as "NAOS") of 25 February 1954[85] under which the user States through ICAO defrayed the cost of services provided by the ocean ships.

The Agreements with Denmark on the Joint Financing of Certain Air Navigation Services in Greenland and the Faeroe Islands in 1956,[86] and a similar Agreement with Iceland[87] (commonly referred to as "the DEN/ICE Agreements") amended in 1982,[88] established a system managed by ICAO under which 5% of the cost of services was absorbed by the governments of Denmark and Iceland in recognition of the special benefits they derived from it and the remaining 95% was to be recovered from the users. The air navigation facilities are provided for flights north of the 45 degrees North latitude; Annexes to the Agreements define the facilities and services available.

g) Determine the emoluments of the President of the Council.

Unlike the presiding official of other international bodies, the President of the Council is a salaried employee of the Organization. His salary, emoluments and representation allowance are determined by the Council in a closed session, the working papers are "restricted", minutes of the closed meetings are also restricted and the information is not publicly available. The President absents himself from such a closed session and one of the Vice Presidents presides. However, it is public knowledge that the President's base salary is equal to that of an Under-Secretary-General (USG) of the United Nations.[89]

---

84   Doc 7248-C/839, p. 57. Under this agreement a number of ships were permanently anchored in strategic locations of the North Atlantic providing meteorological information to overflying aircraft.
85   Doc 8080-JS/579; By 1 July 1975, the NAOS Agreement was terminated and the project was taken over by the WMO as serving primarily maritime transport.
86   Doc 7726-JS/563.
87   Doc 7727-JS/564.
88   Doc 9585-JS/681 and Doc 9586-JS/682.
89   On 1 January 2022, USG's base salary is USD 207.368 (plus "post adjustment" amounting currently to additional more than USD 100,000). ICAO Secretary General receives salary equivalent to that of an Assistant Secretary-General (ASG) of the United Nations (by 1 January 2022, USD 188.253 + post adjustment of some additional $100.000). Moreover, the President and the Secretary General receive generous representation allowance, health and pension benefits, education grant for children, travel on home leave, etc., free from Canadian taxation and including fiscal privileges such as tax and duty-free purchases and imports. Compared with top executive salaries in private enterprise in developed countries, these emoluments are admittedly high but not exorbitant.

h) Appoint a chief executive officer who shall be called the Secretary General, and make provision for the appointment of such other personnel as may be necessary, in accordance with the provisions of Chapter XI.

Unlike the President of the Council, the Secretary General is not "elected" but "appointed" indicating the administrative nature of the action rather than a policy decision. Nevertheless, the appointment of the Secretary General always involved a political decision and concern for the geographic rotation in the function. The Secretary General is currently appointed for a term of three years and may be reappointed; however, in the light of the UN General Assembly recommendation in Resolution 51/241 ICAO Assembly at its 36th Session in September 2007 limited the tenure in the post of Secretary General to two terms and made him ineligible for the position of the President of the Council.[90]

Since the time of PICAO the following persons have filled the post of the Secretary General:
- Albert Roper (France) – 1944-1951
- Carl Ljungberg (Sweden) – 1952-1959
- Ronald MacAllister Macdonnel (Canada) – 1959-1964
- Bernardus Tieleman Twigt (the Netherlands) – 1964-1970
- Assad Kotaite (Lebanon) – 1970-1976
- Yves Lambert (France) – 1976-1988
- Shivinder Singh Sidhu (India) – 1988-1991
- Philippe Rochat (Switzerland) – 1991-1997
- Renato Claudio Costa Pereira (Brazil) – 1997-2003
- Taieb Cherif (Algeria) – 2003-2009
- Raymond Benjamin (France) – 2009-2015
- Fang Liu (China) – 2015-2021
- Juan Carlos Salazar (Colombia) – 2021-

Under Article 58 of the Convention, the Council determines the method of appointment and of termination of appointment, the training and the salaries, allowances and conditions of service of the Secretary General and other personnel of the Organization, and may employ or make use of the services of nationals of any contracting State.[91] With respect to the position of the Secretary General the Council determined[92] that the Secretary General should be appointed for a specified term of from three to five years, the exact duration to

---

90 Resolution A36-28.
91 In practice, it has been interpreted that ICAO is not at liberty to employ a citizen of a non-contracting State or a stateless person. The general issues of the ICAO personnel will be addressed below under the heading "Secretariat".
92 Doc 8665-C/970, pp. 2-3, 16 December 1966.

be determined by the Council on each occasion. The appointment should take place approximately five months before the termination of the period for which the incumbent was appointed. The established practice is three years' appointment.

> i) Request, collect, examine and publish information relating to the advancement of air navigation and the operation of international air services, including information about the costs of operations and particulars of subsidies paid to airlines from public funds.
> j) Report to contracting States any infraction of this Convention, as well as any failure to carry out recommendations or determinations of the Council.
> k) Report to the Assembly any infraction of this Convention where a contracting State has failed to take appropriate action within a reasonable time after notice of the infraction.

There is so far no record of decisions by the Council under paragraphs i), j) and k) of Article 54 of the Convention. The Council could have availed itself of the provisions of paragraphs j) and k) in cases where States failed to comply with the international standards and did not notify a departure from them under Article 38 of the Convention but it took decades before the Organization formulated a policy of "safety oversight audit" under which it could report to States or to the Assembly any failures of a State in compliance with any recommendations of the audit procedures.[93] It may be open to discussion whether under these provisions the Council could also report on the failure of a State to correct any shortcomings identified during the security oversight audit on matters not governed by the Convention but it should be assumed that the Council will always see aviation security against unlawful interference as an overriding priority and will exercise this function.

> l) Adopt, in accordance with the provisions of Chapter VI of this Convention, international standards and recommended practices; for convenience, designate them as Annexes to this Convention; and notify all contracting States of the action taken.

This is arguably the most important mandatory function of the ICAO Council. The Council is vested with the law-making function that is outlined in Chapter VI of the Convention. That Chapter consists of Articles 37 and 38 that set forth the ICAO function in adopting and amending the international standards and recommended practices and procedures dealing with a wide spectrum of matters dealing with the safety, regularity and

---

93 This will be addressed below under the heading "Law-making Function of the ICAO Council" (See Section 7.3.5.2).

efficiency of air navigation; contracting States have accepted an undertaking to collaborate in securing the highest practicable degree of uniformity but under Article 38 of the Convention States may depart from international standards and procedures under prescribed conditions. The procedure for the adoption and amendment of Annexes is prescribed in Article 90 of the Convention. A more detailed analysis of this function of the ICAO Council and on the legal status of Annexes to the Convention will be given below.

> m) Consider recommendations of the Air Navigation Commission for amendment of the Annexes and take action in accordance with the provisions of Chapter XX.

The Council is obliged to "consider" (not to "approve") recommendations of the ANC with respect to amendment of Annexes to the Convention. Chapter XX contains a single Article 90 that governs the procedure for the adoption and amendment of Annexes.

> n) Consider any matter relating to the Convention which any contracting State refers to it.

This is a wide open *omnibus* provision under which a contracting State may bring to the Council any issues relating to the Convention and the Council is obliged to consider it. In the history of ICAO such requests sometimes related to the interpretation of the Convention[94] but more often they implied a complaint against another State or a pending dispute that has not yet reached the stage for the settlement of disputes under Chapter XVIII of the Convention.

A typical example of such issues was the request of the United Kingdom relating to Article 9 of the Convention, in fact complaining against the declaration by Spain of a prohibited area near Gibraltar.[95]

A similar case was the complaint by Nigeria against Portugal for alleged unlawful flights and support of rebels in the province of Biafra[96] and also the complaint of Lebanon against Israel concerning an attack against Beirut airport and the destruction of many civil aircraft.[97]

Another case presented to the Council under Article 54 n) was the complaint by the Islamic Republic of Iran against the United States concerning the shooting down of the

---

[94] *E.g.*, request of Sweden for interpretation of Article 7 of the Chicago Convention, 58th and 59th Sessions of the Council, Doc 8596-C/964 and 8629-C/967; request of the League of Arab States for determination under Article 77 of the Convention, Doc 8106-C/927, etc.
[95] Doc 8678-C/972, pp. 14-32, 34-48, 50-55.
[96] Discussions were spread between the 63rd to 66th Sessions of the Council in 1968 and 1969.
[97] Doc 8793-C/982 – Extraordinary Session of the Council, 1969.

Iranian Airbus A300 Flight 665 in the Gulf on 3 July 1988 that resulted in 290 fatalities; the Council considered the matter in several meetings, initiated its own investigation and on 17 March 1989 adopted a resolution *inter alia* deploring the incident;[98] later the Government of Iran brought the case to the International Court of Justice in a manner that appeared to be an appeal against the ICAO Council decision.[99]

It should be noted that under Article 54 n) the Council is obliged to consider any matter brought to it by a contracting State; it is not obliged to take a decision on the matter. That principle has been confirmed in 1967 during the discussion of the United Kingdom request concerning the prohibited area in the vicinity of Gibraltar; after extensive discussions a stage was reached when there was no proposal for action and no request for the floor. The President then declared that the debate has been "exhausted" and proceeded to another agenda item; when an objection was raised by the representative of the United Kingdom that the Council did not comply with the mandatory duty, it was explained that the duty was to "consider" and that the Convention did not impose a duty on the Council to "decide".[100] The United Kingdom then proceeded to the settlement of differences under Chapter XVIII of the Convention.

The Convention refers to other mandatory functions of the Council that are not mentioned in Article 54. Among them are:

– Article 56: appointment of the members of the ANC and appointment of its President;
– Article 58: determination of the personnel appointment and policy;
– Article 61: submission of annual budgets, annual statements of accounts, etc. to the Assembly;
– Article 65: agreements with other international bodies for the maintenance of common services and for common arrangements concerning personnel;
– Article 77: determination in what manner the provisions of the Convention relating to nationality of aircraft shall apply to aircraft operated by international operating agencies;
– Articles 81 and 83: arrangements for the registration of aeronautical agreements and arrangements;
– Article 83*bis* b): arrange for the registration of agreements on transfer of certain functions and duties from the State of Registry to the State of the operator;
– Article 84: settlement of disputes;
– Article 90: adoption and amendment of Annexes.

---

98   C-DEC 126/20, PIO 4/89.
99   Under Article 84 of the Chicago Convention, compulsory jurisdiction in an appeal to the ICJ is foreseen only from decisions under Chapter XVIII of the Convention. Iran later withdrew the case from the ICJ. *Islamic Republic of Iran v. United States of America* – ICJ (Case Concerning the Aerial Incident of 3 July 1988), 2001.
100 Doc 8678-C/972, pp. 50-55.

Permissive Functions of the ICAO Council

Article 55 of the Convention lists a series of functions that the Council "may" assume, although it is not "obliged" to do so. Over the years of practical application of the Convention the Council may have tacitly acted under different provisions of Article 55 without expressly mentioning it. The article states:

> Article 55
> *Permissive functions of the Council*
> The Council may:
> a. Where appropriate and as experience may show to be desirable, create subordinate air transport commissions on a regional or other basis and define groups of states or airlines with or through which it may deal to facilitate the carrying out of aims of this Convention.
> b. Delegate to the Air Navigation Commission duties additional to those set forth in the Convention and revoke or modify such delegation of authority at any time.
> c. Conduct research into all aspects of air transport and air navigation which are of international importance, communicate the results of its research to the contracting States, and facilitate the exchange of information between contracting states on air transport and air navigation matters.
> d. Study any matters affecting the organization and operation of international air transport, including the international ownership and operation of international trunk routes and submit to the Assembly plans in relation thereto.
> e. Investigate, at the request of any contracting state any situation which may appear to present avoidable obstacles to the development of international air navigation; and, after such investigation, issue such reports as may appear to it desirable.

The legal impact of Article 55 is not easy to analyse. It should definitely not be interpreted as an exhaustive list of matters that the Council is permitted to deal with and beyond which the Council is not permitted to go. Some elements of Article 55 were never invoked in practice. Thus. under paragraph a) the Council never created any regional air transport commissions; again, under paragraph b) the Council could not possibly delegate to the Air Navigation Commission (ANC) any of its own functions. Paragraph d) may be just a token lip service to the Australian-New Zealand's proposal at the Chicago Conference for the international ownership and operation of trunk routes – a proposal that received minimal support and to which the Council never returned. Council "investigation" under paragraph e) may have been applied – without express reference to Article 55 – in a few

7 INTERNATIONAL CIVIL AVIATION ORGANIZATION (ICAO)

cases when the Council decided on "fact finding" after the use of weapons against civil aircraft in flight.[101]

Law-Making Function of the ICAO Council: International Standards and Recommended Practices

Since the very infancy of international civil aviation, the international community has understood the unavoidable need for worldwide uniformity of aviation safety standards, practices and procedures. The international aviation cannot operate in a safe and orderly manner unless all essential aspects of international aircraft operation and air navigation are governed in a transparent, uniform and predictable manner. Different national standards, requirements, procedures or practices would create conflicts and jeopardize safety.

When aircraft cross the national boundaries they must be assured of uniform standards for personnel training and licensing, rules of the air, units of measurement, certification of airworthiness, aeronautical communications, characteristics of airports, aircraft operation and many other aspects.

The first attempt at international standardization of aviation practices and procedures was made in the Paris Convention on Regulation of International Air Navigation (1919).[102] That Convention contained eight "Annexes" (A to H)[103] that were an integral part of the Convention. Article 39 of the Paris Convention states:

> *Article 39*
> The provisions of the present Convention are completed by the Annexes A to H, which, subject to Article 34 c), shall have the same effect and shall come into force at the same time as the Convention itself.[104]

This approach had an apparent advantage that the standards had the same binding power as the Convention itself and the process of their amendment by the ICAN was easier, faster and more flexible than an amendment of the Convention itself. There was no need for the laborious process of an amendment of the Convention – a process requiring a Diplomatic Conference, authentication of the text and its ratification by the national

---

101 Destruction of Libyan B-727 over Sinai on 21 February 1973; Korean B-747 on 1 September 1983 off the island of Sakhalin; Iran Air Airbus A300 in 3 July 1988 in the Gulf.
102 Text in the League of Nations Treaty Series, Vol. XI, p. 173; see Section 2.2 in this book..
103 *Ibid*. 2.2, 26.
104 Article 34 c) gives the International Commission on Air Navigation (ICAN) – an organ similar to the ICAO Council – the power and duty to amend the provisions of Annexes A to G. Annex H dealt with customs and its provisions were subject of a special agreement.

authorities. Moreover, such a solution could respond fast and effectively to any new technical and operational requirements.

On the other hand, this solution had a serious legal disadvantage: many States could not constitutionally accept an open-ended Convention, an integral part of which could be amended by the ICAN without explicit consent or even against the opposition of the State concerned. It has been stated that this aspect of the Paris Convention was one of the reasons why the United States did not consider ratification of the Convention and why Spain, in 1926, denounced the Paris Convention and initiated the Iberian-American Convention.

The Chicago Conference in 1944 considered the precedent of the Paris Convention (1919), maintained the concept of "Annexes" to the Convention but radically changed their legal status.

The Council of ICAO has a unique position and jurisdiction among the various bodies of the United Nations system. It has a function to adopt international standards and recommended practices aimed at worldwide application under specified conditions. In one specific case – the rules of the air over the high seas (in the international airspace) – the standards adopted by the Council are mandatory to all States without exception. This is a sole example that an executive body of an international organization is empowered to legislate with binding force over some 46% of the surface of the Earth.[105]

It has been already stated that the Council of ICAO has a mandatory function to adopt international standards and recommended practices.[106] Their adoption requires a two-thirds majority vote of all members of the Council (currently 24 out of 36; in fact with very rare exceptions, the Standards are adopted by the Council by unanimity) at a meeting called for that purpose and they come into force unless disapproved by a majority of ICAO contracting States.[107]

It is interesting to note that in the history of ICAO such a "collective veto" has never taken place; this is a reflection of the fact that the adoption and amendment of the standards is always the result of extensive consultations and dialogue with States through the regional or divisional meetings and consultations by exchange of letters and questionnaires conducted by the Air Navigation Commission and by the Council itself.

The Standards and Recommended Practices are grouped into "Annexes" to the Convention. When Article 54 l) refers to the adoption of international standards and recommended practices by the Council, it adds: "for convenience designate them as Annexes to this Convention". From this wording it is apparent that the Annexes are not an

---

105 Article 12 of the Chicago Convention, third sentence: "Over the high seas, the rules in force shall be those established under this Convention."
106 Article 54 l) of the Chicago Convention.
107 Article 90 of the Chicago Convention; the "disapproval" would have to come from 97 States (out of 193).

integral part of the Convention but that they are so designated only "for convenience" – perhaps to perpetuate in the terminology the tradition of the Paris Convention (1919). In substance, however, the legal status of the Annexes represents a clear departure from the previous practice under the Paris Convention.

If the Annexes are not an integral part of the Convention, they do not have the same legal force as the Convention itself and they are not subject to the general international law of treaties.[108]

The analysis of the legal status of the standards and recommended practices must start with Article 37 of the Convention:

Article 37
Adoption of international standards and procedures
Each contracting State undertakes to collaborate in securing the highest practicable degree of uniformity in regulations, standards, procedures and organization in relation to aircraft, personnel, airways and auxiliary services in all matters in which such uniformity will facilitate and improve air navigation. To this end the International Civil Aviation Organization shall adopt and amend from time to time, as may be necessary, international standards and recommended practices and procedures dealing with:
a. Communications systems and air navigation aids, including ground marking;
b. Characteristics of airports and landing areas;
c. Rules of the air and air traffic control practices;
d. Licensing of operating and mechanical personnel;
e. Airworthiness of aircraft;
f. Registration and identification of aircraft;
g. Collection and exchange of meteorological information;
h. Log books;
i. Aeronautical maps and charts;
j. Customs and immigration procedures;
k. Aircraft in distress and investigation of accidents;

and such other matters concerned with the safety, regularity, and efficiency of air navigation as may from time to time appear appropriate.

---

108 The provisions on the interpretation of the treaties formulated in the Vienna Convention on the Law of Treaties (1969) should be, *mutatis mutandis*, applicable to the interpretation of the Annexes. However, this issue has not been addressed in ICAO practice.

Article 37 of the Convention is open-ended and there is no limitation of the subjects that may be addressed in the Standards and Recommended Practices. In fact, the Council many times exceeded the subjects listed in Article 37, *e.g.*, when dealing with aircraft noise and engines emissions, aviation security or the carriage of dangerous goods, etc.

The Convention does not provide a definition of the "standards" and "recommended practices". A definition was formulated in several subsequent resolutions of the ICAO Assemblies, the current text being:[109]

> Standard – any specification for physical characteristics, configuration, materiel, performance, personnel or procedure, the uniform application of which is recognized as *necessary* for the safety or regularity of air navigation and to which contracting States *will conform* in accordance with the convention; in the event of impossibility of compliance, *notification to the Council is compulsory* under Article 38 of the Convention.
>
> Recommended Practice – any specification for physical characteristics, configuration, material, performance, personnel or procedure, the uniform application of which is recognized as *desirable* in the interest of safety, regularity or efficiency of international air navigation and to which contracting States *will endeavour to conform* in accordance with the Convention.[110]

Under Article 37 of the Convention States have accepted an international commitment but it is not an absolute one. The obligation accepted is not "to comply" with the standards but "to collaborate in the highest practicable degree of uniformity". Each contracting State is the sole authority to determine what is "practicable" and what is not. No State may be expected or forced to do what is not possible for it or not "practicable".[111] However, if a State finds it impossible to comply with an international standard, it has an international legal obligation formulated in Article 38 of the Convention:

> *Article 38*
> *Departures from international standards and procedures*
> Any State which finds it impracticable to comply in all respects with any such international standard or procedure, or to bring its own regulations or practices into full accord with any international standard or procedure after amendment of the latter, or which deems it necessary to adopt regulations or practices

---

109 Resolution A36-13, Appendix A.
110 Emphasis added.
111 The maxim of Roman law *ultra posse nemo tenetur* is equally applicable in international law.

differing in any particular respect from those established by an international standard, shall give immediate notification to the International Civil Aviation Organization of the differences between its own practice and that established by the international standard. In the case of amendments to international standards, any State which does not make the appropriate amendments to its own regulations or practices shall give notice to the Council within sixty days of the adoption of the amendment to the international standard, or indicate the action which it proposes to take. In any such case, the Council shall make immediate notification of the difference that exists between one or more features of an international standard and the corresponding national practice of that State.

The "filing of differences" to international standards is enabled by Article 38 with respect to international standards; the Recommended Practices are by their legal nature only "desirable", States should only "endeavour" to conform to them and there is no legal duty to notify a non-compliance with the recommended practices. Nevertheless, it appears that the Organization expects that States notify it of any differences that exist between their national regulations and practices and "the provisions of SARPs".[112]

The reason for the unconditional legal obligation of States to notify any differences from the international standards is evident: there must be full international transparency as to which standards are not implemented in a particular location and other States must receive a timely warning in the interest of safety of air navigation that certain standards, procedures, facilities or services are not available. Without such notification the flight safety of foreign aircraft could be seriously jeopardized, if they were to rely on the existence of particular facilities and services which in fact were unavailable. A question could arise whether a State that failed to notify its departure from international standards would face international responsibility if that failure caused or attributed to damage; such a contingency has not yet been recorded in the history of ICAO, but it need not be only an abstract theoretical concern.

The summary of the features of the ICAO Council law-making function presents some intrinsic contradictions and difficulties that lead some commentators to express doubts about the legal force of the ICAO SARPs and to call the function of the Council at best as "quasi-legislative".[113]

---

112 SARPs is an established acronym for "Standards and Recommended Practices"; Resolution A36-13 in Appendix D (Implementation of SARPs and PANS), Associated practices, paragraphs 3 and 4 refers to differences from the "provisions of SARPs" thus encompassing also the recommended practices. In more recent practice, the Council's Resolution of Adoption of an Annex expressly invites States to notify also any differences from the recommended practices.

113 Among others: Jaques Naveau and M. Godfroid, "Precis de droit aerien", Bruyland, Brussels, 1988.

A majority of States can disapprove of the standards.[114] States accepted the obligation to cooperate only "to the highest practicable measure"[115] and States have the right (and the corresponding duty) to notify differences between their national practices and the international standards. That would appear to make the SARPs legally "weak" and the unconvincing term "soft law" is also frequently used. From the firmly positivistic approach to international law the SARPs do not qualify as part of the international law, they are not subject to the law of treaties and represent rather guidance to desirable conduct of States than a formal legal obligation.

On the other hand, it is convincing that the international standards are not devoid of legal significance. Under Article 37 of the Convention, States have accepted an international obligation to collaborate in securing the highest practicable degree of uniformity and this obligation must be fulfilled in good faith.

Moreover, States are strongly motivated to implement international standards by the sheer realities of international life: non-compliance with SARPs could eliminate the State concerned from any meaningful participation in international air navigation and air transport – any deficiency in pilot licensing or airworthiness of aircraft would prevent the aircraft of the defaulting State to operate into other States; any deficiency in the characteristics of airports or in the Air Traffic Services (ATS), communications and navigational aids would compel foreign operators to avoid the airspace and airports of a particular country for safety reasons and risk that their insurance coverage would not be applicable; non-compliance with the aviation security standards would disqualify the airline and airports concerned from international operations, etc.

Another strong argument for full compliance with the minimum ICAO standards is made explicit in the Convention: certificates of airworthiness and certificates of competency and licenses issued or rendered valid in a contracting State of an aircraft's registry must be recognized as valid by all other States if they were issued or rendered valid under requirements which are equal to or higher than the minimum ICAO standards.[116] Certificates of airworthiness or licenses falling below such minimum standards need not be recognized as valid and could eliminate the State concerned from international air navigation and transport.

During its existence ICAO elaborated 19 Annexes to the Convention that amount to hundreds of pages of regulatory materials. It is beyond the resources of one person to achieve the full command of all those Annexes the subjects of which cover vastly different spectra of technical subjects and each of them requires specialized knowledge. The

---

114 Article 90 of the Chicago Convention.
115 Article 37 of the Chicago Convention.
116 Article 33 of the Chicago Convention.

Annexes are drafted in uniform pattern, and it is essential to understand the different components of the Annexes and their legal significance:[117]

1) Material comprising the Annex proper:
a. *Definitions*: the Annexes contain definitions of the terms used in the SARPs which are not self-explanatory in that they do not have accepted dictionary meanings. A definition does not have an independent status but is an essential part of each standard or recommended practice in which the term is used, since a change in the meaning of the term would affect the specification.
b. *SARPs*: the essential part of each Annex are the Standards and Recommended Practices arranged in numbered Chapters, subchapters and paragraphs and subparagraphs; the provisions are numbered by the number of the Chapter with decimal subdivisions (for example 2.3.9.1).
c. *Appendices*: comprise material grouped separately for convenience but forming part of the Standards and Recommended Practices adopted by the Council; there must be an enabling clause in a standard relating to the Appendix.

2) Material approved by the Council for publication in association with the SARPs:
a. *Forewords* that comprise historical and explanatory material based on the action of the Council and including an explanation of the obligation of States with regard to the application of the SARPs ensuing from the Convention and the Resolution of Adoption.
b. *Introductions* comprising explanatory material introduced at the beginning of parts, chapters or sections of the Annexes to assist in the understanding of the application of the text.
c. *Notes* included in the text, where appropriate, to give factual information or references or cross-references bearing on the SARPs in question but not constituting part of the SARPs.
d. *Attachments* (distinct from Appendices!) comprising material supplementary to the SARPs or included as a guide to their application.

The typographical presentation of the text of the SARPs facilitates understanding at a glance the status of each part of the text. *Standards* are printed in light face Roman font; *Recommended Practices* are printed in light face italics and their status is indicated by the

---

117 The points below are paraphrased from the typical Annexes.

words *Recommended Practice*; Notes are printed in light face italics and their status is indicated by the prefix *Note*.

This practice is followed in all language versions of the Annexes – Arabic, Chinese, English, French, Russian and Spanish.

Table 2.1 The following Annexes to the Convention have been adopted:

Annex 1	Personnel Licensing
Annex 2	Rules of the Air*
Annex 3	Meteorological Service for International Air Navigation
Annex 4	Aeronautical Charts
Annex 5	Units of Measurement to be Used in Air and Ground Operations
Annex 6	Operation of Aircraft
	Part I – International Commercial Air Transport – Aeroplanes
	Part II – International General Aviation – Aeroplanes
	Part III – International Operations – Helicopters
Annex 7	Aircraft Nationality and Registration Marks
Annex 8	Airworthiness of Aircraft
Annex 9	Facilitation
Annex 10	Aeronautical Telecommunications
	Volume I – Radio Navigational Aids
	Volume II – Communication Procedures including those with PANS status
	Volume III – Communication Systems
	Volume IV – Surveillance Radar and Collision Avoidance Systems
	Volume V – Aeronautical Radio Frequency Spectrum Utilization
Annex 11	Air Traffic Services
Annex 12	Search and Rescue
Annex 13	Aircraft Accident and Incident Investigation
Annex 14	Aerodromes
	Volume I – Aerodromes Design and Operations
	Volume II – Heliports
Annex 15	Aeronautical Information Services
Annex 16	Environmental Protection
	Volume I – Aircraft Noise
	Volume II – Aircraft Engine Emissions
Annex 17	Security: Safeguarding International Civil Aviation Against Acts of Unlawful Interference

Annex 18   The Safe Transport of Dangerous Goods by Air
Annex 19   Safety Management

* The special feature of Annex 2 is that it contains only Standards and no Recommended Practices; its application over the high seas is obligatory and no difference can be filed by any State; this Annex also contains provisions relating to interception of civil aircraft.

Analysis of each of these Annexes could require a separate book specialized in a particular technical discipline and the national aviation administrations must have on their staff experts in the various disciplines to assure the national implementation of the SARPs or timely filing of a difference. The task of a lawyer specializing in international air law is not to have a profound knowledge of the substance of each of the Annexes; however, a lawyer must be able to locate the relevant sources of regulation and assist in their interpretation and application in the overall context of the Convention and other Annexes. Legal professionals also take an important part in the drafting of the Annexes to safeguard their clarity and consistency with the Convention and harmony with other Annexes.

ICAO produces, in addition to the standards and recommended practices, some other regulatory documents that have a lower legal status than the SARPs. They are the Procedures for Air Navigation Services (PANS) and may be designed for "world-wide application" (*i.e.*, without regional limitation); PANS fall short of the status of the SARPs since they may be considered "immature" for the status of SARPs. The PANS "comprise, for the most part, operating practices as well as material considered too detailed for SARPs. PANS often amplify the basic principles in the corresponding SARPs contained in Annexes to assist in the application of those SARPs".[118]

Among the current PANS are PANS-OPS: Procedure for Air Navigation Services – Aircraft Operations, Vol. I: Flight Procedures, Vol. II: Construction of Visual and Instrument Flight Procedures,[119] PANS – Air Traffic Management[120] and PANS – ICAO Abbreviations and Codes.[121]

In addition, there are ICAO Regional Supplementary Procedures (SUPPs)[122] that are not applicable world-wide but only for specific regions. With the advent of long-range aircraft the regional specificities are further to diminish.

The PANS and SUPPs are not expressly foreseen in the Convention and their legal force is not equal to that of the SARPs. The SARPs are "adopted" by the Council within its

---

118   See paragraph 3.1 of the Directives to the Divisional-type Air Navigation Meetings and Rules of Procedure for their Conduct, ICAO Doc 8143-AN/873/3; See also paragraph 3.2 of the introduction to Doc 4444 ATM/501.
119   ICAO Doc 8168, OPS/611.
120   ICAO Doc 4444, ATM/501.
121   ICAO Doc 8400.
122   ICAO Doc 7030.

specific constitutional jurisdiction and in the prescribed constitutional procedure[123] while the PANS and SUPPs are "approved" by the Council. Their force is that of a guidance material, but their practical importance cannot be underestimated – they represent the best collective knowledge, expertise and experience available in the international aviation community and the "approval" by the Council gives them a formal seal of recognition by a recognized international aviation authority.

Even the SARPs do not represent "hard law" in view of the conditions stipulated in the Convention. They do not possess a legal force equal to that of the Convention and they are not subject to the international law of treaties;[124] however, the weak international commitment in Article 37 of the Convention must be complied with in good faith by all States and the duty to notify any differences under Article 38 is an unconditional legal obligation.

In practice, there is a powerful motivation for all States wishing to participate in international air transport to comply with the standards as closely as possible. While it may be argued that the SARPs represent only "soft law" they cannot be disregarded with impunity. A phrase has been coined that the force of the SARPs could be compared with that of the "law of gravity": compliance is simply unavoidable in practice and non-compliance would have serious consequences.

ICAO has accomplished a most impressive work in the adoption and constant updating of the 19 Annexes to the Convention, fifteen of which, with the exception of Annex 9 (Facilitation), Annex 17 (Security), Annex 18 (Carriage of dangerous goods) and Annex 19 (Safety management), deal directly with aspects of air navigation and are essential to its safety.

Implementation of SARPs – Need for Enforcement?
Since the adoption of the first Annexes in ICAO in 1947, the number of differences filed by States under Article 38 of the Convention has been relatively low and all ICAO Member States appeared to be endeavouring to align their national practices and procedures on the ICAO SARPs. The fast development of aviation technology after World War II was also accompanied by the process of decolonization that brought to ICAO membership scores of new Member States. The complex law-making process required harmonization of the conflicting interests and disparate economic potential of the ICAO membership.

It would be normal to expect that the new SARPs would in fact reflect the lowest achievable common denominator acceptable to most States, both developed and developing, but in reality this was not the case. The technically advanced and economically powerful States exercised a logical and overwhelming leadership in matters of safety of

---

123 Articles 37, 54 l) and 90 of the Chicago Convention.
124 Vienna Convention on the Law of Treaties (1969), 1155 U.N.T.S. 331.

7 INTERNATIONAL CIVIL AVIATION ORGANIZATION (ICAO)

civil aviation and other States did not find it possible to object to such justifiable concern for increased safety, in spite of their limited technical and economic resources.

A negative trend has developed over the time that fewer and fewer States participated in the relevant conferences and meetings or answered questionnaires from ICAO or sent comments on new proposed standards. What is worse, many States failed to file notification under Article 38 of the Convention that they were not able to implement the standards. For a long time, ICAO knowingly tolerated this "silent treatment" of the SARPs – perhaps as a political convenience or opportunism and not to cause an irritation. Silence of States – lack of notified differences – with respect of new or amended SARPs cannot be interpreted as consent.

In 1995, the situation reached a level when a Secretariat paper had to admit that "it is at present time impossible to indicate with any degree of accuracy or certainty what the status of the implementation of regulatory Annex material really is, because a large number of States have not notified ICAO of their compliance with or differences to the standards in the Annexes for some considerable time".[125] This was a problem of serious proportions – if the Secretariat at ICAO Headquarters did not know what was the real situation of aviation safety in the world was, who else should know it and what level of safety exists in different parts of the world?[126]

The maxim "law without enforcement is not law" has its validity – without transparent view of the actual implementation of the ICAO SARPs and without any consequences for their non-implementation the SARPs would remain ineffective. Yet, the Chicago Convention did not create any machinery or procedures for the "enforcement" of compliance with the SARPs.

The issue was first brought into the open by a unilateral action of the United States. In 1992, following a series of accidents and findings of shortcomings of foreign carriers during "ramp inspections" at US airports, the US FAA (Federal Aviation Administration) established the International Aviation Safety Assessment Program (IASA)[127] focusing on the foreign States' ability (not that of individual airlines) to adhere to international SARPs for aircraft operations and maintenance established by ICAO. The purposes of the IASA program were to ensure that each foreign air carrier that operate or wish to operate to or from the US is licensed under conditions meeting ICAO SARPs and receive adequate continuing safety oversight from a competent civil aviation authority (CAA). The safety

---

125 C-WP/10218, 26 May 1995, p. 5.
126 This subject was first commented on in M. Milde, "Enforcement of Aviation Safety Standards – Problems of Safety Oversight" in 1995, and later published in *ZLW*, 1/1996 at pp. 1-17. At that time, the author's views also appeared in the local press, which reflects the author's deep commitment to the need for a harmonized international action in order to audit the level of implementation of the SARPs. This commitment was finally accorded the highest priority in the work programme.
127 For history and background of IASA, see www.faa.gov/avr/iasa/iasabrl15.

assessment includes, with the consent and cooperation of the other State, on-site visits to the foreign State and are mostly concentrated on the legal and administrative infrastructures of civil aviation – the underlying national aviation law, existence of appropriate regulatory structures empowered and competent to issue air operator certification, oversight of continuing airworthiness of aircraft and the work of adequately trained flight operations inspectors.

The FAA employed two ratings for the status of countries at the time of assessment:

> Category 1: Does comply with ICAO Standards: A country's civil aviation authority has been assessed by FAA inspectors and has been found to license and oversee air carriers in accordance with ICAO aviation safety standards.
> Category 2: Does not comply with ICAO Standards: The FAA assessed this country's civil aviation authority (CAA) and determined that it does not provide safety oversight of its air carrier operators in accordance with the minimum safety oversight standards established by ICAO.[128]

Category 2 rating is applied if the country lacks laws or regulations necessary to support the certification and oversight of air carriers, or lacks the technical expertise, resources and organization to license and oversee air carrier operations, does not have adequately trained and qualified technical personnel, etc.

Operators from States in Category 2 that do not have air carriers with existing operations to the United States will not be permitted to commence service to the US. Operators from States with existing operations to the US may continue operations at current level under heightened FAA surveillance but are not permitted to expand their operations while the rating in Category 2 continues.

According to the current data, some 100 States have been subject to the US FAA safety assessment, and over time several of them were listed in Category 2.[129] The high number of States listed as not complying with ICAO SARPs is a matter of concern.

The US initiative gave rise to vocal criticism as a "strong arm" tactic, yet nobody questioned that the US action has been fully lawful – it was carried out only with the consent and cooperation of the States concerned and was in full harmony with Articles 1, 11, 16 and 33 of the Chicago Convention. However, it was rather infelicitous that the

---

128 www.faa.gov/safety/programs_initiatives/oversight/iasa/definition.
129 The names of states/territories in this category are kept for four years, and any of them is deleted if that state's airline does not operate to and from the US territory; currently (December 2022), the following States/territories are listed in Category 2: Bangladesh, Venezuela, Thailand, Russia, Pakistan, Organization of Eastern Caribbean States, Mexico.

results of the assessments have been announced with media publicity leading to public embarrassment or humiliation of the States concerned.

The actual effect of the US action was also limited – it protected the specific US interests in bilateral relations with other States and did not have a global impact on the aviation safety; the carriers of the defaulting countries continue with impunity their operations in their respective regions, and are only prevented from entering the US territory.

The European Union also took a unilateral step to "blacklist" airlines deemed to be unsafe. Scores of minor air carriers from Africa and Asia have been subject to operational ban within the European Community.[130]

ICAO did not show initial leadership in the enforcement of the SARPs. For decades, ICAO silently and passively tolerated an alarming fact that many States did not implement ICAO safety standards and failed in their legal duty to notify their departure from or non-implementation of the SARPs pursuant to their explicit legal obligation under Article 38. While the ICAO Secretariat experts were for years aware of the shortcomings in implementation of the SARPs and of the deplorable lack of transparency in the attitude of States, the ICAO leadership was too "diplomatic" and timid to bring the problem into the open and to address it. Eventually, the experience of the US FAA and the attention of the EU to the problem prompted the execution of the ICAO safety oversight program.

The program in its first form was initiated by the ICAO Council in 1995,[131] and became operational in March 1996. It offered to States – that specifically requested this assistance – to send to them a team of experts (either ICAO staff members or experts seconded from national administrations) to make an on-the-spot evaluation of the implementation of ICAO safety standards and of the oversight capability of the State concerned. In this original form, the program was strictly voluntary and was mostly financed from extra-budgetary means granted by donor States. It focused on the implementation of Annex 1 (Personnel Licensing), Annex 6 (Operation of Aircraft) and Annex 8 (Airworthiness of Aircraft).

One of the stumbling blocks in the initial form of the program was the issue of "confidentiality" or "publicity" of findings by the oversight teams, some States showing reluctance or outright opposition to any publicity of the findings. In the light of the obligation of States under Article 38 of the Convention to notify publicly any differences from the SARPs the insistence on "confidentiality" of the findings lacked credibility.

---

130 http://ec.europa.eu/transport/air-ban/pdf/list_en.pdf. All the banned operators are minor enterprises of very marginal importance. Decree No. 2111/2005 (EC) of 14 December 2005, Community list of air carriers subject to an operating ban within the Community and on informing air transport passengers about the identity of the operator, and repealing Article 9 of Directive 2004/36/EC, HL L 344., 27 December 2005, p. 15.
131 C-DEC 145/7.

At the insistence of some States, the results of the assessments were strictly confidential but a new awareness developed gradually in ICAO signalling the determination of the most influential States that matters of aviation safety are of global interest and concern and should not be treated as an internal matter within the exclusive jurisdiction of the State concerned. Visible steps have been taken towards the "empowerment" of ICAO to conduct safety audits of States – going beyond the safety oversight on a strictly voluntary basis. A proposal was considered by the Council,[132] which contemplated "audits" to be carried out by ICAO upon its own initiative (not only at the request of a State).

On 10-12 November 1997, ICAO convened at Montreal a Conference of the Directors General of Civil Aviation on "Global Strategy for Safety Oversight".[133] The purpose of the Conference was to chart new vigorous strategies for safety audits of States in general (not only on request), with confidentiality of the findings only for the period set for correction of the identified shortcomings and closely correlated to the need to provide technical assistance to States in need.

Such a global conference of Directors General of Civil Aviation (DGCAs) had no precedent in ICAO history and there is no provision for such a body in the Chicago Convention. Moreover, the DGCAs are national civil servants and not politicians or diplomats with full powers for important decision-making. Nevertheless, the DGCA's Conference could be taken as an expert body concerned with aviation safety as opposed to diplomatic or policy considerations.

The Conference adopted unanimously thirty-eight recommendations calling for regular, mandatory, systematic and harmonized safety audits of all States to be carried out by ICAO. While the Conference had no law-making power, its unanimous recommendations carried important weight as *opinion iuris ac necessitatis* expressed by the aviation experts of the world responsible for the national administration of civil aviation. The recommendations in fact formulated, by implication, a principle that matters of aviation safety are a subject of global international concern and that the international community should be empowered to verify the national implementation of safety standards and procedures.

The recommendations of the Conference were endorsed by the Council and the 32nd Session of the ICAO Assembly unanimously resolved[134] "that a universal safety oversight audit programme be established, comprising regular, mandatory, systematic and harmonized safety audits, to be carried out by ICAO; that such universal safety oversight audit programme shall apply to all contracting States; and that greater transparency and increased disclosure be implemented in the release of audit results".

---

132 C-WP/10612.
133 DGCA/97-WP/1.
134 Resolution A32-11: "Establishment of an ICAO Universal Safety Oversight Audit Program (USOAP)".

The audits' scope was extended to 17 of the 19 Annexes (*i.e.*, all safety related provisions, except Annexes 9 and 16). In March 2006, another Conference of DGCAs was held in Montreal and unanimously decided to allow the Organization to post results of the audits on its public website

In 2010, the 37th Session of the ICAO Assembly adopted Resolution "Universal Safety Oversight Audit Programme (USOAP) – Continuous Monitoring Approach (CMA)".[135] The USOAP is a long term program to be phased into the Regular Programme budget. The CMA incorporates the analysis of safety risk factors and be applied on a universal basis in order to asses States' oversight capabilities.[136] The Resolution directs the Secretary General to ensure that the CMA continues to maintain as core elements the key safety provisions contained in Annex 1 (Personnel Licensing), Annex 6 (Operation of Aircraft), Annex 8 (Airworthiness of Aircraft), Annex 11 (Air Traffic Services), Annex 13 (Aircraft Accident and Incident Investigation) and Annex 14 (Aerodromes).

The USOAP is a significant development in international practice and international law. The ICAO SARPs (that in legal theory do not have a strong legal power) have been elevated to the level of global concern that is to be "enforced" by the international organization – not by any "force" but by the implied threat of publicly revealing any shortcomings and failures in the implementation of SARPs. The power of publicity, embarrassment and loss of credibility within the international community cannot be underestimated – it could be a very powerful "enforcement measure", possibly eliminating the defaulting State's carriers from international operations. ICAO just seems to have acquired an unprecedented power of enforcement of the safety standards of international civil aviation.

Another High-Level Safety Conference was held at Montreal from 29 March to 1 April 2010,[137] and in its Recommendation 2/5 recommended that the Council adopt a new Annex compiling all provisions of the safety management under the States' Safety Programmes (SSP).

So far the entire program has hinged on the unanimous views of the DGCAs and "High-Level" Conferences and Unanimous Resolution of the Assembly – neither of which is a source of international law in the proper sense of the word. The adoption of the new Annex 19 – Safety Management – elevates, with applicability from 14 November 2013, the issue of safety programmes and their oversight to the level of international standards.

Would States be willing to accept the "enforcement" program or "empowerment" of ICAO in a formal legal form? Would they be ready to ratify it in some future amendment of the Chicago Convention or in another legal instrument? There is no precedent of such

---

135 Resolution A37-5.
136 ICAO Doc 9807 Universal Security Audit Programme Continuous Monitoring Manual. 3rd ed., 2021.
137 Report in Doc 9935, HLSC 2010-WP/86.

a development within any international organization of the UN system and ICAO may well be a forerunner of some future developments of international law and of a new vision of the sovereignty of States in the globalized and interdependent world. Safety and security are a global concern transcending national boundaries, and the political will of States is united in the common interest.

7.3.5.3 ICAO Secretariat

In the United Nations, the Secretariat is designated as one of the principal organs of the Organization.[138] In the Chicago Convention there is no such designation and the word "Secretariat" is not used even once. Yet, a permanent Secretariat has been an integral feature of all intergovernmental organizations since the time of the very first such organization – the Universal Postal Union (UPU) in 1874.

The League of Nations established by the Covenant of the League of Nations[139] did not obtain clear guidance as to the composition of the Secretariat and two concepts were competing: first concept would insist that the staff members must be appointed by the governments of the Member States and represent them politically. The second and victorious concept was presented as a personal initiative by the first Secretary General of the League – Sir Eric Drummond: he advocated the concept of an autonomous international civil service that would be recruited on the basis of merit and on an international basis but remain independent and impartial, with loyalty to the Organization and its constitutional principles.

This concept of international civil service was practiced by the League and by all organizations affiliated with it. It is further developed in the United Nations Charter that embodied the following principles:

- In the performance of their duties, the Secretary General and the staff shall not seek or receive instructions from any government or from any other authority external to the Organization.
- They shall refrain from any action which might reflect on their position as international officials responsible only to the Organization.
- As a corollary – each Member State of the United Nations undertakes to respect the exclusively international character of the responsibilities of the Secretary General and the staff and not to seek to influence them in the discharge of their responsibilities.
- The paramount consideration in the employment of the staff and in the determination of the conditions of service shall be the necessity of securing the highest standards of efficiency, competence and integrity.

---

138 Article 7 of the UN Charter.
139 Articles 1-26 of the Versailles Peace Treaty (1919).

– Due regard shall be paid to the importance of recruiting the staff on as wide a geographical basic as possible.[140]

The Agreement between the United Nations and the International Civil Aviation Organization[141] that came into force on 14 May 1947, provides for uniformity in the conditions of service of the staff of ICAO and the UN. Moreover, on 13 June 1975, ICAO accepted the Statute of the International Civil Service Commission (ICSC)[142] – an advisory body of the United Nations for the regulation and coordination of personnel matters in the UN system.

The role of the Secretariat is "to serve" the Organization and the staff members are "international civil servants". Their task is to provide the required services to the representative bodies and to the contracting States by preparing studies of specific problems, analyses, documentation for the meetings, translation services and interpretation at meetings, implementation of the decisions of the representative bodies. They have no decision-making power of their own and must loyally and impartially serve the Organization and all its Member States. The standards of conduct for international civil service are very exacting and stress the loyalty to the Organization, impartiality, tolerance, international outlook and respect of dignity of all human beings.[143]

The Chicago Convention deals with issues of personnel in Chapter XI, Article 58, 59 and 60.

Article 58

Appointment of personnel

Subject to any rules laid down by the Assembly and to the provisions of this Convention, the Council shall determine the method of appointment and termination of appointment, the training, and the salaries, allowances, and conditions of service of the Secretary General and other personnel of the Organization, and may employ or make use of the services of national of any contracting State.

---

140 Articles 100 (1-2) and 101 (3) of the UN Charter.
141 ICAO Doc 7970, Article XII.
142 Statute and the Rules of Procedure of the ICSC; approved by the UN General Assembly Resolution 3357 (XXIX) of 18 December 1974. icsc.un.org-english.pdf.
143 The Standards of Conduct for International Civil Service in the current version were approved by the UN General Assembly in its Resolution 56/244, 5 February 2002.

Article 59
International character of personnel
The President of the Council, the Secretary General and other personnel shall not seek or receive instruction in regard to the discharge of their responsibilities from any authority external to the Organization. Each contracting State undertakes fully to respect the international character of the responsibilities of the personnel and not seek to influence any of its nationals in the discharge of their responsibilities.

Article 60
Immunities and privileges of personnel
Each contracting state undertakes, so far as possible under its constitutional procedure, to accord to the President of the Council, the Secretary General, and other personnel of the Organization, the immunities and privileges which are accorded to corresponding personnel of other public international organizations. If a general agreement on the immunities and privileges of international civil servants is arrived at, the immunities and privileges accorded to the President, Secretary General, and other personnel of the Organization shall be the immunities and privileges accorded under that international agreement.

The terms and condition of the appointment of ICAO staff are laid down in the ICAO Service Code, approved and amended from time to time by the ICAO Council. The Service Code in essence reflects the Staff Regulations and Staff Rules of the United Nations.[144]

As in other organizations of the UN system, the staff of ICAO is divided into Professional category (P) and General Service category (GS). Each of these categories is divided into "levels" and within those levels the "steps" in salary increases according to length of service or merit increments.

In the professional category, there are the following levels: P-1 Assistant Officer; P-2 Associate Officer; P-3 Officer; P-4 First Office; P-5 Senior Officer; P-O Principal Officer; D Director[145]. The salaries of the professional category staff are determined by the ICSC and are supplemented by "post adjustment" – sometimes in very substantial amounts representing a very high proportion of the base salary – according to the cost of living in a particular duty station. In the general service there are nine levels – while in the UN and other agencies there are only seven such levels.

---

144   UN document ST/SGB/Staff Rules/1, New York, 2018.
145   In the UN and other specialized agencies such as the ICAO, P-O is designated as D-1 and ICAO D as D-2.

Salaries and emoluments in the professional category are paid in US dollars,[146] in the general service in the local currency of the duty station. Staff in the general category is recruited "locally" and their salary is determined by comparison with the best local employers.

The appointment of staff is an administrative act of the Secretary General and by accepting the "letter of appointment" the staff member is to make a declaration undertaking to be impartial and not to seek or receive instructions from any authority outside the Organization.

Immunities and privileges of the staff of the United Nations system are outlined in the Convention on the Privileges and Immunities of the Specialized Agencies adopted by the UN General Assembly on 21 November 1947. Section 19 of the Agreement refers to officials of specialized agencies and States that they shall:

a. Be immune from legal process in respect of words spoken or written and all acts performed by them in their official capacity;
b. Enjoy the same exemptions from taxation in respect of salaries and emoluments paid to them by the specialized agencies and on the same conditions as are enjoyed by officials of the United Nations;
c. Be immune, together with their spouses and relatives dependent on them, from immigration restrictions and alien registration;
d. Be accorded the same privileges in respect of exchange facilities as are accorded to officials of comparable rank of diplomatic missions;
e. Be given, together with their spouses and relatives dependent on them, the same repatriation facilities in time of international crises as officials of comparable rank of diplomatic missions;
f. Have the right to import free of duty their furniture and effects at time of first taking up their post in the country in question.

Canada, the host State of the Headquarters of ICAO, did not accede to the UN Convention but concluded with ICAO a special Headquarters Agreement in 1951 that was replaced by a new one in 1992, which extended another 20 years on 2013 (from 2016-2036);[147] the scope of immunities and privileges accorded by Canada to ICAO staff is more generous than that offered by the UN agreement; it offers, *inter alia*, full range of diplomatic immunities and privileges to senior ICAO staff from P-4 up. Similar, Headquarters Agreements have been concluded with the host States of the ICAO Regional Offices.

---

146 Starting with the budget for 2008-2009-2010 in Doc 9895, the overall budget is expressed in Canadian dollars (CAD).
147 *Idem.* 7.3.3.

The Headquarters Agreement stresses that it is the duty of all persons enjoying the privileges and immunities to respect the laws and regulations of Canada; they also have the duty not to interfere in the internal affairs of Canada. It also emphasizes that the immunities and privileges are granted in the interests of the Organization and not for the personal benefit of the individuals themselves.[148]

The Organization itself enjoys immunity from legal process and the staff cannot bring their grievances to a local court of law. The Service Code provides machinery for the settlement of such grievances or claims against the decision of the Secretary General in the form of the Advisory Joint Appeals Board (AJAB) composed of the nominees of the Secretary General and of the Staff Association. The AJAB considers the claim, often after an oral hearing and testimony of witnesses, and gives an advisory opinion to the Secretary General. If the Secretary General rejects an opinion favourable to the staff member, there is a possibility of an appeal to the United Nations Administrative Tribunal (UNAT) for a final decision.[149]

According to the latest data,[150] ICAO's total workforce, including all staff, consultants, seconded personnel, gratis personnel and interns comprised 908 individuals representing 108 nations. 285 persons are working in the Professional or higher categories; some of the established posts remain vacant for extended periods of time due to budgetary reasons. By far the largest part of the ICAO budget goes towards the Secretariat services and among them to the language services (translation and interpretation). After the 36th Session of the Assembly in September 2007 a major reduction of the staff and outsourcing of some language functions were accomplished.

The structure of the ICAO Secretariat contains five Bureaus headed by Directors:

Air Navigation Bureau (ANB) – the main "substantive" Bureau that is in charge of technical studies and analyses for the updating the Annexes to the Convention relating to the safety and regularity of air navigations. It provides relevant secretarial services to the Council, Air Navigation Commission, regional and divisional meetings as well as the technical Commission of the Assembly.

Air Transport Bureau (ATB) – studies matter of economic policy, statistics, forecasting, joint financing, facilitation and also – not very logically – matters of aviation security and environment. It provides secretarial services to the Air Transport Committee (ATC), Committee on Unlawful Interference (UIC) and the Joint Support of Air Navigation Services Committee (JSC), and to special conferences and meetings in the air transport

---

148 Article 21 of the Headquarters Agreement with Canada.
149 United Nations Administrative Tribunal – Statute and Rules, UNAT Publication, untreaty.un.org/unat.
150 Annual Report of the Council, Human Resources Management and Gender Equity. 31 December 2021.

field. Similarly, with little logic, this Bureau is in charge of issues related to the environment and to climate change.

Legal Affairs Bureau (LAB) – serves as "in house" legal advisor to the President of the Council, Secretary General and through him to the representative bodies of the Organization and Member States on all constitutional and legal issues, problems of international law and its codification and unification. It conducts research in relevant matters of international law and practice, private law and other items on the General Work Program of the Legal Committee. It provides secretarial services and documentation to the Legal Committee, Diplomatic Conferences, Assemblies, Council and its subordinate bodies. It also performs the depositary functions and registers international agreements on aviation. It also coordinates external relations and legal activities with the UN and the specialized agencies.

Technical Cooperation Bureau (TCB) – is in charge of managing and implementing the technical cooperation/assistance program of the Organization in the "field operations", fellowships and procurement.

Bureau of Administration and Services (ADM) – is by far the largest bureau encompassing Personnel Branch, Conference Services and the Language and Publications Branch. It also provides Assembly and Council secretariat services, information and telecommunications technology, registry, distribution and sales, WEB, library and archives.

Separate from the Bureaus is the Office of the Secretary General (OSG) that is not headed by a Director but is directly responsible to the Secretary General. The OSG includes the Finance Branch, as well as the Regional Affairs Office coordinating the work of the seven Regional offices.

The methods of work of the Secretariat have developed over the years by adopting modern methods of management and electronic data processing. The policy of "zero growth" budget advocated by several States will further keep the personnel establishment at a conservative level, most probably reducing the overall number of staff. The External Auditor controls the proper management policies and their cost effectiveness and makes suggestions for the improvement of the management practices. Similarly, the Joint Inspection Unit of the United Nations makes from time to time a review of the management and administration at ICAO.[151]

In its previous report of 2007, the Joint Inspection Unit[152] noted as undesirable practice that the ICAO Council participates in the appointment of the professional staff at the

---

151 Review of Management and Administration in the International Civil Aviation Organisation (ICAO), JIU/REP/2019/1, www.unjiu.org/news/jiurep20191---review-management-and-administration-international-civil-aviation-organization.
152 JIU/REP/2007/5.

Director (D-2) level and plans to participate also in the appointment at the level of Principal Officer – this practice essentially allows the Council to enter even further into the management responsibilities that would be clearly beyond its mandate. In spite of the JIU position, the Council established, in 2007, the Human Resources Committee and the Council's mandate was extended to include appointments at D-1 category and, since early 2009, any appointment above the P-4 level must be approved in writing by the President of the Council.[153] It is unlikely that the President of the Council would act in such matters without consulting with the representatives on the Council. This approach tends to politicize the recruitment of the staff and, on occasions, favour the applicants from among the representatives on the Council or their protégés. It diminishes the constitutional responsibility of the Secretary General in the selection for senior posts, the choices he can make, as well as his accountability before the Council for his choices.[154]

ICAO has been successful in maintaining a wide geographic representation on the staff and substantive success has also been achieved in the employment of women – even in the most senior positions. As at 31 December 2021, women held 32.28% of posts in the Professional and higher categories and the percentage of women in the General Service category was 75%.[155]

7.3.5.4 ICAO Legal Committee

Over the years of its existence ICAO has become a catalyst and forum for a vast scope of codification and unification of both private and public international air law. Many international instruments – Conventions and Protocols – have been adopted by Diplomatic Conferences of plenipotentiaries convened and held under the auspices of ICAO. Some of these instruments now belong to the most widely accepted instruments of unified international law and are practically universally applicable around the world. In some cases – in particular in the pioneering field of aviation security – the legal work of ICAO commanded universal respect and admiration for its speed and efficiency and became a model for the work in other fields.

In view of the success, international impact and publicity of the legal work in ICAO, it may come as a surprise that the Chicago Convention does not contain any single provision on the legal work of the Organization, does not foresee the existence of the ICAO Legal Committee or the procedure for the adoption of international instruments in the framework of ICAO. The legal work is not mentioned among the objectives of ICAO in Article 44 of the Convention, in Article 49 on the powers and duties of the ICAO Assembly or in Article 54 on the mandatory functions of the Council.

---

153 Quoted from A37-WP/306, EX/71 presented by Saudi Arabia.
154 *Idem.*
155 *Ibid.*, note 151.

There is an obvious historical reason for this *lacuna*, although it is not expressly spelled out in the records of the Chicago Conference of 1944. Since 1926 there has been in existence the CITEJA[156] created on the recommendation of the First International Conference on Private Air Law held in Paris in 1925; the diplomats assembled at that Conference found it out of their depth to draft an instrument on liability in international carriage by air and recommended that it be first considered by "technical experts". CITEJA, composed of experts nominated by States but acting in their personal capacity, made a considerable contribution to the codification of private law and had before it several pending projects when the work was interrupted for many years by the outbreak of World War II.

The Chicago Conference (1944) refrained from drafting specific provisions on the legal work of the future Organization out of respect for the continuing existence of CITEJA and its work in progress. Nevertheless, the Conference adopted a Resolution attached to its Final Act[157] recommending an early resumption of the work of CITEJA and also recommending that "consideration also is given … to the desirability of coordinating the activities of CITEJA with those of the international organization within the field of public international law provided for by this International Civil Aviation Conference".

The 1st Interim Assembly of the Provisional International Civil Aviation Organization (PICAO) on 8 June 1946 adopted a more radical and far-reaching resolution foreseeing the establishment of a "Permanent Committee on International Air Law" after the creation of ICAO; the resolution stated that "it is undesirable that questions of international law, being of intimate concern for the Permanent Organization, should be handled by a body divorced from such Organization".[158]

CITEJA fully agreed with the view of the PICAO Assembly and it held its last working meeting in Cairo in 1946 where it recommended that a Committee on International Air Law be established within ICAO and decided to transmit its archives to the future ICAO. In 1947, at the time of the 1st Session of the ICAO Assembly, CITEJA held its final meeting where it decided on its dissolution.[159]

The 1st Session of the ICAO Assembly adopted Resolution A1-46[160] creating the Legal Committee as "permanent body of the Organization constituted by the Assembly", and approving its Constitution.[161] In Resolution A1-48, the Assembly approved the procedure for approval of draft Conventions.

---

156 *Comite International Technique d'Experts Juridiques Aeriens* (International Technical Committee of Aeronautical Legal Experts).
157 Proceedings, Vol. I, p. 551.
158 Doc 1843, A/47 Resolution XXXI, p. 31; see also A1-LE/1, 21/3/47.
159 R.A. Draper, "Transition from CITEJA to the Legal Committee of ICAO", 42 *AJIL*, (1948) p. 155.
160 Doc 4411, A1-P/45, 3/6/47.
161 The year 2022 marks the 75th anniversary of the establishment of the ICAO Legal Committee by the First Session of the ICAO Assembly (Montreal, 6-27 May 1947). LC/38-WP/7-2, Legal Committee 38th Session,

Under the original Constitution of 1947 the Legal Committee enjoyed considerable independence similar to that of CITEJA. However, the 7th Session of the Assembly held in June-July 1953 in Brighton adopted a revised Constitution of the Legal Committee[162] and a new Procedure for the Approval of Draft Conventions.[163] While the Constitution of the Legal Committee (1953) is still in force, the Procedure for Approval of Draft Conventions on International Air Law was reformulated by the Assemblies.[164] The revised Constitution of the Legal Committee strengthened the authority of the ICAO Council over the Committee and restricted its autonomy.

The Constitution of the ICAO Legal Committee now stipulates (in Articles 1-8):

1. The Legal Committee shall be a permanent Committee of the Organization constituted by the Assembly and responsible to the Council except as otherwise specified herein.
2. The duties of the Committee shall be:
    a. to advise the Council on matters relating to the interpretations and amendment of the Convention on International Civil Aviation, referred to it by the Council;
    b. to study and make recommendations on such matters relating to public international air law as may be referred to it by the Council or the Assembly;
    c. by direction of the Assembly or the Council, or on the initiative of the Committee and subject to prior approval of the Council, to study problems relating to private air law affecting international civil aviation, to prepare drafts of international air law conventions and submit reports and recommendations thereon;
    d. to make recommendations to the Council as to the representation at sessions of the Committee of non-contracting States and other international organizations, as to the coordination of the work of the Committee with that of other representative bodies of the Organization and of the secretariat and also as to such other matters as will be conducive to the effective work of the Organization.
3. The Committee shall be composed of legal experts designated as representatives of and by contracting States and shall be open to participation by all contracting States.

75th Anniversary of the Legal Committee of the ICAO. 10 March 2022.
162 Resolution A7-5.
163 Resolution A7-6; now Resolution A39-11, Appendix B; Doc 7669-LC/139/6.
164 See Resolution A41-4, Appendix B, October 2022.

4. Each contracting State represented in meetings of the Committee shall have one vote.
5. The Committee shall determine, subject to approval of the Council, the general work programme of the Committee and the provisional agenda of each session, provided that the Committee may, during a session, modify the provisional agenda for the better conduct of its work consistently with the provisions of this Constitution. Sessions of the Committee shall be convened at such places and times as may be directed or approved by the Council.
6. The Committee shall adopt rules of procedure. Such rules, and any amendment thereof which affect the relationship of the Committee with other bodies of the Organization or with States or other organizations, shall be subject to approval by the Council.
7. The Committee shall elect its own officers.
8. The Committee may appoint Sub-Committees either to meet concurrently with the Committee or, subject to approval of the Council, at other times and places as it may deem fit.

The text of the Constitution makes it clear that the Legal Committee is fully subject to the authority of the Council – it cannot decide on its work program, cannot meet at a time and place of its preference, and there is in fact very little that is not subject to direction or approval by the Council. The creative freedom and theoretical thinking that prevailed in the CITEJA is now a matter of history.

While the Committee does not have limited membership and is open to all contracting States, the usual participation at the sessions of the Committee is only a fraction of the total number of contracting States.

The Committee should be composed of legal experts and in the earlier years of the Organization some outstanding lawyers made a significant contribution to the legal work of ICAO – among them the renowned legendary Great "G's" – A. Garnault (France), W. Guldimann (Switzerland), C. Gomez Jara (Spain), D.A. Gutiez (Argentina) and G. Guillaume (France) and the longest serving and impressively erudite A.W.G. Kean (United Kingdom). Two of the ex-Chairmen of the Legal Committee – W. Guldimann (Switzerland) and A.W.G. Kean (United Kingdom) – were awarded the "Edward Warner Award" – the highest distinction given by the Council of ICAO for exceptional contribution to international civil aviation. G. Guillaume (France) rose to become Judge and later President of the International Court of Justice. In the evident process of politicization of the law-making functions, in more recent times States have been frequently sending to the Legal Committee, diplomats or other civil servants who are not necessarily experts in air law or even lawyers.

Under Rule 1 of its Rules of Procedure,[165] the Committee shall normally hold an annual session, and additional sessions may be held, if necessary. Under Rule 2, special sessions may be convened by direction of the Council or the Assembly. The reality is different – during the last years the Committee was not convened for extended periods of time and sometimes its legitimate functions were referred to special bodies not foreseen in the Convention, not representative or transparent but more amenable to reach "pragmatic" decisions.[166]

Any Sub-Committee of the Legal Committee is expected to include in its report on a draft Convention an assessment of the measure of agreement reached and capable of being reached between the States upon the problem under consideration, together with its view whether the subject is ripe for consideration by the Legal Committee.[167] This approach permits a mature assessment and direction for further consideration.

The ICAO procedure for approval of draft conventions on international air law prescribes the following steps to be taken:[168]

> 1. Any draft convention which the Legal Committee considers as ready for presentation to States as a final draft shall be transmitted to the Council, together with a report thereon. 2. The Council may take such action as it deems fit, including the circulation of the draft to the contracting States and to such other States and international organizations as it may determine. 3. In circulating the draft convention, the Council may add comments and afford States and organizations an opportunity to submit comments to the Organization within a period of no less than four months. 4. Such draft convention shall be considered with a view to its approval, by a conference which may be convened in conjunction with a session of the Assembly. The opening date of the conference shall be not less than six months after the date of transmission of the draft as provided in paragraphs 2 and 3 above. The Council may invite to such a conference any non-contracting State whose participation it considers desirable, and shall decide whether such participation

---

165 Doc 7669-LC/139/6. 2018.
166 One such example was the Special Group on Modernization and Consolidation of the Warsaw Convention, (SGMW) that bypassed the Legal Committee and whose draft was presented to the Montreal Diplomatic Conference (1999). The 30th Session of the Legal Committee (Report in Doc 9693-LC/190) did not reach convincing conclusions, and there was a need to have its subject studied first by a new Legal Sub-Committee and then again by the Committee itself, but pressure and "political convenience" took the subject from the hands of lawyers representing all contracting States and gave the authority to a group essentially selected by the President of the Council in his discretion.
167 Doc 8704-LC/155, p. 22.
168 Resolution A31-15, Appendix B, most recently A39-11, Appendix B; Doc 7669-LC/139/6.

carries the right to vote. The Council may also invite international organizations to be represented at the conference by observers.

This procedure is based on practical experience, and it should be noted how important the time limits are to give full opportunity to States to give due consideration to any draft and to permit any pre-conference mutual consultations.

The "conference" contemplated by this procedure and many times tested in ICAO's history is not a part of the ICAO constitutional structure. It is a separate and distinct body that – once it meets – is sovereign in all its decisions. ICAO would provide the facilities and services, including documentation and language services, but the conference is composed of plenipotentiaries of special designation, the conference is fully autonomous and is not bound by any drafts presented to it as the result of ICAO studies.

The representatives of States to a conference must present credentials issued by the Head of State, Head of Government or Minister for External Affairs entitling them to participate in the deliberations of the Conference and in the decisions. If a resulting instrument is open for signature at the close of the Conference, it could be signed only by those representatives who present in addition to their credentials also full powers to do so – again issued by the Head of State, Head of Government or the Minister for External Affairs. Some Governments combine the credentials and full powers in one single document.

There have been many conferences of this type in ICAO's history – some time called "International Conference on Air Law" or simply known as "Diplomatic Conference". In the past practice the Secretary General acted as Secretary General of the Conference and the Director of the Legal Bureau as "Executive Secretary".

ICAO has been very productive in international law-making and the Legal Committee since 1947 has prepared drafts which led to the adoption of the following instruments (in chronological order):[169]

– *Convention on the International Recognition of Rights in Aircraft*, signed at Geneva on 19 June 1948.[170]
– *Convention on Damage Caused by Foreign Aircraft to Third Parties on the Surface*, signed at Rome on 7 October 1952.[171]
– *Protocol to Amend the Convention for the Unification of Certain Rules Relating to International Carriage by Air*, signed at Warsaw on 12 October 1929, done at The Hague on 28 September 1955.[172]

---
169 See all in Dick van het Kaar: *International Civil Aviation: Treaties, Institutions and Programmes*, Eleven International Publishing, The Hague, 2019. pp. 1-320.
170 ICAO Doc 9740.
171 ICAO Doc 7364.
172 ICAO Doc 7632.

- *Convention, Supplementary to the Warsaw Convention, for the Unification of Certain Rules Relating to International Carriage by Air Performed by a Person Other than the Contracting Carrier*, signed at Guadalajara on 18 September 1961.[173]
- *Convention on the Offences and Certain Other Acts Committed on Board Aircraft*, signed at Tokyo on 14 September 1963.[174]
- *Convention on the Suppression of Unlawful Seizure of Aircraft*, signed at The Hague on 16 December 1970.[175]
- *Protocol to Amend the Convention for the Unification of certain Rules Relating to International Carriage by Air*, signed at Warsaw on 12 October 1929 as amended by the Protocol done at The Hague on 28 September 1955, signed at Guatemala City on 8 March 1971.[176]
- *Convention for the Suppression of Unlawful Acts Against the safety of Civil Aviation*, signed at Montreal on 23 September 1971.[177]
- *Additional Protocol No. 1 to Amend the Convention for the Unification of Certain Rules Relating to International Carriage by Air*, signed at Warsaw on 12 October 1929, signed at Montreal on 25 September 1975.[178]
- *Additional Protocol No. 2 to Amend the Convention for the Unification of Certain Rules Relating to International Carriage by Air*, signed at Warsaw on 12 October 1929 as Amended by the Protocol done at The Hague on 28 September 1955, signed at Montreal on 25 September 1975.[179]
- *Additional Protocol No. 3 to Amend the Convention for the Unification of Certain Rules Relating to International Carriage by Air*, signed at Warsaw on 12 October 1929 as Amended by the Protocols done at The Hague on 28 September 1955 and at Guatemala City on 8 March 1971, signed at Montreal on 25 September 1975.[180]
- *Montreal Protocol No. 4 to Amend the Convention for the Unification of Certain Rules Relating to International Carriage by Air*, signed at Warsaw on 12 October 1929 as amended by the Protocol done at The Hague on 28 September 1955, signed at Montreal on 25 September 1975.[181]

---

173 ICAO Doc 8181.
174 ICAO Doc 8364.
175 ICAO Doc 8920.
176 ICAO Doc 8932.
177 ICAO Doc 8966.
178 ICAO Doc 9145.
179 ICAO Doc 9146.
180 ICAO Doc 9147.
181 ICAO Doc 9148.

- *Protocol to Amend the Convention on Damage Caused by Foreign Aircraft to Third Parties on the Surface,* signed at Rome on 7 October 1952, signed at Montreal on 23 September 1978.[182]
- *Protocol for the Suppression of Unlawful Acts of Violence at Airports Serving International Civil Aviation, Supplementary to the Convention for the Suppression of Unlawful Acts Against the Safety of Civil Aviation,* done at Montreal on 23 September 1971, signed at Montreal on 24 February 1988.[183]
- *Convention on the Marking of Plastic Explosives for the Purpose of Detection,* done at Montreal on 1 March 1991.[184]
- *Convention for the Unification of Certain Rules for International Carriage by Air,* signed at Montreal on 28 May 1999.[185]
- *Convention on International Interests in Mobile Equipment,* signed at Cape Town on 16 November 2001.[186]
- *Protocol to the Convention on International Interests in Mobile Equipment on Matters Specific to Aircraft Equipment,* signed at Cape Town on 16 November 2001.[187]
- *Convention on Compensation for Damage to Third Parties, Resulting from Acts of Unlawful Interference Involving Aircraft,* done at Montreal on 2 May 2009.[188]
- *Convention on Compensation for Damage to Third Parties,* done at Montreal on 2 May 2009.[189]
- *Convention on the Suppression of Unlawful Acts Relating to International Civil Aviation,* done at Beijing on 10 September 2010.[190]
- *Protocol Supplementary to the Convention for the Suppression of Unlawful Seizure of Aircraft,* done at Beijing on 10 September 2010.[191]
- *Protocol to Amend the Convention on Offences and Certain Other Acts Committed on Board Aircraft,* done at Montreal on 4 April 2014.[192]

Legal work in the framework of ICAO deserves a more formal recognition and regulation in the basic constitutional structure of ICAO – perhaps in a future amendment of the

---

182 ICAO Doc 9257.
183 ICAO Doc 9518.
184 ICAO Doc 9571.
185 ICAO Doc 9740.
186 ICAO Doc 9793; the Conference at Cape Town was held jointly with the International Institute for the Unification of Private Law (UNIDROIT).
187 ICAO Doc 9794.
188 ICAO Doc 9920.
189 ICAO Doc 9919.
190 ICAO Doc 9960.
191 ICAO Doc 9959.
192 ICAO Doc 10034.

Chicago Convention. It also deserves a much higher profile in the Strategic Action Plan of the Organization.

7.3.5.5 Settlement of Differences in ICAO

In the field of civil aviation, like in other international activities conflicts of interests of the States are bound to occur. Conflicting interests may clash to amount to a conflict – a dispute. In general, a dispute may be defined as a situation where one party asserts a claim (entitlement, fact creating liability...) while the other party denies such claim. Peaceful settlement of international disputes has been, at least since the times of the League of Nations, one of the basic aims of the international community.

The Paris Convention Relating to the Regulation of Aerial Navigation (1919) contemplated, for its time, an innovative method of the settlement of disagreements between two or more States.[193] Differences relating to the interpretation of the Convention were to be referred to the Permanent Court of International Justice (to be established by the League of Nations and, until it was established, by arbitration); this amounts to acceptance of compulsory jurisdiction of the Permanent Court of International Justice. Disagreements relating to the technical regulations annexed to the Convention were to be settled by the decision of the International Commission for Air Navigation (ICAN) by a majority of votes.

The Paris Convention thus made a difference between interpretation of the Convention and interpretation of the technical Annexes to the Convention. This difference seems to be justifiable – interpretation of the Convention is a "legal" dispute to be properly adjudicated by a "judicial" (independent, impartial, non-political) body. The current Statute of the International Court of Justice includes among the "legal disputes":[194]

> a) the interpretation of a treaty; b) any question of international law; c) the existence of any fact which, if established, would constitute a breach of an international obligation; d) the nature or extent of the reparation to be made for the breach of an international obligation.

Nevertheless, it must be admitted that even a disagreement on the interpretation of the technical Annexes may amount to a "legal" issue. Any preliminary question whether the difference involves interpretation of the Convention or that of a regulation was to be decided, under the Paris Convention, by arbitration.

The Chicago Convention devotes to the settlement of disputes Chapter XVIII – Articles 84-88. It will be noted that the Convention gives a mandatory power to decide on the

---

193 Article 37 of the Paris Convention (1919).
194 Article 36 (2) (a-d) of the Statute of the International Court of Justice, 26 June 1945.

disputes to the ICAO Council. The Convention does not make any difference between the interpretation of the Convention and the interpretation of the Annexes. The Council of ICAO is thus – unlike the governing bodies of other specialized agencies – also a quasi-judicial body. Only an appeal from the Council's decision would be referred to the International Court of Justice which is thus vested with obligatory jurisdiction.[195]

Article 84
Settlement of disputes
If any disagreement between two or more contracting States relating to the interpretation or application of this Convention and its Annexes cannot be settled by negotiation, it shall, on the application of any State concerned in the disagreement, be decided by the Council. No member of the Council shall vote in the consideration by the Council of any dispute to which it is a party. Any contracting State may, subject to Article 85, appeal from the decision of the Council to an ad hoc arbitral tribunal agreed upon with the other parties to the dispute or to the Permanent Court of International Justice. Any such appeal shall be notified to the Council within sixty days of receipt of notification of the decision of the Council.

Article 85
Arbitration procedure
If any contracting State party to a dispute in which the decision of the Council is under appeal has not accepted the Statute of the Permanent Court of International Justice and the contracting States parties to the dispute cannot agree on the choice of the arbitral tribunal, each of the contracting states parties to the dispute shall name a single arbitrator who shall name an umpire. If either contracting State party to the dispute fails to name an arbitrator within a period of three months from the date of the appeal, an arbitrator shall be named on behalf of that State by the President of the Council from a list of qualified and available persons maintained by the Council. If, within thirty days, the arbitrators cannot agree on an umpire, the President of the Council shall designate the umpire from the list previously referred to. The arbitrators and the umpire shall then jointly constitute an arbitral tribunal. Any arbitral tribunal established under this or preceding Article shall settle its own

---

195 Since the Chicago Convention was drafted prior to the acceptance of the UN Charter, it refers to the Permanent Court of International Justice. Article 37 of the Statute of the International Court of Justice explains: "Whenever a treaty or convention in force provides for reference of a matter to a tribunal to have been instituted by the League of Nations, or to the Permanent Court of International Justice, the matter shall, as between the parties to the present Statute, be referred to the International Court of Justice."

procedure and give its decisions by majority vote, provided that the Council may determine procedural questions in the event of any delay which in the opinion of the Council is excessive.

Under Article 66 of the Convention, the Organization also assumes functions placed upon it by the International Air Services Transit Agreement and by the International Air Transport Agreement drawn up at Chicago on 7 December 1944[196] that refer to the ICAO machinery for the settlement of differences. Similar functions have been assumed by ICAO under the Joint Financing agreements with Denmark and with Iceland.[197] The Paris Multilateral Agreement on Commercial Rights of Non-scheduled Air Services in Europe (1956)[198] also referred to the ICAO machinery for the settlement of differences.

Even some very early post-war bilateral agreements on air services – perhaps in the euphoria favouring international organizations by the end of World War II – provided for the settlement of any differences by the Council of ICAO. However, the Chicago Convention does not contain any constitutional basis for the settlement of differences arising from bilateral agreements and on the basis of the Convention the Council would not be competent to consider disputes based on bilateral agreements. This matter was addressed by the very first Session of the Assembly in 1947 in Resolution A1-23[199] named "Authorization to the Council to act as an arbitral body". That Resolution authorized the Council to act as an arbitral body on any differences arising among contracting States relating to civil aviation matters submitted to it, when expressly requested to do so by all parties to such difference. On such occasions the Council would be authorized to render an advisory report, or a decision binding upon the parties, if the parties expressly decide to obligate themselves in advance to accept the decision of the Council as binding. It is interesting to note that in the more than sixty years of ICAO's existence no dispute was ever referred to the Council for arbitration under the terms of Resolution A1-23.

It is an imperative function of the Council to decide on the disputes referred to it. The words "shall ... be decided" in Article 84 make this role of the Council mandatory – however, as will be seen later – it may not always be practicable. The Convention does not define the procedure to be followed by the Council in the consideration of the disputes and the Council's Rules of Procedure would not adequately cover the necessary specifics. The Council realized the lack of proper procedural guidance in this respect when the very first case under Article 84 of the Convention was brought before it in April 1952 by India against Pakistan.[200] Apart from exhorting the parties to negotiate further and reach an

---

196 ICAO Doc 7500 and PICAO Doc 2187, pp. 71-75.
197 Docs. 9585-JS/681 and 9586-JS/682.
198 ICAO Doc 7695, 30 April 1956.
199 Doc 9848, I. Constitutional and General Policy Matters, p. 19.
200 Doc 7367, p. 74.

amicable solution, the Council did nothing but engaged in long discussions of the proper procedure; finally it agreed on the need to draft special Rules for the Settlement of Differences and such Rules were adopted on 9 April 1957 – five years after India filed its case with the Council![201]

It is a matter of opinion whether the Rules for the Settlement of the Differences are most appropriate for the Council of ICAO. They have been drafted in close alignment with the Rules of the Court of the International Court of Justice[202] and that may be a problem. The Rules of the Court of the ICJ are rules for a truly judicial body composed of independent and (arguably) impartial Judges bound by their oath of office and obliged to follow international law and their conscience. Such is not the situation in the Council of ICAO. The "members" of the Council are sovereign States elected by the Assembly; their representatives on the Council are not independent individuals acting in their personal capacity, but they are diplomatic agents of their respective States and are obliged to follow any instructions received from their States. There is no "judicial detachment" in the Council of ICAO and the Council cannot be compared with the International Court of Justice. Under Article 84 (which is unnecessarily duplicated in the last sentence of Article 53 of the Convention), no representative may vote on a dispute to which his State is a party. Under Article 66 (b), members of the Council whose State is not a party to the Transit or Transport Agreements cannot vote in the Council on matters relating to those Agreements. Moreover, in the Council members may abstain from a decision or absent themselves from a meeting – a liberty not available to the Judges of the Court. It could thus happen that the Council would not even have a sufficient quorum to take any decision.

The Rules for the Settlement of Differences provide a detailed, formal and legalistic procedure suitable for a court of law. The procedure is initiated by the applicant State by filing an application to which is attached a "memorial" indicating the name of the "applicant" and the name of the "respondent", name of the plenipotentiary agent for the applicant, statement of the facts with supporting data, statement of law, the relief desired by action of Council on the specific points submitted and a statement that negotiations to settle the disagreement had taken place between the parties but were not successful. Thereafter, within the time-limit determined by the Council, the respondent State is expected to file a "counter-memorial" answering the points raised in the applicant's memorial, listing additional facts and supporting data and its statement of law. The counter-memorial may also present a counter-claim directly connected with the subject matter of the application.

The respondent is entitled to question the jurisdiction of the Council to handle the matter presented by the applicant and may file a preliminary objection. When such a

---

201 Doc 7782, amended on 10 November 1975. See the full text in Appendix 4 of this book.
202 www.icj-cij.org/documents/index.php?pl=4&p2=3&p3=0.

preliminary objection is filed, the proceedings on the merits are to be suspended until the objection is decided by the Council after hearing the parties.

After the filing of the counter-memorial by the respondent, the Council should decide whether the parties should be invited to enter into direct negotiation. In fact, throughout the procedure and prior to the final decision of the Council the parties are to be urged to engage in direct negotiation to settle their dispute or to narrow the issues.[203]

The written proceedings follow the submission of the counter-memorial by additional pleadings which may be filed by the parties within the time-limits determined by the Council: reply to be filed by the applicant and rejoinder to be filed by the respondent. These filings should include copies or originals of all relevant documents which the parties wish to have considered – and the experience shows that the files of the written proceedings can be extremely voluminous. After the last written pleading no further documents may be submitted by any party except with the consent of the other party or by permission of the Council granted after hearing the parties.

There may follow an oral hearing with testimonies of witnesses or experts and oral arguments of the parties. The decision of the Council should summarize the proceedings and spell out the conclusions of the Council together with its decisions and the reasons for reaching them and a statement of the voting. A member of the Council who voted against the majority opinion may have its views recorded in the form of a dissenting opinion which shall be attached to the decision of the Council.

While the Rules for the Settlement of Differences appear to be rigid, there is one element of flexibility: the Council, subject to agreement of the parties, may suspend or amend the Rules if in its opinion such act would lead to a more expeditious or effective disposition of the case.[204]

It is submitted, with reference to Article 85 of the Convention, that any appeal can be directed only to the International Court of Justice since all ICAO Member States are also members of the United Nations, parties to the Charter of the UN and thus have accepted the Statute of the International Court of Justice; the arbitration alternative is no longer available.

The Convention contains, in Articles 87 and 88, very rigorous sanctions. Under Article 87 contracting States accepted an obligation not to allow the operation of an airline of a contracting State through the airspace above its territory if the Council has decided that the airline concerned is not conforming to a final decision rendered by the Council or, on appeal, by the ICJ. There has not been any instance when this provision would be applied.

---

203 Article 14 of the Rules for the Settlement of Differences.
204 Article 32 of the Rules for the Settlement of Differences.

Under Article 88 the Assembly "shall" (*i.e.*, must) suspend the voting power in the Assembly and in the Council of any contracting State that is found in default under the provisions of Chapter XVIII of the Convention. Again, this provision was never tested in the practice of ICAO, and it would have to be taken by the majority of the Assembly and would be undoubtedly motivated by many policy considerations.

Some commentators have asserted that the Council of ICAO has a true judicial power under Chapter XVIII of the Chicago Convention and that "the Council must consider itself an international judicial organ and act in accordance with rules of international law governing judicial proceedings. Thus, *inter alia*, members of the Council, even though they may be national representatives nominated by Governments must, when functioning under Chapter XVIII of the Chicago Convention, act in an impartial and judicial capacity".[205]

Although this is a view of the most distinguished authority in international law and air law, it cannot be shared since it overlooks not only the wording of the Convention but also the working realities of all international organizations, including those specific for ICAO as observed over the years by this author. In the first place, members of the Council are the sovereign States, not the physical individuals representing them. Such representatives cannot act in an "impartial and judicial capacity"; they are obliged to follow the instructions of their Government.

In any case, a predominant majority of the representatives on the ICAO Council are diplomats or aviation experts rather than lawyers. The Council cannot be considered to be a true judicial body composed of judges who would be acting in their personal capacity and deciding strictly and exclusively on the basis of international law. Since the Council is a policy making body composed of States, the procedure for the settlement of differences under Chapter XVIII of the Convention is not and cannot be a true international adjudication on the basis of international law but rather a sort of "qualified international arbitration" – arbitration *sui generis* – "diplomatic arbitration" conducted by sovereign States. Their decisions may be based on policy or political considerations or equity, rather than on strictly legal rules.

Support for such conclusion comes from the first President of the ICAO Council – Edward Warner – who wrote in April 1945 – full two years before ICAO came into existence: "No international agency composed of representatives of States could be expected to bring judicial detachment to the consideration of particular cases in which large national interests were involved… The Council as a whole can hardly be expected to act judicially".[206] His successor as President of the Council – Walter Binaghi – stated in his farewell speech to the Council in June 1976 that he "had always had doubts about the role

---

205 B. Cheng, *The Law of International Air Transport* (1961), p. 101.
206 Dr E.P. Warner, "The Chicago Air Conference", *Foreign Affairs*, April 1945.

assigned to the Council by Chapter XVIII of the Convention".[207] These views are also shared by leading scholars in the field of international law and air law.[208]

A convincing illustration that the Representatives on the Council do not act in "an impartial and judicial capacity" may be found, *e.g.*, in the Minutes of the Council Meeting held on 29 July 1971, where several Representatives requested a postponement of a vote (in re *Pakistan v. India*) to consult with their respective administrations to obtain instructions.[209] It would be unthinkable for a judge to request "instructions" from a national administration or anybody else.

The history of the attempts within ICAO to apply the machinery of Chapter XVIII during the past more than sixty years is not encouraging. It may be said that the mechanism does not work to anybody's satisfaction and that it has been a failure. Only seven cases were presented to the Council during nearly eighty years of ICAO under Chapter XVIII and in none of them did the Council issue a decision on the merits of the case. The brief history of the cases is as follows:

India v. Pakistan (1952): the Government of Pakistan established in early 1952 a prohibited zone along its western border with Afghanistan and thereby effectively prevented Indian aircraft from flying from the Indian territory to Kabul over Pakistani territory. The Indian Government claimed that the Pakistani action was discriminatory since the airline of Iran was permitted to cross the prohibited area and to fly between Teheran, Kabul and points in Western Pakistan. The Government of India in its submission alleged that Pakistan violated Article 5 (Right of non-scheduled flight), Article 9 (Prohibited areas) of the Convention and the Transit Agreement. It must have been clear to the Council that it was not faced with a simple aeronautical problem but with an issue originating from the tense political relations between India and Pakistan. At the time of the dispute the Council did not have any rules of procedure for the settlement of differences under Chapter XVIII of the Convention and its first step was to create a Working Group to elaborate such Rules, and in the meantime, invited the Governments of Pakistan and India to negotiate an amicable settlement with the assistance, if required, of the Council members. Such a settlement was reached in early 1953 and the Council was informed accordingly. The substance of the settlement was the establishment by Pakistan of special corridors leading across the prohibited zone and enabling Indian aircraft to reach Kabul with minimum re-routement. On 19 January 1953, the Council noted that the disagreement had been

---

207 C-Min. 88/5, pp. 40-41.
208 The priority in this respect belongs to Professor D. Goedhuis – see his "Questions of Public International Air Law" in *Recueil des Cours*, Academie de Droit International (1952-II), p. 205 and pp. 222-225.
209 C-Min 74/6, 29 July 1971.

settled.[210] While the Council took no steps or decisions on the merits of the case, its good offices to bring the parties together could be credited with some success.

U.K. v. Spain (1967): the application and memorial submitted by the Government of the United Kingdom claimed that the Government of Spain established a prohibited zone in the Bay of Algeciras directly opposite to the British airport of Gibraltar and that the extent and location of the prohibited zone would effectively prevent safe take-off and landing manoeuvres to and from the airport of Gibraltar; that was claimed to be a violation of Article 9 of the Chicago Convention since the extent and location of the prohibited zone was not "reasonable" and that it interfered unnecessarily with air navigation. The root of the dispute was a political problem and the prevailing tension between the United Kingdom and Spain with respect to the legal status of Gibraltar that was dealt with also on a bilateral basis and in other fora, including the United Nations.

The ICAO Council was well aware of the underlying political problem and proceeded very slowly, without discussing the substance, through all the formal written proceedings – Memorial by the United Kingdom, Counter-Memorial by Spain, Reply by the United Kingdom and Rejoinder by Spain with additional written submissions. It must have been clear to the parties that due to the patently political nature of the issue underlying the "aeronautical" aspects no decision could be expected from the ICAO Council. In November 1969, the Council noted the following statement by its President: "At the request of the United Kingdom and Spain consideration of the disagreement between those two States relating to the interpretation and application of Article 9 of the Convention would be deferred *sine die*; the question would not be included in the work program for any future session unless there was a request to that effect by a Council member and the Council agreed to it."[211]

This 'inconclusive conclusion" is very unorthodox and technically this case is still pending before the Council; it could be revived at any time. It would have been more appropriate for the parties and for the Council to record discontinuance of the proceedings or to adopt a decision on the merits of aeronautical nature regardless of any political underlying elements. Again, the policy considerations prevailed, and the adversarial type of proceedings were not pressed by the parties or by the Council. This procedure may appear to be incorrect in theory, but the prudent approach of the Council in this matter helped to achieve or preserve an acceptable international *modus vivendi* in the matter without a direct confrontation which any adjudication based exclusively on legal considerations would have undoubtedly entailed. The political sensitivities between the

---

210 Doc 7388-C/860, pp. 30-31.
211 Doc 8903-C/994, p. 27.

Pakistan v. India (1971): in this submission Pakistan in fact presented two cases as one – case I: Application under Article 84 of the Convention and Section 2 of the Transit Agreement; case II: Complaint under Section 1 of Article II of the Transit Agreement. The underlying facts – apart from the continuing political tensions between Pakistan and India were as follows: on 4 February 1971, India suspended all overflight rights of the Indian territory by Pakistani aircraft. Thereby, India effectively cut off any economically feasible air communications between West and East Pakistan (as then existing).

This situation arose against the background of armed hostilities between the two neighbouring countries in 1965 (terminated by the Tashkent Declaration in 1966), continuing tensions relating to the Indian State of Jammu and Kashmir and flared up as a result of a "hijacking", on 30 January 1971, of an Indian aircraft flying on a domestic flight to Jammu (India) and landing it in Lahore (Pakistan). The hijackers were pro-Pakistan Kashmiri nationalists, they asked asylum in Pakistan and requested the release of Kashmiri nationalists imprisoned in India. The hijackers released the passengers and crew of the Indian aircraft but threatened to blow up the aircraft if their demands were not met. It was alleged that the hijackers were actually granted asylum in Pakistan, the local authorities gave them full support, aid and comfort and allegedly supplied them with explosives. Eventually, the hijackers blew up the aircraft with full view and publicity on Pakistani television – a serious provocation for India.

In this case, India did not file a counter-memorial but lodged a preliminary objection questioning the jurisdiction of the ICAO Council to handle the matter. The main contention of India was that the operation of the basic treaties (Chicago Convention and Transit Agreement) had been suspended because of the hostilities in 1965 and their application was not fully revived after the Tashkent Declaration. Furthermore, India relied on Article 89 of the Convention that would grant it "freedom of action" in case of war or national emergency. India also submitted that there was no "dispute" on the interpretation or application of the Conventions since the suspension of those legal instruments was not a matter of "interpretation" or "application". The Council considered this preliminary objection during five tedious meetings in July 1971 and eventually decided to reject the Indian preliminary objection and to confirm that it had jurisdiction to consider the matter.[212] The decision is reflected only in the Minutes of the Council meeting, not in a special document as a "decision" under Article 84 of the Convention. The Minutes indicate the result of the vote but do not spell out any arguments or reasons for the decision.

---

212 C-Min. 74/6.

India appealed this decision on the preliminary objection to the International Court of Justice which issued its decision on 18 August 1972.[213] The Court did not deal with the merits of the case but, by a vote of 14 to 2, held that the ICAO Council was competent to deal with the merits of the Application and Complaint since there was a disagreement on the interpretation and application of the legal instruments; the decision is also critical of the ICAO procedure, in particular the lack of reasons for the Council's decision.[214] India in due course filed its Counter-Memorial on the merits accompanied by a counter-claim; however, the proceedings did not continue. In the meantime, Bangladesh emerged as a new State replacing East Pakistan and the case became to a large degree moot. On 20 July 1976 India and Pakistan by a joint statement discontinued the proceedings before the Council and the case is closed without any decision of the Council or the ICJ on the merits.

Like in the previous two cases, it is apparent that the centre of gravity of the dispute was of a political nature and that the "aviation" aspect could not be meaningfully addressed without a more general solution of the underlying political issues. That, of course, is not within the purview of the ICAO Council.

Cuba v. United States (1998): the decades of tense relations between Cuba and the United States brought about one of the crises on 26 February 1996. On that day, Cuban Air Force MIG-29 and MIG-23 shot down two US registered Cessna 337 over the high seas killing three US citizens and one US resident. The light US aircraft were operated by "Hermanos al Rascate" (Brothers to the Rescue) – an organization of Cuban émigrés who from time to time operated flights over Cuba to distribute anti-Castro leaflets; however, on this particular day the aircraft did not enter the Cuban airspace.

Reprisals followed in the form of legislation tightening the commercial embargo and overflights of US territory by Cuban aircraft were prohibited. That patently violated Article 5 of the Chicago Convention and the International Air Services Transit Agreement, to which both Cuba and the United States are parties. In fact, in spite of the tense relations over a long time, US carriers have been operating scores of flights daily over Cuban airspace and duly paid for the air navigation services rendered. Cuba filed a complaint under the Transit Agreement with the Council of ICAO.

On the request of the UN Security Council, ICAO investigated the incident of 26 February 1996 and reached a conclusion that the US aircraft were destroyed over the high seas and not in the Cuban airspace. However, that was unrelated to the substance of the Cuban claim before the Council. The political overtones of the situation discouraged

---

213 International Court of Justice, Reports of Judgments, *Appeal Relating to the Jurisdiction of the ICAO Council (India v. Pakistan)*, Judgement of 18 August 1972.
214 Paragraph 44 of the Judgment and opinions of Judges Lachs and Petren.

the Council from direct dealing with the dispute and it called on and the parties agreed to discontinuation of the proceedings.[215] It is gratifying to note that in spite of this isolated incident Cuba has, by the turn of the century, adhered to all aviation security conventions and ratified Article 3*bis* of the Chicago Convention.[216]

Yet another example that Chapter XVIII does not offer an effective mechanism for the settlement of international disputes within ICAO!

United States v. European Union (2000): the last formal dispute so far presented to the ICAO Council under Chapter XVIII of the Convention was directed by the United States against (then) all fifteen members of the European Union since the EU itself could not be a respondent under Article 84 of the Chicago Convention, although it was the EU Regulation that triggered the dispute.[217] That Regulation had a long name "…on the registration and operation within the Community of certain types of civil subsonic jet aeroplanes which have been modified and recertified as meeting the standards of volume I, Part II, Chapter 3 of Annex 16 to the Convention on International Civil Aviation, third edition (July 1993)". In plain language, the subject of the Regulation was a flagrant departure from ICAO Annex 16 that would not prevent aircraft of "Chapter 2" noise level to be modified (*e.g.*, through the so called "hush kitting") to achieve the "Chapter 3" noise certification. The EU wished to eliminate from its airspace as of 1 April 2002 any "recertified civil subsonic jet aeroplanes" that it defined as "civil subsonic jet aeroplane initially certified to Chapter 2 or equivalent standards or initially not noise-certified which has been modified to meet Chapter 3 standards either directly through technical measures or indirectly through operational restrictions".[218] While the direct idea may have been to reduce the noise level in the European airspace, it did not concern the aircraft fleets of European States manufactured by European manufacturers specifically to meet Chapter 3 standards.

On the other hand, all B-707, most B-727 and the initial B-737 and DC-9 of US manufacture – although hush kitted to comply with Chapter 3 noise certification and having still a long, economic and meaningful operational life – would not be admissible in Europe if their engines' by-pass ratio was lower that "three to one". The core of the dispute in fact was whether the "by-pass" ratio of the engines was the real benchmark for the assessment of the noise level. Many US air carriers' aircraft would have been directly facing elimination from the European airspace; similarly, some US manufacturers of aircraft, engines and hush kits would have suffered economic losses.

---

215 C-Min/161-6, C-Min 163-17, C-Min 164-11 and C-Min 166-12.
216 See icao.int/secretariat/legal/status%20individual%States/Cuba_es.pdf.
217 Council Regulation (EC) No. 925/1999 of 29 April 1999; Official Journal of the European Communities L.115/1-4.
218 Article 2 (2) of the Council Regulation 925/1999.

The States of the EU filed a preliminary objection to the jurisdiction of the Council, *inter alia* claiming that negotiations have not been exhausted. The Council unanimously asserted its jurisdiction; European States did not appeal that decision and submitted their counter-memorial on the merits. However, negotiations continued with the "good offices" of the President of the Council and the parties reached an agreement. The EU repealed the Regulation 925/1999 by Directive 2002/30 0f 26 March 2002 and the parties agreed to discontinuation of the proceedings.[219] Global policy on the matter of noise was adopted by the 33rd Session of the ICAO Assembly[220] that called for "balanced approach" to issues of noise that would take account of the underlying economic implications.

Thus again, the ICAO machinery did not produce a decision in the dispute of major proportions and economic and operational implications. Did Chapter XVIII of the Convention prove useless? Should it be drastically amended if and when a review conference is convened? Could the current machinery of the Council be replaced by a body of elected arbitrators or judges who would be able to act with due judicial detachment? In theory many variants can be considered but it is in practice quite unlikely that States would be ready to submit their differences to any form of final adjudication on a compulsory basis. However, imperfect the current machinery may be, it is available to States and its existence can act as a "deterrent" that it could be used with all the undesirable publicity and further inflame the adversarial attitudes – unless States use their best effort to find a solution through their direct negotiation. Even under the current deficient machinery the Council can act in a positive manner if it provides "good offices" or acts as a quasi-mediator.

Brazil v. United States (2016): There were intensive negotiations in the dispute between the Brazilian Applicant and the Respondent from the United States relating to the collision of the Gol Transportes Aéreos (G3) Brazil air carrier – operating a regular flight with a brand new B-737-8EH, – and the ExcelAire Services, Inc. company – operating a flight with a brand new executive Embraer Legacy 600 (N600XL) jet – on 29 September 2006. The two aircraft collided as they were flying at the same altitude (FL370 = 11.277,6 m) in opposite directions and the transponder of the Embraer Legacy was not functioning so the equipment of the traffic collision avoidance system (TCAS) on neither of the planes alerted the crew. In the catastrophe, the passengers and the crew of the G3 airline, altogether 154 persons lost their lives. The private jet performed a safe emergency landing.[221]

The Parties had a long dispute about "the interpretation and application of the Chicago Convention and its Annexes". On 27 March 2017, the Respondent submitted a Statement

---

219 C-Min/161-6, C-Min 163-17, C-Min 164-11 and C-Min 166-12.
220 Resolution A33-7.
221 Aviation Safety Network, aviation-safety.net/database/record.php?id=20060929-0.

of preliminary objection to the Application. On 19 May 2017, the Applicant submitted Comments on the Statement of preliminary objection. After hearing the Parties, the Council Representatives decided with 4 votes in favour, 19 against and 11 abstentions not to accept the Respondent's preliminary objection.[222] The Parties continued to make progress but later suspended the process and at the 40th Session of the ICAO Assembly (2019), Brazil and the United States submitted a paper on State cooperation under Article 12 of the Chicago Convention.[223] The dispute has not been finally settled.

Qatar v. Bahrain, Egypt, Saudi Arabia and United Arab Emirates (2017): The dispute arose due to the acts of four States (Respondents) ordaining the full blockade on 5 June 2017 against Qatar (Applicant) on water, land and in the national airspace.[224] It implied that from the viewpoint of aviation, Qatar could not use the national airspaces of the neighbouring States and was obliged to fly towards Iran and Turkey.

The ICAO Council considered and approved the request submitted by Qatar pursuant to Article 54 n) of the Chicago Convention[225] to schedule an Extraordinary Session for the consideration of the activities of the closure of their airspaces before aircraft registered in Qatar by Bahrain, Egypt, Saudi Arabia and the United Arab Emirates.[226] Qatar instituted legal proceedings with reference to the Chicago Convention (Articles 1, 4, 57, 84) and to the International Air Services Transit Agreement (IASTA) (Section 2 of Article II), while later, in relation to the blockade Qatar sued the United Arab Emirates before the International Court of Justice for the violation of human rights (mainly discrimination).[227] The Respondents submitted a preliminary complaint vis-a-vis the proceedings to be conducted before the ICAO Council, which was dismissed. Against the decision of the Council, the Respondent States took recourse to the International Court of Justice (ICJ) and pleaded for the establishment of the nullity of the ICAO decision. On 14 July 2020, the International Court of Justice dismissed the action of the Respondent States unanimously and established that the final ruling can be brought by the ICAO Council as a body with jurisdiction.[228] Finally, the Council of ICAO does not need to bring a decision as the

---

222 ICAO Annual Report 2017, ICAO Council 211th and 212th Sessions, www.icao.int/annual-report-2017.
223 Legal Commission A40-WP/101, LE/3, 24 July 2019.
224 The announcement said: "with immediate effect and without any previous negotiation or warning that Qatar-registered aircraft are not permitted to fly to or from the airports within their territories and would be barred not only from their respective national airspaces, but also from their Flight Information Regions (FIRs) extending beyond their national airspaces, even over the high seas violates the Chicago Convention".
225 Consider any matter relating to the Convention which any contracting State refers to it.
226 The 10th Meeting of the Council on ICAO, 211th Session, 31 July 2017.
227 International Convention on the Elimination of All Forms of Racial Discrimination (ICERD). UN, New York, 21 December 1965.
228 ICJ – Appeal Relating to the Jurisdiction of the ICAO Council under Article 84 of the Convention on International Civil Aviation *(Bahrain, Egypt, Saudi Arabia and United Arab Emirates v. Qatar)*. The Hague, 14 July 2020, www.icj-cij.org/en/case/173.

blockade was lifted due to the agreement reached at the 41ˢᵗ Gulf Cooperation Council Summit in Al Ula[229] on 5 January 2021.

7.4 Does the Chicago Convention Require Modernization?

The Convention was drafted with foresight that commands full respect. It endured – without substantive amendments – for over seventy-eight years. However, each international instrument is no more than a "snapshot" of a particular time of its drafting, of the social relations existing at that time and of the specific agreed balance of the conflicting interests achieved by the original parties at that time. During the last more than seventy years the world has changed dramatically in many fields – geopolitical, technical, social and economic. Many new States have emerged on the map of the world that did not exist as independent entities by 1944. Cold War marked the world relations for over forty years and its end offers many new opportunities and challenges. The aviation technology leaped ahead from the DC-3 – the workhorse of civil aviation by 1944 – to jet aircraft of several generations succeeding each other at a fast pace, including the wide-bodied aircraft capable of reaching any point on the Earth without refuelling; supersonic flight has been tested as technically feasible, albeit not yet economical as a means of mass transport. Hypersonic and suborbital flights are also slowly becoming the part of the life of humankind. The world progresses towards globalized economy in which the national borders and the nationality marks of aircraft will have only diminishing relevance. New problems and challenges have arisen that could not be foreseen more than seventy years ago – criminal acts against the safety of civil aviation, growing concern for the environmental protection, application of space technology for air traffic management, growing need for technical cooperation or assistance to assure global safety of civil aviation, electronic data processing that finds its application in airline management processes and also could change the working methods of the ICAO Secretariat, etc.

In 1944, the Convention was adopted by only fifty-two States out of the current 193 Parties; that means that only some 27% of the current membership had any direct influence on the drafting of the Convention while the remaining 141 States (73%) adhered to the Convention without having any role in its drafting.

The UN Charter drafted only few months after the Chicago Convention has a provision on the convening of a General Conference of the Members of the United Nations for the purpose of reviewing the Charter.[230] There is no similar provision in the Chicago Convention but nothing prevents the ICAO Member States from convening such a general

---

229 Al Ula one of the oldest cities in the Arabian Peninsula and home to Saudi Arabia's first UNESCO World Heritage Site: Hegra.
230 Article 108 of the UN Charter.

review Conference or to devote one of its Assemblies to a general revision and updating of the Convention.

It may be argued that on the one hand, there is no need for any general review of the Convention since it has served ICAO well for almost 80 years and can flexibly accommodate the interpretation of any new developments or contingencies. On the other hand, it can be argued that any "creative" interpretation could go contrary to the original meaning of the Convention, distort the scope of the consensus of States or lead to a lack of the legal certainty that it is supported by all contracting States.

The constitutional framework of ICAO would evidently benefit from major modernization both in the practice and in amended provisions of the Convention.

The Assembly should be restored to the true position of the main body of the organization. ICAO is the only organization within the UN system that maintains a triennial cycle for the Assembly. Some empowering of the Assembly can be achieved by arranging for a regular session of the Assembly every two years for a period of three weeks,[231] in line with other United Nations system organizations – a proposal strongly formulated also by the Joint Inspection Unit of the United Nations after its evaluation of ICAO in May 2007[232] for several reasons: in the first place, the Assembly would be more in charge of the Organization's effective decision-making and general governance, supervise the program and control the work of the Council; contracting States would get more frequently together to discuss their mutual problems and formulating the ICAO policy; the budgets would be prepared for a more reasonable period of two years – the current budgeting for three years in advance could often be a blind exercise that cannot take realistically into account the currency fluctuations or urgent exigencies arising for the work of the Organization. More frequent use should be made of the extraordinary sessions of the Assembly rather than of various "Conferences" or "High-Level Conferences" that have no constitutional status under the Convention and, unlike the Assembly, cannot give binding instructions to the Council.[233]

Similarly, the sessions of the Council – a rare "permanent" body within the UN system – and of the subordinate bodies should be limited to no more than two sessions per year and the Council should not waste its time by considering matters that are traditionally within the purview of the executive management (*i.e.*, Secretary General).

---

231 In 2013, the Council Permanent Representative of Saudi Arabia raised this issue, but it was not supported. ICAO Assembly A37-WP/305, Proposal to hold ICAO Assembly Sessions Every Two Years, under Agenda Item 21: Increasing the efficiency and effectiveness of the ICAO and Proposal to hold Assembly Sessions every two years. A38-WP/18 EX 13, Item 20, 2013.
232 JIU/REP/2007/5.
233 Under Article 54 b) of the Chicago Convention the Council is obliged "to carry out the directions of the Assembly".

The high number of meetings of the Council and the subordinate bodies and the vast amount of documentation prepared for them also lead to exorbitant language translation and interpretation expenses and high cost of conference services. The 2007 Joint Inspection Unit's Report critically indicated that 21.5% of ICAO's budget accounts for language services and publication.[234] According to the latest report, the overall budget allocated for conference and language services has been reduced from 16.7% in the budget for the triennium 2008-2010 to 13.6% in that of 2017-2019. Still, language services remain by far the largest expenditure for the organization in terms of programme support.[235]

The time has also come that ICAO may consider redefining the role of the President of the Council. He should not be a salaried international civil servant with ill-defined jurisdictional delimitation from the Secretary General but one of the Representatives elected – possibly on a rotational basis – who would not interfere with the performance of the executive functions of the Organization but remain strictly within the powers defined in the Convention's Article 51. The Organization did not benefit from the thirty years with one President who accumulated powers and influence not foreseen in the Chicago Convention and relegated the Secretary General to the position of a "glamorous" Director of Administration (even that under President's supervision and authority).

Any future revision of the Convention should attempt to fill some evident "lacunae" issues that were not foreseen or were even unforeseeable by 1944 when the Convention was drafted but that have become an essential part of the work of the Organization:

Technical assistance/Cooperation: technical assistance (now, for political correctness called "technical cooperation") has become over the years an integral part and "permanent priority of ICAO that complements the role of the Regular programme in providing support to States in the effective implementation of SARPs and Air Navigation Plans (ANPs), as well as in the development of their civil aviation administration infrastructure and human resources".[236] Although there is no word about technical assistance in the Convention, this activity is administered by a self-standing Bureau headed by a Director (Technical Cooperation Bureau – TCB) and some seventy-three staff members that required, in 2003, additional office space in a building adjacent to ICAO Headquarters.

The origins of the technical cooperation program within ICAO are obscured to most delegations and even the senior members of the Secretariat since the program started slowly and almost invisibly through a very vague patchwork of decisions taken more than

---

234 JIU/REP/2007/5, p. 13, paragraph 77.
235 JIU/REP/2019/1, Review of Management and Administration in the International Civil Aviation Organization (ICAO), p. vii; *Ibid.*, note 151.
236 Resolution A35-20, Update of the new policy on technical cooperation, October 2004.

fifty years ago – by the UN Economic and Social Council (ECOSOC),[237] the UN General Assembly, the ICAO Council[238] and ICAO Assembly[239] approving Council's decision that ICAO should participate in the EPTA (Expanded Program of Technical Assistance) as an executing agency.

The projects were initially funded by the United Nations Development Program (UNDP) and ICAO costs were refunded to it in the form of the Administrative and Operational Services Costs (AOSC) – a determined percentage amount of each project to cover ICAO "overhead" and, at times, creating a healthy surplus for the TCB that gave it the best equipment and amenities within the Secretariat. There were instances of cash flow problems for the organization and the Secretary General was able to borrow money for salaries of the staff from the AOSC funds.

The UNDP funding has gradually decreased to the current insignificant portion to be replaced by funds provided by the assisted States themselves. The TCB went into major deficits on the AOSC that were temporarily covered from the accumulated surplus of the previous years. When that surplus was exhausted, the ICAO Assembly intervened by succeeding resolutions[240] essentially approving measures that would cover any shortfalls in the TCB financing from the regular budget and aim at progressive integration of the TCB into the organizational regular structure of the Secretariat.

The gradual step-by-step "creeping" of the Technical Cooperation Program into the Regular Program and Budget – with financial implications for States – seems to have gone almost unnoticed by the States. It is important to stress that the Technical Cooperation Program under whatever name is very important in assisting States to implement their obligations under the SARPs. However, there is no constitutional and legal basis for this program and no amount of alleged "flexibility" in the interpretation of the Convention could possibly accommodate this additional activity, financial obligations and institutional structure. The Convention should be modernized and updated to give a formal constitutional basis to technical assistance/cooperation.

Aviation security: at the Chicago Conference (1944) the delegations were aware of the ongoing war in Europe and in the Pacific and were anticipating that international peace would be achieved soon. Unlawful acts committed by individuals (not by States) against the safety of civil aviation and its facilities – in the form of unlawful seizure of aircraft

---

237 ECOSOC *Expanded Program of Technical Assistance for Economic Development of Under-Developed Countries*, ECOSOC Doc 222 (IX), 15 August 1949.
238 8th Session of the Council, December 1949.
239 Resolution A4-20, ICAO Doc 7017 (1950) – declared to be no longer in force by the 16th Session of the Assembly in 1968.
240 Resolutions A29-20, A31-14, A32-21, A35-20, A40-24 and A41-21, Consolidated statement of ICAO policies on technical cooperation and technical assistance, Appendix A, 8, 2022.

("hijacking"), sabotage of aircraft or of aeronautical facilities, communication of false information endangering safety of aircraft, violent acts at airports serving international civil aviation, misuse of civil aviation for criminal purposes, etc. – were not even imagined during the drafting of the Convention in 1944.

However, in the second half of the 20th century such acts became a critical and worldwide challenge for civil aviation and was capable to undermine the public confidence in the safety of this vital means of transport. ICAO Member States responded to the challenge by initiating a spectrum of aviation security instruments adopted with maximum dispatch and in a rare harmony by diplomatic conferences convened by ICAO. These legal instruments currently belong to the most widely accepted unifications of law on the global level.[241] Moreover, the SARPs and the Security Manual were developed with urgent priority and are constantly being updated and modernized.

An abortive attempt was made in 1973 to adopt a) either an additional Convention or Protocol that would provide for sanctions against States not respecting their obligations under the aviation security conventions; or b) a major amendment of the Chicago Convention that would make the security obligations an integral part of the Chicago Convention. This alternative was presented because the Legal Committee was not able to decide clearly for one or the other course of action. For that reason, two types of meetings were convened simultaneously in Rome on 28 August-21 September 1973:

– the 20th (Extraordinary) Session of the Assembly to consider the amendments of the Chicago Convention under Article 94 of the Convention; and
– separate Diplomatic Conference to consider any new Convention or protocol on aviation security.

The Diplomatic Conference was a complete failure since it did not adopt any instrument. The Assembly did not fare better: it had for consideration draft amendment to the Chicago Convention that would have inserted into the Convention a new Chapter XVI *bis* entitled: "Supplementary Provisions to Improve the Safety of International Civil Aviation" and that new Chapter would have included new Articles 79*bis*, 79*ter*, 79*quarter*, 79*quinquies*, 79*sexies* and 79*septies* dealing with the duties of States to prevent acts against the safety of civil aviation, to suppress them, to cooperate with other States and with ICAO and that would eventually make The Hague Convention on the Suppression of Unlawful Seizure of Aircraft of 1970 and the Montreal Convention for the Suppression of Unlawful Acts Against the Safety of Civil Aviation of 1971 an integral part of the Chicago Convention by reference. Two of the proposed new Articles obtained the required majority of two-thirds of the Assembly, the other did not; a vote on the proposal as a whole also failed.[242]

---

241 See Chapter 8 below, Legal Management of Aviation Security.
242 ICAO Doc 9087, A20-Res, P-Min.

It must be understood that 1973 was not an easy time in international relations and the Cold War was an acutely sore reality. Moreover, the 20th (Extraordinary) Session of the Assembly was marred by the fact, that a few days prior to the opening of the Assembly – on 10 August 1973 – Israeli military aircraft violated the Lebanese airspace and forcibly seized a Lebanese civil aircraft chartered by Iraqi Airways. The ICAO Council condemned Israel for its action on 20 August 1973 and the Assembly placed this item on its agenda and after extensive and animated discussions adopted Resolution A20-1 strongly condemning Israel.[243] The atmosphere of the session was not conducive to quiet drafting and seeking compromise. Nevertheless, the underlying idea was sound and did not lose its validity even now.

It should be also remembered that the 17th Extraordinary Session of the Assembly in Montreal adopted resolution A17-21 in which it requested the Council "to arrange for a study, taking account of existing conventions or conventions to be concluded, on the desirability of revising the Convention on International Civil Aviation with a view to including therein specific provisions covering acts of unlawful interference in order to afford better protection to international civil aviation".[244] There is no record that the Council ever took an action on this resolution. During any revision of the Chicago Convention new provisions should be considered defining the commitment of States to prevent and suppress acts of unlawful interference with civil aviation, to cooperate mutually among them and with ICAO in matters of aviation security. The principles of the aviation security instruments prepared under the auspices of ICAO should be an integral part of the renewed Chicago Convention. The security provisions are set forth in Annex 17 (taking effect in 1975).[245]

Protection of the environment: environmental protection is gradually becoming one of the top priorities in the work program of ICAO. These issues were not foreseeable at the time of the Chicago Conference and they gained their importance with the swift evolution of the industrial activities and output in the second half of the 20th century all around the world, including the former colonial countries.

The production of electric energy by thermal power plants together with refineries, chemical and metallurgical industry and with the millions of new automobiles on the roads resulted in growing pollution of the human environment, clouds of smoke in industrial areas and smog in the cities endangering the quality of life and threatening the health of the population. The "green" initiatives gained growing political weight in many

---

243 A20-WP/12. Draft Resolution, 29 August 1973; Resolution A20-1, Diversion and seizure by Israeli military aircraft of a Lebanese civil aircraft (1973).
244 Doc 8895, Resolution A17-21, Revision of the Convention on International Civil Aviation, p. 31.
245 Annex 17 on Security was adopted by the ICAO Council in March 1974. ICAO Annex 17, Security – Safeguarding International Civil Aviation against Acts of Unlawful Interference, 11th ed., March 2020.

countries and the international community started taking active interest in the protection of the environment.

The United Nations addressed the environmental issues for the first time on 30 July 1968 at the 45th Session of ECOSOC that recommended to the General Assembly to convene a conference on "problems of the human environment".[246]

The first identified problem of environmental pollution connected with aviation was the noise, in particular in the vicinity of airports. ICAO took an early initiative at the 16th Session of the Assembly in Buenos Aires in September 1968 addressing the subject of aircraft noise in the vicinity of airports and urging the Council to convene an international conference and to adopt international specifications and guidance materials relating to aircraft noise.[247]

The Special Meeting on Aircraft Noise in the Vicinity of Aerodromes met in Montreal in November-December 1969 and made recommendations on the measurement of aircraft noise, aircraft noise certification, noise abatement procedures and land use control. The Council then adopted Annex 16 – Aircraft Noise, which was later expanded under the title "Environmental Protection" to encompass also provisions on aircraft engine emissions.

Since its 35th Session, the ICAO Assembly has been adopting a "Consolidated statement of continuing ICAO policies and practices related to environmental protection"[248] such as outlining the policies on the development of SARPs, land-use planning and management, environmental impact of civil aviation on the atmosphere, later added to new resolutions about noise and local air quality,[249] climate change,[250] Carbon Offsetting and Reduction Scheme for International Aviation (CORSIA),[251] etc. Special emphasis is placed on "balanced approach"[252] opposing unilateral or uncoordinated noise restrictions and taking into account the economic impact of premature forced replacement of earlier types of aircraft, in particular for the operators from developing countries. Engine emissions will become a matter for heightened attention since the carbon dioxide and oxides of nitrogen ("greenhouse gas") contained in the engine emissions are considered the chief cause of ozone layer depletion and growing global warming. A unilateral action of the European Union to introduce an "Emission Trading Scheme" (ETS)[253] faced a negative reaction from

---

246 On 3 December 1968, the General Assembly adopted Resolution 2398 (XXIII) convening the UN Conference on the Human Environment in Stockholm in 1972 and creating the United Nations Environment Programme (UNEP).
247 Resolution A16-3: Aircraft Noise in the Vicinity of Airports.
248 Resolution A35-5.
249 Resolution A41-20, Appendixes A-H (2022).
250 Resolution A41-21.
251 Resolution A41-22.
252 Guidance material in ICAO Doc 9829.
253 The European Union Emissions Trading Scheme (EU ETS) is the world's first and so far the largest installation-level 'cap and trade' system for cutting greenhouse gas (GHS) emissions.

many non-European States and, as a face-saving operation, was "temporarily suspended" in 2012.[254]

However, among ICAO Member States there is no clear consensus yet on the methods of controlling the impact of civil aviation on the environment and minimizing the carbon footprint. The cleavage of opinions was manifested at the 37th Session of the Assembly,[255] 56 delegations filed a reservation to a resolution that exhorted States to take specific action, albeit in a differentiated manner according to their capabilities and circumstances. It was unprecedented that a Resolution of the Assembly would be accompanied by a long list of reservations. The situation did not change at the Assembly Session in 2013,[256] where 62 delegations filed reservations.[257] The 2016 Session of the Assembly made progress towards a general acceptance of some market-based system in the form of an "emission trading system". Much was expected from the 39th Session of the Assembly, for which a "High-level Group" had been preparing an "Aviation Global Market-Based Measure"; a draft Resolution for the Assembly was prepared by another "High-level Meeting" open to all ICAO States, which was scheduled for 11-13 May 2016. (It must be noticed that the creation of "high-level" groups and Conferences with fancy titles have no constitutional basis in the Chicago Convention. An Extraordinary Session of the Assembly would be the proper constitutional forum for issues of such importance.)

Aviation – domestic, international, both civil and military – is responsible for only about more than 2% of the CO2 emissions, a small but potentially growing part of overall emissions.[258] Environmental protection is a matter of general concern and any revision of the Chicago Convention should confirm as a legal commitment of States the duty to protect the environment from aircraft noise and engine emissions in a coordinated and balanced manner determined by the Organization; at the same time States should accept an obligation not to introduce unilateral measures that would in any manner jeopardize the operation of foreign aircraft. Alternatively, ICAO should prepare a separate Convention in which States would accept specific obligations for the protection of the environment, as well as procedures for the market-based measures.[259] Eventually, at the 39th ICAO Assembly the Member States adopted the Global Market-Based Measure (GMBM) Scheme, which

---

254 M. Milde, "The EU Emissions Trading Scheme – Confrontation or Compromise?", 61 ZLW, 2012, pp. 173-186.
255 Resolution A37-19.
256 Resolution A38-18, Consolidated statement of continuing ICAO policies and practices related to environmental protection – Climate change, September 2013.
257 In spite of the vast differences of opinions and reservations to the Resolution, on 12 May 2016, an ICAO source labelled the 2013 Resolution as a "landmark Resolution" (Air Transport News, 12/0-5/2016).
258 IATA has a "tongue-in-cheek" message "Danger CO2W" message with a picture of a cow on the webpage iata.org/whatwedo/environment/campaign/cow.htm, accessed on 7 December 2007; it claims that the share of airlines to atmospheric pollution is "less than the CO2 produced worldwide by cattle …".
259 Extensive and up-to-date analysis will be found in A. Piera Valdes, "*Greenhouse Gas Emissions from International Aviation*", Eleven International Publishing, The Hague, 2015, 498 pages.

after 2020 requires the Member States to force back carbon-dioxide (CO2) emissions in aviation in several phases (in the first phase voluntarily). Thus, the representatives of the air transport industry reached consensus for the design of aviation Market-Based Measures as an emissions mitigation tool, aviation with these steps has become the first among the major industry sectors to initiate meaningful global action.[260]

CNS/ATM – Global Navigation Satellite Systems (GNSS): the communication, navigation and surveillance (CNS) technology has developed fast after 1944, but the terrestrial systems have reached their limits of range and precision and new solutions had to be found in the "Future Air Navigation Systems" (FANS) now defined in the satellite-based system for the CNS and Air Traffic Management (ATM).

The GNSS is an electronic type of radio-navigation and positioning based on a range measurement from a satellite signal (timed by a precise atomic clock) whose arrival timing is measured by high precision GNSS receivers on board the aircraft or on the ground; by measuring the arrival time of the signal from three or more satellites (the position of which is known with precision), the receiver can determine its range from those satellites and hence its position in three dimensions and in real time. The GNSS is considered the backbone of the CNS/ATM system and is expected to evolve as the sole means of navigation on the global basis for terminal, en route, non-precision approach and landing and – with appropriate augmentations and overlays (provided by a Wide Area Augmentation System, Local Area Augmentations and differential readings) – for precision approach and landing, possibly in zero visibility.

If the GNSS is to become the "sole" means of navigation, would it replace other electronic aids, including VOR/DME, Loran-C, Omega, Inertial Navigation System, Inertial Reference System, etc.? Would it replace them on a "global" scope? Only time will show whether some "back-up" system will not be always needed since the GNSS signal could be vulnerable.

At present there are two systems of the GNSS, one provided by the United States (NAVSTAR GPS), the other by the Russian Federation (Global Orbiting Satellite Navigation System – GLONASS). Both systems were originally designed for military uses and the US GPS vastly dominates among the various users (aviation is deemed to amount to some 2% of GPS use). A third system – Galileo – is planned by the European Union and the European Space Agency (ESA), which should rival the GPS in precision and continuing availability (the full Galileo constellation will consist of 24 active satellites); however, it was plagued by financial uncertainties and its full operational availability is expected with the next generation of satellites after 2025. The GNSS are a new development unforeseeable

---

260 Resolution A39-3, Consolidated statement of continuing ICAO policies and practices related to environmental protection, Global Market-based Measure (MBM) Scheme, September 2016.

at the time of the Chicago Conference in 1944.[261] The ICAO Legal Committee concluded that there was "no fundamental legal obstacle to the implementation and achievement of the CNS/ATM concept" and that there was "nothing inherent in the CNS/ATM concept which was inconsistent with the Chicago Convention".[262]

This conclusion means no more than that the Chicago Convention is "neutral" or "void" as to the GNSS. No State has the duty to provide the GNSS services and no State is obliged to make use of such technology in its sovereign airspace if it is available from whatever source. The State or States providing the GNSS are free to design the system characteristics and there are no pre-existing ICAO standards that should be observed – on the contrary, any ICAO SARPs relating to GNSS take account of the paradigm of the existing design.

The need to formulate some legal principles relevant to GNSS inspired the Council of ICAO to adopt, on 9 March 1994, a "Statement of ICAO Policy on CNS/ATM Systems Implementation and Operation"[263] formulating several "precepts" that have no legal force but could be indicative of the incipient international consensus concerning the desirable legal principles for CNS/ATM.

In October 1998, the 32nd Session of the ICAO Assembly adopted Resolution A32-19, somewhat bombastically and improperly called "Charter on the Rights and Obligations of States Relating to GNSS Services";[264] the term "Charter" should be reserved to international treaties of fundamental importance while an ICAO Assembly Resolution is not a source of international law but at best an indication of an opinion or developing consensus.

Resolution A32-19 "solemnly declares" that certain principles shall apply in the implementation and operation of GNSS. Among them is the principle of universal access and non-discrimination, no restriction on the sovereignty of States, safeguard of continuity, availability, integrity, accuracy and reliability of the services, highest practicable degree of uniformity in the provision of the GNSS services, any charges for the services to be in accordance with Article 15 of the Chicago Convention, principle of cooperation and mutual assistance on a bilateral or multilateral basis and due regard for the interests of other States.

These principles go beyond the current scope of the Chicago Convention and in any perspective revision of the Convention such principles should be embodied directly in the Convention. On the other hand, there is no urgency for such a revision prior to full implementation of the GNSS services and before extensive experience is gained on the social relations created by the GNSS that require legal regulation. GNSS as technology

---

261 See M. Milde, "Solutions in Search of a Problem. Legal Problems of the GNSS", *Annals of Air and Space Law*, Vol. XXII, Part II (1997), pp. 195-219.
262 ICAO Doc 9630-LC/189 – Report of the 28th Session of the Legal Committee (1994).
263 ICAO Doc LC/29-WP/3-2, 28 March 1994.
264 ICAO Doc 9848, Legal matters, pp. V 3-4.

does not require international legal regulation before potentially conflicting interests of States create a need for a legal balancing of such conflicting interests. In that sense it would appear premature that the Resolution of ICAO Assembly A32-20 (1998) called for the "Development and elaboration of an appropriate long-term legal framework to govern the implementation of GNSS"; this Resolution recognized "the urgent need for the elaboration, both at the regional and global level, of the basic legal principles that should govern the provision of the GNSS".[265] Not only is this Resolution premature but it also takes away much of the credibility of Resolution A32-19 – the "Charter" that was deemed to have already formulated such basic principles in a very solemn form. ICAO also provides information and support to the operational implementation of GNSS in order to assist States to introduce GNSS-based services via Manual, which is used in conjunction with the relevant provisions in Annex 10, Volume I, and with the Performance Based Navigation Manual.[266]

Regional Air Navigation Conferences and Air Navigation Plans: over the years the Regional Air Navigation Conferences have become an important instrument of ICAO Member States for regional planning and coordination of air navigation facilities and services. Such Conferences have been drafting, subject to approval by the Council of ICAO, the Regional Air Navigation Plans (RANPs) listing the facilities and services that are to be available in the given Region and assigning the authority over the designated Flight Information Regions (FIR). This regional planning frequently reveals conflicting interests of States, conflicting claims and sensitive political implications on the delimitation of the respective boundaries, exercise of jurisdiction or economic interests in providing the services.

The legal status of the RANPs has never been formally defined but States are led to believe that they have a legally binding force. However, there is no legal authority for such a conclusion and the RANPs have no legal status whatsoever under the Chicago Convention. Yet, even the United Nations Secretariat at the highest level was made to believe, in 1999 and again in 2003, that they were obliged to request the President of the Council of ICAO to suspend the European RANP[267] in relation to the UN administered territory of Kosovo to exempt it from the jurisdictional ambit of Serbia-Montenegro as it then existed.[268] The presumed "authority" of the President of the Council to suspend the RANP for a particular territory had no basis in law.

The practical importance of the RANPs cannot be underestimated but there is no constitutional basis in the Chicago Convention that would define their legal status, as well

---

265 *Idem.* p. V 4.
266 ICAO Doc 9849, Global Navigation Satellite System (GNSS) Manual, 3rd ed., 2017; ICAO Doc 9613.
267 EUR ANP ICAO Doc 7754.
268 Letter of the President of the ICAO Council to Secretary-General of the UN Kofi Atta Annan, AN13/14.2 (open) dated 24 December 1999.

as the authority of the Council to "approve" them. In practice, the RANPs were frequently "approved", suspended or amended by the President of the Council under his "delegated authority". It would be highly desirable to define a clear legal foundation for this field of ICAO activity in any update of the Convention. The current "legal vacuum" could lead to uncertainties, disputes or confusions.

Legal work of the Organization: the work of the ICAO Legal Committee and of the Diplomatic Conferences convened under the auspices of ICAO over the years has become a highly visible, important and successful feature of the ICAO programs. Among the number of the international instruments drafted by the Legal Committee and its Sub-Committees are some that are decidedly in the forefront of the progressive development of international law and its codification. Among such instruments a particular place belongs to the aviation security conventions adopted with unprecedented speed and efficiency in response to the global challenges of aviation terrorism.

The legal principles and approaches developed in ICAO have been closely followed in other instruments adopted in different fora. Yet, for historical reasons (due to the then existing CITEJA) the Chicago Convention did not make any reference to the legal work of the Organization and the existence and Constitution of the Legal Committee, and the Procedure for Approval of Draft Conventions are based only on Assembly Resolutions[269] that do not represent a source of international law. That leads to some disregard of the proper procedures of the Legal Committee; long periods without a session of the Committee and improper referral of the legal issues to different bodies (*e.g.*, "Secretariat Study Groups") for which there is no constitutional basis, which worked without the proper international representation and without transparency and whose composition was too often fully at the discretion of the President of the Council. In any perspective, updating of the Chicago Convention the legal work of the Organization should be given appropriate constitutional basis and recognition.

"Empowerment" of ICAO: perhaps the most far reaching innovation in the law and practice of international organizations is the ICAO's determined approach to the enforcement of the safety and security standards. Enforcement is one of the rather blurred areas of international law; individual or collective enforcement of obligations is acceptable under strict limits in extreme cases – such as threat to international peace and security (*e.g.*, armed attack) – justifying "right of individual and collective self-defence" under the UN Charter.[270]

---

269 Resolution A7-5 *"Constitution of the Legal Committee"* and Resolution A31-15, Appendix B.
270 Article 51 of the UN Charter.

There is no precedent in international practice that an international organization would be granted the power of inspecting and assessing a State's implementation of certain obligations, instruct on the remedial action to be taken with the implied threat that non-implementation of the corrective action would lead to damaging public disclosure of the shortcomings. But that is exactly what ICAO has done in its unprecedented quest for the global safety and security oversight – regular, mandatory, systematic and harmonized safety audit carried out by the Organization.[271]

The system is now firmly established in the practice of ICAO and so far there are no recorded difficulties, conflicts or complaints by States. However, the practice is based only on shaky and dubious legal grounds that could at any time be open to challenge – recommendation of a meeting of the Directors General of Civil Aviation[272] and a resolution of the ICAO Assembly are not sources of international law. If there is in fact a true unity of the political will among States on such an "empowerment" of ICAO, the authority for ICAO to carry out safety and security oversight audits with potential "sanctions" as consequences should be included in due course in a revised version of the Chicago Convention or in a separate new Convention.

Regional economic integration organizations: a novel phenomenon that was not foreseeable at the time of the drafting of the Chicago Convention is the trend towards economic integration of sovereign States and their gradual integration in matters of policy and law. The European Union (EU) is the most advanced example of such a trend that may be in due course followed in other geographic areas.

The EU developed its own extensive legislation binding on its 27 members and among such legislation are detailed regulations on the creation of a single aviation market and a host of regulations on a multitude of aspect of civil aviation. The EU has become a party to the *Convention for the Unification of Certain Rules for International Carriage by Air* of 28 May 1999 (Montreal Convention 1999)[273] as expressly permitted by Article 53 (2) of that Convention. The Convention states that it is open for signature by "Regional Economic Integration Organizations" – *i.e.*, organizations created by sovereign States of a given region which have competence in respect of certain matters governed by the Convention and have been duly authorized to sign and to ratify the Convention. An identical provision will be found in the *Convention on International Interests in Mobile Equipment* and the *Protocol* to that Convention "*on Matters Specific to Aircraft Equipment*", both signed at Cape Town on 16 November 2001.[274] However, this practice was not followed by the

---

271 See Section 7.3.5.2 to this book, ICAO Council, Implementation of SARPs – Need for enforcement?
272 ICAO Doc 9866, ICAO DGCA Conference on a global strategy for aviation safety. Report, 2006.
273 ICAO Doc 9740.
274 ICAO Docs. 9793 and 9794.

Diplomatic Conference held in September 2010 in Beijing that adopted the Beijing Convention and Beijing Protocol.

The Regional Economic Integration Organizations may have competence in other matters of international civil aviation activities and voices have been heard that such organizations should have a formal status within ICAO. On the other hand, views have been expressed that giving any decision-making status in ICAO to such organizations would unduly enhance and duplicate the power of the component States of such organization.

The role of regional organizations within ICAO deserves consideration and should be addressed in any future review of the Convention. In its past, ICAO readily adjusted itself to "disintegration" of the colonial empires and of several States by adjusting the Convention's Article 50 a) on the size of the Council. The Organization may have to adjust itself to the growing trends of "integration" of States. In the meantime, there should be no obstacle for the EU to be represented as an Observer in the meetings of the Council (so far not admitted); the Council has the power to adjust its Standing Rules of Procedure to admit such representation – if supported by the political will of States.

8 Legal Management of Aviation Security

Vim vi defendere omnes leges permittunt

Aviation is statistically the safest means of transport but it will never be absolutely safe. It is undeniable that aviation is and will remain vulnerable. The complex aviation technology is required to defy the law of gravity, reach very high speed, use highly flammable fuel and face sometimes unpredictable adverse weather conditions. Highly qualified human element is in control of the operations and that human element is not immune to failure at different levels of the chain of operational control and for a variety of reasons.

"Safety" – the primary requirement in aviation – could be defined as absence of danger to human life, to property and to the environment. The term "safety" covers also the concept of "security",[1] *i.e.*, protection from man-made criminal acts against the safety of civil aviation.

In the development and codification of international air law at the Paris Conference in 1919 or at the Chicago Conference in 1944, no mention was made of "security" to protect international aviation against criminal acts by individuals. In the first place, there were no recorded incidents of such criminal acts at that time; moreover, it would have been believed that such acts are to be dealt with under domestic criminal laws and not by international regulations.

The experience of later years proved the vulnerability of civil aviation to different types of unlawful acts, in particular
– unlawful seizure of an aircraft in flight ("hijacking");
– sabotage of an aircraft in flight or of the air navigation facilities and services;
– attack against the aircraft on the ground or against persons at an airport;
– unruly passengers on board.

8.1 Unlawful Seizure of Aircraft

Several commentators repeatedly assert that the first recorded "hijacking" was in 1931 when Peruvian revolutionaries commandeered a Ford Tri-motor.[2] The facts are somewhat

---

[1] There is some terminological confusion since in French the word "securite" is equivalent to English "safety"; the English word "security" in French is "surete". Spanish language uses the expression "securidad" both for "safety" and "security" and Russian also use a single word "bezopasnost".
[2] Among many, see P.S. Dempsey, "Aviation Security: the role of law in the war against terrorism", *Columbia Journal of Transnational Law*, Vol. 41, 2003, No. 3, p. 654.

different: on 21 February 1931, American pilot Byron Richards flew from Lima to Arequipa; on landing his Panagra Ford Tri-Motor was surrounded by armed soldiers and he was told that he and the aircraft are detained and are to be available to revolutionaries and follow their orders; Richards refused and kept refusing until 2 March 1931, when the soldiers informed him that the revolution succeeded and he was free to return to Lima as long as he takes one of the junta with him. This almost comic event does not have any of the features of the later "hijackings" – it did not occur on board and in flight and the soldiers did not take over the control of the aircraft. (Byron Richards had another similar "abortive" experience 30 years later as a pilot of Continental Airlines B-707 flying from Phoenix to El Paso: as his aircraft started to move on the runway, an armed man and his son ordered him to fly to Cuba where they naively expected to get a reward for bringing to Fidel Castro a valuable aircraft; FBI agents shot the aircraft tires off and disabled its take-off; the perpetrators were overpowered and arrested.)[3]

The situation developed into a true problem only shortly after the end of World War II after the beginning of the Cold War (1947-1991). With the appearance of the "Iron Curtain" in Europe came a series of seizures of aircraft from several Eastern European States that were forced to fly to Turkey, West Germany or other territories not under communist domination. In many of these cases, acts of brutal violence were committed on board against the crew to force them to fly to a different destination. Between 1947 and 1953, there were 15 successful and 2 unsuccessful incidents of seizure of aircraft in Eastern Europe. There is no doubt that a serious danger was created for the flight and all persons on board during such acts but due to the political motive of such acts the perpetrators were often welcomed as "heroes" and were given sympathy and encouragement.

In 1958, Raul Castro masterminded a successful seizure of two DC-3 aircraft from Havana to an improvised air strip in the rebel-held Oriente province; a later attempt to seize a Viscount aircraft led to a crash on the primitive air strip, loss of life and a temporary loss of sympathy for the rebels.

Between 1959 and 1960, there were eleven successful and five unsuccessful seizures of Cuban aircraft to the US territory by opponents of the Castro regime. Then the situation changed – on 1 May 1960 came the first seizure of a US aircraft to Cuba that grew into an epidemic: from that time until 1973 some 133 US aircraft were seized and brought to Cuba. The most hijacks in the history of civil aviation occurred in 1969, accurately on 86 occasions.[4]

By the same time, the Israeli airline El-Al became a target of a series of seizures by the fighters of the Popular Front for the Liberation of Palestine, several of El-Al aircraft being

---

3   "Crime: The Skywayman", 11 August 1961, www.content.time.com/time/subscriber/article/.
4   Hugh Morris, "The strangest stories from the golden age of plane hijacking", *Travel News Editor*, 5 July 2019, www.telegraph.co.uk/travel.

brought to Algiers where the aircraft and its Israeli passengers were kept for an extensive period of time for alleged "unlawful entry". Aircraft of the United States and some other Western countries flying to or from Israel were similarly targeted.

Since the historically first incident of unlawful seizure of aircraft there have been hundreds and hundreds of similar incidents culminating eventually in the deadliest incident of aviation terrorism on 11 September 2001 when the seized aircraft were used in a suicidal act as giant flying bombs in New York and Washington, D.C.

Since the disaster of "911" attention has been focused on "aviation terrorism" as the chief danger to civil aviation but a great majority of previous incidents of seizure of aircraft were not attributable to acts of terrorism, yet represented a serious danger. The underlying causes of these acts were very varied and included:
– acts by refugees, defectors or "returning refugees" seeking a destination which they cannot reach, for whatever reason, by legitimate means;
– criminal acts without political overtones (*e.g.*, extortion of money);
– taking of hostages to achieve concessions of political nature (*e.g.*, publicity for political statements, release of prisoners);
– acts of mentally deranged persons confused or seeking personal prominence;
– acts connected with illicit drugs ("narcoterrorism").

There could be various other underlying causes for such acts and that also calls for varied methods of prevention and suppression of the unlawful seizure of aircraft.

National legislation in many States could prosecute the act of unlawful seizure of aircraft under many existing rules of the penal law, *e.g.*, assault, kidnapping, extortion, unlawful possession of firearms, etc. One of the first specific laws addressing these acts was the US amendment, on 5 September 1961, of the Federal Aviation Act of 1958 imposing penalties at least of twenty years imprisonment or imprisonment for life or even the death penalty (if the death of another individual results from the commission or attempt) for the act of "aircraft piracy".[5]

The term "aircraft piracy" is rather infelicitous; in international law the term "piracy" is well-established as an act committed on the high seas by the crew of one ship against another ship while – if the maritime terms are to be used by analogy – the act on board an aircraft in flight would be rather comparable to a mutiny on board a ship.[6] Even less fortunate is the journalistic term "hijacking" which appears to be a neologism coined by the criminal underworld during the time of prohibition in the United States designating

---

5   49 U.S. Code, paragraph 46502, 1 (A-B) and 2 (A-B).
6   "Aircraft piracy" means seizing or exercising control of an aircraft in the special aircraft jurisdiction of the United States by force, violence, threat of force or violence, or any form of intimidation, and with wrongful intent, 49 U.S. Code, paragraph 46502, 1 (A).

the act of stopping a bootleggers' vehicle on the road and stealing its contraband liquor, robbers robbing other criminals. It may not be the most fortunate term, but the journalistic usage has established itself for almost half a century. The appropriate legal term coined within ICAO is "unlawful seizure of aircraft" but even that term is not perfect – a creditor may "seize" an aircraft by a judicial action that on appeal is proved "unlawful"…; moreover, the term is too long for common use and we may have to live with the term "hijacking" overlooking its historic roots.

International law was slow in developing any responses to unlawful seizure of aircraft. The initial welcoming of hijackers as "heroes" subsided but no action was taken. The problem was that the predominant international opinion considered the acts to be of a "political" nature and organizations like ICAO avoided them for fear of political confrontation; similar hesitation was apparent in the UN and even in ICPO-INTERPOL. However, it was obvious that acts of unlawful seizure of aircraft endangered the safety of the aircraft, its occupants, other aircraft in the air and third persons and property on the surface and undermined the confidence of the international community in the safety of civil aviation.

The "turning point" in the ICAO attitude is not formally recorded but is not "anecdotal" either and is here described faithfully from the personal memory of the author. The 16th Session of the ICAO Assembly was held in Buenos Aires from 3 to 26 September 1968. The issue of aviation security was not on the agenda of the session. Early in the session the Chief Delegate of Cuba – R. Del Pino Diaz, Deputy Minister of Transport – requested a private meeting with the President of the ICAO Council, Walter Binaghi, "on a legal issue" and this author participated in that meeting as the Legal Officer in the Secretariat. To a great surprise, the Delegate of Cuba urged the President that ICAO should take a determined action against "hijacking" that endangers the safety of civil aviation; he stated specifically that the frequent forced arrivals of US registered aircraft to Cuba gave Cuba a bad reputation, although such actions were in no way encouraged by Cuban authorities, were even kept secret from the domestic media and not used for any propaganda, disrupt the operations of the Havana airport, force the military to scramble some fighter jets to identify the incoming unknown aircraft, etc. Most importantly, the seized aircraft had to be refuelled prior to their return to the US and Cuba suffered serious shortage of aviation fuel and fully depended on imports from the then USSR.

The President of the Council understood and welcomed the initiative of the Cuban delegate but the problem was how to include the item on the agenda of the Assembly that was already advancing in its work and the delegation of Cuba did not wish to be publicly seen as the initiator of this subject and to face the procedure of reopening the debate on the approved Agenda of the Assembly. Fortunately, under item 29 of the agenda there was already a point for the Legal Commission "Status of international conventions on air law" the intent of which was to encourage States to greater participation in international instruments – among them the Tokyo Convention on Offences and Certain Other Acts Committed on Board Aircraft (1963);[7] that Convention was at that time – erroneously – considered to be directly applicable to unlawful seizure of aircraft; again, the Convention was not yet in force.

Thus unexpectedly, the Assembly adopted not only Resolution A16-36 on "Participation of States in International Conventions on Air Law" but also Resolution A16-37 "Unlawful Seizure of Civil Aircraft". That resolution for the first time recognizes that "unlawful seizure of civil aircraft has a serious adverse effect on the safety, efficiency and regularity of air navigation".[8] The Resolution also noted that Article 11 of the Tokyo Convention (1963) "provides certain remedies" but not "a complete remedy" for the problem and urged States to ratify and implement the Convention "as soon as possible". The real progress is in the last clause of the Resolution A16-37 that "Requests the Council, at the earliest possible date, to institute a study of other measures to cope with the problem of unlawful seizure". The Council was thus given not only a green light to address the problem but a specific order to do so fast.

The view of the Council was that a solution has to be found in the legal field and intensive studies were initiated in the ICAO Secretariat, a Special Sub-Committee of the Legal Committee and the 17th Session of the ICAO Legal Committee. It all culminated in the December 1970 Diplomatic Conference at The Hague which adopted the "Convention for the Suppression of Unlawful Seizure of Aircraft".

However, before discussing the Hague Convention (1970), it is unavoidable first to comment on the Tokyo Convention (1963) that was also deemed to have some relevance to the unlawful seizure of aircraft and that is till today an important part of the mosaic of international instruments for the protection of civil aviation against unlawful acts. The very fact that 187 States[9] have ratified the Tokyo Convention makes it an important part of the general international law.

8.2 Tokyo Convention on Offences and Certain Other Acts Committed on Board Aircraft 1963

This Convention has a rather chequered history. It originated as a very theoretical and "academic" project on the "legal status of aircraft". Under this title a Sub-Committee of the Legal Committee and the Committee itself considered potential problems of the applicable

---

7   ICAO Doc 8364.
8   Doc 8779, Resolution A16, (1968), p. 92.
9   By December 2022

law for contracts concluded on board aircraft in flight, the possibility of concluding marriages on board aircraft and similar remote and unlikely events.

The debate eventually narrowed on the legal status of the aircraft commander ("pilot in command" in the language of the ICAO SARPs). That was a legitimate subject since the international air law did not include any provisions giving the aircraft commander a similar status and jurisdiction that centuries of international maritime custom have conferred on the master of a ship. In the maritime practice the master of the ship that may be for long periods of time on the high seas has a distinct status ("first after God" in the popular parlance) with many jurisdictional attributes as a "magistrate", "notary" and to some degree enforcer of law and order on board. No such attributes were contemplated for the aircraft commander in the evolution of the international air law – undoubtedly because there did not appear any need for such a status and jurisdiction in view of the short duration of the flight.

One problem identified in the deliberations was the question which State should exercise jurisdiction over criminal acts committed on board aircraft, in particular when such aircraft is over the high seas. Attention was drawn to the case *United States v. Diego Cordova*[10] dating back to 1948: passenger Diego Cordova was on American Airlines flight from San Juan, Puerto Rico to New York; he was heavily inebriated and somewhere over the Atlantic he assaulted and injured three passengers. He was brought to trial in New York and found guilty but he was not sentenced because at that time the United States had no jurisdiction to punish an assault committed over the high seas.[11]

The issue of which State should exercise the criminal jurisdiction over acts committed on board aircraft was retained for further study. The disparity of national laws relating to criminal jurisdiction was evident – some States based jurisdiction on the principle of personality (*i.e.*, State had criminal jurisdiction over its citizen wherever the criminal act was committed), other States based it on the principle of territoriality (criminal jurisdiction over all acts committed in its territory) and in some rare cases the principle of universality was applied (jurisdiction over an act regardless of where and by whom it was committed). Another issue that was dealt with related to the powers and rights of the aircraft commander with respect to acts committed on board aircraft.

On 14 September 1963 a Diplomatic Conference convened under the auspices of ICAO in Tokyo adopted and opened for signature the Convention on Offences and Certain Other Acts Committed on Board Aircraft. The Convention was slow in attracting

---

10 US District Court E.D. New York, 1950.89 F. Supp. 298.
11 As the crime was committed on the high seas, and at that time the court of the United States only had jurisdiction if the crime was committed on board a ship registered by US authorities. This gap was soon filled by a law on Crimes of Violence over the High Seas in American Aircraft. See G.F. Fitzgerald, "Toward Legal Suppression of Acts Against Civil Aviation" in *Air Hijacking, An International Perspective*, International Conciliation, November 1971, No. 585, pp. 42-78.

attention of States and came into force only on 4 December 1969 upon ratification by ten States (the 12th State bringing the Convention into force happened to be the United States) but the epidemic wave of unlawful interferences with civil aviation that followed by 1970 accelerated its wide acceptance. Today it may be stated that the Tokyo Convention, with 187 Parties, has become part of the general international law.

Article 1 of the Convention defines the scope of applicability of the Convention as follows:

> *Scope of the Convention*
> *Article 1*
> 1. This Convention shall apply in respect of: a) offences against penal law; b) acts which, whether or not they are offences, may or do jeopardize the safety of the aircraft or of persons or property therein or which jeopardize good order and discipline on board.
> 2. Except as provided in Chapter III, this Convention shall apply in respect of offences committed or acts done by a person on board any aircraft registered in a Contracting State, while that aircraft is in flight or on the surface of the high seas or of any other area outside the territory of any State.
> 3. For the purposes of this Convention, an aircraft is considered to be in flight from the moment when power is applied for the purpose of take-off until the moment when the landing run ends.
> 4. This Convention shall not apply to aircraft used in military, customs or police services.

The Convention applies in respect of any offence whatsoever against penal law and it does not create a separate new concept or definition of a specific criminal act (such as unlawful seizure of aircraft). Moreover, it applies to any act regardless whether it is an "offence" that may or actually does jeopardize safety or good order and discipline on board. It would thus apply, *e.g.*, to unruly conduct such as smoking on board when it is prohibited, use of electronic equipment when prohibited, rude behaviour, etc. The Convention is applicable only to aircraft registered in a State party to the Convention while that aircraft is "in flight" as defined in paragraph 3 of Article 1 and is not applicable to aircraft used in military, customs or police services.

The first substantial provision of the Convention refers to the criminal jurisdiction of States as follows:

Jurisdiction

Article 3

1. The State of registration of the aircraft is competent to exercise jurisdiction over offences and acts committed on board.

2. Each Contracting State shall take such measures as may be necessary to establish its jurisdiction as the State of registration over offences committed on board aircraft registered in such State.

3. This Convention does not exclude any criminal jurisdiction exercised in accordance with national law.

It appeared logical that the State of Registry of the aircraft had the closest relation to that aircraft and should be competent to exercise criminal jurisdiction over acts committed on board that aircraft and was to be obliged to establish its jurisdiction; that would, however, not exclude the criminal jurisdiction of other States in accordance with their national laws, except as stated in Article 4 below. Two problems arise from this provision that weaken the impact of the Convention. First, a great proportion of the fleets of aircraft in international air transport are registered in one State and operated by an operator in another State due to financing, leasing or other arrangements; the State of Registry may be so detached from the actual operation of the aircraft as to have little interest in exercising criminal jurisdiction over acts committed on board that aircraft. The second weakness of this provision is that the Convention only recognizes the competence of the State of Registry to exercise the criminal jurisdiction but does not impose the duty to actually use that competence in any specific case.

A State that is not a State of Registry may interfere with an aircraft in flight in order to exercise its criminal jurisdiction only in limited cases stipulated in Article 4:

Article 4

A contracting State which is not the State of registration may not interfere with an aircraft in flight in order to exercise its criminal jurisdiction over an offence committed on board except in the following cases: a) the offence has effect on the territory of such State; b) the offence has been committed by or against a national or permanent resident of such State; the offence is against the security of such State; c) the offence consists of a breach of any rules or regulations relating to the flight or manoeuvre of aircraft in force in such State; d) the exercise of jurisdiction is necessary to ensure the observance of any obligation of such State under a multilateral international agreement.

The second substantive provision of the Convention refers to the powers of the aircraft commander – an important innovation because international law prior to this Convention did not deal with the status and powers of the aircraft commander. The powers of the aircraft commander under the Convention are applicable only for an international flight as stipulated in Article 5, paragraph 1. Paragraph 2 of that Article modifies the definition of "in flight" differently than Article 1, paragraph 3 and the criterion is that the external doors of the aircraft are closed and the aircraft becomes a "closed universe" where no outside authority can come to assistance. Article 5 stipulates:

> *Powers of the aircraft commander*
> *Article 5*
> 1. The provisions of this Chapter shall not apply to offences and acts committed or about to be committed by a person on board an aircraft in flight in the airspace of the State of registration or over the high seas or any other area outside the territory of any State unless the last point of take-off or the next point of intended landing is situated in a State other than that of registration, or the aircraft subsequently flies in the airspace of a State other than that of registration with such person still on board.
> 2. Notwithstanding the provisions of Article 1, paragraph 3, an aircraft shall for the purposes of this Chapter, be considered to be in flight at any time from the moment when all its external doors are closed following embarkation until the moment when any such door is opened for disembarkation. In the case of a forced landing, the provisions of this Chapter shall continue to apply with respect to offences and acts committed on board until competent authorities of a State take over the responsibility for the aircraft and for the persons and property on board.

The specific powers of enforcement are given to the aircraft commander in Articles 6-10 of the Convention. They include the right to restrain a person, disembark a person in any State upon landing or, in case of a serious offence, "deliver"[12] the person to the competent authorities of any contracting State upon landing. The commander may require or authorize assistance of other crew members and may request or authorize (but not require) assistance of passengers. Article 10 grants "immunity" from claims against the commander, members of the crew or passengers and the owner or operator of the aircraft on account of the treatment undergone by the person against whom the actions under the Convention were taken. For convenience of reference Articles 6-10 are reproduced:

---

12 This action, sometimes called "rendition", would amount to an informal "extradition". There is no record that this provision was ever used.

Article 6

1. The aircraft commander may, when he has reasonable grounds to believe that a person has committed, or is about to commit, on board the aircraft, an offence or act contemplated in Article 1, paragraph 1, impose upon such person reasonable measures including restraint which are necessary: a) to protect the safety of the aircraft, or of persons or property therein; or to maintain good order and discipline on board; or b) to enable him to deliver such person to competent authorities or c) to disembark him in accordance with the provisions of this Chapter.

2. The aircraft commander may require or authorize the assistance of other crew members and may request or authorize, but not require, the assistance of passengers to restrain any person whom he is entitled to restrain. Any crew member or passenger may also take reasonable preventive measures without such authorization when he has reasonable grounds to believe that such action is immediately necessary to protect the safety of the aircraft or of persons or property therein.

Article 7

1. Measures of restraint imposed upon a person in accordance with Article 6 shall not be continued beyond any point at which the aircraft lands unless: a) such point is in the territory of a non-Contracting State and its authorities refuse to permit disembarkation of that person or those measures have been imposed in accordance with Article 6, paragraph 1 (c) in order to enable his delivery to competent authorities; b) the aircraft makes a forced landing and the aircraft commander is unable to deliver c) that person to competent authorities; or that person agrees to onward carriage under restraint.

2. The aircraft commander shall as soon as practicable, and if possible before landing in the territory of a State with a person on board who has been placed under restraint in accordance with the provisions of Article 6, notify the authorities of such State of the fact that a person on board is under restraint and of the reasons for such restraint.

Article 8

1. The aircraft commander may, in so far as it is necessary for the purpose of subparagraph (a) or (b) or paragraph 1 of Article 6, disembark in the territory of any State in which the aircraft lands any person who he has reasonable grounds to believe has committed, or is about to commit, on board the aircraft an act contemplated in Article 1, paragraph 1(b).

2. The aircraft commander shall report to the authorities of the State in which he disembarks any person pursuant to this Article, the fact of, and the reasons for, such disembarkation.

Article 9
1. The aircraft commander may deliver to the competent authorities of any Contracting State in the territory of which the aircraft lands any person who he has reasonable grounds to believe has committed on board the aircraft an act which, in his opinion, is a serious offence according to the penal law of the State of registration of the aircraft.
2. The aircraft commander shall as soon as practicable and if possible before landing in the territory of a Contracting State with a person on board whom the aircraft commander intends to deliver in accordance with the preceding paragraph, notify the authorities of such State of his intention to deliver such person and the reasons therefor.
3. The aircraft commander shall furnish the authorities to whom any suspected offender is delivered in accordance with the provisions of this Article with evidence and information which, under the law of the State of registration of the aircraft, are lawfully in his possession.

Article 10
For actions taken in accordance with this Convention, neither the aircraft commander, any other member of the crew, any passenger, the owner or operator of the aircraft, nor the person on whose behalf the flight was performed shall be held responsible in any proceeding on account of the treatment undergone by the person against whom the actions were taken.

By the time of the drafting of the Tokyo Convention there were relatively few incidents of unlawful seizure of aircraft and it was still believed that domestic criminal law would cover them and that the Convention itself should only clearly settle the question of the criminal jurisdiction. For that reason there was no specific mention of the unlawful seizure of aircraft. Another point is that by the time of the drafting of the Tokyo Convention there was not yet a clear consensus among States about the nature of the act of unlawful seizure of aircraft and several States felt that the act was of a "political" nature and thus beyond the purview of ICAO.

Towards the end of the deliberations the delegations of Venezuela and of the United States drew attention of the Conference to the fact that after some acts of unlawful seizure of aircraft the aircraft and its crew and passengers were held in the country of landing for unduly long periods and were exposed to various forms of difficulties or harassment.

Following this initiative, Article 11 was inserted into the Convention that mentions "unlawful seizure of aircraft".[13] However, the Convention still does not deal directly with the act of unlawful seizure of aircraft and Article 11 addresses only the aftermath of such act and stipulates the duties of the State of landing:

> *Unlawful seizure of aircraft*
> *Article 11*
> 1. When a person on board has unlawfully committed by force or threat thereof an act of interference, seizure, or other wrongful exercise of control of an aircraft in flight or when such an act is about to be committed, Contracting States shall take all appropriate measures to restore control of the aircraft to its lawful commander or to preserve his control of the aircraft.
> 2. In the cases contemplated in the preceding paragraph, the Contracting State in which the aircraft lands shall permit its passengers and crew to continue their journey as soon as practicable, and shall return the aircraft and its cargo to the persons lawfully entitled to possession.

This provision proved to have practical impact since it established a rule of international law – now almost generally accepted – that following an unlawful seizure of aircraft contracting States have the duty to restore the control of the aircraft to the lawful commander and the State of landing must permit the crew and passengers to continue their journey as soon as possible and return the aircraft and its cargo to persons entitled to their possession.

The practice of States differed as to whether to permit the landing in its territory of an aircraft subject to an act of unlawful interference. Some States were concerned that such a landing would lead to critical security concerns on the ground, violent acts or acts of extortion, disruption of the operation of the airport, etc. There were incidents when the local authorities blocked the runway by trucks or fuel cisterns to prevent the landing of an aircraft.[14] Later the opinion prevailed that an aircraft under unlawful seizure was "in distress" in the terms or Article 25 of the Chicago Convention and deserved all assistance. It was recognized that the safest place for aircraft in such situation was on the ground and

---

13   This was the first time when agreement was reached on this term rather than "hijacking" or "air piracy".
14   In 1977, Lufthansa Flight 181 on a route from Mallorca to Frankfurt was seized and taken around different places in the Middle East where the plane was not permitted to land. In Mogadishu, Somalia the fuel was close to exhaustion, and it was necessary to land. However, the runway was blocked by heavy obstacles, the "hijackers" killed the pilot and the young co-pilot (only on his second flight!) miraculously landed the aircraft on rough ground next to the blocked runway. A German commando of the border police force later successfully stormed the plane, killed three hijackers and freed 86 hostages.

that all necessary steps should be taken to keep it on the ground and not to tolerate its departure while still under seizure.

A clear policy statement on this problem is now reflected in Assembly Resolution A33-2,[15] that recognized that "the safety of flights of aircraft subjected to an act of unlawful seizure may be further jeopardized by the denial of navigational aids and air traffic services, the blocking of runways and taxiways and the closure of airports". It also recognized that "the safety of passengers and crew of an aircraft subjected to an act of unlawful seizure may also be further jeopardized if the aircraft is permitted to take off while still under seizure". States are urged to ensure that "an aircraft subjected to an act of unlawful seizure which has landed in its territory is detained on the ground unless its departure is necessitated by the overriding duty to protect human life". These principles also found their regulatory reflection in Annex 17 – Security, Standards 5.2.1 to 5.2.5.

In practice, there have been several ways how to detain such an aircraft on the ground – block the runway for take-off, refuse to refuel the aircraft, shoot off the tires of the landing gear, storm the aircraft by a commando,[16] arranging for the flight crew to escape from the aircraft and thus disable its operation, etc. Each case must be judged by its particular features and the protection of human life must be paramount.

Contracting States have accepted in the Tokyo Convention duties that are correlated to the powers of the aircraft commander – to allow the commander to disembark any person pursuant to Article 8, paragraph 1 and to take delivery of any person whom the aircraft commander delivers pursuant to Article 9, paragraph 1.

Article 16 of the Convention provides that offences committed on aircraft registered in a contracting State shall be treated, for the purpose of extradition, as if they had been committed not only in the place in which they have occurred but also in the territory of the State of Registration of the aircraft. Nevertheless, nothing in the Convention is to be deemed to create an obligation to grant extradition. Another provision weakening the Convention is in Article 2 that states that "no provision of this Convention shall be interpreted as authorizing or requiring any action in respect of offences against penal laws of a political nature or those based on racial or religious discrimination".

The Tokyo Convention must be evaluated as a positive contribution to the development of international law in that it confirmed the criminal jurisdiction of the State of Registry of the aircraft, vested important powers in the aircraft commander and addressed the aftermath of an unlawful seizure of aircraft. However, the Convention was not drafted with a special aim to prevent and suppress any specific acts against the safety of civil

---

15 Resolution A33-2, Appendix E, Action of States with respect to unlawful seizure of aircraft in progress, (2001); Updated Resolutions A37-17, Appendix D, (2010), A38-15, Appendix D (Act in unlawful interference), (2013).
16 Such action could backfire – in 1985, EgyptAir Flight 648 was seized and brought to Malta. Sixty persons died when the Egyptian commando stormed the aircraft and caused fire and explosion.

aviation. By 1963, consensus had not yet been reached in the international community that unlawful seizure of aircraft and similar acts should not be deemed to be "political" acts, that such acts seriously endanger the safety of flight and undermine the confidence in the safety of this vital means of communication.

The Convention does not define any specific act as "criminal" and does not oblige any State to actually assume jurisdiction or to proceed to extradition of the alleged offender. The impact of the Convention is also limited by vesting the jurisdiction only in the State of Registry (that may be different from the State of the actual operator) and by not recognizing that safety of civil aviation against criminal acts is a matter of a global concern and deserves universal jurisdiction.

8.3 The Hague Convention for the Suppression of Unlawful Seizure of Aircraft 1970

ICAO Assembly Resolution A16-37, adopted in Buenos Aires in September 1968, urged States to ratify the Tokyo Convention in spite of its perceived insufficiency; it also exhorted the Council "to institute a study of other measures to cope with the problem of unlawful seizure". This was the first occasion that ICAO decided to directly address the issue of violent acts against civil aviation. Until that moment there was some hesitation that seizures of aircraft were essentially acts of a "political" nature and should be beyond the scope of ICAO's jurisdiction.

The Council decided without hesitation that the "other measures" should be sought in the legal field and should go beyond the scope of the Tokyo Convention. The subject was studied by two sessions of a Special Sub-Committee of the Legal Committee in 1969 and by the Legal Committee in early 1970 that prepared a draft Convention considered ripe to be presented to a Diplomatic Conference.[17] In the history of international law-making, the Convention was prepared with unprecedented speed and gained fast and wide acceptance – currently (December 2022) by 185 States making its scope practically universal worldwide. This success was due to the prevailing unity of the political will of States achieved at that time that unlawful seizure of aircraft endangers the safety of international civil aviation, cannot be justified by any (political) aims or other reasons and must be suppressed. This universal support was reached in spite of the prevailing atmosphere of Cold War at that time.

The study of the subject started with a "clean slate", no relevant precedents and only with vague ideas that the acts of unlawful seizure of aircraft must be considered a criminal

---

17 Text of the Convention in Doc 8920; Minutes and Documents of the International Conference on Air Law, The Hague, December 1970 in Doc 8979.

act by all States and must be duly prosecuted. International law offered few precedents in the field of criminal acts and their prosecution. Piracy on the high seas was historically the oldest recognized crime that international customary law defined and authorized all States to punish such acts. War crimes, crimes against peace, crimes against humanity and the crime of genocide offered some remote precedents but did not lead to a specific solution.

Closer analogies were found in the International Convention for the Suppression of Trade in Women and Children,[18] the International Convention for the Suppression of Circulation of Obscene Publications,[19] the Slavery Convention[20] and the International Convention for the Suppression of Counterfeiting Currencies.[21] At the first glance it would appear that these different instruments had no relation or similarity with the act of unlawful seizure of aircraft but there was an important lesson to be learned from these multilateral conventions: they all defined a specific and distinct act that was to be considered an "ordinary" (*i.e.*, non-political) crime because it involved the important common interests of the contracting States, provided for penalties to be imposed by the contracting States and determined the jurisdiction and conditions for extradition of the alleged offenders. The establishment of universal jurisdiction was another feature to be learned from these conventions.

Inspired by the approach and structure of such conventions, the special Sub-Committees of the Legal Committee painstakingly discussed and polished the draft and agreed that it should contain the following elements:
– definition of the act of unlawful seizure of aircraft;
– declaration that such act constitutes an "offence";
– declaration that States shall make the offence punishable by "severe penalties";
– declaration that the offence is an "ordinary" offence not meriting the right of asylum;
– establishment of wide jurisdiction of States amounting to universal jurisdiction;
– dealing with the issue of extradition.

All these elements were accepted during the preparation of the 1970 Diplomatic Conference. The mid-1970 brought about a critical series of ruthless criminal acts against international civil aviation in the form of sabotage and destruction of aircraft[22] and an Extraordinary Session of the ICAO Assembly met at Montreal from 16 to 30 June 1970 to address the crisis.

---

18   Geneva, 30 September 1921, League of Nations Treaty Series, Vol. 9, p. 415.
19   Geneva, 12 September 1923, League of Nations Treaty Series, Vol. 27, p. 213.
20   Geneva, 25 September 1926, League of Nations Treaty Series, Vol. 60, p. 253.
21   Geneva, 20 April 1929, League of Nations Treaty Series, Vol. 112, p. 231.
22   On 21 February 1970, a Swissair Flight 330 from Zurich to Tel Aviv crashed after explosion of a bomb on board; on 6 September 1970 four jets were seized and taken to a desert strip at Dawson Field, Jordan with 310 hostages; on 12 September 1970 (so-called in "the Black September") three aircraft were destroyed by explosive in full view of the media, the fourth was destroyed in Cairo.

It was apparent that there was an urgent need to develop additional rules of international law that would deal not only with the unlawful seizure of aircraft but also with the acts of sabotage of aircraft and of the aviation facilities and services.

However, by that time the Diplomatic Conference was already convened to meet at The Hague in December 1970 to consider, with a view to adoption, a draft Convention dealing with the suppression of unlawful seizure of aircraft. A strong momentum had already been gained for the adoption of that Convention and it was agreed not to risk losing that momentum and to delay the subject of aircraft sabotage until a later stage. This tactical consideration is the only cause why there had to be a separate Montreal Convention of 1971 dealing with sabotage of aircraft and why the subjects were not consolidated in one single instrument.

The Extraordinary Session of the Assembly adopted Resolution A17-20[23] requesting the Council to convene the Legal Committee before the end of the year 1970 to prepare a new Convention so that it can be adopted by a Diplomatic Conference "not later than the summer 1971 in the Northern Hemisphere". The Assembly thus gave no more than one calendar year for the preparation of an additional new convention. The history of international law-making never saw a similar speed in the creation of multilateral instruments!

8.3.1   Definition of the "Offence"

The critical drafting point was to agree on a universally acceptable definition of a new and distinct criminal act of "unlawful seizure of aircraft" that would be recognized by the contracting States as an "offence" and be subject to a wide criminal jurisdiction and possibly extradition. The aim of the drafting was to make sure that the alleged offender would not find a "safe haven" anywhere in the world but would face prosecution or extradition everywhere.

The resulting consensus is reflected in Article 1 of the Convention:

> Article 1
> Any person who on board an aircraft in flight: a) unlawfully, by force or threat thereof, or by any other form of intimidation, seizes, or exercises control of, that aircraft, or attempts to perform any such act, or b) is an accomplice of a person who performs or attempts to perform any such act commits an offence (hereinafter referred to as "the offence").

---

23   Doc 8895, Resolution A17-20, Proposed convention on acts of unlawful interference against international civil aviation, pp. 30-31.

The act is to be committed on board an aircraft in flight. Under the terms of Article 3, paragraph 1 the aircraft is deemed to be "in flight"

> at any time from the moment when all its external doors are closed following embarkation until the moment when any such door is opened for disembarkation. In the case of a forced landing, the flight shall be deemed to continue until the competent authorities take over the responsibility for the aircraft and for persons and property on board.

For the purposes of the Convention, the aircraft is "in flight" when it becomes separated from the outside and becomes a "closed universe" where the competent outside authorities do not have open access to come to assistance.

The act of seizure is to be committed "on board" and it must be "unlawful"– it would not be unlawful, *e.g.*, if a qualified person were to take over the control of the aircraft for an incapacitated crew member. The terms "force" or "threat of force" would be interpreted under the domestic law and in general would mean a use of a physical assault against the bodily integrity or a threat of such force. "Any other form of intimidation" would include any type of threat of physical or other harm causing fear, including harm that could have effect on other persons or property on the ground (*e.g.*, a threat that accomplices would harm the pilot's family or burn his house).

The term "offence" encompasses an attempt to commit such act and complicity in such act or in an attempt.

Article 2 contains the fundamental commitment of States:

> *Article 2*
> Each Contracting State undertakes to make the offence punishable by severe penalties.

During the preparation of the Convention there was considerable discussion whether the text should include specific penalties for the offence. There was a great difference of opinions because some States' legislation provided for death penalty while others excluded capital punishment, some included jail term for life, others a maximum of twenty or twenty-five years' term, etc. It should be noted that international law nowhere stipulates specific penalties and that even the international tribunals (*e.g.*, Nuremberg or Tokyo) were given full discretion in determining the penalties. While a consensus was reached on the term "severe penalties", it will obviously lead to different interpretations in different legal cultures and traditions.[24] (A controversial example was the case of Thomas Michael Hoare, an Irish mercenary who led and attempted coup in Seychelles in November 1981 and then commandeered an Air India aircraft to Durban, South Africa; only after international pressure was he sentenced to ten years in prison but released after three years and died at the age of 100 – a penalty internationally criticized as not being sufficiently "severe").[25]

The scope of applicability of the Convention is limited – as all instruments of international air law it does not apply "to aircraft used in military, customs or police services".[26] In interpreting this provision, it is appropriate to use the functional approach to the character of an aircraft that is expressed by the term "used in … services". The type of the aircraft, its registration marks and the crew may be "military" but it is the actual *use* of the aircraft determined by its accepted flight plan (*e.g.*, humanitarian assistance after a natural disaster) that will define the status of the aircraft.

A further limitation of the applicability of the Convention is given by the wish of the drafters to apply the Convention only to incidents containing an "international element" and to exclude its applicability to strictly "domestic" incidents that should remain governed by the applicable domestic law. The Convention expresses this principle in Article 3, paragraph 3 as follows:

> 3. This Convention shall apply only if the place of take-off or the place of actual landing of the aircraft on board which the offence is committed is situated outside the territory of the State of registration of that aircraft; it shall be immaterial whether the aircraft is engaged in an international or domestic flight.

The reference to the State of registration is gradually losing its relevance since many aircraft are registered in a State other than the State of the actual operator. However, regardless of the limitation in Article 3, paragraph 3 the jurisdictional provisions of the Convention apply if the offender or alleged offender is found in the territory of a State other than the State of the registration of that aircraft.[27]

---

24 What does *severe* (in the Russian version "*brutal*") mean? In some nations this may mean capital punishment, while in other places it does not.
25 P. Beaumont, "Mercenary 'Mad Mike' Hoare dies in South Africa aged 100", *The Guardian*, 3 February 2020.
26 Article 3, paragraph 2.
27 Article 3, paragraph 5.

8.3.2 Jurisdiction of Courts and Extradition of Offenders

In the drafting of the Convention States wished to go beyond the concepts of the Tokyo Convention (1963) that vested jurisdiction only in the State of registration of the aircraft. The aim was to extend the jurisdiction as wide as possible – to the level of universal jurisdiction – to make sure that the offender could not find a "safe haven" anywhere in the world.

While the Tokyo Convention stated only that the State of registration of the aircraft is "competent" to exercise criminal jurisdiction over the offence committed on board, this Convention committed States to take the necessary measures to actively establish their jurisdiction in a wide spectrum of circumstances defined in Article 4 as follows:

> *Article 4*
> 1. Each Contracting State shall take such measures as may be necessary to establish its jurisdiction over the offence and any other act of violence against passengers or crew committed by the alleged offender in connection with the offence, in the following cases: a) when the offence is committed on board an aircraft registered in that State; b) when the aircraft on board which the offence is committed lands in its territory with the alleged offender still on board; c) when the offence is committed on board an aircraft leased without crew to a lessee who has his principal place of business or, if the lessee has no such place of business, his permanent residence, in that State.
> 2. Each Contracting State shall likewise take such measures as may be necessary to establish its jurisdiction over the offence in the case where the alleged offender is present in its territory, and it does not extradite him pursuant to Article 8 to any of the States mentioned in paragraph 1 of this Article.
> 3. This Convention does not exclude any criminal jurisdiction exercised in accordance with national law.

Each contracting State is thus obliged to establish its criminal jurisdiction when the act took place on board an aircraft of its registration, when any aircraft with the offender on board lands in its territory, when the offence took place on a leased aircraft of an operator having his principal place of business or residence in that State and also in all cases when the alleged offender is present in its territory and is not extradited. In practice, this amounts to universal jurisdiction from which the offender cannot escape.

The procedural steps to be taken by a State in a specific case are set in Article 6 as follows:

Article 6

1. Upon being satisfied that the circumstances so warrant, any Contracting State in the territory of which the offender or the alleged offender is present, shall take him into custody or take other measures to ensure his presence. The custody and other measures shall be as provided in the law of that State but may only be continued for such time as is necessary to enable any criminal or extradition proceedings to be instituted.

2. Such State shall immediately make a preliminary enquiry into the facts.

3. Any person in custody pursuant to paragraph 1 of this Article shall be assisted in communicating immediately with the nearest appropriate representative of the State of which he is a national.

4. When a State, pursuant to this Article, has taken a person into custody, it shall immediately notify the State of registration of the aircraft, the State mentioned in Article 4, paragraph 1(c), the State of nationality of the detained person and, if it considers it advisable, any other interested States of the fact that such person is in custody and of the circumstances which warrant his detention. The State which makes the preliminary enquiry contemplated in paragraph 2 of this Article shall promptly report its findings to the said States and shall indicate whether it intends to exercise jurisdiction.

The issue of extradition became hotly debated in the preparation of the Convention – all the way to the closing hours of the Diplomatic Conference in December 1970.[28] It was felt imperative that the Convention must be drafted in a manner that would attract its universal acceptance world-wide across the complicated political spectrum of the Cold War that was at its peak. Surprisingly, the most unlikely allies at that period – United States, USSR and Israel – advocated identical positions with respect to extradition of the alleged offenders: they were proposing unconditional extradition of the alleged offenders to the State of registration of the aircraft. It must be admitted that this would have been the most effective approach creating a powerful deterrent of prospective extradition to the directly involved States known for their severe penalties.

Shortly before the end of the Conference the problem became critically divisive and almost led to a failure of the Conference. Some African delegations objected that unconditional extradition might in a particular case lead to extradition of an African to the "apartheid regime" of South Africa and such a condition would make the Convention absolutely unacceptable for African States. Similarly, some Arab States found it unacceptable that under such provision of the Convention an Arab or Moslem might face extradition to Israel. There were other delegations that expressed doubts about

---

28　The debates are recorded in Doc 8979-LC/165, Vol. I: Minutes and Vol. II: Documents.

unconditional extradition due to many existing constitutional provisions that may prevent extradition of own citizens.

At an advanced stage of the debates, salvation was found in the Roman law practice *aut dedere aut prosequi* (or *judicare*) – either extradite or prosecute – that was to be applied by provincial magistrates (praetors): either to extradite the accused to Rome or to assume jurisdiction. This alternative was found acceptable to assure that no offender could escape justice – he would be either extradited to a State directly interested or subject to the jurisdiction of the State holding him.

The discussion did not terminate at this point. Some delegations insisted that the alternative should be between extradition and *punishment (aut dedere aut punire)* but others objected that punishment may be meted out only if the alleged offender is found guilty after a due process.

Another proposal was to set the alternative between extradition and obligatory *prosecution* but that was also rejected with an argument that State authorities cannot be obliged to prosecute in any and all circumstances – *e.g.*, in the case of a minor or a mentally deranged person or in case the authorities invoke their prerogative to refrain from prosecution *(nolle prosequi)*; the obligation should not go beyond the duty to present the case to the competent authorities for the purpose of prosecution. The resulting compromise is reflected in Article 7 of the Convention that reads as follows:

> *Article 7*
> The Contracting State in the territory of which the alleged offender is found shall, if it does not extradite him, be obliged, without exception whatsoever and whether or not the offence was committed in its territory, to submit the case to its competent authorities for the purpose of prosecution. Those authorities shall take their decision in the same manner as in the case of any ordinary offence of a serious nature under the law of that State.

There was a clear understanding that no priority has been established by the Convention between extradition and prosecution. This Article also clearly stresses that the offence is to be treated as any "ordinary offence of serious nature", hence it should not be treated as a "political" offence for the purposes of justifying a claim for immunity or asylum.

The Convention also deals in Article 9 with the aftermath of an act of unlawful seizure in terms similar to Article 11 of the Tokyo Convention but it goes further in requiring not only to "permit" the passengers to continue the journey but to "facilitate" such continuation of the journey:

Article 9

1. When any of the acts mentioned in Article 1(a) has occurred or is about to occur, Contracting States shall take all appropriate measures to restore control of the aircraft to its lawful commander or to preserve his control of the aircraft.

2. In the cases contemplated by the preceding paragraph, any Contracting State in which the aircraft or its passengers or crew are present shall facilitate the continuation of the journey of the passengers and crew as soon as practicable, and shall without delay return the aircraft and its cargo to the persons lawfully entitled to possession.

Additional provisions of the Convention oblige the States to provide one another the greatest measure of assistance (Article 10) and to report to the Council of ICAO information on the circumstances of the offence and the measures taken under the Convention (Article 11).

A special attention had to be paid to the question of the depositary of the Convention due to the political cleavage in the recognition or non-recognition of certain entities at that point of the Cold War. A solution was found in the precedent established by the *Treaty Banning Nuclear Weapons Tests in the Atmosphere, in Outer Space and Under Water* signed at Moscow on 5 August 1963 (PTBT).[29] That treaty provided that the instruments of ratification or accessions are to be deposited in London, Moscow or Washington.

Following closely this precedent the Convention states in Article III, paragraph 2:

2. This Treaty shall be subject to ratification by the signatory States. Instruments of ratification and instruments of accession shall be deposited with the Governments of the Union of Soviet Socialist Republics, the United Kingdom of Great Britain and Northern Ireland, and the United States of America, which are hereby designated the Depositary Governments.

In the history of ICAO, this Convention is the first instrument adopted not only in English, French and Spanish but also in Russian. ICAO did not have its own Russian language services at that time, and the expert staff had to be brought from UNESCO in Paris at very short notice.

This Convention represents a substantial contribution to the development of international law and proves that common interests, unity of the political will and the sense of urgency can speed up the international law-making. Nevertheless, The Hague Convention was a fabulous compromise between the Parties and it made a success. However, the wave of unlawful seizures of aircraft substantially subsided over the years

---

29 www.state.gov/t/ac/trt/4797.htm#treaty, accessed on 31 December 2022.

but it would not be realistic to attribute this result to The Hague Convention. Criminal law is only an instrument of general prevention – a warning to the would-be criminals that they would face either prosecution or extradition and would not find a welcome or safe haven anywhere in the world. International civil aviation requires a high level of physical protection by searching and screening passengers and baggage to prevent the introduction of potential weapons on board.

The most serious incident of unlawful seizure of aircraft occurred on 11 September 2001 when four wide-bodied and fully fuelled aircraft on domestic flights were seized almost simultaneously in the Eastern United States and three of them were intentionally crashed – two against the World Trade Towers in New York and the third on the premises of Pentagon in Washington, D.C., the fourth crashed in Pennsylvania after valiant resistance and self-sacrifice of the passengers. Law alone could not have prevented this act of suicidal mass murderers but truly effective screening of all passengers and properly locked doors of the cockpits of the aircraft would have made a difference. No deficiency in The Hague Convention exists that could have contributed to the catastrophe of "911". Nevertheless, in the light of the policy pressure a visible action had to be taken also in the legal field in the "post 911" ICAO work program and at a Diplomatic Conference in Beijing on 10 September 2010 the scope of The Hague Convention (1970) was complemented by a Protocol purporting to define additional acts as offences in the light of "new" dangers.

8.4 Montreal Convention for the Suppression of Unlawful Acts Against the Safety of Civil Aviation 1971[30]

While an unlawful seizure of aircraft creates a serious danger for the flight and all persons on board, a far greater danger could be created by acts of sabotage of the aircraft or of the essential air navigation facilities. A typical example of an act of sabotage of an aircraft is causing an explosive charge (bomb) to detonate on board the aircraft in flight – such an act would in most cases lead to a complete destruction of the aircraft, death of all on board and possibly loss of life and material damage on the surface.

Incidents of this type also have a long history. The first recorded case appears to be the crash of Imperial Airways Argosy plane at Dixmude (or Diksmuide), Belgium on 28 March 1933 caused by fire started by a passenger on board.[31] On 10 October 1933, United Airlines B-247 crashed with 7 fatalities at Chesterton, Indiana after a nitro-

---

30 ICAO Doc 8966; the Minutes and Documents of the Conference are in ICAO Doc 9081 (in CD).
31 www.planecrashinfor.com/cause.htm.

glycerine charge exploded on board.³² Also the explosion of LZ Hindenburg Zeppelin on 6 May 1937 at Lakehurst, New Jersey was sometimes attributed to an act of sabotage.

A clearly criminal act was committed on 7 May 1949 against Philippine Airlines DC-3 on board of which 13 persons perished – a bomb was placed on board by two ex-convicts in a contract killing of the husband of a woman involved with another man.

A very similar act was committed on 9 September 1949 at Sault-au-Cochon, Quebec, Canada on board a Canadian Pacific Airlines DC-3 when a bomb placed in the baggage compartment caused the death of 23 persons; the main accused planned to murder his wife after insuring her life for USD 10,000 while his mistress helped to place a time bomb on board; her brother – a watchmaker – construed the timing mechanism; all three were sentenced to death and executed; M. Pitre was hanged on 9 January 1953 – the last woman ever to be hanged in Canada.³³

Serious political implications were involved in the explosion and crash, on 11 April 1955, of Air India "Princess of Kashmir" Lockheed Constellation flight from Hong Kong to Jakarta in the context of the Bandung Conference of non-aligned nations; the planned target of the bomb placed in the wheel well were apparently some senior Chinese politicians but they changed their travel plans and the victims were mostly journalists.

On 21 February 1970, Swissair Convair CV-990 on a flight from Zurich to Tel Aviv experienced an explosion on board shortly after take-off and the valiant effort of the captain to execute emergency landing was thwarted when acrid smoke filled the cockpit and electrical systems failed; all nine crew members and 38 passengers were killed.³⁴

Among other major instances of sabotage of aircraft with extensive loss of life was the explosion on Air India B-747 on 23 June 1985 in the Irish Sea, sabotage of the Korean Air plane in the Andaman Sea on 29 November 1985, explosion on Pan Am B-747 Flight 103 on 21 December 1988 over Lockerbie, Scotland, Union de Transports Aériens (UTA) Flight 772 on 19 September 1989 in Niger, etc.

The task of the ICAO Legal Committee in the preparation of a new instrument dealing, *inter alia*, with sabotage of aircraft in conformity with Assembly Resolution A17-20 was greatly facilitated by the consensus reached in The Hague Convention on issues of unlawful seizure of aircraft. The task was to formulate a sufficiently exhaustive and precise definition of an unlawful act against the safety of civil aviation to be designated as an "offence", stipulate a severe penalty for such offence, determine the jurisdiction of States to prosecute the alleged offender or offenders as widely as possible to achieve practically universal jurisdiction and to agree on conditions of extradition and related provisions.

---

32   www.wikipedia.org/wiki/United_Airlines_Chesterton_crash.
33   www.planecrashinfo.com/unusual.htm and www.mysteriesofcanada.com/Quebec/mass_murder.htm.
34   www.planecrashinfo.com/1970/1970-21.htm.

The Diplomatic Conference held in Montreal in August-September 1971 was more "relaxed" than the previous Conference at The Hague in December 1970. The most contentious problems of extradition have been solved by an acceptable compromise at The Hague and the new resulting Montreal Convention is now (December 2022) accepted by 188 States – an absolute record among Conventions for the unification of law!

The most difficult problem in discussions proved to be the definition of the "offence". While many delegations wished to make the definition as wide and all-encompassing as possible, others cautioned that the convention should not go beyond incidents with a distinct "international element" and that the incidents to be covered by the definition of the "offence" had to be directly related to the safety of civil aviation.

The cautious drafting of the definition of the "offence" is reflected in Article 1 as follows:

> *Article 1*
> 1. Any person commits an offence if he unlawfully and intentionally: a) performs an act of violence against a person on board an aircraft in flight if that act is likely to endanger the safety of that aircraft; or b) destroys an aircraft in service or causes damage to such an aircraft which renders it incapable of flight or which is likely to endanger its safety in flight; or c) places or causes to be placed on an aircraft in service, by any means whatsoever, a device or substance which is likely to destroy that aircraft, or to cause damage to it, which renders it incapable of flight, or to cause damage to it which is likely to endanger its safety in flight; or d) destroys or damages air navigation facilities or interferes with their operation, if any such act is likely to endanger the safety of aircraft in flight; or e) communicates information which he knows to be false, thereby endangering the safety of an aircraft in flight.
> 2. Any person also commits an offence if he: a) attempts to commit any of the offences mentioned in paragraph 1 of this Article; or b) is an accomplice of a person who commits or attempts to commit any such offence.

Some elements of this definition require more detailed interpretation based on the true intentions of the drafters. In the first place, the act must be "unlawful", *i.e.*, must be contrary to a general duty imposed by law. The act must be "intentional" – this specific offence under the Montreal Convention (1971) cannot be committed by negligence; the Conference did not discuss whether the intention must be "direct" (*i.e.*, true intent to cause the harmful result) or whether an "indirect" or "eventual" interest would suffice (the offender did not intend to cause the harmful result but was aware that such result may occur and that did not stop him from acting) – that would be left to interpretation by the Courts of law.

Not every act of violence against a person on board an aircraft in flight would constitute an "offence" under the Convention – it would qualify as an "offence" only "if that act is likely to endanger the safety of that flight" – and that would be a matter of evidence in each particular case for consideration by a Court of law. A physical attack by a passenger against another passenger would be relevant under the Tokyo Convention (1963) for the establishment of jurisdiction or powers of the aircraft commander (restraint, disembarkation, delivery ...) but in itself would not be an "offence" under the Montreal Convention (1971) unless the act is likely to endanger the safety of that aircraft.

Much thought was given during the drafting process to the act of destruction of an aircraft on the ground (as occurred in 1970 at the Dawson Field or elsewhere when a stationary aircraft was attacked by a bomb, hand grenade or anti-tank missile). Many delegations believed that an aircraft on the ground was just another piece of property and would not merit international legal protection against an attack unless there is a distinct danger to the safety of that aircraft in flight. The Conference finally decided to give international protection only to "aircraft in service" in case of its destruction or damage which would render it incapable of flight or which is likely to endanger its safety in flight. The term "in service" was defined in Article 2, paragraph b) as follows:

> b) an aircraft is considered to be in service from the beginning of the pre-flight preparation of the aircraft by ground personnel or by the crew for a specific flight until twenty-four hours after any landing; the period of service shall, in any event, extend for the entire period during which the aircraft is in flight as defined in paragraph a) of this Article.

This definition aimed at making sure that the aircraft is not just an object but that it is close to actual operation that could be endangered. The definition is not very fortunately formulated – in particular the twenty-four hours period after any landing is highly improbable for any airline because the commercial airlines cannot afford to keep the aircraft idle for such a long period of time – the typical aircraft would be "in service" practically all the time except for periods of extensive maintenance or repairs.

The very act of placing or causing to be placed on board an aircraft in service a "device or substance" (explosive or corrosive material ...) which is likely to destroy or damage the aircraft is an offence, regardless of any actual resulting damage; even an attempt to do so or complicity in the act or attempt would be qualified as an offence.

The destruction of or damage to air navigation facilities or interference with their operation is an offence only if it is likely to endanger the safety of aircraft in flight. There was an extensive debate about this provision since some delegations believed that the air navigation facilities (*e.g.*, radio transmission towers, radar stations) were localized in a particular State and did not possess an appropriate "foreign element" justifying inclusion into an international instrument. A provision limiting the applicability of subparagraph d) of paragraph 1 of Article 1 was then included in Article 4, paragraph 5 as follows:

> 5. In the cases contemplated in subparagraph d) of paragraph 1 of Article 1, this Convention shall apply only if the air navigation facilities are used in international air navigation.

This is not a very good and precise drafting – all system of electronic air navigation facilities, such as the HF, VHF, DME, VOR[35] and radar or GNSS facilities are generally available to aircraft at a very great distance from the originating transmitters and serve both domestic and international flights; the lawyers should have taken better advice from the technical experts.

Communication of a knowingly false message ("hoax") could endanger the safety of aircraft in flight. A malicious warning that there is a bomb on board the aircraft which is timed to explode at a determined moment cannot be disregarded and may force the pilot to seek fastest possible landing, possibly without proper maps, instrumentation, ATC or at an unsuitable airport. The pilot-in-command may also order emergency evacuation of the aircraft and in such actions the safety may be seriously jeopardized.

As in The Hague Convention the concept "in flight" is defined in Article 2 a) as a "closed universe", *i.e.*, when the external doors are closed to separate the aircraft from the possibility of an intervention by any external authority:

> a) an aircraft is considered to be in flight at any time from the moment when all its external doors are closed following embarkation until the moment when any such door is opened for disembarkation; in the case of a forced landing, the flight shall be deemed to continue until the competent authorities take over the responsibility for the aircraft and for persons and property on board;

Article 3 expresses the undertaking of each contracting State to make the offences punishable by "severe penalties". The Conference accepted the compromise reached in The Hague Convention and there was no extensive discussion on what the term "severe" is to mean.

Article 4, paragraph 1 repeats the now standard provision that the Convention shall not apply to aircraft used in military, customs or police services. The rest of Article 4 deals with additional aspects of the scope of applicability of the Convention and the somewhat convoluted text proves how anxious the authors of the Convention were to make sure that

---

35 High Frequency (HF), Very High Frequency (VHF), Distance Measuring Equipment (DME), Very-high-frequency Omnidirectional Radio (VOR).

only situations with a distinct "foreign element" would be governed by the new international instrument:

> 2. In the cases contemplated in subparagraphs a), b), c) and e) of paragraph 1 of Article 1, this Convention shall apply, irrespective of whether the aircraft is engaged in an international or domestic flight, only if: a) the place of take-off or landing, actual or intended, of the aircraft is situated outside the territory of the State of registration of that aircraft; or b) the offence is committed in the territory of a State other than the State of registration of the aircraft.
> 3. Notwithstanding paragraph 2 of this Article, in the cases contemplated in subparagraphs a), b), c) and e) of paragraph 1 of Article 1, this Convention shall also apply if the offender or the alleged offender is found in the territory of a State other than the State of registration of the aircraft.
> 4. With respect to the States mentioned in Article 9 and in the cases mentioned in subparagraphs a), b), c) and e) of paragraph 1 of Article 1, this Convention shall not apply if the places referred to in subparagraph a) of paragraph 2 of this Article are situated within the territory of the same State where that State is one of those referred to in Article 9, unless the offence is committed or the offender or alleged offender is found in the territory of a State other than that State.
> 5. In cases contemplated in subparagraph d) of paragraph 1 of Article 1, this Convention shall apply only if the air navigation facilities are used in international air navigation.
> 6. The provisions of paragraphs 2, 3, 4 and 5 of this Article shall also apply in the cases contemplated in paragraph 2 of Article 1.

The "foreign element" triggering the applicability of the Convention is, even in the case of a domestic flight, the place of take-off or landing (actual or intended) in a State other than the State of registration or the offence is committed in a State other than the State of registration; in any case, the Convention applies if the offender (or alleged offender) is found in a State other than the State of registration. The strict reference to the State of registration is gradually becoming less relevant in practice since aircraft are often registered in a State other than the State of the operator.

The provisions relating to jurisdiction of States fall short of universal jurisdiction with respect to some acts defined in Article 1. Universal jurisdiction would have been established if every State where the offender may be found would have to establish its jurisdiction. However, as will be seen in Article 5, paragraph 2 of the Convention, such universal jurisdiction is foreseen only with respect to acts defined in subparagraphs a), b) and c) of paragraph 1 of Article 1 and not for the acts defined in subparagraphs d) and e) (which refer to damage to air navigation facilities and to communication of false information):

Article 5
1. Each Contracting State shall take such measures as may be necessary to establish its jurisdiction over the offences in the following cases: a) when the offence is committed in the territory of that State; b) when the offence is committed against or on board an aircraft registered in that State; when the aircraft on board which the offence is committed lands in its territory with the alleged offender still on board; c) when the offence is committed against or on board an aircraft leased without crew to a lessee who has his principal place of business or, if the lessee has no such place of business, his permanent residence, in that State.
2. Each Contracting State shall likewise take such measures as may be necessary to establish its jurisdiction over the offences mentioned in Article 1, paragraph 1 a), b) and c), and in Article 1, paragraph 2, in so far as that paragraph relates to those offences, in the case where the alleged offender is present in its territory and it does not extradite him pursuant to Article 8 to any of the States mentioned in paragraph 1 of this Article.
3. This Convention does not exclude any criminal jurisdiction exercised in accordance with national law.

The procedural steps to be taken by the State having jurisdiction are described in Article 6:

Article 6
1. Upon being satisfied that the circumstances so warrant, any Contracting State in the territory of which the offender or the alleged offender is present, shall take him into custody or take other measures to ensure his presence. The custody and other measures shall be as provided in the law of that State but may only be continued for such time as is necessary to enable any criminal or extradition proceedings to be instituted.
2. Such State shall immediately make a preliminary enquiry into the facts.
3. Any person in custody pursuant to paragraph 1 of this Article shall be assisted in communicating immediately with the nearest appropriate representative of the State of which he is a national.
4. When a State, pursuant to this Article, has taken a person into custody, it shall immediately notify the States mentioned in Article 5, paragraph 1, the State of nationality of the detained person and, if it considers it advisable, any other interested States of the fact that such person is in custody and of the

circumstances which warrant his detention. The State which makes the preliminary enquiry contemplated in paragraph 2 of this Article shall promptly report its findings to the said States and shall indicate whether it intends to exercise jurisdiction.

The possibly controversial and divisive issue of extradition was solved in the Montreal Convention without any substantive discussion and the model adopted in The Hague Convention was accepted – *aut dedere aut prosequi* without establishing any mutual priority between extradition or assumption of jurisdiction:

Article 7
The Contracting State in the territory of which the alleged offender is found shall, if it does not extradite him, be obliged, without exception whatsoever and whether or not the offence was committed in its territory, to submit the case to its competent authorities for the purpose of prosecution. Those authorities shall take their decision in the same manner as in the case of any ordinary offence of a serious nature under the law of that State.

The format is the same as in The Hague Convention: the State concerned is only obliged to present the case to the appropriate authorities for the purpose of prosecution and the offence is to be addressed as an "ordinary" (*i.e.*, non-political) offence of a serious nature and there is no obligation to extradite the alleged offender.

This seemingly clear provision became strongly contested after the Lockerbie disaster of Pan Am Flight 103 on 21 December 1988 in which 270 people were killed after the explosion of a SEMTEX[36] bomb on board. The United Kingdom and the United States after their investigation claimed that the bomb was planted on board by security agents of the Libyan Arab Jamahiriya and requested extradition of the alleged offenders.

The Libyan authorities refused extradition with reference to Article 7 of the Montreal Convention (1971) and professed willingness to prosecute the alleged offenders if the US and UK authorities provide the relevant evidence.

The matter was presented to the UN Security Council as a subject of "international terrorism" endangering international peace and security. The Security Council adopted a Resolution on 21 January 1992[37] requesting Libya to cooperate in the suppression of international terrorism; when Libya failed to comply, the Security Council adopted

---

36 Semtex is an extraordinarily dangerous and powerful explosive developed in Czechoslovakia in the 1960s. It is difficult to find, dogs cannot smell it, X-ray does not detect it, the density of the material is low; finally, it is plastic and heat and water resistant. It can be used for 20 years, see Section 8.6.
37 UN S/RES 731 (1992).

another resolution shortly thereafter – on 31 March 1992[38] – in which it determined that the failure by the Libyan Government "to demonstrate, by concrete actions its renunciation of terrorism ... constitutes a threat to international peace and security" and declared as of 15 April 1992 sanctions against Libya under Chapter VII of the UN Charter.

The sanctions included denial by States of "permission to any aircraft to take off from, land in or overfly their territory if it is destined to land or has taken off from the territory of Libya", prohibition to supply any aircraft or aircraft components to Libya, etc. An even stricter measure was imposed on Libya by Security Council Resolution of 11 November 1993[39] that called for the freezing of all Libyan funds abroad. Libya brought the case to the International Court of Justice.[40] The case became to a large degree moot after the Security Council adopted, on 12 September 2003, a Resolution lifting the sanctions.[41]

However, the case raised a fundamental question whether the decisions of the Security Council under Chapter VII of the UN Charter are subject to a review by another body of the UN. The ICJ is not positioned above the Security Council!

According to Article 103 of the UN Charter "in the event of a conflict between the obligations of the Members of the United Nations under the present Charter and their obligations under any other international agreement, their obligations under the present Charter shall prevail". The Lockerbie case went beyond the scope of the Montreal Convention once it was qualified by the Security Council – a body with "primary responsibility for the maintenance of international peace and security" – as a threat to international peace and security and once the Security Council invoked measures under Chapter VII of the Charter.[42]

Like The Hague Convention (1970) the Montreal Convention has three depositories – the Soviet Union, the United Kingdom and the United States.

Like The Hague Convention (1970) the Montreal Convention was also revisited in the ICAO legal work program in the "post 911" efforts to address all acts and offences of concern to the international aviation community. The intended expansion of the scope of offences to be covered by international instruments did not make it feasible to solve the task by a protocol to the Montreal Convention (1971); the ICAO-sponsored Diplomatic Conference in Beijing adopted and opened for signature, on 10 September 2010, a new

---

38 UN S/RES 748 (1992).
39 UN S/RES/883 (1983).
40 Case Concerning Questions of Interpretation and Application of the Montreal Convention (1971) arising from the Aerial Incident at Lockerbie (*Libyan Arab Jamahiriya v. United Kingdom* and *Libyan Arab Jamahiriya v. United States of America*, Judgment of 27 February 1998).
41 UN S/RES/1506 (2003).
42 The title of that Chapter is "Action with Respect to Threats to the Peace, Breaches of the Peace, and Acts of Aggression". The Resolutions of the Security Council in this case were based on Article 41 of the Charter that deals with "measures not involving the use of armed force".

Convention that would – as among the parties to this new Convention – replace the Montreal Convention (1971) (see Section 8.11). The venerable Convention of 1971 remains untouched for its 188 current Parties, and it is to be seen whether the new 2010 instrument ever achieves such a wide acceptance. Anyhow, the Beijing Convention (2010) came into force on 1 July 2018.

8.5 MONTREAL PROTOCOL FOR THE SUPPRESSION OF UNLAWFUL ACTS OF VIOLENCE AT AIRPORTS SERVING INTERNATIONAL CIVIL AVIATION 1988, SUPPLEMENTARY TO THE CONVENTION FOR THE SUPPRESSION OF UNLAWFUL ACTS AGAINST THE SAFETY OF CIVIL AVIATION 1971[43]

At the 26th Session of the ICAO Assembly in 1986, Canada, supported by several other delegations, proposed[44] that a new instrument should be elaborated dealing with the unlawful acts of violence at airports serving international civil aviation. Particular attention was given to the bomb explosion at Narita airport in June 1985 and the armed attacks at the Rome and Vienna airports in December 1985.

During 1973-1985, there were twenty-five armed attacks committed at different airports. While none of them took place in Canada, the authorities of Canada were anxious to come up with a new initiative in the field of aviation security due to some implicit international criticism of the allegedly ineffective screening of passengers and baggage in Canada that may have contributed to the sabotage of Air India B-747 in the Irish Sea and the explosion at the Narita airport on 23 June 1985.

At the first glance there is no prominent "foreign element" in the acts of violence at airports – the airport is clearly situated in a particular sovereign territory where the local law applies and where the local authorities exercise full authority and jurisdiction. There is no visible "legal vacuum" that would have to be filled by an international instrument. An exceptional situation would be if the offenders or alleged offenders managed to escape from the place where the act was committed and be eventually found in another State – that would justify new provisions on prosecution or extradition.

The concept "airport serving international civil aviation" is not a "foreign element" because of its location in the territory of a particular State and within its full jurisdiction.

Resolution A26-4 allocated to the subject the highest degree of priority in the work program of the ICAO Legal Committee. The Council convened a Special Sub-Committee of the Legal Committee from 20 to 30 January 1987 to implement the Resolution A26-4. That Sub-Committee, on the basis of the rapporteur's report, concluded that the issue

---

43   Doc 9518; generally referred to as "Montreal Protocol 1988".
44   A26-WP/41, EX/9, 14/7/86.

should not be dealt with in a separate instrument but in the form of a protocol to the Montreal Convention (1971) – extending its applicability and the correlated jurisdiction to additional elements of the "offences".

The 26th Session of the Legal Committee met at Montreal from 28 April to 13 May 1987 and finalized the draft Protocol.[45] The Diplomatic Conference met at Montreal from 9 to 24 February 1988[46] and adopted by consensus the Protocol to the Montreal Convention. Currently (December 2022), the Protocol has been ratified by 176 States. It is unprecedented in international practice of law-making that a new multilateral instrument was prepared and adopted in less than 18 months after the first initiative! The Protocol contains only two substantive provisions, but they were not easy to draft and will not be easy to interpret in practice. In general, it may be fair to say that the Protocol is not a masterpiece of legal drafting.

The scope of application is defined in Article I of the Protocol:

> *Article I*
> This Protocol supplements the Convention for the Suppression of Unlawful Acts against the Safety of Civil Aviation, done at Montreal on 23 September 1971, and, as between the Parties to this Protocol, the Convention and the Protocol shall be read and interpreted together as one single instrument.

Article I thus clarifies that the Protocol is not a self-standing instrument but that it only supplements the Montreal Convention (1971) and, between the parties thereto, is to be read and interpreted together as one single instrument.

Like in The Hague and Montreal Conventions the centre of gravity of the Protocol is in the definition of the offence and the jurisdiction related thereto. The addition to the definition of the offence is in Article II that adds paragraph 1*bis* to Article 1 of the Montreal Convention (1971):

> *Article II*
> 1. In Article 1 of the Convention, the following shall be added as new paragraph 1*bis*:
> "1*bis*. Any person commits an offence if he unlawfully and intentionally, using any device, substance or weapon: a) performs an act of violence against a person at an airport serving international civil aviation which causes or is likely to cause serious injury or death; or b) destroys or seriously damages the

---
45 Doc 9502-LC/186.
46 Doc 9823-DC/5.

facilities of an airport serving international civil aviation or aircraft not in service located thereon or disrupts the services of the airport,
if such an act endangers or is likely to endanger safety at that airport."
2. In paragraph 2 a) of Article 1 of the Convention, the following words shall be inserted after the words "paragraph 1":
"or paragraph 1*bis*".

Each element of this additional definition of an "offence" was subject to exhaustive discussions but that still cannot guarantee full mutual understanding and unity of interpretation. Several issues remain open to interpretation.

The act must be "unlawful", *i.e.*, contrary to a binding legal standard of behaviour. It must be "intentional", not committed by negligence. Whether the intention must be "direct" or "eventual" would remain for interpretation by a competent court of law.

The act must be committed with the use of "any device, substance or weapon" – evidently not by bare hands only – even hands qualified in lethal martial arts. The expression "weapon" would have been sufficient since most legal system interpret this term as meaning "any object that can make the attack against a body or object more effective"; "device" and "substance" make the concept much wider but not more precise.

"Act of violence against a person" should mean any attack against the bodily integrity of a person and the intensity of such an act must be such as to cause or be likely to cause serious injury or death. Could a "mental trauma" be interpreted as a "serious injury"?

The act must be committed "at an airport serving international civil aviation". No definition is offered of what means "airport" and which areas of an aerodrome are still to be considered "airport" – the public parking lot or restaurant close to or within the terminal building? What is an airport "serving international civil aviation"? Should it be interpreted as a customs airport designated by the State concerned?[47] Could it be any airport where foreign civil aircraft may be permitted to land in emergency?

Much debated point was the so-called "private" crime – a crime that is unrelated to civil aviation and could have been committed anywhere: the frequently discussed hypothesis was a passenger murdering his mother-in-law at an airport. It was correctly considered absurd that such type of a crime would be the subject of an international instrument and the strict qualification was added: "if such an act endangers or is likely to endanger safety at that airport" – a concept open to interpretation.

Destruction or serious damage of "facilities" at such an airport also call for interpretation: a real example was discussed when the striking employees of the parking service were throwing bricks and broke glass in the airport restaurant and disrupted the movement of the passengers – an act hardly to be considered an international "offence".

---

47   Article 10 of the Chicago Convention.

Again, this provision had to be qualified by the condition that the act endangers or is likely to endanger safety at that airport.

In a substantial departure from the Montreal Convention (1971) the Protocol also refers to "aircraft not in service" the damage or destruction of which would be an offence but only if such act does or is likely to endanger the safety at that airport.

The jurisdiction of courts had to be extended by the Protocol to take account of the extended definition of the offence. It was achieved in Article III of the Protocol which would add an additional paragraph 2*bis* into Article 5 of the Convention:

> *Article III*
> In Article 5 of the Convention, the following shall be added as paragraph 2*bis*:
> "2*bis*. Each Contracting State shall likewise take such measures as may be necessary to establish its jurisdiction over the offences mentioned in Article 1, paragraph 1*bis*, and in Article 1, paragraph 2, in so far as that paragraph relates to those offences, in the case where the alleged offender is present in its territory and it does not extradite him pursuant to Article 8 to the State mentioned in paragraph 1 a) of this Article."

For symmetry with the Montreal Convention (1971) the Protocol also has three depositaries – USSR, United Kingdom and the United States – although by 1988 most of the protocolar irritants of the Cold War were overcome.

The Protocol may be criticized for not being of substantial international importance, not containing a strong "international element" and for not being perfectly drafted. However, it is a useful addition to the global mosaic of aviation security instruments.

8.6 Montreal Convention on the Marking of Plastic Explosives for the Purpose of Detection 1991

The investigation concluded that the Lockerbie disaster of Pan Am Flight 103 over Lockerbie on 21 December 1988 was caused by the plastic explosive SEMTEX.[48] Similar conclusion was reached in the case of the disaster of UTA Flight 772 on 19 September 1989 in Niger. In many other terrorist attacks against other targets (*e.g.*, Israeli Embassy in Buenos Aires, the USS Cole in the Gulf, the IRA murder of Lord Mountbatten) plastic explosives were also used.

---

48 This explosive was manufactured by the firm Explosia Semtin. a.s. in (then) Czechoslovakia; a comparable substance is C-4 (Composition 4) of the US armed forces, UK's DEMTEX, France's PE-4. See explosia.cz/app/uploads/2020/05/Explosia_100_let_kniha_210x210_n4.pdf, accessed on 31 December 2022.

Plastic explosives belong to the most powerful explosives short of nuclear power. They have unique physical characteristics – they are stable at different temperatures, waterproof, flexible and hand malleable into different shapes that are easily concealed in letters, books, toys, small appliances, etc. They are inert to shock or flame, safe to handle and require a fuse to trigger detonation.

Plastic explosives are a legitimate substance widely used by the armies of the world and in the mining, landscaping and construction industries. However, in the hands of terrorists they become very dangerous not only for their enormous power but because they are hard to detect.

They have a low mass and thus are not detectable by X-rays. Moreover, they have a very low "vapor pressure", do not issue any perceptible "smell" and cannot be detected by the traditional means (sniffing dogs, explosive detection sensors).

The Lockerbie disaster, with its 270 fatalities on 21 December 1988, drew urgent attention to the special danger of plastic explosives for aviation and already on 30 January 1989, the Council of ICAO established an ad hoc Group of Experts on the Detection of Explosives that met at Montreal from 6 to 10 March 1989 and these experts concluded that it was technically possible to "mark" the plastic explosives by a specific additive that would make them detectable.

On 14 June 1989, the UN Security Council[49] unanimously "urged ICAO to intensify its work aimed at preventing all acts of terrorism against international civil aviation, and in particular its work on devising an international regime for the marking of plastic or sheet explosives for the purpose of detection".

At the 27th Session of the ICAO Assembly in September-October 1989 the delegations of the United Kingdom and Czechoslovakia jointly made a proposal[50] that an international instrument on the marking of plastic explosives should be expeditiously drafted and that a session of the ICAO Legal Committee should be convened in the first half of 1990 to prepare such draft. The Assembly unanimously accepted this proposal.[51] The UN General Assembly in December 1989 adopted a unanimous resolution[52] noting the ongoing work of ICAO on this problem.

While the subject was so urgently in the focus of ICAO, of the UN Security Council and the UN General Assembly, the legal work progressed effectively but strictly in harmony with the established procedures: a Rapporteur was duly appointed and presented his report in September 1989; a special Sub-Committee of the Legal Committee met at Montreal from 9 to 19 January 1990 and prepared a preliminary draft Convention.[53] The

---

49 UN S/RES 635 (1989).
50 A27-WP/115, EX/37.
51 Resolution A27-8.
52 A44/29.
53 LC/SC-MEX-REPORT.

27th Session of the Legal Committee met at Montreal from 27 March to 17 April 1990 and prepared a final draft that it considered mature for presentation to a Diplomatic Conference.[54] Thus in some six months since the formal proposal by the United Kingdom and Czechoslovakia the draft Convention was ready and only the procedural rules and the scheduling logistics required some delay in the convening of the Diplomatic Conference.

The Conference met at Montreal from 11 February to 1 March 1991[55] and was attended by the then UN Secretary-General Javier Perez de Cuellar. It adopted by consensus and opened for signature the Convention for the Marking of Plastic Explosives for the Purpose of Detection that has by now (December 2022) been ratified by 156 States.

The general concept of the Convention is very simple: plastic explosives could be made detectable by a "marker" – a small quantity of an additive substance added to them. The fundamental obligation of States under the Convention should be to prohibit and prevent the manufacture in their territory of unmarked explosives, and to prohibit and prevent the movement into and out of its territory of unmarked explosives. Those simple principles are set forth in Article II and III of the Convention:

> *Article II*
> Each State Party shall take the necessary and effective measures to prohibit and prevent the manufacture in its territory of unmarked explosives.
>
> *Article III*
> 1. Each State Party shall take the necessary and effective measures to prohibit and prevent the movement into or out of its territory of unmarked explosives.
> 2. The preceding paragraph shall not apply in respect of movements for purposes not inconsistent with the objectives of this Convention, by authorities of a State Party performing military or police functions, of unmarked explosives under the control of that State Party in accordance with paragraph 1 of Article IV.

There appeared one technical difficulty: the plastic explosives can be effectively marked only during the process of their manufacture and the vast existing stock of such explosives that is in the hands of the military, police or industrial or other holders cannot be effectively marked. The Conference had to find agreement on how to deal with such existing stock. In the first place it would be necessary to prevent the diversion of such unmarked explosives for illegitimate purposes. The legitimate industrial holders would be given three years from the entry into force of the Convention to mark (if that proves feasible),

---
54 Doc 9556-LC/187.
55 Doc 9801-DC/4.

destroy, consume or render permanently ineffective the exiting stock of unmarked explosives.

A greater problem for the Conference was the existing stock of unmarked plastic explosives that are in the possession of military or police authorities. The Conference heard an argument that the purpose of the new convention was not "disarmament" and that it was not possible to have an international obligation to destroy the vast stockpiles of military ammunition, shells, grenades, bombs, etc. that do contain unmarked plastic explosives. It was also believed that a sudden "destruction" (*i.e.*, explosion) of all existing stocks of plastic explosives could cause unforeseeable environmental consequences. All such military devices had to be excluded from the scope of the Convention on the assumption that the military and police authorities were able to prevent any diversion of their materials to unlawful use. Military and police plastic explosives not incorporated integrally into some devices are to be marked or rendered permanently ineffective within a period of fifteen years from the entry into force of the Convention.

The difficult compromise concerning the existing stock of plastic explosives is reflected in Article IV of the Convention:

Article IV
1. Each State Party shall take the necessary measures to exercise strict and effective control over the possession and transfer of possession of unmarked explosives which have been manufactured in or brought into its territory prior to the entry into force of this Convention in respect of that State, so as to prevent their diversion or use for purposes inconsistent with the objectives of this Convention.
2. Each State Party shall take the necessary measures to ensure that all stocks of those explosives referred to in paragraph 1 of this Article not held by its authorities performing military or police functions are destroyed or consumed for purposes not inconsistent with the objectives of this Convention, marked or rendered permanently ineffective, within a period of three years from the entry into force of this Convention in respect of that State.
3. Each State Party shall take the necessary measures to ensure that all stocks of those explosives referred to in paragraph 1 of this Article held by its authorities performing military or police functions and that are not incorporated as an integral part of duly authorized military devices are destroyed or consumed for purposes not inconsistent with the objectives of this Convention, marked or rendered permanently ineffective, within a period of fifteen years from the entry into force of this Convention in respect of that State.

4. Each State Party shall take the necessary measures to ensure the destruction, as soon as possible, in its territory of unmarked explosives which may be discovered therein and which are not referred to in the preceding paragraphs of this Article, other than stocks of unmarked explosives held by its authorities performing military or police functions and incorporated as an integral part of duly authorized military devices at the date of the entry into force of this Convention in respect of that State.

5. Each State Party shall take the necessary measures to exercise strict and effective control over the possession and transfer of possession of the explosives referred to in paragraph II of Part 1 of the Technical Annex to this Convention so as to prevent their diversion or use for purposes inconsistent with the objectives of this Convention.

6. Each State Party shall take the necessary measures to ensure the destruction, as soon as possible, in its territory of unmarked explosives manufactured since the coming into force of this Convention in respect of that State that are not incorporated as specified in paragraph II d) of Part 1 of the Technical Annex to this Convention and of unmarked explosives which no longer fall within the scope of any other sub-paragraphs of the said paragraph II.

In spite of its apparent simplicity, the Montreal Convention (1991) introduced some pioneering and creative elements to international law-making. This was to a large degree attributable to the complex technical nature of the subject: it is not easy to formulate an all-encompassing definition of plastic explosives because the technology is in constant process of development and any definition may soon become obsolete. Similarly, the current knowledge of the suitable marking agents may evolve in time and new techniques may become available. The resulting drafting approach was not to include the definitions of plastic explosives and of the "detection agents"[56] into the main body of the Convention but into a Technical Annex that is subject to an innovative and simplified amendment procedure – by "silence" (non-objection).

In Article I of the Convention only the following general definitions appear with cross-reference to the Technical Annex that forms an integral part of the Convention:

Article I
For the purposes of this Convention:
1. "Explosives" mean explosive products, commonly known as "plastic explosives", including explosives in flexible or elastic sheet form, as described in the Technical Annex to this Convention.

---

56   The "detection agents" are in fact miniscule quantities (0.1-0.5%) of some known and detectable explosives.

2. "Detection agent" means a substance as described in the Technical Annex to this Convention which is introduced into an explosive to render it detectable.

3. "Marking" means introducing into an explosive a detection agent in accordance with the Technical Annex to this Convention.

The Convention in Article V and VI provides for the establishment of an International Explosive Technical Commission of 15-19 experts appointed by the ICAO Council; the experts should have direct and substantial experience in matters relating to the manufacture or detection of, or research in, explosives. The Commission should evaluate the technical developments relating to the manufacture, marking and detection of explosives, report to States through the ICAO Council and make recommendations for amendments to the Technical Annex. The Council of ICAO may then, on the recommendation of the Commission, propose to States Parties amendments to the Technical Annex.

The novel element in international treaties is the procedure for the amendment of the Technical Annex: if a proposed amendment has not been objected to by five or more States Parties by written notification within ninety days of the Council's proposal, it shall be deemed to have been adopted and shall enter into force one hundred and eighty days thereafter or after such other period as specified in the proposed amendment.[57] In the absence of any further qualification it has to be understood that such an amendment will be applicable *erga omnes*. If five or more States have objected to the proposed amendment, the Council shall refer it to the Commission for further consideration and may also convene a conference of all States Parties.

This creative approach may assure speedy and effective updating and modernization of the Technical Annex. The Convention by its scope and impact exceeds the interests of international civil aviation and its benefits will be felt in all situations where the detection of plastic explosives may prevent an unlawful act.

The fact that the UN Security Council and the UN General Assembly specifically entrusted ICAO with the preparation of an instrument of a general interest not restricted to civil aviation is a sign of respect and recognition that the ICAO law-making mechanism proved to be expeditious and efficient.

8.7   Annex 17 – Security

ICAO Standards and Recommended Practices are another source of international regulations relevant to aviation security. Following Assembly Resolutions A17-10 and

---

57   The first such amendment under the procedure set out in Articles VI and VII of the Convention came into force on 19 December 2005. See ICAO Doc 9571, 2nd ed., 2007.

A18-10 and extensive studies in the ICAO Council, Air Transport Committee, Air Navigation Commission and the Unlawful Interference Committee a new set of security Standards and Recommended Practices was adopted on 22 March 1974 and designated as Annex 17.

That Annex was amended and updated on several occasions to reflect the practical experience and the changing character of the threats to civil aviation. The amendments of 7 December 2001 – in the wake of "911" – gave that Annex a unique character among the others by making it applicable not only to international aviation but also to domestic flights. This amendment – the 14th since 1974 – became applicable on 14 November 2014.

Annex 17 is complemented by the *Security Manual for Safeguarding Civil Aviation Against Acts of Unlawful Interference*.[58]

Annex 17 provides that each State must establish in written form a national aviation security program and designate an appropriate authority responsible for the development, implementation and maintenance of the national aviation security program. Similarly, each airport must establish, implement and maintain in written form airport security program. Moreover, each commercial air transport operator providing service from that State must have such a program. All persons involved in the aviation security program must be certified according to the national security requirements to ensure reliability and consistency.

While the international multilateral Conventions (The Hague 1970 and Montreal 1971) have their centre of gravity in the *suppression* of the acts against the security of aviation by criminal prosecution and penalty, Annex 17 focuses on the preventive measures. It established the duty of each State to take measures to prevent weapons, explosives or any other dangerous devices, articles or substances, which may be used to commit an act of unlawful interference, from being introduced, by any means whatsoever, on board an aircraft engaged in civil aviation.

One of the essential preventative elements is to control the access to airside areas of the airports and to prevent unauthorized access. Security restricted areas must be established at the airports and a proper identification system must be established in respect of persons and vehicles in order to prevent unauthorized access to airside areas and security restricted areas. Background checks should be conducted on persons granted unescorted access to security restricted areas and their identity should be verified at designated checkpoints.

With respect to the aircraft the prescribed *security check* or aircraft *security search* should be performed. Measures should be taken that disembarking passengers of commercial flights do not leave items on board the aircraft. (This provision was added after the destruction of Korean Air B-707 on a flight from Abu Dhabi to Bangkok on

---

58 ICAO Doc 8973, Restricted (The designation "Restricted" does not make the document "secret" but it means that ICAO restricts the distribution of this document only to the appropriate national authorities!).

29 November 1987 over the Andaman Sea; two passengers (posing as Japanese tourists but in fact agents of North Korea) disembarked in Abu Dhabi and left a radio/alarm clock and liquor bottles with explosives in the overhead rack; there were 115 victims).[59]

Contracting States have the duty to establish measures to ensure that originating passengers of commercial air transport operations and their cabin baggage are screened prior to boarding an aircraft departing from a security restricted area. The screening of passengers and their hand baggage is a universal international practice and has been intensified and professionalized in particular after "911".

The "culture" of the screening differs from country to country – from gentle and polite to intrusive and hostile and the passenger has no choice but to submit to it. After some alarming suspicious activities identified in London in 2005 the airlines had to prohibit the carriage of any liquids in the cabin baggage, later mitigated to tolerate liquids not exceeding 100 ml. The baggage that is to be carried in the hold must be screened prior to being loaded onto an aircraft engaged in commercial air transport operations.

States must also ensure that commercial air transport operators do not transport the baggage of passengers who are not on board;[60] this provision was formulated after the disaster of Air India B-747 Flight 182 from Montreal to London on 23 June 1985 over the Irish Sea with 329 fatalities; a bomb was planted in a piece of luggage checked in Vancouver whose owner did not board the flight; simultaneously, unaccompanied luggage from Canadian Pacific Flight 003 exploded at the Narita airport, Japan killing two baggage handlers. The Lockerbie disaster of Pan Am Flight 103 on 21 December 1988 was caused by an explosive device hidden in an unaccompanied transfer luggage apparently originating in Malta.

Security controls must be applied to cargo and mail prior to their being loaded onto an aircraft engaged in passenger commercial air transport.[61] No such requirement exists so far with respect to "all cargo" flights but in practice such controls are applied in most countries. Appropriate security controls must be applied also to catering, stores and supplies intended for carriage on passenger commercial flights.[62]

States should develop requirements for air carriers for the carriage of potentially disruptive passengers who are obliged to travel because they have been the subject of judicial or administrative proceedings. This applies, in particular, to persons who are being deported against their will. The aircraft operator and the pilot-in-command must be informed of such passengers in order that appropriate security procedures can be applied.[63]

---

59 ICAO ADREP Summary 4/88 (#11); ICAO Circular 259-AN/153 (234-243) (1998).
60 Annex 17, Standard 4.5.3.
61 Annex 17, Standard 4.6.1.
62 Annex 17, Standard 4.6.5.
63 Annex 17, Standard 4.7.3.

While the carriage of weapons on board aircraft is generally prohibited, a special authorization in accordance with the law of the State involved may be given to law enforcement officers but they may travel on board with the weapons only subject to approval of all States involved.[64] The deployment of armed security officers on board ("air marshals") continues to be a controversial matter and many States do not approve such practice.

In the confined space of an aircraft any use of firearms may hurt innocent passengers or cause damage to sensitive equipment of the aircraft – such as the wiring controlling the operation of some vital components; the piercing of the pressurized hull of the aircraft could possibly lead to explosive decompression.

Such tragic event was experienced on 23 November 1985 by EgyptAir Flight 648 from Athens to Cairo; when the Abu Nidal terrorists hijacked the plane, an air marshal shot one terrorist dead and he himself was killed a moment later. In the exchange of fire, the plane's fuselage was punctured causing a rapid depressurization and the aircraft had to descend to 10,000 feet to allow the crew and passengers to breathe. The aircraft eventually landed in Malta, some passengers were murdered by the hijackers and 56 out of the remaining 88 passengers perished during a bungled rescue attempt by Egyptian military that caused not only an indiscriminate shootout but also an explosion and fire.[65]

In spite of the lack of consensus on the deployment of air marshals some States insisted that all aircraft with destination to a particular airport in their territory must have armed marshals on board.[66] The air marshals must be "government personnel" who are specially selected and trained and their deployment must be kept strictly confidential.

The pilot-in-command must be notified of the number of armed persons and their seat location.[67] It remains questionable whether the pilot-in-command can give orders to or override the decision of the armed marshals, and it should be argued that the aircraft commander should be the ultimate authority in charge of the aircraft.

The security arrangements and procedures are very costly and in most cases it is the passenger who pays for the in the form of special charges or within the overall airport charges. Moreover, the preventive security measures are very time consuming and require

---

64 Annex 17, Standard 4.7.4.
65 en.wikipedia.org/wiki/EgyptAir_Flight_648, accessed on 31 December 2022.
66 Air Canada normally did not use air marshals but was obliged to do so for flights to Ronald Reagan Washington National Airport that is within sight of the landmarks of the US capital. In late 2007, in response to heightened perceived threat, US started requesting all airlines flying to the US to have armed Federal Air Marshals on board. It was not generally clear who is to pay for the carriage of such persons and who is to be responsible for their acts. Therefore, the Montreal Protocol (2014) to Amend the Convention on Offences and Certain Acts Committed on Board Aircraft (Tokyo Convention, 1963) deals with the In-Flight Security Officers' (IFSO) rights and obligations. Besides, the States can conclude bilateral Agreements regarding IFSO's activity on international flights. See Section 8.8.1.
67 Annex 17, Standard 4.7.8.

the passengers to be at the airport in some cases up to 3 hours before departure of their flight. This apparent but unavoidable conflict with the interest of facilitation of international civil aviation is not mitigated by a general Recommended Practice 2.3 of Annex 17 which reads as follows:

> 2.3 Each Contracting State should whenever possible arrange for the security controls and procedures to cause a minimum of interference with, or delay to the activities of, civil aviation provided that the effectiveness of these controls and procedures is not compromised.

This is only a recommended practice and its cautious wording clearly indicates that the interests of aviation security have an overriding priority over any other interests. In Annex 9 dealing with facilitation a similar position is reflected in Standard 3.2:

> 3.2 In developing procedures aimed at efficient application of border controls of passengers and crew, Contracting States shall take into account the application of aviation security, border integrity, narcotics control and immigration control measures, where appropriate.

The Attachment to Annex 17 consolidates the provisions of other Annexes that specifically address the issues of aviation security.

Standard 3.7 of Annex 2 (Rules of the Air) provides that an aircraft under unlawful seizure should endeavour to communicate this fact and any deviation from the flight plan to the appropriate Air Traffic Service (ATS); this is essential to coordinate the new flight path with other traffic to prevent a possible collision.

Standard 13.2.1 of Annex 6 – Part I (Operation of the Aircraft – International Commercial Air Transport – Aeroplanes) provides that the crew compartment door of the aircraft should be capable of being locked; moreover, Standard 13.2.2 adopted after "911" provides that as of 1 November 2003, all airplanes with a seating capacity over 60 passengers must have crew compartment doors designed to resist small arms fire and grenade shrapnel and resist forcible intrusion. The implementation of this requirement proved to be extremely costly for the airlines at a time of serious drop in air transport demand.

Standard 11.2 of Annex 8 (Airworthiness of Aircraft) requires that during the design of aircraft consideration should be given to the provision of a "least-risk" location so as to minimize the effect of a bomb to the aeroplane and its occupants; under Standard 11.4 of the same Annex the design should deter any easy concealment of explosives or weapons on board and should facilitate the search procedures.

During an act of unlawful interference in flight it may be impossible for the crew to use voice communication to inform the ground services of its situation. For that reason, Annex 10 (Aeronautical Communications, Vol. IV – Surveillance and Collision Avoidance Systems, Secondary Surveillance Radar [SSR]) specifies Mode A reply code (information pulse) 7700 for any emergency on board and code 7500 specifically for unlawful interference on board.[68]

Annex 11 (Air Traffic Services) provides for maximum assistance and priority to aircraft subjected to unlawful interference, Annex 14 (Aerodromes) sets forth aspects of airport design and operation to prevent unlawful interference.

Recommended Practice 2.4.6 in Annex 17 states that each State should include in each of its bilateral agreements on air transport a clause related to aviation security, taking into account the model clause developed by ICAO. This recommendation has received a large acceptance and the security clause can now be deemed to be an integral part of the mutual exchange of traffic rights.

In general, it should be concluded that the technical specifications in the ICAO SARPs, in particular in Annex 17, have accomplished a high level of preventive security in civil aviation on a world-wide basis. The SARPs are constantly updated – mostly as a response to new threats and methods used by the perpetrators.

8.8 Unruly/Disruptive Passengers

Aviation security may be compromised also by the conduct of the passengers on board and their actions against the crew, against other passengers or property on board or otherwise endangering the safety of the aircraft.

Aircraft in flight represents a very special environment and inherent risks. The number and gravity of incidents involving unruly or disruptive passengers on board has been growing in an alarming manner[69] and "air rage" has become as common as "road rage". It is important to analyse the causes of the disruptive behaviour on board in order to prevent it or mitigate its impact.

One of the leading causes of the unruly conduct on board is stress. The passengers come on board tired by the travel to the airport, long waiting at the airport, intrusive security checks, looking for their seat and trying to find space for their hand luggage in competition with other passengers. The confined space on board, long periods of waiting without explanation of the delays, long flight with dry air and poor ventilation, poor food

---

68   Standard 2.1.4.
69   www.faa.gov./data_statistics/passengers_cargo/unruly_passengers, accessed on 31 December 2022. More than two thousands unruly passenger incidents were reported by the crew of US airlines in the first 10 months of 2022.

or no food service, nicotine withdrawal – all these elements add to the level of stress that may result in unsuppressed rage and aggressiveness.

The cabin crew are not exempt and their own stress may provoke negative reaction of the passengers. Stress and anxiety of persons suffering from the "fear of flying" may trigger serious consequences – *e.g.*, effort to open the door and leave the aircraft. "Inflated ego" of some individuals may turn into aggression when their expectations of seating, quality of food or service are not met or when they feel snubbed by the crew or another passenger. Physical molestation or verbal assault has been experienced frequently in the confined space of the aircraft and the lights off.

Excessive consumption of alcohol during the flight is also a potential cause of antisocial behaviour on board. It should be the duty of the cabin crew to limit the serving of alcohol and deny any further serving to intoxicated passengers but such a denial itself may trigger aggressive reaction. Use of drugs or psychoactive substances prior to or during the flight could also influence the conduct of the user and make him aggressive. Nicotine withdrawal on long flights due to the general prohibition of smoking on board has also been cited as causing irrational behaviour.

It could be rightly argued that all such acts would be covered by the Tokyo Convention (1963) as "certain other acts committed on board aircraft". Nevertheless, the Tokyo Convention itself cannot be a sufficient instrument to suppress or punish unruly or disruptive behaviour on board – while its field of applicability is wide, it does not oblige any State to actually assume jurisdiction and, in any case, restricts the jurisdiction solely to the State of Registry of the aircraft.

ICAO has prepared by a "Model Legislation on Certain Offences Committed on Board Civil Aircraft" (1999)[70] and it is now for States to implement the model in their national legislation. Such model legislation could contribute to the unification of law on a wide basis without the adoption of a new instrument or amendment of an existing Convention.

The key issue of the Model Legislation is that the State implementing it would extend its jurisdiction and actually exercise it in cases when the offence took place on board any civil aircraft registered in that State, on an aircraft leased without crew to an operator having his principal place of business in that State, on any aircraft on or over the territory of that State, on any aircraft in flight outside its territory if the next landing is in that State and in cases the aircraft commander has delivered the suspected offender to that State with assurance that similar request will not be made to another State. Thus, the legislation would make the assumption of jurisdiction mandatory and would considerably extend the territorial application compared with the Tokyo Convention.

The offences defined in the Model Legislation are divided into three groups:
– assault or other acts of interference against a crew member on board a civil aircraft;

---

[70] Doc 10117, Manual on the Legal Aspects of Unruly and Disruptive Passengers, 1st ed., Appendix A, 2019.

- assault and other acts endangering safety or jeopardizing good order and discipline on board a civil aircraft; and
- other offences committed on board a civil aircraft.

In the first group are assault, intimidation or threat, whether physical or verbal, against a crew member if such act interferes with the performance of the duties of the crew member or lessens the ability of the crew member to perform those duties; furthermore, offence is also defined as refusal to follow a lawful instruction given by the aircraft commander, or on behalf of the aircraft commander by a crew member, for the purpose of ensuring the safety of the aircraft or of any person or property on board or for the purpose of maintaining good order and discipline on board.

In the second group without further qualification or conditions is the offence of physical violence against a person or sexual assault or child molestation.

Additional acts in the second group are deemed to be offences if an act is likely to endanger the safety of the aircraft or any person on board or if such act jeopardizes the good order and discipline on board the aircraft:
- assault, intimidation or threat whether physical or verbal, against another person;
- intentionally causing damage to, or destruction of, property;
- consuming alcoholic beverages or drugs resulting in intoxication.

The third group includes as offences:
- smoking in a lavatory, or smoking elsewhere in a manner likely to endanger the safety of aircraft;
- tampering with a smoke detector or any other safety-related device on board the aircraft;
- operating a portable electronic device when such act is prohibited.

Several States have adopted national legislation defining as offences certain acts committed on board aircraft in flight that may or do jeopardize the safety of flight. Moreover, many States now assume jurisdiction over such acts even when the acts were committed beyond their territory and on board a foreign aircraft. Actual prosecutions are known in cases of smoking on board and tampering with the smoke detectors, drunkenness and aggression on board as well as operation of cell phones, remote control gadgets or other electronic devices that could interfere with on board avionics, in particular during the take-off and landing operations.

The practice of States just confirms the understanding that aviation security is a global concern. Several airlines have also established a "black list" of passengers who should be excluded in the future from air transport; the legality of such measures has not yet been tested against the status of the air carrier as a public service available to everyone.

In a different class are the "no-fly" lists established by some governments excluding from air transport persons suspected of terrorist links; the legality of such measures is also questionable if the governments concerned are unwilling to disclose the evidence on which they base their allegation and do not enable a review. Media reports indicate that this system is unreliable, and they point to multiple incidents when a small child was considered "blacklisted" just because of coincidence of names or other programming error. There is so far no evidence that the "no-fly" list ever prevented any specific planned criminal act.

Some airlines have resorted to an educational practice – they distribute to passengers leaflets outlining the rights of passengers and their duties of proper conduct on board and informing of the possible legal consequences of any defined misconduct. Some States (*i.e.*, Singapore, Malaysia) warn the passengers on board that they may face death penalty if they try to bring into the country narcotic drugs.

If a large number of States implemented in their national legislation the "Model" prepared by ICAO, it would, in practice, extend the scope of applicability of the Tokyo Convention and make the assumption of criminal or administrative justice mandatory. Regrettably, there are no reliable statistics to show how many States have actually implemented this model legislation, which would ensure that no offender would escape justice. It appears that many legislators were reluctant to extend their mandatory jurisdiction without some basis in an international convention. Hence, there was pressure to revisit the Tokyo Convention and make it more effective in suppressing unruly conduct on board.

8.8.1 Montreal Protocol to Amend the Tokyo Convention 1963

After the Post-"9/11" frenzy, the attention of the ICAO Legal Committee turned to new issues deemed to be of sufficient magnitude, proven practical importance and requiring urgent international solution. The issue of "unruly passengers", "disruptive passengers" or "air rage" does not generate a high political appeal, but the airlines, individually and through the IATA, have been expressing mounting concern that such conduct on board endangers the safety and security of international aviation.

The data collected by IATA indicated a troubling growth in the number of incidents; in 2016 there was one unruly passenger for every 1,424 flights, but in 2017 this number was 1,053 flights. The marked weakness of these statistics is that they do not distinguish between incidents on domestic[71] and international flights – an international legal solution

---

71 According to the FAA, the year 2021 was the worst on record for unruly passenger behaviour in the United States. A whopping 5,981 cases involving unruly passengers were reported as of December 31. Of those,

is needed only for incidents with an international element; more convincing data would have demonstrated the true magnitude of the problem and urgency of its international solution. ICAO addressed the issue with impressive speed and finally in 2019 published a new Manual on the Legal Aspects of Unruly and Disruptive Passengers.[72] Before this, the 34th Session of the Legal Committee in 2009 agreed on the establishment of the Secretariat Study Group on Unruly Passengers; that group met twice in 2011 and was followed by a Special Subcommittee of the Legal Committee that met at Montreal from 22 to 25 May 2012[73] and from 3 to 7 December 2012,[74] and by the 35th Session of the Legal Committee (Montreal, 6-15 May 2013).[75] The documentation of the Legal Committee was unusually sparse – only one State (United Arab Emirates), IATA and the International Union of Aerospace Insurers (IUAI) presented a working paper, and it is surprising that States did not offer more comments, views or suggestions, an obvious sign that the subject was not in the forefront of States' interests, while for the airlines it creates a practical problem, often on a daily basis. However, the States' attention was attracted by the possibility that a new unification of law could not only address the extension of criminal jurisdiction but also establish the legal status and the powers of the in-flight Security Officer (IFSO) – the newly coined term for air marshals on board aircraft used by some States.

There was a general agreement that there was no need for a new convention and that a protocol for the amendment of the Tokyo Convention was preferable. The Diplomatic Conference convened by ICAO adopted the *Protocol to Amend the Convention on Offences and Certain Other Acts Committed on Board Aircraft*, done at Montreal on 4 April 2014.[76] The amendments introduced by the Protocol would extend the jurisdiction of States over any offence also to the State of the operator and to the State of landing of the aircraft with the alleged offender still on board. While these States are supposed to establish their jurisdiction, no State is obliged to actually exercise such jurisdiction. Moreover, the Protocol did not attempt to define any "offences" or "acts", and only in a new Article 15*bis* "encouraged" States to initiate criminal proceedings in cases of physical assault or refusal to follow lawful instructions issued on behalf of the commander of the aircraft. It is doubtful whether such "encouragement" has any legally meaningful value.

The status and jurisdiction of the In-flight Security Officer (IFSO) was controversial at all stages of the consideration of the draft. Some States preferred to give the IFSO status

---

4,290 – nearly 72% – were mask-related incidents in the context of Covid-19. www.faa.gov/data_research/passengers_cargo/unruly_passengers/2021_archive.
72 Doc 10117.
73 LC/SC-MOT Report; the Subcommittee had for consideration a Rapporteur's Report, see Appendix 4 to the Report.
74 LC/SC-MOT2 Report.
75 LC/35 Report.
76 ICAO Doc 10034.

equal to that of the aircraft commander and entitle him to take action without authorization of the aircraft commander. Other States maintained the absolute supremacy of the aircraft commander, who is, under the terms of Annex 6 (Part I, 4.5.1) to the Chicago Convention responsible for the operation and safety of the aeroplane and for the safety of all persons on board, during the flight. The solution finally adopted in amended Article 6.3 in the first place clarifies that the IFSO must be deployed "pursuant to a bilateral agreement or arrangement" between the relevant Contracting States. The IFSO may take reasonable preventive measures without the commander's authorization "when he has reasonable grounds to believe that such action is immediately necessary to protect the safety of the aircraft or persons therein from an act of unlawful interference, and, if the agreement or arrangement so allows, from the commission of serious offence". The vagueness of the terms "reasonable grounds" and "serious offence" without a definition is bound to create difficulties in practical application. It seems clear that the Diplomatic Conference avoided the substance of the issue and relegated it to the agreements or arrangements between the relevant States.

A new Article 18*bis* states that nothing in the Convention shall preclude "any right to seek recovery, under national law, of damages incurred, from a person disembarked or delivered" pursuant to the Convention. IATA stated[77] that diversion of an aircraft, depending on its type and the airport involved, may cost the airline anything from USD 6000 to USD 200,000. Naturally, the practical likelihood of recovery will depend on the ability of the passenger to pay. Another practical difficulty concerns the availability of proper evidence – the aircraft and its crew spend a minimum time on the ground after disembarking or delivering the passenger, and that may not be sufficient to record full evidence of the case for recovery.

While the Diplomatic Conference was attended by 100 States, little enthusiasm was exhibited for the Protocol; it is to enter into force upon ratification by 22 States. At the Conference the Protocol was signed by only 22 States, but later it was ratified by more, so on 1 January 2020 the Protocol came into force.

8.9 MANPADS

The Man Portable Air Defence Systems (MANPADS) are surface-to-air missiles that are easily portable (less than 20 kg) and could be effectively used against aircraft in flight at a low altitude by a single person without particular training. These weapons have proliferated world-wide and the numbers are growing constantly. Many States are known to manufacture MANPADS for their military needs but the missiles appear to be widely

---

77 LC/35-WP/2-3, p. 4.

available on the black markets around the world and have been found in the hands of different terrorist groups.

The best known types of MANPADS are the US "Stinger", the Russian SA-2 (Strela-2), SA-14 (Strela-3), SA-16/18 (Igla-1), the European Javelin and Mistral,[78] but several other types are manufactured by China, the UK, Sweden, Serbia, Turkey and other States. These weapons are self-guiding to the targeted aircraft either with the help of infrared sensors that aim at the heat emanating from the engines or with the help of more sophisticated laser systems and proximity fuses. They are fired from the shoulder and do not require any preparations or installations.

A massive stockpile of the MANPADS existed in Afghanistan, where the mujahedeen is reported to have shot down 269 Soviet aircraft with 340 such missiles[79] – mostly by the US Stingers but a large supply of the Russian rockets remained also in the country. The proliferation of MANPADS beyond the effective control of governmental bodies presents a serious danger to aviation security. All civil aircraft in the landing or take-off configuration are an easy target for the MANPADS and their vulnerability could be only diminished but not completely eliminated. Flares released by the aircraft could confuse the heat seeking missiles and costly laser equipment could similarly change the trajectory of the missile. The aircraft in such landing or take-off configuration has very limited possibility to employ any escape manoeuvres and the incoming missile does not give any advance warning.

The first recorded example of attempted terrorist uses of MANPADS against civil aircraft occurred in 1973 in Italy (Rome), where the "Black September" group had smuggled to the country 14 Soviet SA-7 MANPADS that they intended to fire from the rooftops against a landing Israeli aircraft bringing the prime Minister Golda Meier for a State visit; however, the plot was uncovered in time and the conspirators were arrested.[80]

On 8 November 1983, a B-737 airplane of the Angolan Airlines was destroyed by a shoulder-fired missile with all 130 occupants killed. On 9 February 1984, a B-737 of the same airline was struck by a missile and seriously damaged – no fatalities were recorded. On 21 September 1984, an Afghan Ariana Airlines DC-10 was hit by a missile and suffered substantial damage. On 10 October 1998, in the Democratic Republic of Congo a Congo Airlines B-727 was destroyed by a missile with 41 fatalities. On 28 November 2002 in Mombasa, Kenya a B-757 of the Arkia Israeli Airlines was targeted by two Russian SA missiles during the climb out, but they missed. On 22 November 2004, a DHL Airbus A300 in Iraq was hit by a missile on departure from Baghdad but in spite of loss of all hydraulic power managed to return to the runway.[81]

---

78 www.globalsecurity.org/military/intro/manpads/htm, accessed on 31 December 2022.
79 *Idem.*
80 MANPADS – A Terrorist Threat to Civilian Aviation?, www.files.ethz.ch/isn/160759/BICC_brief_47.pdf, accessed on 31 December 2022.
81 sgp.fas.org/crs/terror/RL31741.pdf, accessed on 31 December 2022.

One of the earliest governmental responses to the danger of proliferation of MANPADS was the "Wassenaar Arrangement on Export Controls for Conventional Arms and Dual-Use Goods and Technologies"[82] that at its plenary meeting on 2-3 December 1998 noted the concerns regarding the threat to civil aviation posed by the illicit possession of MANPADS and recognized the need for appropriate measures to prevent such possession.

The United Nations General Assembly adopted Resolutions A58/241 on the illicit trade in small arms and light weapons in all its aspects and A58/54 on transparency in armaments.

ICAO first addressed the problem of MANPADS in Assembly Resolution A32-23: *MANPADS Export Control* and again in 2003 in Resolution A35-11: *Threat to civil aviation posed by man-portable air defence systems (MANPADS)*. That Resolution urges contracting States to take the necessary measures to exercise strict and effective controls on the import, export, transfer or retransfer, as well as storage of MANPADS. It also calls upon the States to take the necessary measures to ensure the destruction of non-authorized MANPADS in their territory, as soon as possible. In September 2007, the 36th Session of the ICAO Assembly repeatedly called for an action by States in Resolution A36-19 and in 2010 MANPADS were again mentioned in resolution A37-17.

Only governments can take an effective action to eliminate the black market with these destructive weapons and seize and destroy those held by unauthorized persons.

8.10 "Bonn Declaration" 1981

The collective political will of States to use joint effort to combat international terrorist acts against civil aviation found its early expression in the Declaration adopted on 17 July 1978 in Bonn by the members of the (then) Group of Seven (G7).[83] Their aim was to impose effective sanctions on any State that would disregard its duties under The Hague Convention (1970) to prosecute or extradite the alleged offenders and to return the aircraft.

The "Bonn Declaration" affirmed that

> in cases where a country refuses extradition or prosecution of those who have hijacked an aircraft and/or does not return such aircraft, the heads of State and government are jointly resolved that their governments should take immediate action to cease all flights to that country. At the same time, their governments will initiate action to halt all incoming flights from that country or from any

---

82   www.wassenaar.org/guidelines/index.html, accessed on 31 December 2022.
83   Canada, France, Germany, Italy, Japan, the United Kingdom and the United States; 17 International Legal Materials, 1285 (1978).

country by the airlines of the country concerned. The heads of state and government urge other governments to join them in this commitment.

The "Bonn Declaration" was complemented, in July 1981, by the "Montebello Summit Statement on Terrorism".[84] It followed one of the most dramatic hijackings in history – on 2 March 1981 three attackers seized a Pakistani B-720 on domestic flight from Karachi to Peshawar with 141 persons on board; the aircraft was diverted to Kabul where negotiations started on the release of hostages in exchange for the release of prisoners from Pakistan. During the five days of negotiations the hijackers murdered a Pakistani diplomat and dumped his body on the tarmac – all in the view of the TV cameras and support from the Afghani authorities; the aircraft eventually was permitted to leave for Damascus and the hijackers were equipped with Afghani documents. The incident lasted thirteen days before the hostages were released, the hijackers finally obtained safe haven in Afghanistan.

The heads of State and government in Montebello were

> convinced that, in the case of hijacking of a Pakistan International Airlines aircraft in March, the conduct of the Babrak Karmal regime of Afghanistan, both during the incident and subsequently in giving refuge to the hijackers, was and is in flagrant breach of its international obligations under the Hague Convention to which Afghanistan is a party and constitutes a serious threat to air safety. Consequently, the heads of state and government propose to suspend all flights to and from Afghanistan in implementation of the Bonn Declaration unless Afghanistan immediately takes steps to comply with its obligations. Furthermore, they call upon all states which share their concern for air safety to take appropriate action to persuade Afghanistan to honour its obligations.

Afghani authorities took no action in response to the Montebello Declaration and the G7 members denounced their bilateral agreements on air services with Afghanistan. However, none of them denounced the agreement with immediate effect but with one year's notice …; that, in the light of further developments in Afghanistan, made the G7 gesture meaningless.

There is media evidence that the threat to apply the Bonn/Montebello enforcement motivated the government of South Africa to prosecute and sentence some 34 mercenaries who staged, on 25 November 1981, a farcical "coup" in Seychelles and after its failure seized Air India Flight 224 and forced it to take them to Durban, South Africa. Upon landing there, the mercenaries led by the "Mad Colonel" Michael Hoare were free, gave their stories to the media and were signing their photographs and alleged that their act

---

84   20 International Legal Materials, 956 (1981).

was fully approved by South African intelligence services. After some international pressure the mercenaries were prosecuted in 1982 and most of them received light penalties of six months prison term; Michael Hoare was sentenced to ten years in prison but was released three years later.[85]

The Bonn Declaration is at present only a reminder of history without any practical relevance.

8.11 Other Acts or Offences of Concern Addressed after "911"

In September 2007, the 36th Session of the ICAO Assembly had on its agenda as Item 46 the subject "Acts and offences of concern to the international aviation community and not covered by existing air law instruments".[86]

The origin of this subject is to be found in Assembly Resolution A33-1[87] that requested urgent studies of the new and emerging threats to civil aviation, in particular, to review the adequacy of the existing ICAO aviation security conventions. This resolution, adopted in the wake of "911", is symptomatic of the frantic search for any conceivable prevention that would protect aviation against the repetition of a similar tragedy. This Resolution for the first recorded time used the term "terrorism" that was previously only "whispered" within ICAO. The Resolution declared that using civil aircraft as weapons of destruction was "contrary to the letter and spirit of the Convention on International Civil Aviation, in particular its preamble and Articles 4 and 44" and that "such acts and other terrorist acts involving civil aviation or civil aviation facilities constitute grave offences in violation of international law". The ICAO Assembly thus unanimously confirmed that there was no void in the scope of the applicable international law and that the acts of "911" were in fact "grave offences in violation of international law. A sober analysis would suggest that more international law or better international law is not a sufficient safeguard against the criminal acts aimed at international civil aviation. Law can offer only a "general prevention" – a message that a particular act will be prosecuted and severely punished everywhere in the world and that there will be no safe haven anywhere in the world for the perpetrators; that may not be an effective deterrent for determined suicidal maniacs and effective "physical" prevention is more important than additional provisions of criminal law and jurisdiction.

The ICAO Secretariat Working Group came up with the idea of criminalization of certain acts independent of motive and a Special Subcommittee of the ICAO Legal

---

85 *Ibid.* 8.3.1; 25. www.military-history.fandom.com/wiki/Mike_Hoare, accessed on 31 December 2022.
86 A36-WP/12, LE/4, 14 August 2007.
87 "Declaration on misuse of civil aircraft as weapons of destruction and other terrorist acts involving civil aviation".

Committee further elaborated on them during its session from 3 to 6 July 2007. Among them were:

a. use of civil aircraft as a weapon as was in the case of 11 September 2001; the Group believed that the gravity of using civil aircraft as a weapon calls for its explicit criminalization as an independent offence under an international convention, in order to protect the safety of civil aircraft and to maintain public confidence in air transport.[88]

Nevertheless, it can be argued that the elements of such an act are covered by the existing instruments and applicable laws and that this course of action would have only a declaratory significance.

b. use of civil aircraft to unlawfully spread biological, chemical and nuclear substances.

Here it could be argued that such acts would have nothing in common with aviation security, aviation as such would not be the target of such acts and the acts would not necessarily jeopardize the safety of the aircraft or of persons on board; the means of delivery of the biological, chemical and nuclear substances are not relevant and nobody would propose a separate instrument for instances when such noxious substances would be spread from an automobile, a ship or even a bicycle…; the substance of this offence is not related to the security of civil aviation. Moreover, the issues of biological, chemical and nuclear (BCN weapons) substances could be meaningfully addressed only by the United Nations in a global scope not limited to aviation.

c. attacks against civil aviation using biological, chemical and nuclear substances.

It could be argued that such attacks would be fully covered by the existing conventions that use the terms "weapon", "any device, substance or weapon" or "any means whatsoever".

d. acts of organizing or directing offences specified in the Conventions; the Group argued that in cases of suicide attacks in the air or on the ground, while the attackers perish during the attacks and can no longer be punished under criminal law, those masterminds remaining on the ground should not be allowed safe haven.

---

88 A36-WP/12, paragraph 2.1.2.1 a).

An argument against this initiative would be that the existing instruments – The Hague (1970) and Montreal (1971) Conventions – specifically penalize the act of being an "accomplice" to the defined offences.

> e. wilful contribution to an offence specified in the Conventions; the Group states that such acts "should be criminalized even if such contribution did not lead to actual commission of an unlawful act".

Under the existing instruments the accomplice of a person who attempts to commit an offence also commits the offence. The national laws implementing the existing international instruments mostly include a "conspiracy" as an offence.

> f. credible threat to commit an offence specified in a Convention. The Group observed that, under certain circumstances, a threat to commit an act, without the actual commission of the act contemplated, may cause grave adverse consequences to civil aviation.

This concern appears justified but how would such a threat differ from a false information ("hoax") punishable as an offence under Article 1, paragraph 1 e) of the Montreal Convention (1971)?

By the decision of the 36th Session of the ICAO Assembly the approved Work Programme of the Organization in the legal field by the end of 2007 included as item No. 2 in the order of priorities the subject "Acts and offences of concern to international aviation community and not covered by existing air law instruments".[89]

It is difficult to believe that this subject is truly suitable for an international solution and whether it requires an urgent action; much likely, this initiative was mostly political posturing in the wake of "911" while self-analysis of own omissions that contributed to "911" would have been more appropriate.

Further proliferation of the legal instruments does not appear to offer an effective safeguard of aviation security and the energy of States within ICAO should be rather geared to physical prevention of the criminal acts.

In spite of such justifiable misgivings the prevailing frenzy of "Post- 9/11" policy pressure motivated expedited work in the ICAO Secretariat, a Study group and a Special Subcommittee of the ICAO Legal Committee and the Legal Committee itself at its 34th Session (9-17 September 2009).[90] These studies have not identified any patent flaw in the existing aviation security conventions or any urgent need to revisit the substance of the

---

89 A36-WP/297, LE/14, paragraph 47.11.
90 Doc 9926-LC/194.

The Hague (1970) and Montreal (1971) Conventions; nevertheless, it had been recognized that both Conventions could be refined and expanded to cover new or emerging threats, although it was not even suggested that an urgent international solution was necessary.

After extensive deliberations the Legal Committee recommended that a Diplomatic Conference should consider a Draft protocol for the amendment of The Hague Convention (1970); such a protocol would refine the definition of the "offence" and expand it to organizing or directing such act or assisting the perpetrator of the offence to evade investigation, prosecution or punishment; the revised Convention would apply not only to aircraft "in flight" but also to aircraft "in service" aligning it with the Montreal Convention (1971). A novel and highly controversial concept was the introduction of the "military exclusion clause" that would specify that the Convention would not apply to the activities of the armed forces during an armed conflict, and the activities undertaken by the military forces of a State in the exercise of their official duties – such legal immunity for the actions of armed forces was not acceptable to several States.

The Montreal Convention (1971) was subject to a much wider proposed expansion to cover and criminalize the use of aircraft as a weapon, the use of aircraft to unlawfully spread biological, chemical or nuclear substances (BCN weapons) and the attacks against civil aviation using such substances. Further proposed amendments included provisions prohibiting intentional and unlawful transport of the dangerous biological, chemical or nuclear substances and the transport of fugitives. Again, the "military exclusion clause" was proposed for the amended Convention. These proposals for the amendment of the Montreal Convention were supported under the prevailing policy pressure – albeit not unanimously – even though the use of an aircraft as a weapon had been already declared an international offense by Assembly declaration and there was no proven need to amend the Convention for this purpose – apart from the "post-911" posturing and determination to take a strong and highly visible action. The issue of transport or use of BCN weapons is definitely not a subject specific for international air law and ICAO should be handled in a more general UN-sponsored context.

The ICAO Council accepted the invitation of the Government of China and the Diplomatic Conference met at Beijing from 30 August to 10 September 2010. The participation by 76 States – just 40% of the total ICAO membership – is not impressive and does not indicate that all States considered this subject to be of utmost urgency.[91]

As a result of its deliberations the Conference approved the text of the *Protocol Supplementary to the Convention for the Suppression of Unlawful Seizure of Aircraft*[92]

---

91 In a questionable positive spin ICAO Journal Vol. 66, No. 1 states that "some 400 participants from more than eighty States and international organizations" took part in the Conference; however, the Final Act lists only seventy-six States that were properly accredited; the final official List of delegates No. 5 (10 September 2010, 11:00 hours) lists 333 delegates; such flagrant exaggeration is neither professional, nor dignified.
92 ICAO Doc 9959.

amending the pioneering Hague Convention (1970) that has stood for forty years. Unlike at the 1970 Conference – there was no consensus at Beijing on this instrument and the vote in the "Commission of the Whole" was fifty-seven votes in favour, thirteen votes not in favour. It was in particular the "military exclusion clause" that some States found objectionable – it is for them not a formal legal issue, but a deeply divisive political point and they objected to the granting of blanket "immunity" to State actions and the military forces.

The Protocol is "authentic" in English, Arabic, Chinese, French, Russian and Spanish versions – a daring proposition when the essential drafting work was done predominantly in English. According to the Final Act of the Conference, the texts were "subject to verification by the Secretariat of the Conference under the authority of the President of the conference within a period of ninety days from [10 September 2010] as to the linguistic changes requires bringing the texts of the different languages into conformity with one another". An objection could be raised that the process of "authentication" is left in the care of the Secretariat and not in the sovereign decision-making power of the Diplomatic Conference but it must be assumed that the Secretariat acted under delegated power granted by the Conference.

To facilitate the practical implementation the Final Act attaches a "user friendly" consolidated text of the 1970 Convention as Amended by the Beijing Protocol in six languages – another audacious proposition since the underlying text of the 1970 Convention did not exist in authentic Arabic and Chinese versions.

The original Hague Convention (1970) continues in force for its 185 parties; the Convention as amended by the Beijing Protocol will be applicable only among States that will have ratified the Beijing Protocol and it is most unlikely that such States would denounce the original unamended 1970 Convention upon ratification of the Beijing Protocol. The protocol shall come into force on the first day of the second month following the deposit of the 22nd instrument of ratification. Uganda deposited an instrument of ratification as a 22nd Member State, so the Protocol came into force on 1 January 2018. The revision of the Montreal Convention (1971) proved to be more complicated and wider in scope. The Legal Committee proposed to consolidate its text with the Montreal Protocol (1988) and wished to add new provisions to expand the definition of the "offense", to add definitions of several new terms, to include the "military exclusion clause" and to refine the provisions on jurisdiction. The extent of such changes made it unsuitable for a protocol supplementary to the Convention and it was agreed to draft a new Beijing *Convention for the Suppression of Unlawful Acts Relating to International Civil Aviation* (2010).[93] The Commission of the Whole again failed to obtain consensus and the text was approved by

---

93   ICAO Doc 9960.

fifty-five votes in favour, fourteen votes not in favour. The split was due to strong objection by some States to the "military exclusion clause" immunizing the "acts of States".[94]

Article 1 of the Beijing Convention contains an expanded definition of the "offences" covered by the new Convention; the Article is subdivided into five lengthy paragraphs, each with numerous subparagraphs. The definition now includes, *inter alia*, using aircraft as a weapon, or organizing, directing and financing acts of aviation terrorism, transporting or using BCN weapons and transporting fugitives from justice.

The following unlawful acts to be punished:
- the use of a civil aircraft as a weapon for the purpose of causing death, serious personal injury or considerable material damage;
- using a civil aircraft so that biological, chemical and nuclear (BCN – Biological, Chemical, Nuclear) weapons reach their destinations with the purpose of the extermination of lives, causing injury or incurring damages;
- assault on civil aircraft using BCN weapons;
- unlawful delivery of BCN weapons using civil aircraft;
- unlawful delivery of explosives and fissionable materials by civil aircraft for terrorist purposes; and
- attack (such as cyberattacks)[95] against the IT infrastructure of airports or air navigational services.

An equally lengthy Article 2 is fully dedicated to the definitions of the numerous terms used in Article 1. A more general and abstract drafting in a simple language without casuistic enumeration of each conceivable detail would have been preferable. The text could have highlighted in more abstract form any type of unlawful activity or participation therein that is deemed dangerous for international aviation and that should be determined to be an "offence" and should have been lighter and give more flexibility to the prosecuting authorities and discretion to the judges.

Article 7 fine-tunes the jurisdictional provisions of the Montreal Convention (1971) to adjust them to the newly defined "offences".

Like the Beijing Protocol, the Beijing Convention is supposed to be authentic in English, Arabic, Chinese, French, Russian and Spanish, subject to the "verification" by the Conference Secretariat.[96] The new Convention shall enter into force on the first day of the second month following the deposit of the 22nd instrument of ratification. Turkey deposited an instrument of ratification as a 22nd Member States so the Convention came into force in

---

94 See Article 6, paragraph 2 of the Beijing Convention.
95 I. Benjamin Scott, *Aviation Cybersecurity: Regulatory Approach in the European Union*, Eleven International Publishing, The Hague, 2019, pp. 1-245.
96 The verified text can be found at www.icao,int/DCAS2010/restr/docs/beijing_convention_multi_pdf.

1 July 2018. The Beijing Convention (2010) is a new, separate and distinct instrument of international law. It has no impact whatsoever on the original Montreal Convention (1971) which remains in force for its 188 parties. The new instrument will apply only to States that will have ratified it and will prevail among them over the original Montreal Convention (1971) and the Montreal Protocol (1988).

In general, it may be concluded that these two new international instruments were drafted under policy pressure to produce determined and visible responses to the horrid crime of "911". These instruments expand quantitatively (incrementally) the scope of application of the original 1970 and 1971 Conventions but – unlike these venerated instruments – did not make a qualitative creative contribution to international law. The aviation security is not made more vulnerable by the lack of entry into force of the Beijing instruments and will not improve by the mere fact of their entry into force – their declaratory power reflects the determined policy of States but does not solve any specific problem and does not enrich the codified international law.

9   International Unification of Private Air Law through ICAO

Obligatio est iuris vinculum

Aviation is by its nature an international activity that easily crosses international boundaries and enters foreign territories where different private laws apply. Private law relations – *i.e.*, relations between non-sovereign subjects that act as equals (persons or corporate bodies) – may contain a multitude of "foreign elements" that may create a question which law should be applied and which court could assume jurisdiction.

An easy example may be the purchase of aircraft by an airline – a costly decision in the order of hundreds of millions of dollars requiring often international financing and insurance: an airline in State A buys aircraft from a manufacturer in State B, negotiates bank loans in States C, D and E and arranges for insurance in States F and G; then the airline decides to let one aircraft by lease to an operator in State H. How about if one of the creditors disagrees with the lease of the aircraft and wishes to repossess that aircraft? A multitude of private law systems is encountered in such a transaction and a question may arise whether some action taken under one legal system could be recognized and enforced by another and which court would be competent to make the decision.

Similarly complicated may be a contract of international carriage between a passenger and an airline or a series of airlines in successive international carriage. Which law would be applicable if a US citizen and resident contracts (on a single ticket) for a flight by Swiss International from Toronto to Zurich, from there by Singapore Airlines to Singapore and from there by Qantas to Sydney, return by Gulf Air from Sydney to Manama, by British Airways from Manama to London and from there by Air Canada to Toronto? Such complicated flights were not uncommon in international practice (mostly in cases of sequential missions to different destinations, otherwise direct point-to-point flights are more common at present) and the question of the applicable law does not even arise if no problems are encountered. But how about if the passenger somewhere during the travel loses his luggage or during a transfer to another flight in one of the countries concerned sprains his ankle? Which law would be applicable to the claim for compensation and which court would be competent to consider the claim?

If a foreign aircraft causes damage to third parties on the surface (impact damage caused by a falling part of the aircraft or the aircraft itself crashing on the surface) which court is competent to assume jurisdiction on the claims and would the judgment be recognized in other countries?

Next to international aviation there is probably no other human activity that would produce a comparable vast spectrum of conflicts of laws and conflicts of jurisdiction.

Unification of law is the only method how to remove such conflicts and bring into the respective social relations the elements of predictability and security. Unification of law replaces in its field of applicability the disparate conflicting rules of substantive law and jurisdiction, clarifies between the parties their mutual rights and obligations and makes the social relation transparent and predictable.

Unification of private law on a multilateral basis is achieved by the adoption of an international instrument governed by the international law of treaties in which the contracting States stipulate the rules of private law in a defined field and commit themselves to adopt such rules as their national law. Depending on the specific constitutional frameworks, most States have to "transform" the international law into the domestic law by special legislation.

Each of the unifications of private air law would deserve a separate dedicated book to analyse the provisions as well as the diverse applications and interpretations by different courts of law. The purpose of this compact treatise is only to give a brief general outline of each instrument with some critical comments on the merits and flaws of each of them, a substantial analysis has to be sought in specialized monographs.

9.1 Geneva Convention on the International Recognition of Rights in Aircraft 1948

9.1.1 Background

Aircraft is an object – movable property – of very high value. Its acquisition and possession are usually circumscribed by rights of other persons – creditors, lessors, holders of mortgages, hypothecs and other similar rights created as security for the payment of the debt. Very complicated problems of the applicable law may arise partly due to the mobility of the aircraft; movable objects are normally governed by the law of the place where they are located *(lex rei sitae)* but that could not be applicable in view of the "mobility" of the aircraft changing its *situs* constantly. Another category of problems arises due to the different location of the creditors and potential conflicting assertions of the relative privilege or priority of their claims under different laws and before different courts.

The issue of aircraft ownership and related rights *(ius in rem* - real rights) attracted attention within CITEJA between 1927 and 1931 and two draft conventions were prepared – one to define aircraft ownership and aeronautical register and the second to deal with "real rights" (mortgages, other securities and other privileged claims) but the drafts were not presented to an international conference with a view of their approval. It could be only assumed that at that time the limited interest in the unification of law in this field was caused by the very limited market for aircraft as well as by the then relatively low price of aircraft.

During the Chicago Conference on International Civil Aviation in November-December 1944 the US delegation – expecting extensive sales of aircraft after the war – initiated Resolution V that the Conference adopted in its Final Act.[1]

That Resolution noted that

> the sale of aircraft to be used in international operations will render it desirable for the various governments to reach a common understanding on the legal questions invoked in the transfer of title.

The resolution recommended to governments

> to give consideration to the early calling of an international conference on private international air law for the purpose of adopting a convention dealing with the transfer of title to aircraft and that such private law conference includes in the bases of discussion: a) The existing draft convention relating to mortgages, other real securities, and aerial privileges; and b) the existing draft Convention on the ownership of aircraft and aeronautical register,
> both of which were adopted by the Comite International Technique d'Experts Juridiques Aeriens (CITEJA) in 1931.

The CITEJA drafts were transmitted to PICAO by 1946 and updated by 1947 and in September 1947 the draft was studied by the ICAO Legal Committee in Brussels. The resulting draft was further modified by the Legal Commission of the 2nd Session of the ICAO Assembly held in Geneva in 1948 and on 19 June 1948 that Assembly adopted the "Convention on the International Recognition of Rights in Aircraft".[2] It is the only international Convention adopted directly by the Assembly of ICAO but it was signed only by those delegates to the Assembly who possessed the appropriate full powers for that purpose.

The Convention came into force on 17 September 1953 and by December 2022, 91 States became parties and made it a very important instrument for the unification of international private air law.

---

1 See Proceedings, Vol. I, p. 125.
2 ICAO Doc 7620.

9.1.2 Outline of the Convention

Under Article XVI of the Convention, the term "aircraft" includes the airframe, engines, propellers, radio apparatus, and all other articles intended for use in the aircraft, whether installed therein or temporarily separated there from. It is important to understand what the Convention did not intend to achieve: it did not wish to unify the substantive law of property/ownership of aircraft and the related issues of mortgages and other securities or aerial privileges. It wished to achieve only the recognition of such rights if such rights were established in a contracting State under specified conditions. This fundamental obligation of contracting States is expressed in Article I as follows:

> Article I
> 1. The Contracting States undertake to recognize: a) rights of property in aircraft; b) rights to acquire aircraft by purchase coupled with possession of the aircraft; c) rights to possession of aircraft under leases of six months or more; mortgages, hypotheques and similar rights in aircraft which are contractually created as security for payment of indebtedness;
> *provided that such rights* (i) have been constituted in accordance with the law of the Contracting State in which the aircraft was registered as to nationality at the time of their constitution, and (ii) are regularly recorded in a public record of the Contracting State in which the aircraft is registered as to nationality.
> The regularity of successive recordings in different Contracting States shall be determined in accordance with the law of the State where the aircraft was registered as to nationality at the time of each recording.
> 2. Nothing in this Convention shall prevent the recognition of any rights in aircraft under the law of any Contracting State; but Contracting States shall not admit or recognize any right as taking priority over the rights mentioned in paragraph 1 of this Article.

These provisions seem to be self-explanatory. In Article I, 1 b) the expression "rights to acquire aircraft by purchase coupled with possession of the aircraft" refers to the different practices in common law and civil law in which possession and use of the aircraft is granted but the transfer of the title is deferred until defined conditions are met (conditional sale, hire purchase, equipment trust, etc.) – usually upon the full payment of the debt. Article I, 1 d) refers to all types of securities that may exist under different legal systems.

The condition of the international recognition of the enumerated rights is that they have been constituted in harmony with the law of a Party to the Convention in which the aircraft is registered as to nationality and that they have been regularly recorded in the public record of that Party. This may be a weakness of the Convention since currently – in view of frequent use of lease, charter and interchange of aircraft – the State of Registry is less relevant than the State of the operator.

The Convention does not prescribe the format of the public record; Article II states:

> Article II
> 1. All recordings relating to a given aircraft must appear in the same record.
> 2. Except as otherwise provided in this Convention, the effects of the recording of any right mentioned in Article I, paragraph 1, with regard to third parties shall be determined according to the law of the Contracting State where it is recorded.
> 3. A Contracting State may prohibit the recording of any right which cannot validly be constituted according to its national law.

All secured claims and privileges are to be recorded in one single register that will indicate their chronological order and relative priority; the record is to be open to the public and any person may request from the appropriate authority a certified copy or extract of the particulars recorded.[3]

The Convention accords priority to claims arising out of compensation for salvage or for extraordinary expenses essential for the preservation of the aircraft. To give an incentive to those who provide either salvage or other extraordinary expenses their claims enjoy not only priority over any other claims but are to be satisfied in the inverse order of their priority[4] so that the last essential expenditure is satisfied first. Article IV states about it:

> Article IV
> 1. In the event that any claims in respect of: a) compensation due for salvage of the aircraft, or b) extraordinary expenses indispensable for the preservation of the aircraft give rise, under the law of the Contracting State where the operations of salvage or preservation were terminated, to a right conferring a charge against the aircraft, such right shall be recognised by Contracting States and shall take priority over all other rights in the aircraft.
> 2. The rights enumerated in paragraph 1 shall be satisfied in the inverse order of the dates of the incidents in connexion with which they have arisen.
> 3. Any of the said rights may, within three months from the date of the termination of the salvage or preservation operations, be noted on the record.

---

3 Article III of the Geneva Convention (1948).
4 In this case it is not priority of the recording but the date of the incident that gave rise to the claim.

> 4. The said rights shall not be recognised in other Contracting States after expiration of the three months mentioned in paragraph 3 unless, within this period, a) the right has been noted on the record in conformity with paragraph 3, and b) the amount has been agreed upon or judicial action on the right has been commenced. As far as judicial action is concerned, the law of the forum shall determine the contingencies upon which the three months period may be interrupted or suspended.
>
> 5. This Article shall apply notwithstanding the provisions of Article I, paragraph 2.

It should be noted that the priority rights for salvage and essential expenses are secured only for the period of three years unless they have been within that period recorded in the register (Article V).

In the case of attachment or sale in execution of the aircraft the rights of the creditors are protected against the actions of the other parties purporting to establish rights under Article I, 1 with the knowledge of the sale or execution proceedings by a person against whom the proceedings are directed. It is formulated in Article VI as follows:

> *Article VI*
> In case of attachment or sale of an aircraft in execution, or of any right therein, the Contracting States shall not be obliged to recognize, as against the attaching or executing creditor or against the purchaser, any right mentioned in Article I, paragraph 1, or the transfer of any such right, if constituted or effected with knowledge of the sale or execution proceedings by the person against whom the proceedings are directed.

Under Article VIII of the Convention sale of aircraft in execution in conformity with the Convention shall effect the transfer of property in such aircraft free from all rights which are not assumed by the purchaser. Further protection is provided to the creditors in Article IX that prohibits transfer of the aircraft from the nationality register of a contracting State to the nationality register of another State unless all holders of recorded rights have been satisfied or consent to the transfer.

The Geneva Convention (1948) is the first international instrument adopted in the framework of ICAO. Its ratification progressed rather slowly but the current ninety-one parties to this Convention are a confirmation of its practical importance. With the progress of decolonization and the growth of new national airlines requiring new airplanes the manufacturers of aircraft and the financing creditors expressly insisted that the new States ratify the Geneva Convention before any aircraft financing deals are approved.

The Convention has its centre of gravity in the protection granted to the creditors – be they the manufacturers, banks or other financial institutions or lessors. However, the protection is not very effective – it only assures that properly recorded rights of the creditor will be recognized in the contracting States.

Legal recognition of such rights is possibly still far away from the actual assertion of such rights through repossession of the aircraft or its sale in execution of the claims. It took more than half a century before a new convention was prepared that went beyond the mere recognition of rights but aimed at the creation of an international title and facilitation of the repossession of an aircraft.[5]

9.2 "Warsaw System" and the Montreal Convention 1999

9.2.1 Background of the Warsaw Convention 1929

Unification of private air law of international carriage by air became a priority very early in the history of aviation. The first airlines capable to carry passengers, mail and freight were established very shortly after WW I. On 8 February 1919, the first French airline was established – Lignes Aeriennes Farman – starting irregular flights between Paris and London; on 25 August 1919 the first international scheduled service was established between London and Paris by the Aircraft Transport and Travel Ltd. (AT&T) – the forerunner of Imperial Airways, and eventually, British Airways.[6]

At that time there was no established international machinery for the adoption of international conventions and the initiative was in the hands of the interested governments. The government of France by 1923 attempted to adopt national laws relating to liability in the carriage by air and realized that the complex foreign elements of such issue called for unification of law on a wide international level to prevent the unforeseeable conflicts of law and conflicts of jurisdiction. According to the international practice of that time the government of France convened the First International Conference of Air Law in October 1925 in Paris.

The diplomats assembled at the Conference did not feel comfortable with the issues of liability and unification of law; they agreed that such problems must be first studied by "technical legal experts". The Conference decided to create the "Comite International Technique d'Experts Juridiques Aeriens" (CITEJA) – a body of legal experts appointed by

---

[5] Convention on International Interests in Mobile Equipment and Protocol to that Convention on Matters Specific to Aircraft Equipment, signed at Cape Town on 16 November 2001; See Section 9.5 to this book.
[6] www.aerosociety.com/news/one-hundred-years-of-international-passenger-flights, accessed on 31 December 2022.

different governments but acting in their individual capacity. CITEJA in several sessions prepared a draft convention that was then presented for consideration to the Second International Conference of Private Air Law that met in Warsaw from 4 to 12 October 1929.[7]

CITEJA went well beyond the initiative of the French government and dealt not only with the problem of liability in international carriage by air; it established also uniform rules regarding the documents of carriage and their link with liability, rules of liability and limitation of liability and rules on the jurisdiction of courts. The resulting "Warsaw" *Convention for the Unification of Certain Rules Relating to International Carriage by Air* was signed on 13 October 1929 and became soon the widest accepted unification of private law; even today – more than two generations later – it must be recognized as a monumental piece of international law-making that pioneered new legal principles and enabled a smooth development of international carriage by air.

The unification of law introduced transparency and security to the legal relations created by international carriage by air and enabled realistic risk management through insurance. It must be recognized that the Convention was adopted in the early infancy of international air transport just two years after Charles Lindbergh accomplished the first solo flight across the Atlantic, a daring adventure at that time. By December 2022, there are still technically 152 parties to the original Warsaw Convention (1929) but its actual scope of applicability has been reduced by succeeding instruments and the Convention proved its viability through complex steps towards its updating and modernization and through tortuous interpretations by different courts of law that tried to circumvent the limitation of liability. Many of its principles survived beyond 1999 when the Convention was replaced – among the consenting parties – by a new modern instrument.

9.2.2   Basic Elements of the Warsaw Convention

The basic provisions of the Warsaw Convention achieved unity of law in the following fields.

9.2.2.1   The Format and Legal Significance of the Documents of Carriage (Passenger Ticket, Baggage Check, Air Waybill)[8]

The format and the particulars of these documents have been used by the airlines for several decades. They have been modelled on the established maritime models and were rather formalistic and eventually proved to be an obstacle to electronic data processing and growing use of electronic documents.

---

7   ICAO Doc 7838-CD, the Minutes and Documents are available in CD-ROM format, French only.
8   Articles 3-16 of the Warsaw Convention.

Strict compliance with the formalities of the documents (in particular the provision that the passenger or shipper must be given a "notice" that the Convention with its limitation of liability will apply to the carriage in question) was sanctioned by loss of limitation of liability for the carrier – a rich minefield for litigation and a source of decisions perverting the meaning of the Convention to avoid the limitation of liability.

There have been decisions based on the timeliness of the delivery of the notice advising the passengers of the applicability of the Convention with its limits of liability, effectiveness of the notice and even the size of the fonts in which the notice was printed.[9] The linkage between the liability and the formalities of the ticket has at present no justification and there was urgent need to simplify the formalities of the documents and to enable their electronic processing.

The airlines aim at completely "ticketless" travel to minimize the cost of documentation. The IATA airlines achieved 100% electronic ticketing by 31 May 2008, saving the industry up to USD 3 billion annually![10] However, the passenger will always need some document or access to the data as evidence of the contract of carriage for accounting and taxation purposes, for immigration (to prove that return passage is available), for successive carriage and other purposes. Such a "document" need not in practice be anything more than an "alpha-numeric" code enabling the access to the central database of the airline.

9.2.2.2 Regime of Liability

Liability represents the core subject of the unification of law by the Warsaw Convention which governs air carrier's liability for death, wounding and other bodily injury of the passenger,[11] destruction or loss of or damage to baggage and cargo[12] and liability for damage caused by delay in the carriage by air of passengers, baggage and cargo.[13]

The liability of the carrier under the Convention is based on his fault (intention or negligence), but the Convention adopted a boldly progressive attitude for its time by embodying a presumption of such fault. That was achieved by reversing the burden of proof – it is not for the passenger/claimant to prove the fault of the carrier,[14] but the carrier is presumed to be guilty of fault and can be exonerated only if he proves that he and his

---

9 *Mertens v. Flying Tiger*, 341 F.2d, 851 (1965), *Warren v. Flying Tiger*, 352 F.2d 494 (1965) when the passengers received ticket "too late" and not "effectively" to arrange for personal insurance – one at the ramp of the aircraft, the other only when he was seated on board. In the *Lisi v. Alitalia*, 370 F.2.d 508 (1966) case the ticket was delivered well in advance of the departure but the notice was printed in 4 point font and the court found the notice "camouflaged in Lilliputian print in a thicket of conditions of carriage… in simple truth concealed".
10 www.iata.org/en/pressroom/pr/2008-31-05-01, accessed on 31 December 2022.
11 Article 17 of the Warsaw Convention.
12 Article 18 of the Warsaw Convention.
13 Article 19 of the Warsaw Convention.
14 The traditional legal principle is that the claimant bears the burden of proof – "*actori incumbit probatio*".

agents have *taken all necessary measures* to avoid the damage or that it was impossible for him or them to take such measures.[15]

This was truly a progressive legislative step since by 1929 the protection of the consumer was less firmly established in the legal systems and the innovative reversal of the burden of proof was a positive step toward a better protection of the claimants. In any case, in view of the technical and operational complexity of aviation the claimant would find it very difficult to marshal the necessary evidence. However, this element favourable for the claimant was counterbalanced by the imposition of monetary limits of liability.

9.2.2.3 Limitation of Liability

This has been the central point of contention for decades; limitation of liability to fixed maximum monetary amounts goes contrary to the general principles of liability that compensation should amount to restitution *(status quo ante)* or equivalent monetary compensation. Yet, aviation as a nascent industry urgently needed a limitation of liability to survive and develop through the period of gradually improving safety its record and financial viability. The limitation of liability was also presented as an equitable *quid pro quo* for the aggravated regime of liability of the air carrier with its presumption of fault of the carrier. Among other justifications for the limitation of liability was to enable the air carrier to negotiate a realistic insurance coverage within such limits; however, the practice proved that the carriers could not restrict their risk management by insurance only to the limits of liability under the Warsaw Convention but had to count with the worst possible scenario when the limits could not be invoked (*e.g.*, in cases when the Convention would not be applicable to the particular carriage, in case of a fault in ticketing or in case of the "qualified fault"[16]).

The most likely reason for the introduction of the limits of liability was the protection of the infant industry that could not sustain its development without such protection; moreover, since at that time most internationally operating airlines[17] were State-owned and State-operated, the States party to the Convention were in fact protecting their own interests. Whatever other justifications may be formulated, limitation of liability is a departure from the common law of liability and from the concept of natural justice.

Taking into account the devastating mega-inflation of some currencies after WW I, the monetary limits of liability were expressed in a "gold clause", since at that time gold was a recognized and stable yardstick of values. The currency unit for the limits of liability was the 1927 "Poincaré" (French) gold franc consisting of 65.5 mg of gold of 900/1000 fineness. The limit of liability for death, wounding or other bodily injury of a passenger was set at

---

15 Article 20 of the Warsaw Convention.
16 Wilful misconduct under Article 25 of the Warsaw Convention.
17 With the exception of the United States and Japan and some minor private operators.

125,000 francs – between 1929 and 1968 (when the US dollar was pegged at USD 35 per Troy ounce of pure gold) that represented USD 8,300, after the 1969 devaluation some USD 10,000.[18]

It is to be stressed that these amounts were not "lump sums" payable under any circumstances – the claimant had to prove that the damage equalled or exceeded the amount of the limit, otherwise only the proven amount was payable.

The liability for loss of or damage to baggage and cargo was limited to 250 francs per kilogram, equivalent to some USD 17 (USD 20 after devaluation). For objects of which the passenger takes charge himself (hand luggage) the limit was set at 5000 francs (USD 332 or USD 400 after devaluation).[19]

No separate specific limit was set for the delay and the jurisprudence accepted that the respective passenger and cargo limitation would apply. These limits could be exceeded only under the conditions stipulated by the Convention.[20]

It is not surprising that most cases considered over the decades by the courts of law focused on the provisions enabling to exceed the limits of liability and the Courts showed a benevolent attitude to such claims. The air carriers were deemed to have "deeper pockets" and adequate insurance and that perhaps motivated the courts (in particular in the US) to resort to very flexible interpretations of the Convention to give satisfaction to the claimants.

9.2.2.4   Jurisdiction of Courts

The unification of the substantive private law would not achieve its purpose without the determination of the courts which may be seized of any claims. This is another field where CITEJA went far beyond the original proposals of the French government. While trying to restrict "forum shopping", the Convention left a considerable flexibility in the selection of the court. Article 28 of the Convention stipulates that an action for damages must be brought, at the option of the plaintiff, in the territory of one of the High Contracting Parties, either before the Court having jurisdiction

1. where the carrier is *ordinarily resident*; or
2. has his (the air carrier) *principal place of business*; or
3. has an establishment by which the *contract has been made*; or
4. at the *place of destination*.

---

18   By August 2011, during a speculative hysteria, the price of gold reached a historic maximum of USD 1,950.000 per oz., soon to fall to USD 1,650.000. At present gold cannot serve as a stable yardstick of values and is traded as any other commodity based on supply and demand.
19   Article 22 of the Warsaw Convention.
20   The relevant provisions are Articles 3 (2), 4 (4) and 9 with respect to shortcomings of the documentation of carriage and Article 25 of the Warsaw Convention with respect to wilful misconduct.

In matters of procedural law the Convention further states that questions of procedure shall be governed by the law of the Court seized of the case *(lex fori)* and that the right to damages shall be extinguished if an action is not brought within two years, reckoned from the date of arrival at the destination, or from the date on which the aircraft ought to have arrived or from the date on which the carriage stopped.

It should be noted that in the Warsaw Convention (1929) was drafted under the predominant influence of European ("civil law") concepts and its text is authentic only in the French language, all other existing texts prepared by different governments for domestic use are unofficial translations and cannot serve as a basis of interpretation of the text.

Soon after the Convention came into force many States realized a major flaw in this unification of law – it went far beyond the unification of substantive law when imposing the strict and uniform limits of liability and thereby in fact attempted to "unify" the cost of living in a widely divergent spectrum of States. The limits of liability established by the Convention soon proved inadequate and economically unrealistic for many States and the Courts often accepted a "creative" interpretation of the Convention – a most undesirable judicial "amendment" of the real aim of the Convention. With the vastly improving safety record of the airlines, privatization of most airlines in the world and with the economic strength of the industry the low limits of liability lost any justification and steps were taken for the improvement and updating of the Convention, most of them half-hearted.

9.2.3 Steps in the Amendment of the Warsaw Convention

Under Article 41 of the Warsaw Convention (1929) it was for the Government of France to take any steps for the amendment of the Convention and the convening of a diplomatic conference. However, after World War II this task was assumed by ICAO and the French government *de facto* renounced its role in favour of the ICAO Legal Committee and of Diplomatic Conferences convened by the ICAO Council.[21]

9.2.3.1 The Hague Protocol 1955

After extensive studies in the Subcommittees of the Legal Committee and of the Legal Committee itself a certain compromise was reached on the amendment of the Convention. The Council of ICAO convened a diplomatic conference at The Hague that adopted, on 28 October 1955 the *Protocol to Amend the Convention for the Unification of Certain Rules*

---

21 An explicit notice of renunciation of its role was given by France only on the very eve of The Hague Conference in 1955 when the ICAO Secretariat started to worry about the impact of Article 41 of the Convention on the Conference that was already convened.

Relating to International Carriage by Air signed at Warsaw on 12 October 1929, done at The Hague, 28 October 1955[22] generally referred to as The Hague Protocol of 1955.

The Conference – out of deference to the Warsaw Convention – did not wish to adopt a new convention and agreed on the form of a Protocol that would insert new text into the original Convention, modify some provisions and delete some other.

The result is that the Protocol cannot stand by itself but must be read together with the original Convention. Nevertheless, a new instrument of international law was created by The Hague Protocol – *Warsaw Convention as amended at The Hague*, (1955)[23] that is separate and distinct from the original Warsaw Convention. The Protocol and the Convention are to be read and interpreted together as one single instrument.

A peculiar feature is that the Protocol was drafted in English, French and Spanish, each text being of equal authenticity, while the underlying Warsaw Convention exists only in one authentic language – French. Consequently, apart from the composite French text of the Warsaw Convention as amended at The Hague Protocol (1955), no such composite authentic text exists in English and Spanish. Again, the Convention as amended by the Protocol applies only between the parties thereto – a State party only to the original Warsaw Convention and another State party only to that Convention as amended at The Hague have no common denominator and neither of the two instruments applies in their mutual relation.

The primary object of the amendment was to increase the limits of liability with respect to passengers. These limits were considered, in particular in the United States, to be outdated and unrealistically low. The US delegation wished to have the limit of liability with respect to passengers increased at least to the equivalent of USD 25,000 but most delegations from the developing world considered such amount excessive.

A compromise was reached to double the "Warsaw" limit of 125,000 francs to 250,000 francs,[24] equivalent to some USD 16,600 (and USD 20,000 after devaluation). Such limit did not meet the needs of the United States with their high cost of living and other States in due course came to the same position as the United States. No change was made in the amount of limits with respect to baggage, personal effects and cargo.

In other respects the Protocol made only minor amendments. It contributed to some simplification of the documents of carriage and stipulated that only the absence of a notice (and not any other defect) would lead to the loss of limits of liability. The vague wording of Article 25 dealing with qualified fault ("wilful misconduct") was clarified by specifying that limit of liability could be exceeded if it is proved that the carrier or his agents acted

---

22 ICAO Doc 7632.
23 See Article XIX of The Hague Protocol.
24 While the Warsaw Convention refers to "French franc", that currency was no longer in circulation by 1955. The Protocol refers to a "franc" as an abstract currency unit consisting of 65.5 mg of gold of 900/1000 fineness.

with intent to cause a damage or recklessly and with knowledge that damage would probably result.[25] An additional Article 25 A) clarifies that the limits also protect the servants or agents of the carriers acting within the scope of their employment.

The Protocol gradually achieved wide acceptance, and by December 2022, 137 States were party to it. Its continuing coexistence with the original Warsaw Convention is unexpected – there are States that are party both to the original Convention and the Convention as amended at The Hague Protocol; there are States that were not party to the Warsaw Convention or have denounced it and are party only to the Convention as amended at the Hague Protocol; since the original Convention and the Convention as amended at The Hague Protocol are two separate and distinct instruments, it is important to determine which of the two instruments, if any, applies as common denominator to any two States. The practical scope of applicability of the amended Convention has been vastly reduced by the wide acceptance of the Montreal Convention (1999) and also by the fact that many international airlines have accepted the terms of the Montreal Convention into their conditions of carriage even in situations when the Montreal Convention would not be applicable.

9.2.3.2   Guadalajara Convention 1961

The next step in the evolution of what was now called the "Warsaw system" came in 1961 after extensive studies by the ICAO Legal Committee and its Subcommittees. On 18 September 1961 an International Conference on Air Law held in Guadalajara, Mexico from 29 August to 18 September 1961[26] adopted the *Convention, Supplementary to the Warsaw Convention, for the Unification of Certain Rules Relating to International Carriage by Air Performed by a Person Other than the Contracting Carrier*.[27]

A possible legal loophole was identified in the Warsaw Convention (1929) and that Convention as amended at The Hague Protocol (1955). It referred to some innovative practices in international air transport – in particular in the case of lease, charter or interchange of aircraft, in the practice of freight-forwarding and more recently in the practice of code-shared flights.

In such modalities of air transport the passenger or shipper concludes a contract of carriage with one entity (charterer, freight forwarder, a carrier which is not actually performing the code shared flight), while the actual carriage is performed by another entity – the actual carrier. It was perceived that such situations may make the Convention inapplicable since Article 1 (2) of the Warsaw Convention and that Convention as

---

25 This clarification puts on equal level the Roman law concepts of *dolus malus* and *culpa lata* – *culpa lata dolo equiparatur*.
26 ICAO Doc 8301-CD, the Minutes and Documents are available in CD-ROM format.
27 ICAO Doc 8181.

amended at The Hague Protocol (1955) makes the Convention system applicable only if there is a contract with the air carrier; in the modalities listed above the passenger or shipper enters into a contract with one "carrier" while the actual carriage is performed by another carrier and the Convention would not be applicable.

It is noteworthy that this new instrument was not adopted in the form of a Protocol to the Warsaw Convention but as a separate Convention supplementary to the Warsaw Convention. Much speculation was directed to this question but the memory of the participants of the Conference will confirm the "political" nature of this decision: if the instrument were to be Protocol, it would have to be deposited – like the Warsaw Convention and The Hague Protocol – with the Government of Poland. The communist government of Poland at that time proved to be "less than impartial" in the performance of its duties as the depositary in the controversial matters of that time (*e.g.*, siding with North Korea against South Korea, with the German Democratic Republic against the Federal Republic of Germany and Peoples Republic of China against the Republic of China – refusing to accept the ratification of one entity and giving priority to the other). The separate Convention was deposited with the host government of the Conference – Mexico.[28]

The substance of the Guadalajara Convention is simple: it extends the applicability of the Warsaw Convention or that Convention as amended at The Hague Protocol beyond the carrier identified in the contract of carriage ("contracting carrier") and grants the Convention's regime also to the "actual carrier" defined as

> a person other than the contracting carrier, who, by virtue of authority from the contracting carrier, performs the whole or part of the carriage contemplated [in the contract of carriage – added by ed.] but who is not with respect to such part a successive carrier within the meaning of the Warsaw Convention. Such authority is presumed in the absence of proof to the contrary.[29]

According to the information from the depositary Government, by December 2022 there were 86 States party to the Guadalajara Convention. However, all substantive provisions of the Convention have now been incorporated in the Montreal Convention (1999) [30] and it will gradually lose its meaning, together with the rest of the "Warsaw system".

---

[28] The Mexican government did not prove to be impartial either – due to continuing tension with the Vatican, it refused to accept the instruments coming directly from the Holy See and they had to be forwarded through ICAO.
[29] Article I c) of the Guadalajara Convention.
[30] Montreal Convention for the Unification of Certain Rules for International Carriage by Air (1999), Chapter V, Articles 39-48.

9.2.3.3 Montreal Agreement 1966

A Crisis of the "Warsaw System" resulted from the sudden denunciation of the Convention by the US Government. Dissatisfied by the low limit on recovery for passengers' death or injury, the US Department of State sent the notice of denunciation to the Polish Government on 18 October 1965; however, the US Government expressed hope that a new agreement could be reached before the notice of denunciation was to take effect six months later and it promised to withdraw the notice of denunciation if the limits of liability per passenger could be increased to between USD 75,000 and 100,000.

This notice was perceived as a serious crisis of the unification of private air law. Without the US participation in the Convention a large proportion of all international traffic would not be covered by unified law but would be subject to unpredictable conflicts of law, conflicts of jurisdiction and to unforeseeable difficulties in trying to obtain reasonable insurance coverage.

In February 1966, ICAO convened a "special meeting" in Montreal to which all contracting States were invited and that was to consider a solution that would avert the impending US denunciation of the Convention.[31] The meeting faced unusual acrimony ("a peasant should not pay for the bowl of soup for the Emperor"...) and the expectation of the US delegation to reach agreement on limit in the order of USD 100,000 was not supported by any other delegation. The forum of States within ICAO failed to find any solution.

The initiative was taken over by the airlines within the IATA and they reached an "interim solution" known as "Agreement Relating to Liability Limitation of the Warsaw Convention and The Hague Protocol" that is referred to as "Montreal Agreement 1966"[32] and was accepted by the US Civil Aeronautics Board (CAB). Just two days before the expiry of the deadline, the US notice of denunciation of the Convention was withdrawn. Where ICAO failed, a non-governmental body of the airlines succeeded in reaching a workable compromise.

The "Montreal Agreement 1966" is not an instrument of international law and is not a formal amendment of the Warsaw system. It is no more than a private agreement between the airlines and the US authorities under which the airlines accepted the regime of strict liability (renouncing their defence under Article 20 of the Convention) and a limit of USD 75,000 per passenger's death or injury for any flights to, from or through the territory of the US. It is just a private agreement of the airlines that on the flights involving US territory they will accept a particular interpretation and application of the Warsaw regime.

---

31 "Special ICAO Meeting on Limits for Passengers under the Warsaw Convention and Hague Protocol", ICAO Doc 8584/LC/154-1 and 2 (1966).
32 In the United States it is referred to as Agreement CAB 18900, approved by Order E-23680, 13 May 1966, (Docket 17325).

The agreement represents a *de facto* amendment of the Convention between particular subjects and with respect to particular flights. It undoubtedly eroded the unification of law and was contrary to the general precepts of the international law of treaties. The term "Agreement" would indicate a voluntary acceptance of the conditions but the airlines operating to, from or through the US territory had no choice if they wished to keep their operating permit. The "interim" nature of the agreement proved to be a mockery – it persisted for over thirty years!

9.2.3.4   Guatemala City Protocol 1971

ICAO had no alternative but to note this "interim" solution and it started to work on a permanent solution without delay. The matter was studied by two sessions of a special Panel of Experts on Limits of Liability in January and July 1967,[33] two sessions of the Subcommittee of the ICAO Legal Committee and the 17th Session of the Legal Committee.[34] These studies did not concentrate only on the issue of limits of liability but attempted to modernize the Warsaw system in several other aspects as part of a "package". The results were formulated in the format of a Protocol-to-Protocol and adopted at an International Conference on Air Law on 8 March 1971 as *Protocol to Amend the Convention for the Unification of Certain Rules Relating to International Carriage by Air*[35] signed at Warsaw on 12 October 1929 as amended by the Protocol, done at The Hague on 28 September 1955, signed at Guatemala on 8 March 1971.

The Guatemala City Protocol did not focus only on the increase of the limit of liability but attempted a radical modernization of the Warsaw system and pioneered new ideas that have later formed the basis of the Montreal Convention (1999). The Protocol was confined only to the urgent issues relating to passengers and left for later consideration all aspects relating to baggage and cargo.

One of the fundamental innovations was the simplification of the passenger ticket that could be substituted by "any other means" and thus enable electronic data processing; that innovation was a remarkable progress considering the legal practices of 1971. Moreover, the formalities of the documentation were completely separated from the regime of liability and any shortcoming in the ticketing had no influence on the limit of liability.

The Protocol also introduced the regime of strict liability regardless of fault and removed the exoneration clause in former Article 20. Strict liability regardless of fault was a bold innovation for the time.

---

33 Doc 8839-LC/158.
34 Doc 8877-LC/162, Montreal, 9 February-11 March 1970.
35 ICAO Doc 8932.

The Protocol expanded the conditions of recovery by referring to "personal injury" rather than "bodily injury", thus opening the door to compensation for mental trauma, post-traumatic shock syndrome, etc. that so far was at least questionable.

All those "improvements" of the regime of liability were predicated on the existence of a limit – admittedly a very high limit of 1,500,000 "francs" of the gold value of 65.5 mg of gold of 900/1000 fineness – a sum twelve times higher than the sum in the original Warsaw Convention and at that time equivalent to USD 100,000. It is important that this limit with respect to passengers was to be an absolute limit and that it was to be unbreakable under any circumstance – be it for any shortcomings in the documents of carriage or "wilful misconduct" (Article 25 was deleted). The authors of the text thus wished to prevent the frequently used "legal" techniques to exceed the limits of liability under the old system.[36]

The Guatemala City Conference was essentially a dialogue between the United States and the rest of the world, all States being sincerely anxious to accommodate the understandable economic needs of the United States. However, without previous preparation the US came at the last minutes of the Conference with additional demands.

One of them was to provide in the instrument for permission to States to operate in their territory a "national supplement" to the limit in the form of additional insurance that would not add anything to the liability of the carrier. This request was accommodated in a new Article 35.

The second additional request of the United States was to add to the four jurisdictions in Article 28 of the Warsaw Convention a "fifth jurisdiction" in the place of carrier's establishment if the passenger has his domicile or permanent residence in the territory of the same State. Other delegations believed that this additional jurisdiction would give an unfair advantage to US passengers who would have almost always access to US courts – notorious for their relatively high compensation awards compared with the courts in other States. In spite of serious doubts even this wish of the US was accepted with the understanding that regardless of the choice of the court the absolute limit of liability cannot be ever exceeded.

Since the Protocol was drafted to meet the needs and requirements of the US, the Conference believed that the Protocol should require for its entry into force not only ratification by thirty States, but specifically also the ratification by the United States. This is the idea behind the otherwise incomprehensible provision of Article XX of the Protocol that does not mention the United States but refers to 1970 statistics of passenger-kilometres of five States that represent at least 40% of all international carriage. There could not be any such five States unless the United States are among them.

---

36 It remains questionable whether the unbreakability of the limit would not be against the "public order" in many States when it would be supposed to apply even in case of intentional damage, even in case of a criminal act.

The Guatemala City Protocol was a bold and honest effort to modernize private international air law and introduced several progressive elements valid at present. However, it never came into force since the United States did not ratify it and it is now a dead letter. The fatal flaw of the Protocol was its absolutely unbreakable limit of liability – such a condition even in the case of criminal intent was hardly acceptable not only to the US (who could have bypassed it by a "national supplement") but also to the civil law countries as it would contradict their constitutional concepts of "public order". In any case, many States avoided ratification of the Protocol waiting – in vain – for the first such step by the United States.

9.2.3.5 Additional Protocols of Montreal Nos. 1-3 and Montreal Protocol No. 4 1975

Soon after the Guatemala City Conference attention was drawn to the "unfinished business" – the problem of cargo that was not dealt with in the Guatemala City Protocol. The Legal Committee of ICAO prepare d a draft protocol and a Diplomatic Conference was convened in Montreal in September 1975.[37] Against all expectations the main task of the Conference was embodied only in what is now "Montreal Protocol No. 4"[38] while the preceding "Additional Protocols of Montreal" Nos. 1, 2 and 3 deal with a problem that was not even on the agenda of the Conference when it convened.

The problem singled out by the US delegation was the expression of the limits of liability in the "gold clause" in French gold franc or in "francs" as an abstract currency unit defined by their gold content. This clause was meaningful and convincing as long as gold was a steady yardstick of values and a Troy ounce of gold (31,1 grams) was officially worth USD 35. However, by 1968-1969 de Gaulle's France requested exchange of their vast stock of "Eurodollars" for gold at the standard parity and that caused devaluation of the US dollar as well as creation of a free market for gold. Many countries followed the US example and abolished the gold par value of their currency and gold was thus "demonetized" and became just another commodity the price of which was determined by the market laws of supply and demand. Gold is no longer a stable yardstick of values and frequently reaches unrealistic speculative price in response to political events or general economic downturn.

In the light of these developments the "gold clause" in the Warsaw system lost its relevance. The International Monetary Fund by that time also abolished the gold parity of currencies and created the concept of "Special Drawing Right" (SDR) as a new yardstick of values. The SDR is not a real currency but a measure of values defined every day from a floating basket of the leading trading currencies – often called "paper gold". Those leading currencies are the EURO, Japanese yen, Pound Sterling, Chinese renminbi (yuan) and the

---

37 ICAO Doc 9154-CD, the Minutes and Documents are available in CD-ROM format.
38 ICAO Doc 9148.

US dollar. Originally in 1969, one SDR equalled one US dollar. The SDR currency code is XDR. The current rate (December 2022) is 1 USD = 0,75 SDR (or 1 SDR = USD 1.33) but it is subject to daily changes.[39]

The Conference adopted "Additional Protocols of Montreal" Nos. 1, 2 and 3[40] that have the sole purpose of replacing the "gold clause" in the original 1929 Warsaw Convention, in that Convention as amended at The Hague 1955 and in that Convention as amended at The Hague and by the Guatemala City Protocol (1971) by translating the limits of liability from the gold clause into the SDR.[41]

Protocols Nos. 1 and 2 came into force for 49 and 50 States, respectively but their practical relevance has been overshadowed by the Montreal Convention (1999).

Protocol No. 3 is a peculiar instrument – it is a Protocol-to-Protocol-to-Protocol that was to be a separate and distinct instrument to be known as the *Warsaw Convention as amended at The Hague 1955, at Guatemala City, 1971 and by Additional Protocol No. 3 of Montreal, 1975*; it could have come into force by ratification by any thirty States without the condition that the United States must be among them; however, other States did not show interest to join such instrument without the support of the US, so Protocol 3 never came into force and remains only a historic landmark of the efforts to modernize the "Warsaw system".

The proper work assigned to the Montreal Diplomatic Conference in 1975 was to adopt updated rules for the carriage of cargo. That was accomplished with a remarkable success in the Montreal Protocol No. 4[42] of 25 September 1975 with a full title *Additional Protocol No. 4 to Amend the Convention for the Unification of Certain Rules Relating to international Carriage by Air* signed at Warsaw on 12 October 1929 as amended by the Protocol done at The Hague on 28 September 1955, signed at Montreal on 25 September 1975.

The Protocol was ratified by 61 States by December 2022, but all its substantive provisions have been adopted in the Montreal Convention (1999) and enjoy wide applicability.

The Protocol left the limit of liability for loss of or damage of cargo at the same level as the original Warsaw Convention (1929), the equivalent of the 250 francs being 17 SDR per kilogram and that limit cannot be exceeded under any circumstances. There was no pressure to increase this amount since the carriage of cargo normally involves business entities carrying adequate insurance.

---

39 The values quoted are from the IMF web page and apply for 31 December 2022.
40 ICAO Docs. 9145, 9146 and 9147.
41 Thus 125,000 francs became 8,300 SDR, 250 francs 17 SDR, 5,000 francs 332 SDR, 250,000 francs 16,600 SDR and 1,500,000 francs 100,000 SDR.
42 ICAO Doc 9148.

Of great importance is the adoption of the regime of strict liability of the air carrier for the loss of or damage to cargo regardless of fault; the only exoneration of the carrier could be transport industry and of the consignors and offered the first ray of hope that in due course the entire liability system in international air transport could be modernized.

After the Montreal Conference (1975) ICAO (or, more precisely, its Member States) made no further effort to modernize the Warsaw system for over twenty years; all action was limited to the "flogging of a dead horse" by repeated exhortation to States to ratify Protocols Nos. 3 and 4. The Assembly Resolutions on this subject were adopted by full unanimity, but no action by States followed.[43]

The lack of any progress in the modernization of the Convention caused major dissatisfaction and frustration to governments and airlines alike. The main concern, although never openly expressed at the ICAO meetings, has been the possibility that the United States and other developed countries might denounce the unsatisfactory Convention owing to its unsatisfactory limits and thus throw international air transport into the unpredictable and uninsurable maze of conflict of laws and conflict of jurisdictions.

9.2.3.6 Japanese Initiative 1992

A series of unilateral actions were taken for practical application to bridge the deadlock reached in international law-making:

– many airlines, in particular in the developed countries, unilaterally increased in their tariffs the limit of liability to passenger's death or injury to 100,000 SDR (currently some USD 133,000);

– Italy adopted this limit of 100,000 SDR by law for all Italian carriers and for all other carriers operating to, from or through Italy;[44]

– the *Japanese initiative* is the name usually given to the decision of all Japanese air carriers, with the approval of the Government of Japan, to waive, as of 20 November 1992, the limit of liability in the international carriage by air in a two-tier system: up to 100,000 SDR strict liability for proven damage would be accepted without defence and beyond that sum, without any monetary limitation, liability would be based on presumed fault with reversed burden of proof (*i.e.*, with the defence of "all necessary measures" have taken under Article 20 (1) of the Warsaw Convention.[45]

---

43 The last such Resolution was adopted in October 1995 (A-31, Appendix C, A31-WP/61, Recent developments concerning the modernisation of the Warsaw System of Airline liability). By that time deliberations had progressed within IATA and only four weeks after the ICAO Assembly Resolution the IATA Kuala Lumpur Annual General Meeting adopted a new initiative of its member airlines on the subject that was a harbinger of a generally satisfactory solution.

44 Italian Law No. 274 of 7 July 1988; this law was adopted in the wake of a ruling by the Constitutional Court of Italy that the Warsaw/The Hague limit of liability was violating the constitutional rights of passengers.

45 Text in *Lloyd's Aviation Law*, Vol. 11, p. 22 (1992).

The "Japanese initiative" was a major historic innovation, indicating the industry's willingness and ability to accept liability without any monetary limits. Moral reasons have motivated the Japanese Government – how to justify limitation of liability for passengers in international carriage by air when there is no such limitation under domestic law for domestic carriage by air, accidents in the automobile operations, etc.; moreover, the level of operational safety and the possibility of effective risk management by insurance made the limitation of liability unjustifiable.[46]

- The Japanese initiative was followed by other airlines within IATA and on 31 October 1995, the IATA Annual General Meeting in Kuala Lumpur adopted the *Intercarrier Agreement on Passenger Liability* followed by the *Measures to Implement the IATA Intercarrier Agreement*.[47] Like the Japanese initiative, the IATA Agreement was to be included in the carriers' tariffs and would waive the limit of liability for recoverable compensatory damages for death or bodily injury of a passenger; the airlines also agreed not to use the defence under Article 20 of the Convention for claims up to 100,000 SDR. The IATA Passenger Liability Agreement came into force on 14 February 1997 and it was claimed that it came into force for airlines carrying some 80% of all international air passengers at that time.

- A multilateral (regional) legislative step was taken by the European Union which adopted, as a law applicable to both international and domestic carriage by air of its Member States, as of 17 October 1998, a *Council Regulation on Air Carrier Liability*.[48] The essence of the Regulation is waiver of the limits of liability for death and bodily injury of a passenger, coupled with the strict liability up to 100,000 SDR.

The unilateral actions of airlines, States or group of States created a *de facto* massive amendment of the Warsaw system but had a fundamental flaw: they could modify the practical application of the provisions relating to the limit of liability (which is permitted by Article 22 (1) of the Convention as a "special contract"). However, they cannot amend any substantive provision of the Convention that in itself has "imperative" nature.[49] Thus the unilateral actions would remain "attached" to the underlying existence and peremptory provisions of the Warsaw/Hague system. That Convention can be amended only in accordance with the rules of international law.[50] No amount of unilateral or collective

---

46 The intellectual father of the "Japanese Initiative" was an outstanding aviation law practitioner George N. Tompkins Jr. from the United States.
47 Text in *Annals of Air and Space Law*, Vol. XXI-1, pp. 293-303 (1996).
48 Council Regulation (EC) No. 2027/97 on Air Carrier Liability in the Event of Accidents, OJ L 285 of 17 October 1997.
49 Article 32 of the Warsaw Convention declares "null and void" any special agreements or clauses purporting to infringe the rules laid down by the Convention.
50 Vienna Convention on the Law of Treaties (1969), Part IV, Amendments and Modifications of Treaties, Articles 39-41.

"patchwork" can replace the appropriate process of amendment of the Convention and establish a solid international legal regime to be applied uniformly by the courts of law.

9.3 MONTREAL CONVENTION 1999[51]

ICAO was initially a reluctant player in any effort to modernize the system after 1975; yet, it was the only forum in which the modernized unification of law could be accomplished.

The ICAO Council initiated new action on 15 November 1995,[52] just two weeks after the IATA Annual General Meeting that had adopted the Passenger Liability Agreement. Without any reference or credit to the IATA action, the Council amended the general work program of the Legal Committee by inserting a new item "The modernization of the Warsaw System and review of the ratification of international air law instruments".

The work progressed in an unusual procedure: instead of appointing a Rapporteur and a Special Subcommittee of the Legal Committee, a "Secretariat Working Group" was established – a non-representative body not foreseen in the applicable rules and established practices and composed of "experts" selected by the President of the Council in his personal discretion.

The 30th Session of the Legal Committee met at Montreal from 28 April to 9 May 1997 and after chaotic discussions prepared three alternative drafts of the liability regime – a sure prescription for a failure of the Diplomatic Conference where a two-thirds majority vote is required. In spite of its confusing conclusions the Committee considered this draft to be "final" and ready for presentation to a Diplomatic Conference.

The Council did not follow the unconvincing recommendation of the Committee but in a clear "censure" of the Committee's views convened two more meetings of the "Secretariat Study Group" and later another unprecedented body appointed by the President – the "Special Group on Modernization and Consolidation of the 'Warsaw System'" (SGMW). That body met at Montreal from 14 to 18 April 1998 and produced a consolidated text daringly called "Text approved by the 30th Session of the ICAO Legal Committee and refined by the Special group on the modernization and consolidation of the Warsaw system".

The expression "refined" is an audacious understatement – the SGMW in fact substantially changed the Legal Committee's text, aligned the draft fully on the IATA Passenger Liability Agreement and the EC Council Regulation (1997) and removed all

---

51 P.S. Dempsey and M. Milde, *International Air Carrier Liability: The Montreal Convention of 1999*, McGill University Centre for Research in Air & Space Law, Montreal, 2005, pp. 1-463.
52 C-DEC 146/3.

alternatives. It also accepted the US requirement to create a "5th jurisdiction" as was provided for in the Guatemala City Protocol (1971).[53]

The Diplomatic Conference met in Montreal from 11 to 28 May 1999 and faced some firmly established benchmarks that appeared non-negotiable – those were the principles of the Japanese initiative with the two-tier regime of liability, those principles as embodied and already widely applied under the IATA Passenger Liability Agreement and under the EC Regulation.

Although there was a deep cleavage of opinions on the complete removal of a liability limit and on the 5th jurisdiction, a "Consensus package"[54] concocted by a closed group called "Friends of the Chairman" was presented to the session, met with thunderous applause and was declared to be accepted "by consensus" without any vote.

The procedure under which the new Convention was adopted may be open to severe criticism and the "pressure for consensus" left some bitterness in several delegations. However, the result was the *Convention for the Unification of Certain Rules for International Carriage by Air*, signed at Montreal on 28 May 1999.[55]

In spite of the seriously flawed procedure, the resulting Montreal Convention (1999) is a good international instrument that achieved several positive aims:

- It consolidated into one single instrument the components of the fragmented "Warsaw System" (fragmented by a Protocol, then Protocol-to-Protocol and finally Protocol-to-Protocol-to Protocol) and took – almost verbatim – the best elements of the "old" system, the Guatemala City Protocol of 1971, Protocol Nos. 3 and 4 of 1975 and the Guadalajara Convention of 1961, including the modernization and simplification of the documents of carriage.
- The text of the new instrument is authentic in Arabic, Chinese, English, French, Russian and Spanish.[56]
- It accepted the industry's progressive initiative to apply, for death or injury of a passenger, strict liability up to 100,000 SDR with no monetary limit of liability above that amount subject to "reversed burden of proof"; this is expected to expedite recovery and avoid lengthy and costly litigation.
- It introduced the 5th jurisdiction – not a revolutionary change but a logical jurisdiction of the claimant if it were not for the peremptory condition of the "old" Article 28.

---

53 Text in DCW No. 3.
54 DCW Doc No. 50.
55 ICAO Doc 9740.
56 In fact, all drafting during the Conference was done only in English and the other versions are just translations prepared by the professional language officers of the Secretariat, most of them non-lawyers.

- It requires the air carrier to submit a proof of adequate insurance guaranteeing the availability of financial resources in case of aircraft accident.[57]

The Montreal Convention (1999) is a new, separate and independent instrument, not an amendment of the "Warsaw system". Its provisions will prevail over any other rules of international carriage by air between States who are also parties to the "old" instruments.[58] It came into force on 4 November 2003, and by December 2022 it was ratified by 139 States, making it applicable for a predominant proportion of international carriage by air.

Its actual scope of applicability is *de facto* extended because any return flight from a State party to a State that is not party to the Convention is covered by the Convention;[59] that can lead to absurd situations when two passengers sitting next to each other can be subject to different systems of liability depending on their different points of origin and destination. Nevertheless, there are still some dwindling situations where between the non-parties the Warsaw/The Hague system would be applicable.

On the proposal of the delegation of China, the Conference adopted an innovative provision in Article 56 of the Montreal Convention that enables a State composed of territorial units with different legal systems to accept the Convention either for the entire territory or only one of them; the intention obviously was to address the issue of the special administrative territories of Hong Kong and Macau and the term "Hong Kong clause" was coined.[60] It was expected that for Hong Kong, the Convention would be applicable first while China may require some time to accept it. In reality, China ratified the Convention well before it became applicable for Hong Kong.

The Montreal Conference of 1999 was a success but several "missed opportunities" must be noted. The Convention failed to clarify the vague and imprecise term "accident" that is the key trigger of liability for the death or injury to passenger. The proper and logical interpretation of this term should be that "accident" is an event closely connected with the operation of the aircraft; however, some judicial decisions have interpreted the term in a rather "creative" manner[61] bordering on the absurd and placing the carrier into

---

57 The Convention does not define what "adequate insurance" is; in practice operators of large aircraft carry insurance in excess of USD 1 billion; it is also a reality that the operators of the developing countries frequently pay higher insurance premiums than those from the developed world who own more modern fleet and have years of damage-free record.
58 Article 55 of the Montreal Convention.
59 Article 1, paragraph 2 of the Montreal Convention (international carriage).
60 M. Milde, "Liability in International Carriage by Air: The New Montreal Convention" in *Uniform Law Review*, NS – Vol. IV, 1999/4, p. 859.
61 In *Husain v. Olympic Airways* the fact that the stewardess did not locate another seat in the non-smoking compartment for an asthmatic passenger was considered to constitute an "accident" causing the death of that passenger. *Husain v. Olympic Airways*, 316 F.3d 829 (9th Cir.) 2002.

the position of an insurer of any conceivable risk. The Montreal Convention failed to accept the term "event" adopted by the Guatemala City Conference in 1971.

The Montreal Conference also, perhaps by oversight, failed to extend the 5th jurisdiction to claims with respect to baggage, cargo and delay.

It is also to be regretted that the Guatemala City reference to "personal injury" was not retained and that the Convention keeps the expression "bodily injury" with its ambiguity whether or not it applies also to "mental trauma", "post-traumatic shock syndrome", etc.

Much leeway has been left to jurisprudence and that is not conducive to uniform interpretation of the unified law. The jurisprudence will have to lead the way and the Montreal Convention (1999) may be expected to stay in force at least for a generation.

Long-term continuing relevance of the Convention is supported by its mechanism for the review of the limits of liability to respond to the inflationary trends.[62] The first such review took effect as of 30 December 2022 as follows:

- liability in the first tier for each passenger for damage sustained in case of death or bodily injury was increased from 100,000 SDR to 128,821 SDR;
- liability for each passenger in case of destruction, loss, damage or delay with respect to baggage was increased from 1,000 SDR to 1,288 SDR;
- liability for each passenger in relation to damage caused by delay in the carriage of persons was increased from 4,150 SDR to 5,346 SDR;
- liability in the case of destruction, loss, damage or delay in relation to the carriage of cargo was increased from 17 SDR per kilogram to 22 SDR per kilogram.

9.4 Rome Convention on Damage Caused by Foreign Aircraft to Third Parties on the Surface 1952

The operation of aircraft could cause damage on the surface to persons who are not in any contractual relation with the operator of the aircraft. The physical impact of a crashing aircraft or parts or objects falling from it could have a devastating effect on the ground for persons and property. The worst such incident – caused by criminal acts – was the intentional crashing of wide-bodied aircraft against the World Trade Centre in New York and the Pentagon in Washington, D.C. on 11 September 2001 causing the death of almost 3,000 persons and enormous material damage.

---

62 Article 24 of the Montreal Convention; the Depositary (ICAO) is to adjust the limits at five-years intervals if the inflation factor exceeds 10%. The upper limit was changed first in 2009, there was no change in 2014, and then, in 2019 the amounts in Articles 21-23 were amended again. Revised Limits of Liability Under the Montreal Convention of 1999, www.icao.int/secretariat/legal/Pages/2019_Revised_Limits_of_Liability_Under_the_MC.

Many incidents of damage on the ground have been recorded and the proximity of airports to densely populated urban centers increases the likelihood of such disasters that occur mostly at take-off or landing.[63]

Damage to third parties on the surface was the subject of the very first recorded judicial decision in the field of "air law" in a colourful case *Guille v. Swan* in 1822.[64] The case is also important as a source of law with respect to torts. Guille's balloon went out of control and landed on Swan's property causing some damage in the vegetable garden; moreover, scores of onlookers rushed to the garden – either in an effort to help or simply out of curiosity – and damaged the fences, flowers and vegetables. Guille was found strictly liable (regardless of fault) not only for the damage caused directly by his balloon but also for the damage caused by the crowd since it was a logical consequence that the uncontrolled landing would attract a curious crowd.

At the first glance, this type of accidents does not create difficult problems of applicable law or jurisdiction that would have to be solved by unification of law. In the theory of conflict of laws this type of damage would be governed by the law of the place where the damage was caused *(lex loci damni commissi)* and the court in that place would have jurisdiction.

However, problems could arise if the damage is caused by a foreign airline; would the judgment of the local court be recognized and enforced in the country of the aircraft operator's residence or principal place of business? Would there be a guarantee that sufficient funds would be available to compensate for the damage?

The problem attracted the attention of CITEJA by 1930 and the Third International Conference on Private Air Law in Rome adopted, on 29 May 1933 the *Convention for the Unification of Certain Rules Relating to Damage Caused by Foreign Aircraft to Third Parties on the Surface*.[65]

---

63 Examples: on 4 November 2007 in Sao Paulo a Learjet crashed into two houses and six persons were killed; on 17 October 2007 in Bogota a Beechcraft crashed into four buildings killing two persons on the ground; on 4 October 2007 in Kinshasa, Democratic Republic of Congo, Antonov 26 of El Sam Airlift crashed on take-off, destroying three houses and causing twenty-eight fatalities on the ground; on 25 July 2000 in Paris an Air France Concorde aircraft crashed into the hotel causing four fatalities and six seriously injured victims on the ground; on 17 July 2007 in Sao Paulo an Airbus A320 crashed on landing killing twelve persons on the ground. Among the earlier incidents are: on 5 December 1997 Russian air force Antonov 124 – at that time the largest aircraft in the world – in Irkutsk suffered engine failure on take-off and crashed into a residential area causing forty-five fatalities on the ground; on 4 October 1992 a cargo B-747 of El Al lost two engines on take-off in Amsterdam (Bijlmer), the falling engines causing vast damage and the hull crashed into a eleven-floor apartment building in the suburb of Amsterdam and scores of tenants were killed.
64 Referred to as *Guille v. Swan*, 19 Johns, 381 (N.Y. 1822).
65 ICAO Doc 106-CD, the Minutes and Documents are available in CD-ROM format, French only.

The Rome Convention (1933) did not achieve wide acceptance and is now obsolete.[66] Nevertheless, it remains interesting since it determined some fundamental principles on which further considerations and decisions could build. Among them were:
– liability attaches to the operator (not owner) of the aircraft;
– strict liability is imposed on the operator of the aircraft from which he could be exonerated only if he proves intervention of a third party;
– liability is limited to sums depending on the weight of the aircraft; it is expressed in gold clause (French gold franc), one third of the compensation to be reserved for material damage, two-thirds to persons with a limit of 200,000 francs per person killed or injured;
– a financial guarantee must be obtained by each aircraft operator in international air operations.

These points had their merit by 1933: the operator is in control of the flight and liability rightly attaches to him; strict liability was very rare by 1933 and its acceptance here was a progress since the victim would have great difficulties in proving fault of the operator; a *quid pro quo* for this "advantage", the claimant has to accept limits of liability and the amount of 200,000 francs was only marginally above the Warsaw limit of 125,000 francs for passengers – persons who knowingly and willingly entered into the contract of carriage with its intrinsic risks. The financial guarantee of ability to compensate the victims was to be a safeguard against bankruptcy of the operator.

CITEJA prepared a further document complementing the Rome Convention (1933) on matters of insurance guarantees and the Fourth International Private Air Law Conference adopted it in Brussels on the eve of World War II on 29 September 1938 as the *Protocol Supplementary to the Convention for the Unification of Certain Rules Relating to Damage Caused by Foreign Aircraft to Third Parties on the Surface*, signed in Rome on 29 May 1933, done at Brussels on 29 September 1938.[67]

The Brussels Protocol (1938) was ratified only by two countries (Brazil and Guatemala) and the war interrupted further development of the international unification of private air law.

ICAO returned to this subject at the 1st Session of its Assembly in 1947 when it requested the ICAO Legal Committee to resume the studies of liability to third parties. After several meetings of the "Rome" Subcommittee of the Legal Committee the Committee itself considered a draft new Convention at its meetings in Taormina and Mexico City and the draft was presented to a Diplomatic Conference held in Rome

---

66 It was expressly overtaken under Article 29 of the Rome Convention (1952).
67 ICAO Doc 107-CD, the Minutes and Documents are available in CD-ROM format, French only.

between 9 September – 7 October 1952, which adopted the *Convention on Damage Caused by Foreign Aircraft to Third Parties on the Surface*, signed at Rome on 7 October 1952.[68]

The Convention did not achieve wide acceptance. By December 2022, there were 51 parties to the Convention; some earlier parties (Australia, Canada and Nigeria) have denounced it (and other States would be well-advised to denounce the Convention since its application would lead to economically unrealistic consequences). The Convention represents a modernization and drafting improvement of the 1933 text and encompasses also the subjects covered by the Brussels Protocol (1938). The positive aspects of this unification of law are:

- strict liability that attaches to the operator of the aircraft; the victim on the surface is entitled to compensation upon proof only that the damage was caused by an aircraft in flight or by any person or thing falling therefrom;
- the liability is guaranteed by detailed provisions on security or operator's liability;
- single forum jurisdiction: all claims must be brought to courts in the State where the damage occurred, and all claims are to be consolidated for disposal in a single proceeding before the same court; and
- the judgment is to be recognized and enforced in other contracting States.

The negative element of the Convention is the severe limitation of liability. That was in fact the very purpose of the Convention which in the Preamble declares "desire to ensure adequate compensation for persons who suffer damage caused on the surface by foreign aircraft, while limiting in a reasonable manner the extent of the liability incurred for such damage in order not to hinder the development of international air transport …".

Limitation of liability is thus clearly aimed at the protection of the infant industry and it is the innocent victims on the ground that are expected to "subsidize" the development of international air transport.

Like in the 1933 Convention, the Rome Convention (1952) limits are tied to the weight of the aircraft – a very unconvincing benchmark because even a very light aircraft may cause extensive damage if it crashes against a sensitive target (gas works, oil refinery, nuclear plant, etc.).

The typical aircraft in today's international transport are heavier than 50 tons, the highest category under Article 11, paragraph 1 d) of the Convention; there the limit is determined as 10,500,000 francs plus 100 francs for each additional kilogram. According to the parities applicable in 1952 that was USD 773, 850 plus USD 7.37 for each additional kilogram. The limit of liability for a crashed B-747 would be less than USD 3 million – an unrealistically low amount if we consider the scenario of a crash in populous downtown area or on an industrial plant.

---

68 ICAO Doc 7364.

The specific limit for death or personal injury is 500,000 francs – only twice the limit for passengers under the Warsaw/The Hague system that is now obsolete. Moreover, this sum may be reduced "proportionately" if the sum of all claims exceeds the overall limit.

With the exception of Italy, Russia and the United Arab Emirates, no major aviation country is party to the Convention and the Convention does not reflect the current needs of the international community.

ICAO continued studies related to the Rome Convention (1952). One of the initiatives that failed to get support was to enhance the scope of the Convention to refer not only to physical impact damage but also to damage caused by noise and sonic boom. There were serious doubts whether any solution may be found because it was believed that problems of noise damage arise only in the vicinity of airports, that the aircraft operators have no choice but to land and take-off from that designated airport and that, in any case, it would be impossible to single out one operator responsible for the damage caused by noise since such damage is caused by a cumulative effect of many flights. Further studies of this subject were abandoned.

A Subcommittee of the Legal Committee considered the Rome Convention (1952) further in an effort to simplify its text, increase the limits of liability and, in general, make the Convention more acceptable to a wider scope of States. The Subcommittee presented its report in 1975 for consideration by the 22nd Session of the Legal Committee.[69] In a surprise motion a proposal was made to recommend to the Council the convening of a Diplomatic Conference for the revision of the Rome Convention (1952). The Legal Committee is supposed to make such a proposal if there is a draft instrument that the Committee considered "final" and mature for consideration by a Diplomatic Conference. There was no such draft at the time of adjournment of the Legal committee's session, only a record of vague discussions!

The Conference met at Montreal from 6 to 23 September 1978[70] and focused its attention on the amounts of limits of liability. There were no solid economic data or statistics available to support any proposed solution and the results of the deliberations do not marshal much credibility. The delegations of the major aeronautical countries were reticent to accept any decision on the limits of liability but decided not to vote against the text but to abstain; the Conference takes its decision by two-thirds majority of those present and voting and the massive abstentions permitted to adopt the *Protocol to Amend the Convention on Damage Caused by Foreign Aircraft to Third Parties on the Surface*, signed at Montreal on 23 September 1978.[71]

---

69 ICAO Doc 9183.
70 ICAO Doc 9357-CD, the Minutes and Documents are available in CD-ROM format.
71 ICAO Doc 9257.

At the end of the Diplomatic Conference this Protocol was signed by nine delegations. By December 2022, the Protocol was in force for twelve States, among them only Brazil is a major aviation State. It is justified to state that this effort to enhance the international unification of private air law was a failure – a predictable failure due to the insufficient and unconvincing preparation, lack of interest among States and lack of any convincing urgency of the subject.

One of the positive contributions of the Protocol is the adoption of the SDR as the yardstick of values. However, the limit of 125,000 SDR in respect of loss of life or personal injury per person killed or injured falls far short of the expectations of most States; by 1978 many leading airlines unilaterally increased their liability to passengers to 100,000 SDR and the passengers, unlike the third party victims on the ground, are willingly by contract part of the flight and its risk and could manage their share of the risk by additional personal insurance.

With the Montreal Convention (1999) there is no monetary limit of liability for passenger's death or injury. Third parties on the surface have no relationship with the operator of the aircraft and it is difficult to justify why they should share the operator's risk by having their right of compensation limited. It appears contrary to natural justice to limit the liability with respect to innocent third parties on the surface while the passengers – who willingly contracted with the operator to become part of the flight, a venture the risk of which they knowingly assumed, may enjoy unlimited compensation.

9.4.1 After "9/11"

The problem of liability to third parties on the surface attracted renewed attention after the unprecedented damage caused by the terrorist acts of 11 September 2001. It was the worst man-made disaster on US territory in history and the loss of life and material damage reached unparalleled levels.[72]

The nature of the 11 September 2001 disaster was purely domestic and did not involve any "international element" that would necessitate international regulation. The aircraft involved were registered in the United States, were operated by airlines with principal place of business in the US and were on domestic flights; the damage occurred on US territory. An event of this nature and the claims for compensation resulting from it would not attract the application of foreign law or need for an international instrument for the unification of private law.

---

72 The loss of life on 11 September 2001 was higher than that caused by the Japanese attack on Pearl Harbour on 7 December 1941; 2996 persons died in New York and Washington D.C., while the number of victims at Pearl Harbour was 2403.

However, the impact of "9/11" was felt throughout the world and has thrown the airlines of the world into a crisis threatening the future viability of aviation and insurance industries. The airlines lost billions of dollars in the years that followed "9/11" and many governments had to bail out their national airlines from the brink of bankruptcy by massive cash and loan subsidies.

The situation was aggravated by the steep increases in the price of fuel that accounted for 13% of the airlines' operating costs prior to "9/11" and by May 2011 reached over 35%, and remained between 20-25% in 2022. Intrusive and time-consuming preventive measures, insensitive searches and the screening of passengers coupled often with intimidating attitudes of the security officers turned away for a long time many passengers from air transport or from some airports.

Risk management became a major problem for the airlines around the world. As of 23 September 2001, the aviation insurers invoked the often overlooked "seven-day-clause" in the policies and cancelled all war and terrorism clauses from the aviation insurance policies; later they re-introduced such coverage but for limited amounts. The insurance market – underfunded and overexposed over many years – could have completely collapsed. The lack of available insurance for third party risk would have grounded many airlines but some States stepped in with governmental guarantees.

ICAO attempted to facilitate the availability of third party insurance with the unsuccessful effort to find an alternative to commercial insurance for airlines.

The planned proposal of an "ICAO Global Scheme on Aviation War Risk Insurance" – generally referred to as "Globaltime"[73] – would have set up a non-profit Insurance Entity collecting premiums payable by passengers and any pay-out for damage caused to third parties on the surface in cases of aviation terrorism would be guaranteed by the participating governments. The scheme was supposed to become operational when agreement on participation is reached from States responsible for 51% of the contributions to the ICAO budget; that target was not achieved since, *inter alia*, it was not mandatory and the largest potential contributors (United States and Japan) did not join.

The actions within ICAO included the establishment of the Special Group on Aviation War Risk Insurance (SGWI), Council Study Group on Aviation War Risk Insurance (CGWI) and a Review Group (SGWI-RG), Council Special Group on the Modernization of the Rome Convention of 1952 (SGMR) – all *ad hoc* bodies not foreseen in the applicable rules or established practice.[74]

A Rapporteur of the Legal Committee was appointed in early 2002 and the issue was considered at the 32nd Session of the Legal Committee held in Montreal from 15 to 21 March 2004; its only conclusion was that the problem required more work. Little

---

73 C-WP/12003, Appendix A, www.icao.int/secretariat/legal/Documents/sl_02_55_atte_en.pdf.
74 A35-WP/18.

enthusiasm was indicated for any "modernization" of the Rome Convention (1952), although the special problem of incidents caused by terrorist acts proved to be somewhat more attractive.[75]

The result of these studies were two draft conventions – one dealing with liability and compensation in cases of damage caused by unlawful interference and the other dealing with liability and compensation where there is no unlawful interference. It would appear that the draft "Convention on Compensation for Damage Caused by Aircraft to Third Parties, in case of Unlawful Interference" (referred to as "the Unlawful Interference Compensation Convention") had more support at the 36th Session of the Assembly in September 2007 than the draft "Convention on Compensation for Damage Cause by Aircraft to Third Parties" (referred to as "the General Risk Convention").[76] The majority of the Legal Commission of the Assembly agreed that the work on both drafts was sufficiently mature to go to the Legal Committee early in 2008. The Council convened the 33rd Session of the Legal Committee in Montreal from 21 April to 2 May 2008 and decided that the Committee should accord equal priority to each of the draft conventions. The Committee completed the work at that session, prepared two separate draft conventions and considered them as final drafts ready for transmittal to the Council and for presentation to States and ultimately to a Diplomatic Conference.[77]

The wish of some States to go ahead and attempt to adopt yet another instrument along the lines of the Rome Convention (1952) is perplexing. The trigger of "9/11" for this initiative is not convincing – that tragedy was not an attack on the operators of the aircraft – American Airlines and United – it was an attack against the United States and their iconic symbols, the World Towers, the White House (it was set back) and the Pentagon; the airlines themselves were victims of these attacks and it seems improper to attach or channel any liability for compensation to or through the aircraft operators. The authorities of the United States recognized, after "9/11" that the airlines should not be liable beyond the extent of their existing insurance and thereafter vast amounts of compensation to victims – without any monetary limitation – were paid to the victims directly by the US government. States should compensate the victims of terrorism in the same manner as the US did in the wake of "9/11" and that should apply regardless whether the terrorism involved aviation or not, the problem of compensation to victims of terrorism should not be restricted to aviation operators alone.

In the light of this experience it appeared most unlikely that many States would be willing to adopt and ratify a Convention or Conventions containing monetary limits of compensation to victims on the surface or channelling the compensation from

---

75 591 Report is in ICAO Doc 9907-LC/193.
76 A36-WP/297, LE/14.
77 ICAO Doc 9907-LC/103.

international or national resources through the airlines. "9/11" was a tragic incident but so far an isolated one, purely domestic and without international elements. It is more important to look for new ways and means how to prevent similar terrorist acts than to calculate how to protect the Governments or airlines against extreme liability and shift a share of the risk on the innocent victims on the ground.

"Special cases make bad law" and a dismal failure of the new codification attempt was foreseen by some commentators.[78] Nevertheless, ICAO convened a Diplomatic Conference in Montreal from 20 April to 2 May 2009 and it adopted and opened for signature with little enthusiasm two instruments:

- "*Convention on Compensation for Damage to Third Parties, Resulting from Acts of Unlawful Interference Involving Aircraft*", signed on 2 May 2009;[79] and
- "*Convention on Compensation for Damage Caused by Aircraft to Third Parties*", signed on 2 May 2009.[80]

Both instruments avoid in their title the word 'liability,' but the essence deals predominantly with the liability of the operator. Strict liability attaches to the operator upon condition only that the damage was caused by an aircraft in flight.

The first – "Unlawful Interference Convention" – was the main task of the Diplomatic Conference, the "general risk" Convention was a secondary task of no proven importance but considered useful guidance for some States that do not have any domestic legislation dealing with third party liability of aircraft operators.

The first instrument is applicable in the case of an "event" – defined as an occurrence when damage results from an act of unlawful interference involving an aircraft in flight on an international flight. That narrows the applicability of the instrument to hypothetical future events never experienced so far.

In spite of its neutral title, the Convention does not avoid the issue of liability and deals with it in detail. The operator is liable for direct consequences of the "event" and damages due to death, bodily injury and mental injury are compensable. Damage to property is also compensable. In a creative contribution that was missed in the Montreal Convention (1999) damages due to mental injury are expressly compensable but "only if caused by a recognizable psychiatric illness resulting either from bodily injury or from direct exposure to the likelihood of imminent death or bodily injury".

---

78 G.N. Tompkins Jr., "Some Thought to Ponder when Considering Whether to Adopt the New Aviation General Risks and Unlawful Interference Conventions Proposed by ICAO", *Air and Space Law*, Vol. XXX-III, Issue 2, 2008, pp. 81-84; M. Milde, "Liability for Damage Caused by Aircraft on the Surface: Past and Current Efforts to Unify the Law", *ZLW*, 2008/4, pp. 532-558.
79 ICAO Doc 9920.
80 ICAO Doc 9919.

Liability of the operator is limited based on the mass of the aircraft involved, the highest limit for aircraft having maximum mass over 500,000 kilograms reaching 700,000,000 SDRs. Although this appears to be a very high sum of money (but still deemed "insurable"), it is only a small fraction of the overall compensations paid as a consequence of "9/11". It remains questionable why the aircraft operator should be held liable at all in case of a terrorist act of which he is himself a victim and which is in fact aimed at a State.

Since the limit of liability of the operator would be insufficient to compensate fully all victims the Convention created a complex and convoluted mechanism called the "International Civil Aviation Compensation Fund", in fact an international organization possessing international legal personality and made of Conference of the Parties (consisting of the States Parties) and a Secretariat headed by a Director.

The "International Fund" would be financed by contributions collected by the operators in respect of each passenger and each metric ton of cargo departing on an international commercial flight from an airport in a State Party. States are even bound to impose sanctions to ensure that an operator fulfils its obligation to collect and remit the contributions to the International Fund. The Convention would thus impose on the aircraft operators a new and tedious duty that is unrelated to their primary task to provide transportation services. Passengers and shippers of the cargo would be by their contributions carrying the burden of financing the compensation to victims not only in their own country but anywhere in the world where an "event" could take place.

The maximum amount of compensation available from the Fund would be 3,000,000,000 SDR for each event – a very high amount of money but not even one third of the overall compensations paid by the US authorities after "9/11". That could still result in incomplete compensation of the victims of a major "event", leaving innocent third parties in a less advantageous position compared with the passengers under the Montreal Convention (1999) who can expect compensation without any monetary limit.

To make the complex regime of liability and compensation and the International Fund effective, the Convention would enter into force only after some rigorous conditions are met: it would enter into force on the 180th day after the deposit of the 35th instrument of ratification, acceptance, approval or accession on condition that the total number of passengers departing in the previous year from airports of such ratifying States is at least 750,000,000 (pax) as appears from the declarations made by such States. That means that the Convention could enter into force only if the thirty-five ratifying States would account for at least one-third of the entire world passenger traffic.[81] The conditions for the entry into force were made very difficult as if the authors wished the Convention never to enter into force…

---

81 In 2009, the total scheduled passenger traffic amounted to about 2,280,000,000 passengers. See Annual Report of the ICAO Council for 2009, ICAO Doc 9921, p. 7.

The reluctant support of States for the Convention is illustrated by the fact that at the close of the Conference, the Convention was signed by six States; by December 2022 the total number of signatories rose to 11; 14 years after its adoption at the Diplomatic Conference the Convention was ratified by three States and adhered to by six. The Convention will probably never enter into force and will be quietly forgotten.

The second Convention – the "General Risk Convention" – does not represent a contribution to the progress of codified international air law either. It is just a modernized Rome Convention (1952) as amended in 1978 at Montreal and there was no convincing reason for its adoption. It attaches liability for damage sustained by third parties upon condition only that the damage was caused by an aircraft in flight on an international flight, other than as a result of an act of unlawful interference. The operator's liability is limited in the same manner as in the first Convention based on the mass of the aircraft involved up to 700,000,000 SDR for the heaviest aircraft. There is no provision on an additional international compensation fund and the compensation of victims remains limited – a situation contrary to natural justice when liability for passengers is unlimited under the Montreal Convention (1999). The conditions for the entry into force of the Convention are less exacting than the first Convention – it would enter into force on the 60th day following the deposit of the 35th instrument of ratification, acceptance, approval or accession.

The limited interest of States in the "General Risk Convention" caused that at the end of the Diplomatic Conference this Convention was signed by six States; by fourteen years after its adoption, the Convention is still under ratified and not coming into force.

These two instruments did not contribute to the development of codified international air law. In all probability, they will remain only a monument to good intentions that were misdirected.

9.5 Cape Town Convention on International Interests in Mobile Equipment 2001

The Geneva Convention on the International Recognition of the Rights in Aircraft (1948) made a substantial contribution towards securing the interests of the creditors and lessors of aircraft equipment by providing for the national registration of their rights to such assets and the international recognition of such registered rights and their relative priority. However, in practice there could be a very long way from the recognition of the rights to their enforcement by way of repossession, sale in execution, etc. The risk of a complicated, time-consuming and expensive process of repossession of the asset is calculated as part of the cost of the creditor and is charged to the debtor in the form of higher interest rate.

Among the manufacturers of aircraft, lessors of aircraft and financial institutions a need for an international instrument was felt that would facilitate asset-based financing in order to reduce the risk assessment and, as a consequence, increase the availability of credit and lower the finance cost of aviation credit.[82]

The International Institute for the Unification of Private Law (UNIDROIT)[83] in Rome studied for some time a "high value mobile assets convention" and a non-governmental "Aviation Working Group" (AWG) was established representing the interested stakeholders.[84]

The AWG cooperated with UNIDROIT, attracted the IATA and later ICAO to form, in 1997, the Aircraft Protocol Group (APG), IATA perhaps hoping to become the "registrar" and enhance its functions under the draft instrument and ICAO – initially a reluctant partner – to add to the deliberations international and institutional credibility. The interests of the potential creditors were thus well represented but there was no noticeable presence of any representatives of the debtors' interests.

A Subcommittee of the ICAO Legal Committee was appointed in late 1998 "to study the subject of a draft instrument or draft instruments relating to international interests in mobile equipment, with particular regard to aircraft equipment". That Subcommittee held three sessions together with a Committee of Governmental Experts of UNIDROIT. The text of the draft Convention on International Interests in Mobile Equipment and the draft Protocol on Matters Specific to Aircraft Equipment was presented to the 31st Session of the ICAO Legal Committee held in Montreal from 28 August to 8 September 2000 which adopted, with many modifications, a consolidated text of the two instruments.[85]

The Convention was to create "international interests" in
a. airframes, aircraft engines and helicopters;
b. railway rolling stock; and
c. space assets.

So far only provisions on airframes and aircraft engines and helicopters were adopted in the form of a special Protocol.

---

82 A32-WP/71 LE/6 presented by IATA.
83 UNIDROIT is an independent intergovernmental organization established in 1926 as an auxiliary organ of the League of Nations. It has 64 State Members and its mission is to study the needs and methods to modernize and harmonize private – and in particular commercial – law among States or groups of States. Its work is highly academic and devoid of political controversies.
84 A32-WP/71; Airbus Industrie, Boeing Company, Bombardier, Boullion Aviation Services, Chase Manhattan Bank, CIBC Wood Gundy, Credit Agricole Indosuez, Deutsche VerkehrsBank, GE Capital Aviation Services, General Electric Aircraft Engines, International Lease Finance Corporation, Kreditanstalt für Wiederaufbau, Pratt & Whittney, Rolls Royce, Singapore Aircraft Leasing Enterprise and SNECMA.
85 A33-WP/30.

It is surprising that ICAO permitted the use of its scarce resources for extensive work on the Convention going far beyond the aviation interests to railway rolling stock and space assets. Supportive work on the Protocol specifically relating to aircraft equipment would have been justified but ICAO went further: on 13 March 2001 the Council convened the Diplomatic Conference in Cape Town from 29 October to 16 November 2001 under the joint auspices of ICAO and UNIDROIT, before unprecedented in ICAO's practice. ICAO gave the international authority to the Conference and the Government of South Africa acted as the host of the Conference.

On 16 November 2001 the Conference adopted and opened for signature two instruments:

i) *Convention on International Interests in Mobile Equipment*;[86] and
ii) *Protocol to the Convention on International Interests in Mobile Equipment on Matters Specific for Aircraft Equipment.*[87]

The text is deposited with UNIDROIT in Rome and is authentic in Arabic, Chinese, English, French, Spanish and Russian.[88] The Convention, as applied to aircraft equipment, came into force on 1 March 2006 and by December 2022 was in force for 84 States. Like the Montreal Convention (1999), the Cape Town Convention is open for signature, acceptance, approval or accession to "Regional Economic Integration Organizations"[89] and the EU accepted the Convention in 2009 but several EU States have not ratified it yet.[90]

The International registration system under the Convention and the Protocol provides for the establishment of the "International Registry" or different "Registries" for different categories of object and associated rights.[91]

The Convention foresees the "Supervisory Authority" as provided by the Protocol;[92] ICAO has been designated as the Supervisory Authority for the Protocol specific for aircraft equipment. On the basis of a world-wide tender the Council of ICAO selected, in

---

86   ICAO Doc 9793.
87   ICAO Doc 9794.
88   Such authenticity had to be verified by the Joint (ICAO/UNIDROIT) Secretariat within ninety days of the signature of the instruments and took effect only upon such verification under the authority of the President of the Conference – an open admission that the Conference did not have the resources and time to complete the work to perfection.
89   Article 48 of the Cape Town Convention.
90   The Community's accession does not mean that the whole Convention automatically applies to all EU Member States. 2009/370/EC: Council Decision of 6 April 2009 on the accession of the European Community to the Cape Town Convention ant its Protocol. Doc JOL 2009, 121 R 0003 01, OJ L 121, 15/5/2009, pp. 3-36.
91   Article 16 (2) of the Cape Town Convention.
92   Article 17 of the Cape Town Convention and Article XVII of the Protocol.

June 2004, AVIARETO, Ltd.[93] of Ireland to establish the International Registry and to act as Registrar.[94]

The drafting language of the Convention and of the Protocol is "heavy" and it will not be easy for some States to transform it into national legislation. The text of the Convention required 39 definitions of terms that do not have an ordinary dictionary meaning, and the Protocol has 15 such definitions. The context and application cannot be understood without reference to the Regulations and Procedures for the International Registry.[95] The Convention and the Protocol must be read together and are to be known as the "Convention on International Interests in Mobile Equipment as Applied to Aircraft Objects".[96]

Unlike the Chicago Convention on International Civil Aviation (1944), the Cape Town instruments treat separately and make a distinction between "airframe", "aircraft engine" and "helicopter".

The Convention/Protocol applies to the sale, financing and leasing of an aircraft to an operator if either the aircraft is registered as to nationality in a contracting State or the purchaser or lessee of the aircraft of the aircraft is located in a contracting State. With respect to the engines the Convention applies only if the purchaser or the lessee of the engine is located in a contracting State.

The key contribution of the Convention and the Protocol is the creation of the concept of "international interest" that enjoys protection. The term "international interest" is not synonymous with the term "title" but in effect its creation and proper registration offer the creditor special international protection. For the purpose of the Convention an "international interest" in mobile equipment is an interest in a uniquely identifiable object (airframe, aircraft engines and helicopter):

a. granted by the chargor under a security agreement;
b. vested in a person who is the conditional seller under a title reservation agreement; or
c. vested in a person who is the lessor under a leasing agreement.[97]

Such interest is constituted as an international interest under the Convention where the agreement creating or providing for the interest:

a. is in writing;
b. relates to an object of which the chargor, conditional seller or lessor has the power to dispose;

---

93 AVIARETO, Ltd. of Dublin is a joint venture between SITA SC and the Irish Government; Société Internationale de Télécommunications Aéronautiques (SITA) is a global communications service integrator since 1949, www.sita.aero.
94 ICAO News Release, PIO 06/04.
95 Uniform Law Review, Vol. XI, 2006-1, p. 60.
96 Article I (2) of the Protocol.
97 Article 2 (2) of the Cape Town Convention.

c. enables the object to be identified in conformity with the Protocol; and
d. in the case of a security agreement, enables the secured obligations to be determined, but without the need to state a sum or maximum sum secured.[98]

The Cape Town Convention and Protocol protect the creditor against default of the debtor. The creditor and debtor may at any time agree in writing as to the events that constitute a default and where there is no such agreement the term "default" means a default that substantially deprives the creditor of what it is entitled to expect under the agreement.[99]

The remedies available to the creditor in case of default include the right to take possession or control of the object, sell the object or grant a lease to the object or collect or receive any income or profits arising from the management or use of any such object. Moreover, under the Protocol the creditor may procure the de-registration of the aircraft and procure the export and physical transfer of the aircraft object from the territory in which it is situated; however, such creditor must act only with a written consent of the holder of any registered interest ranking in priority to his own.[100]

In the absence of his default the debtor is entitled to "quiet possession" and use of the object in accordance with the agreement as against its creditor or creditors of its creditor; thus, *e.g.*, the lessee would enjoy protection of the lease even in case of bankruptcy of the lessor.

It will take some time before the Cape Town Convention and Protocol are fully understood by a wider scope of States and transformed into their national legislation. Perhaps ICAO and UNIDROIT could develop a model legislation implementing the Cape Town instruments or direct drafting assistance could be offered to some national administration. There is a general expectancy that all the 27 States of the European Union will soon enlarge the scope of the parties to the instruments, and it is gratifying that the fast expanding aviation economies of China and India already became party to the instrument.

Nevertheless, it cannot be overlooked that initially there was an apparent hesitation among many States about the merits of the Cape Town instruments. It is noticeable that the instruments are largely "one-sided" in their protection of the creditors – aircraft and engine manufacturers, banks and other financing institutions and leasing companies. In the text of the instruments it would be difficult to find provisions that are favouring the debtors – essentially the airlines, in particular those in the developing world.

In spite of such doubts it is argued that the increased protection of the creditors' interests coupled with easy repossession of their assets in case of default of the debtor, will

---

98 Article 7 of the Cape Town Convention.
99 Article 11 of the Cape Town Convention.
100 Article 8 of the Cape Town Convention and Article IX of the Protocol.

decrease the financial risk of the creditors and will lead to lower rate of interest in aviation financing and easier availability of funds.

It has been partly proved by the decision of the United States Export Import Bank (EXIM Bank) to reduce the risk premium it charges on financing for new large commercial aircraft and engines from 3% to 2% for airlines based in countries that have ratified the instruments;[101] it has been estimated that, in certain cases, aircraft operators could save tremendous amount of money per aircraft on lease finance costs.

The Cape Town instruments will not be a *panacea* and will not assure an automatic flow of funds to anybody who happens to need them. The protection of the creditors' interests and the ease of repossession of the assets are but one consideration in the decision whether or not to grant the credit or enter into a lease. The creditors wish to be assured first of all that the debtor (airline) has a sound business plan and guaranteed cash flow to avoid any default.

ICAO has special functions under the Convention and Protocol to act as the Supervisory Authority, among such functions is to supervise the Registrar and the International Registry and to report periodically to Contracting States concerning the discharge of its obligations under the Cape Town Convention and Protocol.

The Cape Town Convention demonstrates thoroughly how a uniform international regulation can be created in a relatively brief time with close cooperation of the civil aviation industry and the international organizations, under the leadership and guidance of the ICAO.

---

101 This refers to US-manufactured new large commercial aircraft; preferential financing terms are also extended to leasing companies if such company and the lessee airline are situated in a "Cape Town Treaty country". See ExIm Bank Extends Offer of Reduced Exposure Fee Through December 2010 for Buyers in Countries www.exim.gov/news/ex-im-bank-extends-offer-reduced-exposure-fee-through-december-2010-for-buyers-countries. Implementing the Cape Town Treaty | EXIM.GOV, accessed on 31 December 2022.

APPENDICES

APPENDIX 1　CONVENTION ON INTERNATIONAL CIVIL AVIATION, CHICAGO 1944

CONVENTION ON INTERNATIONAL CIVIL AVIATION[1]

Signed at Chicago, on 7 December 1944

Source: ICAO Doc. 7300/9 (Ninth Edition, 2006)

PREAMBLE

WHEREAS the future development of international civil aviation can greatly help to create and preserve friendship and understanding among the nations and peoples of the world, yet its abuse can become a threat to the genera security; and

WHEREAS it is desirable to avoid friction and to promote that cooperation between nations and peoples upon which the peace of the world depends;

THEREFORE, the undersigned governments having agreed on certain principles and arrangements in order that international civil

---

[1] Came into force on 4 April 1947, the thirtieth day after deposit with the Government of the United States of America of the twenty-sixth instrument of ratification thereof or notification of adherence thereto, in accordance with Article 91(b).

The present text contains the text adopted and signed at Chicago on 7 December 1944, amended as indicated in the footnotes. All amendments made to the Convention which were in force on 1 June 2005 are incorporated, i.e., Article 3*bis* (non-use of weapons against civil aircraft in flight); Article 45 (permanent seat of the Organization); Article 48(a) (frequency of Assembly Sessions); Article 49(e) (powers of Assembly relating to annual budgets); Article 50(a) (composition and election of the Council); Article 56 (membership of the Air navigation Commission); Article 61 (budget and apportionment of expenses); Article 83*bis* (transfer of certain functions and duties in case of lease, charter or interchange of aircraft); Article 93*bis* (expulsion from the International Civil Aviation Organization or suspension of membership in it); the final paragraph, adding Russian to the authentic texts of the Convention.

Further amendments to the Convention have been adopted but have not been incorporated in this document as they have not yet entered into force, namely: the final paragraph of the Convention, adding Arabic to the authentic texts of the Convention, adopted by the 31st Session of the ICAO Assembly on 29 September 1995; the final paragraph of the Convention, adding Chinese to the authentic texts of the Convention, adopted by the 32nd Session of the ICAO Assembly on 10 October 1998.

aviation may be developed in a safe and orderly manner and that international air transport services may be established on the basis of equality of opportunity and operated soundly and economically;

Have accordingly concluded this Convention to that end.

PART I
AIR NAVIGATION

CHAPTER I
GENERAL PRINCIPLES AND APPLICATION OF THE CONVENTION

Article 1
Sovereignty

The contracting States recognize that every State has complete and exclusive sovereignty over the airspace above its territory.

Article 2
Territory

For the purposes of this Convention the territory of a State shall be deemed to be the land areas and territorial waters adjacent thereto under the sovereignty, suzerainty, protection or mandate of such State.

Article 3
Civil and state aircraft

(a) This Convention shall be applicable only to civil aircraft, and shall not be applicable to state aircraft.
(b) Aircraft used in military, customs and police services shall be deemed to be state aircraft.
(c) No state aircraft of a contracting State shall fly over the territory of another State or land thereon without authorization by special agreement or otherwise, and in accordance with the terms thereof.
(d) The contracting States undertake, when issuing regulations for their state aircraft, that they will have due regard for the safety of navigation of civil aircraft.

Article 3bis[2]

(a) The contracting States recognize that every State must refrain from resorting to the use of weapons against civil aircraft in flight and that, in case of interception, the lives of persons on board and the safety of aircraft must not be endangered. This provision shall not be interpreted as modifying in any way the rights and obligations of States set forth in the Charter of the United Nations.

(b) The contracting States recognize that every State, in the exercise of its sovereignty, is entitled to require the landing at some designated airport of a civil aircraft flying above its territory without authority or if there are reasonable grounds to conclude that it is being used for any purpose inconsistent with the aims of this Convention; it may also give such aircraft any other instructions to put an end to such violations. For this purpose, the contracting States may resort to any appropriate means consistent with relevant rules of international law, including the relevant provisions of this Convention, specifically paragraph (a) of this Article. Each contracting State agrees to publish its regulations in force regarding the interception of civil aircraft.

(c) Every civil aircraft shall comply with an order given in conformity with paragraph (b) of this Article. To this end each contracting State shall establish all necessary provisions in its national laws or regulations to make such compliance mandatory for any civil aircraft registered in that State or operated by an operator who has his principal place of business or permanent residence in that State. Each contracting State shall make any violation of such applicable laws or regulations punishable by severe penalties and shall submit the case to its competent authorities in accordance with its laws or regulations.

(d) Each contracting State shall take appropriate measures to prohibit the deliberate use of any civil aircraft registered in that State or operated by an operator who has his principal place of business or permanent residence in that State for any purpose inconsistent with the aims of this Convention. This provision shall not affect paragraph (a) or derogate from paragraphs (b) and (c) of this

---

[2] On May 1984 the ICAO Assembly amended the Convention by adopting the Protocol introducing Article 3*bis*. Under Article 94(b) of the Convention, the amendment came into force on 1 October 1998 in respect of those States which have ratified it.

Article.

Article 4
Misuse of civil aviation

Each contracting State agrees not to use civil aviation for any purpose inconsistent with the aims of this Convention.

CHAPTER II
FLIGHT OVER TERRITORY OF CONTRACTING STATES

Article 5
Right of non-scheduled flight

Each contracting State agrees that all aircraft of the other contracting States, being aircraft not engaged in scheduled international air services shall have the right, subject to the observance of the terms of this Convention, to make flights into or in transit non-stop across its territory and to make stops for non-traffic purposes without the necessity of obtaining prior permission, and subject to the right of the State flown over to require landing. Each contracting State nevertheless reserves the right, for reasons of safety of flight, to require aircraft desiring to proceed over regions which are inaccessible or without adequate air navigation facilities to follow prescribed routes, or to obtain special permission for such flights.

Such aircraft, if engaged in the carriage of passengers, cargo, or mail for remuneration or hire on other than scheduled international air services, shall also, subject to the provisions of Article 7, have the privilege of taking on or discharging passengers, cargo, mail, subject to the right of any State where such embarkation or discharge takes place to impose such regulations, conditions or limitations at it may consider desirable.

Article 6
Scheduled air services

No scheduled international air service may be operated over or into the territory of a contracting State, except with the special permission or other authorization of that State, and in accordance with the terms of such permission or authorization.

Article 7
Cabotage

Each contracting State shall have the right to refuse permission to the aircraft of other contracting States to take on in its territory passengers, mail and cargo carried for remuneration or hire and destined for another point within its territory. Each contracting State undertakes not to enter into any arrangements which specifically grant any such privilege on an exclusive basis, to any other State or an airline of any other State, and not to obtain any such exclusive privilege from any other State.

Article 8
Pilotless aircraft

No aircraft capable of being flown without a pilot shall be flown without a pilot over the territory of a contracting State without special authorization by that State and in accordance with the terms of such authorization. Each contracting State undertakes to insure that the flight of such aircraft without a pilot in regions open to civil aircraft shall be so controlled as to obviate danger to civil aircraft.

Article 9
Prohibited areas

(a) Each contracting State may, for reasons of military necessity or public safety, restrict or prohibit uniformly the aircraft of other States from flying over certain areas of its territory, provided that no distinction in this respect is made between the aircraft of the State whose territory is involved, engaged in international scheduled airline services, and the aircraft of the other contracting States likewise engaged. Such prohibited areas shall be of reasonable extent and location so as not to interfere unnecessarily with air navigation. Descriptions of such prohibited areas in the territory of a contracting State, as well as any subsequent alterations therein, shall be communicated as soon as possible to the other contracting States and to the International Civil Aviation Organization.

(b) Each contracting State reserves also the right, in exceptional circumstances or during a period of emergency, or in the interest of public safety, and with immediate effect, temporarily to restrict or prohibit flying over the whole or any part of its territory, on condition that such restriction or prohibition shall be applicable without distinction of nationality to aircraft of all other States.

(c) Each contracting State, under such regulations as it may prescribe, may require any aircraft entering the areas contemplated in subparagraphs (a) or (b) above to effect a landing as soon as practicable thereafter at some designated airport within its territory.

Article 10
Landing at customs airport

Except in a case where, under the terms of this Convention or a special authorization, aircraft are permitted to cross the territory of a contracting State without landing, every aircraft which enters the territory of a contracting State shall, if the regulations of that State so require, land at an airport designated by that State for the purpose of customs and other examination. On departure from the territory of a contracting State, such aircraft shall depart from a similarly designated customs airport. Particulars of all designated customs airports shall be published by the State and transmitted to the International Civil Aviation Organization established under Part II of this Convention for communication to all other contracting States.

Article 11
Applicability of air regulations

Subject to the provisions of this Convention, the laws and regulations of a contracting State relating to the admission to or departure from its territory of aircraft engaged in international air navigation, or to the operation and navigation of such aircraft while within its territory, shall be applied to the aircraft of all contracting States without distinction as to nationality, and shall be complied with by such aircraft upon entering or departing from or while within the territory of that State.

Article 12
Rules of the air

Each contracting State undertakes to adopt measures to insure that every aircraft flying over or maneuvering within its territory and that every aircraft carrying its nationality mark, wherever such aircraft may be, shall comply with the rules and regulations relating to the flight and maneuver of aircraft there in force. Each contracting State undertakes to keep its own regulations in these respects uniform, to the greatest possible extent, with those established from time to time under this Convention. Over the high seas, the rules in force shall be those established under this Convention. Each contracting State undertakes to insure the prosecution of all persons violating the regulations applicable.

Article 13
Entry and clearance regulations

The laws and regulations of a contracting State as to the admission to or departure from its territory of passengers, crew or cargo of aircraft, such as regulations relating to entry, clearance, immigration, passports, customs, and quarantine shall be complied with by or on behalf of such passengers, crew or cargo upon entrance into or departure from, or while within the territory of that State.

Article 14
Prevention of spread of disease

Each contracting State agrees to take effective measures to prevent the spread by means of air navigation of cholera, typhus (epidemic), smallpox, yellow fever, plague, and such other communicable diseases as the contracting States shall from time to time decide to designate, and to that end contracting States will keep in close consultation with the agencies concerned with international regulations relating to sanitary measurer, applicable to aircraft. Such consultation shall be without prejudice to the application of any existing international convention on this subject to which the contracting States may be parties.

Article 15
Airport and similar charges

Every airport in a contracting State which is open to public use by its national aircraft shall likewise, subject to the provisions of Article 68, be open under uniform conditions to the aircraft of all the other contracting States. The like uniform conditions shall apply to the use, by aircraft of every contracting State, of all air navigation facilities, including radio and meteorological services, which may be provided for public use for the safety and expedition of air navigation.

Any charges that may be imposed or permitted to be imported by a contracting State for the use of such airports and air navigation facilities by the aircraft of any other contracting State shall not be higher,

(a) As to aircraft not engaged in scheduled international air services, than those that would be paid by its national aircraft of the same class engaged in similar operations, and

(b) As to aircraft engaged in scheduled international air services, than those that would be paid by its national aircraft engaged in similar international air services.

All such charges shall be published and communicated to the International Civil Aviation Organization: provided that, upon representation by an interested contracting State, the charger, imposed for the use of airports and other facilities shall be subject to review by the Council, which shall report and make recommendations thereon for the consideration of the State or States concerned. No fees, dues or other charges shall be imposed by any contracting State in respect solely of the right of transit over or entry into or exit from its territory of any aircraft of a contracting State or persons or property thereon.

Article 16
Search of aircraft

The appropriate authorities of each of the contracting States shall have the right, without unreasonable delay, to search aircraft of the other contracting States on landing or departure, and to inspect the certificates and other documents prescribed by this Convention.

CHAPTER III
NATIONALITY OF AIRCRAFT

Article 17
Nationality of aircraft

Aircraft have the nationality of the State in which they are registered.

Article 18
Dual registration

An aircraft cannot be validly registered in more than one State, but its registration may be changed from one State to another.

Article 19
National laws governing registration

The registration or transfer of registration of aircraft in any contracting State shall be made in accordance with its laws and regulations.

Article 20
Display of marks

Every aircraft engaged in international air navigation shall bear its appropriate nationality and registration marks.

Article 21
Report of registrations

Each contracting State undertakes to supply to any other contracting State or to the International Civil Aviation Organization, on demand, information concerning the registration and ownership of any particular aircraft registered in that State. In addition, each contracting State shall furnish reports to the International Civil Aviation Organization, under such regulations as the latter may prescribe, giving such pertinent data as can be made available concerning the ownership and control of aircraft registered in that State and habitually engaged in international air navigation. The data thus obtained by the International Civil Aviation Organization shall be made available by it on request to the other contracting States.

CHAPTER IV
MEASURES TO FACILITATE AIR NAVIGATION

Article 22
Facilitation of formalities

Each contracting State agrees to adopt all practicable measures, through the issuance of special regulations or otherwise, to facilitate and expedite navigation by aircraft between the territories of contracting States, and to prevent unnecessary delays to aircraft, crews, passengers and cargo, especially in the administration of the laws relating to immigration, quarantine, customs and clearance.

Article 23
Customs and immigration procedures

Each contracting State undertakes, so far as it may find practicable, to establish customs and immigration procedures affecting international air navigation in accordance with the practices which may be established or recommended from time to time, pursuant to this Convention. Nothing in this Convention shall be construed as preventing the establishment of customs-free airports.

Article 24
Customs duty

(a) Aircraft on a flight to, from, or across the territory of another contracting State shall be admitted temporarily free of duty, subject to the customs regulations of the State. Fuel, lubricating oils, spare parts, regular equipment and aircraft stores on board an aircraft of a contracting State, on arrival in the territory of another contracting State and retained on board on leaving the territory of that State shall be exempt from customs duty, inspection fees or similar national or local duties and charges. This exemption shall not apply to any quantities or articles unloaded, except in accordance with the customs regulations of the State, which may require that they shall be kept under customs supervision.

(b) Spare parts and equipment imported into the territory of a contracting State for incorporation in or use on an aircraft of another contracting State engaged in international air navigation shall be admitted free of customs duty, subject to compliance with the regulations of the State concerned, which may provide that the articles shall be kept under customs supervision and control.

Article 25
Aircraft in distress

Each contracting State undertakes to provide such measures of assistance to aircraft in distress in its territory as it may find practicable, and to permit, subject to control by its own authorities, the owners of the aircraft or authorities of the State in which the aircraft is registered to provide such measures of assistance as may be necessitated by the circumstances. Each contracting State, when undertaking search for missing aircraft, will collaborate in coordinated measures which may be recommended from time to time pursuant to this Convention.

Article 26
Investigation of accidents

In the event of an accident to an aircraft of a contracting State occurring in the territory of another contracting State, and involving death or serious injury, or indicating serious technical defect in the aircraft or air navigation facilities, the State in which the accident occurs will institute an inquiry into the circumstances of the accident, in accordance, so far as its laws permit, with the procedure which may be recommended by the International Civil Aviation Organization. The State in which the aircraft is registered shall be given the opportunity to appoint observers to be present at the inquiry and the State holding the inquiry shall communicate the report and findings in the matter to that State.

Article 27
Exemption from seizure on patent claims

(a) While engaged in international air navigation, any authorized entry of aircraft of a contracting State into the territory of another contracting State or authorized transit across the territory of such State with or without landings shall not entail any seizure or detention of the aircraft or any claim against the owner or operator thereof or any other interference therewith by or on behalf of such State or any person therein, on the ground that the construction, mechanism, parts, accessories or operation of the aircraft is an infringement of any patent, design, or model duly granted or registered in the State whose territory is entered by the aircraft, it being agreed that no deposit of security in connection with the foregoing exemption from seizure or detention of the aircraft shall in any case be required in the State entered by such aircraft.

(b) The provisions of paragraph (a) of this Article shall also be applicable to the storage of spare parts and spare equipment for the aircraft and the right to use and install the same in the repair of an aircraft of a contracting State in the territory of any other contracting State, provided that any patented part or equipment so stored shall not be sold or distributed internally in or exported commercially from the contracting State entered by the aircraft.

(c) The benefits of this Article shall apply only to such States, parties to this Convention, as either (1) are parties to the International Convention for the Protection of Industrial Property and to any amendments thereof; or (2) have enacted patent laws which recognize and give adequate protection to inventions made by the nationals of the other States parties to this Convention.

Article 28
Air navigation facilities and standard systems

Each contracting State undertakes, so far as it may find practicable, to:

(a) Provide, in its territory, airports, radio services, meteorological services and other air navigation facilities to facilitate international air navigation, in accordance with the standards and practices recommended or established from time to time, pursuant to this Convention;

(b) Adopt and put into operation the appropriate standard systems of communications procedure, codes, markings, signals, lighting and other operational practices and rules which may be recommended or established from time to time, pursuant to this Convention;

(c) Collaborate in international measures to secure the publication of aeronautical maps and charts in accordance with standards which may be recommended or established from time to time, pursuant to this Convention.

CHAPTER V
CONDITIONS TO BE FULFILLED WITH RESPECT TO AIRCRAFT

Article 29
Documents carried in aircraft

Every aircraft of a contracting State, engaged in international navigation, shall carry the following documents in conformity with the conditions prescribed in this Convention:

(a) Its certificate of registration;
(b) Its certificate of airworthiness;
(c) The appropriate licenses for each member of the crew;
(d) Its journey log book;
(e) If it is equipped with radio apparatus, the aircraft radio station license;
(f) If it carries passengers, a list of their names and places of embarkation and destination;
(g) If it carries cargo, a manifest and detailed declarations of the cargo.

Article 30
Aircraft radio equipment

(a) Aircraft of each contracting State may, in or over the territory of other contracting States, carry radio transmitting apparatus only if a license to install and operate such apparatus has been issued by the appropriate authorities of the State in which the aircraft is registered. The use of radio transmitting apparatus in the territory of the contracting State whose territory is flown over shall be in accordance with the regulations prescribed by that State.

(b) Radio transmitting apparatus may be used only by members of the flight crew who are provided with a special license for the purpose, issued by the appropriate authorities of the State in which the aircraft is registered.

Article 31
Certificates of airworthiness

Every aircraft engaged in international navigation shall be provided with a certificate of airworthiness issued or rendered valid by the State in which it is registered.

Article 32
Licenses of personnel

(a) The pilot of every aircraft and the other members of the operating crew of every aircraft engaged in international navigation shall be provided with certificates of competency and licenses issued or rendered valid by the State in which the aircraft is registered.

(b) Each contracting State reserves the right to refuse to recognize, for the purpose of flight above its own territory, certificates of competency and licenses granted to any of its nationals by another contracting State.

Article 33
Recognition of certificates and licenses

Certificates of airworthiness and certificates of competency and licenses issued or rendered valid by the contracting State in which the aircraft is registered, shall be recognized as valid by the other contracting States, provided that the requirements under which such certificates or licenses were issued or rendered valid are equal to or above the minimum standards which may be established from time to time pursuant to this Convention.

Article 34
Journey log books

There shall be maintained in respect of every aircraft engaged in international navigation a journey log book in which shall be entered particulars of the aircraft, its crew and of each journey, in such form as may be prescribed from time to time pursuant to this Convention.

Article 35
Cargo restrictions

(a) No munitions of war or implements of war may be carried in or above the territory of a State in aircraft engaged in international navigation, except by permission of such State. Each State shall determine by regulations what constitutes munitions of war or implement, of war for the purposes of this Article, giving due consideration, for the purposes of uniformity, to such recommendations as the International Civil Aviation Organization may from time to time make.

(b) Each contracting State reserves the right, for reasons of public order and safety, to regulate or prohibit the carriage in or above its territory of articles other than those enumerated in paragraph (a): provided that no distinction is made in this respect between its national aircraft engaged in international navigation and the aircraft of the other States so engaged; and provided further that no restriction shall be imposed which may interfere with the carriage and use on aircraft of apparatus necessary for the operation or navigation of the aircraft or the safety of the personnel or passengers.

Article 36
Photographic apparatus

Each contracting State may prohibit or regulate the use of photographic apparatus in aircraft over its territory.

CHAPTER VI
INTERNATIONAL STANDARDS AND RECOMMENDED PRACTICES

Article 37
Adoption of international standards and procedures

Each contracting State undertakes to collaborate in securing the highest practicable degree of uniformity in regulations, standards, procedures, and organization in relation to aircraft, personnel, airways and auxiliary services in all matters in which such uniformity will facilitate and improve air navigation.

To this end the International Civil Aviation Organization shall

adopt and amend from time to time, as may be necessary, international standards and recommended practices and procedures dealing with:
(a) Communications systems and air navigation aids, including ground marking;
(b) Characteristics of airports and landing areas;
(c) Rules of the air and air traffic control practices;
(d) Licensing of operating and mechanical personnel;
(e) Airworthiness of aircraft;
(f) Registration and identification of aircraft;
(g) Collection and exchange of meteorological information;
(h) Log books;
(i) Aeronautical maps and charts;
(j) Customs and immigration procedures;
(k) Aircraft in distress and investigation of accidents;
and such other matters concerned with the safety, regularity, and efficiency of air navigation as may from time to time appear appropriate.

Article 38
Departure from international standards and procedures

Any State which finds it impracticable to comply in all respects with any such international standards or procedure, or to bring its own regulations or practices into full accord with any international standard or procedure after amendment of the latter, or which deems it necessary to adopt regulations or practices differing in any particular respect from those established by an international standard, shall give immediate notification to the International Civil Aviation Organization of the differences between its own practice and that established by the international standard. In the case of amendments to inter national standards, any State which does not make the appropriate amendments to its own regulations or practices shall give notice to the Council within sixty days of the adoption of the amendment to the international standard, or indicate the action which it proposes to take. In any such case, the Council shall make immediate notification to all other States of the difference which exists between one or more features of an international standard and the corresponding national practice of that State.

Article 39
Endorsement of certificates and licenses

(a) Any aircraft or part thereof with respect to which there exists an international standard of airworthiness or performance, and which failed in any respect to satisfy that standard at the time of its certification, shall have endorsed on or attached to its airworthiness certificate a complete enumeration of the details in respect of which it so failed.

(b) Any person holding a license who does not satisfy in full the conditions laid down in the international standard relating to the class of license or certificate which he holds shall have endorsed on or attached to his license a complete enumeration of the particulars in which he does not satisfy such conditions.

Article 40
Validity of endorsed certificates and licenses

No aircraft or personnel having certificates or licenses so endorsed shall participate in international navigation, except with the permission of the State or States whose territory is entered. The registration or use of any such aircraft, or of any certificated aircraft part, in any State other than that in which it was originally certificated shall be at the discretion of the State into which the aircraft or part is imported.

Article 41
Recognition of exiting standards of airworthiness

The provisions of this Chapter shall not apply to aircraft and aircraft equipment of types of which the prototype is submitted to the appropriate national authorities for certification prior to a date three years after the date of adoption of an international standard of airworthiness for such equipment.

Article 42
Recognition of exiting standards of competency of personnel

The provisions of this Chapter shall not apply to personnel whose licenses are originally issued prior to a date one year after initial adoption of an international standard of qualification for such personnel; but they shall in any case apply to all personnel whose licenses remain valid five years after the date of adoption of such standard.

PART II
THE INTERNATIONAL CIVIL AVIATION ORGANIZATION

CHAPTER VII
THE ORGANIZATION

Article 43
Name and composition

An organization to be named the International Civil Aviation Organization is formed by the Convention. It is made up of an Assembly, a Council, and such other bodies as may be necessary.

Article 44
Objectives

The aims and objectives of the Organization are to develop the principles and techniques of international air navigation and to foster the planning and development of international air transport so as to:

(a) Insure the safe and orderly growth of international civil aviation throughout the world;
(b) Encourage the arts of aircraft design and operation for peaceful purposes;
(c) Encourage the development of airways, airports, and air navigation facilities for international civil aviation;
(d) Meet the needs of the peoples of the world for safe, regular, efficient and economical air transport;
(e) Prevent economic waste caused by unreasonable competition;
(f) Insure that the rights of contracting States are fully respected and that every contracting State has a fair opportunity to operate international airlines;
(g) Avoid discrimination between contracting States;
(h) Promote safety of flight in international air navigation;
(i) Promote generally the development of all aspects of international civil aeronautics.

Article 45[3]
Permanent seat

The permanent seat of the Organization shall be at such place as shall be determined at the final meeting of the Interim Assembly of the Provisional International Civil Aviation Organization set up by the Interim Agreement on International Civil Aviation signed at Chicago on December 7, 1944. The seat may be temporarily transferred elsewhere by decision of the Council, and otherwise than temporarily by decision of the Assembly, such decision to be taken by the number of votes specified by the Assembly. The number of votes so specified will not be less than three-fifths of the total number of contracting States.

Article 46
First meeting of Assembly

The first meeting of the Assembly shall be summoned by the Interim Council of the above-mentioned Provisional Organization as soon as the Convention has come into force, to meet at a time and place to be decided by the Interim Council.

Article 47
Legal Capacity

The Organization shall enjoy in the territory of each contracting State such legal capacity as may be necessary for the performance of its functions. Full juridical personality shall be granted wherever compatible with the constitution and laws of the State concerned.

---

[3] This is the text of the Article as amended by the Eighth Session of the Assembly on 14 June 1954; it entered into force on 16 May 1958. Under Article 94(a) of the Convention, the amended text is in force in respect of those States which have ratified the amendment. In respect of those States which have not ratified the amendment, the original text is still in force and, therefore, that text is reproduced below:

> The permanent seat of the Organization shall be at such place as shall be determined at the final meeting of the Interim Assembly of the Provisional International Civil Aviation Organization set up by the Interim Agreement on International Civil Aviation signed at Chicago on December 7, 1944. The seat may be temporarily transferred elsewhere by decision of the Council.

CHAPTER VIII
THE ASSEMBLY

Article 48
Meetings of the Assembly and voting

(a) The Assembly shall meet annually and shall be convened by the Council at a suitable time and place. Extraordinary meetings of the Assembly may be held at any time upon the call of the Council or at the request of any ten contracting States addressed to the Secretary General.

(b) All contracting States shall have an equal right to be represented at the meetings of the Assembly and each contracting State shall be entitled to one vote. Delegates representing contracting States may be assisted by technical advisers who may participate in the meetings but shall have no vote.

(c) A majority of the contracting States is required to constitute a quorum for the meetings of the Assembly. Unless otherwise provided in this Convention, decisions of the Assembly shall be taken by a majority of the votes cast.

Article 49
Powers and duties of the Assembly

The powers and duties of the Assembly shall be to:

(a) Elect at each meeting its President and other officers;
(b) Elect the contracting States to be represented on the Council, in accordance with the provisions of Chapter IX;
(c) Examine and take appropriate action on the reports of the Council and decide on any matter referred to it by the Council;
(d) Determine its own rules of procedure and establish such subsidiary commissions as it may consider to be necessary or desirable;
(e) Vote an annual budget and determine the financial arrangements of the Organization, in accordance with the provisions of Chapter XII;
(f) Review expenditures and approve the accounts of the Organization;
(g) Refer, at its discretion, to the Council, to subsidiary commissions or to any other body any matter within its sphere of action;
(h) Delegate to the Council the powers and authority necessary or desirable for the discharge of the duties of the Organization and

revoke or modify the delegations of authority at any time;
(i) Carry out the appropriate provisions of Chapter XIII;
(j) Consider proposals for the modification or amendment of the provisions of this Convention and, if it approves of the proposals, recommend them to the contracting States in accordance with the provisions of Chapter XXI;
(k) Deal with any matter within the sphere of action of the Organization not specifically assigned to the Council.

CHAPTER IX
THE COUNCIL

Article 50
Composition and election of Council

(a) The Council shall be a permanent body responsible to the Assembly. It shall be composed of thirty-six contracting States elected by the Assembly. An election shall be held at the first meeting of the Assembly and thereafter every three years, and the members of the Council so elected shall hold office until the next following election.[4]

(b) In electing the members of the Council, the Assembly shall give adequate representation to (1) the States of chief importance in air transport; (2) the States not otherwise included which make the largest contribution to the provision of facilities for international civil air navigation; and (3) the States not otherwise included whose designation will insure that all major geographic areas of the world are represented on the Council. Any vacancy on the Council shall be filled by the Assembly as soon as possible; any contracting State so elected to the Council shall hold office for the unexpired portion of its predecessor's term of office.

---

[4] This is the text of the Article as amended by the 28th (Extraordinary) Session of the Assembly on 25 October 1990; it entered into force on 28 November 2002. The original text of the Convention provided for twenty-one Members of the Council. The text was subsequently amended to the 13th (Extraordinary) Session of the Assembly on 19 June 1961; that amendment entered into force on 17 July 1962 and provided for twenty-seven Members of the Council; a further amendment was approved by the 17th(A) (Extraordinary) Session of the Assembly on 12 March 1971 providing for thirty Members of the Council; this amendment entered into force on 16 January 1973; a further amendment was approved by the 21st Session of the Assembly on 14 October 1974 providing for thirty-three Members of the Council; this amendment entered into force on 15 February 1980.

(c) No representative of a contracting State on the Council shall be actively associated with the operation of an international air service or financially interested in such a service.

Article 51
President of Council

The Council shall elect its President for a term of three years. He may be reelected. He shall have no vote. The Council shall elect from among its members one or more Vice Presidents who shall retain their right to vote when serving as acting President. The President need not be selected from among the representatives of the members of the Council but, if a representative is elected, his seat shall be deemed vacant and it shall be filled by the State which he represented. The duties of the President shall be to:

(a) Convene meetings of the Council, the Air Transport Committee, and the Air Navigation Commission;
(b) Serve as representative of the Council; and
(c) Carry out on behalf of the Council the functions which the Council assigns to him.

Article 52
Voting in Council

Decisions by the Council shall require approval by a majority of its members. The Council may delegate authority with respect to any particular matter to a committee of its members. Decisions of any committee of the Council may be appealed to the Council by any interested contracting State.

Article 53
Participation without a vote

Any contracting State may participate, without a vote, in the consideration by the Council and by its committees and commissions on any question which especially affects its interests. No member of the Council shall vote in the consideration by the Council of a dispute to which it is a party.

Article 54
Mandatory functions of Council

The Council shall:
(a) Submit annual reports to the Assembly;

(b) Carry out the directions of the Assembly and discharge the duties and obligations which are laid on it by this Convention;
(c) Determine its organization and rules of procedure;
(d) Appoint and define the duties of an Air Transport Committee, which shall be chosen from among the representatives of the members of the Council, and which shall be responsible to it;
(e) Establish an Air Navigation Commission, in accordance with the provisions of Chapter X;
(f) Administer the finances of the Organization in accordance with the provisions of Chapters XII and XV;
(g) Determine the emoluments of the President of the Council;
(h) Appoint a chief executive officer who shall be called the Secretary General, and make provision for the appointment of such other personnel as may be necessary, in accordance with the provisions of Chapter XI;
(i) Request, collect, examine and publish information relating to the advancement of air navigation and the operation of international air services, including information about the costs of operation and particulars of subsidies paid to airlines from public funds;
(j) Report to contracting States any infraction of this Convention, as well as any failure to carry out recommendations or determinations of the Council;
(k) Report to the Assembly any infraction of this Convention where a contracting State has failed to take appropriate action within a reasonable time after notice of the infraction;
(l) Adopt, in accordance with the provisions of Chapter VI of this Convention, international standards and recommended practices; for convenience, designate them as Annexes to this Convention; and notify all contracting States of the action taken;
(m) Consider recommendations of the Air Navigation Commission for amendment of the Annexes and take action in accordance with the provisions of Chapter XX;
(n) Consider any matter relating to the Convention which any contracting State refers to it.

Article 55
Permissive functions of Council

The Council may:
(a) Where appropriate and as experience may show to be desirable, create subordinate air transport commissions on a regional or other basis and define groups of states or airlines with or through which it may deal to facilitate the carrying out of the aims of this

Convention;
(b) Delegate to the Air Navigation Commission duties additional to those set forth in the Convention and revoke or modify such delegations of authority at any time;
(c) Conduct research into all aspects of air transport and air navigation which are of international importance, communicate the results of its research to the contracting States, and facilitate the exchange of information between contracting States on air transport and air navigation matters;
(d) Study any matters affecting the organization and operation of international air transport, including the international ownership and operation of international air services on trunk routes, and submit to the Assembly plans in relation thereto;
(e) Investigate, at the request of any contracting State, any situation which may appear to present avoidable obstacles to the development of international air navigation; and, after such investigation, issue such reports as may appear to it desirable.

CHAPTER X
THE AIR NAVIGATION COMMISSION

Article 56[5]
Nomination and appointment of Commission

The Air Navigation Commission shall be composed of nineteen members appointed by the Council from among persons nominated by contracting States. These persons shall have suitable qualifications and experience in the science and practice of aeronautics. The Council shall request all contracting States to submit nominations. The President of the Air Navigation Commission shall be appointed by the Council.

Article 57
Duties of the Commission

The Air Navigation Commission shall:
(a) Consider, and recommend to the Council for adoption,

---

[5] This is the text of the Article as amended at the 27th Session of the Assembly on 6 October 1989; it entered into force on 18 April 2005. The original text provided for twelve members of the Commission. The text was subsequently amended by the 18th session of the assembly on 7 July 1971; this amendment entered into force on 19 December 1974 and provided for fifteen members of the Commission.

modifications of the Annexes to this Convention;
(b) Establish technical subcommissions on which any contracting State may be represented, if it so desires;
(c) Advise the Council concerning the collection and communication to the contracting States of all information which it considers necessary and useful for the advancement of air navigation.

CHAPTER XI
PERSONNEL

Article 58
Appointment of personnel

Subject to any rules laid down by the Assembly and to the provisions of this Convention, the Council shall determine the method of appointment and of termination of appointment, the training, and the salaries, allowances, and conditions of service of the Secretary General and other personnel of the Organization, and may employ or make use of the services of nationals of any contracting State.

Article 59
International character of personnel

The President of the Council, the Secretary General, and other personnel shall not seek or receive instructions in regard to the discharge of their responsibilities from any authority external to the Organization. Each contracting State undertakes fully to respect the international character of the responsibilities of the personnel and not to seek to influence any of its nationals in the discharge of their responsibilities.

Article 60
Immunities and privileges of personnel

Each contracting State undertakes, so far as possible under its constitutional procedure, to accord to the President of the Council, the Secretary General, and the other personnel of the Organization, the immunities and privileges which are accorded to corresponding personnel of other public international organizations. If a general international agreement on the immunities and privileges of international civil servants is arrived at, the immunities and privileges accorded to the President, the Secretary General, and the other personnel of the Organization shall be the immunities and privileges accorded under that general international agreement.

CHAPTER XII
FINANCE

Article 61[6]
Budget and apportionment of expenses

The Council shall submit to the Assembly annual budgets, annual statements of accounts and estimates of all receipts and expenditures. The Assembly shall vote the budgets with whatever modification it sees fit to prescribe, and, with the exception of assessments under Chapter XV to States consenting thereto, shall apportion the expenses of the Organization among the contracting States on the basis which it shall from time to time determine.

Article 62
Suspension of voting power

The Assembly may suspend the voting power in the Assembly and in the Council of any contracting State that fails to discharge within a reasonable period its financial obligations to the Organization.

Article 63
Expenses of delegations and other representatives

Each contracting State shall bear the expenses of its own delegation to the Assembly and the remuneration, travel, and other expenses of any person whom it appoints to serve on the Council, and of its nominees or representatives on any subsidiary committees or commissions of the Organization.

---

[6] This is the text of the Article as amended by the Eighth Session of the Assembly on 14 June 1954; it entered into force on 12 December 1956. Under Article 94(a) of the Convention, the amended text is in force in respect of the States which have ratified the amendment. In respect of the States which have not ratified the amendment, the original text is still in force and, therefore, that text is reproduced below:

> The Council shall submit to the Assembly an annual budget, annual statements of accounts and estimates of all receipts and expenditures. The Assembly shall vote the budget with whatever modification it sees fit to prescribe, and, with the exception of assessments under Chapter XV to States consenting thereto, shall apportion the expenses of the Organization among the contracting States on the basis which it shall from time to time determine.

CHAPTER XIII
OTHER INTERNATIONAL ARRANGEMENTS

Article 64
Security arrangements

The Organization may, with respect to air matters within its competence directly affecting world security, by vote of the Assembly enter into appropriate arrangements with any general organization set up by the nations of the world to preserve peace.

Article 65
Arrangements with other international bodies

The Council, on behalf of the Organization, may enter into agreements with other international bodies for the maintenance of common services and for common arrangements concerning personnel and, with the approval of the Assembly, may enter into such other arrangements as may facilitate the work of the Organization.

Article 66
Functions related to other agreements

(a) The Organization shall also carry out the functions placed upon it by the International Air Services Transit Agreement and by the International Air Transport Agreement drawn up at Chicago on December 7, 1944, in accordance with the terms and conditions therein set forth.

(b) Members of the Assembly and the Council who have not accepted the International Air Services Transit Agreement or the International Air Transport Agreement drawn up at Chicago on December 7, 1944 shall not have the right to vote on any questions referred to the Assembly or Council under the provisions of the relevant Agreement.

PART III
INTERNATIONAL AIR TRANSPORT

CHAPTER XIV
INFORMATION AND REPORTS

Article 67
File reports with Council

Each contracting State undertakes that its international airlines shall, in accordance with requirements laid down by the Council, file with the Council traffic reports, cost statistics and financial statements showing among other things all receipts and the sources thereof.

CHAPTER XV
AIRPORTS AND OTHER AIR NAVIGATION FACILITIES

Article 68
Designation of routes and airports

Each contracting State may, subject to the provisions of this Convention, designate the route to be followed within its territory by any international air service and the airports which any such service may use.

Article 69
Improvement of air navigation facilities

If the Council is of the opinion that the airports or other air navigation facilities, including radio and meteorological services, of a contracting State are not reasonably adequate for the safe, regular, efficient, and economical operation of international air services, present or contemplated, the Council shall consult with the State directly concerned, and other States affected, with a view to finding means by which the situation may be remedied, and may make recommendations for that purpose. No contracting State shall be guilty of an infraction of this Convention if it fails to carry out these recommendations.

Article 70
Financing of air navigation facilities

A contracting State, in the circumstances arising under the provisions of Article 69, may conclude an arrangement with the Council for giving effect to such recommendations. The State may elect to bear all of the costs involved in any such arrangement. If the States does not so elect, the Council may agree, at the request of the State, to provide for all or a portion of the cost.

Article 71
Provision and maintenance of facilities by Council

If a contracting State so requests, the Council may agree to provide, man, maintain, and administer any or all of the airports and other air navigation facilities, including radio and meteorological services, required in its territory for the safe, regular, efficient and economical operation of the international air services of the other contracting States, and may specify just and reasonable charges for the use of the facilities provided.

Article 72
Acquisition or use of land

Where land is needed for facilities financed in whole or in part by the Council at the request of a contracting State, that State shall either provide the land itself, retaining title if it wishes, or facilitate the use of the land by the Council on just and reasonable terms and in accordance with the laws of the State concerned.

Article 73
Expenditure and assessment of funds

Within the limit of the funds which may be made available to it by the Assembly under Chapter XII, the Council may make current expenditures for the purposes of this Chapter from the general funds of the Organization. The Council shall assess the capital funds required for the purposes of this Chapter in previously agreed proportions over a reasonable period of time to the contracting States consenting thereto whose airlines use the facilities. The Council may also assess to States that consent any working funds that are required.

Article 74
Technical assistance and utilization of revenues

When the Council, at the request of a contracting State, advances funds or provides airports or other facilities in whole or in part, the arrangement may provide, with the consent of that State, for technical assistance in the supervision and operation of the airports and other facilities, and for the payment, from the revenues derived from the operation of the airports and other facilities, of the operating expenses of the airports and the other facilities, and of interest and amortization charges.

Article 75
Taking over of facilities from Council

A contracting State may at any time discharge any obligation into which it has entered under Article 70, and take over airports and other facilities which the Council has provided in its territory pursuant to the provisions of Articles 71 and 72, by paying to the Council an amount which in the opinion of the Council is reasonable in the circumstances. If the State considers that the amount fixed by the Council is unreasonable it may appeal to the Assembly against the decision of the Council and the Assembly may confirm or amend the decision of the Council.

Article 76
Return of funds

Funds obtained by the Council through reimbursement under Article 75 and from receipts of interest and amortization payments under Article 74 shall, in the case of advances originally financed by States under Article 73, be returned to the States which were originally assessed in the proportion of their assessments, as determined by the Council.

CHAPTER XVI
JOINT OPERATING ORGANIZATIONS AND POOLED SERVICES

Article 77
Joint operating organizations permitted

Nothing in this Convention shall prevent two or more contracting States from constituting joint air transport operating organizations or international operating agencies and from pooling their air services on any routes or in any regions, but such organizations or agencies and such pooled services shall be subject to all the provisions of this Convention, including those relating to the registration of agreements with the Council. The Council shall determine in what manner the provisions of this Convention relating to nationality of aircraft shall apply to aircraft operated by international operating agencies.

Article 78
Function of Council

The Council may suggest to contracting States concerned that they form joint organizations to operate air services on any routes or in any regions.

Article 79
Participation in operating organizations

A State may participate in joint operating organizations or in pooling arrangements, either through its government or through an airline company or companies designated by its government. The companies may, at the sole discretion of the State concerned, be state-owned or partly state-owned or privately owned.

PART IV
FINAL PROVISIONS

CHAPTER XVII
OTHER AERONAUTICAL AGREEMENTS AND ARRANGEMENTS

Article 80
Paris and Habana Conventions

Each contracting State undertakes, immediately upon the coming into force of this Convention, to give notice of denunciation of the Convention relating to the Regulation of Aerial Navigation signed at Paris on October 13, 1919 or the Convention on Commercial Aviation signed at Habana on February 20, 1928, if it is a party to either. As between contracting States, this Convention supersedes the Conventions of Paris and Habana previously referred to.

Article 81
Registration of exiting agreements

All aeronautical agreements which are in existence on the coming into force of this Convention, and which are between a contracting State and any other State or between an airline of a contracting State and any other State or the airline of any other State, shall be forthwith registered with the Council.

Article 82
Abrogation of inconsistent arrangements

The contracting States accept this Convention as abrogating all obligations and understandings between them which are inconsistent with its terms, and undertake not to enter into any such obligations and understandings. A contracting State which, before becoming a member of the Organization has under taken any obligations toward a non-contracting State or a national of a contracting State or of a non-contracting State inconsistent with the terms of this Convention, shall take immediate steps to procure its release from the obligations. If an airline of any contracting State has entered into any such inconsistent obligations, the State of which it is a national shall use its best efforts to secure their termination forthwith and shall in any event cause them to be terminated as soon as such action can lawfully be taken after the coming into force of this Convention.

Article 83
Registration of new arrangements

Subject to the provisions of the preceding Article, any contracting State may make arrangements not inconsistent with the provisions of this Convention. Any such arrangement shall be forthwith registered with the Council, which shall make it public as soon as possible.

Article 83bis[7]
Transfer of certain functions and duties

(a) Notwithstanding the provisions of Articles 12, 30, 31 and 32(a), when an aircraft registered in a contracting State is operated pursuant to an agreement for the lease, charter or interchange of the aircraft or any similar arrangement by an operator who has his principal place of business or, if he has no such place of business, his permanent residence in another contracting State, the State of registry may, by agreement with such other State, transfer to it all or part of its functions and duties as State of registry in respect of that aircraft under Articles 12, 30, 31, and 32(a). The State of registry shall be relieved of responsibility in respect of the functions and duties transferred.

---

[7] On 6 October 1980 the Assembly decided to amend the Chicago Convention by introducing Article 83*bis*. Under Article 94(b) of the Convention, the amendment came into force on 20 June 1997 in respect with those States which have ratified it.

(b) The transfer shall not have effect in respect of other contracting States before either the agreement between States in which it is embodied has been registered with the Council and made public pursuant to Article 83 or the existence and scope of the agreement have been directly communicated to the authorities of the other contracting State or States concerned by a State party to the agreement.

(c) The provisions of paragraphs (a) and (b) above shall also be applicable to cases covered by Article 77.

CHAPTER XVIII
DISPUTES AND DEFAULT

Article 84
Settlement of disputes

If any disagreement between two or more contracting States relating to the interpretation or application of this Convention and its Annexes cannot be settled by negotiation, it shall, on the application of any State concerned in the disagreement, be decided by the Council. No member of the Council shall vote in the consideration by the Council of any dispute to which it is a party. Any contracting State may, subject to Article 85, appeal from the decision of the Council to an ad hoc arbitral tribunal agreed upon with the other parties to the dispute or to the Permanent Court of International Justice. Any such appeal shall be notified to the Council within sixty days of receipt of notification of the decision of the Council.

Article 85
Arbitration procedure

If any contracting State party to a dispute in which the decision of de Council is under appeal has not accepted the Statute of the Permanent Court of International Justice and the contracting States parties to the dispute cannot agree on the choice of the arbitral tribunal, each of the contracting States parties to the dispute shall name a single arbitrator who shall name an umpire. If either contracting State party to the dispute fails to name an arbitrator within a period of three months from the date of the appeal, an arbitrator shall be named on behalf of that State by the President of the Council from a list of qualified and available persons maintained by the Council. If, within thirty days, the arbitrators cannot agree on an umpire, the President of the Council shall designate an umpire from the list previously referred to. The arbitrators and the umpire shall then jointly constitute an arbitral tribunal. Any arbitral tribunal established under this or the preceding Article shall settle its own procedure and give its decisions by majority vote, provided that the Council may determine procedural questions in the event of any delay which in the opinion of the Council is excessive.

Article 86
Appeals

Unless the Council decides otherwise, any decision by the Council on whether an international airline is operating in conformity with the provisions of this Convention shall remain in effect unless reversed on appeal. On any other matter, decisions of the Council shall, if appealed from, be suspended until the appeal is decided. The decisions of the Permanent Court of International Justice and of an arbitral tribunal shall be final and binding.

Article 87
Penalty for non-conformity of airline

Each contracting State undertakes not to allow the operation of an airline of a contracting State through the airspace above its territory if the Council has decided that the airline concerned is not conforming to a final decision rendered in accordance with the previous Article.

Article 88
Penalty for non-conformity by State

The Assembly shall suspend the voting power in the Assembly and in the Council of any contracting State that is found in default under the provisions of this Chapter.

CHAPTER XIX
WAR

Article 89
War and emergency conditions

In case of war, the provisions of this Convention shall not affect the freedom of action of any of the contracting States affected, whether as belligerents or as neutrals. The same principle shall apply in the case of any contracting State which declares a state of national emergency and notifies the fact to the Council.

CHAPTER XX
ANNEXES

Article 90
Adoption and amendment of Annexes

(a) The adoption by the Council of the Annexes described in Article 54, subparagraph (I), shall require the vote of two-thirds of the Council at a meeting called for that purpose and shall then be submitted by the Council to each contracting State. Any such Annex or any amendment of an Annex shall become effective within three months after its submission to the contracting States or at the end of such longer period of time as the Council may prescribe, unless in the meantime a majority of the contracting States register their disapproval with the Council.

(b) The Council shall immediately notify all contracting States of the coming into force of any Annex or amendment thereto.

CHAPTER XXI
RATIFICATIONS, ADHERENCES, AMENDMENTS, AND DENUNCIATIONS

Article 91
Ratification of Convention

(a) This Convention shall be subject to ratification by the signatory States. The instruments of ratification shall be deposited in the archives of the Government of the United States of America, which shall give notice of the date of the deposit to each of the signatory and adhering States.

(b) As soon as this Convention has been ratified or adhered to by twenty six States it shall come into force between them on the thirtieth day after deposit of the twenty-sixth instrument. It shall come into force for each State ratifying thereafter on the thirtieth day after the deposit of its instrument of ratification.

(c) It shall be the duty of the Government of the United States of America to notify the government of each of the signatory and adhering States of the date on which this Convention comes into force.

Article 92
Adherence to Convention

(a) This Convention shall be open for adherence by members of the United Nations and States associated with them, and States which remained neutral during the present world conflict.

(b) Adherence shall be effected by a notification addressed to the Government of the United States of America and shall take effect as from the thirtieth day from the receipt of the notification by the Government of the United States of America, which shall notify all the contracting States.

Article 93
Admission of other States

States other than those provided for in Articles 91 and 92 (a) may, subject to approval by any general international organization set up by the nations of the world to preserve peace, be admitted to participation in this Convention by means of a four-fifths vote of the Assembly and on such conditions as the Assembly may prescribe: provided that in each case the assent of any State invaded or attacked during the present war by the State seeking admission shall be necessary.

Article 93bis[8]

(a) Notwithstanding the provisions of Articles 91, 92 and 93 above:
   (1) A State whose government the General Assembly of the United Nations has recommended be debarred from membership in international agencies established by or brought into relationship with the United Nations shall automatically cease to be a member of the International Civil Aviation Organization;
   (2) A State which has been expelled from membership in the United Nations shall automatically cease to be a member of the International Civil Aviation Organization unless the General Assembly of the United Nations attaches to its act of expulsion a recommendation to the contrary.

(b) A State which ceases to be a member of the International Civil Aviation Organization as a result of the provisions of paragraph (a) above may, after approval by the General Assembly of the

---

[8] On 27 May 1947 the Assembly decided to amend the Chicago Convention by introducing Article 93*bis*. Under Article 94(a) of the Convention, the amendment came into force on 20 March 1961 in respect of States which have ratified it.

United Nations, be readmitted to the International Civil Aviation Organization upon application and upon approval by a majority of the Council.

(c) Members of the Organization which are suspended from the exercise of the rights and privileges of membership in the United Nations shall, upon the request of the latter, be suspended from the rights and privileges of membership in this Organization.

Article 94
Amendment of Convention

(a) Any proposed amendment to this Convention must be approved by a two-thirds vote of the Assembly and shall then come into force in respect of States which have ratified such amendment when ratified by the number of contracting States specified by the Assembly. The number so specified shall not be less than two-thirds of the total number of contracting States.

(b) If in its opinion the amendment is of such a nature as to justify this course, the Assembly in its resolution recommending adoption may provide that any State which has not ratified within a specified period after the amendment has come into force shall thereupon cease to be a member of the Organization and a party to the Convention.

Article 95
Denunciation of Convention

(a) Any contracting State may give notice of denunciation of this Convention three years after its coming into effect by notification addressed to the Government of the United States of America, which shall at once inform each of the contracting States.

(b) Denunciation shall take effect one year from the date of the receipt of the notification and shall operate only as regards the State effecting the denunciation.

CHAPTER XXII
DEFINITIONS

Article 96

For the purpose of this Convention the expression:

(a) "Air service" means any scheduled air service performed by air craft for the public transport of passengers, mail or cargo.

(b) "International air service" means an air service which pas through

the air space over the territory of more than one State.
(c) "Airline" means any air transport enterprise offering or operating an international air service.
(d) "Stop for non-traffic purposes" means a landing for any purpose other than taking on or discharging passengers, cargo or mail.

SIGNATURE OF CONVENTION

IN WITNESS WHEREOF, the undersigned plenipotentiaries, having been duly authorized, sign this Convention on behalf of their respective governments on the dates appearing opposite their signatures.

DONE at Chicago the seventh day of December 1944, in the English language. The text of this Convention drawn up in the A text drawn up in the English, French, Russian and Spanish languages are of equal authenticity. These texts shall be deposited in the archives of the Government of the United States of America, and certified copies shall be transmitted by that Government to the Governments of all the States which may sign or adhere to this Convention. This Convention shall be open for signature at Washington, D.C.[9]

---

[9] This is the text of the final Paragraph as amended by the 22nd Session of the Assembly on 30 September 1977. It entered into force on 17 August 1999. Under Article 94(a) of the Convention, the amended text is in force in respect of those States which have ratified the amendment. In respect of the States which have not ratified the amendment, the original text is still in force and, therefore, that text is reproduced below:

> DONE at Chicago the seventh day of December 1944, in the English language. A text drawn up in the English, French and Spanish languages, each of which shall be of equal authenticity, shall be open for signature at Washington, D.C. Both texts shall be deposited in the archives of the Government of the United States of America, and certified copies shall be transmitted by that Government to the governments of all the States which may sign or adhere to this Convention.

Appendix 2　Standing Rules of Procedure for the Assembly of ICAO

STANDING RULES OF PROCEDURE
OF THE ASSEMBLY
OF THE
INTERNATIONAL CIVIL AVIATION
ORGANIZATION*

SECTION I.　SESSIONS

Rule 1

The Assembly shall meet not less than once in three years and shall be convened by the Council at a suitable time and place [Convention on International Civil Aviation (hereinafter "Convention"), Article 48 a)].

Ordinary Sessions

Rule 2

The Assembly may hold extraordinary sessions at any time upon the call of the Council or at the request of not less than one-fifth of the total number of Contracting States addressed to the Secretary General [Convention, Article 48 a)].

Extraordinary Sessions

---

* Adopted by the Assembly in 1952 (Resolution A6-12; Doc 7670) and amended by the Assembly in 1953 (Doc 7409, A7-P/2), 1959 (Resolution A12-4; Doc 7998, A12-P/3), 1962 (Resolution A14-1; Doc 8268, A14-P/20), 1971 (Doc 8963, A18-P/16), 1974 (Doc 9119, A21-P/4), 1977 (Doc 9216, A22-P/10), 1980 (Doc 9317, A23-P/12), 1989 (Doc 9550, A27-P/12), 2007 (Doc 9891, A36-P/9), 2010 (Doc 9982, A37-P/1) and 2013 (Doc 10023, A38-P/6).

SECTION II. COMPOSITION

Delegations and their Credentials

Rule 3

All Contracting States shall have an equal right to be represented at the sessions of the Assembly [Convention, Article 48 b)]. No person shall represent more than one State.

<small>Representation of Contracting States</small>

Rule 4

Delegations of Contracting States may be composed of delegates, alternates and advisers. One of the delegates shall be designated as the Chief Delegate. In case of his absence the Chief Delegate may designate another member of his delegation to serve in his stead.

<small>Delegations of Contracting States</small>

Rule 5

Non-Contracting States and international organizations duly invited by the Council, or by the Assembly itself, to attend a session of the Assembly may be represented by observers. Where a delegation consists of two or more observers, one of them shall be designated as "Chief Observer".

<small>Observers of non-Contracting States and International Organizations</small>

Rule 6

a) Delegations shall be provided with credentials signed on behalf of the State or organization concerned, by a person duly authorized thereto, specifying the name of each member of the delegation and indicating the capacity in which he is to serve. The credentials shall be deposited with the Secretary General.

<small>Credentials and Credentials Committee</small>

b) A Credentials Committee shall be established at the beginning of the session. It shall consist of five members representing five Contracting States nominated by the President of the Assembly, and the representative of each such State shall be designated by the Chief Delegate concerned. The committee shall elect its own chairman. It shall examine the credentials of members of delegations and report to the Assembly without delay.

Rule 7

Any member of a delegation shall be entitled, pending the presentation of a report by the Credentials Committee and Assembly action thereon, to attend meetings and to participate in them, subject, however, to the limits set forth in these Rules. The Assembly may bar from any further part in its activities any member of a delegation whose credentials it finds to be insufficient.
Eligibility for Participation in Meetings

SECTION III. OFFICERS

Rule 8

The Assembly, as soon as practicable after the commencement of a session, shall elect its President, who shall preside over the plenary meetings of the Assembly. Until such election, the President of the Council shall act as President of the Assembly.
President

Rule 9

The Assembly shall elect four vice-presidents and the chairmen of the commissions referred to in Section V.
Vice-Presidents and Chairmen of Commissions

SECTION IV.   AGENDA

Rule 10

a) The provisional agenda prepared by the Council for an ordinary session shall be communicated to Contracting States so as to reach them at least ninety days before the opening of the session. Subject to paragraph d) hereof, the basic documentation including budget proposals, Council's Report to the Assembly, and supporting documentation on questions of general policy, air transport matters and air navigation matters, shall be communicated by such means as will ensure, apart from unforeseen contingencies, that they will be received by Contracting States at least fifty days before the date of the opening of the session.

b) Subject to the requirements of paragraph d), any Contracting State may, at least forty days before the date fixed for the opening of an ordinary session, propose to the Secretary General the addition of items to the provisional agenda. Such items, together with any explanatory documentation furnished by the Contracting State, and, time permitting, additional comments, if any, made by the Secretary General thereon, shall be communicated to Contracting States so as to reach them, apart from unforeseen circumstances, at least twenty-one days before the opening of the session.

c) The provisional agenda prepared by the Council or by the requesting Contracting States, as the case may be, for an extraordinary session shall be communicated to Contracting States so as to reach them at least fourteen days before the opening of the session, and the supporting documentation shall be communicated as soon as possible prior to the opening of the session.

d) Proposals for the amendment of the Convention, together with any comments or recommendations of the Council

Provisional Agenda and Addition of Items thereon

thereon, shall be communicated to Contracting States so as to reach them at least ninety days before the opening of the session.

Rule 11

Failure of a State to receive the provisional agenda or supporting documentation in accordance with the provisions of these Rules shall not invalidate the session of the Assembly.

Delay in Receipt of Agenda or Documentation

Rule 12

At each session, the provisional agenda prepared as provided in Rule 10, together with any additional item that the United Nations may request or that any Contracting State may propose for inclusion in the agenda, shall be submitted to the Assembly for approval as soon as possible after the opening of the session.

Approval of the Agenda

Rule 13

The Assembly in plenary meeting, or the Executive Committee, may at any time add any item to the agenda or otherwise amend it.

Amendments to the Agenda

SECTION V.   COMMITTEES AND COMMISSIONS

Rule 14

The Assembly shall establish, in addition to the Credentials Committee referred to in Rule 6, the following committees and commission:

Establishment of Committees and Commissions

a)   Executive Committee;

b) Coordinating Committee (in the case of sessions including two or more commissions);

c) Administrative Commission; and may establish such other committees and commissions as it deems desirable for the conduct of its business.

Rule 15

The Executive Committee shall consist of the President of the Assembly, the Chief Delegates of Contracting States and the President of the Council. Each Chief Delegate may be accompanied at meetings of the Executive Committee by not more than one member of his delegation, unless otherwise agreed by the committee. The committee shall be convened by the President of the Assembly, who shall be its chairman.

Executive Committee

The functions of the Executive Committee shall include:

a) the submission to the Assembly, when necessary, of a list of Contracting States desirous of being considered for election to the Council;

b) the consideration of amendments to, or the addition of items to, the Assembly's agenda, under the terms of Section IV;

c) the consideration of and report on such items of the agenda as the Assembly may refer to it;

d) the submission of recommendations to the Assembly on the organization and conduct of the business of the Assembly;

e) the giving of advice to the President of the Assembly, on his request, on matters requiring his decision.

Rule 16

If established, the Coordinating Committee shall consist of the President of the Assembly, who shall be its chairman, the vice-presidents, the President of the Council and the chairmen of the commissions. The function of the Coordinating Committee shall be to coordinate the activities of the commissions.

Coordinating Committee

Rule 17

The membership and functions of any other committees appointed by the Assembly shall be determined by the Assembly and such committees shall appoint their own chairmen, and, if necessary, vice-chairmen.

Other Committees

Rule 18

The Assembly may establish such commissions as it may consider to be necessary or desirable.

Establishment of Commissions

Rule 19

Any commission may create subcommissions and any commission, committee, or subcommission may create working groups.

Subcommissions and Working Groups

Rule 20

The Assembly may refer items of the agenda or parts of such items to commissions and other committees for consideration and report. These commissions and committees shall not, on their own initiative, add new items to their agenda.

Reference of Subjects to Commissions and Committees

Rule 21

Any Contracting State may be represented on any commission or subcommission by a member or members of its delegation. A working group shall consist of a limited number of members appointed by the chairman of the commission, committee or subcommission by which it is created, not more than one member being appointed from any one delegation.

Representation of Contracting States on Commissions, Subcommissions and Working Groups

Rule 22

The chairmen of commissions shall be elected by the Assembly. The commissions shall elect their own vice-chairmen.

Each subcommission and working group shall elect its own officers.

Officers of Commissions, Subcommissions and Working Groups

SECTION VI. SECRETARIAT

Rule 23

The Secretary General of the International Civil Aviation Organization shall act as Secretary General of the Assembly and shall provide and direct the staff required by the Assembly and its committees, commissions, subcommissions and working groups.

Duties of the Secretary General

SECTION VII. CONDUCT OF BUSINESS

Rule 24

Meetings of the Assembly, its commissions and subcommissions shall be held in public unless any such body decides that any of its meetings shall be held in private.

General Principles

Meetings of committees and working groups shall not be open to the public except by decision of the committee or working group concerned.

Rule 25

Observers may participate without vote in the deliberations of the Assembly, its commissions and subcommissions when their meetings are not held in private. In the case of meetings of bodies of limited membership, observers may also attend and participate without vote in the meetings of such a body if invited by that body or by the officer by whom the members of that body were originally appointed. With respect to private meetings, individual observers may be invited by the body concerned to attend and be heard. — **Participation of Observers**

Rule 26

Notwithstanding any of these Rules, observers of the United Nations may attend the meetings of the Assembly and its commissions and committees and may participate without vote in the deliberations of these bodies. — **United Nations Representation**

Rule 27

Members of delegations of Contracting States not represented in a body of limited membership may attend and participate without vote in the meetings of such body, except when the officer by whom the members of that body were originally appointed authorizes the body to meet with attendance limited to its membership and to such other persons as that body may invite. — **Bodies of Limited Membership**

Rule 28

A majority of the Contracting States shall constitute a quorum for the plenary meetings of the Assembly. A majority of the — **Quorum**

Contracting States represented in the Assembly shall constitute a quorum for meetings of the Executive Committee. The Executive Committee shall determine the quorum for other committees and commissions in any case when it is considered necessary that a quorum be established.

Rule 29

The presiding officer in the Assembly and any of its bodies shall declare the opening and closing of each meeting, direct the discussion, ensure observance of these Rules, accord the right to speak, put questions and announce decisions. He shall rule on points of order and, subject to these Rules, shall have complete control of the proceedings of the body concerned and over the maintenance of order at its meetings. **Powers of Presiding Officers**

Rule 30

The President of the Council, the Secretary General, or a member of the Secretariat designated by him as his representative, may, at any time, make either oral or written statements to the Assembly or any body thereof concerning any question under consideration by it. **Statements by President of the Council and by Secretary General**

Rule 31

Plenary meetings shall be held on the call of the President of the Assembly or on the direction of the Executive Committee. **Calling of Plenary Meetings**

Rule 32

If the President of the Assembly finds it necessary to be absent during the whole or part of a plenary meeting of the Assembly or during the whole or part of a meeting of the Executive Committee or Coordinating Committee, he shall appoint one of the vice-presidents to take his place. **Acting President**

Rule 33

Except as otherwise specifically provided, the subsequent Rules of this section shall not apply to subcommissions and working groups, which shall conduct their deliberations informally.

Non-application of Certain Rules to Subcommissions and Working Groups

Rule 34

a) The presiding officer shall call upon speakers in the order in which they have expressed their desire to speak; he may call a speaker to order if his observations are not relevant to the subject under discussion.

b) Generally, no representative should be called to speak a second time on any question except for clarification, until all other representatives desiring to speak have had an opportunity to do so.

Speakers

Rule 35

At plenary meetings, the chairman of a committee or commission may be accorded precedence for the purpose of explaining the conclusions arrived at by the body concerned. In commission meetings, a similar precedence may be given to the chairmen of subcommissions and working groups.

Precedence

Rule 36

During the discussion of any matter, and notwithstanding the provisions of Rule 34, a member of the delegation of a Contracting State may at any time raise a point of order, and the point of order shall be immediately decided by the presiding officer. Any member of a delegation representing a Contracting State may appeal against the ruling of the presiding officer. The appeal shall be immediately put to vote, and the ruling of the presiding officer shall stand unless

Points of Order

overruled by a majority of votes cast. A member of a delegation raising a point of order may speak only on this point, and may not speak on the substance of the matter under discussion before the point was raised.

Rule 37

A presiding officer may, with the approval of the Assembly or of the body concerned, limit the time allowed to each speaker. **Time Limit on Speeches**

Rule 38

A motion or amendment shall not be discussed until it has been seconded. Motions and amendments may be presented and seconded only by members of delegations of Contracting States. **Motions and Amendments**

Rule 39

No motion may be withdrawn if an amendment to it is under discussion or has been adopted. **Withdrawal of Motion**

Rule 40

Any member of the delegation of a Contracting State may move at any time the suspension or adjournment of the meeting, the adjournment of the debate on any question, the deferment of discussion of an item, or the closure of the debate on an item. After such a motion has been made and explained by its proposer, only one speaker shall normally be allowed to speak in opposition to it, and no further speeches shall be made in its support before a vote is taken. Additional speeches on such a motion may be allowed at the discretion of the presiding officer, who shall decide the priority of recognition. **Procedural Motions**

Rule 41

Subject to the provisions of Rule 36, the following motions shall have priority over all other motions, and shall be taken in the following order: *Order of Procedural Motions*

a) to suspend the meeting;

b) to adjourn the meeting;

c) to adjourn the debate on an item;

d) to defer the debate on an item;

e) for closure of the debate on an item.

Rule 42

Reopening within the same body and at the same session of a debate already completed by a vote on a given item shall require a majority of votes cast. Permission to speak on a motion to reopen shall normally be accorded only to the proposer and to one speaker in opposition, after which it shall be immediately put to vote: when a larger number of speeches is allowed by the presiding officer, priority of recognition shall be given to the leading participants in the debate affected by the motion, or in the sponsorship of or opposition to the proposal that would be affected. Speeches on a motion to reopen shall be limited in content to matters bearing directly on the justification of reopening. Discussion of the substance of the question at issue will be in order only if, and after, the motion to reopen prevails. *Reconsideration of Proposal*

Rule 42A

a) No resolution or other form of action involving expenditure not provided for in the budget estimates shall be recommended by a commission or committee for approval by the Plenary before the Secretary General *Proposals Involving Expenditure Outside Budget Estimates* presents to such commission or committee his estimate of the expenditure involved.

b) If a commission or a committee decides to recommend to the Assembly approval of a proposal of the type described in paragraph a) above, it shall accompany its recommendation with an estimate of expenditure prepared by the Secretary General and it shall inform the Administrative Commission that it is making that recommendation to the Assembly.

c) No recommendation of a commission or a committee which would involve expenditure not provided for in the budget estimates shall be voted by the Assembly until the Administrative Commission has had an opportunity of stating the repercussions of the recommendation upon those budget estimates.

SECTION VIII. VOTING

Rule 43

a) At meetings of any body of the Assembly other than bodies of limited membership, each Contracting State represented by an accredited delegation shall be entitled to one vote, unless the voting power of such State has been suspended by the Assembly under the terms of the Convention. Advisers shall not be entitled to cast a vote on behalf of their delegations in plenary meetings of the Assembly, but may do so elsewhere. *Voting Rights*

b) In meetings of bodies of limited membership each duly appointed member thereof shall be entitled to one vote.

c) Observers representing non-Contracting States or international organizations shall not be entitled to vote.

Rule 44

The presiding officer of the Assembly, or of any of its bodies, shall have the right to cast the vote of his State.

Voting of Presiding Officer

Rule 45

Except as otherwise provided in the Convention, decisions shall be by a majority of the votes cast [Convention, Article 48 c)]. An abstention shall not be considered as a vote.

Majority Required

Rule 46

Voting shall normally be by voice, by show of hands, or by standing, but at the request of any delegation of a Contracting State there shall be a roll-call, which shall be taken in the English alphabetical order of the names of the Contracting States, beginning with the State whose name is drawn by lot by the presiding officer. The vote of each delegation participating in a roll-call shall be recorded in the minutes, as required by Rule 65.

Method of Voting

Rule 47

The vote on any question shall be by secret ballot if the delegations of two or more Contracting States so request and the request is not opposed. In case of opposition the question whether there shall be a secret ballot shall be decided by a majority of votes cast in secret ballot. The provisions of this Rule shall prevail over those of Rule 46.

Secret Ballot

Rule 48

On request of the delegation of any Contracting State and unless opposed by a majority of those voting, parts of a motion shall be voted on separately. The resulting motion shall then be put to a final vote in its entirety.

Division of Motions

Rule 49

Any amendment to a motion shall be voted on before a vote is taken on the motion. When two or more amendments are moved to a motion, the vote should be taken on them in their order of remoteness to the original motion, commencing with the most remote. The presiding officer shall determine whether a proposed amendment is so related to the motion as to constitute a proper amendment thereto, or whether it must be considered as an alternative or substitute motion; this ruling may be reversed by a majority of votes cast.

Voting on Amendments

Rule 50

Alternative or substitute motions shall, unless the meeting otherwise decides, be put to vote in the order in which they are presented, and after the disposal of the original motion. The presiding officer shall decide whether it is necessary to put such alternative or substitute motions to vote in the light of the vote on the original motions and any amendments thereto; this ruling may be reversed by a majority of votes cast.

Voting on Alternative or Substitute Motions

Rule 51

A vote on any motion or amendment shall be postponed upon request of any member of the delegation of a Contracting State until copies of the motion have been available to all delegations for at least twenty-four hours. Such postponement may be denied by a majority of votes cast.

Postponement of Voting

Rule 52

In the event of a tie vote, a second vote on the motion concerned shall be taken at the next meeting, unless the body concerned decides that such second vote be taken during the

Tie Vote

meeting at which the tie vote took place. Unless there is a majority in favour of the motion on this second vote, it shall be considered lost.

Rule 53

The four-fifths and two-thirds vote of the Assembly required under Articles 93 and 94 a) respectively of the Convention shall be construed as meaning four-fifths and two-thirds of the total number of Contracting States represented at the Assembly and qualified to vote at the time the vote is taken. For the purpose of establishing this total, there shall be excluded from the total number of Contracting States for which delegations had, at any time either immediately prior to or during the Assembly, filed their credentials:

_{Voting under Articles 93 and 94 a) of the Convention}

a) Contracting States whose delegations had given notice in writing or otherwise of their withdrawal or departure from the Assembly prior to the time when the vote is taken;

b) Contracting States whose delegations' credentials or instructions, filed with the Secretary General, expressly deprive them of the right to vote on the question with respect to which the required majority is being determined; and

c) Contracting States whose voting power is under suspension at the time the vote is taken.

SECTION IX. VOTING ON ELECTION OF THE COUNCIL

Rule 54

Each Contracting State which intends to stand for election to the Council may at any time so inform, in writing, the Secretary General who shall, at the opening of the session,

_{Information List of Candidates}

publish a list showing the names of all the States which have so notified him. This list shall serve the purpose of information only. The official notification of candidacy may be given only at the times specified in Rules 56 and 58 and the official lists of candidatures shall be only those specified in Rules 56 b) and 58 b).

Rule 55

a) The election of the Council shall be so conducted as to enable adequate representation on the Council to be given to the Contracting States described in Article 50 b) of the Convention and shall be held in three parts as follows:

    i) The first part — election of States of chief importance in air transport — shall be held within four days of the opening of the session.

    ii) The second part — election of States not already elected in the first part but which make the largest contribution to the provision of facilities for international civil air navigation — shall be held immediately after the first part of the election.

    iii) The third part — election of States not elected in either the first or the second part, and whether or not they were candidates in either of those parts, and whose designation will ensure that all the major geographical areas of the world are represented on the Council — shall be held as soon as possible after the expiry of twenty-four hours following the publication of the list of candidates mentioned in Rule 58 b).

b) As early as possible after the opening of the session, the Assembly shall fix the maximum number of Contracting States to be elected in each part of the election and fix also the day on which the first two parts of the election shall be held.

Marginal note: Principle of Adequate Representation

Rule 56

a) Each Contracting State which desires to stand for election in either the first or the second part shall so notify the Secretary General in writing during the period of forty-eight hours following the opening of the session.

List of Candidates for First and Second Parts of Election

b) At the end of the period of forty-eight hours mentioned above, the Secretary General shall publish a list of the States which have notified him, in accordance with paragraph a) above, of their candidacy for the first or the second part of the election.

c) All States entered in the aforesaid list shall be deemed to be available for consideration for the first part as well as for the second part, if necessary, of the election unless a Contracting State notifies the Secretary General that it does not wish to be considered in the first part or the second part of the election. Accordingly, and subject to the foregoing, any Contracting State included in the said list and not elected in the first part of the election will automatically be included amongst those to be considered in the second part of the election.

Rule 57

After the second part of the election the President of the Assembly shall declare an interval of approximately forty-eight hours specifying the hour at which that interval will expire, in order that candidatures may be presented for the third part of the election.

Interval

Rule 58

a) Any Contracting State not elected in the first or the second part of the election, and whether or not it was a candidate in either of those parts, shall, if it wishes to be a

List of Candidates for Third Part of Election

candidate for the third part, so notify the Secretary General in writing after the commencement, but before the expiry, of the interval mentioned in Rule 57.

b) A list showing the names of the States which are candidates in accordance with this Rule for the third part of the election shall be published at the end of the aforesaid interval.

Rule 59

a) The election in each of the three parts shall be conducted by secret ballot.   *Balloting*

b) Arrangements shall be made by the Secretary General for voting on each ballot. The names of all Contracting States which are to be considered for the purpose of the particular ballot concerned as well as a statement of the maximum number of Contracting States to be elected in that ballot shall be provided. A Contracting State may vote for any number of candidates up to, but not exceeding, the number of vacancies to be filled by the ballot concerned. An affirmative vote shall be indicated by selecting the name of the Contracting State for which the vote is cast.

c) Voting procedures may be effected through manual or electronic means with the understanding that manual votes remain in place as a fall-back position where electronic voting is used.

d) Any ballot submission shall be rejected if the number of affirmative votes therein exceed the number to be elected in that particular ballot.

e) The results of each ballot shall be announced by the President of the Assembly.

Rule 60

To be elected a member of the Council, a Contracting State must receive the affirmative vote of a majority of the total number of Contracting States voting. The submission of a ballot shall constitute the act of voting. If the number of Contracting States receiving such majority on any ballot is in excess of the number of places to be filled, those receiving the highest numbers of votes shall be chosen. If the number of Contracting States receiving such majority is less than the number of places to be filled, those which have obtained this majority shall be considered to be elected and there shall be another ballot, and, if necessary, additional ballots to fill the remaining places. In these ballots only those Contracting States which were unsuccessful in obtaining the required majority in the previous ballot shall be considered. Following any such ballot in which no Contracting State receives the required majority, the list of Contracting States in the next ballot shall be restricted to a number not more than twice the number of vacancies to be filled and these Contracting States shall be those which received the highest numbers of votes in the previous ballot. However, in the case where two or more Contracting States are tied for the last place on such a restricted list, such Contracting States shall all be included in the list.

Majority Required

Rule 61

In the event of a tie between two or more Contracting States for the last place or places in a part of the election as described in Rule 55, a further ballot shall be held in which only those thus tied shall be considered. If such a ballot results in another tie, the Contracting State to be eliminated from the list for the next ballot shall be determined by a drawing of lots by the President of the Assembly; and the Contracting State so eliminated shall not be eligible for consideration in any subsequent ballot for election in that part.

Balloting in Case of Tie Vote

Rule 62

For an election to fill a vacancy or vacancies on the Council: **Election to Fill a Vacancy**

a) the name of any Contracting State desiring to be elected shall be notified in writing to the Secretary General within the forty-eight hours following the opening of the Assembly, and the Secretary General shall, without delay, publish a list of all such names;

b) the election shall be held at an early date following such publication;

c) the principle concerning adequate representation, specified in Article 50 b) of the Convention, shall apply;

d) the voting shall be by secret ballot;

e) the provisions of paragraphs b), c) and d) of Rule 59 and those of Rules 60 and 61 shall apply to the election.

SECTION X. LANGUAGES

Rule 63

All preparatory documentation for or at the Assembly as well as recommendations, resolutions and decisions of the Assembly shall be prepared and circulated in the English, Arabic, Chinese, French, Russian and Spanish languages. **Languages of Documentation**

Rule 64

The English, Arabic, Chinese, French, Russian and Spanish languages may be used in the deliberations of the Assembly and its bodies. Speeches made in any of six languages shall be interpreted into the other five languages, except where such interpretation is dispensed with by common consent. **Languages of Deliberations**

SECTION XI. RECORDS OF PROCEEDINGS

Rule 65

Unless otherwise decided by the Assembly, minutes of plenary meetings and of meetings of the Executive Committee shall be distributed as soon as possible after each meeting, in such form as the body concerned may decide. **Records**

SECTION XII. AMENDMENT OF THE RULES OF PROCEDURE

Rule 66

Subject to the provisions of the Convention, these Rules may be amended, or any portion of the Rules may be suspended, at any time by the Assembly. **Amendment or Suspension of Rules**

— END —

APPENDIX 3   RULES OF PROCEDURE FOR THE ICAO COUNCIL

RULES OF PROCEDURE FOR THE COUNCIL[*]

PRELIMINARY SECTION

DEFINITIONS

For the purpose of these Rules, the expression:

Alternate — means a person designated and authorized by a Member of the Council to act on its behalf in the absence[**] of the Representative, and holding credentials as evidence thereof.

Convention — means the Convention on International Civil Aviation.

Majority of the Members of the Council — means more than half of the total membership of the Council.

Meeting — means a single sitting of the Council from the time the Council comes to order until it adjourns.

Member of the Council — means a Contracting State elected by the Assembly to form part of the Council in accordance with Article 50 of the Convention.

---

[*] Revised on 28 November 1969, entered into force on 27 April 1970; amended by the Council on 12 May 1971 (Rule 50), 17 March 1976 (Rules 56 and 57), 13 April 1976 (Rule 16 a)), 12 September 1980 (Rule 56), 9 June 1999 (Rule 56), 9 June 2006 (entered into force on 1 August 2006), 16 March 2007, 20 June 2013 (Rule 12), 7 June 2021 (Rules 26, 57 and Appendix J), 26 April 2021 (Appendices G, H and I), 13 September 2021 (Rule 17), 25 October 2021 (Definitions, Rules 4, 7, 9, 11, 15, 19, 20, 31, 34, 35, 39, 49, 53, 54 and Appendix E) and 13 December 2021 (Appendices G and H).

[**] This does not require the Representative to leave the room in the case of a Council meeting.

Observer — means a person representing a Contracting State not represented on the Council, a non-Contracting State, an inter-national organization or other body, designated and authorized by the State or organization to participate in one or more of the meetings of the Council without the right to vote or to move or second motions or amendments, under such further conditions as the Council may determine and holding credentials as evidence of appointment.

Order of business — means a list of items of business for consideration at one meeting.

President — means the President of the Council.

Representative — means a person designated and authorized by a Member of the Council to act on the Council, and holding credentials as evidence thereof.

Secret Ballot — means a ballot where the marking of the ballot paper by a Representative takes place in private and cannot be overseen by any person other than the Representative's Alternate. All ballot papers distributed should be exactly alike so that it cannot be determined how any one Representative voted.

Work Programme — means the list of items to be considered during a session of the Council.

Working Day — means a weekday on which the Organization conducts business at Headquarters and does not observe a public holiday.

Working paper — means a paper proposing Action by the Council.

SECTION I

REPRESENTATIVES, ALTERNATES AND OBSERVERS, AND THEIR CREDENTIALS

Rule 1

Each Member of the Council shall have one Representative, whose place may be taken by an Alternate. No person may represent more than one State.

Rule 2

Credentials of Representatives, of their Alternates and of Observers shall be signed on behalf of the State, organization or body concerned and indicate the capacity in which the individual is to serve, and shall be deposited with the Secretary General.

Rule 3

The credentials shall be examined by the President, one of the Vice-Presidents and the Secretary General, who shall report to the Council.

Rule 4

Representatives, Alternates or Observers shall be entitled, pending the presentation of the reports on their credentials and Council action thereon, to attend meetings and to participate in them subject, however, to the limits set forth in these Rules. The Council may bar from any further part in the activities of the Council, Commissions, Committees and Working Groups any Representative, Alternate or Observer whose credentials it finds to be insufficient.

SECTION II

OFFICERS OF THE COUNCIL AND THE SECRETARY GENERAL

Rule 5

The Council shall elect its President for a term of three years, the exact dates of commencement and termination of which will be determined by the Council. Candidates shall be nominated by Contracting States. The rules and procedures governing the election of the President are set out in Appendix A.

Rule 6

The President of the Council may be removed from office at any time by a decision of the Council taken by a majority of its Members, provided that the motion for that purpose is introduced in writing and is moved jointly by not less than one third of the Members of the Council. Upon the introduction of such a motion, the meeting shall be adjourned. As soon as practicable thereafter, a meeting to consider the motion shall be called by the Vice-President entitled to act under Rule 10. Pending the decision of the Council, the President shall refrain from carrying out the normal functions of the President.

Rule 7

In the event of the President's death, removal from office, or resignation, or if the President is otherwise unable to complete the term of office, a new President shall be elected by the Council as soon as possible thereafter and the latter shall hold office for the remainder of the term of the President's predecessor. If the President gives prior notice of resignation, the election shall be held on a date to be decided by the Council, if possible before the resignation takes effect.

Rule 8

The Council shall elect from among Representatives a First, a Second and a Third Vice-President. Candidates shall be nominated by one or more Council Members. The rules set out in Appendix B shall govern the election of each Vice-President.

Rule 9

The term of office of a Vice-President shall extend for one year from the date of the election, but the Vice-President may continue to hold office thereafter until a successor is elected, provided that the term of office shall not extend beyond the end of the term of the Council unless the State which the Vice-President represents continues to be a Member of the Council.

Rule 10

In the absence of the President, the First Vice-President, the Second Vice-President or the Third Vice-President in that order shall exercise the functions vested in the President by these Rules of Procedure.

Rule 11

A Vice-President when acting in the absence of the President shall retain the right to vote.

Rule 12

The Council shall appoint the Secretary General for a term of three years. Candidates shall be nominated by Contracting States. A Secretary General who has served for two terms shall not be appointed for a third term. The rules and procedures governing the appointment of the Secretary General are set out in Appendix C.

Rule 13

The Secretary General of the Organization shall be the Secretary of the Council.

Rule 14

The Secretary General may be removed from office by a decision of the Council taken by a majority of its Members, provided that the motion for that purpose is introduced in writing and is moved jointly by not less than one third of the Members of the Council. As soon as practicable thereafter, a meeting to consider the motion shall be called by the President. Pending the decision of the Council, the Secretary General shall refrain from carrying out the normal functions of the Secretary General.

Rule 15

In the event of the Secretary General's death, removal from office, or resignation, or if the Secretary General is otherwise unable to complete the term of office, the Council shall, notwithstanding the procedure in Appendix C, draw up an appropriate timetable for appointing a successor. If the Secretary General gives prior notice of resignation, the appointment shall be held on a date to be decided by the Council, if possible before the resignation takes effect.

SECTION III

COMMISSIONS, COMMITTEES AND WORKING GROUPS OF THE COUNCIL

Rule 16

a) The Council shall appoint the Members of the Air Navigation Commission from candidates nominated by Contracting States. Such appointment shall be for a term of three years, or for the remainder of the term of a predecessor.

APPENDICES

b) The Council may appoint Alternates to act in the absence of a member of the Air Navigation Commission.

c) The Council shall appoint the President of the Air Navigation Commission in accordance with the Guidelines set out in paragraph 4 of Appendix D.

d) The rules and procedures governing the appointment of the Members, Alternates and President of the Air Navigation Commission are set out in Appendix D.

Rule 17

a) In addition to the Air Navigation Commission, the Air Transport Committee and the Finance Committee, the Council may establish other Commissions, Committees or Working Groups, either Standing or Temporary. The Council shall appoint the Members and Alternates of standing bodies and shall specify at the time of establishing such bodies whether the body shall also elect its own Chairperson. Standing bodies shall elect their own Vice-Chairpersons.

b) The Council may appoint an Alternate who may act and vote on behalf of a Member of the Standing Commission, Committee or Working Group who is absent or who is discharging the functions of Chairperson.

c) The rules and procedures for cases where the Council elects the Members, Alternates and Chairpersons of Commissions (other than the Air Navigation Commission), Committees and Working Groups are set out in Appendix E.

d) The temporary bodies mentioned in paragraph a) shall elect their own officers, unless the Council decides otherwise.

e) The method of selection, terms of reference and working methods of Temporary Commissions, Committees or Working Groups shall be determined by the Council in each case.

SECTION IV

SESSIONS OF THE COUNCIL

Rule 18

The Council shall meet at such times and for such periods as it deems necessary for the proper discharge of its responsibilities. The Council shall determine the dates of the opening and termination of each session.

Rule 19

a) Between two consecutive sessions of the Council, at the President's initiative or at the request of a Contracting State, after consulting the Members of the Council and with the approval of the majority of the Members of the Council, the President shall call an extra-ordinary session or change the date which the Council has set for the opening of the next session. No such action shall result in a Council Meeting being held on less than seven days' notice.

b) When the President considers that the urgency of a situation so warrants, the President may, after consultation with the most senior Vice-President available, convene a special session of the Council provided that no less than 48 hours' notice is given.

Rule 20

If a part of a Council session is devoted primarily to Committee meetings, the President may, when considered necessary, call Council meetings. No such meetings shall be called on less than 48 hours' notice without the approval of the majority of the Council.

Rule 21

The Council shall meet at the seat of the Organization unless the Council decides that a particular session or meeting shall take place elsewhere.

SECTION V

WORK PROGRAMME AND ORDER OF BUSINESS

Rule 22

A Provisional Work Programme of each session of the Council shall be prepared by the Secretary General after consultation with the President and presented to the Council for approval. The presentation to the Council should normally, and wherever practicable, be made during the preceding session. The Council should indicate the priority which it attaches to the consideration of the various items in the Provisional Work Programme.

Rule 23

In preparing the Provisional Work Programme, the Secretary General shall include therein:

a) subjects which require consideration by the Council by virtue of provisions of the Convention or other international agreement;

b) subjects to be considered by virtue of decisions of the Assembly or decisions taken by the Council at a previous session;

c) reports presented or references made to the Council by bodies of the Organization or other international bodies;

d) any subject proposed by a Member of the Council and transmitted directly to the President or the Secretary General;

e) any subject referred by a Contracting State for consideration by the Council;

f) any subject which the President or the Secretary General desires to bring before the Council;

g) a report on action carried out to implement the decisions of the Council taken at its previous session;

h) a report on the financial situation of the Organization; and

i) a report on the progress made by the Organization towards its strategic objectives and the objectives of the Business Plan.

Rule 24

a) Supplementary items may be placed on the Work Programme during a session at the request of any Member of the Council, or of the President or the Secretary General, subject to the approval of the Council.

b) Any additional subject which fulfils the conditions specified in Rule 26, paragraph d), shall be deemed to be included in the Work Programme of the session concerned.

c) Supplements to the Work Programme should be issued by the Secretary General showing results of the application of paragraphs a) and b) of this Rule.

Rule 25

The Order of Business for each meeting shall be prepared by the Secretary General and approved by the President.

Rule 26

a) The Order of Business shall be distributed to all Representatives at least two working days before the meeting of the Council.

b) All documents listed in the Order of Business shall be distributed to all Representatives in advance of the meeting of the Council to which the Order of Business relates as follows:

i) for working papers containing proposals for adopting or amending the Annexes under Article 90 of the Convention — at least ten working days before the meeting;

ii) for other working papers — at least five working days before the meeting;

iii) for reports from Standing Commissions or Committees of the Council or reports of other bodies established under Rule 17 — at least three working days before the meeting; and

iv) for all other documents — at least 24 hours before the meeting.

c) A revised Order of Business may be distributed less than 24 hours before the meeting of the Council to include, without substantial change, items of business included in the Order of Business already distributed for that meeting or an item carried over from the immediately preceding meeting provided that the revised Order of Business shall not list any documents not distributed in accordance with paragraph b) of this Rule.

d) If the Secretary General, or the President, or a Contracting State requests that a new subject, whether or not included in the Work Programme, be considered at a meeting of the Council, such subject shall be listed in an Addendum to the Order of Business to be issued by the Secretary General. Any such additional item shall be considered only if the Council so decides by a majority of its Members.

e) Notwithstanding paragraphs a) and b), for special sessions of the Council convened pursuant to Rule 19 b), the Order of Business and other documents shall be distributed as soon as practicable, but not less than three working days in advance of the meeting.

Rule 27

Any subject on the Work Programme of the Council and any document presented in connection therewith may be referred by the Council to an appropriate existing Committee, Commission or Working Group for consideration and report before its consideration by the Council.

Rule 28

Any Member of the Council may have placed on the Order of Business any item of the Work Programme which it wishes to be considered forthwith by the Council. This right is subject to the provisions of the second sentence of paragraph d) of Rule 26, and subject also to the proviso contained in clause b) of Rule 30.

Rule 29

a) Any Member of the Council, the President or the Secretary General may introduce for the consideration of the Council documents bearing upon any item on the Council Work Programme, or present any recommendations with respect thereto.

b) The Council shall, as necessary, issue guidelines on the structure and presentation of working papers and other documents.

Rule 30

The Council may at any time:

a) amend the Work Programme of a session; or

b) decide, by a majority of its Members, to amend the Order of Business of a meeting, provided that no item or other matter which was not included in the Order of Business as distributed in accordance with the provisions of Rule 26, shall be brought to final action at that meeting except by the unanimous consent of all the Members of the Council represented at the meeting.

SECTION VI

CONDUCT OF BUSINESS

Rule 31

Any Contracting State may participate, without a vote, in the consideration by the Council and by its Committees and Commissions of any question which especially affects its interests (Article 53 of the Convention). Subject to the approval of the Council, the President may invite such participation when considering that the condition of special interest is fulfilled. If a Contracting State requests permission to participate on the grounds of special interest, the President shall refer the request to the Council for decision.

Rule 32

a) The Council may invite non-Contracting States and international organizations or other bodies to be represented at any of its meetings by one or more Observers.

b) The President shall invite the United Nations to be represented by Observers at meetings of the Council.

c) Subject to the approval of the Council, the President may invite Specialized Agencies in relationship with the United Nations to be represented by Observers at meetings of the Council in which matters of special interest to them are to be discussed.

Rule 33

A majority of the Members of the Council shall constitute a quorum for the conduct of the business of the Council.

Rule 34

a) The President shall convene meetings of the Council (Article 51 a) of the Convention); the President shall preside at, and declare the opening and closing of each meeting, direct the discussion in a structured and focused way, accord the right to speak, put questions and announce the decisions.

b) The President shall ensure the observance of these Rules.

c) During the discussion of any matter, a Representative may raise a point of order or any other matter related to the interpretation or application of these Rules. The point of order or matter related to the interpretation or application of these Rules shall be decided immediately by the President, in accordance with these Rules. A Representative raising a point of order may only speak in relation to that point of order.

Rule 35

a) The President shall call upon speakers in the order in which, in the opinion of the President, they have expressed their desire to speak, taking into account the desirability of maintaining a structured and focused discussion; a speaker may be called to order if the President considers that the speaker's observations are not relevant to the subject under discussion, or for any other appropriate reason.

b) Generally, no speaker shall be called to intervene a second time on any question, except for clarification, until all others desiring to intervene have had the opportunity to do so.

c) The President of the Air Navigation Commission and the Chairperson of a Commission, Committee or Working Group may be accorded precedence for the purpose of explaining the conclusions arrived at by the body concerned.

Rule 36

Rulings given by the President during a meeting of the Council on the interpretation or application of these Rules of Procedure may be appealed by any Member of the Council and the appeal shall be put to vote immediately. The ruling of the President shall stand unless over-ruled by a majority of the votes cast.

Rule 37

Meetings of the Council shall be open to the public unless the Council rules by a majority of votes cast that any particular meeting or part thereof be closed. Guidelines on when Council meetings should be held in closed session and when Council documents should be marked "Restricted" are found in Appendix F.

Rule 38

Closed meetings of the Council shall be open to the Alternates and Advisers accompanying the Representatives; to Observers from any other Contracting State, unless the Council decides otherwise; to the members of the Secretariat whose attendance is necessary to the conduct of the meeting or is desired by the Secretary General; and to any other persons invited by the Council. Closed meetings shall not be broadcast by the Organization's monitoring exchange.

Rule 39

Subject to the approval of the Council, the President may invite the President of the Air Navigation Commission and the Chairpersons of Commissions, Committees or Working Groups who are not Representatives to attend any open or closed meeting of the Council and participate in its discussion without the right to vote when business relating to the work of their Commission, Committee or Working Group, or to any documentation connected therewith, is before the Council.

Rule 40

Any Member of the Council may introduce a motion or amendment thereto, subject to the following rules:

a) with the exception of motions and amendments relative to nominations, no motion or amendment shall be discussed unless it has been seconded;

b) no motion or amendment may be withdrawn by its author if an amendment to it is under discussion or has been adopted;

c) if a motion has been moved, no motion other than one for an amendment to the original motion shall be considered until the original motion has been disposed of. The President shall determine whether such additional motion is so related to the motion already before the Council as to constitute a proper amendment thereto, or whether it is to be regarded as an alternative motion, consideration of which shall be postponed as stipulated above;

d) if an amendment to a motion has been moved, no amendment other than an amendment to the original one shall be moved until the original amendment has been disposed of. The President shall determine whether such additional amendment is so related to the original one as to constitute an amendment thereto, or whether it is to be regarded as an alternative amendment, consideration of which shall be postponed as stipulated above.

Rule 41

a) The following motions shall have priority over all other motions and shall be taken in the following order:

1) a motion to reverse a ruling by the President;

2) a motion to adjourn the meeting;

3) a motion to fix the time to adjourn the meeting;

4) a motion to suspend the meeting for a limited time;

5) a motion to defer further debate on a particular question, either indefinitely or for a limited period greater than that covered by Rule 42;

6) a motion to refer the matter to a Commission, Committee or Working Group;

7) a motion to invite the opinions of Contracting States on a matter, and to postpone final action thereon until reasonable time for the receipt of such opinions has been allowed;

8) a motion to terminate the debate on a particular motion and to take at once a decision thereon.

b) Action on these matters will be determined by a majority of the votes cast.

Rule 42

Upon the request of any Member of the Council, and unless objection is raised by the majority of the Members of the Council, further debate on any item of business shall be deferred for a period of not over two working days, or until the next Council meeting following the second day; but no such action under this paragraph shall be admissible when it would have the effect, due to the anticipated adjournment of a Council session, of making it impossible to resume consideration of the deferred item by the seventh day following the action of deferment. Any such request shall be privileged, and shall be considered immediately on its presentation.

Rule 43

The Council may decide, by a majority of its Members, to reopen the discussion of an item already disposed of by the Council in the same session. In that event, and unless the Council by a majority of its Members decides that the item be dealt with forthwith, the item concerned shall be placed on the Order of Business of the next meeting.

SECTION VII

VOTING

Rule 44

Each Member of the Council has one vote.

Rule 45

With the exception of motions and amendments relative to nominations, no motion or amendment shall be voted on, unless it has been seconded.

Rule 46

Upon the request of any Member of the Council, and unless a majority of its Members decide otherwise:

a) final action on any motion or amendment thereto shall be delayed until the proposed text of the motion or amendment thereto has been available to Representatives for at least 24 hours;

b) a vote or final action on any item which has been considered shall, after any initial discussion of the item, be postponed for a period not exceeding that indicated in Rule 42.

Rule 47

Any amendment shall be voted on before the motion or amendment to which it refers.

Rule 48

On the request of any Member of the Council, and unless opposed by a majority of the votes cast, parts of a motion shall be voted on separately. The resulting motion shall then be put to a final vote in its entirety.

Rule 49

Except in the case of a secret ballot, upon request by a Member, the vote or the abstention from voting of any Member of the Council shall be recorded. Subject to the same exception, upon the request of any Member of the Council, the individual votes of all the Members of the Council shall be recorded. In the latter case, the roll-call shall be taken in the English alphabetical order of the names of the Members, beginning with the Member whose name is drawn by lot by the President.

Rule 50

Unless opposed by a majority of the Members of the Council, the vote shall be taken by secret ballot if a request to that effect is supported, if made by a Member of the Council, by one other Member, and, if made by the President, by two Members.

Rule 51

A vote received by correspondence or electronically shall not be counted unless, in a particular case, the Council has previously decided otherwise. In the latter event, a communication approved by the Council or under its authority shall be sent to the Member of the Council concerned for the purpose of ensuring that due consideration is given to the major points of view expressed on the question before the vote is sent, and reasonable time shall be allowed for a reply.

Rule 52

In the event of a tie vote, a second vote on the motion concerned shall be taken at the next meeting of the Council, unless by a majority of the votes cast the Council decides that such second vote be taken during the meeting at which the tie vote took place. Unless there is a majority in favour of the motion on the second vote, it shall be considered lost.

Rule 53

The President may take a preliminary informal vote or poll of the Members of the Council on any issue, in terms to be phrased by the President, for the purpose of facilitating the subsequent framing of a motion. Such informal procedure shall not commit the Council or any Member thereof. The results of such informal procedure may be recorded in the Minutes, but no mention of the vote of any Member of the Council shall be made.

SECTION VIII

APPROVAL OF PROPOSALS WITH RESPECT TO ADMINISTRATIVE MATTERS

Rule 54

Notwithstanding the other provisions of these Rules of Procedure, proposals of the Secretary General with respect to such administrative matters including amendments to administrative regulations as require approval of the Council may be approved in accordance with the following procedure:

1) the Secretary General shall distribute to the Representatives of the Members of the Council a paper explaining the proposals, and the existence of this paper shall be noted on the Orders of Business of two Council meetings, the first of which shall be held at least one week after the date of the distribution of the paper;

2) upon the request of any Member of the Council, filed with the President at least 24 hours before either of these two meetings, the paper shall be brought before the Council for consideration under the normal procedure;

3) in the absence of a request for discussion under the provisions of paragraph 2) of this Rule, the proposal of the Secretary General shall be deemed to have been approved on the date of the second of the two Council meetings in the Orders of Business of which the existence of the paper has been noted.

SECTION IX

LANGUAGES OF THE COUNCIL

Rule 55

The discussions of the Council shall be conducted in the English, Arabic, Chinese, French, Russian and Spanish languages, and interpretation shall take place accordingly. By unanimous agreement, the Council may decide that interpretation into one or more of such languages shall be waived.

Rule 56

The Council shall decide from time to time in which language or languages, specified in Rule 55, the documentation for the Council shall be drawn up.

SECTION X

RECORDS OF PROCEEDINGS

Rule 57

a) The Secretary General shall prepare Draft Decisions taken at each meeting within five working days of the meeting to which they relate based on the summary of the President. These Draft Decisions shall be submitted to the President for agreement and shall be distributed to Representatives who shall have three working days to comment thereon. If there are no objections raised by Representatives to the content of the Draft Decisions, the President shall declare them approved. If any objections are raised, the President shall attempt to resolve them with the Representative concerned. If the objections are not so resolved, the matter shall be considered by the Council, without reopening the substance of the debate, if at least two Representatives ask for it to be so.

b) The Secretary General shall prepare Draft Minutes of each meeting within six weeks of the session of the Council to which they relate. These shall be submitted to the President for agreement, distributed to Representatives who shall have ten working days to comment thereon and adopted by the Council either through written procedure or at a subsequent meeting.

c) After adoption, the text of Decisions and Minutes shall be made available to Representatives and to Contracting States.

Rule 58

Council documents other than the Minutes of closed meetings may be provided to non-Contracting States, to international organizations and to the public, unless otherwise directed by the Council or, between sessions of the Council, by the President.

Rule 59

The final texts of all resolutions and decisions of the Council, together with Council working and other papers, shall be made available by the Secretary General to all Contracting States as soon as possible.

Rule 60

Press releases concerning the proceedings of the Council shall be prepared by the Secretary General and shall be approved by the President after consulting with the most senior Vice-President available, before being made public.

SECTION XI

INTERPRETATION, REVOCATION, SUSPENSION AND AMENDMENT OF THE RULES OF PROCEDURE

Rule 61

Any Member of the Council may request that any application or interpretation of these Rules by the President otherwise than during a meeting of the Council, be reviewed by the Council. Such request shall be considered by the Council at its next regular meeting, unless the President considers it advisable to call a special meeting for that purpose under Rule 20 of these Rules of Procedure. The action taken by the President shall stand confirmed unless decided otherwise by a majority of the votes cast.

Rule 62

In the case of any provision herein which does not specify the majority by which a decision shall be taken, it is understood that a majority of the votes cast will be sufficient, provided that if a Member of the Council has requested that the decision be taken by a majority of Members of the Council, the latter majority shall apply.

Rule 63

a) These Rules of Procedure or any portion thereof may be revoked, temporarily suspended or amended by Council decision taken by a majority of its Members, provided that no such action is in conflict with the Convention or with any direction given or decision taken by the Assembly. The Secretary General shall maintain and make available to Council Members a central record of all such temporary suspensions.

b) Notwithstanding Rule 26, proposals to amend or revoke these Rules of Procedure shall be circulated to Representatives at least ten working days in advance of the meeting of the Council in which they will be considered.

APPENDIX A

Rules and Procedures for the election of the President of the Council

1. The Council shall, not less than three months before the opening of the ordinary session of the Assembly which will elect a new Council, inform Contracting States that the Council to be elected at that Session of the Assembly will elect the President of the Council. The communication should also:

   a) invite attention to the provisions of Article 51 of the Convention;

   b) set out the qualifications, experience and abilities which candidates are expected to demonstrate; and

   c) indicate the date by which the names of candidates for the Presidency should be in the hands of the Secretary General.

2. The names of the candidates shall be circulated by the Secretary General to all Contracting States as soon as they are received.

3. The Council shall invite candidates, at an appropriate date before the election, to present their views and ideas to a meeting of Representatives, and to answer any questions which may be posed.

4. The election of the President shall require a majority of the Members of the Council.

5. If no candidate receives the majority on the first ballot, a second and, if necessary, subsequent ballots shall be held on the two candidates who received the largest number of votes in the preceding ballot. Candidates tying for the last qualifying place in a ballot shall all be included in the next ballot.

6. The election shall take place by secret ballot, unless waived by unanimous decision of the Members represented at the meeting.

APPENDIX B

Rules and Procedures for the election of the Vice-Presidents of the Council

1. The election of each Vice-President shall require a majority of the Members of the Council.

2. If no candidate receives the majority on the first ballot, a second and, if necessary, subsequent ballots shall be held on the two candidates who received the largest number of votes in the preceding ballot. Candidates tying for the last qualifying place in a ballot shall all be included in the next ballot.

3. The election shall take place by secret ballot, unless waived by unanimous decision of the Members represented at the meeting.

APPENDIX C

Rules and Procedures for the appointment of the Secretary General

1. The appointment of the Secretary General will take place approximately five months before the termination of the period for which the incumbent was appointed.

2. Ten months before the termination of that period, the Council shall inform Contracting States that it will proceed to the appointment of the Secretary General. The communication should also:

   a) invite attention to the provisions of Articles 54 (h), 58 and 59 of the Convention;

   b) set out the qualifications, experience and abilities which candidates are expected to demonstrate; and

   c) indicate the date by which the names of candidates for the Secretary General should be in the hands of the President; that date to provide Contracting States three full months for reply.

3. The names of the candidates shall be circulated by the President to all Contracting States as soon as they are received.

4. The Council shall invite candidates, at an appropriate date before the election, to present their views and ideas to a meeting of Representatives, and to answer any questions which may be posed.

5. The appointment of the Secretary General shall require a majority of the Members of the Council.

6. If no candidate receives the majority on the first ballot, a second and, if necessary, subsequent ballots shall be held on the two candidates who received the largest number of votes in the preceding ballot. Candidates tying for the last qualifying place in a ballot shall all be included in the next ballot.

7. The election shall take place by secret ballot, unless waived by unanimous decision of the Members represented at the meeting.

APPENDIX D

Rules and Procedures governing the appointment of the Members, Alternates and President of the Air Navigation Commission

1. The appointment of the Members, Alternates and President of the Air Navigation Commission shall require a majority of the Members of the Council and, unless waived by unanimous agreement of the Members represented at the meeting, shall be by secret ballot.

Appointment of Members and Alternates

2. If the number of candidates receiving the required majority on the first ballot is in excess of the number of places to be filled, those receiving the highest number of votes shall be appointed. If the number of candidates appointed on the first ballot is less than the number of places to be filled, additional ballots shall be held as necessary. In each ballot subsequent to the first one, the names considered shall be those having received the highest number of votes in the previous ballot, up to a total number of candidates equal to twice the total number of places to be filled. Candidates tying for the last qualifying place in a ballot shall all be included in the next ballot.

Appointment of President

3. If no candidate receives the majority on the first ballot, a second and, if necessary, subsequent ballots shall be held on the two candidates who received the largest number of votes in the preceding ballot. Candidates tying for the last qualifying place in a ballot shall all be included in the next ballot.

4. Pursuant to Rule 16 c), the following constitutes the Guidelines relating to the appointment of the President of the Air Navigation Commission:

a) the candidacies to the post of the President of the Commission should be declared to the President of the Council;

b) the Commission should indicate to the Council what is expected of its future President, the major tasks to be performed during its mandate, and the main qualities needed by its future President in this context;

c) the Commission should refrain from voting on this issue.

APPENDIX E

Rules and Procedures governing the appointment of the Members, Alternates and Chairpersons of Commissions (other than the Air Navigation Commission), Committees and Working Groups

1. In cases where the Council has to elect Members, Alternates or a Chairperson of a Standing Commission (other than the Air Navigation Commission), Committee or Working Group, each Member of the Council may present names from among the Representatives or Alternates, with their consent, for inclusion in a list to be presented to the Council by the President. Not more than one Representative or Alternate of any State may be elected.

2. The election of Members, Alternates and Chairpersons of such Commissions, Committees and Working Groups shall require a majority of the Members of the Council and, unless waived by unanimous agreement of the Members represented at the meeting, shall be by secret ballot.

Election of Members, Alternates and Chairpersons

3. If the number of candidates receiving the required majority on the first ballot is in excess of the number of places to be filled, those receiving the highest number of votes shall be elected. If the number of candidates elected on the first ballot is less than the number of places to be filled, additional ballots shall be held as necessary. In each ballot subsequent to the first one, the names considered shall be those having received the highest number of votes in the previous ballot, up to a total number of candidates equal to twice the total number of places to be filled. Candidates tying for the last qualifying place in a ballot shall all be included in the next ballot.

APPENDIX F

Guidelines on when Council meetings should be held in closed session (Rule 37) and when Council documents should be marked "Restricted"

1. Meetings of the Council should normally be open to the public. In general, meetings should only be held in closed session if discussion involves the following:

   a) the level of aviation security in specified States or in general;

   b) current or future provisions concerning aviation security;

   c) salaries or allowances of an individual member of staff or of a category of staff;

   d) disputes between Contracting States; and

   e) issues where Representatives' personal security could be endangered if their statements were made public.

2. Normally, only documents relating to meetings considering the subjects listed under a) to e) above should be marked "Restricted".

APPENDIX G

Rules and Procedures to address allegations of misconduct or retaliation against the Secretary General of ICAO

Scope

1. In conformity with paragraph 1 of the ICAO Framework on Ethics (Annex I to the ICAO Service Code), these Rules and Procedures for addressing allegations of misconduct or retaliation against the Secretary General of ICAO shall apply to all staff members of ICAO. They shall also apply mutatis mutandis to all non-staff personnel of ICAO, including, but not limited to, gratis personnel, consultants, experts, interns and individuals working for ICAO under a contractual relationship.

Investigative entity

2. ICAO shall enter into an agreement with an investigative entity within the United Nations system, such as the Office of Internal Oversight Services (OIOS), or a similar expert entity, to establish a mechanism for the reporting and handling of allegations of misconduct committed by the Secretary General. In principle, this should be the same investigative entity engaged as a mechanism for the reporting and handling of all cases of misconduct committed by staff members of the Organization, as defined in the ICAO Framework on Ethics (Annex I to the ICAO Service Code). The agreement should address inter alia the issue of access by the investigative entity to documents and records.

3. The Council delegates to the investigative entity the responsibility to receive, assess, investigate, close and report on any allegations of misconduct against the Secretary General, without the need to request further authorization from the Council.

External ethics entity

4. ICAO shall enter into an agreement with an external ethics entity within the United Nations system, such as the Ethics Office, or similar expert entity, to establish a mechanism for the direct reporting and handling of complaints of retaliation committed by the Secretary General. In principle, this should be the same external ethics entity engaged to review determinations by the Ethics Officer that there was no prima facie case of retaliation or threat of retaliation.

5. The Council delegates to the external ethics entity the responsibility to receive, assess, close and report on any requests by staff members for protection against retaliation by the Secretary General, without the need to request further authorization from the Council.

Misconduct

6. For the purposes of these Rules and Procedures, misconduct is defined as the non-compliance, through acts or omissions, with the Secretary General's obligations under the Convention on International Civil Aviation (Chicago Convention), the Code of Conduct for the President of the Council and the Secretary General of ICAO and the principles and values of the ICAO Framework on Ethics. Misconduct is also defined as disregard for the standards of conduct expected from an international civil servant, as defined by the International Civil Service Commission (ICSC) and other relevant administrative issuances such as those on anti-fraud and anti-corruption, protection against sexual exploitation and abuse, and prevention of sexual harassment.

Reporting alleged cases of misconduct by the Secretary General

7. Staff members should report any allegations of misconduct against the Secretary General directly to the investigative entity according to instructions provided on the public websites of the investigative entity and ICAO.

8. Notwithstanding the provisions of paragraph 7, staff members reporting allegations of misconduct in relation to any administrative decisions taken by the Secretary General that are of direct concern to them shall, as a rule, first avail themselves of the appropriate appeal mechanisms

available to them under Article XI of the ICAO Service Code, before reporting such cases to the investigative entity. Non-staff personnel, as defined in paragraph 1, reporting allegations of misconduct in relation to any contractual disputes with the Organization shall, as a rule, first avail themselves of the contractual remedies available to them before reporting such cases to the investigative entity.

Protection against retaliation by the Secretary General

9. Staff members should submit any requests for protection against retaliation by the Secretary General directly to the external ethics entity according to instructions provided on the public websites of the external ethics entity and ICAO. Staff members should consider that the primary objective of the provisions on retaliation is to provide enhanced protection to individuals who have reported behaviour that poses a significant risk to the Organization, i.e. a report that, if established, would be manifestly harmful to the interests, operations or governance of the Organization. Such reports should be made in the public interest and not stem from personal disagreements over policy or management decisions or individual grievances.

Responsibilities of staff reporting allegations of misconduct

10. Staff members reporting allegations of misconduct by the Secretary General, or requesting protection against retaliation, should only do so in good faith and must provide credible arguments supporting their claims. Claims must be supported by evidence that includes documents and records, verbal statements and even tangible items, or the physical condition of those items. Staff members reporting complaints of misconduct shall adhere to the confidentiality of the process and cooperate in good faith with a subsequent investigation.

11. Reporting shall not be used to transmit or disseminate unsubstantiated rumours and must respect the appropriate reporting channels as outlined in paragraphs 7, 8 and 9 above. Making a report or providing information that is deliberately false or misleading constitutes misconduct. The transmission or dissemination of unsubstantiated rumours is not a protected activity. Making a report or providing information that is intentionally false or misleading constitutes misconduct and may result in disciplinary or other appropriate action.

Responsibilities of the investigative entity in cases of misconduct

12. The investigative entity will receive, promptly log, assess and take appropriate action on all incoming complaints of misconduct, while ensuring the confidentiality and integrity of the entire process.

13. Upon receiving and assessing allegations of misconduct against the Secretary General, the investigative entity shall, where possible within three weeks of receiving such reports or information:

   a) close the case due to insufficient information, obviously frivolous claims, or because the matter falls outside the scope of a typical investigation conducted by the investigative entity and inform the complainant; or

   b) notify the President of the Council of its intention to launch an investigation into the allegations. Where there is a credible allegation of misconduct, the investigative entity shall interview the Secretary General and offer an opportunity to comment on the transcript of that interview before closing the case, or completing the investigation and delivering its report.

14. After investigating the allegations, the investigative entity shall:

   a) close the case when misconduct is not substantiated, provide a closure notice to the President of the Council and inform the complainant; or

   b) refer the matter, including an investigation report and supporting documentation, to the President of the Council for further consideration by the Council.

15. The investigative entity shall, on or before 31 January of each year, provide to the Council an annual report of all cases of misconduct handled on behalf of ICAO within the preceding year. The annual report shall contain sufficient details of the cases, while respecting the utmost confidentiality and privacy rights. It shall contain a redacted summary of investigations, and the findings and recommendations arising from such investigations pertaining to systemic improvement. The annual report should also contain information on the timelines, as appropriate, from initial intake to assessment, investigation, closure and reporting.

Responsibilities of the external ethics entity in cases involving retaliation by the Secretary General

16. The provisions on protection against retaliation are without prejudice to the legitimate application of regulations, rules and administrative procedures, including those governing evaluation of performance, non-extension or termination of appointment.

17. Upon receiving and assessing a request for protection against retaliation, the external ethics entity shall, where possible within three weeks of receiving such a request:

a) close the case if there is no prima facie case of retaliation and inform the complainant; or

b) refer the case for investigation by the investigative entity, notify the President of the Council and, where appropriate, make recommendations for interim protection measures.

18. Upon completion of the investigation into retaliation, normally within 90 calendar days of referral, the investigative entity shall submit its investigation report to the external ethics entity. The external ethics entity shall conduct an independent review of the investigation report and supporting documentation and determine whether:

a) retaliation did not occur, in which case it shall close the case, provide a closure notice to the President of the Council and inform the complainant; or

b) retaliation occurred, in which case it shall refer the matter to the President of the Council for further consideration by the Council, including a reasoned determination and recommendations, accompanied by the investigation report and supporting documentation released by the investigative entity.

Responsibilities of the President of the Council

19. The President of the Council shall inform the Council and the Secretary General of complaints reported by the investigative entity and/or the external ethics entity, according to paragraphs 13b, 14a, 17b and 18a above. Details of any case, including the identities of claimants and witnesses, shall be kept strictly confidential.

20. Following consultations with the ICAO Ethics Officer on interim protection measures recommended by the external ethics entity, the President of the Council shall consider:

   a) taking immediate action to protect the complainant; and

   b) calling a meeting of the Council to consider any action to protect the interests of the Organization pending completion of the investigation by the investigative entity.

Action taken pursuant to this paragraph shall be appropriate, proportionate and restricted with regard to scope and duration to what is strictly necessary.

21. In cases referred to the Council for further consideration, pursuant to paragraphs 14b and 18b above, the President of the Council shall call a meeting of the Council, as soon as possible and no later than four weeks after referral. The President of the Council shall ensure that Council members receive, as soon as possible and no later than two weeks after referral, the investigation report delivered by the investigative entity and, where applicable, the reasoned determination and recommendations of the external ethics entity. Council members will be offered an opportunity, upon request, to confidentially review, a redacted version of the supporting documentation released by the investigative entity, before the Council meets to discuss the matter.

22. The President of the Council shall ensure that the Secretary General is given appropriate opportunity to reflect and comment on the investigation report delivered by the investigative entity and, where applicable, the reasoned determination and recommendations of the external ethics entity, before the Council commences its deliberations on substance.

Decision by the Council

23. The Council shall carefully consider the findings of the investigative entity and any recommendations from the external ethics entity, as well as the written response from the Secretary General to those findings and recommendations. The Council may call in assistance from an independent expert third party to review the findings and recommendations.

24. The Council shall deliberate in a closed session of Council members and/or their alternates only. The Council may decide to invite the external ethics entity and the investigative entity to attend the meeting. The Secretary General and the complainant shall each be afforded time and appropriate opportunity to present their case, verbally and in writing, before the Council takes a decision.

25. The Council shall decide on appropriate and proportionate action. The Council shall also substantiate and record its decision. The President of the Council shall separately inform the Secretary General and the complainant of the outcome. Decisions of the Council, as well as any closure notices received from the investigative entity and the external ethics entity pursuant to paragraphs 14a and 18a, shall be kept in the Office of the President of the Council.

26. Decisions taken by Council in such matters are final.

APPENDIX H

Rules and Procedures to address allegations of misconduct or retaliation against the President of the Council

The President of the Council shall be recused from any involvement in cases involving allegations of misconduct or retaliation against the President. The First Vice-President of the Council shall have the authority and duty to convene meetings of the Council regarding such cases. The First Vice-President of the Council shall pass on this responsibility to the Second Vice-President of the Council in cases where there may be a conflict of interest between the First Vice-President's own interests and the interests of the Organization.

Scope

1. In conformity with paragraph 1 of the ICAO Framework on Ethics (Annex I to the ICAO Service Code), these Rules and Procedures for addressing allegations of misconduct or retaliation against the President of the Council shall apply to all staff members of ICAO. They shall also apply mutatis mutandis to all non-staff personnel of ICAO, including, but not limited to gratis personnel, consultants, experts, interns and individuals working for ICAO under a contractual relationship.

Investigative entity

2. ICAO shall enter into an agreement with an investigative entity within the United Nations system, such as the United Nations Office of Internal Oversight Services (OIOS), or a similar expert entity, to establish a mechanism for the reporting and handling of allegations of misconduct committed by the President of the Council. In principle, this should be the same investigative entity engaged as a mechanism for the reporting and handling of all cases of misconduct committed by staff members of the

Organization, as defined in the ICAO Framework on Ethics (Annex I to the ICAO Service Code). The agreement should address inter alia the issue of access by the investigative entity to documents and records.

3. The Council delegates to the investigative entity the responsibility to receive, assess, investigate, close, and report on any allegations of misconduct against the President of the Council, without the need to request further authorization from the Council.

External ethics entity

4. ICAO shall enter into an agreement with an external ethics entity within the United Nations system, such as the United Nations Ethics Office, or similar expert entity, to establish a mechanism for the direct reporting and handling of complaints of retaliation committed by the President of the Council. In principle, this should be the same external ethics entity engaged to review determinations by the Ethics Officer that there was no prima facie case of retaliation or threat of retaliation.

5. The Council delegates to the external ethics entity the responsibility to receive, assess, close and report on any requests by staff members for protection against retaliation by the President of the Council, without the need to request further authorization from the Council.

Misconduct

6. For the purposes of these Rules and Procedures, misconduct is defined as the noncompliance, through acts or omissions, with the President's obligations under the Convention on International Civil Aviation (Chicago Convention) and the Code of Conduct for the President of the Council and the Secretary General of ICAO and the principles and values of the ICAO Framework on Ethics. Misconduct is also disregard for the standards of conduct expected from an international civil servant as defined by the International Civil Service Commission (ICSC) and other relevant administrative issuances such as those on anti-fraud and anti-corruption, protection against sexual exploitation and abuse and prevention of sexual harassment.

Reporting alleged cases of misconduct by the President of the Council

7. Staff members should report any allegations of misconduct against the President of the Council directly to the investigative entity according to instructions provided on the public websites of the investigative entity and ICAO.

8. Notwithstanding the provisions of paragraph 7, staff members reporting allegations of misconduct in relation to any administrative decisions in which the President of the Council is involved that are of direct concern to them shall as a rule first avail themselves of the appropriate appeal mechanisms available to them under Article XI of the ICAO Service Code, before reporting such cases to the investigative entity.

Protection against retaliation by the President of the Council

9. Staff members should submit any requests for protection against retaliation by the President of the Council directly to the external ethics entity according to instructions provided on the public websites of the external ethics entity and ICAO. Staff members should consider that the primary objective of the provisions on retaliation is to provide enhanced protection to individuals who have reported behaviour that poses a significant risk to the Organization, i.e. a report that, if established, would be manifestly harmful to the interests, operations or governance of the Organization. Such reports should be made in the public interest and not stem from personal disagreements over policy or management decisions or individual grievances.

Responsibilities of staff reporting allegations of misconduct

10. Staff members reporting allegations of misconduct by the President of the Council, or requesting protection against retaliation, should only do so in good faith and must provide credible arguments supporting their claims. Claims must be supported by evidence that includes documents and records, verbal statements and even tangible items, or the physical condition of those items. Staff members reporting complaints of misconduct shall adhere to the confidentiality of the process and cooperate in good faith with a subsequent investigation.

11. Reporting shall not be used to transmit or disseminate unsubstantiated rumours and must respect the appropriate reporting channels as outlined in paragraphs 7, 8 and 9 above. Making a report or providing information that is deliberately false or misleading constitutes misconduct. The transmission or dissemination of unsubstantiated rumours is not a protected activity. Making a report or providing information that is intentionally false or misleading constitutes misconduct and may result in disciplinary or other appropriate action.

Responsibilities of the investigative entity in cases of misconduct

12. The investigative entity will receive, promptly log, assess and take appropriate action on all incoming complaints of misconduct, while ensuring the confidentiality and integrity of the entire process.

13. Upon receiving and assessing allegations of misconduct against the President of the Council, the investigative entity shall, where possible within three weeks of receiving such reports or information:

a) close the case due to insufficient information, obviously frivolous claims, or because the matter falls outside the scope of a typical investigation conducted by the investigative entity and inform the complainant; or

b) notify the First Vice-President of the Council of its intention to launch an investigation into the allegations. Where there is a credible allegation of misconduct, the investigative entity shall interview the President of the Council and offer an opportunity to comment on the transcript of that interview before closing the case, or completing the investigation and delivering its report.

14. After investigating the allegations, the investigative entity shall:

a) close the case when misconduct is not substantiated, provide a closure notice to the First Vice-President of the Council and inform the complainant; or

b) refer the matter, including an investigation report and supporting documentation, to the First Vice-President of the Council for further consideration by the Council.

15. The investigative entity shall, on or before 31 January of each year, provide to the Council an annual report of all cases of misconduct handled on behalf of ICAO within the preceding year. The annual report shall contain sufficient details of the cases, while respecting the utmost confidentiality and privacy rights. It shall contain a redacted summary of investigations, and the findings and recommendations arising from such investigations pertaining to systemic improvement. The annual report should also contain information on the timelines, as appropriate, from initial intake to assessment, investigation, closure and reporting.

Responsibilities of the external ethics entity in cases involving retaliation by the President of the Council

16. The provisions on protection against retaliation are without prejudice to the legitimate application of regulations, rules and administrative procedures, including those governing evaluation of performance, non-extension or termination of appointment.

17. Upon receiving and assessing a request for protection against retaliation, the external ethics entity shall, where possible within three weeks of receiving such a request:

a) close the case if there is no prima facie case of retaliation and inform the complainant; or

b) refer the case for investigation by the investigative entity, notify the First Vice-President of the Council and, where appropriate, make recommendations for interim protection measures.

18. Upon completion of the investigation into retaliation, normally within 90 calendar days of referral, the investigative entity shall submit its investigation report to the external ethics entity. The external ethics entity shall conduct an independent review of the investigation report and supporting documentation and determine whether:

a) retaliation did not occur, in which case it shall close the case, provide a closure notice to the President of the Council and inform the complainant; or

b) retaliation occurred, in which case it shall refer the matter to the First Vice-President of the Council for further consideration by the Council, including a reasoned determination and recommendations, accompanied by the investigation report and supporting documentation released by the investigative entity.

Responsibilities of the First Vice-President of the Council

19. The First Vice-President of the Council shall inform the Council and the President of the Council of complaints reported by the investigative entity and/or the external ethics entity, according to paragraphs 13b, 14a, 17b and 18a above. Details of any case, including the identities of claimants and witnesses, shall be kept strictly confidential.

20. Following consultation of the ICAO Ethics Officer on interim protection measures recommended by the external ethics entity, the First Vice-President of the Council shall consider:

a) taking immediate action to protect the complainant; and

b) calling a meeting of the Council to consider any action to protect the interests of the Organization pending completion of the investigation by the investigative entity.

Action taken pursuant to this paragraph shall be appropriate, proportionate and restricted with regard to scope and duration to what is strictly necessary.

21. In cases referred to the Council for further consideration, pursuant to paragraphs 14b and 18b above, the First Vice-President of the Council shall call a meeting of the Council, as soon as possible and no later than four weeks after referral. The First Vice-President of the Council shall ensure that Council members receive, as soon as possible and no later than two weeks after referral, the investigation report by the investigative entity and, where applicable, the reasoned determination and recommendations of the external ethics entity. Council members will be offered an opportunity, upon request, to confidentially review, a redacted version of the supporting documentation released by the investigative entity, before the Council meets to discuss the matter.

22. The First Vice-President of the Council shall ensure that the President of the Council is given appropriate opportunity to reflect and comment on the investigation report delivered by the investigative entity and, where applicable, the reasoned determination and recommendations of the external ethics entity, before the Council commences its deliberations on substance.

Decision by the Council

23. The Council shall carefully consider the findings of the investigative entity and any recommendations from the external ethics entity, as well as the written response from the President of the Council to those findings and recommendations. The Council may call in assistance from an independent expert third party to review the findings and recommendations.

24. The Council shall deliberate in closed session of Council members and/or their alternates only. The Council may decide to invite the external ethics entity and the investigative entity to attend the meeting. The President of the Council and the complainant shall each be afforded time and appropriate opportunity to present their case, verbally and in writing, before the Council takes a decision.

25. The Council shall decide on appropriate and proportionate action. The Council shall also substantiate and record its decision. The First Vice-President of the Council shall separately inform the President of the Council and the complainant of the outcome. Decisions of the Council, as well as any closure notices received from the investigative entity and the external ethics entity pursuant to paragraphs 14a and 18a, shall be kept in the Office of the President of the Council.

26. Decisions taken by Council in such matters are final.

APPENDIX I

Code of Conduct for the President of the Council and the Secretary General

1. The ICAO Council attaches utmost importance to promoting the highest standards of ethical behaviour and leadership in ICAO.

2. The Council recognizes that the legitimacy and credibility of the work undertaken by ICAO depends heavily on public trust and confidence. The heads of the Organization must lead by example. Their behaviour must be beyond reproach and promote an organizational culture of transparency, integrity and accountability.

3. The President of the Council and the Secretary General play a critical role in building a healthy and safe working environment, projecting a positive image of the Organization, and safeguarding its staff, resources and reputation.

4. Accordingly, the President of the Council and the Secretary General should respect and promote the highest standards of ethical behaviour. This includes observing and applying the present Code of Conduct and adhering to the principles and values of the ICAO Framework on Ethics (Annex I to the ICAO Service Code).

5. Allegations of misconduct or retaliation against the President of the Council and the Secretary General shall be handled according to the procedures outlined in Appendices G and H to these Rules of Procedure.

6. The President of the Council and the Secretary General shall perform their duties and responsibilities in an impartial and equitable manner, in full honesty and good faith.

7. The President of the Council and the Secretary General shall respect the same principles and values, standards of conduct, and ethical aspects of working relations, as outlined in the ICAO Service Code, with due consideration to their respective roles and leadership responsibilities within the Organization.

8. The President of the Council and the Secretary General shall avoid any action that might result in:

a) giving unwarranted preferential treatment to any State, organization, staff member, or third party;

b) taking a preferential, biased or prejudged approach in performing their duties;

c) affecting adversely the confidence of Member States, or of the public at large, in the integrity of the work of the Organization.

9. The President of the Council and the Secretary General shall avoid any situation involving a conflict between their own personal or private interests and the interests of the Organization.

10. The President of the Council and the Secretary General shall discharge their functions and regulate their conduct in the interest of ICAO only, engaging with Member States and other third parties in a cooperative manner, while at the same time refraining from receiving or accepting instructions from any government or third parties.

11. The President of the Council and the Secretary General shall ensure the greatest possible transparency and prudence in the utilization of ICAO property, premises, services and resources and shall ensure that they are used only in the interest of the Organization.

12. The President of the Council and the Secretary General shall commit themselves to issuing a statement of no conflict of interest on assuming their duties and respect the obligation to file an annual conflict of interest declaration and financial disclosure statement.

APPENDIX J

Approval of proposals by written procedure

1. Notwithstanding the other provisions of these Rules of Procedure, proposals of the President of the Council on routine matters, urgent matters and other matters to be tabled during the period between Sessions of the Council that require action by the Council, may be approved in accordance with the following:

   a) the President shall distribute to the Members of the Council a memorandum explaining the proposal;

   b) the Members of the Council shall be given a period of not less than five working days to indicate if they support or object to the proposal;

   c) in the absence of an objection by any Member of the Council, the proposal shall be deemed to have been approved by the Council;

   d) Should there be an objection by a Member of the Council, the President of the Council may:

      i) place the proposal on the Order of Business for the Council meeting subject to the relevant provisions of these Rules of Procedure; or

      ii) revise the proposal taking into account the reasons for the objection.

2. If the President decides to revise the proposal in terms of paragraph 1 (d) (ii), the proposal shall follow the same process as outlined in paragraph 1.

3. Notwithstanding the provisions of paragraph 2, and subject to paragraph 4), the proposal revised in terms of paragraph 1 (d) (ii) shall be deemed to have been approved by the Council if it is supported by the majority of the Members of the Council.

4. A Member of the Council may request a Council discussion on the matter resolved in terms of paragraph 3 within three working days of the formal notification. Such a request shall suspend the approval when supported by two or more other Members of the Council and the item shall be placed on the Order of Business of the ensuing Council meeting for consideration in accordance with the relevant provisions of these Rules of Procedure.

— END —

APPENDIX 4   RULES FOR THE SETTLEMENT OF DIFFERENCES

RULES
FOR THE
SETTLEMENT OF DIFFERENCES
Approved by the Council on 9 April 1957 and amended on 10 November 1975*

CHAPTER I

SCOPE OF RULES

Article 1

(1) The Rules of Parts I and III shall govern the settlement of the following disagreements between Contracting States which may be referred to the Council:

(*a*) Any disagreement between two or more Contracting States relating to the interpretation or application of the Convention on International Civil Aviation (hereinafter called "the Convention") and its Annexes (Articles 84 to 88 of the Convention);

(*b*) Any disagreement between two or more Contracting States relating to the interpretation or application of the International Air Services Transit Agreement and of the International Air Transport Agreement (hereinafter respectively called "Transit Agreement" and "Transport Agreement") (Article II, Section 2 of the Transit Agreement; Article IV, Section 3 of the Transport Agreement).

(2) The Rules of Parts II and III shall govern the consideration of any complaint regarding an action taken by a State party to the Transit Agreement and under that Agreement, which another State party to the same Agreement deems to cause injustice or hardship to it (Article II, Section 1), or regarding a similar action under the Transport Agreement (Article IV, Section 2).

Part I

CHAPTER II

DISAGREEMENTS

Article 2

Any Contracting State submitting a disagreement to the Council for settlement (hereinafter referred to as "the applicant") shall file an application to which shall be attached a memorial containing:

---

* *Amendment of Article 29 approved by the Council on 10 November 1975.*

(a) The name of the applicant and the name of any Contracting State with which the disagreement exists (the latter hereinafter referred to as "the respondent");

(b) The name of an agent authorized to act for the applicant in the proceedings, together with his address, at the seat of the Organization, to which all communications relating to the case, including notice of the date of any meeting, should be sent;

(c) A statement of relevant facts;

(d) Supporting data related to the facts;

(e) A statement of law;

(f) The relief desired by action of Council on the specific points submitted;

(g) A statement that negotiations to settle the disagreement had taken place between the parties but were not successful.

Chapter III

Action upon Receipt of Applications

Article 3

Action by Secretary General

(1) Upon receipt of an application, the Secretary General shall:

(a) Verify that it complies in form with the requirements of Article 2, and, if necessary, require the applicant to supply any deficiencies appearing therein;

(b) Immediately thereafter notify all parties to the instrument the interpretation or application of which is in question, as well as all Members of the Council, that the application has been received;

(c) Forward copies of the application and of the supporting documentation to the respondent, with an invitation to file a counter-memorial within a time-limit fixed by the Council.

(2) Copies of all subsequent pleadings or other documents submitted by a party to the Council shall similarly be forwarded by the Secretary General to the other party or parties in the case.

(a) The name of the applicant and the name of any Contracting State with which the disagreement exists (the latter hereinafter referred to as "the respondent");

(b) The name of an agent authorized to act for the applicant in the proceedings, together with his address, at the seat of the Organization, to which all communications relating to the case, including notice of the date of any meeting, should be sent;

(c) A statement of relevant facts;

(d) Supporting data related to the facts;

(e) A statement of law;

(f) The relief desired by action of Council on the specific points submitted;

(g) A statement that negotiations to settle the disagreement had taken place between the parties but were not successful.

CHAPTER III

ACTION UPON RECEIPT OF APPLICATIONS

Article 3

Action by Secretary General

(1) Upon receipt of an application, the Secretary General shall:

(a) Verify that it complies in form with the requirements of Article 2, and, if necessary, require the applicant to supply any deficiencies appearing therein;

(b) Immediately thereafter notify all parties to the instrument the interpretation or application of which is in question, as well as all Members of the Council, that the application has been received;

(c) Forward copies of the application and of the supporting documentation to the respondent, with an invitation to file a counter-memorial within a time-limit fixed by the Council.

(2) Copies of all subsequent pleadings or other documents submitted by a party to the Council shall similarly be forwarded by the Secretary General to the other party or parties in the case.

(2) If it is decided not to invite direct negotiations at this stage, without prejudice to a later invitation as provided in Article 14, the Council shall decide which procedure under these Rules is applicable. Unless the Council decides to undertake the preliminary examination of the matter itself, it shall appoint a Committee (hereinafter referred to as "the Committee") of five individuals who shall be Representatives on the Council of Member States not concerned in the disagreement, and shall designate one of them as Chairman.

(3) The decisions under (2), in cases where negotiations are invited, may be postponed until the parties have either refused to enter into negotiations or reported that the negotiations have failed to solve the dispute.

CHAPTER IV

PROCEEDINGS

Article 7

Written proceedings

(1) The additional pleadings which may be filed by the parties shall consist of:

— Reply to be filed by the applicant,

— Rejoinder to be filed by the respondent.

(2) The pleadings shall be filed with the Secretary General within time-limits fixed.

(3) There shall be annexed to every pleading, copies or originals of all the relevant documents which the party filing the pleading may wish to have considered.

(4) After the filing of the last pleading, save in the case of the submission of written evidence pursuant to Article 9 or of observations in writing pursuant to Article 19 (5), no further documents may be submitted by any party except with the consent of the other party or by permission of the Council granted after hearing the parties.

Article 8

Investigations by Council

(1) The Council may at any time, but after hearing the parties, entrust any individual, body, bureau, commission, or other organization that it may select, with the task of carrying out an enquiry or giving an expert opinion. In such cases it shall define the subject of enquiry or expert opinion and prescribe the procedure to be followed.

(2) A report incorporating the results of the investigation, together with the record of the enquiry and any expert opinion, shall be submitted to the Council in such form, if any, as the Council may have prescribed, and shall be communicated to the parties.

Article 9

Evidence

If the parties should desire to produce evidence in addition to any evidence produced with the pleadings, such evidence, including testimony of witnesses and experts, shall be submitted in writing, within a time-limit fixed by the Council, but on special application the Council may agree to receive oral testimony. The Council may also request the parties to call witnesses or experts to give testimony before it at an oral hearing.

Article 10

Declaration by witnesses and experts

(1) The testimony of a witness shall be verified by the following declaration:

"I solemnly declare upon my honour and conscience that my testimony contains the truth, the whole truth and nothing but the truth."

(2) The statement of an expert shall be verified by the following declaration:

"I solemnly declare upon my honour and conscience that my statement is in accordance with my sincere belief."

Article 11

Questions

At the oral hearing, any Member of the Council not a party to the dispute may put questions, through the President, to the agents of the parties or to any counsel or advocate appearing for them. Such questions, if any, may be answered immediately or at a later date to be fixed by the Council.

Article 12

Arguments

(1) Upon completion of the evidence, and after a reasonable period for preparation by the parties, they may present arguments to the Council within time-limits fixed by it.

(2) The final arguments shall be in writing, but oral arguments may be admitted at the discretion of the Council.

Article 13

Procedure before the Committee

(1) If under Article 6 of the present Rules a Committee has been appointed, it shall, on behalf of the Council, receive and examine all documents submitted in accordance with these Rules and, in its discretion, hear evidence or oral arguments, and generally deal with the case with a view to action being taken by the Council under Article 15. The procedures governing the examination of the case by the Committee shall be those prescribed for the Council when it examines the matter itself. While the Committee has charge of the proceedings, the functions of the President of the Council under these Rules shall be exercised by the Chairman of the Committee.

(2) Thereafter the Committee shall, without undue delay, present to the Council a report which shall be a part of the record of the proceedings. The report shall include a summary of the evidence and other matters on record and the findings of facts and the recommendations of the Committee.

(3) The Council shall cause a copy of the report of the Committee to be delivered to each party in the case and each of the parties may, within a time-limit fixed by the Council, submit to the Council its written observations on the said report or, if permitted by the Council, its oral observations.

(4) When considering the report of the Committee, the Council may make such further enquiries as it may think fit or obtain additional evidence.

Article 14

Negotiations during proceedings

(1) The Council may, at any time during the proceedings and prior to the meeting at which the decision is rendered as provided in Article 15 (4), invite the parties to the dispute to engage in direct negotiations, if the Council deems that the possibilities of settling the dispute or narrowing the issues through negotiations have not been exhausted.

(2) If the parties accept the invitation to negotiate, the Council may set a time-limit for the completion of such negotiations, during which other proceedings on the merits shall be suspended.

(3) Subject to the consent of the parties concerned, the Council may render any assistance likely to further the negotiations, including the designation of an individual or a group of individuals to act as conciliator during the negotiations.

(4) Any solution agreed through negotiations shall be recorded by Council. If no solution is found the parties shall so report to Council and the suspended proceedings shall be resumed.

Article 15
Decision

(1) After hearing arguments, or after consideration of the report of the Committee, as the case may be, the Council shall render its decision.

(2) The decision of the Council shall be in writing and shall contain:

    (*i*) the date on which it is delivered;

    (*ii*) a list of the Members of the Council participating;

    (*iii*) the names of the parties and of their agents;

    (*iv*) a summary of the proceedings;

    (*v*) the conclusions of the Council together with its reasons for reaching them;

    (*vi*) its decision, if any, in regard to costs;

    (*vii*) a statement of the voting in Council showing whether the conclusions were unanimous or by a majority vote, and if by a majority, giving the number of Members of the Council who voted in favour of the conclusions and the number of those who voted against or abstained.

(3) Any Member of the Council who voted against the majority opinion may have its views recorded in the form of a dissenting opinion which shall be attached to the decision of Council.

(4) The decision of the Council shall be rendered at a meeting of the Council called for that purpose which shall be held as soon as practicable after the close of the proceedings.

(5) No Member of the Council shall vote in the consideration by the Council of any dispute to which it is a party.

Article 16
Default of appearance or in defending

(1) If one of the parties does not appear before the Council or the Committee, if any, set up under Article 6, or fails to defend its case, the other party may call upon the Council to decide in favour of its claim.

(2) The Council must, before doing so, satisfy itself not only that it has jurisdiction in the matter but also that the claim is well founded in fact and law.

Article 17
Discontinuance

(1) If in the course of the proceedings the applicant informs the Council in writing that it is not going on with the proceedings, and if, at the date on which this communication is received by the Secretary General, the respondent has not yet taken any step in the proceedings, the Council, or its President if the

Council is not in session, will officially record the discontinuance of the proceedings, and the Secretary General shall inform the respondent accordingly.

(2) If, at the time when the notice of discontinuance is received, the respondent has already taken some step in the proceedings, the Council, or its President if the Council is not sitting, shall fix a time-limit within which the respondent must state whether it objects to the discontinuance of the proceedings. If no objection is so made, acquiescence will be presumed and the Council, or its President if the Council is not sitting, will officially record the discontinuance of the proceedings. If objection is made, the proceedings shall continue.

Article 18
Notification and appeal

(1) The decision of the Council shall be notified forthwith to all parties concerned and shall be published. A copy of the decision shall also be communicated to all States previously notified under Article 3 (1) (*b*).

(2) Decisions rendered on cases submitted under Article 1 (1) (*a*) and (*b*) are subject to appeal pursuant to Article 84 of the Convention. Any such appeal shall be notified to the Council through the Secretary General within sixty days of receipt of notification of the decision of the Council.

Article 19
Intervention

(1) Any State which is a party to the particular instrument, the interpretation or application of which has been made the subject of a dispute under these Rules, and which is directly affected by the dispute, has the right to intervene in the proceedings, but if it uses this right it shall undertake that the decision of the Councill will be equally binding upon it.

(2) Any State which desires to intervene in a disagreement shall forthwith file a declaration to that effect with the Secretary General.

(3) Such declaration shall be communicated to the parties to the instrument concerned. If within a month of the despatch of this communication, any objection has been notified to the Secretary General with respect to the admissibility of an intervention under paragraph (1) of this Article, the decision shall rest with the Council.

(4) If no objection has been notified within the above-mentioned period or if the Council decides in favour of the admissibility of an intervention, as the case may be, the Secretary General shall take the necessary steps to make the documents of the case available to the intervening party who may file a memorial within a time-limit to be fixed by the Council, in no event later than the date fixed for the filing of the last pleading referred to in Article 7 (4).

(5) Any such memorial shall be communicated to the other parties to the disagreement who shall send to the Secretary General their observations in writing within a time-limit to be fixed by the Council. The memorial and observations may be discussed by the parties in the course of the subsequent proceedings in which the intervening party shall take part.

Article 20
Dismissal of proceedings

(1) (a) If at any time before a decision is reached the parties conclude an agreement for the settlement of the dispute, or agree to discontinue the proceedings, they shall so inform the Council in writing. The Council shall then officially record the conclusion of the settlement or the discontinuance of the proceedings.

(b) In the event that the original parties to a dispute conclude such an agreement, the Council shall terminate the proceedings notwithstanding the fact that additional parties have intervened. This provision does not affect the right of an intervening party to file an application on its own behalf respecting the subject matter of the original dispute.

(2) In case the termination of the proceedings is pursuant to a settlement between the parties, the terms of the settlement shall be transmitted to the President of the Council and he shall communicate such terms to all States previously notified under Article 3 (1) (b).

Part II

CHAPTER V
COMPLAINTS

Article 21
Form of request

Any Contracting State submitting a complaint to the Council regarding a situation defined in Article 1 (2) of these Rules shall file a request to which shall be attached a memorial containing the same particulars as in the case of an application submitted under Article 2.

Article 22
Action upon receipt of requests

Articles 3 (1) (a) and (c), 4 and 5 of Chapter III of Part I (*Action upon receipt of Applications*) shall apply correspondingly to a request submitted under the preceding Article.

Article 23

Appointment of Committee

(1) Upon the filing of the counter-memorial the Council shall meet and formally decide whether the matter falls under the category of complaints under the provisions listed in Article 1 (2).

(2) The Council shall, if the answer under (1) is in the affirmative, appoint a Committee composed as the Committee described in Article 6 (2) of these Rules.

Article 24

Proceedings before Committee

(1) The Committee shall thereupon inquire into the matter on behalf of the Council and shall call the States concerned into consultation.

(2) The Committee shall arrange the procedures for the consultation as far as possible in agreement with the parties, and on an informal basis in accordance with the circumstances of each case. It may request additional information and summon representatives of the parties to meet with the Committee at the seat of the Organization or in any other place.

Article 25

Report of Committee

(1) The Committee shall report to Council on the outcome of the consultation held as expeditiously as possible.

(2) If the consultation has failed to resolve the difficulty the report may include proposed findings and recommendations to the States concerned.

Article 26

Council Action

(1) After receiving the report of the Committee the Council shall consider it.

(2) If a settlement has been reached through consultation the terms of the settlement shall be recorded and communicated to all States notified of the proceedings.

(3) If consultation has failed to resolve the difficulty the Council may make appropriate findings and recommendations to the States concerned. Article 15 shall apply, *mutatis mutandis*, in this case.

Part III

CHAPTER VI

GENERAL PROVISIONS

Article 27

Agents

(1) A State which becomes a party to the proceedings on disagreements or complaints under these Rules shall name an agent authorized to represent it and to act for it in the proceedings, provided that a Representative on the Council of any Member State shall not be nominated as an agent.

(2) The agent may have the assistance of counsel or advocates. The name of any assisting counsel or advocate shall be communicated to the Council in advance of any meeting where he will be present.

(3) The agents shall be invited to attend any meeting convened to discuss the case.

Article 28

Procedural measures

(1) The Council shall determine the time-limits to be applied, and other procedural questions related to the proceedings. Any time-limit fixed pursuant to these Rules shall be so fixed as to avoid any possible delays and to ensure fair treatment of the party or parties concerned.

(2) The Council may at any time extend any time-limit that has been fixed under these Rules, either at the request of any of the parties or at its own discretion. It may also in special circumstances and after hearing objections from any party, decide that any step taken after the expiration of a time-limit shall be considered as valid.

(3) In respect of fixing or extending a time-limit under these Rules, the President of the Council shall act on behalf of the Council when it is not in session.

Article 29

Languages

(1) A party may make its submissions, written or oral, in any of the four working languages of the Organization and, at the request of any of the other parties, these shall be translated into each of the other languages under arrangements to be made by the Secretary General. The Council may at the request of any party authorize another language to be used by that party, in which case the necessary arrangements for translation shall be made by the party concerned.

(2) The text of the decision of the Council in case of a disagreement, or its findings and recommendations in case of a complaint, shall be rendered in the four working languages, and each of such texts shall be of equal authenticity unless all the parties agree that any of the texts shall be considered as the authentic one.

Article 30

Records and publicity

(1) The Secretary General shall keep a full record of the proceedings.

(2) A verbatim transcript shall be made of any oral testimony and any oral arguments and incorporated into the record of the proceedings.

(3) The record of the proceedings shall, unless otherwise ordered by the Council, be open to the public. The Council may open to the public any part of the record previously ordered to be withheld from the public.

Article 31

Costs

(1) Unless otherwise decided by the Council, each party shall bear its own costs.

(2) All other costs may be assessed to the parties in proportions fixed by the Council.

Article 32

Suspension of the Rules

Subject to agreement of the parties, any of these Rules may be varied or their application suspended when, in the opinion of the Council, such action would lead to a more expeditious or effective disposition of the case.

Article 33

Amendments to the Rules

The present Rules may, at any time, be amended by the Council. No amendment shall apply to a pending case except with the agreement of the parties.

END

Appendix 5   List of the Nationality Marks of Aircraft

**AIRCRAFT NATIONALITY MARKS, NATIONAL EMBLEMS
AND COMMON MARKS**

1. Aircraft nationality marks as notified to ICAO

Nationality marks arranged alphabetically by State

State	Mark
Afghanistan	YA
Algeria	7T
Angola	D2
Antigua and Barbuda	V2
Argentina	LQ, LV
Armenia	EK
Australia	VH
Austria	OE
Azerbaijan	4K
Bahamas	C6
Bahrain	A9C
Bangladesh	S2
Barbados	8P
Belarus	EW
Belgium	OO
Belize	V3
Benin	TY
Bhutan	A5
Bolivia (Plurinational State of)	CP
Bosnia and Herzegovina	E7
Botswana	A2
Brazil	PP, PR, PS, PT, PU
Brunei Darussalam	V8
Bulgaria	LZ
Burkina Faso	XT
Burundi	9U
Cabo Verde	D4
Cambodia	XU
Cameroon	TJ
Canada	C, CF
Central African Republic	TL
Chad	TT
Chile	CC
China (including Hong Kong SAR and Macao SAR)	B
Colombia	HJ, HK
Comoros	D6
Congo	TN
Cook Islands	E5
Costa Rica	TI
Côte d'Ivoire	TU
Croatia	9A
Cuba	CU
Cyprus	5B
Czechia	OK
Democratic People's Republic of Korea*	P
Democratic Republic of the Congo	9Q
Denmark	OY
Djibouti	J2
Dominica	J7
Dominican Republic	HI
Ecuador	HC
Egypt	SU
El Salvador	YS
Equatorial Guinea	3C
Eritrea	E3
Estonia	ES
Eswatini	3DC
Ethiopia	ET
Fiji	DQ
Finland	OH
France	F
Gabon	TR
Gambia	C5
Georgia	4L
Germany	D
Ghana	9G, 9GR
Greece	SX
Grenada	J3
Guatemala	TG
Guinea	3X
Guinea-Bissau	J5
Guyana	8R
Haiti	HH
Honduras	HR
Hungary	HA
Iceland	TF

* This mark differs from the provision in 3.3 of this Annex.

1/12/22

India	VT	Netherlands Antilles	PJ
Indonesia	PK	New Zealand	ZK, ZL, ZM
Iran (Islamic Republic of)	EP	Nicaragua	YN
Iraq	YI	Niger	5U
Ireland	EI, EJ	Nigeria	5N
Israel	4X, 4Z	North Macedonia	Z3
Italy	I	Norway	LN
Jamaica	6Y	Oman	A4O
Japan	JA		
Jordan	JY	Pakistan	AP
		Palau	T8
Kazakhstan	UP	Panama	HP
Kenya	5Y	Papua New Guinea	P2
Kuwait	9K	Paraguay	ZP
Kyrgyzstan	EX	Peru	OB
		Philippines*	RP
Lao People's Democratic Republic*	RDPL	Poland	SP
Latvia	YL	Portugal	CR, CS
Lebanon	OD		
Lesotho	7P	Qatar	A7
Liberia	A8		
Libya	5A	Republic of Korea	HL
Liechtenstein	HB plus national emblem	Republic of Moldova	ER
Lithuania	LY	Romania	YR
Luxembourg	LX	Russian Federation	RA
		Rwanda	9XR
Madagascar	5R		
Malawi	7Q	Saint Kitts and Nevis	V4
Malaysia	9M	Saint Lucia	J6
Maldives	8Q	Saint Vincent and the Grenadines	J8
Mali	TZ	Samoa	5W
Malta	9H	San Marino	T7
Marshall Islands	V7	Sao Tome and Principe	S9
Mauritania	5T	Saudi Arabia	HZ
Mauritius	3B	Senegal	6V, 6W
Mexico	XA, XB, XC plus national emblem	Serbia	YU
Micronesia (Federated States of)	V6	Seychelles	S7
Monaco	3A	Sierra Leone	9L
Mongolia	JU	Singapore	9V
Montenegro	4O	Slovakia	OM
Morocco	CN	Slovenia	S5
Mozambique	C9	Solomon Islands	H4
Myanmar	XY, XZ	Somalia	6O
		South Africa	ZS, ZT, ZU
Namibia	V5	Spain	EC
Nauru	C2	Sri Lanka	4R
Nepal	9N	Sudan	ST
Netherlands	PH	Suriname	PZ
Aruba	P4	Sweden	SE

---

* This mark differs from the provision in 3.3 of this Annex.

1/12/22

Switzerland	HB plus national emblem	Gibraltar	VP-G
Syrian Arab Republic	YK	Isle of Man	M
		Jersey	ZJ
Tajikistan	EY	Montserrat	VP-M
Thailand	HS	St. Helena/Ascension	VQ-H
Togo	5V	Turks and Caicos	VQ-T
Tonga	A3	Virgin Islands	VP-L
Trinidad and Tobago	9Y	United Republic of Tanzania	5H
Tunisia	TS	United States	N
Türkiye	TC	Uruguay	CX
Turkmenistan	EZ	Uzbekistan	UK
Uganda	5X	Vanuatu	YJ
Ukraine	UR	Venezuela (Bolivarian Republic of)	YV
United Arab Emirates	A6	Viet Nam	XV
United Kingdom	G		
Anguilla	VP-A	Yemen	7O
Bailiwick of Guernsey	2		
Bermuda	VP-B, VQ-B	Zambia	9J
Cayman Islands	VP-C	Zimbabwe*	Z
Falkland Islands (Malvinas)	VP-F		

Nationality marks arranged alphanumerically

AP	Pakistan	D	Germany
A2	Botswana	DQ	Fiji
A3	Tonga	D2	Angola
A4O	Oman	D4	Cabo Verde
A5	Bhutan	D6	Comoros
A6	United Arab Emirates		
A7	Qatar	EC	Spain
A8	Liberia	EI, EJ	Ireland
A9C	Bahrain	EK	Armenia
		EP	Iran (Islamic Republic of)
B	China (including Hong Kong SAR and Macao SAR)	ER	Republic of Moldova
		ES	Estonia
C, CF	Canada	ET	Ethiopia
CC	Chile	EW	Belarus
CN	Morocco	EX	Kyrgyzstan
CP	Bolivia (Plurinational State of)	EY	Tajikistan
CR, CS	Portugal	EZ	Turkmenistan
CU	Cuba	E3	Eritrea
CX	Uruguay	E5	Cook Islands
C2	Nauru	E7	Bosnia and Herzegovina
C5	Gambia		
C6	Bahamas	F	France
C9	Mozambique		

---

* This mark differs from the provision in 3.3 of this Annex.

G	United Kingdom
HA	Hungary
HB plus national emblem	Liechtenstein
HB plus national emblem	Switzerland
HC	Ecuador
HH	Haiti
HI	Dominican Republic
HJ, HK	Colombia
HL	Republic of Korea
HP	Panama
HR	Honduras
HS	Thailand
HZ	Saudi Arabia
H4	Solomon Islands
I	Italy
JA	Japan
JU	Mongolia
JY	Jordan
J2	Djibouti
J3	Grenada
J5	Guinea-Bissau
J6	Saint Lucia
J7	Dominica
J8	Saint Vincent and the Grenadines
LN	Norway
LQ, LV	Argentina
LX	Luxembourg
LY	Lithuania
LZ	Bulgaria
M	Isle of Man (United Kingdom)
N	United States
OB	Peru
OD	Lebanon
OE	Austria
OH	Finland
OK	Czechia
OM	Slovakia
OO	Belgium
OY	Denmark
P	Democratic People's Republic of Korea*
PH	Netherlands
PJ	Netherlands Antilles (Netherlands)
PK	Indonesia
PP, PR, PS, PT, PU	Brazil
PZ	Suriname
P2	Papua New Guinea
P4	Aruba (Netherlands)
RA	Russian Federation
RDPL	Lao People's Democratic Republic*
RP	Philippines*
SE	Sweden
SP	Poland
ST	Sudan
SU	Egypt
SX	Greece
S2	Bangladesh
S5	Slovenia
S7	Seychelles
S9	Sao Tome and Principe
TC	Türkiye
TF	Iceland
TG	Guatemala
TI	Costa Rica
TJ	Cameroon
TL	Central African Republic
TN	Congo
TR	Gabon
TS	Tunisia
TT	Chad
TU	Côte d'Ivoire
TY	Benin
TZ	Mali
T7	San Marino
T8	Palau
UK	Uzbekistan
UP	Kazakhstan
UR	Ukraine
VH	Australia
VP-A	Anguilla (United Kingdom)
VP-B, VQ-B	Bermuda (United Kingdom)
VP-C	Cayman Islands (United Kingdom)
VP-F	Falkland Islands (Malvinas) (United Kingdom)
VP-G	Gibraltar (United Kingdom)
VP-L	Virgin Islands (United Kingdom)
VP-M	Montserrat (United Kingdom)
VQ-B, VP-B	Bermuda (United Kingdom)
VQ-H	St. Helena/Ascension (United Kingdom)
VQ-T	Turks and Caicos (United Kingdom)
VT	India

---

* This mark differs from the provision in 3.3 of this Annex.

1/12/22

V2	Antigua and Barbuda	4O	Montenegro
V3	Belize	4R	Sri Lanka
V4	Saint Kitts and Nevis	4X, 4Z	Israel
V5	Namibia		
V6	Micronesia (Federated States of)	5A	Libya
V7	Marshall Islands	5B	Cyprus
V8	Brunei Darussalam	5H	United Republic of Tanzania
		5N	Nigeria
XA, XB, XC plus national emblem	Mexico	5R	Madagascar
XT	Burkina Faso	5T	Mauritania
XU	Cambodia	5U	Niger
XV	Viet Nam	5V	Togo
XY, XZ	Myanmar	5W	Samoa
		5X	Uganda
YA	Afghanistan	5Y	Kenya
YI	Iraq		
YJ	Vanuatu	6O	Somalia
YK	Syrian Arab Republic	6V, 6W	Senegal
YL	Latvia	6Y	Jamaica
YN	Nicaragua		
YR	Romania	7O	Yemen
YS	El Salvador	7P	Lesotho
YU	Serbia	7Q	Malawi
YV	Venezuela (Bolivarian Republic of)	7T	Algeria
Z	Zimbabwe*	8P	Barbados
ZJ	Jersey (United Kingdom)	8Q	Maldives
ZK, ZL, ZM	New Zealand	8R	Guyana
ZP	Paraguay		
ZS, ZT, ZU	South Africa	9A	Croatia
Z3	North Macedonia	9G, 9GR	Ghana
		9H	Malta
2	Bailiwick of Guernsey (United Kingdom)	9J	Zambia
		9K	Kuwait
3A	Monaco	9L	Sierra Leone
3B	Mauritius	9M	Malaysia
3C	Equatorial Guinea	9N	Nepal
3DC	Eswatini	9Q	Democratic Republic of the Congo
3X	Guinea	9U	Burundi
		9V	Singapore
4K	Azerbaijan	9XR	Rwanda
4L	Georgia	9Y	Trinidad and Tobago

---

* This mark differs from the provision in 3.3 of this Annex.

Appendix 6   ICAO Illustration of the "Freedoms of the Air"

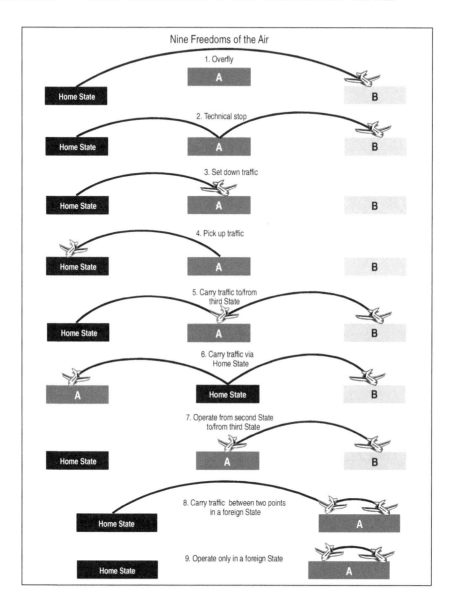

* Compare ICAO Doc. 9626, 3rd. edition (2018) at Part IV. Chapter 2, IV-2-11.

Bibliography of Documents

1   General Public Law Treaties

- Covenant of the League of Nations (Versailles, 28 June 1919), 1 UNTS
- Convention Relating to the Regulation of Aerial Navigation (Paris, 13 October 1919), LNTS, 173
- Proceedings of the International Civil Aviation Conference, Chicago, Illinois, November 1-December 7, 1944, Vol. I and II (Washington D.C., The Department of State, 1948)
- Charter of the United Nations and Statute of the International Court of Justice (San Francisco, 26 June 1945)
- Antarctic Treaty (Washington, D.C., 1 December 1959)
- Vienna Convention on the Law of Treaties (23 May 1969), 1155 UNTS 331 (1980)
- UN Convention on the Law of the Sea (Montego Bay, 10 December 1982), 1833 UNTS 3
- Agreement between the United Nations and ICAO, (New York, 3 October 1947), ICAO Doc 7970

2   ICAO Public and Private Air Law Treaties

a) International Instruments

- Convention on International Civil Aviation (Chicago, 7 December 1944, ICAO Doc 7300/9
- International Air Services Transit Agreement (Chicago, 7 December 1944) ICAO Doc 7500
- International Air Transport Agreement (Chicago, 7 December 1944), Proceedings of the International Civil Aviation Conference, Vol. I
- Convention for the Unification of Certain Rules relating to International Carriage by Air (Warsaw, 12 October 1929), ICAO Doc 7838
- Convention on the International Recognition of Rights in Aircraft (Geneva, 19 June 1948) ICAO Doc 7620
- Convention on Damage Caused by Foreign Aircraft to Third Parties on the Surface (Rome, 7 October 1952), ICAO Doc 7364

- Protocol to Amend the Convention for the Unification of Certain Rules Relating to International Carriage by Air Signed at Warsaw on 12 October 1929 (The Hague, 28 September 1955), ICAO Doc 7632
- Convention, Supplementary to the Warsaw Convention, for the Unification of Certain Rules Relating to International Carriage by Air Performed by a Person Other than the Contracting Carrier (Guadalajara, 18 September 1961), ICAO Doc 8181
- Convention on Offences and Certain Other Acts Committed on Board Aircraft (Tokyo, 14 September 1963), ICAO Doc 8364
- Convention for the Suppression of Unlawful Seizure of Aircraft (The Hague, 16 December 1970), ICAO Doc 8920
- Protocol to Amend the Convention for the Unification of certain Rules Relating to International Carriage by Air signed at Warsaw on 12 October 1929 as amended by the Protocol done at The Hague on 28 September 1955 (Guatemala City, 8 March 1971), ICAO Doc 8932
- Convention for the Suppression of Unlawful Acts Against the Safety of Civil Aviation (Montreal, 23 September 1971), ICAO Doc 8966
- Additional protocol No. 1 to amend the Convention for the Unification of Certain Rules Relating to International Carriage by Air signed on 12 October 1929 (Montreal, 25 September 1975), ICAO Doc 9145
- Additional Protocol No. 2 to Amend the Convention for the Unification of Certain Rules Relating to International Carriage by Air signed at Warsaw on 12 October 1929 as amended by the Protocol done at The Hague on 28 September 1975 (Montreal, 25 September 1975), ICAO Doc 9146
- Additional Protocol No. 3 to Amend the Convention for the Unification of Certain Rules Relating to International Carriage by Air signed at Warsaw on 12 October 1929 as amended by the Protocols done at The Hague on 28 September 1955 and Guatemala City on 8 March 1971 (Montreal, 25 September 1975), ICAO Doc 9147
- Additional Protocol No. 4 to Amend the Convention for the Unification of Certain Rules Relating to International Carriage by Air signed at Warsaw on 12 September 1929 as amended at The Hague on 28 September 1955 (Montreal, 25 September 1975), ICAO Doc 9148
- Protocol for the Suppression of Unlawful Acts of Violence at Airports Serving International Civil Aviation, Supplementary to the Convention for the Suppression of Unlawful Acts Against the Safety of Civil Aviation, done at Montreal on 23 September 1971 (Montreal, 24 February 1988), ICAO Doc 9518
- Protocol to Amend the Convention on Damage Caused by Foreign Aircraft to Third Parties on the Surface (Montreal, 23 September 1978), ICAO Doc 9257
- Agreement on the Joint Financing of Certain Air Navigation Services in Greenland (1956) as amended by the Montreal Protocol of 1982, ICAO Doc 9585

- Agreement on the Joint Financing of Certain Air Navigation Services in Iceland (1956) as amended by the Montreal Protocol of 1982, ICAO Doc 9586
- Convention on the Marking of Plastic Explosives for the Purpose of Detection (Montreal, 1 March 1991), ICAO Doc 9571
- Convention on the Unification of Certain Rules for the International Carriage by Air (Montreal, 28 May 1999), ICAO Doc 9740
- Convention on International Interests in Mobile Equipment (Cape Town, 16 November 2001), ICAO Doc 9793
- Protocol to the Convention on International Interests in Mobile Equipment on Matters Specific to Aircraft Equipment (Cape Town, 16 November 2001), ICAO Doc 9794
- Consolidated Text of the Convention on International Interests in Mobile Equipment and the Protocol to the Convention on International Interests in Mobile Equipment on Matters Specific to Aircraft Equipment (Cape Town, 16 November 2001), ICAO Doc 9795
- Convention on Compensation for Damage Caused by Aircraft to Third Parties (Montreal, 2 May 2009), ICAO Doc 9919
- Convention on Compensation for Damage to Third Parties, Resulting from Acts of Unlawful Interference Involving Aircraft (Montreal, 2 May 2009), ICAO Doc 9920
- Convention on the Suppression of Unlawful Acts Relating to International Civil Aviation (Beijing, 10 September 2010), ICAO Doc 9960
- Protocol Supplementary to the Convention for the Suppression of Unlawful Seizure of Aircraft (Beijing, 10 September 2010), ICAO Doc 9959
- Protocol to Amend the Convention on Offences and Certain Other Acts Committed on Board Aircraft (Montreal, 4 April 2014), ICAO Doc 10034

b) ICAO Standards and Recommended Practices (SARPs)

- ICAO SARPs in Annexes 1-19 to the Convention on International Civil Aviation are available on ICAO CD-ROM ANX-CD updated annually

c) ICAO Assembly Resolutions in Force

- Assembly Resolutions in Force (as of 7 October 2022), ICAO Doc 10184

d) Procedures for Air Navigation Services (PANS)

- ABC – ICAO Abbreviations and Codes, ICAO Doc 8400
- ATM – Air Traffic Management, ICAO Doc 4444

- OPS – Aircraft Operations, ICAO Doc 8168
- Training, ICAO Doc 9868
- Regional Supplementary Procedures, ICAO Doc 7030

e) Annual Reports of the Council to the Assembly

- CD-ROM AR
  Vol. I. 1945-1969
  Vol. II 1970-1999
- www.icao.int/about-icao/Pages/annual-reports.aspx
  2000-2012 Docs. format
  2013- Online format

f) ICAO Rules

- Standing Rules of Procedure of the Assembly of ICAO, Doc 7600
- Rules of Procedure for the Council, Doc 7559
- Rules of Procedure for the Air Navigation Commission, Doc 8229
- Rules for the Settlement of Differences, Doc 7782
- Legal Committee Constitution, Procedure for Approval of Draft Conventions, Rules of Procedure, Doc 7669
- ICAO Financial Regulations, Doc 7515
- ICAO Publication Regulations, Doc 7231

3 INTERNET LINKS

- www.icao.int
- www.un.org
- untreaty.un.org
- www.iata.org
- www.aci.aero
- www.faa.gov
- www.transport.ec.europa.eu
- www.aviation-safety.net
- www.planecrashinfo.com/
- www.avherald.com

4   GENERAL BIBLIOGRAPHY OF AIR LAW

- Wybo P. Heere: *International Bibliography of Air Law 1900-1971*, 1972; Supplements 1972-1976. Leyden, Sijthoff, 1976.
- Dick van het Kaar: *International Civil Aviation: Treaties, Institutions and Programmes*, International Eleven Publishing, 2019. pp. 1-320.

Index

A

Accident Data Report (ADREP) 106
accidents 82, 100, 101, 103, 107, 185, 312
Additional Protocol No. 1 202, 309, 310, 462
Additional Protocol No. 2 73, 202, 309, 310, 462
Additional Protocol No. 3 73, 202, 309, 310, 462
Additional Protocol No. 4 73, 202
adequate representation 157, 158
aerial navigation 5
aerodrome 54
aeronautical communications 11, 42, 82, 175
aeronautical law 1
Agreement on North Atlantic Ocean Weather Stations (NAOS) 168
Air Afrique 87
aircraft 3, 6, 7, 9, 10, 13, 14, 15, 17, 35, 41, 42, 46, 47, 48, 49, 50, 51, 52, 53, 55, 56, 57, 58, 60, 62, 65, 66, 67, 68, 69, 70, 71, 72, 76, 231, 232, 233, 235, 236, 237, 238, 239, 240, 242, 243, 244, 246, 247, 248, 249, 250, 252, 253, 254, 255, 256, 257, 258, 259, 317
Aircraft Accident Investigation 100, 104
aircraft commander 236, 238, 239, 240, 241, 243, 256, 257, 272
– pilot-in-command 257
aircraft documents carried in aircraft 1, 7, 10, 65
aircraft in distress 52
aircraft noise 178, 223, 224

aircraft piracy 233
Aircraft Protocol 203
air cushion vehicles 65
air law 1, 2, 3, 5, 11, 12, 14, 35, 36, 39, 66, 67, 68, 71, 231, 236, 248
air marshals 273
air navigation 3, 5, 8, 9, 11, 26, 39, 42, 46, 47, 48, 51, 52, 53, 67, 231, 235, 253, 255, 256, 257, 258, 259
Air Navigation Commission (ANC) 153, 160, 168, 176, 271
Air Operators Certificate (AOC) 91
airport 14, 41, 43, 47, 51, 54, 242, 243, 257
airport customs procedures 9, 264
air services agreement (ASA) 46
air space 1, 3, 5, 6, 9, 11, 16, 17, 36, 38, 39, 40, 42, 44, 45, 46, 50, 51, 53, 54, 55, 57, 58, 60, 61, 66, 67, 68, 70, 75
Air Traffic Services 53, 243
air transport 3, 15, 17, 31
Air Transport Committee (ATC) 160, 271
airworthiness 9, 13, 52
amendment 13, 19, 21, 23, 24, 26, 27, 28, 30, 31, 34, 42, 59, 62, 75, 233
Annexes to Chicago Convention 13, 14, 42, 50, 59, 65, 73, 74, 75
Antarctica 45
Antarctic Treaty 45
Arab Air Cargo 87
arbitration 141, 204, 206, 208, 209
archipelagic sea lane passage 42
archipelagic waters 38, 40, 42
Atlantic Charter 15
authentic texts 19, 21, 24

aviation security 234
– program 92, 271

B
baggage 72, 253, 254
balloon
– hot air balloon 6
Beijing Convention 230, 290
Beijing Protocol 230, 288, 289
Bermuda I 97, 122, 126
Bermuda II 122
blacklist 187, 278
Bonn Declaration 282
Briand-Kellogg Pact 51
Brussels Protocol 1938 318

C
cabotage 9, 13, 46, 124
capacity 16, 17, 73
Cape Town Convention 203, 229, 328
certificate of airworthiness 88, 91, 109
Certificate of Registration 85
certification of aircraft 9
change of gauge 124
Charter of GNSS 226
Charter of the United Nations 15, 28, 30, 31
Chicago Conference 15, 16, 17, 19, 20, 21, 22, 26, 31, 36, 231
Chicago Convention 1944 3, 18, 19, 20, 22, 23, 24, 25, 26, 28, 29, 31, 32, 34, 36, 38, 39, 40, 42, 45, 46, 50, 51, 52, 53, 54, 56, 58, 59, 60, 62, 65, 66, 69, 70, 71, 73, 75, 242
CITEJA 197, 228, 292, 293, 297, 301, 317
civil aircraft 41, 46, 48, 53, 55, 56, 57, 58, 60, 62, 63, 66, 69, 70, 74, 235

civil aviation 3, 13, 16, 17, 18, 36, 40, 43, 45, 46, 51, 54, 58, 62, 65, 67, 69, 74, 231, 233, 234, 235, 245, 253, 254
coastal State 37, 38, 41, 42, 43
cockpit voice recorder (CVR) 58
code-sharing 127
Commission internationale de la navigation aerienne (CINA) 13
common mark 87
communicable diseases 51
communication, navigation and surveillance (CNS) 225
community carrier 99
complete and exclusive sovereignty 11, 35, 36, 37, 47
computer reservation system (CRS) 126
Contiguous Zone 41
continental shelf, air space over 44
Convention on International Civil Aviation 18
Corfu Channel Case 61
countertrails 45
Covenant of the League of Nations 133, 190
Cuba v. United States (1988) 213
customary law 37, 39, 67, 245
customs airport 48

D
danger area 48, 54
Declaration of the United Nations 15
DEN/ICE Agreements (Joint Financing Agreements) 169, 206
denunciation 116, 306
depositary 19, 20, 21, 22, 252
designation 85, 96, 120, 126, 131, 157, 190, 201
Diplomatic Conference 13, 22, 23, 25, 73, 235, 236, 244, 245, 246, 250, 253, 255

Directors General of Civil Aviation (DGCAs) 147, 188, 229
dirigibles 1
double disapproval 124
drone 46, 47, 65
dual registration 84

E
enemy States 32
engine emissions 45, 83, 223, 224
environmental protection 83, 215, 217, 222, 223, 224
established air route 53, 66
Exclusive Economic Zone (EEZ) 38, 40, 41, 42, 43
expulsion 19, 33
extradition 243, 244, 245, 246, 249, 250, 251, 253, 254
Extraordinary Sessions 58

F
facilitation 107, 110, 167, 194, 274, 297
fifth jurisdiction 308
filing of differences 179
flight data recorder (FDR) 82
Flight Information Regions (FIR) 82, 227
flight number 123
force, threat or use of 36, 54, 56, 60, 62, 63, 70, 247
foreign aircraft 10, 37, 38, 41, 46, 47, 48, 51, 52, 62
freedom of flight 10, 114
freedom of the high seas 40
freedoms of the air 14, 17, 115, 116, 117, 118
free transit 41
frequency 30, 42

G
Galileo 225
Garcia and Garza Case 61
General Agreement on Tariffs and Trade (GATT) 129
General Agreement on Trade in Services (GATS) 129
general aviation
– private flights 67
Geneva Convention on the International Recognition of Rights in Aircraft 1948 71
glider 66
Global Navigation Satellite Systems (GNSS) 225
– Charter of 226, 227
Globaltime 322
GLONASS 225
GPS 225
Guadalajara Conference 1961 95
Guadalajara Convention 1961 304
Guatemala City Protocol 1971 73, 307

H
Hague Convention 1907 61
Hague Convention 1970 72, 235, 244, 253
Hague Protocol 1955 72, 302, 304
hard rights 126
Havana Convention 1928 14, 17, 20
high seas, air space over 40, 43, 44, 50, 58
hijacking 231, 233, 234
Hong Kong clause 315
hovercraft 65
hydroplane 41

I
Ibero-American Air Navigation Convention 14

Ibero-American Aviation Congress 1926 14
ICAO xii
ICAO Air Navigation Commission (ANC) 74, 153, 160, 168, 176, 271
ICAO Air Transport Committee (ATC) 160, 271
ICAO Assembly 20, 21, 22, 23, 25, 31, 54, 58, 59, 62, 74, 75, 144, 146, 234, 244, 245, 246
ICAO Code of Conduct on operation of CRS 128
ICAO Council 40, 46, 54, 55, 56, 59, 69, 73, 74
ICAO Council President 234
ICAO Headquarters Agreement 140, 141, 193, 194
ICAO law-making functions 156
ICAO Legal Committee 31, 235, 244, 245, 246, 254
ICAO Secretary General 21, 144, 155, 163, 165, 170, 190, 194, 195, 196, 201, 219
ICAO Standing Rules of Procedure 25, 147, 149, 150, 151, 157, 158
immunities and privileges 140, 141, 192, 193
immunity 239, 251
implementation
– enforcement 185, 187, 189, 228
incidents 8, 54, 231, 232, 233, 241, 242, 248, 253
India v. Pakistan (1952) 210
innocent passage 9, 12, 38, 41, 42, 68
interception of aircraft 62
internal waters and lakes 37
International Air Services Transit Agreement (Two Freedoms Agreement) 18, 97

international air transport 37, 46, 238
International Air Transport Agreement (Five Freedoms Agreement) 18
International Aviation Safety Assessment Program (FAA IASA) 185
international carriage by air 73
International Civil Aviation Organization (ICAO) 3, 20, 41
International Commission for Air Navigation (ICAN) 13
International Court of Justice (ICJ) 55, 61, 62
international interest 133, 327, 329
international operating agencies 86, 87, 155, 173
international routes 14
international standards and recommended practices 81
International Telecommunications Union (ITU) 30
international treaty 24, 29
Iran Air flight IR655 56

J

Japanese initiative 311, 312, 314
Joint and International Registration of Aircraft 86
Joint Financing agreements with Denmark and with Iceland 206
journey log book 81, 109
jurisdiction, exclusive 36

K

Korean Airlines Flight 007 54, 56, 57

L

land area 37
law of the sea 39
League of Nations 13, 14, 21, 28, 37

legal capacity 139
limitation of liability 298, 299, 300, 319
Lockerbie disaster 260

M

Madrid Convention 1926 13, 14
mail 46
Man Portable Air Defence Systems (MANPADS) 280
maritime law 39
meteorological services 52
military aircraft 35, 40, 54, 55, 56, 67, 68, 69, 70, 73, 74, 75
military, customs or police aircraft 68
Montgolfier 6
Montreal Agreement 1966 306
Montreal Convention 1971 72, 246, 253
Montreal Convention 1991 203, 265, 269
Montreal Convention 1999 313, 314
Montreal Protocol 2014 203, 279
Montreal Protocol No. 4 (1975) 202, 309, 310, 462

N

narcoterrorism 233
nationality 12, 22, 47, 49, 62, 68, 80, 250
nationality marks 455
nationality of aircraft 9, 85, 87, 155, 173
nationality of the airline 96, 118
no-fly lists 278
non-scheduled flights 115

O

offence 235, 237, 238, 239, 240, 241, 243, 245, 246, 247, 248, 249, 251, 252, 254, 255, 256, 257, 258
open skies agreements 99, 124
open skies cases 99

opinio juris ac necessitatis 8, 10, 12, 67, 69, 242
outer space 1, 39

P

Pakistan v. India 210, 212
PANAM Flight 103 260, 265, 272
Paris Conference 1910 8, 10, 35
Paris Conference 1919 35, 231
Paris Convention 1919 11, 12, 14, 20, 68
passengers 14, 40, 46, 49, 52, 55, 56, 57, 233, 236, 239, 240, 241, 243, 249, 251, 252, 253, 254
pilotless aircraft 46, 51, 70
plastic explosives 266, 267, 269
Plenary 27
police and customs aircraft 68
practice of States 8
pricing 124, 126
private aircraft 68
private air law 3, 73
private law 2
Procedures for Air Navigation Services (PANS) 74
prohibited area 47, 48, 51, 53, 57
prohibited zones 9, 12
prosecution 70, 245, 246, 251, 253
Protocols 21
Provisional Civil Aviation Organization (PICAO) 18
public and private aircraft 9

Q

quasi-judicial 156
quasi-legislative 156

R

radio services 52

ratification 20, 22, 24, 26, 28, 30, 32, 237, 252
Regional Air Navigation Plans (RANPs) 227
Regional Offices of ICAO 139
Regional Supplementary Procedures (SUPPs) 74
registration 83
registration marks 80, 87, 248, 455
registration of aircraft 83, 84, 85, 86
Rendition flights 80, 81
restricted area 47, 48, 53
right to fly 113, 116
roman law 5
Rome Convention 1933 317, 318
Rome Convention 1952 63, 71
Rules for the Settlement of Differences 207, 208, 443
rules of the air 9, 13, 40, 41, 49, 50, 51, 66, 75, 82, 176

S

sabotage 231, 245, 246, 253, 254
safety 3, 7, 40, 46, 54, 59, 62, 66, 74, 75, 231, 234, 235, 237, 240, 244, 254, 255, 256, 257
– audits 188
scheduled air services 45
search and rescue 77, 82, 107
search of aircraft 49
security 10, 15, 36, 41, 53, 67, 231, 238, 242
Security Manual 161, 221
security oversight audits 171, 188, 229
SEMTEX 260, 265
September 11 2001 ('911') 48, 63, 233, 253
serious incident 253
settlement of differences 36, 156, 205

soft law 2
soft rights 126
sovereign rights 9
sovereignty 12
special authorization 46, 68, 69, 70
Special Drawing Right (SDR) 152, 309, 325
special interest 35
specialized agencies 30, 50
special permission or other authorization 45
stand alone cabotage 124
standards 50
Standards and Recommended Practices (SARPs) 58, 69, 73, 74, 81, 171, 236
state aircraft 13, 51, 53, 54, 66, 68, 69, 71, 73, 75
State of Occurrence 103
State of registry 238, 243, 244
State of the occurrence 107
State of the operator 258
state sovereignty 2, 9, 10, 12, 28, 29, 35, 36, 37, 38, 40, 42, 43, 44, 45, 60, 67, 69
stop for non-traffic purposes 114, 117
straits, regime of transit passage 41
substantial ownership and effective control of airlines 96, 97, 99, 100

T

technical cooperation 167, 195, 217, 219
template air services agreements 125
territorial airspace 49
territorial sea 9, 35, 38, 39, 41, 42, 44
territorial sovereignty 6, 36
territorial waters 37
territory 8, 9, 10, 11, 16, 35, 36, 37, 38, 40, 41, 42, 43, 45, 47, 48, 49, 51, 52, 53, 54, 61, 66, 67, 68, 69, 70, 236, 237, 238,

239, 240, 241, 242, 243, 248, 249, 251, 258
terrorism 2
Tokyo Convention 1963 72, 235, 241, 243, 244, 249, 251, 256
trade in services 129
traffic rights 14, 15, 17, 126, 130
type certification 91

U

UK v. Spain (1967) 211
UN Convention on the Law of the Sea 1982 (UNCLOS) 28, 37, 38, 39, 40, 41, 42, 43
UNIDROIT 327, 328, 330
United Nations 15, 32, 33
United States v. Diego Cordova 236
United States v. Fifteen States of the European Union 214
unlawful incursions 53
unlawful interferences 237, 242
unlawful seizure of aircraft 231, 233, 234, 235, 237, 241, 243, 245, 246, 253, 254
unruly passengers 231
US Space Shuttle 66

V

Versailles Peace Conference 133
Versailles Peace Treaty 68
vertical separation 53, 54
Vienna Convention on the Law of Treaties 19, 24, 25, 50

W

Warsaw Convention 72, 73
Warsaw system 73
Wassenaar Arrangement 282
weapons, use against civil aircraft in flight 51, 54, 56, 59, 62

World Trade Organization (WTO) 129, 130, 131

Essential Air and Space Law (Series Editor: Marietta Benkö)

Volume 1: Natalino Ronzitti & Gabriella Venturini (eds.), The Law of Air Warfare – Contemporary Issues, ISBN 978-90-77596-14-2

Volume 2: Marietta Benkö & Kai-Uwe Schrogl (eds.), Space Law: Current Problems and Perspectives for Future Regulations, ISBN 978-90-77596-11-1

Volume 3: Tare Brisibe, Aeronautical Public Correspondence by Satellite, ISBN 978-90-77596-10-4

Volume 4: Michael Milde, International Air Law and ICAO, ISBN 978-90-77596-54-8

Volume 5: Markus Geisler & Marius Boewe, The German Civil Aviation Act, ISBN 978-90-77596-72-2

Volume 6: Ulrich Steppler & Angela Klingmüller, EU Emissions Trading Scheme and Aviation, ISBN 978-90-77596-79-1

Volume 7: Heiko van Schyndel (ed.), Aviation Code of the Russian Federation, ISBN 978-90-77596-80-7

Volume 8: Zang Hongliang & Meng Qingfen, Civil Aviation Law in the People's Republic of China, ISBN 978-90-77596-91-3

Volume 9: Ronald M. Schnitker & Dick van het Kaar, Aviation Accident and Incident Investigation. Concurrence of Technical, ISBN 978-94-90947-01-9

Volume 10: Michael Milde, International Air Law and ICAO, second edition, ISBN 978-90-90947-35-4

Volume 11: Ronald Schnitker & Dick van het Kaar, Safety Assessment of Foreign Aircraft Programme. A European Approach to Enhance Global Aviation Safety, ISBN 978-94-9094-793-4

Volume 12: Marietta Benkö & Engelbert Plescher, Space Law: Reconsidering the Definition/Delimitation Question and the Passage of Spacecraft through Foreign Airspace, ISBN 978-94-6236-076-1

Volume 13: Heiko van Schyndel (ed.), Aviation Code of the Russian Federation, second edition, ISBN 978-94-6236-433-2

Volume 14: Alejandro Piera Valdés, Greenhouse Gas Emissions from International Aviation: Legal and Policy Challenges, ISBN 978-94-6236-467-7

Volume 15: Peter Paul Fitzgerald, A Level Playing Field for "Open Skies": The Need for Consistent Aviation Regulation, ISBN 978-94-6236-625-1

Volume 16: Jae Woon Lee, Regional Liberalization in International Air Transport: Towards Northeast Asian Open Skies, ISBN 978-94-6236-688-6

Volume 17: Tanveer Ahmad, Climate Change Governance in International Civil Aviation: Toward Regulating Emissions Relevant to Climate Change and Global Warming, ISBN 978-94-6236-692-3

Volume 18: Michael Milde, International Air Law and ICAO, third edition, ISBN 978-94-6236-619-0

Volume 19: Nataliia Malysheva, Space Law and Policy in the Post-Soviet States, ISBN 978-94-6236-847-7

Volume 20: Philippe Clerc, Space Law in the European Context, ISBN 978-94-6236-797-5

Volume 21: Benjamyn Scott, Aviation Cybersecurity: Regulatory Approach in the European Union, ISBN 978-94-6236-961-0

Volume 22: Dick van het Kaar, International Civil Aviation: Treaties, Institutions and Programmes, ISBN 978-94-6236-972-6

Volume 23: Lasantha Hettiarachchi, International Air Transport Association (IATA): Structure and Legitimacy of its Quasi-International Regulatory Power, ISBN 978-94-9094-758-3

Volume 24: Masataka Ogasawara & Joel Greer, Japan in Space, ISBN 978-94-6236-203-1

Volume 25: Ronald Schnitker & Dick van het Kaar, Drone Law and Policy, ISBN 978-94-6236-198-0

Volume 26: Marietta Benkö & Kai-Uwe Schrogl (eds.), Outer Space, Future for Humankind – Issues of Law and Policy, ISBN 978-94-6236-225-3

Volume 27: Wu, Xiaodan, China's ambition in Space, Programs, Policy and Law, ISBN 978-94-6236-277-2

Volume 28: Attila Sipos, Michael Milde's International Air Law and ICAO, revised by Attila Sipos, fourth edition, ISBN 978-94-6236-622-0